WRITING COMPILERS AND INTERPRETERS

Second Edition

WRITING COMPILERS AND INTERPRETERS

Second Edition

Ronald Mak

■

Wiley Computer Publishing

John Wiley & Sons, Inc.

New York • Chichester • Brisbane • Toronto • Singapore

Associate Publisher: Katherine Schowalter

Editor: Philip Sutherland

Managing Editor: Mark Hayden

Text Design & Composition: SunCliff Graphic Productions

Designations used by companies to distinguish their products are often claimed as trademarks. In all instances where John Wiley & Sons, Inc. is aware of a claim, the product names appear in initial capital or all capital letters. Readers, however, should contact the appropriate companies for more complete information regarding trademarks and registration.

This text is printed on acid-free paper.

This publication is designed to provide accurate and authoritative information in regard to the subject matter covered. It is sold with the understanding that the publisher is not engaged in rendering legal, accounting, or other professional service. If legal advice or other expert assistance is required, the services of a competent professional person should be sought.

Library of Congress Cataloging-in-Publication Data

ISBN: 0-471-11353-0

Printed in the United States of America

10 9 8 7 6

Dedicated to the memory of my grandmother

TRADEMARKS

CONTENTS ▰▰▰▰

This book teaches you how to write compilers and interpreters by *doing*. We'll write a working Pascal interpreter, an interactive symbolic debugger, and a compiler that generates code for a real computer, one that uses a processor based on the popular 8086 architecture. We'll spend very little time on theory, but instead we'll learn *incrementally* by writing a lot of code. Almost every chapter will have at least one working program that not only illustrates the concepts taught in that chapter, but also does something useful. So besides the interpreter, debugger, and compiler, we'll also write some utility programs that process Pascal programs, such as a program lister, a source file compactor, an interactive calculator, a cross-referencer, a pretty printer, and a syntax checker.

Who Should Read This Book

This book is for the practicing programmer who needs to learn how to write a compiler or an interpreter, but who does not yet want to study a more traditional textbook. Whether you are a professional programmer who needs to write a compiler at work, or a personal programmer who wants to write an interpreter for a language you've just invented, this book will quickly show you what you need to know.

If you're a student taking a computer science course on compiler writing, you'll find that this book can also be a good laboratory text. The programs are all examples of how to apply what you're learning in the classroom, and you can make numerous exercises and projects out of improving them.

The prerequisites for reading this book are a good working knowledge of C++, an understanding of basic data structures such as linked lists and binary trees, and some familiarity with Pascal. A strong desire to learn the subject and the patience to slog through a lot of code are also very helpful!

A Practical Approach Using C++

Writing a compiler or an interpreter is not a simple task. The best way to learn how to do it is to learn the necessary concepts first, and you can best learn these concepts by using them in working programs. This theme runs throughout Chapters 2 through 14. Each chapter contains one, two, or even three working utility programs that use the concepts taught in that chapter.

Each chapter's programs build upon the ones in the previous chapters. The Pascal interpreter we'll complete in Chapter 10 is composed of parts from all the programs that came before it. The interactive debugger in Chapter 11 is built on top of the interpreter. The Pascal compiler we'll complete in Chapter 14 is the culmination of all the previous programs.

The table at the end of this Preface lists all the programs in this book. This practical approach, using many intermediate programs, enables you to see an interpreter and a compiler evolve in stages. If you study the utility programs in each chapter and understand the concepts they illustrate, you will have little trouble moving on to the next chapter.

Even though this book's utility programs process Pascal programs, the utility programs themselves are written in C++. C++ has become a very popular language, and it is proving itself to be well-suited for writing systems programs such as compilers and interpreters. The object-oriented programming techniques supported by C++ enable large complex programs to be developed in a very modular fashion.

This book further exploits object technology by frequently using class diagrams and object diagrams. The class diagrams show how a program's classes are defined and how they relate to one another. The object diagrams show how the objects derived from these classes behave at runtime. When concepts are explained using these diagrams, you aren't distracted by having to look at (often dense) C++ code. When you finally do see the code, you already know what the code says and what it will do. The class and object diagrams in this book are simplified versions of the ones developed by Grady Booch. (See the book *Object-Oriented Analysis and Design with Applications,* 2nd ed., by Grady Booch, published by the Benjamin/Cummings Publishing Company, 1994.) These diagrams will be explained when they first appear in this book. Appendix B also contains a summary.

By design, this book teaches you essentially one way to write a compiler or an interpreter. The techniques you'll learn will not always be the best or most efficient ones, just ones that do the job and are easy to learn and understand. Perhaps you'll be inspired to study more advanced texts and replace the routines with better ones. We'll write the code in a modular fashion to make it easier to do just that.

This book tries to strike a balance between writing compilers and interpreters, and purely object-oriented design. Projects as complex as writing compilers and interpreters certainly lend themselves to such design. We'll resist the temptation to use advanced object-oriented techniques such as deeply nested subclasses or multiple inheritance, or making every possible "thing" into an object. Perhaps a good exercise for a class on object-oriented programming would be to do a full analysis and design of a compiler or an interpreter. Surely this is a subject for another book.

To keep the code relatively simple, this book errs on the conservative side. For example, we never check the result of calling new to ensure that the memory allocation was successful. Real production code should always make this check, perhaps by using the C++ exception handing features (which were not implemented by Microsoft's compiler when this book was being written).

Why Learn to Write Compilers and Interpreters?

As a competent programmer, you can hardly afford not to know something about writing compilers and interpreters. Today's computing environment places increasing emphasis on "user-friendly" software. The languages we use to communicate with the computer play a major part in determining just how friendly the software is.

Any computer language professional is fascinated by the continuing activity in programming language development. In the past few years, we've seen C++ rise in popularity in academia and in industry, and, of course, some other languages begin to fade into obscurity.

At this moment, yet another exciting new language is emerging—the Java language for writing programs that run on the Internet. The language is a simplified form of C++, and Java applets are downloaded to Web browsers that contain Java interpreters to execute them. This book would not exist if it were not for such developments.

Organization

This book is organized into three parts. The first part teaches you the basic concepts of reading a Pascal program and producing a listing, decomposing the program into its elements (scanning), and analyzing the program based on its grammar rules (parsing).

By the second part of the book, you'll know enough to write a Pascal interpreter that can execute actual programs. But we won't stop there. We'll add features to turn the interpreter into a symbolic debugger with an interactive command language that allows you to set breakpoints and watchpoints, single-step and trace the execution flow, and print and modify the values of the program's variables.

In the third part of the book, we'll write a compiler that translates a Pascal program into 8086 assembly language. You can then use an assembler and a linker to run the program on any computer based on the 8086 processor.

In the very last chapter, we'll take a brief look at some advanced concepts that are beyond the scope of this book.

Software Requirements

All the programs in this book were developed using both Borland's C++ (version 4.02) and Microsoft's Visual C++ (version 1.52). You can also use Borland's Turbo C++ (version 3.0). You can assemble the assembly language programs generated by the compiler with Borland's Turbo Assembler (version 4.0) or with Microsoft's Quick Assembler (version 2.51).

You can obtain the source files of the programs, including the "make" files and the test Pascal programs (and their input files) by following the instructions at the beginning of this book.

The Second Edition

The first edition of this book has done surprisingly well during its four years. It has received nice reviews, and there has been positive feedback from readers and from instructors who are using it in their classrooms. A nontheoretical approach to this subject just may be a good idea after all.

Hopefully, this second edition hasn't ruined anything. It keeps the same approach as the first edition, but all the programs have been redesigned and rewritten using C++, and most of the text has been revised. Even though C++ is more complicated than C (the language of the first edition), through the use of class and object diagrams and better modularity, the text is easier to understand.

The major changes in this second edition are:

- The use of C++ and object-oriented programming techniques
- The class diagrams and object diagrams
- An earlier and better integrated discussion of intermediate code
- Better reuse of the front end by the compiler, which now generates assembly code from the intermediate code.

Acknowledgments

Once again, Bill Gladstone and his company, Waterside Productions, Inc., represented me when dealing with my publisher. But they had an easy time, because I had such great editors at Wiley. Paul Farrell encouraged me to do a second edition and got me started, and Phil Sutherland did an excellent job getting me to finish it despite "minor" schedule slips.

The technical reviewer hired by Wiley convinced me to do a better job explaining why I did this or that. (Some things, evidently, were obvious only to me.) I must especially thank my good friend, John Stafford, who volunteered to read and annotate my chapters, and who actually checked my programs and found bugs or ways to improve the code. John and I used to work together writing compilers. He's better at it than I am—I'm lucky he doesn't also write books.

Oh, No, Bugs Again

While going through the C programs of the first edition to write this edition's programs, I found and fixed several nontrivial and somewhat embarrassing bugs. Unfortunately, I'm sure I've introduced some new ones for this edition, except this time they may be obscure C++ bugs.

Once again, I take full responsibility for all my bugs, and I apologize in advance for them. Neither I nor my publisher, however, can be responsible for any consequences if you use the programs for anything but instructional purposes.

If you find a bug, or if you have a suggestion for an improvement, please write to me care of the publisher.

▟▙▟▙ **Table P.1** Table of Programs

Chapter	Name	Title	Description
2	list	Program 2-1: Source Program Lister	Print a listing of a program.
3	tokeniz1	Program 3-1: Simple Tokenizer	Extract and print simple tokens of a Pascal program.
	tokeniz2	Program 3-2: Pascal Tokenizer	Extract and print all the tokens of a Pascal program.
	compact	Program 3-3: Pascal Source Compactor	Compact a Pascal program by removing blanks and comments.
4	xref1	Program 4-1: Cross-Referencer I	Print a cross-reference listing of a Pascal program's identifiers.
	crunch	Program 4-2: Pascal Source Cruncher	Compress a Pascal program into intermediate code.
	decrunch	Program 4-3: Pascal Source Decruncher	Restore a Pascal program from the intermediate code.
5	calc	Program 5-1: Calculator	Interactive calculator.
	execute1	Program 5-2: Simple Executor I	Execute a Pascal program containing assignment and I/O statements.
6	synchek1	Program 6-1: Syntax Checker I	Check the syntax of a simple Pascal program.
	execute2	Program 6-2: Simple Executor II	Execute a Pascal program containing compound and REPEAT statements.
7	xref2	Program 7-1: Cross-Referencer II	Print a cross-reference listing including type information about each identifier.
	synchek2	Program 7-2: Syntax Checker II	Check the syntax of a Pascal program containing declarations.
8	synchek3	Program 8-1: Syntax Checker III	Check the syntax of a complete Pascal program.
	pprint	Program 8-2: Pascal Pretty-Printer	Pretty-print a Pascal program.
9	execute3	Program 9-1: Pascal Executor III	Execute a Pascal program containing assignment statements, procedures, and functions.
10	run	Program 10-1: Pascal Interpreter	Execute a complete Pascal program.
11	debug	Program 11-1: Interactive Debugger	Interactive symbolic debugger for a Pascal program.
13	emit	Program 13-1: Code Emitter	Emit assembly code for a Pascal program containing assignment statements, procedures, and functions.
14	compile	Program 14-1: Pascal Compiler	Compile a complete Pascal program.

WRITING COMPILERS AND INTERPRETERS

Second Edition

1

INTRODUCTION

MISSING SEMICOLON. SYNTAX ERROR.

Well, so much for respect for your latest programming masterpiece! We programmers swear and curse at compilers more than just about any other systems software, yet they enable us to concentrate more on our algorithms than on the intricacies of machine language. But, as we're far too often reminded, compilers also meticulously check our programs for syntactic correctness.

What Are Compilers and Interpreters?

The main purpose of a compiler and of its close cousin, the interpreter, is to translate a program written in a high-level programming language like Pascal into a form that a computer can understand in order to execute the program. In the context of this translation, the high-level language is called the *source language*.

1

A compiler translates a program written in the source language into a low-level *object language*, which can be the assembly language or the machine language of a particular computer. The program that you write in the source language is called the *source program*, which you edit in one or more *source files*. The compiler translates each source file into an *object file*. If the object files contain assembly language, you must next run an *assembler* (yet another type of program translator) to convert them into machine language. You then run a utility program called a *linker* to combine the object files (along with any needed runtime library routines) into the *object program*. Once created, an object program is a separate program in its own right. You can load it into the computer's memory and then execute it.

For example, if you are programming in Pascal or C on an IBM PC, you would edit the source files and save them using names ending in `.pas` or `.c`. The Pascal or C compiler from Microsoft or Borland then translates each source file into a machine language object file, which it saves using a name ending in `.obj`. The linker combines the separate object files into the final object program, which is saved using a name ending in `.com` or `.exe`. Then, you can load and run the object program.

Figure 1.1 summarizes the compiler translation process.

On the other hand, an interpreter does not produce an object program. It may translate the source program into an internal *intermediate code* that it can execute more efficiently, or it may simply execute the source program's statements directly. The net result is that an interpreter translates a program into the actions specified by the program. Interpreters are often used for the BASIC language.

A compiler may also first translate the source program into intermediate code, and then translate the intermediate code into the object language. We'll see shortly how using intermediate code allows an interpreter and a compiler to share many routines.

Differences Between Compilers and Interpreters

What an interpreter does with a source program is very similar to what you would do with the program if you had to figure out what it does without using a computer. Let's suppose that you are handed a Pascal program. You first look it over to check

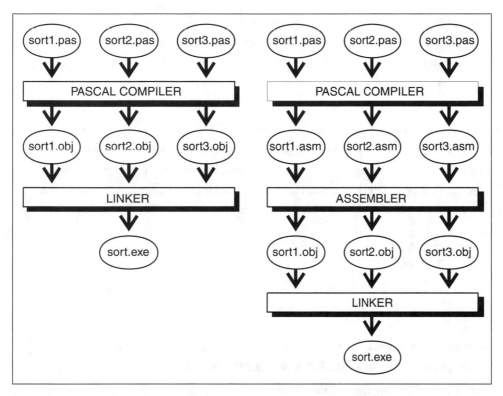

Figure 1.1 The diagram on the left shows how a Pascal program consisting of the three source files is translated by a compiler into three machine-language object files, which are then linked together (along with runtime library routines) into an executable object program. The diagram on the right shows a compiler that generates assembly-language object files. An assembler must translate each object file into machine language before they can be linked.

for syntax errors. You then locate the start of the main program, and from there you execute the statements one at a time by hand. You might use a pencil and a scratch pad to keep track of the values of the variables. For example, if you encounter the statement

```
i := j + k
```

in the program, you would look up the current values of j and k on your scratch pad, add the values, and write down the sum as the new value for i.

An interpreter essentially does what you just did. It is itself a program that runs on the computer. A Pascal interpreter reads in a Pascal source program, looks it over for syntax errors, and executes the source statements one at a time. Using some of its own variables as a scratch pad, the interpreter keeps track of the values of the source program's variables.

A compiler is also a program that runs on the computer. A Pascal compiler reads in a Pascal source program and checks it for syntax errors. But then, instead of executing the source program, it translates the source program into the object program. For example, a compiler that generates an assembly language object program for the IBM PC can translate the above Pascal statement into the assembly statements

```
mov   ax,WORD PTR j
add   ax,WORD PTR k
mov   WORD PTR i,ax
```

If the compiler generates a machine language object program, the output is even more cryptic!

Advantages and Disadvantages of Compilers and Interpreters

Which is better, a compiler or an interpreter?

To execute a source program with an interpreter, you simply feed the source program into the interpreter, and it takes over to check and execute the program. A compiler, however, checks the source program and then produces an object program. After running the compiler, you may need to run the linker, and then you have to load the object program into memory in order to execute it. If the compiler generated an assembly language object program, you must also run an assembler. So, an interpreter definitely has advantages over a compiler when it comes to the effort required to execute a source program.

Interpreters can be more versatile than compilers. Remember that they are themselves programs, and like any other programs, they can be made to run on different computers. You can write a Pascal interpreter that runs on both an IBM PC and an Apple Macintosh so that it will execute Pascal source programs on either computer. A compiler, however, generates object programs for a particular computer. Therefore, even if you took a Pascal compiler originally written for the PC and made it run on the Mac, it would still generate object programs for the PC. To make the compiler generate object programs for the Mac, you would have to rewrite substantial portions of the compiler.

What happens if the source program contains a logic error that doesn't show up until runtime, such as an attempt to divide by a variable whose value is zero? Since an interpreter is in control when it is executing the source program, it can stop and tell you the line number of the offending statement and the name of the variable. It can even prompt you for some corrective action (like changing the value of the variable) before resuming execution. The object program generated by a compiler, on the other hand, usually runs by itself. Information from the source program, such as line numbers and names of variables, might not be present in the object program. When a runtime error occurs, the program may simply abort and perhaps print a message containing the address of the bad instruction. Then it's up to you to figure out which source statement that address corresponds to, and which variable was zero.

When it comes to debugging, an interpreter is generally the way to go. However, many modern program development environments now give compilers debugging capabilities that are almost as good as those of interpreters. You compile a program and then run it under the control of the environment. If a runtime error occurs, you are given the information and control you need to correct the error. Then, you can either resume the execution of the program, or compile and run it again. Such compilers, though, usually generate extra information or instructions in the object program to keep the environment informed of the current state of the program's execution. This often causes the object program to be less efficient than it otherwise could be. Most people turn off the debugging features when they're about to generate the final "production" version of their programs. (This situation has been compared to wearing a life jacket when you're learning to sail on a lake, and then taking the jacket off when you're about to go out into the ocean.)

Suppose you've successfully debugged your program, and now your most important concern is how fast it executes. Remember that an interpreter executes the statements of the source program pretty much the way you would by hand. Each time it executes a statement, it looks it over to figure out what operations the statement says to do. With a compiler, the computer executes a machine-language program, generated either directly by the compiler or indirectly with an assembler. Since a computer executes a machine language program at top speed, such a program can run 10 to 100 times faster than the interpreted source program. A compiler is definitely the winner when it comes to speed. This is certainly true in the case of an optimizing compiler that knows how to generate especially efficient code.

So we see that compilers and interpreters have advantages and disadvantages. It depends on what aspects of program development and execution we consider. A compromise may be to have both a compiler and an interpreter for the same source language. Then we have the best of both worlds, easy development and fast execution.

That's what we'll accomplish in this book. By the time we're finished, we will have written a Pascal interpreter with interactive debugging facilities and a Pascal compiler that generates assembly language object programs.

Writing Compilers and Interpreters

Compilers and interpreters are complex programs. Writing one can be a daunting task, and it is generally believed that only the most advanced systems programmers are privy to this arcane art. That's part of the mystique of being considered the Grand Guru of the programming department.

This book tackles the task with the proven strategy of breaking it up into smaller ones and sharing code among the subtasks. We'll write our Pascal compiler and interpreter using C++ and object-oriented programming (OOP) methodology. OOP gives us the tools to manage the complexity. By carefully defining the right set of classes, we can construct the compiler and interpreter incrementally from its objects. We'll also use class and object diagrams to illustrate how these objects work together, and to show what messages they send to each other while translating a source program.

The incremental approach is important. Instead of trying to write an entire compiler or interpreter all at once, we'll start with just a small set of classes and objects. (Do not confuse the *object* in object program with objects from object-oriented programming!) As we refine existing objects and add new ones, we'll also write utility programs that make use of the objects we have so far. These programs will not only do useful things (such as generate cross-reference listings or pretty-print programs), they'll also give us a chance to test our code and to apply the concepts as we learn them. This incremental approach, and the ability in OOP to reuse and inherit from existing objects, enable us to build up the necessary skills to write full compilers and interpreters.

The goal of this book is *not* to write the best possible compilers and interpreters, but to teach the fundamentals in an understandable way. After reading this book, you should be able to study more advanced compiler textbooks, learn the theory behind the techniques, and then go back to refine the objects we created for this book to incorporate better algorithms.

The Parts of a Compiler and an Interpreter

To see what we're getting ourselves into, let's now take a high-level overview of what compilers and interpreters are made of. In later chapters, we'll examine these parts in much greater detail. At the highest level, we speak of the *front end* and the *back end*. The front end of a compiler or an interpreter reads the source program. An interpreter's back end executes the program, while a compiler's back end generates the object program.

Figure 1.2 shows some of the major objects that make up an interpreter's front and back ends. This figure also introduces us to object diagrams. Each object is represented by a cloud. A line connecting two objects indicates that the two objects send messages to each other, in either or both directions. The messages themselves, along with small arrows indicating direction, are written next to the connecting line.

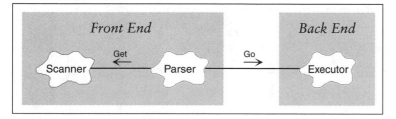

■■■■■■ **Figure 1.2** The major objects of an interpreter.

In the front end, the *parser* object knows the *syntax* of the source language, which is the set of grammar rules that determine how the source statements are written. Armed with such knowledge, the parser controls the translation process. Whenever the parser needs more of the source program to work on, it sends a `Get` message to the *scanner* object. The scanner reads the source program and breaks it apart into a sequence of *tokens*—numbers, identifiers, operators, and so on. It returns the next token to the parser in response to each `Get` message. After it has read the entire source program, the parser sends a `Go` message to the *executor* object in the back end to tell it to run the program.

Sending a message, in object-oriented programming parlance, generally means calling an object's function. In C++, such functions are called *member functions*. So, when we say that the parser object sends the `Get` message to the scanner object to obtain the next token, what really happens is that the parser calls the scanner's `Get` member function, and the function returns a value that represents the next token.

The *semantics* of a programming language determines the meaning of its expressions and statements. So while Pascal's syntax tells us that `i + j` is a correct way to write an expression, its semantics tells us that the values of `i` and `j` should be added together to obtain a new value. The executor's knowledge of the semantics enables it to perform the correct actions.

Figure 1.3 shows the major objects that make up a compiler's front and back ends. It has the same front end as the interpreter. However, a compiler has a *code generator* object in its back end instead of an executor object. The parser sends a `Go` message to the code generator object to generate the correct object code as determined by the semantics of the source program. (The first *object* is from OOP; the second *object* refers to the object program.)

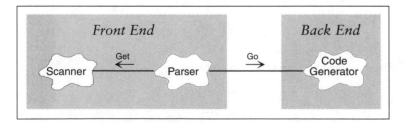

■■■■■■ **Figure 1.3** The major objects of a compiler.

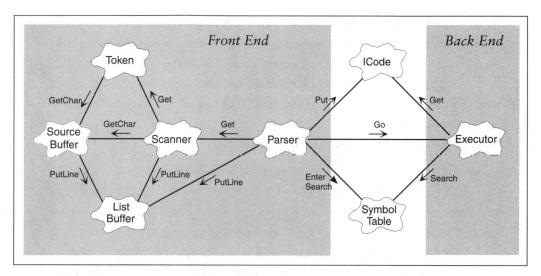

Figure 1.4 A more complete object diagram of an interpreter.

This has been a very simplified view of compilers and interpreters. Figure 1.4 shows a more complete object diagram of an interpreter.

The scanner object sends `Get` messages to the *token* object. Both the scanner and token objects send `GetChar` messages to the *source buffer* object, which fetches characters sequentially from the source program. Whenever the parser sends the scanner a `Get` message, the scanner first sends one or more `GetChar` messages to the source buffer to determine what kind of token (identifier, number, etc.) is next in the source program, and then it sends an `Get` message to the token object to extract that kind of token.

Several interpreter objects send `PutLine` messages to the *list buffer* object. This object takes care of the source listing, error messages, and other printed information.

The parser sends `Enter` and `Search` messages to the *symbol table* object. The symbol table is where the parser keeps track of information about certain tokens, such as identifiers. The parser enters information into the symbol table and then searches for it later.

The parser also sends `Put` messages to the *intermediate code* object (*icode* for short). The icode is a predigested version of the source program that, together with the symbol table object, serves as a clean interface between the interpreter's front and back ends. As we'll see later in the book, the icode also enables the interpreter to execute the source program more efficiently. After the parser has processed the source program and built the icode, it sends the Go message to the executor object. As it runs the program, the executor then sends Get messages to the icode object to fetch the predigested tokens and Search messages to the symbol table object to look up information previously entered by the parser.

Figure 1.5 is a more complete object diagram for a compiler. It's similar to Figure 1.4, except for the back end. After the parser has processed the source program and built the icode, it sends the Go message to the code generator object. As it generates the object program, the code generator then sends Get messages to the icode object to fetch the predigested tokens and Search messages to the symbol table object to look up information previously entered by the parser. It sends Put messages to the *object buffer* object to output the object program.

In this book, we'll first write the common frontend objects and interface objects. Next, we'll write the backend objects for the interpreter, and then we'll add interactive debugging features. Finally, we'll write the backend objects for a compiler that generates assembly language object programs for the IBM PC. You can see from the

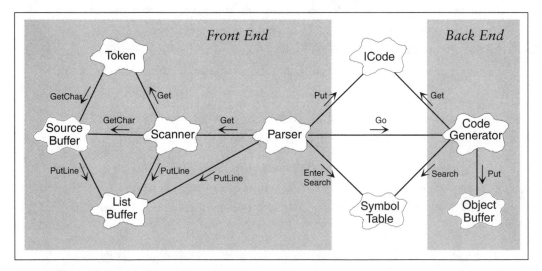

Figure 1.5 A more complete object diagram for a compiler.

object diagrams that we'll be able to reuse many of the objects. As we develop the programs incrementally, we'll use object diagrams that show how the objects we're working on interact with the other objects. We'll also use class diagrams that show how to define the classes from which the objects are instantiated. In the next chapter, we start with two fundamental frontend objects, the source buffer and list buffer objects that read and list (print) the source program.

2

READING AND LISTING THE SOURCE PROGRAM

In this chapter, we begin writing the front end of our Pascal compiler or interpreter by creating two fundamental objects. The first is the source buffer object that represents the source file and contains method functions to read the file. The second is the list buffer object that represents the source program listing and contains member functions print the listing. These objects are part of the front end's buffer module, and they will remain unchanged throughout the rest of the book. To test them, we'll write our first utility program, a source program lister.

The Program Listing

A *program listing* is a printed copy of the source program. To make the listing more useful, we can also add a line number and a nesting level before each printed line, and we can also print a page header at the top of each page. The nesting level of a statement indicates how deeply nested it is within Pascal's BEGIN END blocks. Until we learn how to parse such blocks, we'll just print zero as the nesting level. Figure 2.1 shows a sample listing of a short Pascal program.

```
Page 1    hello.pas    Sat Jul 09 21:48:01 1994

   1 0: PROGRAM hello (output);
   2 0:
   3 0: {Write 'Hello, world.' ten times.}
   4 0:
   5 0: VAR
   6 0:     i : integer;
   7 0:
   8 0: BEGIN {hello}
   9 0:     FOR i := 1 TO 10 DO BEGIN
  10 0:         writeln('Hello, world.');
  11 0:     END;
  12 0: END {hello}.
```

The Buffer Module

Figure 1.4 showed how the source buffer and list buffer objects fit in with the rest of the front end. We now need to define the two classes from which these objects are instantiated, TSourceBuffer and TListBuffer.

Later in this book, there will be other text I/O files. For example, when we write the interactive debugger, we'll need a command buffer object to read the debugger commands that are typed in. When we write the compiler, we'll need an assembly buffer object to write the assembly language object file.

Therefore, we'll anticipate our future needs and define two abstract base classes for text I/O, TTextInBuffer and TTextOutBuffer. We can derive classes TSourceBuffer and TListBuffer from these base classes.

In Figure 2.2, a class diagram illustrates the definition of the base classes and the derived subclasses. Whereas an object diagram shows what objects exist at runtime and the messages they send to each other, a class diagram shows the definitions of the classes from which these objects are instantiated. It shows the data members and member functions of each class. It also shows the relationships among the classes, such as a subclass being derived from a base class, or one class containing (either directly or via pointers) other classes. Each class is represented by a dashed cloud outline.

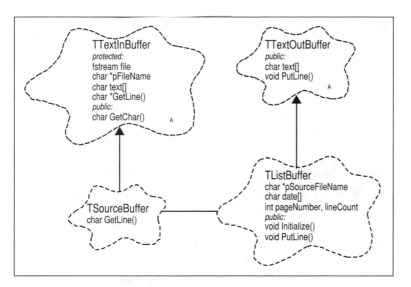

▬▬▬ **Figure 2.2**   Class diagram for the text I/O buffer classes.

In each definition of the base classes TTextInBuffer and TTextOutBuffer, the A in the triangle symbol indicates that the class is abstract. We also see the definitions of the derived subclasses TSourceBuffer and TListBuffer. A line connecting two class definitions indicates an association between the two classes. In particular, a line with an arrowhead points from a subclass to its base class.

Inside each dashed cloud diagram, we show the name of the class and its private, protected, and public members. (The members are private unless otherwise indicated.) Class TTextInBuffer has several protected data members: file is the input file, pFileName points to the file name, and text is the input character buffer. The protected member function GetLine reads a line of characters from the input file into the input buffer. These protected data members and member function will be available to each kind of text input buffer, but we do not want other objects to access them. The public member function GetChar, which we saw in the object diagrams, returns the next character from this buffer. We want it to be available to other objects, such as the scanner and token objects.

Subclass TSourceBuffer redefines GetLine as a private member function. Each subclass of TTextInBuffer will redefine GetLine because each subclass has its own requirements when reading text lines. For example, when we read lines from the source file, we also want to print them to the list file.

Class TTextOutBuffer has a public data member text to contain the characters to be printed, and a public member function PutLine (also shown in the object diagrams) to print a line of characters. We make PutLine public so that it is available to other objects such as the scanner and parser objects (to print error messages) and the source buffer object (to print the source program listing). We also make text public so that other objects can construct their print lines directly in the output buffer. We don't include a file data member in this base class since the output file is often the standard output file.

Subclass TListBuffer adds several private data members: pSourceFileName points to the name of the source file, date contains the current date string, and pageNumber and lineCount keep track of the current page number and line count. Each subclass of TTextOutBuffer will redefine the public member function PutLine to meet its printing requirements.

The class diagram shows an association between the subclasses TSourceBuffer and TListBuffer. When the source buffer object opens a source file, it calls the list buffer object's Initialize member function, passing the name of the source file, so that the list buffer object can later include the name in its page headings. Each time the source buffer object reads a line from the source file, it calls the list buffer object's PutLine member function to print the line to the list file.

We don't try to show all the class attributes in the class diagrams. (Similarly, our object diagrams don't try to show all the messages.) Such diagrams, however, do make it easier to read the C++ header files containing the actual class definitions. Figure 2.3 shows header file buffer.h, where we define the above classes.

■■■■■■■ **Figure 2.3** Header file **buffer.h**.

```
//    ****************************************************************
//    *                                                            *
//    *    I / O   B U F F E R S    (Header)                       *
//    *                                                            *
//    *    CLASSES: TTextInBuffer,  TSourceBuffer                  *
//    *             TTextOutBuffer, TListBuffer                    *
//    *                                                            *
```

```
//  *    FILE:    prog2-1/buffer.h                          *
//  *                                                       *
//  *    MODULE:  Buffer                                    *
//  *                                                       *
//  *    Copyright (c) 1996 by Ronald Mak                   *
//  *    For instructional purposes only.  No warranties.   *
//  *                                                       *
//  ***********************************************************

#ifndef buffer_h
#define buffer_h

#include <fstream.h>
#include <stdio.h>
#include <string.h>
#include "misc.h"
#include "error.h"

//              **********
//              *        *
//              *  Input *
//              *        *
//              **********

extern char eofChar;
extern int  inputPosition;
extern int  listFlag;
extern int  level;

const int maxInputBufferSize = 256;

//------------------------------------------------------------
// TTextInBuffer       Abstract text input buffer class.
//------------------------------------------------------------

class TTextInBuffer {

protected:
    fstream  file;                      // input text file
    char    *const pFileName;           // ptr to the file name
    char     text[maxInputBufferSize];  // input text buffer
    char    *pChar;                     // ptr to the current char
                                        //   in the text buffer

    virtual char GetLine(void) = 0;
```

(continues)

Figure 2.3 Header file **buffer.h**. (*Continued*)

```
public:
    TTextInBuffer(const char *pInputFileName, TAbortCode ac);

    virtual ~TTextInBuffer(void)
    {
        file.close();
        delete pFileName;
    }

    char Char        (void) const { return *pChar; }
    char GetChar     (void);
    char PutBackChar(void);
};

//----------------------------------------------------------------
// TSourceBuffer       Source buffer subclass of TTextInBuffer.
//----------------------------------------------------------------

class TSourceBuffer : public TTextInBuffer {
    virtual char GetLine(void);

public:
    TSourceBuffer(const char *pSourceFileName);
};

//           ***********
//           *         *
//           *  Output *
//           *         *
//           ***********

//----------------------------------------------------------------
// TTextOutBuffer      Abstract text output buffer class.
//----------------------------------------------------------------

class TTextOutBuffer {

public:
    char text[maxInputBufferSize + 16];  // output text buffer

    virtual void PutLine(void) = 0;

    void PutLine(const char *pText)
    {
```

```
            strcpy(text, pText);
            PutLine();
        }
    };

    //-------------------------------------------------------------
    // TListBuffer          List buffer subclass of TTextOutBuffer.
    //-------------------------------------------------------------

    class TListBuffer : public TTextOutBuffer {
        char *pSourceFileName;   // ptr to source file name (for page header)
        char  date[26];          // date string for page header
        int   pageNumber;        // current page number
        int   lineCount;         // count of lines in the current page

        void PrintPageHeader(void);

    public:
        virtual ~TListBuffer(void) { delete pSourceFileName; }

        void Initialize(const char *fileName);
        virtual void PutLine(void);

        void PutLine(const char *pText)
        {
            TTextOutBuffer::PutLine(pText);
        }

        void PutLine(const char *pText, int lineNumber, int nestingLevel)
        {
            sprintf(text, "%4d %d: %s", lineNumber, nestingLevel, pText);
            PutLine();
        }
    };

    extern TListBuffer list;

    #endif
```

In the actual definition of class TTextInBuffer, protected data member pChar points to the current character in the input buffer text. Public member function Char returns this character. The destructor function closes the source file and deletes the file name string. The constructor function and the public member function PutBackChar are explained below.

Class `TTextOutBuffer` overloads public member function `PutLine`. When `Put-Line` is called with a character string, it copies the characters into the `text` buffer and calls the virtual member function `PutLine` without arguments (implemented by the subclasses) to print the characters.

Subclass `TListBuffer` has a private member function `PrintPageHeader`, which is explained below. When its overloaded public member function `PutLine` is called with a pointer to a character string, it simply calls the base class's function. If the function is called also with a line number and nesting level, it constructs a listing line consisting of the text preceded by the line number and nesting level.

Figure 2.4 shows file `buffer.cpp`, which implements these classes.

■■■■■ **Figure 2.4** Implementation file **buffer.cpp**.

```
//      ************************************************************
//      *                                                          *
//      *    I / O   B U F F E R S                                 *
//      *                                                          *
//      *    Process text I/O files.  Included are member functions *
//      *    to read the source file and write to the list file.   *
//      *                                                          *
//      *    CLASSES: TTextInBuffer,  TSourceBuffer               *
//      *             TTextOutBuffer, TListBuffer                  *
//      *                                                          *
//      *    FILE:    prog2-1/buffer.cpp                           *
//      *                                                          *
//      *    MODULE:  Buffer                                       *
//      *                                                          *
//      *    Copyright (c) 1996 by Ronald Mak                     *
//      *    For instructional purposes only.  No warranties.     *
//      *                                                          *
//      ************************************************************

#include <stdio.h>
#include <string.h>
#include <iostream.h>
#include <time.h>
#include "common.h"
#include "buffer.h"

//              **********************
//              *                    *
//              *  Text Input Buffer *
```

```
//                *                    *
//               ***********************

char eofChar = 0x7F;    // special end-of-file character
int  inputPosition;     // "virtual" position of the current char
                        //   in the input buffer (with tabs expanded)
int  listFlag = true;   // true if list source lines, else false


//-------------------------------------------------------------
//  Constructor      Construct a input text buffer by opening the
//                   input file.
//
//      pInputFileName : ptr to the name of the input file
//      ac             : abort code to use if open failed
//-------------------------------------------------------------

TTextInBuffer::TTextInBuffer(const char *pInputFileName, TAbortCode ac)
    : pFileName(new char[strlen(pInputFileName) + 1])
{
    //--Copy the input file name.
    strcpy(pFileName, pInputFileName);

    //--Open the input file.  Abort if failed.
    file.open(pFileName, ios::in|ios::nocreate);
    if (!file.good()) AbortTranslation(ac);
}


//-------------------------------------------------------------
//  GetChar          Fetch and return the next character from the
//                   text buffer.  If at the end of the buffer,
//                   read the next source line.  If at the end of
//                   the file, return the end-of-file character.
//
//  Return: next character from the source file
//          or the end-of-file character
//-------------------------------------------------------------

char TTextInBuffer::GetChar(void)
{
    const int tabSize = 8;  // size of tabs
    char ch;                // character to return

    if      (*pChar == eofChar) return eofChar;  // end of file
    else if (*pChar == '\0')    ch = GetLine();  // end of line
    else {                                       // next char
        ++pChar;
```

(continues)

```
        ++inputPosition;
        ch = *pChar;
    }

    //--If tab character, increment inputPosition to the next
    //--multiple of tabSize.
    if (ch == '\t') inputPosition += tabSize - inputPosition%tabSize;

    return ch;
}

//------------------------------------------------------------
//  PutBackChar      Put the current character back into the
//                   input buffer so that the next call to
//                   GetChar will fetch this character. (Only
//                   called to put back a '.')
//
//  Return: the previous character
//------------------------------------------------------------

char TTextInBuffer::PutBackChar(void)
{
    --pChar;
    --inputPosition;

    return *pChar;
}

//              ******************
//              *                *
//              *  Source Buffer *
//              *                *
//              ******************

//------------------------------------------------------------
//  Constructor      Construct a source buffer by opening the
//                   source file.  Initialize the list file, and
//                   read the first line from the source file.
//
//      pSourceFileName : ptr to name of source file
//------------------------------------------------------------

TSourceBuffer::TSourceBuffer(const char *pSourceFileName)
    : TTextInBuffer(pSourceFileName, abortSourceFileOpenFailed)
```

```
{
    //--Initialize the list file and read the first source line.
    if (listFlag) list.Initialize(pSourceFileName);
    GetLine();
}


//-------------------------------------------------------------
// GetLine          Read the next line from the source file, and
//                  print it to the list file preceded by the
//                  line number and the current nesting level.
//
// Return: first character of the source line, or the
//         end-of-file character if at the end of the file
//-------------------------------------------------------------

char TSourceBuffer::GetLine(void)
{
    extern int lineNumber, currentNestingLevel;

    //--If at the end of the source file, return the end-of-file char.
    if (file.eof()) pChar = &eofChar;

    //--Else read the next source line and print it to the list file.
    else {
        file.getline(text, maxInputBufferSize);
        pChar = text;    // point to first source line char

        if (listFlag) list.PutLine(text, ++currentLineNumber,
                                   currentNestingLevel);
    }

    inputPosition = 0;
    return *pChar;
}


//              ****************
//              *              *
//              *  List Buffer *
//              *              *
//              ****************

const int maxPrintLineLength = 80;
const int maxLinesPerPage    = 50;

TListBuffer list;    // the list file buffer
```

(continues)

█████████ **Figure 2.4** Implementation file **buffer.cpp**. (*Continued*)

```cpp
//---------------------------------------------------------------
//  PrintPageHeader     Start a new page of the list file and
//                      print the page header.
//---------------------------------------------------------------

void TListBuffer::PrintPageHeader(void)
{
    const char formFeedChar = '\f';

    cout << formFeedChar << "Page "  << ++pageNumber
         << "    " << pSourceFileName << "    " << date
         << endl  << endl;

    lineCount = 0;
}

//---------------------------------------------------------------
//  Initialize     Initialize the list buffer.  Set the date
//                 for the page header, and print the first
//                 header.
//
//      pFileName : ptr to source file name (for page header)
//---------------------------------------------------------------

void TListBuffer::Initialize(const char *pFileName)
{
    text[0]    = '\0';
    pageNumber = 0;

    //--Copy the input file name.
    pSourceFileName = new char[strlen(pFileName) + 1];
    strcpy(pSourceFileName, pFileName);

    //--Set the date.
    time_t timer;
    time(&timer);
    strcpy(date, asctime(localtime(&timer)));
    date[strlen(date) - 1] = '\0';  // remove '\n' at end

    PrintPageHeader();
}

//---------------------------------------------------------------
//  PutLine          Print a line of text to the list file.
//---------------------------------------------------------------
```

```
void TListBuffer::PutLine(void)
{
    //--Start a new page if the current one is full.
    if (listFlag && (lineCount == maxLinesPerPage)) PrintPageHeader();

    //--Truncate the line if it's too long.
    text[maxPrintLineLength] = '\0';

    //--Print the text line, and then blank out the text.
    cout << text << endl;
    text[0] = '\0';

    ++lineCount;
}
```

We begin by declaring several global variables, including `inputPosition`. This variable keeps track of the virtual position of the current character in the input text buffer. If the current source line contains no tab characters, then this position equals the array index of the current character. However, if there are tabs, then the position corresponds to the index as if each tab were expanded with the appropriate number of space characters. We'll see in a later chapter why we need to keep track of this position.

Constructor function `TTextInBuffer::TTextInBuffer` makes a copy of the source file name, and then opens the source file. Member function `TTextIn-Buffer::GetChar` fetches and returns the next character from the input buffer. At the end of the input file, it returns the special `eofChar`, and at the end of the current input line, it calls `GetLine` to read the next line. It also updates the pointer `pChar` and the global `inputPosition`.

Member function `TTextInBuffer::PutBackChar` backs up one character so that the current character will be fetched again by the next call to `GetChar`. It will only be called to put back a period character, so it doesn't need to be more general. (We'll see this happen in the next chapter when we scan numbers.)

Constructor function `TSourceBuffer::TSourceBuffer` is passed a pointer to the source file name, which it then passes to its base class's constructor function to open the file. If the open succeeds, the subclass constructor initializes the list buffer and reads the first source line. Member function `TSourceBuffer::GetLine` reads the next source line, and then calls the list buffer object's `PutLine` member function to print the line to the list file preceded by the line number and nesting level.

Note that before we implement the member functions of class `TListBuffer`, we declare the global list buffer object `list`.

Member function `TListBuffer::PrintPageHeader` prints the page header at the top of the next page. `TListBuffer::Initialize` initializes the data members and prints the first page header. Member function `TListBuffer::PutLine` (with no arguments) prints a line from the output buffer to the list file. It first checks to see if the current page is full, in which case it starts a new page by printing the page header.

The Abort Error Function

The constructor function `TSourceBuffer::TSourceBuffer` calls the error function `AbortTranslation`, which is the first of several functions we'll implement for the error module. Figure 2.5 shows the header file `error.h`, and Figure 2.6 shows the implementation file `error.cpp`.

■■■■■ **Figure 2.5** Header file **error.h**.

```
//    ****************************************************************
//    *                                                            *
//    *    E R R O R S    (Header)                                 *
//    *                                                            *
//    *    FILE:    prog2-1/error.h                                *
//    *                                                            *
//    *    MODULE:  Error                                          *
//    *                                                            *
//    *    Copyright (c) 1996 by Ronald Mak                        *
//    *    For instructional purposes only.  No warranties.        *
//    *                                                            *
//    ****************************************************************

#ifndef error_h
#define error_h

extern int errorCount;
```

```
//--------------------------------------------------------------
//  Abort codes for fatal translator errors.
//--------------------------------------------------------------

enum TAbortCode {
    abortInvalidCommandLineArgs     = -1,
    abortSourceFileOpenFailed       = -2,
    abortIFormFileOpenFailed        = -3,
    abortAssemblyFileOpenFailed     = -4,
    abortTooManySyntaxErrors        = -5,
    abortStackOverflow              = -6,
    abortCodeSegmentOverflow        = -7,
    abortNestingTooDeep             = -8,
    abortRuntimeError               = -9,
    abortUnimplementedFeature       = -10,
};

void AbortTranslation(TAbortCode ac);

#endif
```

■■■■■■■ **Figure 2.6** Implementation file **error.cpp**.

```
//    **************************************************************
//    *                                                            *
//    *    E R R O R S                                              *
//    *                                                            *
//    *    Routines to handle translation-time and runtime errors. *
//    *                                                            *
//    *    FILE:    prog2-1/error.cpp                               *
//    *                                                            *
//    *    MODULE:  Error                                          *
//    *                                                            *
//    *    Copyright (c) 1996 by Ronald Mak                        *
//    *    For instructional purposes only.  No warranties.        *
//    *                                                            *
//    **************************************************************

#include <stdlib.h>
#include <iostream.h>
#include "error.h"

int errorCount = 0;     // count of syntax errors

//--------------------------------------------------------------
//  Abort messages      Keyed to enumeration type TAbortCode.
//--------------------------------------------------------------
```

(continues)

■■■■■■■ **Figure 2.6** Implementation file **error.cpp**. (*Continued*)

```
static char *abortMsg[] = {
    NULL,
    "Invalid command line arguments",
    "Failed to open source file",
    "Failed to open intermediate form file",
    "Failed to open assembly file",
    "Too many syntax errors",
    "Stack overflow",
    "Code segment overflow",
    "Nesting too deep",
    "Runtime error",
    "Unimplemented feature",
};

//-------------------------------------------------------------
//  AbortTranslation      A fatal error occurred during the
//                        translation.  Print the abort code
//                        to the error file and then exit.
//
//      ac : abort code
//-------------------------------------------------------------

void AbortTranslation(TAbortCode ac)
{
    cerr << "*** Fatal translator error: " << abortMsg[-ac] << endl;
    exit(ac);
}
```

The Common Module

The object diagrams in the previous chapter showed the interface between the front and back ends consisting mostly of the symbol table and the intermediate code. The common module will contain parts of this interface. Figure 2.7 shows the header file common.h, and Figure 2.8 shows the implementation file common.cpp. As we develop the front and back ends in the rest of this book, we'll add to this module.

■■■■■■ **Figure 2.7** Header file **common.h**.

```
//  ************************************************************
//  *                                                          *
//  *   C O M M O N    (Header)                                *
```

```
// *                                                              *
// *   FILE:     prog2-1/common.h                                 *
// *                                                              *
// *   MODULE:  Common                                            *
// *                                                              *
// *   Copyright (c) 1996 by Ronald Mak                           *
// *   For instructional purposes only.  No warranties.           *
// *                                                              *
// ****************************************************************

#ifndef common_h
#define common_h

#include "misc.h"

extern int currentLineNumber;
extern int currentNestingLevel;

#endif
```

▆▆▆▆▆▆ **Figure 2.8** Implementation file **common.cpp**.

```
// ****************************************************************
// *                                                              *
// *   C O M M O N                                                *
// *                                                              *
// *   FILE:     prog2-1/common.cpp                               *
// *                                                              *
// *   MODULE:  Common                                            *
// *                                                              *
// *   Data and routines common to the front and back ends.       *
// *                                                              *
// *   Copyright (c) 1996 by Ronald Mak                           *
// *   For instructional purposes only.  No warranties.           *
// *                                                              *
// ****************************************************************

#include "common.h"

int currentNestingLevel = 0;
int currentLineNumber   = 0;
```

Figure 2.9 shows header file misc.h, in which we will place miscellaneous definitions needed by other header files.

■■■■■ **Figure 2.9** Header file **misc.h**.

```
// ****************************************************************
// *                                                              *
// *    M I S C E L L A N E O U S    (Header)                     *
// *                                                              *
// *    FILE:    prog2-1/misc.h                                   *
// *                                                              *
// *    MODULE:  Common                                           *
// *                                                              *
// *    Copyright (c) 1996 by Ronald Mak                          *
// *    For instructional purposes only.  No warranties.          *
// *                                                              *
// ****************************************************************

#ifndef misc_h
#define misc_h

const int false = 0;
const int true  = 1;

#endif
```

Program 2-1: Pascal Source Program Lister

Now we're ready to implement our first utility program, a Pascal source program lister. This program, shown in Figure 2.10, exercises the code we've written for the buffer module.

■■■■■ **Figure 2.10** The Pascal source program lister program in file **list.cpp**.

```
// ****************************************************************
// *                                                              *
// *    Program 2-1:  Source File Lister                          *
// *                                                              *
// *    Print the contents of the source file in a format that    *
// *    includes page headings, line numbers, and nesting         *
// *    levels.                                                    *
// *                                                              *
// *    FILE:   prog2-1/list.cpp                                  *
// *                                                              *
// *    USAGE:  list <source file>                                *
```

```
//  *                                                     *
//  *               <source file>  name of source file to list  *
//  *                                                     *
//  *    Copyright (c) 1996 by Ronald Mak                 *
//  *    For instructional purposes only.  No warranties.  *
//  *                                                     *
//  ********************************************************

#include <iostream.h>
#include "error.h"
#include "buffer.h"

//----------------------------------------------------------
//  main
//----------------------------------------------------------

void main(int argc, char *argv[])
{
    char ch;  // character fetched from source

    //--Check the command line arguments.
    if (argc != 2) {
        cerr << "Usage: list <source file>" << endl;
        AbortTranslation(abortInvalidCommandLineArgs);
    }

    //--Create source file buffer.
    TSourceBuffer source(argv[1]);

    //--Loop to fetch each character of the source.
    do {
        ch = source.GetChar();
    } while (ch != eofChar);
}
```

The `main` function validates the command line arguments and calls the error function `AbortTranslation` if there isn't exactly one argument (`argc` always has a value one greater than the number of command line arguments). It then creates the source buffer object, passing the source file name to the constructor function. Finally, `main` loops to send the `GetChar` message to the source buffer object until it reaches the end-of-file character. From the above class definitions, we know this will indeed produce a listing of the source program.

Table 2.1 below shows the modules and files that make up the Lister utility program. The **Directory** column shows where the original version of the file resides, assuming that we create a separate directory for each utility program's source files.

■■■■■■■■■ **Table 2.1** Modules and Files of Program 2-1

Module	File	Status	Directory
Main	list.cpp	*new*	prog2-1
Error	error.h	*new*	prog2-1
	error.cpp	*new*	prog2-1
Buffer	buffer.h	*new*	prog2-1
	buffer.cpp	*new*	prog2-1
Common	common.h	*new*	prog2-1
	common.cpp	*new*	prog2-1
	misc.h	*new*	prog2-1

In the next chapter, we'll see how the parser, scanner, and token objects work together to read and tokenize a source program.

CHAPTER 3

SCANNING

The scanner in the front end of a compiler or an interpreter reads the source program and breaks it apart into small units called tokens. Pascal's syntax defines the following tokens: identifiers, reserved words, numbers, strings, and special symbols (such as semicolons, parentheses, the arithmetic operators, etc.). In our implementation, the parser object requests the next token from the scanner object by sending it a `Get` message.

In this chapter, we'll write the front end's scanner module. We'll see how to:

- Extract word, number, string, and special symbol tokens from the source program text.

- Calculate the value of a number token and determine its type (integer or real).

- Determine which word tokens are identifiers and which are reserved words.

We'll also start the front end's parser module by writing several rudimentary parsers. This chapter makes use of the buffer and error modules that we wrote in the previous chapter. To test everything, we'll write three utility programs, including a handy Pascal source program compactor.

The object diagrams in Figures 1.4 and 1.5 showed the runtime interactions among the scanner object and the other front end objects. Whenever the parser object needs the next token from the source program, it sends a Get message to the scanner object.

Figure 3.1 shows a more detailed object diagram. We've replaced the single token object with several token objects for the different kinds of Pascal tokens. (We'll see later that the token objects are all instantiated from the subclasses of a base token class.)

Upon receiving a Get message from the parser object, the scanner object sends GetChar messages to the source buffer object until it has fetched the first character of the next token. (It may need to skip over one or more blanks between the previous token and the next one.) This character tells the scanner what kind of token is next (word, number, or string), so it can send a Get message to the appropriate

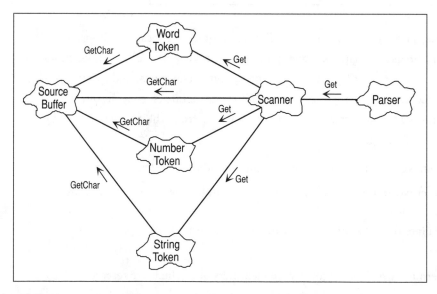

■■■■■ **Figure 3.1** A more detailed object diagram showing the scanner, parser, and multiple token objects.

token object. This token object sends `GetChar` messages to the source buffer object to fetch the rest of the token's characters. When the token object is done, the scanner returns a pointer to the token object to the parser.

How to Scan for Tokens

Scanning is the process of breaking some text apart into its constituent tokens. For example, we can scan the English sentence

```
They cried, "54-40 or fight!"
```

to obtain the tokens

word:	They
word:	cried
comma:	,
quotation mark:	"
number:	54
hyphen:	-
number:	40
word:	or
word:	fight
exclamation mark:	!
quotation mark:	"

Now how do we manage to do that? We visually scan the characters of the sentence from left to right. We know what kind of token we're about to get next from its first character: If it's a letter, we're getting a word, and if it's a digit, we're getting a number. If it's any other character, we're getting a special symbol. As soon as we've have seen enough characters to make up a valid token, we mentally extract it from the sentence. Each time we've extracted a token, we resume scanning the sentence from where we last left off.

The interpreter's scanner will work just like that. To see what is happening in greater detail, we begin with three simple tokens: word, number, and the period special symbol. Suppose we just read the line

```
Add 12 and 34.
```

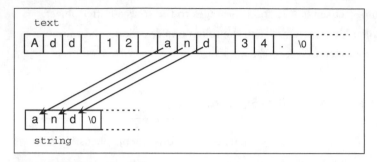

Figure 3.2 Extracting the word token **and** from **text** and placing its characters into **string**.

into the character array `text`. As shown in Figure 3.2, we want to extract each token in turn from `text` and place its characters into the initially empty character array `string`. Note how blanks separate some of the tokens from each other.

If the first character of the next token is a letter, we know that a word token is next. We fetch this first letter from text and put it into `string[0]`. In Pascal, a word such as an identifier begins with a letter, and subsequent characters of the token can be letters and digits. So one after another, we continue to fetch characters from `text`, appending each one to the contents of `string`, until we fetch a character that is neither a letter nor a digit. At that point, we stop and append a terminating null character to `string`. Then `string` contains the characters that make up the word token.

Similarly, if the first character of the next token is a digit, we know that a number token is next. The first digit goes into `string[0]`, and we continue to fetch subsequent characters from `text` and append them to `string` until we fetch a character that's not a digit. We stop, append a null character to `string`, and then `string` contains all the characters that make up the number token.

If the first character of the next token is a period, we just fetch that character, stuff it into `string[0]`, and append a null character. We must then fetch the next character from `text`. (We'll see why shortly.)

Each time we've finished extracting a token from `text`, we can process it in `string`. Afterwards, we can reset `string` to empty to prepare it for the next token.

As soon as we're done extracting a token, we have the first character after the token. (That's why we fetched the next character after a period.) It is this character that told us that we finished extracting the token. If the character is a blank, we skip it and any subsequent blanks until we're looking again at a nonblank character. This character is the start of the next token, which we extract the same way we extracted the previous one. We continue until we've extracted and processed all the tokens from text.

The basic steps to scanning are:

1. Skip any whitespace characters up to the next nonwhitespace character. This is the first character of the next token to extract, and it indicates what kind of token it is. A *whitespace character* is defined by Pascal to be a blank, a tab character, the end-of-line marker, or an entire comment.

2. Fetch characters of the token up to and including the first character that does not belong to that kind of token. You are done extracting the token.

3. Now you have the first character after the token. Process the token you have just extracted, then repeat these steps to extract the next token.

A Simple Scanner Module

The scanner module does all of the above, and more. We'll start with a simple version that we can test with this chapter's first utility program. Figure 3.3 shows the class diagram of the scanner and token classes.

We can think of a scanner as an object that supplies tokens—send it the `Get` message and it returns the next token. Then, Figures 1.4 and 1.5 each showed *two* scanner objects, the other one being the icode object. Send the `Get` message to the icode object and it returns the next token from the intermediate code. This prompts us to define a base `TScanner` class from which we derive a `TTextScanner` subclass. An object instantiated from `TTextScanner` returns tokens from text, such as the source program. We'll derive a `TICode` scanner subclass in the next chapter.

Figure 3.3 also shows the derivation of subclasses `TWordToken`, `TNumberToken`, and `TStringToken` from the abstract base class `TToken`. It also shows subclasses `TEOFToken` and `TErrorToken` that represent the end of the source input and an erroneous token, respectively.

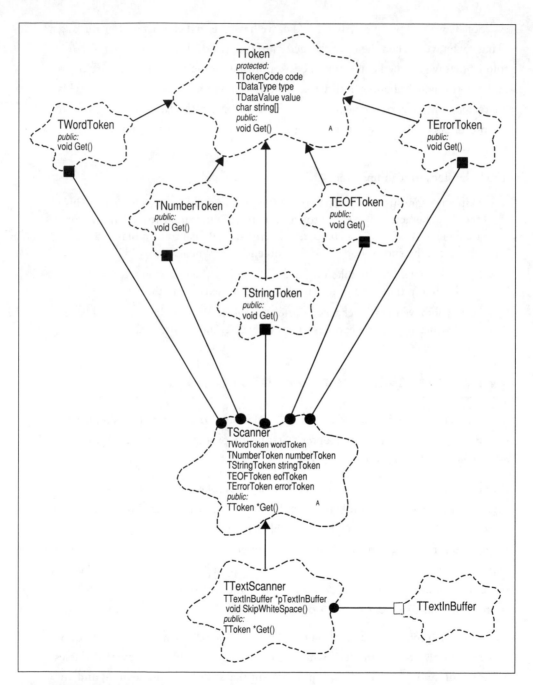

Figure 3.3   Class diagram of the scanner and token classes.

Base class `TScanner` has private `TWordToken`, `TNumberToken`, `TStringToken`, `TEofToken`, and `TErrorToken` class members. This means that any object instantiated from the subclass `TTextScanner` physically contains one of each kind of `TToken` object. In the class diagram, we show this by drawing a line between `TScanner` and each of the `TToken` subclasses. On each line, we place a solid circle at the container end (class `TScanner`) and a solid square at the containee end (a `TToken` subclass). Whenever a scanner object receives a `Get` message, it in turn sends a `Get` message to the appropriate token object that it contains (depending on what's next in the source program) to extract the token string from the source program. The scanner object then returns a pointer to that token object.

Subclass `TTextScanner` has a `TTextInBuffer` pointer data member—each text scanner object points to a text input buffer object. This is containment by reference, which we show in the class diagram with an open square at class `TTextInBuffer`. (Figure 2.2 showed a more complete diagram of class `TTextInBuffer`.) `TTextScanner` also has a private member function `SkipWhiteSpace`.

The abstract base `TToken` class has a protected `TTokenCode` data member `code`. In each token object, this data member indicates what kind of token the object represents. The protected `TDataType` data member `type` indicates the type (integer, real, etc.) of the token, and `TDataValue` data member `value` is its value. The protected data member `string` will contain the characters that make up the token.

Figure 3.4 shows the definitions of these and other new types in header file `misc.h`.

▆▆▆▆▆ **Figure 3.4** New type definitions in header file **misc.h**.

```
//----------------------------------------------------------------
//   TCharCode           Character codes.
//----------------------------------------------------------------

enum TCharCode {
    ccLetter, ccDigit, ccSpecial, ccQuote, ccWhiteSpace,
    ccEndOfFile, ccError,
};

//----------------------------------------------------------------
//   TTokenCode          Token codes.
//----------------------------------------------------------------

enum TTokenCode {
```

(continues)

■■■■■■■■■■■■ **Figure 3.4** New type definitions in header file **misc.h**. (*Continued*)

```
    tcDummy, tcWord, tcNumber, tcPeriod, tcEndOfFile, tcError,
};

//----------------------------------------------------------------
//  TDataType           Data type.
//----------------------------------------------------------------

enum TDataType {
    tyDummy, tyInteger, tyReal, tyCharacter, tyString,
};

//----------------------------------------------------------------
//  TDataValue          Data value.
//----------------------------------------------------------------

union TDataValue {
    int     integer;
    float   real;
    char    character;
    char    *pString;
};
```

The character codes `ccLetter` and `ccDigit` represent a letter and a digit, respectively. Code `ccQuote` represents the single-quote character while `tcWhiteSpace` represents any whitespace character. Code `ccSpecial` represents any other valid character. Code `ccEndOfFile` represents the end-of-file marker, and `ccError` represents any invalid character. The token codes `tcWord`, `tcNumber`, and `tcPeriod` represent the word (identifier or reserved word), number, and period tokens, respectively. Code `tcEndOfFile` represents the end of the file token, and code `tcError` represents any invalid token.

The Scanner Class TScanner

Figure 3.5 shows header file `scanner.h`, where we define the abstract base class `TScanner` and its subclass `TTextScanner`.

■■■■■■■■■■■■ **Figure 3.5** Header file **scanner.h**.

```
//  ****************************************************************
//  *                                                              *
//  *   S C A N N E R   (Header)                                   *
//  *                                                              *
//  *   CLASSES: TScanner, TTextScanner                            *
```

```
//  *                                                            *
//  *    FILE:     prog3-1/scanner.h                             *
//  *                                                            *
//  *    MODULE:   Scanner                                       *
//  *                                                            *
//  *    Copyright (c) 1996 by Ronald Mak                        *
//  *    For instructional purposes only.  No warranties.        *
//  *                                                            *
//  ***************************************************************

#ifndef scanner_h
#define scanner_h

#include "misc.h"
#include "buffer.h"
#include "token.h"

//----------------------------------------------------------------
// TScanner           Abstract scanner class.
//----------------------------------------------------------------

class TScanner {

protected:

    //--Tokens extracted and returned by the scanner.
    TWordToken     wordToken;
    TNumberToken   numberToken;
    TStringToken   stringToken;
    TSpecialToken  specialToken;
    TEOFToken      eofToken;
    TErrorToken    errorToken;

public:
    virtual ~TScanner(void) {}

    virtual TToken *Get(void) = 0;
};

//----------------------------------------------------------------
// TTextScanner       Text scanner subclass of TScanner.
//----------------------------------------------------------------

class TTextScanner : public TScanner {
    TTextInBuffer *const pTextInBuffer;  // ptr to input text buffer
                                         //   to scan
```

(continues)

■■■■■■ **Figure 3.5** Header file **scanner.h**. (*Continued*)

```
    void SkipWhiteSpace(void);

public:
    TTextScanner(TTextInBuffer *pBuffer);
    virtual ~TTextScanner(void) { delete pTextInBuffer; }

    virtual TToken *Get(void);
};

#endif
```

In the abstract base class TScanner, we define Get to be a pure virtual member function so that each subclass must define Get accordingly. In particular, subclass TTextScanner will define Get to extract tokens from the source program.

■■■■■■ **Figure 3.6** The initial version of implementation file **scanner.cpp**.

```
//  ************************************************************
//  *                                                        *
//  *    S C A N N E R                                        *
//  *                                                        *
//  *    Scan the text input file for the Simple Tokenizer    *
//  *    utility program.                                     *
//  *                                                        *
//  *    CLASSES: TTextScanner                               *
//  *                                                        *
//  *    FILE:    prog3-1/scanner.cpp                         *
//  *                                                        *
//  *    MODULE:  Scanner                                     *
//  *                                                        *
//  *    Copyright (c) 1996 by Ronald Mak                    *
//  *    For instructional purposes only.  No warranties.    *
//  *                                                        *
//  ************************************************************

#include "scanner.h"

TCharCode charCodeMap[128];  // maps a character to its code

//--------------------------------------------------------------
//  Constructor     Construct a scanner by constructing the
//                  text input file buffer and initializing the
//                  character code map.
//
```

```
//      pBuffer : text input buffer to scan
//---------------------------------------------------------------

TTextScanner::TTextScanner(TTextInBuffer *pBuffer)
    : pTextInBuffer(pBuffer)
{
    int i;

    //--Initialize the character code map.
    for (i = 0;   i <= 127; ++i) charCodeMap[i] = ccError;
    for (i = 'a'; i <= 'z'; ++i) charCodeMap[i] = ccLetter;
    for (i = 'A'; i <= 'Z'; ++i) charCodeMap[i] = ccLetter;
    for (i = '0'; i <= '9'; ++i) charCodeMap[i] = ccDigit;
    charCodeMap['+' ] = charCodeMap['-' ] = ccSpecial;
    charCodeMap['*' ] = charCodeMap['/' ] = ccSpecial;
    charCodeMap['=' ] = charCodeMap['^' ] = ccSpecial;
    charCodeMap['.' ] = charCodeMap[',' ] = ccSpecial;
    charCodeMap['<' ] = charCodeMap['>' ] = ccSpecial;
    charCodeMap['(' ] = charCodeMap[')' ] = ccSpecial;
    charCodeMap['[' ] = charCodeMap[']' ] = ccSpecial;
    charCodeMap['{' ] = charCodeMap['}' ] = ccSpecial;
    charCodeMap[':' ] = charCodeMap[';' ] = ccSpecial;
    charCodeMap[' ' ] = charCodeMap['\t'] = ccWhiteSpace;
    charCodeMap['\n'] = charCodeMap['\0'] = ccWhiteSpace;
    charCodeMap['\'']    = ccQuote;
    charCodeMap[eofChar] = ccEndOfFile;
}


//---------------------------------------------------------------
//  SkipWhiteSpace      Repeatedly fetch characters from the
//                      text input as long as they're
//                      whitespace.
//---------------------------------------------------------------

void TTextScanner::SkipWhiteSpace(void)
{
    char ch = pTextInBuffer->Char();

    while (charCodeMap[ch] == ccWhiteSpace) {
        ch = pTextInBuffer->GetChar();
    };
}


//---------------------------------------------------------------
//  Get         Extract the next token from the text input,
//              based on the current character.
```

(continues)

■■■■■■■ **Figure 3.6** The initial version of implementation file **scanner.cpp**.
(*Continued*)

```
//
//  Return: pointer to the extracted token
//-------------------------------------------------------------

TToken *TTextScanner::Get(void)
{
    TToken *pToken;  // ptr to token to return

    SkipWhiteSpace();

    //--Determine the token class, based on the current character.
    switch (charCodeMap[pTextInBuffer->Char()]) {
        case ccLetter:    pToken = &wordToken;     break;
        case ccDigit:     pToken = &numberToken;   break;
        case ccQuote:     pToken = &stringToken;   break;
        case ccSpecial:   pToken = &specialToken;  break;
        case ccEndOfFile: pToken = &eofToken;      break;
        default:          pToken = &errorToken;    break;
    }

    //--Extract a token of that class, and return a pointer to it.
    pToken->Get(*pTextInBuffer);
    return pToken;
}
```

We implement these classes in file scanner.cpp, whose initial version is shown in
Figure 3.6. The constructor function TTextScanner::TTextScanner is passed a
pointer to the text input buffer object so it can initialize data member pTextIn-
Buffer. It also initializes charCodeMap, a global array that maps a character to
its character code. The various cc character codes are from the enumeration type
TCharCode, which we saw earlier defined in header file common.h. First, the entire
map is set to ccError, and then selected elements are set to the various other character codes.

Member function TTextScanner::SkipWhiteSpace skips over any whitespace
characters by repeatedly sending the GetChar message to the text input buffer
object until it fetches a nonwhitespace character. (We'll handle comments later,
which are also whitespace.)

The important member function `TTextScanner::Get` extracts and returns a pointer to a token object. It first skips any whitespace characters, and then it sends the `Char` message to the text input object to examine the current (nonwhitespace) input character. This is the first character of the next token. Based on that character's code, the function sets `pToken` to point to the token object representing the appropriate kind of token. Of course, it must extract the rest of the token from the source file, so it sends the `Get` message to the token object, passing a pointer to the text input buffer object.

The Token Class TToken

The token class `TToken` represents the tokens that the scanner extracts and returns. As shown in Figure 3.7, we define it in header file `token.h` as an abstract base class, with a subclass for each kind of token. These are initial definitions; we'll see the complete definitions later.

▐▬▬▬▬▐ **Figure 3.7** The initial version of header file **token.h**.

```
//      ****************************************************************
//      *                                                            *
//      *    T O K E N S    (Header)                                 *
//      *                                                            *
//      *    CLASSES: TToken, TWordToken, TNumberToken,              *
//      *             TStringToken, TSpecialToken, TEOFToken,        *
//      *             TErrorToken                                    *
//      *                                                            *
//      *    FILE:    prog3-1/token.h                                *
//      *                                                            *
//      *    MODULE:  Scanner                                        *
//      *                                                            *
//      *    Copyright (c) 1996 by Ronald Mak                        *
//      *    For instructional purposes only.  No warranties.        *
//      *                                                            *
//      ****************************************************************

#ifndef token_h
#define token_h

#include "misc.h"
#include "error.h"
#include "buffer.h"

extern TCharCode charCodeMap[];
```

(continues)

Figure 3.7 The initial version of header file **token.h**. (*Continued*)

```
//----------------------------------------------------------------
//   TToken                Abstract token class.
//----------------------------------------------------------------

class TToken {

protected:
    TTokenCode  code;
    TDataType   type;
    TDataValue  value;
    char        string[maxInputBufferSize];

public:
    TToken(void)
    {
        code = tcDummy;
        type = tyDummy;
        value.integer = 0;
        string[0]     = '\0';
    }

    TTokenCode  Code()   const { return code;   }
    TDataType   Type()   const { return type;   }
    TDataValue  Value()  const { return value;  }
    char        *String()      { return string; }

    virtual void Get(TTextInBuffer &buffer) = 0;
    virtual void Print(void) const = 0;
};


//----------------------------------------------------------------
//   TWordToken           Word token subclass of TToken.
//----------------------------------------------------------------

class TWordToken : public TToken {

public:
    virtual void Get(TTextInBuffer &buffer);
    virtual void Print(void) const;
};


//----------------------------------------------------------------
//   TNumberToken         Number token subclass of TToken.
//----------------------------------------------------------------
```

```
class TNumberToken : public TToken {

public:
    TNumberToken(void) { code = tcNumber; }

    virtual void Get(TTextInBuffer &buffer);
    virtual void Print(void) const;
};

//-------------------------------------------------------------
//  TStringToken          String token subclass of TToken.
//-------------------------------------------------------------

class TStringToken : public TToken {

public:
    virtual void Get(TTextInBuffer &buffer) {}
    virtual void Print(void) const {}
};

//-------------------------------------------------------------
//  TSpecialToken          Special token subclass of TToken.
//-------------------------------------------------------------

class TSpecialToken : public TToken {

public:
    virtual void Get(TTextInBuffer &buffer);
    virtual void Print(void) const;
};

//-------------------------------------------------------------
//  TEOFToken          End-of-file token subclass of TToken.
//-------------------------------------------------------------

class TEOFToken : public TToken {

public:
    TEOFToken(void) { code = tcEndOfFile; }

    virtual void Get(TTextInBuffer &buffer) {}
    virtual void Print(void) const {}
};

//-------------------------------------------------------------
//  TErrorToken          Error token subclass of TToken.
//-------------------------------------------------------------
```

(continues)

■■■■■■■ **Figure 3.7** The initial version of header file **token.h**. (*Continued*)

```cpp
class TErrorToken : public TToken {

public:
    TErrorToken(void) { code = tcError; }

    virtual void Get(TTextInBuffer &buffer);
    virtual void Print(void) const {}
};

#endif
```

As we saw in the class diagram, the protected data members of the abstract base class TToken are code, type, value, and string. The constructor function initializes these data members, and the public member functions Code, Type, Value, and String return their values. We've seen public member function Get in the object diagrams. It receives a reference to the text input buffer object from which it will extract the tokens. In the base class, it is a pure virtual member function. The other pure public member function, Print, will be redefined in each subclass to print its token in an appropriate format.

Subclasses TWordToken, TNumberToken, TStringToken, TSpecialToken, and TEOFToken represent the different kinds of tokens. Each redefines the virtual public member functions Get and Print.

■■■■■■■ **Figure 3.8** The initial version of implementation file **token.cpp**.

```cpp
//  *************************************************************
//  *                                                          *
//  *    T O K E N S                                           *
//  *                                                          *
//  *    Extract simple word, short integer, and period tokens *
//  *    from the source file for the Simple Tokenizer utility *
//  *    program.                                              *
//  *                                                          *
//  *    CLASSES: TToken, TWordToken, TNumberToken,            *
//  *             TStringToken, TSpecialToken, TEOFToken,      *
//  *             TErrorToken                                  *
//  *                                                          *
//  *    FILE:    prog3-1/token.cpp                            *
//  *                                                          *
//  *    MODULE:  Scanner                                      *
```

```
//  *                                                    *
//  *    Copyright (c) 1996 by Ronald Mak                *
//  *    For instructional purposes only.  No warranties. *
//  *                                                    *
//  ********************************************************

#include <stdio.h>
#include <string.h>
#include "token.h"

//            ****************
//            *              *
//            *  Word Tokens *
//            *              *
//            ****************

//------------------------------------------------------------
// Get         Extract a word token from the source and down-
//             shift its characters.  Check if it's a reserved
//             word.
//
//     buffer : ref to text input buffer
//------------------------------------------------------------

void TWordToken::Get(TTextInBuffer &buffer)
{
    char  ch = buffer.Char();  // char fetched from input
    char *ps = string;

    //--Extract the word.
    do {
        *ps++ = ch;
        ch = buffer.GetChar();
    } while (   (charCodeMap[ch] == ccLetter)
             || (charCodeMap[ch] == ccDigit));

    *ps = '\0';
    strlwr(string);            // downshift its characters
    code = tcWord;
}

//------------------------------------------------------------
// Print       Print the token to the list file.
//------------------------------------------------------------

void TWordToken::Print(void) const
```

(continues)

■■■■■■■ **Figure 3.8** The initial version of implementation file **token.cpp**. (*Continued*)

```cpp
{
    sprintf(list.text, "\t%-18s %-s", ">> word:",
                        string);
    list.PutLine();
}


//                  *******************
//                  *                 *
//                  *  Number Tokens  *
//                  *                 *
//                  *******************


//----------------------------------------------------------------
//  Get         Extract a number token from the source and set
//              its value.
//
//      pBuffer : ptr to text input buffer
//----------------------------------------------------------------

void TNumberToken::Get(TTextInBuffer &buffer)
{
    const int maxDigitCount = 4;

    char  ch = buffer.Char();       // char fetched from input
    char *ps = string;
    int   digitCount     = 0;
    int   countErrorFlag = false;  // true if too many digits,
                                   //    else false

    //--Accumulate the value as long as the total allowable
    //--number of digits has not been exceeded.
    value.integer = 0;
    do {
        *ps++ = ch;

        //--Shift left and add.
        if (++digitCount <= maxDigitCount) {
            value.integer = 10*value.integer + (ch - '0');
        }
        else countErrorFlag = true;  // too many digits

        ch = buffer.GetChar();
    } while (charCodeMap[ch] == ccDigit);

    *ps  = '\0';
```

```
        code = countErrorFlag ? tcError : tcNumber;
    }


    //----------------------------------------------------------------
    //  Print        Print the token to the list file.
    //----------------------------------------------------------------

    void TNumberToken::Print(void) const
    {
        sprintf(list.text, "\t%-18s =%d", ">> number:", value.integer);
        list.PutLine();
    }


    //                    *******************
    //                    *                 *
    //                    *  Special Tokens *
    //                    *                 *
    //                    *******************


    //----------------------------------------------------------------
    //  Get         Extract the period special symbol token from the
    //              source.
    //
    //      pBuffer : ptr to text input buffer
    //----------------------------------------------------------------

    void TSpecialToken::Get(TTextInBuffer &buffer)
    {
        char  ch = buffer.Char();
        char *ps = string;

        *ps++ = ch;
        *ps = '\0';
        buffer.GetChar();

        code = (ch == '.') ? tcPeriod : tcError;
    }


    //----------------------------------------------------------------
    //  Print        Print the token to the list file.
    //----------------------------------------------------------------

    void TSpecialToken::Print(void) const
    {
        sprintf(list.text, "\t%-18s %-s", ">> special:", string);
        list.PutLine();
    }
```

(*continues*)

Figure 3.8 The initial version of implementation file **token.cpp**. (*Continued*)

```
//                ******************
//                *                *
//                *  Error Token   *
//                *                *
//                ******************


//------------------------------------------------------------
// Get          Extract an invalid character from the source.
//
//      pBuffer : ptr to text input buffer
//------------------------------------------------------------

void TErrorToken::Get(TTextInBuffer &buffer)
{
    string[0] = buffer.Char();
    string[1] = '\0';
    buffer.GetChar();
}
```

Figure 3.8 shows file token.cpp, which implements the initial versions of the definitions of the token classes. Each token subclass implements its own version of the public Get and Print member functions. The Print functions are useful for some of our utility programs. They print the kind of token to the list file, followed by either the token string, or for number tokens, the = character and then the number's value.

Member function TWordToken::Get extracts a word token. It first stuffs the initial letter into string[0], and then it fetches letters and digits from the text input buffer object and appends them to string. It downshifts all the letters in the word (we'll see why later) and sets data member code to tcWord.

Member function TNumberToken::Get fetches digits and appends them to string. The function also accumulates the value of the number digit by digit in data member value. We see how this is done below with the sample number token 486:

```
    value:   0
      ch:    4
    value:   10*0 + 4 = 4
```

```
   ch:   8
value:   10*4 + 8 = 48
   ch:   6
value:   10*48 + 6 = 486
```

As we fetch each digit character, we multiply `value` by ten and add the value of the digit character. We obtain the character's value by subtracting `'0'`, which works because the ASCII values for `'0'` through `'9'` are contiguous.

To guard against overflow, `TNumberToken::Get` imposes a limit of four digits—digits after the fourth one are not included in the value, and `code` is set to `tcError`. (Of course, in the full scanner, we'll allow a much greater range of values, including reals.) Otherwise, it sets `code` to `tcNumber`.

For now, member function `TSpecialToken::Get` can only extract and return the period token. If it sees any other character, it sets the token code to `tcError`, otherwise to `tcPeriod`.

A Simple Parser Module

For our simple scanner module, we'll write an equally simple parser module. Figure 3.9 shows a class diagram for class `TParser`.

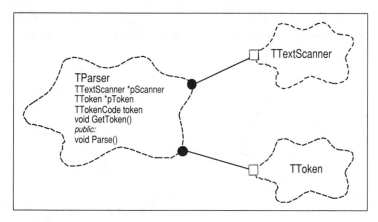

▮▮▮▮▮▮▮ **Figure 3.9** Class diagram for class **TParser**.

Class TParser has three private data members: pScanner and pToken point to
TTextScanner and TToken objects, respectively, and token is of type TToken-
Code. Therefore, a parser object points to its scanner object and to the current
token object. Private member function GetToken will get the current token from
the scanner. Public member function Parse enables us to send a message to the
parser object to tell it to start parsing.

Figure 3.10 shows implementation file parser.h, which contains the initial version
of the definition of class TParser.

■■■■■ **Figure 3.10** The initial version of header file **parser.h**.

```
//    ****************************************************************
//    *                                                              *
//    *     P A R S E R     (Header)                                 *
//    *                                                              *
//    *     CLASSES: TParser                                         *
//    *                                                              *
//    *     FILE:    prog3-1/parser.h                                *
//    *                                                              *
//    *     MODULE:  Parser                                          *
//    *                                                              *
//    *     Copyright (c) 1996 by Ronald Mak                         *
//    *     For instructional purposes only.  No warranties.         *
//    *                                                              *
//    ****************************************************************

#ifndef parser_h
#define parser_h

#include "misc.h"
#include "buffer.h"
#include "token.h"
#include "scanner.h"


//--------------------------------------------------------------
//  TParser      Parser class.
//--------------------------------------------------------------

class TParser {
    TTextScanner *const pScanner;   // ptr to the scanner
    TToken       *pToken;           // ptr to the current token
    TTokenCode    token;            // code of current token

    void GetToken(void)
```

```
    {
        pToken = pScanner->Get();
        token  = pToken->Code();
    }

public:
    TParser(TTextInBuffer *pBuffer)
        : pScanner(new TTextScanner(pBuffer)) {}

    ~TParser(void) { delete pScanner; }

    void Parse(void);
};

#endif
```

Private member function GetToken sends a Get message to the scanner object and sets private data member pToken. It also sets private data member token to the kind of token just returned by the scanner, that is, the current token.

The constructor function receives a pointer to a text input buffer object, and it creates the scanner object by passing this pointer to class TTextScanner's constructor function. (Review TTextScanner::TTextScanner in Figure 3.6.) The destructor function deletes the scanner object. Public member function Parse is the main entry point into the parser module.

████████ **Figure 3.11** The initial version of implementation file **parser.cpp**.

```
//  *****************************************************************
//  *                                                               *
//  *    P A R S E R                                                 *
//  *                                                               *
//  *    Parse the source file for the Simple Tokenizer             *
//  *    utility program.                                           *
//  *                                                               *
//  *    CLASSES: TParser                                           *
//  *                                                               *
//  *    FILE:    prog3-1/parser.cpp                                *
//  *                                                               *
//  *    MODULE:  Parser                                            *
//  *                                                               *
//  *    Copyright (c) 1996 by Ronald Mak                           *
//  *    For instructional purposes only.  No warranties.           *
//  *                                                               *
//  *****************************************************************
```

(continues)

(*Continued*)

```cpp
#include <stdio.h>
#include "common.h"
#include "buffer.h"
#include "error.h"
#include "parser.h"


//-----------------------------------------------------------
//  Parse        Parse the source file.  After listing each
//               source line, extract and list its tokens.
//-----------------------------------------------------------

void TParser::Parse(void)
{
    //--Loop to extract and print tokens
    //--until the end of the source file.
    do {
        GetToken();

        if (token != tcError) pToken->Print();
        else {
            sprintf(list.text, "\t%-18s %-s", ">> *** ERROR ***",
                                pToken->String());
            list.PutLine();
            ++errorCount;
        }
    } while (token != tcEndOfFile);

    //--Print the parser's summary.
    list.PutLine();
    sprintf(list.text, "%20d source lines.",  currentLineNumber);
    list.PutLine();
    sprintf(list.text, "%20d syntax errors.", errorCount);
    list.PutLine();
}
```

Figure 3.11 shows the initial version of implementation file parser.cpp. Member function Parse repeatedly calls GetToken to extract tokens from the source program until the end of the file. It sends the Print message to each valid token object, and for an invalid token, it prints an error message. After processing all the tokens, it prints a summary to the global list file.

▰▰▰▰▰ **Table 3.1** Modules and Files of Program 3-1

Module	File	Status	Directory
Main	tokeniz1.cpp	*new*	prog3-1
Parser	parser.h	*new*	prog3-1
	parser.cpp	*new*	prog3-1
Scanner	scanner.h	*new*	prog3-1
	scanner.cpp	*new*	prog3-1
	token.h	*new*	prog3-1
	token.cpp	*new*	prog3-1
Error	error.h	*unchanged*	prog2-1
	error.cpp	*unchanged*	prog2-1
Buffer	buffer.h	*unchanged*	prog2-1
	buffer.cpp	*unchanged*	prog2-1
Common	common.h	*unchanged*	prog2-1
	common.cpp	*unchanged*	prog2-1
	misc.h	*changed*	prog3-1

Program 3-1: Simple Tokenizer

Let's now look at this chapter's first utility program, which tests the initial version of our scanner. A *tokenizer* is a utility that reads a source program and prints the program's tokens. Our first version can only handle word, number, period, and end-of-file tokens. Table 3.1 indicates which frontend source files are unchanged from the previous program, are modified, or are new.

▰▰▰▰▰ **Figure 3.12** The main file **tokeniz1.cpp** of the Simple Tokenizer utility program.

```
//  *************************************************************
//  *                                                           *
//  *    Program 3-1:  Simple Tokenizer                         *
//  *                                                           *
//  *    List the source file.  After each line, list the       *
//  *    simple word, small integer, and period tokens that     *
//  *    were extracted from that line.                         *
```

(continues)

■■■■■■■ **Figure 3.12** The main file **tokeniz1.cpp** of the Simple Tokenizer utility
program. (*Continued*)

```
//  *                                                              *
//  *    FILE:    prog3-1/tokeniz1.cpp                             *
//  *                                                              *
//  *    USAGE:   tokeniz1 <source file>                           *
//  *                                                              *
//  *                 <source file>  name of source file to       *
//  *                                tokenize                      *
//  *                                                              *
//  *    Copyright (c) 1996 by Ronald Mak                          *
//  *    For instructional purposes only.  No warranties.          *
//  *                                                              *
//  ************************************************************

#include "error.h"
#include "buffer.h"
#include "parser.h"

//-------------------------------------------------------------
//  main
//-------------------------------------------------------------

void main(int argc, char *argv[])
{
    //--Check the command line arguments.
    if (argc != 2) {
        cerr << "Usage: tokeniz1 <source file>" << endl;
        AbortTranslation(abortInvalidCommandLineArgs);
    }

    //--Create the parser for the source file,
    //--and then parse the file.
    TParser parser(new TSourceBuffer(argv[1]));
    parser.Parse();
}
```

Figure 3.12 shows the main file `tokeniz1.cpp` of the Simple Tokenizer utility.
After validating the command line arguments, `main` creates a new source buffer
object with a pointer to the source file name. It then uses the source buffer object to
create a new parser object. It sends the `Parse` message to the parser object to start
parsing the source file.

Figure 3.13 shows the output from some sample input lines. Note that the *values* of the number tokens 2345 and 7890 are printed, and that 11346 is an error because it is too long (over four digits). The + character is also an error because our simple scanner can only handle the period special symbol.

▬▬▬▬ **Figure 3.13** Sample output from the Simple Tokenizer utility program.

```
Page 1    tokeniz1.in   Sun Oct 08 20:10:12 1995

   1 0: The sum of 3456
        >> word:         the
        >> word:         sum
        >> word:         of
        >> number:       =3456
   2 0: + 7890 is 11346.
        >> *** ERROR ***  +
        >> number:       =7890
        >> word:         is
        >> *** ERROR ***  11346
        >> special:       .
   3 0:

                 3 source lines.
                 2 syntax errors.
```

The Complete Scanner Module

Now that the Simple Tokenizer utility has shown how the various objects that make up a scanner work together, we're ready to write the complete Pascal scanner. This scanner will recognize all valid identifiers, reserved words, numbers (integer and real), and every one- and two-character special symbol. It will also treat each comment as a whitespace character. The second utility program of this chapter, Pascal Tokenizer, will test our modifications to the scanner module.

▬▬▬▬ **Figure 3.14** The complete list of token codes in header file **misc.h**.

```
//-------------------------------------------------------------
//  TTokenCode        Token codes.
//-------------------------------------------------------------

enum TTokenCode {
    tcDummy,
```

(continues)

■■■■■■■■ **Figure 3.14** The complete list of token codes in header file **misc.h**.
(*Continued*)

```
    tcIdentifier, tcNumber, tcString, tcEndOfFile, tcError,

    tcUpArrow, tcStar, tcLParen, tcRParen, tcMinus, tcPlus,
    tcEqual, tcLBracket, tcRBracket, tcColon, tcSemicolon, tcLt,
    tcGt, tcComma, tcPeriod, tcSlash, tcColonEqual, tcLe, tcGe,
    tcNe, tcDotDot,

    tcAND, tcARRAY, tcBEGIN, tcCASE, tcCONST, tcDIV,
    tcDO, tcDOWNTO, tcELSE, tcEND, tcFILE, tcFOR, tcFUNCTION,
    tcGOTO, tcIF, tcIN, tcLABEL, tcMOD, tcNIL, tcNOT, tcOF, tcOR,
    tcPACKED, tcPROCEDURE, tcPROGRAM, tcRECORD, tcREPEAT, tcSET,
    tcTHEN, tcTO, tcTYPE, tcUNTIL, tcVAR, tcWHILE, tcWITH,
};
```

Figure 3.14 shows the complete list of token codes in header file misc.h, which
replaces the shortened list we used earlier. This list includes all the special symbol
and reserved word tokens.

■■■■■■■■ **Figure 3.15** A more complete version of header file **token.h**.

```
//    ************************************************************
//    *                                                          *
//    *    T O K E N S    (Header)                                *
//    *                                                          *
//    *    CLASSES: TToken, TWordToken, TNumberToken,            *
//    *             TStringToken, TSpecialToken, TEOFToken,      *
//    *             TErrorToken                                  *
//    *                                                          *
//    *    FILE:    prog3-2/token.h                              *
//    *                                                          *
//    *    MODULE:  Scanner                                      *
//    *                                                          *
//    *    Copyright (c) 1996 by Ronald Mak                      *
//    *    For instructional purposes only.  No warranties.      *
//    *                                                          *
//    ************************************************************

#ifndef token_h
#define token_h

#include "misc.h"
#include "error.h"
#include "buffer.h"
```

```
extern TCharCode charCodeMap[];

//-------------------------------------------------------------
//  TToken              Abstract token class.
//-------------------------------------------------------------

class TToken {

protected:
    TTokenCode code;
    TDataType  type;
    TDataValue value;
    char       string[maxInputBufferSize];

public:
    TToken(void)
    {
        code = tcDummy;
        type = tyDummy;
        value.integer = 0;
        string[0]     = '\0';
    }

    TTokenCode  Code()   const { return code;   }
    TDataType   Type()   const { return type;   }
    TDataValue  Value()  const { return value;  }
    char        *String()      { return string; }

    virtual void Get(TTextInBuffer &buffer) = 0;
    virtual int  IsDelimiter(void) const = 0;
    virtual void Print       (void) const = 0;
};

//-------------------------------------------------------------
//  TWordToken           Word token subclass of TToken.
//-------------------------------------------------------------

class TWordToken : public TToken {
    void CheckForReservedWord(void);

public:
    virtual void Get(TTextInBuffer &buffer);
    virtual int  IsDelimiter(void) const { return false; }
    virtual void Print       (void) const;
};
```

(continues)

■■■■■ Figure 3.15 A more complete version of header file **token.h**. (*Continued*)

```
//----------------------------------------------------------------
//  TNumberToken         Number token subclass of TToken.
//----------------------------------------------------------------

class TNumberToken : public TToken {
    char   ch;              // char fetched from input buffer
    char  *ps;              // ptr into token string
    int    digitCount;      // total no. of digits in number
    int    countErrorFlag;  // true if too many digits, else false

    int AccumulateValue(TTextInBuffer &buffer,
                        float &value, TErrorCode ec);

public:
    TNumberToken() { code = tcNumber; }

    virtual void Get(TTextInBuffer &buffer);
    virtual int  IsDelimiter(void) const { return false; }
    virtual void Print      (void) const;
};

//----------------------------------------------------------------
//  TStringToken         String token subclass of TToken.
//----------------------------------------------------------------

class TStringToken : public TToken {

public:
    TStringToken() { code = tcString; }

    virtual void Get(TTextInBuffer &buffer);
    virtual int  IsDelimiter(void) const { return true; }
    virtual void Print      (void) const;
};

//----------------------------------------------------------------
//  TSpecialToken        Special token subclass of TToken.
//----------------------------------------------------------------

class TSpecialToken : public TToken {

public:
    virtual void Get(TTextInBuffer &buffer);
```

```
    virtual int  IsDelimiter(void) const { return true; }
    virtual void Print      (void) const;
};


//-------------------------------------------------------------
//   TEOFToken           End-of-file token subclass of TToken.
//-------------------------------------------------------------

class TEOFToken : public TToken {

public:
    TEOFToken() { code = tcEndOfFile; }

    virtual void Get(TTextInBuffer &buffer) {}
    virtual int  IsDelimiter(void) const { return false; }
    virtual void Print      (void) const {}
};

//-------------------------------------------------------------
//   TErrorToken         Error token subclass of TToken.
//-------------------------------------------------------------

class TErrorToken : public TToken {

public:
    TErrorToken() { code = tcError; }

    virtual void Get(TTextInBuffer &buffer);
    virtual int  IsDelimiter(void) const { return false; }
    virtual void Print      (void) const {}
};

#endif
```

Figure 3.15 shows a more complete version of header file token.h. The abstract base class TToken has a new public virtual member function IsDelimiter, which is defined by each of the subclasses. We'll discuss later what it means for a token to be a delimiter.

Subclass TWordToken has a new private member function CheckForReserved-Word that distinguishes reserved words from identifiers. Subclass TNumberToken has several new private data members and a private member function Accumulate-Value. We'll examine each of the token subclasses below.

Comments

Pascal's syntax rules state that each comment is to be treated as a whitespace character. Figure 3.16 shows the complete version of member function `TTextScan-`
`ner::SkipWhiteSpace` in file `scanner.cpp`. As it does with the other
whitespace characters, it skips comments. If the function sees a { character, it fetches
characters until it has fetched the first character after the corresponding } character.

■■■■■■■ **Figure 3.16** New version of function **SkipWhiteSpace** in file **scanner.cpp**.

```
//-------------------------------------------------------------
//   SkipWhiteSpace        Repeatedly fetch characters from the
//                         text input as long as they're
//                         whitespace. Each comment is a whitespace
//                         character.
//-------------------------------------------------------------

void TTextScanner::SkipWhiteSpace(void)
{
    char ch = pTextInBuffer->Char();

    do {
        if (charCodeMap[ch] == ccWhiteSpace) {

            //--Saw a whitespace character:  fetch the next character.
            ch = pTextInBuffer->GetChar();
        }
        else if (ch == '{') {

            //--Skip over a comment, then fetch the next character.
            do {
                ch = pTextInBuffer->GetChar();
            } while ((ch != '}') && (ch != eofChar));
            if (ch != eofChar) ch = pTextInBuffer->GetChar();
            else               Error(errUnexpectedEndOfFile);
        }
    } while ((charCodeMap[ch] == ccWhiteSpace) || (ch == '{'));
}
```

With this change, the Pascal tokenizer reads the input lines:

```
{This is a comment
 that spans two lines.}

Two{comments in}{a row}here.
```

and produces the output

```
1 0: {This is a comment
2 0:  that spans two lines.}
3 0:
4 0: Two{comments in}{a row}here.
         >> identifier:     two
         >> identifier:     here
         >> special:        .
```

The Word Token Subclass TWordToken

Pascal word tokens can be either identifiers or reserved words. We'll use a simple technique to distinguish an identifier from a reserved word. Once we have a word token, we'll check it against a list of reserved words. If it's in the list, the token is a reserved word; if it's not in the list, the token must be an identifier.

Figure 3.17 shows the new file `tknword.cpp`, which implements word tokens. We begin with lists of reserved word strings and corresponding token codes, one list per string length. Array `rwTable` collects all the lists so that they are indexed by string length. This will help make searching for a reserved word faster. For example, `rwTable[5]` is the list of all the five-letter reserved words and their token codes.

▌▌▌▌▌▌ **Figure 3.17** Implementation file **tknword.cpp** for word tokens.

```
//  *************************************************************
//  *                                                           *
//  *     T O K E N S    (Words)                                *
//  *                                                           *
//  *     Extract word tokens from the source file.             *
//  *                                                           *
//  *     CLASSES: TWordToken                                   *
//  *                                                           *
//  *     FILE:    prog3-2/tknword.cpp                          *
//  *                                                           *
//  *     MODULE:  Scanner                                      *
//  *                                                           *
//  *     Copyright (c) 1996 by Ronald Mak                      *
//  *     For instructional purposes only.  No warranties.      *
//  *                                                           *
//  *************************************************************

#include <string.h>
#include <stdio.h>
```

(continues)

```cpp
#include "token.h"

//              *************************
//              *                       *
//              *   Reserved Word Table  *
//              *                       *
//              *************************

const int minResWordLen = 2;    // min and max reserved
const int maxResWordLen = 9;    //   word lengths

//--------------------------------------------------------------
//  Reserved word lists (according to word length)
//--------------------------------------------------------------

struct TResWord {
    char        *pString;  // ptr to word string
    TTokenCode  code;      // word code
};

static TResWord rw2[] = {
    {"do", tcDO}, {"if", tcIF}, {"in", tcIN}, {"of", tcOF},
    {"or", tcOR}, {"to", tcTO}, {NULL},
};

static TResWord rw3[] = {
    {"and", tcAND}, {"div", tcDIV}, {"end", tcEND}, {"for", tcFOR},
    {"mod", tcMOD}, {"nil", tcNIL}, {"not", tcNOT}, {"set", tcSET},
    {"var", tcVAR}, {NULL},
};

static TResWord rw4[] = {
    {"case", tcCASE}, {"else", tcELSE}, {"file", tcFILE},
    {"goto", tcGOTO}, {"then", tcTHEN}, {"type", tcTYPE},
    {"with", tcWITH}, {NULL},
};

static TResWord rw5[] = {
    {"array", tcARRAY}, {"begin", tcBEGIN}, {"const", tcCONST},
    {"label", tcLABEL}, {"until", tcUNTIL}, {"while", tcWHILE},
    {NULL},
};

static TResWord rw6[] = {
```

```
    {"downto", tcDOWNTO}, {"packed", tcPACKED}, {"record", tcRECORD},
    {"repeat", tcREPEAT}, {NULL},
};

static TResWord rw7[] = {
    {"program", tcPROGRAM}, {NULL},
};

static TResWord rw8[] = {
    {"function", tcFUNCTION}, {NULL},
};

static TResWord rw9[] = {
    {"procedure", tcPROCEDURE}, {NULL},
};

//-------------------------------------------------------------
//  The reserved word table
//-------------------------------------------------------------

static TResWord *rwTable[] = {
    NULL, NULL, rw2, rw3, rw4, rw5, rw6, rw7, rw8, rw9,
};

//              ****************
//              *              *
//              *  Word Tokens  *
//              *              *
//              ****************

//-------------------------------------------------------------
//  Get     Extract a word token from the source and downshift
//          its characters.  Check if it's a reserved word.
//
//      pBuffer : ptr to text input buffer
//-------------------------------------------------------------

void TWordToken::Get(TTextInBuffer &buffer)
{
    extern TCharCode charCodeMap[];

    char  ch = buffer.Char();  // char fetched from input
    char *ps = string;

    //--Get the word.
    do {
```

(continues)

■■■■■■■■■ **Figure 3.17** Implementation file **tknword.cpp** for word tokens. (*Continued*)

```
            *ps++ = ch;
            ch = buffer.GetChar();
    } while (   (charCodeMap[ch] == ccLetter)
             || (charCodeMap[ch] == ccDigit));

    *ps = '\0';
    strlwr(string);         // downshift its characters

    CheckForReservedWord();
}

//------------------------------------------------------------
//  CheckForReservedWord     Is the word token a reserved word?
//                           If yes, set the its token code to
//                           the appropriate code.  If not, set
//                           the token code to tcIdentifier.
//------------------------------------------------------------

void TWordToken::CheckForReservedWord(void)
{
    int      len = strlen(string);
    TResWord *prw;          // ptr to elmt of reserved word table

    code = tcIdentifier;  // first assume it's an identifier

    //--Is it the right length?
    if ((len >= minResWordLen) && (len <= maxResWordLen)) {

        //--Yes.  Use the word length to pick the appropriate list
        //--from the reserved word table and check to see if the word
        //--is in there.
        for (prw = rwTable[len]; prw->pString; ++prw) {
            if (strcmp(string, prw->pString) == 0) {
                code = prw->code;  // yes: set reserved word token code
                break;
            }
        }
    }
}

//------------------------------------------------------------
//  Print       Print the token to the list file.
//------------------------------------------------------------
```

```
void TWordToken::Print(void) const
{
    if (code == tcIdentifier) {
        sprintf(list.text, "\t%-18s %-s", ">> identifier:", string);
    }
    else {
        sprintf(list.text, "\t%-18s %-s", ">> reserved word:", string);
    }

    list.PutLine();
}
```

Pascal ignores case in its word tokens. The scanner must recognize all of the following to be same identifier:

```
    lastname    LASTNAME   LastName    lastName
```

and all of the following to be the same reserved word:

```
    begin   BEGIN   Begin   BeGiN
```

We have a simple solution to this problem. We always downshift the letters of a word token, so we can then reliably and efficiently compare them against a list of lowercase reserved words.

Public member function `TWordToken::Get` now calls function `CheckForReservedWord`, which checks the newly extracted word against the appropriate reserved word list. If the word is reserved, data member `code` is set to the reserved word token code. Otherwise, the word is an identifier, and `code` is set to `tcIdentifier`.

The Number Token Subclass TNumberToken

The value of a Pascal number token can be either integer or real. It takes a bit more work for the scanner to calculate the value of a real number token. The token string contains a decimal point or the exponent marker E or e, and there may be a decimal fraction or an exponent, or both. This is all handled in the new implementation file `tknnum.cpp`, shown in Figure 3.18.

■■■■■■■■ **Figure 3.18** Implementation file **tknnum.cpp** for number tokens.

```
//    ************************************************************
//    *                                                          *
//    *    T O K E N S    (Numbers)                              *
//    *                                                          *
//    *    Extract number tokens from the source file.           *
//    *                                                          *
//    *    CLASSES: TNumberToken,                                *
//    *                                                          *
//    *    FILE:    prog3-2/tknnum.cpp                           *
//    *                                                          *
//    *    MODULE:  Scanner                                      *
//    *                                                          *
//    *    Copyright (c) 1996 by Ronald Mak                      *
//    *    For instructional purposes only.  No warranties.      *
//    *                                                          *
//    ************************************************************

#include <string.h>
#include <stdio.h>
#include <math.h>
#include "token.h"

//              ******************
//              *                *
//              *  Number Tokens *
//              *                *
//              ******************

//------------------------------------------------------------
// Get         Extract a number token from the source and set
//             its value.
//
//     pBuffer : ptr to text input buffer
//------------------------------------------------------------

void TNumberToken::Get(TTextInBuffer &buffer)
{
    const int maxInteger  = 32767;
    const int maxExponent = 37;

    float  numValue       = 0.0;    // value of number ignoring
                                    //    the decimal point
    int    wholePlaces    = 0;      // no. digits before the decimal point
    int    decimalPlaces  = 0;      // no. digits after  the decimal point
```

```
char    exponentSign  = '+';
float   eValue        = 0.0;        // value of number after 'E'
int     exponent      = 0;          // final value of exponent
int     sawDotDotFlag = false;      // true if encountered '..',
                                    //    else false

ch               = buffer.Char();
ps               = string;
digitCount       = 0;
countErrorFlag   = false;
code             = tcError;      // we don't know what it is yet, but
type             = tyInteger;    //    assume it'll be an integer

//--Get the whole part of the number by accumulating
//--the values of its digits into numValue.  wholePlaces keeps
//--track of the number of digits in this part.
if (! AccumulateValue(buffer, numValue, errInvalidNumber)) return;
wholePlaces = digitCount;

//--If the current character is a dot, then either we have a
//--fraction part or we are seeing the first character of a '..'
//--token.  To find out, we must fetch the next character.
if (ch == '.') {
    ch = buffer.GetChar();

    if (ch == '.') {

        //--We have a .. token.  Back up bufferp so that the
        //--token can be extracted next.
        sawDotDotFlag = true;
        buffer.PutBackChar();
    }
    else {
        type  = tyReal;
        *ps++ = '.';

        //--We have a fraction part.  Accumulate it into numValue.
        if (! AccumulateValue(buffer, numValue,
                              errInvalidFraction)) return;
        decimalPlaces = digitCount - wholePlaces;
    }
}

//--Get the exponent part, if any. There cannot be an
//--exponent part if we already saw the '..' token.
if (!sawDotDotFlag && ((ch == 'E') || (ch == 'e'))) {
```

(continues)

■■■■■ **Figure 3.18** Implementation file **tknnum.cpp** for number tokens.
(*Continued*)

```cpp
    type  = tyReal;
    *ps++ = ch;
    ch    = buffer.GetChar();

    //--Fetch the exponent's sign, if any.
    if ((ch == '+') || (ch == '-')) {
        *ps++ = exponentSign = ch;
        ch    = buffer.GetChar();
    }

    //--Accumulate the value of the number after 'E' into eValue.
    digitCount = 0;
    if (! AccumulateValue(buffer, eValue,
                          errInvalidExponent)) return;
    if (exponentSign == '-') eValue = -eValue;
}

//--Were there too many digits?
if (countErrorFlag) {
    Error(errTooManyDigits);
    return;
}

//--Calculate and check the final exponent value,
//--and then use it to adjust the number's value.
exponent = int(eValue) - decimalPlaces;
if ((exponent + wholePlaces < -maxExponent) ||
    (exponent + wholePlaces >  maxExponent)) {
    Error(errRealOutOfRange);
    return;
}
if (exponent != 0) numValue *= float(pow(10, exponent));

//--Check and set the numeric value.
if (type == tyInteger) {
    if ((numValue < -maxInteger) || (numValue > maxInteger)) {
        Error(errIntegerOutOfRange);
        return;
    }
    value.integer = int(numValue);
}
else value.real = numValue;
```

```
    *ps  = '\0';
    code = tcNumber;
}


//-------------------------------------------------------------
// AccumulateValue      Extract a number part from the source
//                      and set its value.
//
//      pBuffer : ptr to text input buffer
//      value   : accumulated value (from one or more calls)
//      ec      : error code if failure
//
//  Return: true  if success
//          false if failure
//-------------------------------------------------------------

int TNumberToken::AccumulateValue(TTextInBuffer &buffer,
                                  float &value, TErrorCode ec)
{
    const int maxDigitCount = 20;

    //--Error if the first character is not a digit.
    if (charCodeMap[ch] != ccDigit) {
        Error(ec);
        return false;              // failure
    }

    //--Accumulate the value as long as the total allowable
    //--number of digits has not been exceeded.
    do {
        *ps++ = ch;

        if (++digitCount <= maxDigitCount) {
            value = 10*value + (ch - '0');  // shift left and add
        }
        else countErrorFlag = true;         // too many digits

        ch = buffer.GetChar();
    } while (charCodeMap[ch] == ccDigit);

    return true;                 // success
}


//-------------------------------------------------------------
// Print       Print the token to the list file.
//-------------------------------------------------------------
```

(continues)

■■■■■■■■■ **Figure 3.18** Implementation file **tknnum.cpp** for number tokens.
(*Continued*)

```
void TNumberToken::Print(void) const
{
    if (type == tyInteger) {
        sprintf(list.text, "\t%-18s =%d", ">> integer:",
                            value.integer);
    }
    else {
        sprintf(list.text, "\t%-18s =%g", ">> real:",
                            value.real);
    }

    list.PutLine();
}
```

The definition of a Pascal number token begins with the notion of an *unsigned integer*, which consists of one or more consecutive digits. The simplest form of a number token is simply an unsigned integer:

```
3    75    15667
```

A number token may also be an unsigned integer (the whole part) followed by a fraction part. A fraction part consists of a decimal point followed by an unsigned integer, such as:

```
123.45    0.967
```

These numbers have whole parts 123 and 0, and fraction parts .45 and .967, respectively.

A number token may also be a whole part followed by an exponent part. An exponent part consists of the letter E or e followed by an unsigned integer. An optional exponent sign + or − may appear between the letter and the first exponent digit. Examples are:

```
152e3    2E53    345e-12    7825E+5
```

Finally, a number token may be a whole part followed by a fraction part and an exponent part, in that order:

```
163.98E7    0.000123e-45
```

Member function `TNumberToken::Get` keeps track of various values with its local variables. The most important local is `numValue`, whose value eventually will be that of the number token. For each number token, the `Get` extracts up to three unsigned integers. It always extracts the whole part of the number, and then it can extract the fraction part or the exponent part, or both. For each part, it calls private member function `AccumulateValue`.

`Get` makes its first call to `AccumulateValue` to extract and calculate the value of the whole part. It passes `numValue` by reference so that after the call, `numValue` has the value of the whole part. Local variable `wholePlaces` is set to the number of digits in that part.

`Get` then checks if the current input character is a period. If so, it can be looking at either the number's decimal point, or the first character of the `..` special symbol. So `Get` must check if the next input character is another period. If it is, then `Get` is done with the number token (it was an integer), and the next token must be the `..` special symbol. `Get` therefore sends the `PutBackChar` message to the input buffer to put the second period back so that the scanner can next extract the `..` token.

If `Get` did indeed see a decimal point, it calls `AccumulateValue` a second time, again passing `numValue` by reference, to extract the fraction part. After this call, `numValue` will have the value of the whole and fraction parts combined, ignoring the decimal point. However, local variable `decimalPlaces` is set to the number of digits in the fraction part.

Now, if the number token had not been terminated with a `..` token, and the next input character is E or e, `Get` has an exponent part to extract. First, it checks for an exponent sign, and then it calls `AccumulateValue`, this time passing local variable `eValue` by reference. The call sets `eValue` to the value of the exponent. This value is negated if the exponent sign was -.

Finally, after making sure the number doesn't have too many digits (we'll discuss the `Error` function later), `Get` is ready to calculate the final value of the number. First, it sets the final exponent value to the value of `eValue` adjusted by the number of `decimalPlaces`. After a range check on exponent, it sets the final value of numValue by multiplying it by ten raised to the exponent's power. `Get` checks the range of numValue if its type is integer, and then it sets either value.integer or value.real, depending on the type. It sets data member code to tcNumber.

Member function TNumberToken::AccumulateValue extracts an unsigned integer from the input buffer and accumulates its value in whatever variable was passed to it by reference. It keeps track of the number of input digits by incrementing the private data member digitCount.

Let's do an example. Suppose the input buffer contains 386.07e-3. After Get's first call to AccumulateValue, we have:

```
      numValue:   386
   digitCount:   3
  wholePlaces:   3
```

After the second call to AccumulateValue, we have:

```
      numValue:   38607
   digitCount:   5
decimalPlaces:   2
```

Finally, after the third call to AccumulateValue, we have:

```
       eValue:   -3
```

The final exponent value is eValue - decimalPlaces, or -3 - 2 = -5. Multiply numValue by pow(10, -5) to get the final value of 0.386070.

With this new version of subclass TNumberToken, the Pascal tokenizer reads:

```
123 -456 12..34 +123.45 -0.00012 .... 0012.3e001
123.4e27 0 000 00000.100000 -123.4567E-27.
```

and produces the output:

```
1 0: 123 -456 12..34 +123.45 -0.00012 .... 0012.3e001
     >> integer:      =123
     >> special:      -
     >> integer:      =456
     >> integer:      =12
     >> special:      ..
     >> integer:      =34
     >> special:      +
     >> real:         =123.45
     >> special:      -
     >> real:         =0.00012
```

```
                >> special:          ..
                >> special:          ..
                >> real:             =123
      2 0: 123.4e27 0 000 00000.100000 -123.4567E-27.
                >> real:             =1.234e+29
                >> integer:          =0
                >> integer:          =0
                >> real:             =0.1
                >> special:          -
                >> real:             =1.23457e-25
                >> special:          .
```

The String Token Subclass TStringToken

Pascal string tokens are enclosed in single-quote characters. Two consecutive single-quote characters within the string represent one single-quote character in the string. For example, the string token `'don''t'` contains the characters `don't`.

▮▮▮▮▮▮▮▮▮ **Figure 3.19** Implementation file **tknstrsp.cpp** for string, special symbol, and error tokens.

```
//    ************************************************************
//    *                                                          *
//    *    T O K E N S   (Strings and Specials)                  *
//    *                                                          *
//    *    Routines to extract string and special symbol tokens  *
//    *    from the source file.                                 *
//    *                                                          *
//    *    CLASSES: TStringToken, TSpecialToken, TErrorToken     *
//    *                                                          *
//    *    FILE:    prog3-2/tknstrsp.cpp                         *
//    *                                                          *
//    *    MODULE:  Scanner                                      *
//    *                                                          *
//    *    Copyright (c) 1996 by Ronald Mak                      *
//    *    For instructional purposes only.  No warranties.      *
//    *                                                          *
//    ************************************************************

#include <stdio.h>
#include "token.h"

//                    *******************
//                    *                 *
```

(continues)

■■■■■■■■■ **Figure 3.19** Implementation file **tknstrsp.cpp** for string, special symbol, and error tokens. (*Continued*)

```
//              *  String Tokens  *
//              *                 *
//              *******************

//-------------------------------------------------------------
// Get     Get a string token from the source.
//
//       pBuffer : ptr to text input buffer
//-------------------------------------------------------------

void TStringToken::Get(TTextInBuffer &buffer)
{
    char  ch;               // current character
    char *ps = string;   // ptr to char in string

    *ps++ = '\'';   // opening quote

    //--Get the string.
    ch = buffer.GetChar();  // first char after opening quote
    while (ch != eofChar) {
        if (ch == '\'') {      // look for another quote

            //--Fetched a quote.  Now check for an adjacent quote,
            //--since two consecutive quotes represent a single
            //--quote in the string.
            ch = buffer.GetChar();
            if (ch != '\'') break;  // not another quote, so previous
                                    //  quote ended the string
        }

        //--Replace the end of line character with a blank.
        else if (ch == '\0') ch = ' ';

        //--Append current char to string, then get the next char.
        *ps++ = ch;
        ch = buffer.GetChar();
    }

    if (ch == eofChar) Error(errUnexpectedEndOfFile);

    *ps++ = '\'';   // closing quote
    *ps   = '\0';
}
```

```
//----------------------------------------------------------
// Print       Print the token to the list file.
//----------------------------------------------------------

void TStringToken::Print(void) const
{
    sprintf(list.text, "\t%-18s %-s", ">> string:", string);
    list.PutLine();
}


//              ********************
//              *                  *
//              *  Special Tokens  *
//              *                  *
//              ********************


//----------------------------------------------------------
// Get          Extract a one- or two-character special symbol
//              token from the source.
//
//      pBuffer : ptr to text input buffer
//----------------------------------------------------------

void TSpecialToken::Get(TTextInBuffer &buffer)
{
    char  ch = buffer.Char();
    char *ps = string;

    *ps++ = ch;

    switch (ch) {
        case '^':   code = tcUpArrow;     buffer.GetChar();   break;
        case '*':   code = tcStar;        buffer.GetChar();   break;
        case '(':   code = tcLParen;      buffer.GetChar();   break;
        case ')':   code = tcRParen;      buffer.GetChar();   break;
        case '-':   code = tcMinus;       buffer.GetChar();   break;
        case '+':   code = tcPlus;        buffer.GetChar();   break;
        case '=':   code = tcEqual;       buffer.GetChar();   break;
        case '[':   code = tcLBracket;    buffer.GetChar();   break;
        case ']':   code = tcRBracket;    buffer.GetChar();   break;
        case ';':   code = tcSemicolon;   buffer.GetChar();   break;
        case ',':   code = tcComma;       buffer.GetChar();   break;
        case '/':   code = tcSlash;       buffer.GetChar();   break;

        case ':':   ch = buffer.GetChar();      // : or :=
```

(continues)

■■■■■ **Figure 3.19** Implementation file **tknstrsp.cpp** for string, special symbol, and error tokens. (*Continued*)

```
                if (ch == '=') {
                    *ps++ = '=';
                    code  = tcColonEqual;
                    buffer.GetChar();
                }
                else code = tcColon;
                break;

case '<':   ch = buffer.GetChar();      // < or <= or <>
                if (ch == '=') {
                    *ps++ = '=';
                    code  = tcLe;
                    buffer.GetChar();
                }
                else if (ch == '>') {
                    *ps++ = '>';
                    code  = tcNe;
                    buffer.GetChar();
                }
                else code = tcLt;
                break;

case '>':   ch = buffer.GetChar();      // > or >=
                if (ch == '=') {
                    *ps++ = '=';
                    code  = tcGe;
                    buffer.GetChar();
                }
                else code = tcGt;
                break;

case '.':   ch = buffer.GetChar();      // . or ..
                if (ch == '.') {
                    *ps++ = '.';
                    code  = tcDotDot;
                    buffer.GetChar();
                }
                else code = tcPeriod;
                break;

default:    code = tcError;                      // error
                buffer.GetChar();
                Error(errUnrecognizable);
```

```
                break;
    }

    *ps = '\0';
}


//----------------------------------------------------------------
//  Print       Print the token to the list file.
//----------------------------------------------------------------

void TSpecialToken::Print(void) const
{
    sprintf(list.text, "\t%-18s %-s", ">> special:", string);
    list.PutLine();
}


//              *****************
//              *               *
//              *  Error Token  *
//              *               *
//              *****************

//----------------------------------------------------------------
//  Get          Extract an invalid character from the source.
//
//          pBuffer : ptr to text input buffer
//----------------------------------------------------------------

void TErrorToken::Get(TTextInBuffer &buffer)
{
    string[0] = buffer.Char();
    string[1] = '\0';

    buffer.GetChar();
    Error(errUnrecognizable);
}
```

Figure 3.19 shows file tknstrsp.cpp, which implements string, special symbol, and error tokens. Whenever member function TStringToken::Get is called, the current input character is the opening single quote of the string token. The function fetches input characters until it finds another single quote. It then fetches and checks the next character. If it's another single quote, one single-quote character is added to the string, and Get continues to fetch more characters. Otherwise, it saw the closing single quote, so it is done extracting the string token. It fetches the next character after the closing quote. Note that the opening and closing quotes are included in the token string.

With this new version of subclass `TStringToken`, the Pascal tokenizer reads the following input lines:

```
'This is a string.'
'Don''t skip this'.
```

and produces the output

```
1 0: 'This is a string.'
     >> string:          'This is a string.'
2 0: 'Don''t skip this'.
     >> string:          'Don't skip this'
     >> special:         .
```

The Special Symbols Token Subclass TSpecialToken

Most of Pascal's special symbol tokens are one-character, like + and =. Some are two-character, like .. and :=. The two-character ones have an extra bit of complexity: The first character looks just like a one-character special symbol token. If the scanner fetches a character that can either be a one-character special symbol or the first character of a two-character special symbol, it must fetch the following character. From this second character, the scanner can tell whether it has a one- or a two-character special symbol token.

The complete definition of subclass `TSpecialToken` is also in file `tknstrsp.cpp`, shown in Figure 3.19. With this new version, the Pascal tokenizer reads:

```
+ - : = := < <= <> .
```

and produces the output:

```
1 0: + - : = := < <= <> .
     >> special:         +
     >> special:         -
     >> special:         :
     >> special:         =
     >> special:         :=
     >> special:         <
```

```
      >> special:        <=
      >> special:        <>
      >> special:        .
```

Flagging Syntax Errors

What should the scanner do if it encounters a syntax error in the input text? We want it to print an error message to the list file. A nice touch is to point to the error itself. For example, the input:

```
123e99 123456 1234567890.123457890e12
1234.56e.
```

should produce the output:

```
  1 0: 123e99 123456 1234567890.12345789012e34
            ^

*** ERROR: Real literal out of range.


                       ^

*** ERROR: Integer literal out of range.



                                           ^

*** ERROR: Too many digits.

  2 0: 1234.56e.
            ^
*** ERROR: Invalid exponent.

      >> special:        .
```

Figure 3.20 shows a new version of header file error.h, and Figure 3.21 shows a new version of implementation file error.cpp.

▬▬▬▬▬ **Figure 3.20** New version of implementation file **error.h**.

```
// *****************************************************************
// *                                                               *
// *     E R R O R S    (Header)                                   *
// *                                                               *
// *     FILE:    prog3-2/error.h                                  *
// *                                                               *
// *     MODULE:  Error                                            *
// *                                                               *
// *     Copyright (c) 1996 by Ronald Mak                          *
// *     For instructional purposes only.  No warranties.          *
// *                                                               *
// *****************************************************************
```

(continues)

■■■■■■■ **Figure 3.20** New version of implementation file **error.h**. (*Continued*)

```
#ifndef error_h
#define error_h

extern int errorCount;
extern int errorArrowFlag;
extern int errorArrowOffset;

//----------------------------------------------------------------
//  Abort codes for fatal translator errors.
//----------------------------------------------------------------

enum TAbortCode {
    abortInvalidCommandLineArgs     = -1,
    abortSourceFileOpenFailed       = -2,
    abortIFormFileOpenFailed        = -3,
    abortAssemblyFileOpenFailed     = -4,
    abortTooManySyntaxErrors        = -5,
    abortStackOverflow              = -6,
    abortCodeSegmentOverflow        = -7,
    abortNestingTooDeep             = -8,
    abortRuntimeError               = -9,
    abortUnimplementedFeature       = -10,
};

void AbortTranslation(TAbortCode ac);

//----------------------------------------------------------------
//  Error codes for syntax errors.
//----------------------------------------------------------------

enum TErrorCode {
    errNone,
    errUnrecognizable,
    errTooMany,
    errUnexpectedEndOfFile,
    errInvalidNumber,
    errInvalidFraction,
    errInvalidExponent,
    errTooManyDigits,
    errRealOutOfRange,
    errIntegerOutOfRange,
    errMissingRightParen,
    errInvalidExpression,
    errInvalidAssignment,
```

```
errMissingIdentifier,
errMissingColonEqual,
errUndefinedIdentifier,
errStackOverflow,
errInvalidStatement,
errUnexpectedToken,
errMissingSemicolon,
errMissingComma,
errMissingDO,
errMissingUNTIL,
errMissingTHEN,
errInvalidFORControl,
errMissingOF,
errInvalidConstant,
errMissingConstant,
errMissingColon,
errMissingEND,
errMissingTOorDOWNTO,
errRedefinedIdentifier,
errMissingEqual,
errInvalidType,
errNotATypeIdentifier,
errInvalidSubrangeType,
errNotAConstantIdentifier,
errMissingDotDot,
errIncompatibleTypes,
errInvalidTarget,
errInvalidIdentifierUsage,
errIncompatibleAssignment,
errMinGtMax,
errMissingLeftBracket,
errMissingRightBracket,
errInvalidIndexType,
errMissingBEGIN,
errMissingPeriod,
errTooManySubscripts,
errInvalidField,
errNestingTooDeep,
errMissingPROGRAM,
errAlreadyForwarded,
errWrongNumberOfParms,
errInvalidVarParm,
errNotARecordVariable,
errMissingVariable,
errCodeSegmentOverflow,
errUnimplementedFeature,
```

(continues)

■■■■■■■■ **Figure 3.20** New version of implementation file **error.h**. (*Continued*)

```
};

void Error(TErrorCode ec);

#endif
```

■■■■■■■■ **Figure 3.21** New version of implementation file **error.cpp**.

```
//    ************************************************************
//    *                                                          *
//    *    E R R O R S                                           *
//    *                                                          *
//    *    Routines to handle translation-time and runtime errors. *
//    *                                                          *
//    *    FILE:    prog3-2/error.cpp                            *
//    *                                                          *
//    *    MODULE:  Error                                        *
//    *                                                          *
//    *    Copyright (c) 1996 by Ronald Mak                      *
//    *    For instructional purposes only.  No warranties.      *
//    *                                                          *
//    ************************************************************

#include <stdlib.h>
#include <string.h>
#include <stdio.h>
#include <iostream.h>
#include "buffer.h"
#include "error.h"

int errorCount      = 0;       // count of syntax errors
int errorArrowFlag  = true;    // true if print arrows under syntax
                               //    errors, false if not
int errorArrowOffset = 8;      // offset for printing the error arrow

//----------------------------------------------------------------
// Abort messages      Keyed to enumeration type TAbortCode.
//----------------------------------------------------------------

static char *abortMsg[] = {
    NULL,
    "Invalid command line arguments",
    "Failed to open source file",
    "Failed to open intermediate form file",
```

```
        "Failed to open assembly file",
        "Too many syntax errors",
        "Stack overflow",
        "Code segment overflow",
        "Nesting too deep",
        "Runtime error",
        "Unimplemented feature",
};


//-----------------------------------------------------------
//  AbortTranslation     A fatal error occurred during the
//                       translation.  Print the abort code
//                       to the error file and then exit.
//
//      ac : abort code
//-----------------------------------------------------------

void AbortTranslation(TAbortCode ac)
{
    cerr << "*** Fatal translator error: " << abortMsg[-ac] << endl;
    exit(ac);
}


//-----------------------------------------------------------
//  Syntax error messages       Keyed to enumeration type
//                              TErrorCode.
//-----------------------------------------------------------

static char *errorMessages[] = {
    "No error",
    "Unrecognizable input",
    "Too many syntax errors",
    "Unexpected end of file",
    "Invalid number",
    "Invalid fraction",
    "Invalid exponent",
    "Too many digits",
    "Real literal out of range",
    "Integer literal out of range",
    "Missing )",
    "Invalid expression",
    "Invalid assignment statement",
    "Missing identifier",
    "Missing :=",
    "Undefined identifier",
    "Stack overflow",
```

(continues)

Figure 3.21 New version of implementation file **error.cpp**. (*Continued*)

```
        "Invalid statement",
        "Unexpected token",
        "Missing ;",
        "Missing ,",
        "Missing DO",
        "Missing UNTIL",
        "Missing THEN",
        "Invalid FOR control variable",
        "Missing OF",
        "Invalid constant",
        "Missing constant",
        "Missing :",
        "Missing END",
        "Missing TO or DOWNTO",
        "Redefined identifier",
        "Missing =",
        "Invalid type",
        "Not a type identifier",
        "Invalid subrange type",
        "Not a constant identifier",
        "Missing ..",
        "Incompatible types",
        "Invalid assignment target",
        "Invalid identifier usage",
        "Incompatible assignment",
        "Min limit greater than max limit",
        "Missing [",
        "Missing ]",
        "Invalid index type",
        "Missing BEGIN",
        "Missing .",
        "Too many subscripts",
        "Invalid field",
        "Nesting too deep",
        "Missing PROGRAM",
        "Already specified in FORWARD",
        "Wrong number of actual parameters",
        "Invalid VAR parameter",
        "Not a record variable",
        "Missing variable",
        "Code segment overflow",
        "Unimplemented feature",
    };
```

```
//-------------------------------------------------------------
//  Error        Print an arrow under the error and then
//               print the error message.
//
//      ec : error code
//-------------------------------------------------------------

void Error(TErrorCode ec)
{
    const int maxSyntaxErrors = 25;

    int errorPosition = errorArrowOffset + inputPosition - 1;

    //--Print the arrow pointing to the token just scanned.
    if (errorArrowFlag) {
        sprintf(list.text, "%*s^", errorPosition, " ");
        list.PutLine();
    }

    //--Print the error message.
    sprintf(list.text, "*** ERROR: %s", errorMessages[ec]);
    list.PutLine();

    if (++errorCount > maxSyntaxErrors) {
        list.PutLine("Too many syntax errors.  Translation aborted.");
        AbortTranslation(abortTooManySyntaxErrors);
    }
}
```

File error.h now has error codes for syntax errors. The error message corresponding to each error code is in file error.cpp. Global function Error prints error messages to the list file. Just above each error message, it also prints an arrow under the end of the last token that was scanned. We assume this token caused the syntax error.

If the source program contains too many syntax errors, we simply abort. Of course, this is just the sort of action that drives programmers crazy about compilers. We put this in as a last resort and hope that it does not often occur.

■■■■■■■ Figure 3.22 New version of member function **TParser::Parse** in file **parser.cpp**.

```
//-------------------------------------------------------------
//  Parse        Parse the source file.  After listing each
//               source line, extract and list its tokens.
//-------------------------------------------------------------
```

(*continues*)

■■■■■■ **Figure 3.22** New version of member function **TParser::Parse** in file
parser.cpp. (*Continued*)

```
void TParser::Parse(void)
{
    //--Loop to extract and print tokens
    //--until the end of the source file.
    do {
        GetToken();
        if (token != tcError) pToken->Print();
    } while (token != tcEndOfFile);

    //--Print the parser's summary.
    list.PutLine();
    sprintf(list.text, "%20d source lines.",  currentLineNumber);
    list.PutLine();
    sprintf(list.text, "%20d syntax errors.", errorCount);
    list.PutLine();
}
```

Since the error module can now take care of printing all error messages, the parser
module no longer needs to do it. Figure 3.22 shows a new version of member function TParser::Parse that does not print error messages.

Program 3-2: Pascal Tokenizer

Finally, we're ready to see the Pascal Tokenizer utility program that produced the
above output. It is shown in Figure 3.23. Table 3.2 summarizes the changes we
made going from the simple tokenizer to the Pascal tokenizer. Note that file
token.cpp has been replaced by the three new files tknword.cpp, tknnum.cpp,
and tknstrsp.cpp.

■■■■■■ **Figure 3.23**   The main file of the Pascal Tokenizer utility.

```
//    ***************************************************************
//    *                                                             *
//    *    Program 3-2:  Pascal Tokenizer                           *
//    *                                                             *
//    *    List the source file.  After each line, list the Pascal  *
//    *    tokens that were extracted from that line.               *
//    *                                                             *
//    *    FILE: prog3-2/tokeniz2.cpp                               *
//    *                                                             *
```

▮▮▮▮▮ **Table 3.2** Modules and Files of Program 3-2

Module	File	Status	Directory
Main	tokeniz2.cpp	*new*	prog3-2
Parser	parser.h	*unchanged*	prog3-1
	parser.cpp	*changed*	prog3-2
Scanner	scanner.h	*unchanged*	prog3-1
	scanner.cpp	*changed*	prog3-2
	token.h	*changed*	prog3-2
	tknword.cpp	*new*	prog3-2
	tknnum.cpp	*new*	prog3-2
	tknstrsp.cpp	*new*	prog3-2
Error	error.h	*changed*	prog3-2
	error.cpp	*changed*	prog3-2
Buffer	buffer.h	*unchanged*	prog2-1
	buffer.cpp	*unchanged*	prog2-1
Common	common.h	*unchanged*	prog2-1
	common.cpp	*unchanged*	prog2-1
	misc.h	*changed*	prog3-2

```
//  *    USAGE:  tokeniz2 <source file>                            *
//  *                                                              *
//  *                <source file>  name of source file to        *
//  *                               tokenize                       *
//  *                                                              *
//  *    Copyright (c) 1996 by Ronald Mak                          *
//  *    For instructional purposes only.  No warranties.          *
//  *                                                              *
//  ****************************************************************

#include <iostream.h>
#include "error.h"
#include "buffer.h"
#include "parser.h"


//------------------------------------------------------------
// main
//------------------------------------------------------------
```

(continues)

■■■■■■■ **Figure 3.23**   The main file of the Pascal Tokenizer utility. (*Continued*)

```
void main(int argc, char *argv[])
{
    //--Check the command line arguments.
    if (argc != 2) {
        cerr << "Usage: tokeniz2 <source file>" << endl;
        AbortTranslation(abortInvalidCommandLineArgs);
    }

    //--Create the parser for the source file,
    //--and then parse the file.
    TParser parser(new TSourceBuffer(argv[1]));
    parser.Parse();
}
```

Program 3-3: Pascal Source Compactor

We've covered a lot in this chapter. The scanner is a good-sized module, and we built it incrementally from the ground up. At this point, not only the scanner module but also the buffer and error modules are nearly complete, and they will remain mostly unchanged through the rest of this book. We will continue to develop the parser module.

Let's write one more utility to complete this chapter, a handy source program compactor. Pascal programs are written to be read by people, with line breaks, blanks, indentation, and comments to improve readability. But suppose you want to save disk space, even at the expense of readability. You can store a compacted version of the Pascal source file with all comments and unnecessary blanks removed, and with line breaks only to keep line lengths at, say, 80 characters or less. For example, the following Pascal program:

```
PROGRAM hello (output);

{Write 'Hello, world.' ten times.}

VAR
    i : integer;

BEGIN {hello}
    FOR i := 1 TO 10 DO BEGIN
```

```
        writeln ('Hello, world.');
    END;
END {hello}.
```

can be compacted to

```
PROGRAM hello(output);VAR i:integer;BEGIN FOR i:=1 TO 10 DO BEGIN
writeln('Hello, world.');END;END.
```

The output of this utility is a compacted Pascal program that is still syntactically correct. To a Pascal compiler or interpreter, the two versions are equivalent. In fact, the scanner would process the compacted version faster!

Note how the Compactor utility removes all the comments and unnecessary white-space characters. Wherever a whitespace character is still required, it inserts a single blank (or a line break at the end of the line). One blank is required between two words, between two numbers, or between a word and a number. Nothing is required between a word and a special symbol, or between a number and a special symbol. The utility preserves all whitespace characters within strings.

The utility uses the scanner and buffer modules to read in a Pascal source program, and it outputs a compacted version. It needs to classify each token as a delimiter or a nondelimiter. A *delimiter* is a token that establishes a boundary between itself and any adjacent token. Thus, a special symbol is a delimiter. In the expression `alpha*pi`, it is clear that there are three tokens. Words and numbers are not delim-iters. The identifier `alpha` and the number 3 cannot be written together; `alpha3` is scanned as a single identifier token. At least one whitespace character must be inserted between two adjacent nondelimiter tokens.

Recall that in the final version of header file `token.h`, shown in Figure 3.15, each token subclass defines the public member function `IsDelimiter`. For each sub-class, this function returns true if the corresponding token is a delimiter, false if it is not. So, member functions `TWordToken::IsDelimiter` and `TNumberTo-ken::IsDelimiter` both return false, and `TStringToken::IsDelimiter` and `TSpecialToken::IsDelimiter` both return true.

■■■■■■■■■■ **Figure 3.24** Header file **parser.h** for the Compactor utility program.

```
//------------------------------------------------------------
//  TParser      Parser class.
//------------------------------------------------------------
```

(continues)

■■■■■■■■ **Figure 3.24** Header file **parser.h** for the Compactor utility program.
(*Continued*)

```cpp
class TParser {
    TTextScanner      *const pScanner;  // ptr to the scanner
    TToken            *pToken;          // ptr to the current token
    TTokenCode        token;            // code of current token
    TCompactListBuffer *const pCompact; // compact list buffer

    void GetToken(void)
    {
        pToken = pScanner->Get();
        token  = pToken->Code();
    }

public:
    TParser(TTextInBuffer *pBuffer)
        : pScanner(new TTextScanner(pBuffer)),
          pCompact(new TCompactListBuffer) {}

    ~TParser(void)
    {
        delete pScanner;
        delete pCompact;
    }

    void Parse(void);
};
```

We make a small change to the definition of class TParser in header file
parser.h, as shown in Figure 3.24. We add a new private member object pCom-
pact, which points to the buffer object that represents the compact list file. The
constructor function creates both a new scanner object and a new compact list
buffer object. The destructor function deletes them both.

■■■■■■■■ **Figure 3.25** Header file **complist.h**.

```
//   ****************************************************************
//   *                                                              *
//   *   C O M P A C T   L I S T I N G   (Header)                   *
//   *                                                              *
//   *   CLASSES: TCompactListBuffer                                *
//   *                                                              *
//   *   FILE:    prog3-3/complist.h                                *
//   *                                                              *
```

```
//  *    MODULE:  Buffer                                       *
//  *                                                          *
//  *    Copyright (c) 1996 by Ronald Mak                      *
//  *    For instructional purposes only.  No warranties.      *
//  *                                                          *
//  **************************************************************

#ifndef complist_h
#define complist_h

#include "buffer.h"

const int maxCompactTextLength = 72;

//-------------------------------------------------------------
//  TCompactListBuffer      Compact list buffer subclass
//                          of TTextOutBuffer.
//-------------------------------------------------------------

class TCompactListBuffer : public TTextOutBuffer {
    int    textLength;  // length of output text line
    char *pText;        // pointer to end of text

public:
    TCompactListBuffer(void)
    {
        pText      = text;
        *pText     = '\0';
        textLength = 0;
    }

    void PutBlank(void);
    void Put     (const char *pString);
    void PutLine (void);
};

#endif
```

Figure 3.25 shows header file complist.h, where we define TCompactList-
Buffer to be a subclass of TTextOutBuffer. Its private data members are the
current length of the output text line and a pointer to the end of the text. Its public
member functions append a blank or the token string to the output text, or flush the
text to the list file.

■■■■■■■ **Figure 3.26** The parser in implementation file **parser.cpp** for the compactor utility.

```
//----------------------------------------------------------------
//  Parse         Parse the source file.  Output a compacted
//                version with unnecessary blanks and comments
//                removed.
//----------------------------------------------------------------

void TParser::Parse(void)
{
    int currIsDelimiter;        // true if current token is a
                                //   delimiter, else false
    int prevIsDelimiter = true; // likewise for previous token

    //--Loop to extract and process tokens
    //--until the end of the program.
    do {
        GetToken();

        //--Shouldn't see an end of file.
        if (token == tcEndOfFile) {
            Error(errUnexpectedEndOfFile);
            break;
        }

        if (token != tcError) {
            currIsDelimiter = pToken->IsDelimiter();

            //--Append a blank only if both the previous and the
            //--current tokens are not delimiters.  Then append the
            //--token string to the output record.
            if (!prevIsDelimiter && !currIsDelimiter) {
                pCompact->PutBlank();
            }
            pCompact->Put(pToken->String());

            prevIsDelimiter = currIsDelimiter;
        }
        else Error(errUnrecognizable);
    } while (token != tcPeriod);

    //--Flush the last output record.
    pCompact->PutLine();
}
```

Figure 3.26 shows public member function `TParser::Parse` for the Compactor utility in file `parser.cpp`. It keeps track of whether the current and previous tokens are delimiters in local variables `currIsDelimiter` and `prevIsDelimiter`, respectively. It loops once per token, sending the `Put` message to the compact buffer object to append the token string to the compacted text. If there are two adjacent nondelimiters, it also sends the `PutBlank` message to `compact`. Note that the loop stops after processing the period token, since a period ends every Pascal program.

■■■■■■■■ **Figure 3.27** Implementation file **complist.cpp**.

```
//   ***************************************************************
//   *                                                             *
//   *       C O M P A C T     L I S T I N G                       *
//   *                                                             *
//   *       Output a compact source listing.                      *
//   *                                                             *
//   *       CLASSES: TCompactListBuffer                           *
//   *                                                             *
//   *       FILE:    prog3-3/complist.cpp                         *
//   *                                                             *
//   *       MODULE:  Buffer                                       *
//   *                                                             *
//   *       Copyright (c) 1996 by Ronald Mak                      *
//   *       For instructional purposes only.  No warranties.      *
//   *                                                             *
//   ***************************************************************

#include <string.h>
#include "complist.h"


//----------------------------------------------------------------
// PutBlank          Append a blank to the output record,
//                   or print the record if it is full.
//----------------------------------------------------------------

void TCompactListBuffer::PutBlank(void)
{
    if (++textLength >= maxCompactTextLength - 1) PutLine();
    else                                          *pText++ = ' ';
}


//----------------------------------------------------------------
// Put               Append a token string to the output record
```

(*continues*)

■■■■■■■■ **Figure 3.27** Implementation file **complist.cpp**. (*Continued*)

```
//                    if it fits.  If not, print the current
//                    record and append the string to the next
//                    record.
//
//      pString : ptr to the token string to append
//------------------------------------------------------------

void TCompactListBuffer::Put(const char *pString)
{
    int tokenLength = strlen(pString);

    if (textLength + tokenLength >= maxCompactTextLength - 1) {
        PutLine();
    }

    strcpy(pText, pString);
    pText       += tokenLength;
    textLength += tokenLength;
}


//------------------------------------------------------------
//  PutLine          Print the output record.
//------------------------------------------------------------

void TCompactListBuffer::PutLine(void)
{
    if (textLength > 0) {
        *pText = '\0';
        cout << text << endl;

        pText       = text;
        textLength = 0;
    }
}
```

Figure 3.27 shows file complist.cpp, where we implement the compact list buffer. Member functions TCompactListBuffer::PutBlank and TCompactListBuffer::Put append a blank and the token string, respectively, to the compacted text. Each flushes the text to the list file whenever it is near the end of the line and the current token string or a blank will not fit. Member function TCompactListBuffer::PutLine prints the text to the list file and reinitializes the output text buffer.

███████ **Figure 3.28** The main file **compact.cpp** of the Compactor utility program.

```
// ****************************************************************
// *                                                              *
// *    Program 3-3:  Pascal Source Compactor                     *
// *                                                              *
// *    Compact a Pascal source file by removing                  *
// *    unnecessary blanks and all comments.                      *
// *                                                              *
// *    FILE:   prog3-3/compact.cpp                               *
// *                                                              *
// *    USAGE:  compact <source file>                             *
// *                                                              *
// *                   <source file>  name of source file to      *
// *                                  compact                     *
// *                                                              *
// *    Copyright (c) 1996 by Ronald Mak                          *
// *    For instructional purposes only.  No warranties.          *
// *                                                              *
// ****************************************************************

#include <iostream.h>
#include "error.h"
#include "buffer.h"
#include "parser.h"


//---------------------------------------------------------------
// main
//---------------------------------------------------------------

void main(int argc, char *argv[])
{
    //--Check the command line arguments.
    if (argc != 2) {
        cerr << "Usage: compact <source file>" << endl;
        AbortTranslation(abortInvalidCommandLineArgs);
    }

    errorArrowFlag = false;  // don't print arrows under syntax errors
    listFlag       = false;  // don't list the source file

    //--Create the parser for the source file,
    //--and then parse the file.
    TParser parser(new TSourceBuffer(argv[1]));
    parser.Parse();
}
```

■■■■■■■ **Table 3.3** Modules and Files of Program 3-3

Module	File	Status	Directory
Main	compact.cpp	*new*	prog3-3
	complist.h	*new*	prog3-3
	complist.cpp	*new*	prog3-3
Parser	parser.h	*changed*	prog3-3
	parser.cpp	*changed*	prog3-3
Scanner	scanner.h	*unchanged*	prog3-1
	scanner.cpp	*unchanged*	prog3-2
	token.h	*unchanged*	prog3-2
	tknword.cpp	*unchanged*	prog3-2
	tknnum.cpp	*unchanged*	prog3-2
	tknstrsp.cpp	*unchanged*	prog3-2
Error	error.h	*unchanged*	prog3-2
	error.cpp	*unchanged*	prog3-2
Buffer	buffer.h	*unchanged*	prog2-1
	buffer.cpp	*unchanged*	prog2-1
Common	common.h	*unchanged*	prog2-1
	common.cpp	*unchanged*	prog2-1
	misc.h	*unchanged*	prog3-2

Finally, Figure 3.28 shows the main file compact.cpp of the Compactor utility program. Since it doesn't produce a standard source program listing, it must set both global variables errorArrowFlag and listFlag to false.

Table 3.3 shows that we only changed the main and parser modules.

In the next chapter, we'll start on the symbol table and icode objects, which are the interface between the front and back ends.

4

THE SYMBOL TABLE

Compilers and interpreters build and maintain a data structure used throughout the translation process. This structure is commonly called the symbol table, and it is where information about many of the source program's tokens is kept. Almost all symbol tables contain information about identifiers, but, as you'll see, we can also keep information about other tokens, too. As we saw in Figures 1.4 and 1.5, the symbol table object is an important component of the interface between the front and back ends of a compiler or an interpreter.

Maintaining a well-organized symbol table is an important skill for all compiler writers. As a compiler or an interpreter translates a source program, it must be able to enter new information and access and update existing information quickly and efficiently. Otherwise, the translation process is slowed, or worse, produces incorrect results.

In this chapter, we write the symbol table module of our interpreter. We'll learn how to:

- Create a symbol table organized as a binary tree.
- Search for and update information in the symbol table.

We'll also write three useful utility programs to test the new module. The first one reads a Pascal source program and generates a cross-reference listing of all the identifiers. The second utility "crunches" a source program into a compressed binary form that takes up even less disk space than the previous chapter's compacted form, and the third utility "decrunches" a compressed program back into text. These latter two utilities will give us more examples of how a symbol table is used, and they will also introduce us to the intermediate code, which is another important interface component.

Symbol Table Entries and Operations

What information about a token should you keep in the symbol table? Any information that is useful! For example, information about an identifier typically includes its name string, its type, and how it is defined.

No matter what information you keep about a token in a symbol table or how you organize the table, certain operations are fundamental. You store information about a token as an entry in the table. You enter information about a token into the table by creating a new entry. You search the table to look up a token's entry and make available the information stored there. You can then update the entry to modify its information.

Let's assume for now that we're only entering identifiers into the symbol table. Then there can be only one entry per identifier in a symbol table. Therefore, for each identifier, we first search the table to see if it already has an entry, and if so, we just access or update that entry. Otherwise, we must create a new entry.

Binary Tree Organization

How should we organize the symbol table? We can choose from among many different data structures, such as arrays, linked lists, trees, hash tables, and so on. The most common operations that are performed on a symbol table are creating new entries and searching for existing entries. We also want the entries to be sorted

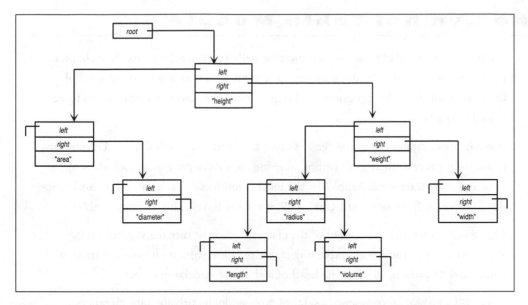

Figure 4.1 A symbol table organized as a binary tree. To keep the node diagrams simple, we show the identifier name strings inside the nodes. Actually, each node contains a pointer to its name string.

alphabetically to aid searching. These operations can be done very efficiently if we organize a symbol table as a binary tree, and also it is not hard to write the functions to perform these operations. Figure 4.1 shows a small symbol table organized as a binary tree.

Each entry of the symbol table is stored as a node of the binary tree. Each node contains a pointer to the identifier's name string and pointers to its left and right subtrees. (To simplify the node diagrams, we show the name string inside each node.) We can then describe the symbol table tree in a recursive manner: at *any* node:

- The node's left subtree is either empty or contains nodes whose name strings are alphabetically *less than* (come before) the node's name string.
- The node's right subtree is either empty or contains nodes whose name strings are alphabetically *greater than* (come after) the node's name string.

We'll see shortly how to build such a tree.

The Symbol Table Module

We'll write the symbol table module incrementally in this and the next few chapters. In this chapter, we start by defining the basic structures that make up the symbol table. Each of the utility programs will require certain additional information to be stored in the table.

A complete compiler or interpreter has more than just one symbol table. During the translation process, there is a symbol table for the source program's global identifiers and a separate symbol table for the local identifiers of each procedure and function. However, from now until Chapter 8, we'll just have a single symbol table.

Figure 4.2 shows a class diagram of the classes that constitute the symbol table. When we refer to the symbol table object, we're talking about an object instantiated from class `TSymtab`, which is the head of a chain of associated objects.

Class `TSymtabNode` represents a symbol table node. Its private data members include pointers to its left and right subtrees and a pointer `pString` to the symbol string (such as an identifier name string). Data member `xSymtab` is a unique index

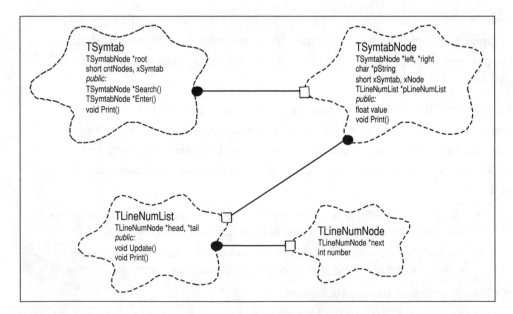

Figure 4.2 Class diagram of the symbol table classes.

number for the symbol table, and xNode is a unique index number for the symbol table node. Since we only have one symbol table so far, xSymtab will always be zero for now. We'll see later how xNode is used. The public data member value contains the value of a number token, and public member function Print prints the contents of the node.

Class TSymtab represents the symbol table itself. It has a private pointer to the root node, a count cntNodes of all its nodes, and a symbol table index xSymtab. The public member functions Search and Enter allow us to search the tree for a node and to enter a new node, respectively. Public member function Print prints the symbol table's nodes.

Since our first utility program for this chapter is a cross-reference listing, we need to keep track of the line numbers of the source program where each identifier appears. Class TSymtabNode also has a private data member pLineNumList that points to a list of line numbers, represented by class TLineNumList. This latter class has private data members that point to the head and tail of a linked list of line numbers, and public member functions Update and Print to update and print the list. The line numbers are represented by class TLineNumNode. It has a private data member that points to the next line number, and a private data member number whose value is a line number.

Figure 4.3 shows the definitions of these classes in the first version of header file symtab.h.

Figure 4.3 The first version of header file **symtab.h**.

```
//  ***************************************************************
//  *                                                             *
//  *     S Y M B O L    T A B L E    (Header)                    *
//  *                                                             *
//  *     CLASSES: TSymtabNode,  TSymtab                          *
//  *              TLineNumNode, TLineNumList                     *
//  *                                                             *
//  *     FILE:    prog4-1/symtab.h                               *
//  *                                                             *
//  *     MODULE:  Symbol table                                   *
//  *                                                             *
//  *     Copyright (c) 1996 by Ronald Mak                        *
//  *     For instructional purposes only.  No warranties.        *
//  *                                                             *
//  ***************************************************************
```

(*continues*)

■■■■■■■■ **Figure 4.3** The first version of header file **symtab.h**. (*Continued*)

```
#ifndef symtab_h
#define symtab_h

#include <string.h>
#include "misc.h"

extern int xrefFlag;
extern int currentLineNumber;

//----------------------------------------------------------------
//   TSymtabNode         Symbol table node class.
//----------------------------------------------------------------

class TLineNumList;

class TSymtabNode {
    TSymtabNode   *left, *right;  // ptrs to left and right subtrees
    char          *pString;      // ptr to symbol string
    short          xSymtab;      // symbol table index
    short          xNode;        // node index
    TLineNumList *pLineNumList;  // ptr to list of line numbers

    friend class TSymtab;

public:
    float value;  // temporary value data member

    TSymtabNode(const char *pStr);
   ~TSymtabNode(void);

    TSymtabNode *LeftSubtree (void) const { return left;    }
    TSymtabNode *RightSubtree(void) const { return right;   }
    char        *String       (void) const { return pString; }
    short        SymtabIndex (void) const { return xSymtab; }
    short        NodeIndex   (void) const { return xNode;   }

    void Print(void) const;
};

//----------------------------------------------------------------
//   TSymtab            Symbol table class.  The symbol table is
//                      organized as a binary tree that is
//                      sorted alphabetically by the nodes'
//                      name strings.
//----------------------------------------------------------------
```

```
class TSymtab {
    TSymtabNode *root;        // ptr to binary tree root
    short        cntNodes;    // node counter
    short        xSymtab;     // symbol table index

public:
    TSymtab()
    {
        root     = NULL;
        cntNodes = 0;
        xSymtab  = 0;
    }

    ~TSymtab() { delete root; }

    TSymtabNode *Search    (const char *pString) const;
    TSymtabNode *Enter     (const char *pString);
    TSymtabNode *Root      (void) const { return root;     }
    int          NodeCount(void) const { return cntNodes; }
    void         Print     (void) const { root->Print();   }
};

//-------------------------------------------------------------
//  TLineNumNode        Line number node class.
//-------------------------------------------------------------

class TLineNumNode {
    TLineNumNode *next;       // ptr to next node
    const int     number;     // the line number

    friend class TLineNumList;

public:
    TLineNumNode(void)
        : number(currentLineNumber) { next = NULL; }
};

//-------------------------------------------------------------
//  TLineNumList        Line number list class.
//-------------------------------------------------------------

class TLineNumList {
    TLineNumNode *head, *tail;  // list head and tail

public:
```

(*continues*)

■■■■■■ **Figure 4.3** The first version of header file **symtab.h**. (*Continued*)

```cpp
    TLineNumList(void) { head = tail = new TLineNumNode; }
    virtual ~TLineNumList(void);

    void Update(void);
    void Print (int newLineFlag, int indent) const;
};

#endif
```

The constructor function TSymtab::TSymtab initializes the root pointer to null
and sets the node counter and symbol table index to zero. Member function
TSymtab::Print sends the Print message to the root symbol table node.

The constructor function TLineNumList::TLineNumList initializes the linked
list of line number nodes by creating the first node. Whenever a line number node is
created, the constructor function TLineNumList::TLineNumList initializes data
member number to the current source line number.

Figure 4.4 shows the implementation file symtab.cpp.

■■■■■■ **Figure 4.4** Implementation file **symtab.cpp**.

```cpp
//      **************************************************************
//      *                                                            *
//      *     S Y M B O L   T A B L E                                *
//      *                                                            *
//      *     Manage a symbol table.                                 *
//      *                                                            *
//      *     CLASSES: TSymtabNode,   TSymtab                        *
//      *              TLineNumNode, TLineNumList                    *
//      *                                                            *
//      *     FILE:    prog4-1/symtab.cpp                            *
//      *                                                            *
//      *     MODULE:  Symbol table                                  *
//      *                                                            *
//      *     Copyright (c) 1996 by Ronald Mak                       *
//      *     For instructional purposes only.  No warranties.       *
//      *                                                            *
//      **************************************************************

#include <stdio.h>
#include <iostream.h>
#include "buffer.h"
```

```
#include "symtab.h"

int xrefFlag = false;   // true = cross-referencing on, false = off

//               ***********************
//               *                     *
//               *   Symbol Table Node  *
//               *                     *
//               ***********************

//------------------------------------------------------------
// Constructor      Construct a symbol table node by initial-
//                  izing its subtree pointers and the pointer
//                  to its symbol string.
//
//      pStr : ptr to the symbol string
//------------------------------------------------------------

TSymtabNode::TSymtabNode(const char *pStr)
{
    left = right = NULL;
    pLineNumList = NULL;
    value = 0.0;
    xNode = 0;

    //--Allocate and copy the symbol string.
    pString = new char[strlen(pStr) + 1];
    strcpy(pString, pStr);

    //--If cross-referencing, update the line number list.
    if (xrefFlag) pLineNumList = new TLineNumList;
}

//------------------------------------------------------------
// Destructor       Deallocate a symbol table node.
//------------------------------------------------------------

TSymtabNode::~TSymtabNode(void)
{
    //--First the subtrees (if any).
    delete left;
    delete right;

    //--Then delete this node's components.
    delete[] pString;
    delete   pLineNumList;
```

(continues)

■■■■■■■ **Figure 4.4** Implementation file **symtab.cpp**. (*Continued*)

```
}

//----------------------------------------------------------------
//  Print       Print the symbol table node to the list file.
//              First print the node's left subtree, then the
//              node itself, and finally the node's right
//              subtree.  For the node itself, first print its
//              symbol string, and then its line numbers.
//----------------------------------------------------------------

void TSymtabNode::Print(void) const
{
    const int maxNamePrintWidth = 16;

    //--First, print left subtree.
    if (left) left->Print();

    //--Print the node:  first the name, then the list of line numbers.
    sprintf(list.text, "%*s", maxNamePrintWidth, pString);
    if (pLineNumList) {
        pLineNumList->Print(strlen(pString) > maxNamePrintWidth,
                            maxNamePrintWidth);
    }
    else list.PutLine();

    //--Finally, print right subtree.
    if (right) right->Print();
}

//                  ******************
//                  *                *
//                  *   Symbol Table  *
//                  *                *
//                  ******************

//----------------------------------------------------------------
//  Search      Search the symbol table for the node with a
//              given name string.
//
//      pString : ptr to the name string to search for
//
//  Return: ptr to the node if found, else NULL
//----------------------------------------------------------------

TSymtabNode *TSymtab::Search(const char *pString) const
```

```
{
    TSymtabNode *pNode = root;  // ptr to symbol table node
    int         comp;

    //--Loop to search the table.
    while (pNode) {
        comp = strcmp(pString, pNode->pString);  // compare names
        if (comp == 0) break;                     // found!

        //--Not yet found:  next search left or right subtree.
        pNode = comp < 0 ? pNode->left : pNode->right;
    }

    //--If found and cross-referencing, update the line number list.
    if (xrefFlag && (comp == 0)) pNode->pLineNumList->Update();

    return pNode;  // ptr to node, or NULL if not found
}


//-------------------------------------------------------------
//  Enter       Search the symbol table for the node with a
//              given name string.  If the node is found, return
//              a pointer to it.  Else if not found, enter a new
//              node with the name string, and return a pointer
//              to the new node.
//
//      pString : ptr to the name string to enter
//
//  Return: ptr to the node, whether existing or newly-entered
//-------------------------------------------------------------

TSymtabNode *TSymtab::Enter(const char *pString)
{
    TSymtabNode  *pNode;          // ptr to node
    TSymtabNode **ppNode = &root;  // ptr to ptr to node

    //--Loop to search table for insertion point.
    while ((pNode = *ppNode) != NULL) {
        int comp = strcmp(pString, pNode->pString);  // compare strings
        if (comp == 0) return pNode;                  // found!

        //--Not yet found:  next search left or right subtree.
        ppNode = comp < 0 ? &(pNode->left) : &(pNode->right);
    }

    //--Create and insert a new node.
```

(continues)

■■■■■ **Figure 4.4** Implementation file **symtab.cpp**. (*Continued*)

```
    pNode          = new TSymtabNode(pString);    // create a new node,
    pNode->xSymtab = xSymtab;                      // set its symtab and
    pNode->xNode   = cntNodes++;                   // node indexes,
    *ppNode        = pNode;                        // insert it, and
    return pNode;                                  // return a ptr to it
}

//             ***********************
//             *                     *
//             *   Line Number List  *
//             *                     *
//             ***********************

//----------------------------------------------------------------
//  Destructor      Deallocate a line number list.
//----------------------------------------------------------------

TLineNumList::~TLineNumList(void)
{
    //--Loop to delete each node in the list.
    while (head) {
        TLineNumNode *pNode = head;    // ptr to node to delete
        head = head->next;             // move down the list
        delete pNode;                  // delete node
    }
}

//----------------------------------------------------------------
//  Update      Update the list by appending a new line number
//              node if the line number isn't already in the
//              list.
//----------------------------------------------------------------

void TLineNumList::Update(void)
{
    //--If the line number is already there, it'll be at the tail.
    if (tail && (tail->number == currentLineNumber)) return;

    //--Append the new node.
    tail->next = new TLineNumNode;
    tail       = tail->next;
}

//----------------------------------------------------------------
//  Print       Print the line number list.  Use more than one
```

```
//              line if necessary; indent subsequent lines.
//
//      newLineFlag : if true, start a new line immediately
//      indent      : amount to indent subsequent lines
//-----------------------------------------------------------

void TLineNumList::Print(int newLineFlag, int indent) const
{
    const int maxLineNumberPrintWidth = 4;
    const int maxLineNumbersPerLine   = 10;

    int          n;        // count of numbers per line
    TLineNumNode *pNode;   // ptr to line number node
    char         *plt = &list.text[strlen(list.text)];
                           // ptr to where in list text to append

    n = newLineFlag ? 0 : maxLineNumbersPerLine;

    //--Loop over line number nodes in the list.
    for (pNode = head; pNode; pNode = pNode->next) {

        //--Start a new list line if the current one is full.
        if (n == 0) {
            list.PutLine();
            sprintf(list.text, "%*s", indent, " ");
            plt = &list.text[indent];
            n   = maxLineNumbersPerLine;
        }

        //--Append the line number to the list text.
        sprintf(plt, "%*d", maxLineNumberPrintWidth, pNode->number);
        plt += maxLineNumberPrintWidth;
        --n;
    }

    list.PutLine();
}
```

The constructor function TSymtabNode::TSymtabNode initializes all the pointers and points to a copy of the symbol string. If there is cross-referencing, the function also creates a new linked list of line number nodes. The destructor function TSymtabNode::~TSymtabNode first deletes the left and right subtrees (which causes this function to be called recursively for each node in the subtrees), and then it deletes the symbol string and the linked list of line number nodes.

Member function `TSymtabNode::Print` recursively prints a node and its subtrees. First it prints the left subtree, then the node itself, and finally the right subtree. For each node, it prints the symbol string. The final result is an alphabetical listing of the nodes.

Member function `TSymtab::Search` searches the symbol table tree for a node with a matching symbol string, beginning with the root node. At each node, it compares the argument symbol string with the node's symbol string. If they match, the function updates the node's line number list and returns a pointer to the node. Otherwise, it searches either the node's left or right subtree, depending on whether the argument string is alphabetically less than or greater than the node string. If the function ever encounters a null node pointer, that means a matching symbol string is not in the symbol table, so the function returns a null pointer.

Member function `TSymtab::Enter` enters a node into the symbol table tree. Of course, it must preserve the alphabetic ordering of the nodes. It must search the tree to see if a node with a matching symbol string isn't already in there. Note that unlike member function `Search`, this function uses a pointer to a node pointer. If it finds an existing matching node, it simply returns a pointer to that node. If it encounters a null node pointer, not only is a matching node not already in the tree, but the null pointer is exactly where the new node should be inserted! This is shown in Figure 4.5. Therefore, `Enter` creates the new node, increments the node counter, and sets the node's symbol table and node indexes. Note that the node index is set to the value of the node counter, and so the nodes are sequentially numbered, in the order they're created, starting from zero. The function inserts the node and returns a pointer to it.

The destructor function `TLineNumList::~TLineNumList` loops to delete each line number node in the linked list. Member function `TLineNumList::Update` updates the list by appending a new line number node to the tail. Member function `TLineNumList::Print` prints the line numbers in the list to the global list file using one or more output lines.

Figure 4.6 shows an object diagram of the objects that constitute a symbol table.

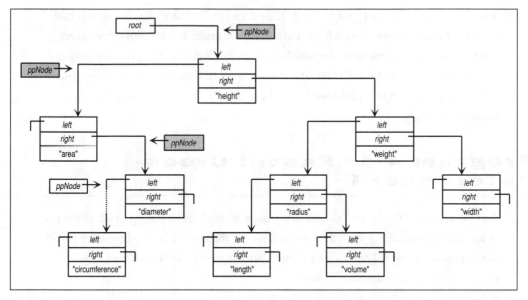

Figure 4.5 How a new node for the identifier name string "**circumference**" is entered into the symbol table tree. Variable **ppNode** is a pointer to a node pointer. After an unsuccessful search for an existing matching node, it points to a null node pointer that is where the new node should be inserted. The null node pointer will be replaced by a pointer to the new node. This diagram also shows the three node pointers that **ppNode** previously pointed to during its search.

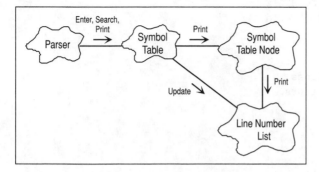

Figure 4.6 Object diagram of the symbol table.

The parser object sends Enter, Search, and Print messages to the symbol table object. After a successful search for a symbol table node, the symbol table object sends an Update message to the node's line number list object. Upon receiving a Print message, the symbol table object sends a Print message to the root symbol table node. Each symbol table node object can send a Print message to its line number list object.

Program 4-1: Pascal Cross-Referencer I

A cross-reference listing of a source program is an alphabetic listing of all of the program's identifiers, along with the line numbers of the source lines where each identifier appears. Figure 4.7 shows an example. Such a listing is useful for us to keep track of where each identifier is used.

■■■■ **Figure 4.7** Sample cross-reference listing.

```
Page 1   hello.pas   Fri Jul 22 22:13:47 1994

  1 0: PROGRAM hello (output);
  2 0:
  3 0: {Write 'Hello, world.' ten times.}
  4 0:
  5 0: VAR
  6 0:     i : integer;
  7 0:
  8 0: BEGIN {hello}
  9 0:     FOR i := 1 TO 10 DO BEGIN
 10 0:         writeln('Hello, world.');
 11 0:     END;
 12 0: END {hello}.

              12 source lines.
               0 syntax errors.

***** Cross-Reference *****

        hello   1
            i   6   9
      integer   6
       output   1
      writeln  10
```

We'll build the Cross-Referencer I utility program using all the modules from the previous chapters, plus the new symbol table module. We'll also need a new parser that enters each new identifier into the symbol table. Each time the parser encounters an identifier, it looks up the identifier's symbol table node, and it enters a new node if necessary. It then updates the new or existing node with the current line number. After processing the source program, it uses the information in the symbol table to print the cross-reference. (We'll write a second version of this utility program in Chapter 7.)

We need to declare the global symbol table. Since the symbol table object is shared by the front and back ends, we add the line

```
TSymtab globalSymtab;  // the global symbol table
```

to implementation file common.cpp, and the lines

```
#include "symtab.h"
```

and

```
extern TSymtab globalSymtab;
```

to header file common.h.

Figure 4.8 shows the new version of member function TParser::Parse for the Cross-Referencer I utility in implementation file parser.cpp. We can use the same header file parser.h from Program 3-2.

Figure 4.8 Member function **TParser::Parse** in file **parser.cpp** for the Cross-Referencer I utility program.

```
//-------------------------------------------------------------
//  Parse       Parse the source file.  Extract each token, and
//              for each identifier, enter it into the symbol
//              table along with its line numbers.
//-------------------------------------------------------------

void TParser::Parse(void)
{
    //--Loop to extract and process tokens
    //--until the end of the program.
    do {
        GetToken();

        //--Shouldn't see an end of file.
```

(continues)

■■■■■ **Figure 4.8** Member function **TParser::Parse** in file **parser.cpp** for the Cross-Referencer I utility program. (*Continued*)

```
    if (token == tcEndOfFile) {
        Error(errUnexpectedEndOfFile);
        break;
    }

    //--Enter each identifier into the symbol table
    //--if it isn't already in there.
    if (token == tcIdentifier) {
        TSymtabNode *pNode = globalSymtab.Search(pToken->String());
        if (!pNode)  pNode = globalSymtab.Enter (pToken->String());
    }
} while (token != tcPeriod);

//--Print the parser's summary.
list.PutLine();
sprintf(list.text, "%20d source lines.",  currentLineNumber);
list.PutLine();
sprintf(list.text, "%20d syntax errors.", errorCount);
list.PutLine();
}
```

The function checks each token that it gets from the scanner. If the token is an identifier, it searches the symbol table for the identifier's name string. If the name is not already in the table, the function enters it. Recall that a successful search sends the Update message to the symbol table node's line number list object, and that creating a new symbol table node also creates a new line number list.

Figure 4.9 shows the main file xref1.cpp of the Cross-Referencer I utility program. It declares the global symbol table object globalSymtab. After main has sent the Parse message to the parser object, it sends the Print message to globalSymtab to produce the cross-reference listing.

■■■■■ **Figure 4.9** The main file **xref1.cpp** of the Cross-Referencer I utility program.

```
//  ****************************************************************
//  *                                                            *
//  *    Program 4-1:  Cross-Referencer I                        *
//  *                                                            *
//  *    After listing the source file, list all of its          *
```

```
//   *    identifiers alphabetically.  For each identifier, list   *
//   *    the line numbers of the source lines that contain it.    *
//   *                                                             *
//   *    FILE:    prog4-1/xref1.cpp                               *
//   *                                                             *
//   *    USAGE:   xref1 <source file> [-x]                        *
//   *                                                             *
//   *                <source file>  name of source file to        *
//   *                               cross-reference               *
//   *                                                             *
//   *                -x             turn on cross-referencing      *
//   *                                                             *
//   *    Copyright (c) 1996 by Ronald Mak                         *
//   *    For instructional purposes only.  No warranties.         *
//   *                                                             *
//   ***************************************************************

#include <iostream.h>
#include <string.h>
#include "common.h"
#include "error.h"
#include "buffer.h"
#include "symtab.h"
#include "parser.h"


//----------------------------------------------------------------
//  main
//----------------------------------------------------------------

void main(int argc, char *argv[])
{
    extern int xrefFlag;

    //--Check the command line arguments.
    if ((argc != 2) && (argc != 3)) {
        cerr << "Usage: xref1 <source file> [-x]" << endl;
        AbortTranslation(abortInvalidCommandLineArgs);
    }

    //--Set the cross-referencing flag.
    xrefFlag = (argc == 3) && (strcmp(argv[2], "-x") == 0);

    //--Create the parser for the source file,
    //--and then parse the file.
    TParser parser(new TSourceBuffer(argv[1]));
```

(continues)

Figure 4.9 The main file **xref1.cpp** of the Cross-Referencer I utility program. (*Continued*)

```
parser.Parse();

//--Print the cross-reference.
if (xrefFlag) {
    list.PutLine();
    list.PutLine("***** Cross-Reference *****");
    list.PutLine();
    globalSymtab.Print();
}
}
```

Table 4.1 shows the status of each module in the utility program.

Program 4-2: Pascal Source Cruncher

In the previous chapter, we wrote a utility that compacts a Pascal source program so that it takes up less disk space. Now we'll write a utility that saves even more disk space by converting ("crunching") a source program into a binary file. Then we'll write another utility that "decrunches" the binary file back to text. The binary file is also the basis for the intermediate code (icode) that both our interpreter and compiler will use, and so we'll also make a start on the icode module.

Here's the basic theory of how to create an icode file from a source program. Since each Pascal token has a token code, we replace each token with its code. Identifier, number, and string tokens need more—the code tcIdentifier by itself, for example, does not tell us *which* identifier. Our solution is to enter into the symbol table not just the identifier name strings, but also the token strings of number and string tokens. Recall that each symbol table node has a unique index xNode. So, after each tcIdentifier, tcNumber, and tcString token code, we also include the symbol table node index. Then, at the end of the icode file, we write out the symbol table nodes in their crunched format.

Later, to convert an icode file back to text, we read in the crunched program and the crunched symbol table, and replace each token code with the token string. For each

▰▰▰▰ **Table 4.1** Modules and Files of Program 4-1

Module	File	Status	Directory
Main	xref1.cpp	*new*	prog4-1
Parser	parser.h	*unchanged*	prog3-2
	parser.cpp	*changed*	prog4-1
Scanner	scanner.h	*unchanged*	prog3-1
	scanner.cpp	*unchanged*	prog3-2
	token.h	*unchanged*	prog3-2
	tknword.cpp	*unchanged*	prog3-2
	tknnum.cpp	*unchanged*	prog3-2
	tknstrsp.cpp	*unchanged*	prog3-2
Symbol table	symtab.h	*new*	prog4-1
	symtab.cpp	*new*	prog4-1
Error	error.h	*unchanged*	prog3-2
	error.cpp	*unchanged*	prog3-2
Buffer	buffer.h	*unchanged*	prog2-1
	buffer.cpp	*unchanged*	prog2-1
Common	common.h	*changed*	prog4-1
	common.cpp	*changed*	prog4-1
	misc.h	*unchanged*	prog3-2

▰▰▰▰

identifier, number, and string token, we can use the symbol table node index to access the appropriate symbol table node to obtain the correct token string.

▰▰▰▰ **Figure 4.10** Header file **icode.h** for the Cruncher and Decruncher utility programs.

```
//  ****************************************************************
//  *                                                            *
//  *     I N T E R M E D I A T E    C O D E    (Header)          *
//  *                                                            *
//  *     CLASSES: TIcode                                        *
//  *                                                            *
//  *     FILE:    prog4-2/icode.h                               *
//  *                                                            *
//  *     MODULE:  Intermediate code                             *
```

(continues)

■■■■■■■ **Figure 4.10** Header file **icode.h** for the Cruncher and Decruncher utility
programs. (*Continued*)

```cpp
//   *                                                              *
//   *    Copyright (c) 1996 by Ronald Mak                          *
//   *    For instructional purposes only.  No warranties.          *
//   *                                                              *
//   ****************************************************************

#ifndef icode_h
#define icode_h

#include <fstream.h>
#include "token.h"
#include "scanner.h"


//----------------------------------------------------------------
// TIcode      Intermediate code subclass of TScanner.
//----------------------------------------------------------------

class TSymtabNode;

class TIcode : public TScanner {
    fstream     file;              // intermediate code file
    const char *const pFileName;   // ptr to the file name
    int        size;               // byte size of file

    char **symtabStrings;  // vector of symbol table strings
    int    symtabCount;    // count of strings in the vector

public:
    enum TMode {input, output};

    TIcode(const char *pTIcodeFileName, TMode mode);
   ~TIcode(void);

    void GoTo(int location) { file.seekg(location, ios::beg); }
    int  Size(void) const    { return size; }

    void Put(int value);
    void Put(TTokenCode tc, short index = -1);
    void Put(const TSymtabNode *pNode);

    virtual TToken *Get      (void);
    int            GetInteger(void);
    void           GetSymtabStrings(void);
```

```
};

#endif
```

Figure 4.10 shows header file `icode.h`, where we define class `TICode`. We define it as a subclass of `TScanner` because, as we first noted in the previous chapter, an icode object is a kind of scanner object. Its private data members include the intermediate file object, a pointer to the file name, and the byte size of the file. Also private are `symtabStrings`, a pointer to a vector of token strings from the symbol table nodes, and `symtabCount`, a count of the strings in this vector. These latter two data members are used by the Decruncher utility, so we'll explain them later. The class's constructor function is passed a pointer to the icode file name and a second argument that indicates whether the file is to be opened for input (by the Decruncher utility) or output (by the Cruncher utility).

The public member function `GoTo` takes a byte offset from the beginning of the icode file and positions the file to that location. Member function `Put` is overloaded. Used by the Cruncher utility, it crunches and writes to the icode file either an integer value, a token code possibly followed by a symbol table node index, or a symbol table node. Member functions `Get`, `GetInteger`, and `GetSymtabStrings` will be used by the Decruncher utility.

We make a small change to the definition of class `TToken` in header file `token.h`. Class `TICode` needs to be a friend of class `TToken`. The reason is that an icode object can act like a scanner and return token objects. So we add the line

```
friend class TICode;
```

to the definition of class `TToken`.

Figure 4.11 shows implementation file `icode.cpp`. It begins with the token string vector `symbolStrings` that corresponds to type `TTokenCode` defined in file `common.h` (see Figure 3.14). This vector will be used by the Decruncher utility.

■■■■■ **Figure 4.11** Implementation file **icode.cpp** for the Cruncher and Decruncher utility programs.

```
//  ************************************************************
//  *                                                        *
//  *    INTERMEDIATE  CODE                                   *
```

(continues)

■■■■■■■ **Figure 4.11** Implementation file **icode.cpp** for the Cruncher and
Decruncher utility programs. (*Continued*)

```
//  *                                                              *
//  *     Create and access the intermediate code implemented as   *
//  *     a file.                                                   *
//  *                                                              *
//  *     CLASSES: TIcode                                           *
//  *                                                              *
//  *     FILE:     prog4-2/iform.cpp                               *
//  *                                                              *
//  *     MODULE:   Intermediate code                               *
//  *                                                              *
//  *     Copyright (c) 1996 by Ronald Mak                          *
//  *     For instructional purposes only.  No warranties.          *
//  *                                                              *
//  ****************************************************************

#include "symtab.h"
#include "icode.h"

//--Vector of special symbol and reserved word strings.
char *symbolStrings[] = {
    NULL,
    NULL, NULL, NULL, NULL, NULL,

    "^", "*", "(", ")", "-", "+",
    "=", "[", "]", ":", ";", "<",
    ">", ",", ".", "/", ":=", "<=", ">=",
    "<>", "..",

    "and", "array", "begin", "case", "const", "div",
    "do", "downto", "else", "end", "file", "for", "function",
    "goto", "if", "in", "label", "mod", "nil", "not", "of", "or",
    "packed", "procedure", "program", "record", "repeat", "set",
    "then", "to", "type", "until", "var", "while", "with",
};

//----------------------------------------------------------------
// Constructor     Open the intermediate code file.
//
//      pIformFileName : ptr to the name of the intermediate
//                       code file
//      mode           : input or output
//----------------------------------------------------------------
```

```
TIcode::TIcode(const char *pIformFileName, TMode mode)
    : pFileName(pIformFileName)
{
    if (mode == input) {
        //--Open the intermediate code file for input.
        //--Abort if failed.
        file.open(pIformFileName, ios::in | ios::binary);
        if (!file.good()) AbortTranslation(abortIFormFileOpenFailed);
    }
    else {
        //--Open the intermediate code file for output.
        //--Abort if failed.
        file.open(pIformFileName, ios::out | ios::binary);
        if (!file.good()) AbortTranslation(abortIFormFileOpenFailed);

        size = 0;
    }

    symtabStrings = NULL;
}

//----------------------------------------------------------------
//  Destructor      Deallocate the intermediate code.
//----------------------------------------------------------------

TIcode::~TIcode(void)
{
    //--Dellocate the symtab strings vector.
    if (symtabStrings) {
        for (int i = 0; i < symtabCount; ++i) delete[] symtabStrings[i];
        delete[] symtabStrings;
    }

    //--Close the intermediate code file.
    file.close();
}

//----------------------------------------------------------------
//  Put(int)                   Append an integer value to the
//                             intermediate code.
//
//      value : the integer value
//----------------------------------------------------------------

void TIcode::Put(int value)
```

```
{
    file.write((const signed char *) &value, sizeof(int));
    size += sizeof(int);
}


//----------------------------------------------------------------
//  Put(TTokenCode, short)     Append a token to the
//                             intermediate code.
//
//      tc    : token code
//      index : -1, or the symbol table node index
//----------------------------------------------------------------

void TIcode::Put(TTokenCode tc, short index)
{
    //--First append the token code.
    char code = tc;
    file.write((const signed char *) &code, sizeof(char));
    size += sizeof(char);

    //--Append the symbol table node index if it's not -1.
    if (index != -1) {
        file.write((const signed char *) &index, sizeof(short));
        size += sizeof(short);
    }
}


//----------------------------------------------------------------
//  Put(TSymtabNode *)          Recursively append a symbol
//                              table's nodes to the
//                              intermediate code.
//
//      pNode : ptr to the root of a symbol table subtree
//----------------------------------------------------------------

void TIcode::Put(const TSymtabNode *pNode)
{
    if (!pNode) return;

    //--First, crunch the left subtree.
    Put(pNode->LeftSubtree());

    //--Then, crunch the subtree root.
```

```
    char  length = strlen(pNode->String()) + 1;
    short index  = pNode->NodeIndex();
    file.write((const signed char *) &index,          sizeof(short));
    file.write((const signed char *) &length,         sizeof(char));
    file.write((const signed char *) pNode->String(), length);
    size += sizeof(short) + sizeof(char) + length;

    //--Finally, crunch the right subtree.
    Put(pNode->RightSubtree());
}


//------------------------------------------------------------
//  Get         Extract the next token from the intermediate
//              code.
//
//  Return: pointer to the extracted token
//------------------------------------------------------------

TToken *TIcode::Get(void)
{
    TToken *pToken;         // ptr to token to return
    char    code;          // token code read from the file
    TTokenCode token;

    //--First extract the token code.
    file.read((signed char *) &code, sizeof(char));
    token = (TTokenCode) code;

    //--Determine the token class, based on the token code.
    switch (token) {
        case tcNumber:  pToken = &numberToken;  break;
        case tcString:  pToken = &stringToken;  break;

        case tcIdentifier: {
            pToken       = &wordToken;
            pToken->code = tcIdentifier;
            break;
        }

        default: {
            if (token < tcAND) {
                pToken       = &specialToken;
                pToken->code = token;
            }
            else {
                pToken       = &wordToken;  // reserved word
```

(continues)

■■■■■■■ **Figure 4.11** Implementation file **icode.cpp** for the Cruncher and
Decruncher utility programs. (*Continued*)

```cpp
                pToken->code = token;
            }
            break;
        }
    }

    //--Extract and set the token string.
    switch (token) {
        case tcIdentifier:
        case tcNumber:
        case tcString: {
            short index;   // symbol table node index

            file.read((signed char *) &index, sizeof(short));
            strcpy(pToken->string, symtabStrings[index]);
            break;
        }

        default: {
            strcpy(pToken->string, symbolStrings[code]);
            break;
        }
    }

    return pToken;
}

//------------------------------------------------------------
// GetInteger          Extract an integer value from the
//                     intermediate code.
//
// Return: the integer value
//------------------------------------------------------------

int TIcode::GetInteger(void)
{
    int value;   // value to extract

    file.read((signed char *) &value, sizeof(int));
    return value;
}

//------------------------------------------------------------
// GetSymtabStrings    Extract the vector of symbol table
```

```
//                      table strings from the intermediate
//                      code.
//
//  Return: pointer to the vector
//-----------------------------------------------------------

void TIcode::GetSymtabStrings(void)
{
    int   count;    // count of symtab strings
    short index;    // symbol table node index
    char  length;   // string length (including final '\0')

    //--First extract the count of strings and allocate
    //--the vector of string pointers.
    file.read((signed char *) &count, sizeof(int));
    symtabStrings = new char *[count];
    symtabCount   = count;

    //--Then extract the strings.
    do {
        file.read((signed char *) &index,  sizeof(short));
        file.read((signed char *) &length, sizeof(char));

        symtabStrings[index] = new char[length];
        file.read((signed char *) symtabStrings[index], length);
    } while (--count > 0);
}
```

The constructor function `TICode::TICode` opens the icode file in binary mode either for input or for output. The destructor function `TICode::~TICode` deallocates the symbol table string vector, and then closes the icode file.

We have three versions of the overloaded member function `Put`. All three write to the icode file and keep track of the file size. The first version writes an integer value. The second version writes either a token code by itself, or if the symbol table node index is not -1, the token code followed by the index value. We'll see below that -1 is passed as the index value if the token is not an identifier, number, or string. The third version recursively writes a symbol table subtree—if we pass it the root of the symbol table tree, it writes the entire tree. For each symbol table node, it writes the node index, the length of the symbol string, and the string itself. Note that all numeric values (including token codes, indexes, and string lengths) are written in binary, whereas symbol strings are written in ASCII.

We'll look at the remaining member functions when we discuss the Decruncher utility.

In header file `parser.h`, we need to add the following two new lines for the Cruncher utility:

```
#include "icode.h"
```

and

```
extern TIcode *pIcode;
```

We'll declare the pointer to the global icode object in the main files of the utility programs.

Figure 4.12 shows the member function `TParser::Parse` for the Cruncher utility in implementation file `parser.cpp`.

■■■■ **Figure 4.12** Member function **TParser::Parse** for the Cruncher utility in implementation file **parser.cpp**.

```
//--------------------------------------------------------------
//  Parse          Parse the source file and build the icode.
//--------------------------------------------------------------

void TParser::Parse(void)
{
    //--Output a placeholder for the size of the crunched program.
    pIcode->Put(0);

    //--Loop to extract and crunch tokens
    //--until the end of the program.
    do {
        GetToken();

        //--Shouldn't see an end of file.
        if (token == tcEndOfFile) {
            Error(errUnexpectedEndOfFile);
            break;
        }

        //--Enter each identifier, number, and string into the
        //--symbol table if it isn't already in there.
        //--Crunch the token.
        switch (token) {
```

```
            case tcIdentifier:
            case tcNumber:
            case tcString: {
                TSymtabNode *pNode = globalSymtab.Search(pToken->String());
                if (!pNode)  pNode = globalSymtab.Enter (pToken->String());
                pIcode->Put(token, (short) pNode->NodeIndex());
                break;
            }

            default: {
                pIcode->Put(token);
                break;
            }
        }
    } while (token != tcPeriod);

    //--Remember the icode size at this point.
    int programSize = pIcode->Size();

    //--Crunch the symbol table.
    pIcode->Put(globalSymtab.NodeCount());  // count of entries
    pIcode->Put(globalSymtab.Root());       // all the entries

    //--Now go back to the beginning of the intermediate code
    //--file and fill in the size of the crunched program.
    pIcode->GoTo(0);
    pIcode->Put(programSize);

    //--Print the parser's summary.
    list.PutLine();
    sprintf(list.text, "%20d source lines.",  currentLineNumber);
    list.PutLine();
    sprintf(list.text, "%20d syntax errors.", errorCount);
    list.PutLine();
}
```

The function first outputs a zero to the icode as a placeholder. Later, after the source program has been processed and we know the byte size of its crunched form, this placeholder will be replaced by that size.

Parse loops to process each token of the source program. For each identifier, number, or string token, it searches the symbol table for the token string, and enters the string if it isn't already in there. It sends the Put message to the icode object to crunch the token code and the symbol table node index. For any other token, Parse sends the Put message to the icode object to crunch the token code only.

After it has crunched the last source token, Parse remembers the byte size of the crunched program. It then sends Put messages to add the symbol table node count to the icode, followed by all the crunched symbol table nodes themselves.

Parse then completes the icode by returning to the beginning and replacing the placeholder with the byte size of the crunched program. This value is, in effect, the offset from the beginning of the icode file to the symbol table node count.

Figure 4.13 shows the main file of the Cruncher utility. Note that the utility requires two file names as command line arguments. The first is the source file name, and the second is the icode file name.

■■■■■■■■■■ **Figure 4.13** The main file **crunch.cpp** of the Cruncher utility program.

```
//    ***************************************************************
//    *                                                             *
//    *    Program 4-2:  Source File Cruncher                       *
//    *                                                             *
//    *    Crunch a Pascal source file into a compressed            *
//    *    intermediate code.  It can be restored later with the    *
//    *    Decruncher utility.                                      *
//    *                                                             *
//    *    FILE:    prog4-2/crunch.cpp                              *
//    *                                                             *
//    *    USAGE:   crunch <source file> <crunch file>              *
//    *                                                             *
//    *                  <source file>  name of source file to      *
//    *                                 crunch                      *
//    *                                                             *
//    *                  <icode file>   name of the intermediate    *
//    *                                 code file                   *
//    *                                                             *
//    *    Copyright (c) 1996 by Ronald Mak                         *
//    *    For instructional purposes only.  No warranties.         *
//    *                                                             *
//    ***************************************************************

#include <iostream.h>
#include "common.h"
#include "error.h"
#include "buffer.h"
```

```
#include "symtab.h"
#include "icode.h"
#include "parser.h"

TIcode *pIcode;   // ptr to the intermediate code

//-------------------------------------------------------------
//  main
//-------------------------------------------------------------

void main(int argc, char *argv[])
{
    //--Check the command line arguments.
    if (argc != 3) {
        cerr << "Usage: crunch <source file> <icode file>" << endl;
        AbortTranslation(abortInvalidCommandLineArgs);
    }

    //--Create the intermediate code.
    pIcode = new TIcode(argv[2], TIcode::output);

    //--Create the parser for the source file,
    //--and then parse the file.
    TParser parser(new TSourceBuffer(argv[1]));
    parser.Parse();

    //--Clean up.
    delete pIcode;
}
```

Table 4.2 shows the modules that make up this utility program.

▰▰▰▰▰ **Table 4.2** Modules and Files of Program 4-2

Module	File	Status	Directory
Main	crunch.cpp	*new*	prog4-2
Parser	parser.h	*changed*	prog4-2
	parser.cpp	*changed*	prog4-2
Intermediate code	icode.h	*new*	prog4-2
	icode.cpp	*new*	prog4-2
Scanner	scanner.h	*unchanged*	prog3-1
	scanner.cpp	*unchanged*	prog3-2

(continues)

■■■■■ **Table 4.2** Modules and Files of Program 4-2 (*Continued*)

Module	File	Status	Directory
	token.h	*changed*	prog4-2
	tknword.cpp	*unchanged*	prog3-2
	tknnum.cpp	*unchanged*	prog3-2
	tknstrsp.cpp	*unchanged*	prog3-2
Symbol table	symtab.h	*unchanged*	prog4-1
	symtab.cpp	*unchanged*	prog4-1
Error	error.h	*unchanged*	prog3-2
	error.cpp	*unchanged*	prog3-2
Buffer	buffer.h	*unchanged*	prog2-1
	buffer.cpp	*unchanged*	prog2-1
Common	common.h	*unchanged*	prog4-1
	common.cpp	*unchanged*	prog2-1
	misc.h	*unchanged*	prog3-2

Program 4-3: Pascal Source Decruncher

Now that we have a Cruncher utility, we need to write a Decruncher utility that converts a crunched source program back to text. We won't be able to reproduce the original source program text. Instead, the output of the Decruncher utility·will be the compact form we saw in the previous chapter.

Table 4.3 shows that for this utility program only, we don't need the parser module, since the main routine takes care of fetching tokens from the icode. This program also requires the compact list buffer class TCompactListBuffer from the previous chapter (files complist.h and complist.cpp in Figures 3.25 and 3.27, respectively).

Figure 4.14 shows the main file decrunch.cpp of the Decruncher utility program.

▬▬▬▬ **Table 4.3** Modules and Files of Program 4-3

Module	File	Status	Directory
Main	decrunch.cpp	*new*	prog4-3
Intermediate code	icode.h	*new*	prog4-2
	icode.cpp	*new*	prog4-2
Scanner	scanner.h	*unchanged*	prog3-1
	scanner.cpp	*unchanged*	prog3-2
	token.h	*changed*	prog4-2
	tknword.cpp	*unchanged*	prog3-2
	tknnum.cpp	*unchanged*	prog3-2
	tknstrsp.cpp	*unchanged*	prog3-2
Symbol table	symtab.h	*unchanged*	prog4-1
	symtab.cpp	*unchanged*	prog4-1
Error	error.h	*unchanged*	prog3-2
	error.cpp	*unchanged*	prog3-2
Buffer	buffer.h	*unchanged*	prog2-1
	buffer.cpp	*unchanged*	prog2-1
Common	common.h	*unchanged*	prog4-1
	common.cpp	*unchanged*	prog2-1
	misc.h	*unchanged*	prog3-2

▬▬▬▬

▬▬▬▬ **Figure 4.14** The main file **decrunch.cpp** of the Decruncher utility program.

```
//  ****************************************************************
//  *                                                            *
//  *    Program 4-3:  Source File Decruncher                    *
//  *                                                            *
//  *    Decrunch a Pascal source file from its intermediate     *
//  *    code to a compacted text form.                          *
//  *                                                            *
//  *    FILE:   prog4-3/decrunch.cpp                            *
//  *                                                            *
//  *    USAGE:  decrunch <icode file>                           *
//  *                                                            *
//  *              <icode file>  name of the intermediate        *
```

(continues)

■■■■■■ **Figure 4.14** The main file **decrunch.cpp** of the Decruncher utility
program. (*Continued*)

```
//   *                          code file                    *
//   *                                                       *
//   *    Copyright (c) 1996 by Ronald Mak                   *
//   *    For instructional purposes only.  No warranties.   *
//   *                                                       *
//   **********************************************************

#include <iostream.h>
#include "common.h"
#include "error.h"
#include "complist.h"
#include "token.h"
#include "icode.h"

//----------------------------------------------------------------
//  main
//----------------------------------------------------------------

void main(int argc, char *argv[])
{
    TToken  *pToken;                    // ptr to the current token
    int      currIsDelimiter;           // true if current token is a
                                        //   delimiter, else false
    int      prevIsDelimiter = true;    // likewise for previous token

    //--Check the command line arguments.
    if (argc != 2) {
        cerr << "Usage: decrunch <icode file>" << endl;
        AbortTranslation(abortInvalidCommandLineArgs);
    }

    //--Create the icode and compact list objects.
    TIcode           icode(argv[1], TIcode::input);
    TCompactListBuffer compact;

    //--Read the location of the crunched symbol table strings,
    //--and then extract the strings.
    int atSymtab = icode.GetInteger();
    icode.GoTo(atSymtab);
    icode.GetSymtabStrings();

    //--Get ready to read the crunched program.
    icode.GoTo(sizeof(int));
```

```
    //--Loop to extract the crunched tokens
    //--until the end of the program.
    do {
        //--Extract the next token.
        pToken         = icode.Get();
        currIsDelimiter = pToken->IsDelimiter();

        //--Append a blank only if both the previous and the
        //--current tokens are not delimiters.  Then append the
        //--token string to the output record.
        if (!prevIsDelimiter && !currIsDelimiter) {
            compact.PutBlank();
        }
        compact.Put(pToken->String());

        prevIsDelimiter = currIsDelimiter;
    } while (pToken->Code() != tcPeriod);

    //--Print the last output record.
    compact.PutLine();
}
```

After checking the command line arguments, the main routine creates the icode and compact list buffer objects. It sends the `GetInteger` message to the icode object to read the offset to the symbol table node count. It sends the `GoTo` message and then the `GetSymtabStrings` message to read the crunched symbol table nodes. The implementations of these member functions of class `TIcode` were shown in Figure 4.11.

`TIcode::GetSymtabStrings` first reads the symbol table node count from the icode file, and then it allocates a symbol table strings vector. It loops to read the crunched symbol table nodes. For each node, the function reads the node index, the token string length, and the token string itself. It uses the node index as a subscript to store the token string into the symbol table strings vector.

After reading the crunched symbol table, `main` goes back to the beginning of the icode file and loops to read the crunched program. It sends the `Get` message to the icode object to obtain the next token. It sends the `PutBlank` message to the compact list buffer object if necessary, and it sends the `Put` message to write the token string.

Member function `TIcode::Get` (again, see Figure 4.11) first reads the next token code from the icode file and points local variable `pToken` to the appropriate token object. If the token is an identifier, number, or string, the function reads the symbol table node index, which it uses to index into the `symtabStrings` vector to obtain the token string. Otherwise, the function uses the token code to index into the `symbolStrings` vector to obtain the token string. Like a scanner, `Get` returns a pointer to the token object.

This concludes our first look at the symbol table module. In the next few chapters, we'll add more information into the symbol table and continue to create the intermediate code as we see how to parse expressions, statements, and declarations. We'll write a pretty-printer utility program in Chapter 8 that can improve the output of the Decruncher utility.

5

PARSING

EXPRESSIONS

Every programming language has a syntax, the set of grammar rules that specify how statements and expressions in that language are correctly written. A language's syntax plays a vital role for compilers and interpreters. Pascal compilers and interpreters must know Pascal's syntax in order to translate Pascal source programs.

The parser is the part of a compiler or an interpreter that knows the source language's syntax. The parser controls the translation process since it analyzes and translates the source program based on the syntax. In the preceding chapters, we've seen the parser in action, albeit in a rudimentary form. The parser object sends `Get` messages to the scanner object to extract tokens from the source program, and it sends `Enter` and `Search` messages to the symbol table object to enter and search for identifiers. It translates the source program into intermediate code and sends `Put` messages to the icode object. After it has translated the entire source program, the parser sends the `Go` message to the backend object. In the case of an interpreter, the back end is an executor object that reads the icode and runs the program. In the case of a compiler, the back end is a code generator object that reads the icode and generates the object program.

The remaining chapters in the first part of this book are about parsing. In this chapter, we write the parts of the parser module that parse assignment statements and expressions. We'll learn how to:

- Represent Pascal's syntax with syntax diagrams.
- Write parsing routines based on these diagrams.
- Parse Pascal assignment statements and expressions, and translate them into intermediate code.
- Execute the statements and expressions from the icode.

We'll do all this in two steps. First, we'll parse elementary expressions containing only a subset of Pascal's operators. We'll write a Calculator utility program in which the parser executes assignment statements directly from the source. In the second step, we'll parse expressions containing nearly all of Pascal's operators. Now the parser will create the intermediate code, and we'll also write a backend executor for these expressions. Our second utility program, Simple Executor I, will execute simple programs consisting of assignment statements. It will also recognize two special variables, `input` and `output`, that prompt the user for a value and print a value, respectively. This utility program is the first of several sneak previews of an interpreter's back end, the main topic of the second part of this book. (We'll write a second version of this utility program in the next chapter.)

Review Figure 1.4 to see how the parser, icode, and executor objects work together in an interpreter.

Syntax Diagrams

Before you can write a parser, you need to be able to describe the source language's syntax. There are several ways to do this, but Pascal's relatively simple syntax lends itself especially well to *syntax diagrams*, which are graphical representations of the syntax rules.

In Chapter 3, we used a written description of what constitutes a Pascal number. Figure 5.1 shows the same description using syntax diagrams. The first diagram says that a *digit* is any of the characters 0 through 9, and the second diagram says that

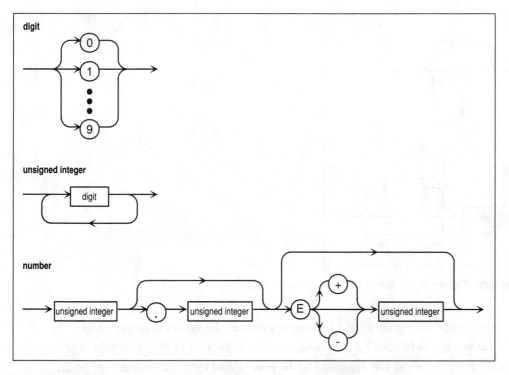

Figure 5.1 Syntax diagrams for Pascal numbers.

an *unsigned integer* consists of one or more consecutive digits. The third diagram gives the definition of a *number*. Figure 5.2 shows the syntax diagram for Pascal identifiers.

In the diagrams, you follow the arrows. Sometimes, as in the diagram for an unsigned integer, there is a loop. There are also alternate paths, as in the diagram for a number. Circles and rounded boxes enclose literal text, and rectangular boxes enclose syntactic entities that are defined by other diagrams. (The rounded boxes enclose the *terminal* symbols of the grammar [since they are not defined further], and the rectangular boxes enclose the nonterminal symbols.) Not all the details of the syntax rules are shown by the syntax diagrams. For example, the diagram for an unsigned integer does not indicate the maximum number of allowable digits, and the diagram for a letter does not indicate that lowercase letters are also accepted by Pascal.

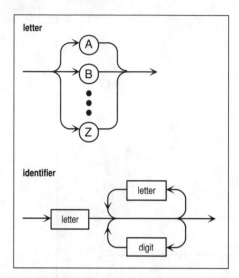

■■■■■■■ **Figure 5.2** Syntax diagrams for Pascal identifiers.

We'll design our parser so that its structure mirrors the syntax diagrams. Thus, the diagrams not only describe the source language's syntax, but they also help us write the parser. The diagrams representing the lowest-level syntactic entities, like identifier and number tokens, help us write the scanner. In Chapter 15, we'll discuss other ways to describe a language's syntax and to design a parser.

Elementary Expressions

We begin our work on the expression parsing member functions by considering elementary expressions. Figure 5.3 shows the syntax diagrams that we'll use to design the parser. The names *simple expression*, *term*, and *factor* are descriptive but are otherwise arbitrary. Such labels often form the basis for the names of the corresponding parsing routines.

The first diagram says that an expression is just a simple expression. (We'll deal with the complete Pascal expression syntax later.) The second diagram says that a simple expression is either a single term (possibly preceded by a unary + or –), or several terms separated by + or – operators. The third diagram says that a term is either a single factor, or several factors separated by * or / operators. The fourth diagram

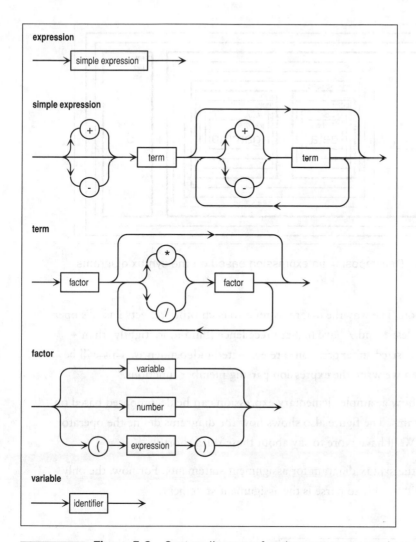

▊▊▊▊▊▊ **Figure 5.3** Syntax diagrams for elementary expressions.

says that a factor is either a variable, a number, or a parenthesized subexpression. Finally, the fifth diagram says that a variable is simply an identifier. (We'll parse variables that have subscripts and record fields in Chapter 7.)

Together, these diagrams show how the definitions are nested: Expressions are made up of simple expressions, simple expressions are made up of terms, and terms are made up of factors. Expressions are also defined recursively, since a factor can con-

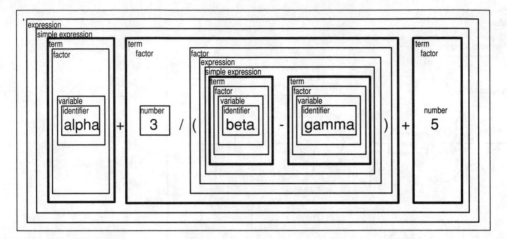

■■■■■■■ **Figure 5.4** Decomposing an expression based on the syntax diagrams.

tain a subexpression. The way the diagrams refer to each other reflects Pascal's operator precedence rules: * and / have higher precedence (bind more tightly) than + and –, and parenthesized subexpressions are evaluated independently. This will be more obvious when we write the expression parsing member functions.

Figure 5.4 shows how a sample elementary expression can be decomposed based on these syntax diagrams. The figure also shows how the diagrams define the operator precedence rules. We'll have more to say about these rules shortly.

Figure 5.5 shows the syntax diagram for assignment statements. For now, the only statement that we'll be able to parse is the assignment statement.

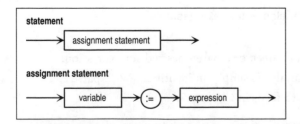

■■■■■■■ **Figure 5.5** Syntax diagram for assignment statements.

Evaluating Expressions with a Runtime Stack

How should expressions be evaluated at runtime? A popular technique uses a push-down stack, similar to the one in a Hewlett-Packard scientific calculator. We push operand values onto the stack. To execute a binary operator (one that takes two operands) like +, we pop off the top two values, add them, and push the sum back onto the stack. To execute a unary operator (one that takes only one operand) like −, we pop off the top value, negate it, and push the new value back onto the stack. All this must done in a way that preserves the operator precedence rules.

For example, Table 5.1 shows how we evaluate the expression

```
((-17 + 49)/4 - 2*3)*(9 - 3 + 2)
```

using a stack (whose top is at the right)

▐▐▐▐▐▐▐ **Table 5.1** Operations and the Stack

Operations	Stack
push 17	17
pop negate push push	-17
push 49	-17 49
pop pop + push	32
push 4	32 4
pop pop / push	8
push 2	8 2
push 3	8 2 3
pop pop * push	8 6
pop pop - push	2
push 9	2 9
push 3	2 9 3
pop pop - push	2 6
push 2	2 6 2
pop pop + push	2 8
pop pop * push	16

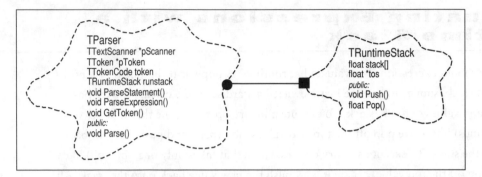

Figure 5.6 Class diagram for classes **TParser** and **TRuntimeStack** of the Calculator utility program.

Note that these stack operations can be performed while parsing the expression strictly from left to right.

We'll define a class TRuntimeStack from which we can instantiate a runtime stack object. Figure 5.6 shows the class diagram for this new class and for class TParser.

Class TRuntimeStack has two private data members, stack, the array of real-valued stack items, and tos, the pointer to the top item of the stack. Public member function Push pushes a new value onto the stack, and public member Pop pops the top value off the stack and returns that value. Until we learn to parse type definitions and variable declarations in Chapter 7, we'll only deal with real values.

We've added to the diagram for class TParser (compare with Figure 3.9). Private data member runStack means that a parser object will contain a runtime stack object. We also show two of several new private member functions, ParseStatement and ParseExpression.

■■■■■■■ **Figure 5.7** Header file **exec.h** of the Calculator utility program.

```
//    ************************************************************
//    *                                                          *
//    *    E X E C U T O R    (Header)                           *
//    *                                                          *
//    *    CLASSES: TRuntimeStack                                *
//    *                                                          *
//    *    FILE:    prog5-1/exec.h                               *
```

```
//  *                                                              *
//  *    MODULE:  Executor                                         *
//  *                                                              *
//  *    Copyright (c) 1996 by Ronald Mak                          *
//  *    For instructional purposes only.  No warranties.          *
//  *                                                              *
//  ****************************************************************

#ifndef exec_h
#define exec_h

#include "common.h"

//-------------------------------------------------------------
//  TRuntimeStack         Runtime stack class.
//-------------------------------------------------------------

class TRuntimeStack {
    enum {stackSize = 32};

    float  stack[stackSize];  // stack elements
    float *tos;               // ptr to the top of the stack

public:
    TRuntimeStack(void) { tos = &stack[-1]; }

    float Pop(void)      { return *tos--; }

    void Push(float value)
    {
        if (tos < &stack[stackSize-1]) *++tos = value;
        else AbortTranslation(abortStackOverflow);
    }
};
```

Figure 5.7 shows a new header file exec.h where we define class TRuntime-
Stack. The constructor function initializes tos to point just below the bottom
item. Member function Push first checks for a stack overflow, and then it adjusts
tos up one stack item before entering the new value. Member function Pop returns
the value at the top of the stack, and then adjusts tos down one item. Stack over-
flows can occur with certain perverse expressions in the source program. Presumably, a properly written executor should *never* have a stack underflow.

■■■■■■ **Figure 5.8** The definition of class **TParser** in header file **parser.h** of the Calculator utility program.

```
#include "misc.h"
#include "buffer.h"
#include "error.h"
#include "symtab.h"
#include "token.h"
#include "scanner.h"
#include "exec.h"

extern TSymtab globalSymtab;

//----------------------------------------------------------------
//  TParser              Parser class.
//----------------------------------------------------------------

class TParser {
    TTextScanner  *const pScanner;  // ptr to the scanner
    TToken        *pToken;          // ptr to the current token
    TTokenCode    token;            // code of current token
    TRuntimeStack runStack;         // runtime stack

    //--Statements.
    void ParseStatement (void);
    void ParseAssignment(void);

    //--Expressions.
    void ParseExpression      (void);
    void ParseSimpleExpression(void);
    void ParseTerm            (void);
    void ParseFactor          (void);

    void GetToken(void)
    {
        pToken = pScanner->Get();
        token  = pToken->Code();
    }

    TSymtabNode *SearchAll(const char *pString) const
    {
        return globalSymtab.Search(pString);
    }

    TSymtabNode *EnterLocal(const char *pString) const
```

```
    {
        return globalSymtab.Enter(pString);
    }

public:
    TParser(TTextInBuffer *pBuffer)
        : pScanner(new TTextScanner(pBuffer)) {}

    ~TParser(void) { delete pScanner; }

    void Parse(void);
};
```

Figure 5.8 shows the new definition of class TParser in header file parser.h for
the Calculator utility program. There is a new private data member runStack, and
several new private member functions for parsing statements and expressions whose
names are derived from the syntax diagrams. The new private member functions
SearchAll and EnterLocal simply send the Search and Enter messages,
respectively, to the global symbol table object. We've chosen the function names in
anticipation of having multiple symbol tables starting in Chapter 8; for now, we
have only the single global symbol table.

The Elementary Expression Parser

The first version of this chapter's parser module, which will be used by the Calculator utility program, both parses and executes elementary assignment statements and
expressions. So not only does the parser perform its syntactic tasks, it also performs
the semantic tasks of the back end. (Recall that *semantics* refers to meaning—what
the expressions say to do.) We also want the parser to do some runtime tracing by
printing the names and values of variables that are used in expressions or are assignment targets. Figure 5.9 shows a sample of the output that we want.

▆▆▆▆▆▆▆ **Figure 5.9** Sample listing and tracing output from the Calculator utility
program.

```
Page 1    calc.in    Wed Aug 31 16:33:16 1994

  1 0: {Temperature conversions.}
  2 0:
```

(continues)

■■■■■■ **Figure 5.9** Sample listing and tracing output from the Calculator utility program. (*Continued*)

```
 3 0: ratio := 5/9;
    >> ratio := 0.555556
 4 0:
 5 0: fahrenheit := 68;
    >> fahrenheit := 68
 6 0: centigrade := (fahrenheit - 32)*ratio;
    >> fahrenheit = 68
    >> ratio = 0.555556
    >> centigrade := 20
 7 0:
 8 0: centigrade := 20;;;
    >> centigrade := 20
 9 0: fahrenheit := centigrade/ratio + 32;
    >> centigrade = 20
    >> ratio = 0.555556
    >> fahrenheit := 68
10 0:
11 0: centigrade := 25
12 0: fahrenheit := celsius/ratio + 32;
    >> centigrade := 25
                 ^
*** ERROR: Missing ;

                      ^
*** ERROR: Undefined identifier
    >> ratio = 0.555556
    >> fahrenheit := 32
13 0:
14 0: dze ratio/(ratio - ratio) := ;
          ^
*** ERROR: Missing :=
    >> ratio = 0.555556
    >> ratio = 0.555556
    >> ratio = 0.555556
*** RUNTIME ERROR: Division by zero.
    >> dze := 0
                           ^
*** ERROR: Unexpected token
15 0: .

              15 source lines.
               4 syntax errors.
```

For now, the parser will store a variable's value in its symbol table node, using public data member value of class TSymtabNode (see Figure 4.3). This can only be a temporary measure until Chapter 8, where we learn how to parse procedures and functions.

██████████ **Figure 5.10** Member function **TParser::Parse** in implementation file **parser.cpp** of the Calculator utility program.

```
//-------------------------------------------------------------
// Parse         Parse the source file.
//-------------------------------------------------------------

void TParser::Parse(void)
{
    //--Extract the first token.
    GetToken();

    //--Loop to parse statements until the end of the program.
    do {
        //--Shouldn't see an end of file.
        if (token == tcEndOfFile) {
            Error(errUnexpectedEndOfFile);
            break;
        }

        //--Parse a statement.
        ParseStatement();

        //--If the current token is not a semicolon or the final
        //--period, we have a syntax error.  If the current token
        //--is an identifier (i.e., the start of the next statement),
        //--the error is a missing semicolon.  Otherwise, the error is
        //--an unexpected token, and so we skip tokens until we find a
        //--semicolon or a period, or until we reach the end of the
        //--source file.
        if ((token != tcSemicolon) && (token != tcPeriod)) {
            if (token == tcIdentifier) Error(errMissingSemicolon);
            else {
                Error(errUnexpectedToken);

                while ((token != tcSemicolon) &&
                       (token != tcPeriod) &&
                       (token != tcEndOfFile)) {
                    GetToken();
                }
```

(continues)

■■■■ **Figure 5.10** Member function **TParser::Parse** in implementation file **parser.cpp** of the Calculator utility program. (*Continued*)

```
        }
    }

    //--Skip over any semicolons before parsing the next statement.
    while (token == tcSemicolon) GetToken();

} while (token != tcPeriod);

//--Print the parser's summary.
list.PutLine();
sprintf(list.text, "%20d source lines.",  currentLineNumber);
list.PutLine();
sprintf(list.text, "%20d syntax errors.", errorCount);
list.PutLine();
}
```

Figure 5.10 shows a new version of member function TParser::Parse in imple-mentation file parser.cpp. It repeatedly calls member function ParseState-ment to parse a statement. After ParseStatement is done, the current token will be the first token after the statement, which should be either a semicolon or a period.

Parse does some simple error checking. If the current token is an identifier, it assumes that it is seeing the beginning of the next assignment statement, and so it flags a missing semicolon error. If it is any other token, Parse flags an unexpected token error, and then it skips the following tokens until it encounters a semicolon, period, or the end of the source file. This search for a reasonable point to resume parsing is called *resynchronizing* the parser. We'll look at error recovery in more detail in the next chapter.

Parse skips over one or more semicolons between statements. It exits its loop upon seeing a period after a statement.

■■■■ **Figure 5.11** Initial version of implementation file **parsstmt.cpp**.

```
//  ************************************************************
//  *                                                          *
//  *     P A R S E R    (Statements)                          *
//  *                                                          *
//  *     Parse statements.                                    *
```

```
//    *                                                           *
//    *    CLASSES: TParser                                       *
//    *                                                           *
//    *    FILE:    prog5.1/parsstmt.cpp                          *
//    *                                                           *
//    *    MODULE:  Parser                                        *
//    *                                                           *
//    *    Copyright (c) 1996 by Ronald Mak                       *
//    *    For instructional purposes only.  No warranties.       *
//    *                                                           *
//    **************************************************************

#include <stdio.h>
#include "parser.h"

//------------------------------------------------------------
//  ParseStatement           Parse a statement.
//------------------------------------------------------------

void TParser::ParseStatement(void)
{
    //--Only assignment statements for now.
    if (token == tcIdentifier) ParseAssignment();
}

//------------------------------------------------------------
//  ParseAssignment          Parse an assignment statement.
//                           Print the assigned value of the
//                           target variable.
//------------------------------------------------------------

void TParser::ParseAssignment(void)
{
    //--Search for the target variable's identifier and enter it
    //--if necessary.
    TSymtabNode       *pTargetNode = SearchAll (pToken->String());
    if (!pTargetNode)  pTargetNode = EnterLocal(pToken->String());

    //-- :=
    GetToken();
    if (token == tcColonEqual) GetToken();
    else                       Error(errMissingColonEqual);

    //--Parse the expression and pop its value into the
    //--target variable's symbol table node.
    ParseExpression();
```

(continues)

■■■■ **Figure 5.11** Initial version of implementation file **parsstmt.cpp**.
(*Continued*)

```
pTargetNode->value = runStack.Pop();

//--Print the target variable's identifier and value.
sprintf(list.text, "\t>> %s := %g", pTargetNode->String(),
                                     pTargetNode->value);
list.PutLine();
}
```

Figure 5.11 shows the initial version of implementation file parsstmt.cpp. Member function ParseStatement only knows about assignment statements.

Whenever member function ParseAssignment is called, the current token is the identifier of the target variable. The function searches the symbol table for the identifier, and enters it if necessary. Then after getting past the := token, the function calls ParseExpression to parse the expression, evaluate it, and leave the value on top of the runtime stack. ParseAssignment pops off this value and sets it into the target variable's symbol table node. It then prints the variable's identifier string and its value as trace output.

■■■■ **Figure 5.12** Initial version of implementation file **parsexpr.cpp**.

```
//   ************************************************************
//   *                                                        *
//   *    P A R S E R    (Expressions)                        *
//   *                                                        *
//   *    Parse expressions.                                  *
//   *                                                        *
//   *    CLASSES: TParser                                    *
//   *                                                        *
//   *    FILE:     prog5-1/parsexpr.cpp                      *
//   *                                                        *
//   *    MODULE:  Parser                                     *
//   *                                                        *
//   *    Copyright (c) 1996 by Ronald Mak                    *
//   *    For instructional purposes only.  No warranties.    *
//   *                                                        *
//   ************************************************************

#include <stdio.h>
#include "parser.h"
```

```
//-----------------------------------------------------------
//   ParseExpression              Parse an expression.
//-----------------------------------------------------------

void TParser::ParseExpression(void)
{
    ParseSimpleExpression();
}


//-----------------------------------------------------------
//   ParseSimpleExpression        Parse a simple expression
//                                (unary operators + or -
//                                and binary operators + and - ).
//-----------------------------------------------------------

void TParser::ParseSimpleExpression(void)
{
    TTokenCode op;                 // binary operator
    TTokenCode unaryOp = tcPlus;   // unary  operator

    //--Unary + or -
    if ((token == tcMinus) || (token == tcPlus)) {
        unaryOp = token;
        GetToken();
    }

    //--Parse the first term and then negate its value
    //--if there was a unary -.
    ParseTerm();
    if (unaryOp == tcMinus) runStack.Push(-runStack.Pop());

    //--Loop to parse subsequent additive operators and terms.
    while ((token == tcMinus) || (token == tcPlus)) {
        op = token;

        GetToken();
        ParseTerm();

        //--Pop off the two operand values, ...
        float operand2 = runStack.Pop();
        float operand1 = runStack.Pop();

        //--... perform the operation, and push the resulting value
        //--    onto the runtime stack.
        runStack.Push(op == tcPlus ? operand1 + operand2
```

(continues)

```
                                    : operand1 - operand2);
    }
}


//-------------------------------------------------------------
//  ParseTerm              Parse a term (binary operators * and /).
//-------------------------------------------------------------

void TParser::ParseTerm(void)
{
    TTokenCode op;   // binary operator

    //--Parse the first factor.
    ParseFactor();

    //--Loop to parse subsequent multiplicative operators and factors.
    while ((token == tcStar) || (token == tcSlash)) {
        op = token;

        GetToken();
        ParseFactor();

        //--Pop off the two operand values, ...
        float operand2 = runStack.Pop();
        float operand1 = runStack.Pop();

        //--... perform the operation, and push the resulting value
        //--    onto the runtime stack.
        if      (op == tcStar)  runStack.Push(operand1*operand2);
        else if (op == tcSlash) {
            if (operand2 != 0.0) runStack.Push(operand1/operand2);
            else {
                //--Division by zero runtime error.
                list.PutLine("*** RUNTIME ERROR: Division by zero.");
                runStack.Push(0.0);
            }
        }
    }
}


//-------------------------------------------------------------
//  ParseFactor           Parse a factor (identifier, number, or a
//                        parenthesized subexpression).  Print the
//                        value of each identifier.
//-------------------------------------------------------------
```

```
    void TParser::ParseFactor(void)
    {
        switch (token) {

            case tcIdentifier: {

                //--Search for the identifier.  If found, push and print
                //--its value.  Undefined identifier error if not found.
                TSymtabNode *pNode = SearchAll(pToken->String());
                if (pNode) {

                    //--Found:  Extract the value from the symbol table
                    //--        node and push it onto the runtime stack.
                    runStack.Push(pNode->value);

                    //--Print the variable's identifier and value.
                    sprintf(list.text, "\t>> %s = %g", pNode->String(),
                                                       pNode->value);
                    list.PutLine();
                }
                else {

                    //--Not found:  Undefined identifier error.
                    Error(errUndefinedIdentifier);
                    runStack.Push(0.0);
                }

                GetToken();
                break;
            }

            case tcNumber:

                //--Push the number's value onto the runtime stack.
                //--First convert and integer value to real.
                runStack.Push(pToken->Type() == tyInteger
                                  ? (float) pToken->Value().integer
                                  : pToken->Value().real);
                GetToken();
                break;

            case tcLParen:

                //--Parenthesized subexpression:  Call ParseExpression
                //--                              recursively ...
                GetToken();
```

(continues)

```
                ParseExpression();

                //-- ... and check for the closing right parenthesis.
                if (token == tcRParen) GetToken();
                else                   Error(errMissingRightParen);

                break;

            default:
                Error(errInvalidExpression);
                break;
        }
    }
```

Figure 5.12 shows the implementation file `parsexpr.cpp`. As suggested by the syntax diagrams for elementary expressions, member function `ParseExpression` simply calls member function `ParseSimpleExpression`.

`ParseSimpleExpression` first parses and remembers any unary + or - operator. It then calls member function `ParseTerm`, which will parse and evaluate the term and leave its value on top of the stack. If there was a unary -, `ParseSimpleExpression` pops off this value, negates it, and pushes the new value back onto the stack. The function then loops to parse and evaluate any subsequent additive operators and terms. After each term, it pops off the top two values, performs the appropriate operation, and pushes the result back onto the stack. Note that the second operand's value is the first one that is popped.

Member function `ParseTerm` is similar. It calls member function `ParseFactor` to parse and evaluate a factor and then loops to parse and evaluate any subsequent multiplicative operators and factors. It performs multiplication or division on the top two stack values and pushes the result back onto the stack. It also checks for and flags the division-by-zero runtime error.

Member function `TParser::ParseFactor` parses and evaluates factors, which can be variable identifiers, numbers, or parenthesized subexpressions. If an identifier is defined (which for now simply means that it was the target of a previously parsed assignment statement), `ParseFactor` pushes its value stored in the symbol table node onto the stack. It then prints the identifier and the value as trace output. The function can flag an error for an undefined identifier.

If the factor is a number, `ParseFactor` pushes its value onto the stack, first converting an integer value to real if necessary. If the factor is a subexpression, the function calls `ParseExpression` recursively and then checks for the closing right parenthesis.

One important thing to note about all of the parsing routines is that just after each routine has been called, the current token is the first token *after* the syntactic entity that the routine parsed. So, for example, after calling `ParseTerm`, the current token is the first token after the term that the function parsed.

Operator Precedence

Now that we've seen the expression parsing member functions of class `TParser`, let's look at how they work together to enforce Pascal's operator precedence rules. Pascal operators have four levels, where higher-level operators are executed before the lower-level ones, and in the absence of parentheses, operators at the same level are executed from left to right:

Level	Operators
1 (highest)	NOT
2	multiplicative: * / DIV MOD AND
3	additive: + - OR
4 (lowest)	relational: = <> < <= > >= IN

Here's how the expression

```
a + b*c
```

is parsed and evaluated. Function `ParseSimpleExpression` calls `ParseTerm`, which calls `ParseFactor`, which parses token a and pushes its value onto the stack. `ParseSimpleExpression` next parses and remembers token +, and then it calls `ParseTerm`, which calls `ParseFactor`, which parses token b and pushes its value onto the stack. However, it is function `ParseTerm` that parses and remembers token *. It calls `ParseFactor`, which parses token c and pushes its value onto the stack. Then `ParseTerm` pops off the values of b and c, multiplies them together, and pushes their product back onto the stack. Finally, `ParseSimpleExpression` pops off the values of a and the product, adds them together, and pushes the sum back onto the stack.

So we see that the operator precedence rules are preserved by how the parsing functions call one another and by which functions perform which operations. In our example, the multiplication was performed by `ParseTerm` before the addition was performed by `ParseSimpleExpression`.

Program 5-1: Calculator

We've now completed the parser module for this chapter's first utility program. Figure 5.13 shows the main file `calc.cpp` of the Calculator utility program. The program reads a series of assignment statements that are separated by semicolons. Each statement is a target variable identifier followed by a `:=` token followed by an elementary expression. The last statement is followed by a period. The parser module both parses and executes each statement as it reads in the statement. It prints the name and value of each variable that is in an expression or that is an assignment target. We saw some sample output in Figure 5.9.

■■■■■■■■ **Figure 5.13** The main file **calc.cpp** of the Calculator utility program.

```
//    ****************************************************************
//    *                                                              *
//    *    Program 5-1: Calculator                                   *
//    *                                                              *
//    *    Execute assignment statements with simple expressions     *
//    *    line-by-line.  Print the name and value of each           *
//    *    variable that is used in an expression or that is the     *
//    *    target of an assignment.                                  *
//    *                                                              *
//    *    FILE:    prog5-1/calc.cpp                                 *
//    *                                                              *
//    *    USAGE:   calc <source file>                               *
//    *                                                              *
//    *                 <source file>  name of the source file       *
//    *                                                              *
//    *    Copyright (c) 1996 by Ronald Mak                          *
//    *    For instructional purposes only.  No warranties.          *
```

```
//   *                                                         *
//   ************************************************************

#include <iostream.h>
#include "error.h"
#include "buffer.h"
#include "parser.h"

//------------------------------------------------------------
//  main
//------------------------------------------------------------

void main(int argc, char *argv[])
{
    //--Check the command line arguments.
    if (argc != 2) {
        cerr << "Usage: calc <source file>" << endl;
        AbortTranslation(abortInvalidCommandLineArgs);
    }

    //--Create the parser for the source file,
    //--and then parse the file.
    TParser parser(new TSourceBuffer(argv[1]));
    parser.Parse();
}
```

Table 5.2 shows the modules in the utility program. The parser module changed, and we began the executor module. The intermediate code module will reappear in the next program.

■■■■■■ **Table 5.2** Modules and Files of Program 5-1

Module	File	Status	Directory
Main	calc.cpp	*new*	prog5-1
Parser	parser.h	*changed*	prog5-1
	parser.cpp	*changed*	prog5-1
	parsstmt.cpp	*new*	prog5-1
	parsexpr.cpp	*new*	prog5-1
Executor	exec.h	*new*	prog5-1
Scanner	scanner.h	*unchanged*	prog3-1
	scanner.cpp	*unchanged*	prog3-2

(continues)

Module	File	Status	Directory
	token.h	*unchanged*	prog4-2
	tknword.cpp	*unchanged*	prog3-2
	tknnum.cpp	*unchanged*	prog3-2
	tknstrsp.cpp	*unchanged*	prog3-2
Symbol table	symtab.h	*unchanged*	prog4-1
	symtab.cpp	*unchanged*	prog4-1
Error	error.h	*unchanged*	prog3-2
	error.cpp	*unchanged*	prog3-2
Buffer	buffer.h	*unchanged*	prog2-1
	buffer.cpp	*unchanged*	prog2-1
Common	common.h	*unchanged*	prog4-1
	common.cpp	*unchanged*	prog2-1
	misc.h	*unchanged*	prog3-2

■■■■ **Table 5.2** Modules and Files of Program 5-1 (*Continued*)

The Need for Intermediate Code

The Calculator utility program executed assignment statements and expressions directly from the source program—it performed the semantic actions as soon as it parsed each statement and expression. Such a scheme is adequate for an interactive calculator that interprets each statement and expression only once, and speed is not so critical.

Speed is more important when interpreting a program. A program can have loops and procedures and functions, so that some statements can be executed many times. Then it is no longer a good idea to execute directly from the source, since doing so means that if a statement is in a loop, each time the interpreter executes the statement, it must rescan and reparse the statement and do a symbol table lookup for each and every identifier in the statement.

The prime motivation for intermediate code is to do all of the scanning, parsing, and symbol table lookups only once. The parser translates the source program into intermediate code. The icode for a source statement contains a byte code for each token and a reference to the symbol table node of each identifier. The scanner object provides the token codes, and the symbol table object provides the nodes. We did something very similar in the previous chapter with the Cruncher and Decruncher utility programs.

Therefore, when the interpreter's backend executor object processes a program in the icode, it does not need to do any scanning or symbol table lookups. If we allow an interpreter to run a program only if it has no syntax errors, then its executor does not need to do any time-consuming syntax checking either.

Our interpreter will use a memory-based intermediate code. We'll design the icode object from the file-based one we used in the previous chapter. Then the Simple Executor I utility program at the end of this chapter will use this icode to interpret "programs" consisting of assignment statements. Figure 5.14 shows the class diagram for the memory-based version of class `TIcode`. We redraw the diagram for the base class `TScanner` to remind ourselves what subclass `TIcode` inherits.

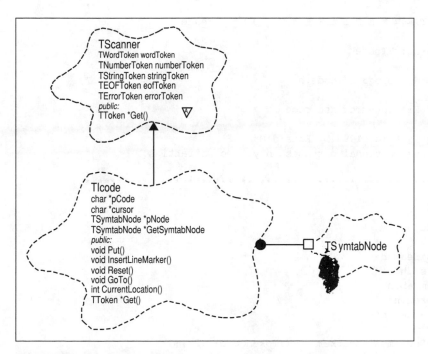

■■■■ **Figure 5.14** Class diagram for class **TIcode**.

Class TIcode has a private data member pCode that points to a *code segment*, which is a block of memory containing the intermediate code. Private data member cursor points to the current byte in the code segment. When the current token from the icode is an identifier, number, or string, private data member pNode points to the token's symbol table node. Private member function GetSymtabNode sets pNode from information extracted from the icode.

Public member function Put appends tokens to the icode, and public member function InsertLineMarker inserts a *line marker*, which we'll explain later. Public member function Reset resets cursor to the beginning of the icode, public member function GoTo sets cursor to a specific location within the icode, and public member function CurrentLocation returns the offset of cursor from the beginning of the icode. Finally, public member function Get extracts the next token from the code segment.

■■■■■■■ **Figure 5.15** A new version of header file **icode.h**.

```
//   ***************************************************************
//   *                                                           *
//   *     I N T E R M E D I A T E   C O D E   (Header)          *
//   *                                                           *
//   *     CLASSES: TIcode                                       *
//   *                                                           *
//   *     FILE:    prog5-2/icode.h                              *
//   *                                                           *
//   *     MODULE:  Intermediate code                           *
//   *                                                           *
//   *     Copyright (c) 1996 by Ronald Mak                      *
//   *     For instructional purposes only.  No warranties.      *
//   *                                                           *
//   ***************************************************************

#ifndef icode_h
#define icode_h

#include <fstream.h>
#include "misc.h"
#include "symtab.h"
#include "token.h"
#include "scanner.h"

const TTokenCode mcLineMarker = ((TTokenCode) 127);
```

```
//-------------------------------------------------------------
//  TIcode          Intermediate code subclass of TScanner.
//-------------------------------------------------------------

class TSymtabNode;

class TIcode : public TScanner {
    enum {codeSegmentSize = 4096};

    char        *pCode;    // ptr to the code segment
    char        *cursor;   // ptr to current code location
    TSymtabNode *pNode;    // ptr to extracted symbol table node

    void         CheckBounds  (int size);
    TSymtabNode *GetSymtabNode(void);

public:
    TIcode(void) { pCode = cursor = new char[codeSegmentSize]; }
    TIcode(const TIcode &icode);  // copy constructor
   ~TIcode(void) { delete[] pCode; }

    void Put(TTokenCode tc);
    void Put(const TSymtabNode *pNode);
    void InsertLineMarker(void);

    void Reset(void)          { cursor = pCode;           }
    void GoTo (int location) { cursor = pCode + location; }

    int          CurrentLocation(void) const { return cursor - pCode; }
    TSymtabNode *SymtabNode     (void) const { return pNode;          }

    virtual TToken *Get(void);
};

#endif
```

Figure 5.15 shows a new version of the header file icode.h. A few member functions were not shown in the class diagram. Private member function CheckBounds guards against running off the end of the code segment. The constructor function allocates the code segment and initializes pCode and cursor. Public member function Put is overloaded — it can append either a token code or symbol table node information to the icode. Note that class TIcode has both a standard and a copy constructor function.

■■■■■■ **Figure 5.16** New version of implementation file **icode.cpp**.

```cpp
// ****************************************************************
// *                                                              *
// *    I N T E R M E D I A T E   C O D E                         *
// *                                                              *
// *    Create and access the intermediate code implemented in    *
// *    memory.                                                    *
// *                                                              *
// *    CLASSES: TIcode                                            *
// *                                                              *
// *    FILE:    prog5-2/icode.cpp                                 *
// *                                                              *
// *    MODULE:  Intermediate code                                *
// *                                                              *
// *    Copyright (c) 1996 by Ronald Mak                           *
// *    For instructional purposes only.  No warranties.          *
// *                                                              *
// ****************************************************************

#include <memory.h>
#include "common.h"
#include "error.h"
#include "symtab.h"
#include "icode.h"

//--Vector of special symbol and reserved word strings.
char *symbolStrings[] = {
    NULL,

    NULL, NULL, NULL, NULL, NULL,

    "^", "*", "(", ")", "-", "+",
    "=", "[", "]", ":", ";", "<",
    ">", ",", ".", "/", ":=", "<=", ">=",
    "<>", "..",

    "and", "array", "begin", "case", "const", "div",
    "do", "downto", "else", "end", "file", "for", "function",
    "goto", "if", "in", "label", "mod", "nil", "not", "of", "or",
    "packed", "procedure", "program", "record", "repeat", "set",
    "then", "to", "type", "until", "var", "while", "with",
};

//----------------------------------------------------------
// Copy constructor    Make a copy of the icode.  Only copy as
//                     many bytes of icode as necessary.
//
```

```
//      icode : ref to source icode
//---------------------------------------------------------------

TIcode::TIcode(const TIcode &icode)
{
    int length = int(icode.cursor - icode.pCode);  // length of icode

    //--Copy icode.
    pCode = cursor = new char[length];
    mcmcpy(pCode, icode.pCode, length);
}


//---------------------------------------------------------------
// CheckBounds          Guard against code segment overflow.
//
//      size : number of bytes to append
//---------------------------------------------------------------

void TIcode::CheckBounds(int size)
{
    if (cursor + size >= &pCode[codeSegmentSize]) {
        Error(errCodeSegmentOverflow);
        AbortTranslation(abortCodeSegmentOverflow);
    }
}


//---------------------------------------------------------------
// Put(TTokenCode)      Append a token code to the intermediate
//                      code.
//
//      tc    : token code
//      pNode : ptr to symtab node, or NULL
//---------------------------------------------------------------

void TIcode::Put(TTokenCode tc)
{
    if (errorCount > 0) return;

    char code = tc;
    CheckBounds(sizeof(char));
    memcpy((void *) cursor, (const void *) &code, sizeof(char));
    cursor += sizeof(char);
}


//---------------------------------------------------------------
// Put(TSymtabNode *)       Append a symbol table node's symbol
```

(continues)

■■■■■ **Figure 5.16** New version of implementation file **icode.cpp**. (*Continued*)

```
//                          table and node indexes to the
//                          intermediate code.
//
//      pNode : ptr to symtab node
//-------------------------------------------------------------

void TIcode::Put(const TSymtabNode *pNode)
{
    if (errorCount > 0) return;

    short xSymtab = pNode->SymtabIndex();
    short xNode   = pNode->NodeIndex();

    CheckBounds(2*sizeof(short));
    memcpy((void *) cursor,
           (const void *) &xSymtab, sizeof(short));
    memcpy((void *) (cursor + sizeof(short)),
           (const void *) &xNode,   sizeof(short));
    cursor += 2*sizeof(short);
}


//-------------------------------------------------------------
// Get              Extract the next token from the
//                  intermediate code.
//
// Return: ptr to the extracted token
//-------------------------------------------------------------

TToken *TIcode::Get(void)
{
    TToken *pToken;          // ptr to token to return
    char    code;            // token code read from the file
    TTokenCode token;

    //--Loop to process any line markers
    //--and extract the next token code.
    do {
        //--First read the token code.
        memcpy((void *) &code, (const void *) cursor, sizeof(char));
        cursor += sizeof(char);
        token = (TTokenCode) code;

        //--If it's a line marker, extract the line number.
        if (token == mcLineMarker) {
```

```
        short number;

        memcpy((void *) &number, (const void *) cursor,
               sizeof(short));
        currentLineNumber = number;
        cursor += sizeof(short);
    }
} while (token == mcLineMarker);

//--Determine the token class, based on the token code.
switch (token) {
    case tcNumber:  pToken = &numberToken;  break;
    case tcString:  pToken = &stringToken;  break;

    case tcIdentifier:
        pToken       = &wordToken;
        pToken->code = tcIdentifier;
        break;

    default:
        if (token < tcAND) {
            pToken       = &specialToken;
            pToken->code = token;
        }
        else {
            pToken       = &wordToken;  // reserved word
            pToken->code = token;
        }
        break;
}

//--Extract the symbol table node and set the token string.
switch (token) {
    case tcIdentifier:
    case tcNumber:
    case tcString:
        pNode = GetSymtabNode();
        strcpy(pToken->string, pNode->String());
        break;

    default:
        pNode = NULL;
        strcpy(pToken->string, symbolStrings[code]);
        break;
}
```

(continues)

```cpp
    return pToken;
}

//----------------------------------------------------------------
//  GetSymtabNode       Extract a symbol table node pointer
//                      from the intermediate code.
//
//  Return: ptr to the symbol table node
//----------------------------------------------------------------

TSymtabNode *TIcode::GetSymtabNode(void)
{
    extern TSymtab **vpSymtabs;
    short xSymtab, xNode;           // symbol table and node indexes

    memcpy((void *) &xSymtab, (const void *) cursor,
            sizeof(short));
    memcpy((void *) &xNode,   (const void *) (cursor + sizeof(short)),
            sizeof(short));
    cursor += 2*sizeof(short);

    return vpSymtabs[xSymtab]->Get(xNode);
}

//----------------------------------------------------------------
//  InsertLineMarker    Insert a line marker into the
//                      intermediate code just before the
//                      last appended token code.
//----------------------------------------------------------------

void TIcode::InsertLineMarker(void)
{
    if (errorCount > 0) return;

    //--Remember the last appended token code;
    char lastCode;
    cursor -= sizeof(char);
    memcpy((void *) &lastCode, (const void *) cursor, sizeof(char));

    //--Insert a line marker code
    //--followed by the current line number.
    char  code   = mcLineMarker;
```

```
    short number = currentLineNumber;
    CheckBounds(sizeof(char) + sizeof(short));
    memcpy((void *) cursor, (const void *) &code, sizeof(char));
    cursor += sizeof(char);
    memcpy((void *) cursor, (const void *) &number, sizeof(short));
    cursor += sizeof(short);

    //--Re-append the last token code;
    memcpy((void *) cursor, (const void *) &lastCode, sizeof(char));
    cursor += sizeof(char);
}
```

Figure 5.16 shows a new version of implementation file `icode.cpp`. The copy constructor make a copy of an existing icode object, except that it copies only as many bytes as are used of the existing code segment.

Member function `CheckBounds` aborts the translation if the code segment is full. Overloaded member function `Put` either appends a token code to the icode, or a symbol table node's symbol table index and node index. Both versions of the function call `CheckBounds` and update `cursor`.

We now introduce the concept of a *line marker*, which the parser inserts into the icode to allow the executor to keep track of the current source line number as it executes the icode. This is very useful for debugging. A line marker consists of a special token code `mcLineMarker`, defined in header file `icode.h` (see Figure 5.15), followed by the current line number.

Member function `InsertLineMarker` inserts a line marker into the icode. We can't simply append it to the icode. As we'll soon see, this function is generally called by the parser whenever it begins to parse a new statement, at which time the first token of the statement has already been translated and appended to the icode. `InsertLineMarker` inserts the line marker just before this token.

Member function `Get` first loops to process any line markers. It sets the global variable `currentLineNumber` each time it encounters one. The rest of the function is the same as before. It determines which token object to return based on the token code extracted from the icode. It calls member function `GetSymtabNode` to point pNode to the symbol table node of an identifier, number, or string token.

Converting the Symbol Table for the Back End

The front end builds the symbol table as a binary tree, which is ideal for the parser to enter and search for nodes. However, back end does not enter new nodes into the symbol table, and it wants to access nodes directly without searching for them. Therefore, the icode must contain information about each symbol table node that allows the back end to access the node directly.

Recall that in the previous chapter, the file form of the icode stored the symbol table nodes as an array. We need to do something similar here. Since each node has an index (private data member TSymtabNode::xNode), we can use it to index into an array of nodes. So, when the front end is finished building the symbol table as a binary tree, we need to "flatten" the tree into an array of pointers to the nodes. We'll also create an array of pointers to the symbol table objects (although for now this array will have but one element). Private data member TSymtab::xSymtab (also copied in private data member TSymtabNode::xSymtab) will index into this latter array.

Member function TIcode::GetSymtabNode extracts the symbol table index and the node index. It first indexes into the symbol table array vpSymtabs to obtain a pointer to the correct symbol table object. It sends the Get message to that symbol table object, passing the node index, to obtain and return a pointer to the correct symbol table node.

■■■■■ **Figure 5.17** New versions of class **TSymtabNode** and class **TSymtab** in header file **symtab.h**.

```
//----------------------------------------------------------------
//  TSymtabNode          Symbol table node class.
//----------------------------------------------------------------

class TLineNumList;

class TSymtabNode {
    TSymtabNode  *left, *right;   // ptrs to left and right subtrees
    char         *pString;        // ptr to symbol string
    short         xSymtab;        // symbol table index
    short         xNode;          // node index
    TLineNumList *pLineNumList;   // ptr to list of line numbers
```

```
        friend class TSymtab;

public:
    float value;   // temporary value data member

    TSymtabNode(const char *pStr);
    ~TSymtabNode(void);

    TSymtabNode *LeftSubtree (void) const { return left;    }
    TSymtabNode *RightSubtree(void) const { return right;   }
    char        *String      (void) const { return pString; }
    short        SymtabIndex (void) const { return xSymtab; }
    short        NodeIndex   (void) const { return xNode;   }
    void         Convert     (TSymtabNode *vpNodes[]);

    void Print(void) const;
};

//-------------------------------------------------------------
//   TSymtab          Symbol table class.  The symbol table is
//                    organized as a binary tree that is
//                    sorted alphabetically by the nodes'
//                    name strings.
//-------------------------------------------------------------

class TSymtab {
    TSymtabNode   *root;       // ptr to binary tree root
    TSymtabNode   **vpNodes;   // ptr to vector of node ptrs
    short          cntNodes;   // node counter
    short          xSymtab;    // symbol table index
    TSymtab       *next;       // ptr to next symbol table in list

public:
    TSymtab()
    {
        extern int      cntSymtabs;
        extern TSymtab *pSymtabList;

        root      = NULL;
        vpNodes   = NULL;
        cntNodes  = 0;
        xSymtab   = cntSymtabs++;

        //--Insert at the head of the symbol table list.
        next        = pSymtabList;
        pSymtabList = this;
```

(continues)

■■■■■■■■ **Figure 5.17** New versions of class **TSymtabNode** and class **TSymtab** in
header file **symtab.h**. (*Continued*)

```
    }

    ~TSymtab()
    {
        delete   root;
        delete[] vpNodes;
    }

    TSymtabNode  *Search(const char *pString) const;
    TSymtabNode  *Enter (const char *pString);

    TSymtabNode  *Root(void)       const { return root;          }
    TSymtabNode  *Get (short xNode) const { return vpNodes[xNode]; }
    TSymtab      *Next(void)        const { return next;          }
    TSymtabNode **NodeVector(void)  const { return vpNodes;       }
    int           NodeCount (void)  const { return cntNodes;      }
    void          Print    (void)   const { root->Print();        }
    void          Convert   (TSymtab *vpSymtabs[]);
};
```

Figure 5.17 shows new versions of the definitions of class TSymtabNode and class
TSymtab in header file symtab.h. Class TSymtabNode has a new public member
function Convert that will flatten a node and its left and right subtrees into the
pointer array vpNodes that is passed to it.

Class TSymtab has several changes. The constructor function now sets the private
data member xSymtab to the value of the global symbol table counter cntSym-
tabs. It also links the new symbol table into the head of a list pointed to by the
global pSymtabList, using the new private data member next. Another new private data member is vpNodes, which will point to an array of the symbol table's
nodes. The destructor function deletes this array.

Class TSymtab also has a public Convert member function. This function will
flatten its tree of nodes into an array pointed to by vpNodes and enter itself into
the symbol table object pointer array vpSymtabs, which is passed to it.

■■■■■■■■ **Figure 5.18** Member function **TSymtab::Convert** in implementation file
symtab.cpp.

```
//------------------------------------------------------------
// Convert      Convert the symbol table into a form suitable
```

```
//              for the back end.
//
//      vpSymtabs : vector of symbol table pointers
//------------------------------------------------------------

void TSymtab::Convert(TSymtab *vpSymtabs[])
{
    //--Point the appropriate entry of the symbol table pointer vector
    //--to this symbol table.
    vpSymtabs[xSymtab] = this;

    //--Allocate the symbol table node pointer vector
    //--and convert the nodes.
    vpNodes = new TSymtabNode *[cntNodes];
    root->Convert(vpNodes);
}
```

Figure 5.18 shows the implementation of the new member function TSymtab::-Convert in file symtab.cpp. It first enters itself into the global vpSymtabs pointer array using data member xSymtab as the index. It next allocates the pointer array vpNodes for the symbol table nodes, and then it sends the Convert message to its root node, passing the pointer array.

■■■■■■■■ **Figure 5.19** Member function **TSymtabNode::Convert** in implementation
file **symtab.cpp**.

```
//------------------------------------------------------------
// Convert      Convert the symbol table node into a form
//              suitable for the back end.
//
//      vpNodes : vector of node ptrs
//------------------------------------------------------------

void TSymtabNode::Convert(TSymtabNode *vpNodes[])
{
    //--First, convert the left subtree.
    if (left) left->Convert(vpNodes);

    //--Convert the node.
    vpNodes[xNode] = this;

    //--Finally, convert the right subtree.
    if (right) right->Convert(vpNodes);
}
```

The new member function `TSymtabNode::Convert` is also implemented in file `symtab.cpp`, as shown in Figure 5.19. It recursively converts its left and right subtrees, and in between, it sets itself into the pointer array using data member `xNode`.

In implementation file `common.cpp`, we need to add the lines

```
int       cntSymtabs  = 0;      // symbol table counter
TSymtab  *pSymtabList = NULL;   // ptr to head of symtab list
TSymtab **vpSymtabs;            // ptr to vector of symtab ptrs

TIcode icode;                   // the intermediate code
```

and in header file `common.h`, we must add

```
#include "icode.h"
```

and

```
extern int       cntSymtabs;
extern TSymtab  *pSymtabList;
extern TSymtab **vpSymtabs;

extern TIcode icode;
```

The global `icode` is the intermediate code object.

Translating the Source Program into Intermediate Code

The parser module of the Calculator utility program both parsed and executed the source statements. We now rewrite the module so that it only does parsing. Instead of executing the source statements, it will translate them into intermediate code. After the parser is done, and if there were no syntax errors, it will send the Go message to the executor object in the back end to execute the icode. The Simple Executor I utility program will use this version of the parser and backend modules. We can think of the utility program as an interpreter for simple programs containing only assignment statements.

■■■■■■ **Figure 5.20** Class **TParser** in header file **parser.h** of the Simple Executor I utility program.

```
#include "misc.h"
#include "buffer.h"
#include "error.h"
```

```
#include "symtab.h"
#include "token.h"
#include "scanner.h"
#include "icode.h"

extern TSymtab globalSymtab;
extern TIcode  icode;

//--------------------------------------------------------------
//  TParser              Parser class.
//--------------------------------------------------------------

class TParser {
    TTextScanner *const pScanner;   // ptr to the scanner
    TToken       *pToken;           // ptr to the current token
    TTokenCode    token;            // code of current token

    //--Statements.
    void ParseStatement (void);
    void ParseAssignment(void);

    //--Expressions.
    void ParseExpression       (void);
    void ParseSimpleExpression(void);
    void ParseTerm             (void);
    void ParseFactor           (void);

    void GetToken(void)
    {
        pToken = pScanner->Get();
        token  = pToken->Code();
    }

    void GetTokenAppend(void)
    {
        GetToken();
        icode.Put(token);  // append token code to icode
    }

    void InsertLineMarker(void) { icode.InsertLineMarker(); }

    TSymtabNode *SearchAll(const char *pString) const
    {
        return globalSymtab.Search(pString);
    }
```

(continues)

```
    TSymtabNode *EnterLocal(const char *pString) const
    {
        return globalSymtab.Enter(pString);
    }

public:
    TParser(TTextInBuffer *pBuffer)
        : pScanner(new TTextScanner(pBuffer))
    {
        //--Enter the special "input" and "output" variable identifiers
        //--into the symbol table.
        EnterLocal("input");
        EnterLocal("output");
    }

    ~TParser(void) { delete pScanner; }

    void Parse(void);
};
```

Figure 5.20 shows a new definition of class `TParser` in header file `parser.h` that
we'll use for the Simple Executor I utility program. We've removed the private `run-
Stack` data member, since the runtime stack now belongs to the back end.

We also have two new private member functions, `GetTokenAppend` and `Insert-
LineMarker`. `GetTokenAppend` calls `GetToken`, and then sends the Put message
to the icode object to append the token to the intermediate code. `InsertLine-
Marker` sends the `InsertLineMarker` message to the icode object. The construc-
tor function now enters two special variables, `input` and `output`, into the symbol
table.

We only need to make a few small changes to the implementation of member function `TParser::Parse` in file `parser.cpp`. First, we replace each of the three
calls to `GetToken` with a call to `GetTokenAppend`. Second, we add the line

```
    list.PutLine();
```

at the end of the function to help separate the source program listing from the output from executing the program.

■■■■■■ **Figure 5.21** New version of implementation file **parsstmt.cpp**.

```
//    **************************************************************
//    *                                                            *
//    *     P A R S E R    (Statements)                            *
//    *                                                            *
//    *     Parse statements.                                      *
//    *                                                            *
//    *     CLASSES: TParser                                       *
//    *                                                            *
//    *     FILE:     prog5-2/parsstmt.cpp                         *
//    *                                                            *
//    *     MODULE:  Parser                                        *
//    *                                                            *
//    *     Copyright (c) 1996 by Ronald Mak                       *
//    *     For instructional purposes only.  No warranties.       *
//    *                                                            *
//    **************************************************************

#include "parser.h"

//-------------------------------------------------------------
//  ParseStatement      Parse a statement.
//-------------------------------------------------------------

void TParser::ParseStatement(void)
{
    InsertLineMarker();

    //--Only assignment statements for now.
    if (token == tcIdentifier) ParseAssignment();
}


//-------------------------------------------------------------
//  ParseAssignment     Parse an assignment statement.
//
//                              <id> := <expr>
//-------------------------------------------------------------

void TParser::ParseAssignment(void)
{
    //--Search for the target variable's identifier and enter it
    //--if necessary.  Append the symbol table node handle
    //--to the icode.
    TSymtabNode        *pTargetNode = SearchAll (pToken->String());
    if (!pTargetNode)  pTargetNode = EnterLocal(pToken->String());
```

(continues)

■■■■■ **Figure 5.21** New version of implementation file **parsstmt.cpp**. (*Continued*)

```
        icode.Put(pTargetNode);
        GetTokenAppend();

        //-- :=
        if (token == tcColonEqual) GetTokenAppend();
        else                       Error(errMissingColonEqual);

        //--<expr>
        ParseExpression();
}
```

Figure 5.21 shows a new version of implementation file parsstmt.cpp. Throughout the file, we've replaced calls to GetToken by calls to GetTokenAppend. Member function ParseStatement inserts a line marker in the icode before it translates the next source statement. Member function ParseAssignment appends the symbol table node of the target variable to the icode. (Remember from Figure 5.16 that TIcode::Put will append the node's symbol table and node indexes to the intermediate code.) We've also removed the semantic actions from ParseAssignment.

Figure 5.22 shows nearly complete syntax diagrams for Pascal expressions. Almost all the operators are now present, although for now, a variable is still just an identifier, and since we will not be implementing sets, the IN operator is missing.

■■■■■ **Figure 5.23** New version of implementation file **parsexpr.cpp**.

```
//   ***************************************************************
//   *                                                           *
//   *     P A R S E R    (Expressions)                          *
//   *                                                           *
//   *     Parse expressions.                                    *
//   *                                                           *
//   *     CLASSES: TParser                                      *
//   *                                                           *
//   *     FILE:     prog5-2/parsexpr.cpp                        *
//   *                                                           *
//   *     MODULE:  Parser                                       *
//   *                                                           *
//   *     Copyright (c) 1996 by Ronald Mak                      *
//   *     For instructional purposes only.  No warranties.      *
//   *                                                           *
//   ***************************************************************
```

(*continues*)

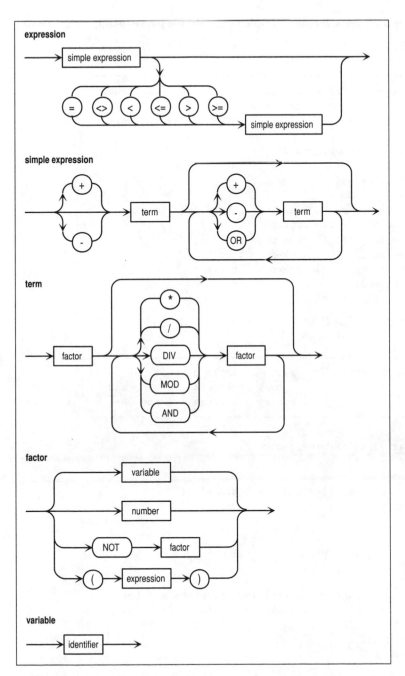

▬▬▬▬▬▬ **Figure 5.22** Syntax diagrams for more nearly complete Pascal expressions.

■■■■■■■■ **Figure 5.23** New version of implementation file **parsexpr.cpp**. (*Continued*)

```cpp
#include "parser.h"

//-------------------------------------------------------------
//  ParseExpression        Parse an expression (binary relational
//                         operators = < > <> <= and >= ).
//-------------------------------------------------------------

void TParser::ParseExpression(void)
{
    ParseSimpleExpression();

    //--If there we now see a relational operator,
    //--parse a second simple expression.
    if ((token == tcEqual) || (token == tcNe) ||
        (token == tcLt)    || (token == tcGt) ||
        (token == tcLe)    || (token == tcGe)) {
        GetTokenAppend();
        ParseSimpleExpression();
    }
}


//-------------------------------------------------------------
//  ParseSimpleExpression       Parse a simple expression
//                              (unary operators + or - , and
//                              binary operators + - and OR).
//-------------------------------------------------------------

void TParser::ParseSimpleExpression(void)
{
    //--Unary + or -
    if ((token == tcPlus) || (token == tcMinus)) {
        GetTokenAppend();
    }

    //--Parse the first term.
    ParseTerm();

    //--Loop to parse subsequent additive operators and terms.
    while ((token == tcPlus) || (token == tcMinus) ||
           (token == tcOR)) {
        GetTokenAppend();
        ParseTerm();
    }
}
```

```
//------------------------------------------------------------
//  ParseTerm              Parse a term (binary operators * / DIV
//                         MOD and AND).
//------------------------------------------------------------

void TParser::ParseTerm(void)
{
    //--Parse the first factor.
    ParseFactor();

    //--Loop to parse subsequent multiplicative operators and factors.
    while ((token == tcStar) || (token == tcSlash) ||
           (token == tcDIV)  || (token == tcMOD)   ||
           (token == tcAND)) {
        GetTokenAppend();
        ParseFactor();
    }
}


//------------------------------------------------------------
//  ParseFactor            Parse a factor (identifier, number,
//                         string, NOT <factor>, or parenthesized
//                         subexpression).
//------------------------------------------------------------

void TParser::ParseFactor(void)
{
    switch (token) {

        case tcIdentifier: {

            //--Search for the identifier.  If found, append the
            //--symbol table node handle to the icode.  If not
            //--found, enter it and flag an undefined identifier error.
            TSymtabNode *pNode = SearchAll(pToken->String());
            if (pNode) icode.Put(pNode);
            else {
                Error(errUndefinedIdentifier);
                EnterLocal(pToken->String());
            }

            GetTokenAppend();
            break;
        }

        case tcNumber: {
```

(continues)

```cpp
        //--Search for the number and enter it if necessary.
        //--Set the number's value in the symbol table node.
        //--Append the symbol table node handle to the icode.
        TSymtabNode *pNode = SearchAll(pToken->String());
        if (!pNode) {
            pNode = EnterLocal(pToken->String());
            pNode->value = pToken->Type() == tyInteger
                                ? (float) pToken->Value().integer
                                : pToken->Value().real;
        }
        icode.Put(pNode);

        GetTokenAppend();
        break;
    }

    case tcString:
        GetTokenAppend();
        break;

    case tcNOT:
        GetTokenAppend();
        ParseFactor();
        break;

    case tcLParen:

        //--Parenthesized subexpression:  Call ParseExpression
        //--                              recursively ...
        GetTokenAppend();
        ParseExpression();

        //-- ... and check for the closing right parenthesis.
        if (token == tcRParen) GetTokenAppend();
        else                   Error(errMissingRightParen);

        break;

    default:
        Error(errInvalidExpression);
        break;
    }
}
```

The new expression parsing member functions, shown in Figure 5.23, is based on these diagrams. Just as in the statement parser above, this parser only translates the source into icode. We've removed all the semantic actions, and we've replaced calls to `GetToken` by calls to `GetTokenAppend`. We can now handle more operators. Member function `ParseExpression` can parse a relational operator between two simple expressions, member function `ParseSimpleExpression` can parse the OR operator, and member function `ParseTerm` can parse the AND operator. Member function `ParseFactor` can now handle string operands and the NOT operator. It enters numeric operands into the symbol table.

Executing Assignment Statements and Expressions

Now that we have a parser module that can create an icode, we need to write a backend module that, for an interpreter, contains an executor object. Since we know that a compiler will contain a code generator object in the back end, we'll create an abstract backend base class `TBackend`. For the interpreter, we'll derive a TExecutor subclass, and later, for the compiler, we'll derive a `TCodeGenerator` subclass. Figure 5.24 shows the class diagram of base class TBackend and its subclass TExecutor. Note that class TRuntimeStack is now associated with class `TExecutor`. We'll start to look at subclass `TCodeGenerator` in Chapter 12.

Class `TBackend` has several protected data members. `pToken` points to the current token object, and `token` is the current token code. Whenever the current token is an identifier, number, or string, `pNode` points to the token's symbol table node. Protected member function `GetToken` will set these data members. Protected member function `GoTo` sets the current location in the intermediate code, and `CurrentLocation` returns the location. Public member function `Go` sets the back end into motion, but it must be overridden by a subclass.

Subclass `TExecutor` has the private `runStack` data member, and also `pInputNode` and `pOutputNode` to point to the symbol table nodes of the special variables `input` and `output`. Private data member `stmtCount` counts the number of executed statements. The subclass has, among others, private member functions `ExecuteStatement` and `ExecuteExpression`. Its public member function `Go` starts the executor.

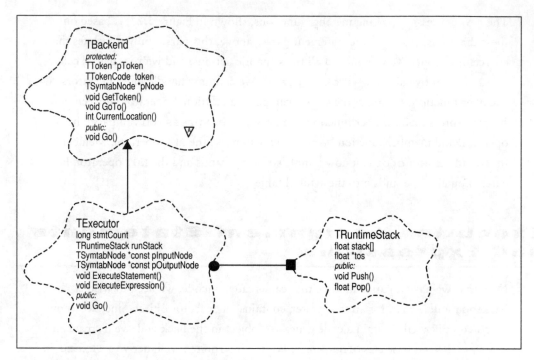

Figure 5.24 Class diagram of base class **TBackend** and its subclass **TExecutor**.

Figure 5.25 Header file **backend.h**.

```
// ***************************************************************
// *                                                             *
// *   B A C K E N D   (Header)                                  *
// *                                                             *
// *   CLASSES: TBackend                                         *
// *                                                             *
// *   FILE:    prog5-2/backend.h                                *
// *                                                             *
// *   MODULE:  Executor                                         *
// *                                                             *
// *   Copyright (c) 1995 by Ronald Mak                          *
// *   For instructional purposes only.  No warranties.         *
// *                                                             *
// ***************************************************************

#ifndef backend_h
```

```
#define backend_h

#include "misc.h"
#include "symtab.h"
#include "token.h"
#include "icode.h"

extern TIcode icode;

//---------------------------------------------------------------
//  TBackend            Abstract back end class.
//---------------------------------------------------------------

class TBackend {

protected:
    TToken      *pToken;   // ptr to the current token
    TTokenCode   token;    // code of current token
    TSymtabNode *pNode;    // ptr to symtab node

    void GetToken(void)
    {
        pToken = icode.Get();
        token  = pToken->Code();
        pNode  = icode.SymtabNode();
    }

    void GoTo(int location) { icode.GoTo(location); }

    int CurrentLocation(void) const {
        return icode.CurrentLocation();
    }

public:
    virtual ~TBackend(void) {}

    virtual void Go(void) = 0;
};

#endif
```

Figure 5.25 shows the definition of the base class TBackend in the new header file backend.h.

■■■■■■■■ **Figure 5-26** New version of header file **exec.h**.

```
// ****************************************************************
// *                                                              *
// *    E X E C U T O R    (Header)                               *
// *                                                              *
// *    CLASSES: TRuntimeStack, TExecutor                         *
// *                                                              *
// *    FILE:    prog5-2/exec.h                                   *
// *                                                              *
// *    MODULE:  Executor                                         *
// *                                                              *
// *    Copyright (c) 1996 by Ronald Mak                          *
// *    For instructional purposes only.  No warranties.          *
// *                                                              *
// ****************************************************************

#ifndef exec_h
#define exec_h

#include "misc.h"
#include "error.h"
#include "symtab.h"
#include "backend.h"

extern TSymtab globalSymtab;

//----------------------------------------------------------------
// TRuntimeStack        Runtime stack class.
//----------------------------------------------------------------

class TRuntimeStack {
    enum {stackSize = 32};

    float  stack[stackSize];  // stack elements
    float *tos;               // ptr to the top of the stack

public:
    TRuntimeStack(void) { tos = &stack[-1]; }

    float Pop(void)     { return *tos--; }

    void Push(float value)
    {
        if (tos < &stack[stackSize-1]) *++tos = value;
        else RuntimeError(rteStackOverflow);
```

```
    }
};

//-------------------------------------------------------------
// TExecutor              Executor subclass of TBackend.
//-------------------------------------------------------------

class TExecutor : public TBackend {
    long          stmtCount;  // count of executed statements
    TRuntimeStack runStack;   // the runtime stack

    //--Pointers to the special "input" and "output"
    //--symbol table nodes entered by the parser.
    TSymtabNode *const pInputNode;
    TSymtabNode *const pOutputNode;

    //--Statements.
    void ExecuteStatement (void);
    void ExecuteAssignment(void);

    //--Expressions.
    void ExecuteExpression(void);
    void ExecuteSimpleExpression(void);
    void ExecuteTerm   (void);
    void ExecuteFactor(void);

public:
    TExecutor(void)
        : pInputNode (globalSymtab.Search("input")),
          pOutputNode(globalSymtab.Search("output")) { stmtCount = 0; }

    virtual void Go(void);
};

#endif
```

Figure 5.26 shows a new version of header file exec.h. Instead of simply aborting the program upon a runtime stack overflow, member function TRuntimeStack::Push now calls RuntimeError. Subclass TExecutor, derived from base class TBackend, is similar to class TParser of the Calculator utility program (see Figure 5.8). Its private member functions have names based on the syntax diagrams (see Figure 5.22). The constructor function searches the symbol table for the variables input and output.

■■■■■■■ **Figure 5.27** Implementation file **exec.cpp**.

```cpp
//   *****************************************************************
//   *                                                               *
//   *    E X E C U T O R                                            *
//   *                                                               *
//   *    Execute the intermediate code.                             *
//   *                                                               *
//   *    CLASSES: TExecutor                                         *
//   *                                                               *
//   *    FILE:    prog5-2/exec.cpp                                  *
//   *                                                               *
//   *    MODULE:  Executor                                          *
//   *                                                               *
//   *    Copyright (c) 1996 by Ronald Mak                           *
//   *    For instructional purposes only.  No warranties.           *
//   *                                                               *
//   *****************************************************************

#include "exec.h"

//---------------------------------------------------------------
//  Go                  Start the executor.
//---------------------------------------------------------------

void TExecutor::Go(void)
{
    //--Reset the icode to the beginning
    //--and extract the first token.
    icode.Reset();
    GetToken();

    //--Loop to execute statements until the end of the program.
    do {
        ExecuteStatement();

        //--Skip semicolons.
        while (token == tcSemicolon) GetToken();

    } while (token != tcPeriod);

    //--Print the executor's summary.
    cout << endl;
    cout << "Successful completion.  " << stmtCount
         << " statements executed." << endl;
}
```

Figure 5.27 shows the new implementation file exec.cpp. Member function TExecutor::Go first resets the intermediate code to its beginning, and then it extracts the first token from the icode by calling GetToken, which is inherited from class TBackend (Figure 5.25). It repeatedly calls ExecuteStatement to execute each statement in the icode.

■■■■■■■■■ **Figure 5.28** Implementation file **execstmt.cpp** of the Simple Executor I utility program.

```
//   ^********************************************************
//   *                                                        *
//   *     E X E C U T O R     (Statements)                   *
//   *                                                        *
//   *     Execute statements.                                *
//   *                                                        *
//   *     CLASSES: TExecutor                                 *
//   *                                                        *
//   *     FILE:     prog5-2/execstmt.cpp                     *
//   *                                                        *
//   *     MODULE:  Executor                                  *
//   *                                                        *
//   *     Copyright (c) 1996 by Ronald Mak                   *
//   *     For instructional purposes only.  No warranties.   *
//   *                                                        *
//   ********************************************************

#include <iostream.h>
#include "exec.h"

//------------------------------------------------------------
// ExecuteStatement     Execute a statement.
//------------------------------------------------------------

void TExecutor::ExecuteStatement(void)
{
    if (token != tcBEGIN) ++stmtCount;

    //--Only assignment statements for now.
    ExecuteAssignment();
}

//------------------------------------------------------------
// ExecuteAssignment    Execute an assignment statement.
//                      Print the assigned value of the
//                      target variable if it is "output".
//------------------------------------------------------------
```

(*continues*)

■■■■■■■■ **Figure 5.28** Implementation file **execstmt.cpp** of the Simple Executor I
utility program. (*Continued*)

```
void TExecutor::ExecuteAssignment(void)
{
    TSymtabNode *pTargetNode = pNode;

    GetToken();  // :=
    GetToken();  // first token of expression

    //--Execute the expression and pop its value into the
    //--target variable's symbol table node.
    ExecuteExpression();
    pTargetNode->value = runStack.Pop();

    //--If the target variable is "output", print its value
    //--preceded by the current source line number.
    if (pTargetNode == pOutputNode) {
        cout << ">> At " << currentLineNumber << ": output = "
             << pTargetNode->value << endl;
    }
}
```

Figure 5.28 shows implementation file execstmt.cpp. Member function ExecuteStatement increments the runtime statement counter and calls member function ExecuteAssignment.

Assignment Statements

Member function ExecuteAssignment calls ExecuteExpression, which evaluates the expression and leaves the value on top of the stack. ExecuteAssignment pops off this value and sets it into the target variable's symbol table node. If this variable happens to be output, the function also prints the current source line number (as determined by the last-encountered line marker in the icode) and the assigned value. Note that the function does not need to do any syntax checking, since the back end is not started if the front end detected any syntax errors.

■■■■■■■■ **Figure 5.29** Implementation file **execexpr.cpp** of the Simple Executor I
utility program.

```
//   ************************************************************
//   *                                                          *
//   *    E X E C U T O R    (Expressions)                      *
//   *                                                          *
```

```
//   *    Execute expressions.                                 *
//   *                                                         *
//   *    CLASSES: TExecutor                                   *
//   *                                                         *
//   *    FILE:    prog5-2/execexpr.cpp                        *
//   *                                                         *
//   *    MODULE:  Executor                                    *
//   *                                                         *
//   *    Copyright (c) 1996 by Ronald Mak                     *
//   *    For instructional purposes only.  No warranties.     *
//   *                                                         *
//   **********************************************************

#include <iostream.h>
#include "exec.h"

//--------------------------------------------------------------
// ExecuteExpression    Execute an expression (binary relational
//                      operators = < > <> <= and >= ).
//--------------------------------------------------------------

void TExecutor::ExecuteExpression(void)
{
    TTokenCode op;

    ExecuteSimpleExpression();

    //--If there we now see a relational operator,
    //--execute a second simple expression.
    if ((token == tcEqual) || (token == tcNe) ||
        (token == tcLt)    || (token == tcGt) ||
        (token == tcLe)    || (token == tcGe)) {

        op = token;

        GetToken();
        ExecuteSimpleExpression();

        //--Pop off the two operand values, ...
        float operand2 = runStack.Pop();
        float operand1 = runStack.Pop();

        //-- ... perform the operation, and push the resulting value
        //--     onto the runtime stack.
        switch (op) {

            case tcEqual:
```

(continues)

■■■■■■■ **Figure 5.29** Implementation file **execexpr.cpp** of the Simple Executor I
utility program. (*Continued*)

```
                    runStack.Push(operand1 == operand2 ? 1.0 : 0.0);
                    break;

                case tcNe:
                    runStack.Push(operand1 != operand2 ? 1.0 : 0.0);
                    break;

                case tcLt:
                    runStack.Push(operand1 <  operand2 ? 1.0 : 0.0);
                    break;

                case tcGt:
                    runStack.Push(operand1 >  operand2 ? 1.0 : 0.0);
                    break;

                case tcLe:
                    runStack.Push(operand1 <= operand2 ? 1.0 : 0.0);
                    break;

                case tcGe:
                    runStack.Push(operand1 >= operand2 ? 1.0 : 0.0);
                    break;
            }
        }
}

//------------------------------------------------------------
//  ExecuteSimpleExpression      Execute a simple expression
//                               (unary operators + or -
//                               and binary operators + -
//                               and OR).
//------------------------------------------------------------

void TExecutor::ExecuteSimpleExpression(void)
{
    TTokenCode op;                   // binary operator
    TTokenCode unaryOp = tcPlus;  // unary  operator

    //-- Unary + or -
    if ((token == tcPlus) || (token == tcMinus)) {
        unaryOp = token;
        GetToken();
    }
```

```
    //--Execute the first term and then negate its value
    //--if there was a unary -.
    ExecuteTerm();
    if (unaryOp == tcMinus) runStack.Push(-runStack.Pop());

    //--Loop to execute subsequent additive operators and terms.
    while ((token == tcPlus) || (token == tcMinus) ||
           (token == tcOR)) {
        op = token;

        GetToken();
        ExecuteTerm();

        //--Pop off the two operand values, ...
        float operand2 = runStack.Pop();
        float operand1 = runStack.Pop();

        //-- ... perform the operation, and push the resulting value
        //--     onto the runtime stack.
        switch (op) {

            case tcPlus:
                runStack.Push(operand1 + operand2);
                break;

            case tcMinus:
                runStack.Push(operand1 - operand2);
                break;

            case tcOR:
                runStack.Push((operand1 != 0.0) || (operand2 != 0.0)
                                 ? 1.0 : 0.0);
                break;
        }
    }
}

//-------------------------------------------------------------
//  ExecuteTerm         Execute a term (binary operators * / DIV
//                      MOD and AND).
//-------------------------------------------------------------

void TExecutor::ExecuteTerm(void)
{
    TTokenCode op;
```

(continues)

```
//--Execute the first factor.
ExecuteFactor();

//--Loop to execute subsequent multiplicative operators and factors.
while ((token == tcStar)  || (token == tcSlash)  ||
       (token == tcDIV)   || (token == tcMOD)    ||
       (token == tcAND)) {
    op = token;

    GetToken();
    ExecuteFactor();

    //--Pop off the two operand values, ...
    float operand2 = runStack.Pop();
    float operand1 = runStack.Pop();

    //-- ... perform the operation, and push the resulting value
    //--     onto the runtime stack.
    int divZeroFlag = false;  // true if division by 0, else false
    switch (op) {

        case tcStar:
            runStack.Push(operand1 * operand2);
            break;

        case tcSlash:
            if (operand2 != 0.0) runStack.Push(operand1 / operand2);
            else                 divZeroFlag = true;
            break;

        case tcDIV:
            if (operand2 != 0.0) runStack.Push(  int(operand1)
                                            / int(operand2));
            else                 divZeroFlag = true;
            break;

        case tcMOD:
            if (operand2 != 0.0) runStack.Push(  int(operand1)
                                            % int(operand2));
            else                 divZeroFlag = true;
            break;

        case tcAND:
```

```
                    runStack.Push((operand1 != 0.0) && (operand2 != 0.0)
                                    ? 1.0 : 0.0);
                break;
        }
        if (divZeroFlag) {

            //--Division by zero runtime error.
            RuntimeError(rteDivisionByZero);
            runStack.Push(0.0);
        }
    }
}

//------------------------------------------------------------
//  ExecuteFactor      Execute a factor (identifier, number,
//                     string, NOT <factor>, or parenthesized
//                     subexpression).  If the identifier is
//                     the variable "input", prompt for its
//                     value.
//------------------------------------------------------------

void TExecutor::ExecuteFactor(void)
{
    switch (token) {

        case tcIdentifier: {

            //--If the variable is "input", prompt for its value.
            if (pNode == pInputNode) {
                cout << ">> At " << currentLineNumber << ":  input ? ";
                cin  >> pNode->value;
                if (!cin.good()) RuntimeError(rteInvalidUserInput);
            }

            //--Push the variable's value onto the runtime stack.
            runStack.Push(pNode->value);
            GetToken();
            break;
        }

        case tcNumber: {

            //--Push the number's value onto the runtime stack.
            runStack.Push(pNode->value);
            GetToken();
            break;
```

(continues)

```
        }

        case tcString:

            //--Just push 0.0 for now.
            runStack.Push(0.0);
            GetToken();
            break;

        case tcNOT:

            //--Execute factor and invert its value.
            GetToken();
            ExecuteFactor();
            runStack.Push((runStack.Pop() != 0.0) ? 0.0 : 1.0);
            break;

        case tcLParen: {

            //--Parenthesized subexpression:  Call ExecuteExpression
            //--                                 recursively.
            GetToken();             // first token after (
            ExecuteExpression();
            GetToken();             // first token after )
        }
    }
}
```

Expressions

Figure 5.29 shows the new implementation file execexpr.cpp. It performs all the semantic actions to evaluate expressions (compare with Figure 5.12). Member function ExecuteExpression evaluates simple expressions with relational operators. Since we are only using real values for now, it pushes 1.0 onto the stack as the true value, or 0.0 for the false value. Member functions ExecuteSimpleExpression, ExecuteTerm, and ExecuteFactor also use 1.0 for true and 0.0 for false for the OR and AND and NOT operators. ExecuteTerm calls the runtime error function RuntimeError. ExecuteFactor prompts for a value if the variable identifier is input. Since we don't have any way yet to handle a string at runtime, the function pushes 0.0 for a string.

■■■■■■■ **Figure 5.30** Runtime error codes and a function prototype in header file
error.h.

```
//-------------------------------------------------------------
//  Runtime error codes.
//-------------------------------------------------------------

enum TRuntimeErrorCode {
    rteNone,
    rteStackOverflow,
    rteValueOutOfRange,
    rteInvalidCaseValue,
    rteDivisionByZero,
    rteInvalidFunctionArgument,
    rteInvalidUserInput,
    rteUnimplementedRuntimeFeature,
};

void RuntimeError(TRuntimeErrorCode ec);
```

Figure 5.30 shows the runtime error codes in the new version of header file
error.h, along with the prototype for the runtime error function RuntimeError.
Figure 5.31 shows the corresponding runtime error messages and the function definition in the new version of implementation file error.cpp. Any runtime error will
immediately terminate program execution. (This will change when we develop the
interactive debugger in Chapter 11.)

■■■■■■■ **Figure 5.31** Runtime error messages and the runtime error function in
implementation file **error.cpp**.

```
//-------------------------------------------------------------
//  Runtime error messages      Keyed to enumeration type
//                              TRuntimeErrorCode.
//-------------------------------------------------------------

char *runtimeErrorMessages[] = {
    "No runtime error",
    "Runtime stack overflow",
    "Value out of range",
    "Invalid CASE expression value",
    "Division by zero",
    "Invalid standard function argument",
    "Invalid user input",
    "Unimplemented runtime feature",
};
```

(continues)

■■■■■■■■■ **Figure 5.31** Runtime error messages and the runtime error function in
implementation file **error.cpp**. (*Continued*)

```
//------------------------------------------------------------
//   RuntimeError        Print the runtime error message and then
//                       abort the program.
//
//      ec : error code
//------------------------------------------------------------

void RuntimeError(TRuntimeErrorCode ec)
{
    extern int currentLineNumber;

    cout << endl;
    cout << "*** RUNTIME ERROR in line " << currentLineNumber << ": "
         << runtimeErrorMessages[ec] << endl;

    exit(abortRuntimeError);
}
```

Program 5-2: Simple Executor I

The Simple Executor I utility program is the prototype for the complete interpreter.
Its parser module in the front end creates the icode, and it has an executor in the
backend module that reads the icode to execute the program.

The utility executes a program of assignment statements separated by semicolons. A
period follows the last statement. The parser module parses the statements and
translates them into icode. Then if there were no syntax errors, the backend module
reads the icode and executes the statements. If the variable input appears in an
expression, the executor prompts for its value, and if the variable output is the
assignment target, the executor prints the assigned value.

Figure 5.32 shows the main file execute1.cpp of the utility program. Note that
after the front end is done, main converts the symbol tables before creating the back
end and sending it the Go message.

■■■■■■■■ **Figure 5.32** The main file **execute1.cpp** of the Simple Executor I utility
program.

```
//   **************************************************************
//   *                                                          *
```

```
//   *    Program 5-2: Simple Executor I                        *
//   *                                                          *
//   *    Execute a "program" of simple assignment statements.  *
//   *    Whenever variable "output" is the assignment target,  *
//   *    print the assigned value.  Whenever variable "input"  *
//   *    appears in an expression, prompt for its value.       *
//   *                                                          *
//   *    FILE:    prog5-2/execute1.cpp                         *
//   *                                                          *
//   *    USAGE:   execute1 <source file>                       *
//   *                                                          *
//   *                 <source file>  name of the source file   *
//   *                                                          *
//   *    Copyright (c) 1995 by Ronald Mak                      *
//   *    For instructional purposes only.  No warranties.      *
//   *                                                          *
//   ***********************************************************

#include <iostream.h>
#include "common.h"
#include "error.h"
#include "buffer.h"
#include "symtab.h"
#include "parser.h"
#include "backend.h"
#include "exec.h"

//------------------------------------------------------------
//  main
//------------------------------------------------------------

void main(int argc, char *argv[])
{
    //--Check the command line arguments.
    if (argc != 2) {
        cerr << "Usage: execute1 <source file>" << endl;
        AbortTranslation(abortInvalidCommandLineArgs);
    }

    //--Create the parser for the source file,
    //--and then parse the file.
    TParser *pParser = new TParser(new TSourceBuffer(argv[1]));
    pParser->Parse();
    delete pParser;

    //--If there were no syntax errors, convert the symbol tables,
    //--and create and invoke the backend executor.
```

(continues)

━━━━━━━ **Figure 5.32** The main file **execute1.cpp** of the Simple Executor I utility program.

```
   if (errorCount == 0) {
      vpSymtabs = new TSymtab *[cntSymtabs];
      for (TSymtab *pSt = pSymtabList; pSt; pSt = pSt->Next()) {
         pSt->Convert(vpSymtabs);
      }

      TBackend *pBackend = new TExecutor;
      pBackend->Go();

      delete[] vpSymtabs;
      delete   pBackend;
   }
}
```

Figure 5.33 shows sample output.

━━━━━━━ **Figure 5.33** Sample output from the Simple Executor I utility program. (User input is underlined.)

```
Page 1    execute1.in   Thu Oct 26 07:31:38 1995

    1 0: {Square roots by Newton's algorithm.}
    2 0:
    3 0: number := input;
    4 0: root    := number;
    5 0:
    6 0: root := (number/root + root)/2;  output := root;
    7 0: root := (number/root + root)/2;  output := root;
    8 0: root := (number/root + root)/2;  output := root;
    9 0: root := (number/root + root)/2;  output := root;
   10 0: root := (number/root + root)/2;  output := root;
   11 0: root := (number/root + root)/2;  output := root;
   12 0: root := (number/root + root)/2;  output := root;
   13 0: root := (number/root + root)/2;  output := root;
   14 0: root := (number/root + root)/2;  output := root;
   15 0: .

                15 source lines.
                 0 syntax errors.

>> At 3:  input ? 4096
>> At 6: output = 2048.5
>> At 7: output = 1025.25
```

```
>> At 8: output = 514.622
>> At 9: output = 261.291
>> At 10: output = 138.483
>> At 11: output = 84.0305
>> At 12: output = 66.3874
>> At 13: output = 64.0429
>> At 14: output = 64

Successful completion.  20 statements executed.
```

Table 5.3 shows that we changed the parser, icode, error, and common modules, and that we began a new backend module.

▰▰▰▰▰▰▰ Table 5.3 Modules and Files of Program 5-2

Module	File	Status	Directory
Main	executor1.cpp	*new*	prog5-2
Parser	parser.h	*changed*	prog5-2
	parser.cpp	*changed*	prog5-2
	parsstmt.cpp	*changed*	prog5-2
	parsexpr.cpp	*changed*	prog5-2
Backend	backend.h	*new*	prog5-2
Executor	exec.h	*changed*	prog5-2
	exec.cpp	*new*	prog5-2
	execstmt.cpp	*new*	prog5-2
	execexpr.cpp	*new*	prog5-2
Intermediate code	icode.h	*changed*	prog5-2
	icode.cpp	*changed*	prog5-2
Scanner	scanner.h	*unchanged*	prog3-1
	scanner.cpp	*unchanged*	prog3-2
	token.h	*unchanged*	prog4-2
	tknword.cpp	*unchanged*	prog3-2
	tknnum.cpp	*unchanged*	prog3-2
	tknstrsp.cpp	*unchanged*	prog3-2
Symbol table	symtab.h	*changed*	prog5-2
	symtab.cpp	*changed*	prog5-2
Error	error.h	*changed*	prog5-2
	error.cpp	*changed*	prog5-2

(continues)

■■■■■■■■ Table 5.3 Modules and Files of Program 5-2 (*Continued*)

Module	File	Status	Directory
Buffer	buffer.h	*unchanged*	prog2-1
	buffer.cpp	*unchanged*	prog2-1
Common	common.h	*changed*	prog5-2
	common.cpp	*changed*	prog5-2
	misc.h	*unchanged*	prog3-2

6

PARSING

STATEMENTS

Every Pascal compiler or interpreter first checks the source program for syntactic correctness. It flags any errors that it finds with an error message in the listing, and only if there are no errors does it then output object code or execute the program. Most programmers must sadly admit that their compilers and interpreters do syntax checking more than anything else.

So, a very important task of the parser of any compiler or interpreter is syntax checking. In this chapter, we first expand the parser module that we wrote in the previous chapter, and we'll see how to:

- Do syntax checking of Pascal statements and expressions.
- Detect, report, and recover from syntax errors.

As a bonus, we'll also expand a bit the previous chapter's backend module, and then we'll be able to:

- Execute compound statements and REPEAT statements.

This chapter's first utility program, Syntax Checker I, will use the new parser module to do syntax checking of Pascal control and assignment statements. The second utility program, Simple Executor II, will interpret programs containing compound, assignment, and REPEAT statements.

Syntax Error Handling

Programmers are very prone to making syntax errors, so it is important to consider how such errors are handled. For each syntax error that a parser detects in the source program, it should

1. Pinpoint the location of the error in the source text.
2. Print a descriptive error message.
3. Recover from the error and continue parsing.

The parser detects a syntax error whenever the source program deviates from the syntax rules as known by the parser. Steps 1 and 2 constitute what is commonly called *flagging* an error, and we have already taken care of these steps by printing an arrow that points to the error and an error message, both right under the erroneous source line in the listing.

Error recovery is a much more difficult matter. We generally don't want a compiler to generate any object code or an interpreter to execute the program if there are any syntax errors. However, we do want the parser to continue syntax checking in a meaningful way despite errors so that it can flag any more errors later in the source program. So what can a parser do after it has flagged an error? Some options are:

- It can terminate, crash, or hang. In other words, no recovery at all is attempted. Thus, at most one syntax error can be uncovered at a time. This option is easy for the compiler writer, but extremely annoying for the programmer.

- It can become hopelessly lost, but still attempt to process the rest of the source program while printing reams of irrelevant error messages. Here, too, there is no error recovery, but the parser doesn't admit it.

- It can skip tokens until it reaches something that it recognizes. The parser resynchronizes itself at that point and then continues syntax checking as though nothing had happened.

The first two options are clearly undesirable. To implement the third option, the parser must look for synchronization points after each error. A synchronization

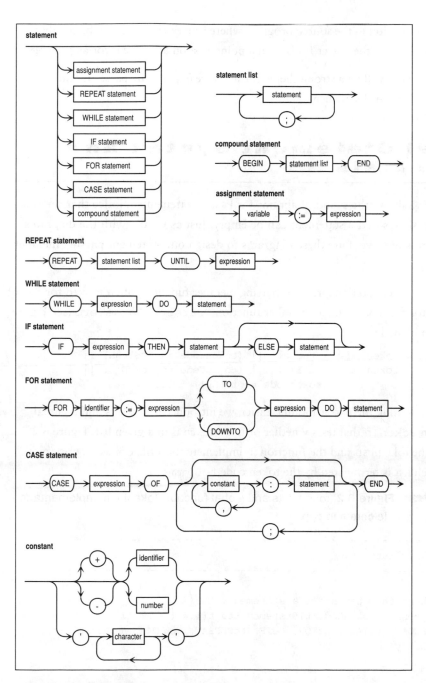

Figure 6.1 Syntax diagrams for Pascal statements.

point is a location in the source program where syntax checking can be reliably restarted. Ideally, the parser finds such a point as soon after the error as possible.

Error recovery will be a strong theme for us as we expand the parser module to handle Pascal's control statements.

Pascal Statement Syntax and Token Lists

Figure 6.1 shows the syntax diagrams for Pascal statements. Notice that the first diagram shows that a statement can be empty. Just as we did with the diagrams for expressions, we'll use these diagrams to design our statement parsing member functions.

The previous chapter's expression parsing member functions often looked for one of several tokens. For example, member function `TParser::ParseTerm` (see Figure 5.23) contained

```
while ((tokenCode == tcStar) || (tokenCode == tcSlash) ||
       (tokenCode == tcDIV) || (tokenCode == tcMOD)   ||
               (tokenCode == tcAND))   ...
```

To make writing the parser module easier, we introduce token lists and a global function `TokenIn` that tests whether or not a token is in a given list. Figure 6.2 shows the token lists and the function in implementation file `common.cpp`. Note how each list is terminated by the token code `tcDummy`.

Figure 6.2 Token lists and global function TokenIn in implementation file **common.cpp**.

```
//-------------------------------------------------------------
//  Token lists
//-------------------------------------------------------------

//--Tokens that can start a statement.
extern const TTokenCode tlStatementStart[] = {
    tcBEGIN, tcCASE, tcFOR, tcIF, tcREPEAT, tcWHILE, tcIdentifier,
    tcDummy
};

//--Tokens that can follow a statement.
```

```
extern const TTokenCode tlStatementFollow[] = {
    tcSemicolon, tcPeriod, tcEND, tcELSE, tcUNTIL, tcDummy
};

//--Tokens that can start a CASE label.
extern const TTokenCode tlCaseLabelStart[] = {
    tcIdentifier, tcNumber, tcPlus, tcMinus, tcString, tcDummy
};

//--Tokens that can start an expression.
extern const TTokenCode tlExpressionStart[] = {
    tcPlus, tcMinus, tcIdentifier, tcNumber, tcString,
    tcNOT, tcLParen, tcDummy
};

//--Tokens that can follow an expression.
extern const TTokenCode tlExpressionFollow[] = {
    tcComma, tcRParen, tcRBracket, tcColon, tcTHEN, tcTO, tcDOWNTO,
    tcDO, tcOF, tcDummy
};

//--Relational operators.
extern const TTokenCode tlRelOps[] = {
    tcEqual, tcNe, tcLt, tcGt, tcLe, tcGe, tcDummy
};

//--Unary + and - operators.
extern const TTokenCode tlUnaryOps[] = {
    tcPlus, tcMinus, tcDummy
};

//--Additive operators.
extern const TTokenCode tlAddOps[] = {
    tcPlus, tcMinus, tcOR, tcDummy
};

//--Multiplicative operators.
extern const TTokenCode tlMulOps[] = {
    tcStar, tcSlash, tcDIV, tcMOD, tcAND, tcDummy
};

//--Tokens that can end a program.
extern const TTokenCode tlProgramEnd[] = {
    tcPeriod, tcDummy
};

//--Individual tokens.
```

(continues)

Figure 6.2 Token lists and global function TokenIn in implementation
file **common.cpp**. (*Continued*)

```
extern const TTokenCode tlColonEqual[] = {tcColonEqual,    tcDummy};
extern const TTokenCode tlDO[]          = {tcDO,           tcDummy};
extern const TTokenCode tlTHEN[]        = {tcTHEN,         tcDummy};
extern const TTokenCode tlTODOWNTO[]    = {tcTO, tcDOWNTO, tcDummy};
extern const TTokenCode tlOF[]          = {tcOF,           tcDummy};
extern const TTokenCode tlColon[]       = {tcColon,        tcDummy};
extern const TTokenCode tlEND[]         = {tcEND,          tcDummy};


//--------------------------------------------------------------
//  TokenIn     Check if a token code is in the token list.
//
//      tc    : token code
//      pList : ptr to tcDummy-terminated token list
//
//  Return:  true if in list, false if not or empty list
//--------------------------------------------------------------

int TokenIn(TTokenCode tc, const TTokenCode *pList)
{
    const TTokenCode *pCode;    // ptr to token code in list

    if (!pList) return false;   // empty list

    for (pCode = pList; *pCode; ++pCode) {
        if (*pCode == tc) return true;   // in list
    }

    return false;   // not in list
}
```

Global function `TokenIn` takes two arguments, a token code and a pointer, to a
token list. It checks the token code against the list and returns true if it found the
code in the list, or false if the code was not in the list or if the list was empty. So,
now we can simply write

```
while (TokenIn(tokenCode, tlMulOps)) ...
```

Figure 6.3 shows an addition we need to make to header file `common.h`.

Figure 6.3 An addition to header file **common.h**.

```
//--------------------------------------------------------------
//  Token lists
//--------------------------------------------------------------
```

```
extern const TTokenCode tlStatementStart[], tlStatementFollow[];
extern const TTokenCode tlCaseLabelStart[];

extern const TTokenCode tlExpressionStart[], tlExpressionFollow[];
extern const TTokenCode tlRelOps[], tlUnaryOps[],
                        tlAddOps[], tlMulOps[];

extern const TTokenCode tlProgramEnd[];

extern const TTokenCode tlColonEqual[];
extern const TTokenCode tlDO[];
extern const TTokenCode tlTHEN[];
extern const TTokenCode tlTODOWNTO[];
extern const TTokenCode tlOF[];
extern const TTokenCode tlColon[];
extern const TTokenCode tlEND[];

int TokenIn(TTokenCode tc, const TTokenCode *pList);
```

Token lists will also play an important role when the parser is looking for synchronization points during error recovery, as we'll soon see.

▰▰▰▰▰▰ **Figure 6.4** New private member functions in the definition of class **TParser**
in header **parser.h** of the Syntax Checker I utility program.

```
void CondGetToken(TTokenCode tc, TErrorCode ec)
{
    //--Get another token only if the current one matches tc.
    if (tc == token) GetToken();
    else             Error(ec);  // error if no match
}

void CondGetTokenAppend(TTokenCode tc, TErrorCode ec)
{
    //--Get another token only if the current one matches tc.
    if (tc == token) GetTokenAppend();
    else             Error(ec);  // error if no match
}

void Resync(const TTokenCode *pList1,
            const TTokenCode *pList2 = NULL,
            const TTokenCode *pList3 = NULL);
```

Figure 6.4 shows new private member functions in the definition of class TParser
in header file parser.h. CondGetToken calls GetToken to extract another token

only if the current token is correct, that is, matches a given token. If there is no match, it flags an error using the given error code. CondGetTokenAppend is similar, except that it also appends the token to the intermediate code. Member function Resync keeps the parser synchronized. We'll see its definition shortly.

We must also add the following private member function prototypes to the definition of class TParser:

```
void ParseStatementList(TTokenCode terminator);
void ParseREPEAT         (void);
void ParseWHILE          (void);
void ParseIF             (void);
void ParseFOR            (void);
void ParseCASE           (void);
void ParseCaseBranch     (void);
void ParseCaseLabel      (void);
void ParseCompound       (void);
```

These are parsing routines for the rest of Pascal's statements. Many of their names are based on the statement syntax diagrams.

■■■■■■■■ **Figure 6.5** Implementation file **parser.cpp** for the Syntax Checker I utility program.

```
//   ***************************************************************
//   *                                                             *
//   *    P A R S E R                                              *
//   *                                                             *
//   *    Parse the source file for the Syntax Checker I utility   *
//   *    program.                                                 *
//   *                                                             *
//   *    CLASSES: TParser                                         *
//   *                                                             *
//   *    FILE:    prog6-1/parser.cpp                              *
//   *                                                             *
//   *    MODULE:  Parser                                          *
//   *                                                             *
//   *    Copyright (c) 1996 by Ronald Mak                         *
//   *    For instructional purposes only.  No warranties.         *
//   *                                                             *
//   ***************************************************************

#include <stdio.h>
#include "common.h"
#include "parser.h"
```

```
//-------------------------------------------------------------
// Parse        Parse the source file.
//-------------------------------------------------------------

void TParser::Parse(void)
{
    //--Extract the first token and append it to the iform.
    //--Parse a statement.
    GetTokenAppend();
    ParseStatement();

    //--Resynchronize at the final period.
    Resync(tlProgramEnd);
    CondGetTokenAppend(tcPeriod, errMissingPeriod);

    //--Print the parser's summary.
    list.PutLine();
    sprintf(list.text, "%20d source lines.",  currentLineNumber);
    list.PutLine();
    sprintf(list.text, "%20d syntax errors.", errorCount);
    list.PutLine();
    list.PutLine();
}


//-------------------------------------------------------------
// Resync          Resynchronize the parser.  If the current
//                 token is not in one of the token lists,
//                 flag it as an error and then skip tokens
//                 up to one that is in a list or end of file.
//-------------------------------------------------------------

void TParser::Resync(const TTokenCode *pList1,
                     const TTokenCode *pList2,
                     const TTokenCode *pList3)
{
    //--Is the current token in one of the lists?
    int errorFlag = (! TokenIn(token, pList1)) &&
                    (! TokenIn(token, pList2)) &&
                    (! TokenIn(token, pList3));

    if (errorFlag) {

        //--Nope.  Flag it as an error.
        TErrorCode errorCode = token == tcEndOfFile
                                    ? errUnexpectedEndOfFile
                                    : errUnexpectedToken;
```

(continues)

```
        Error(errorCode);

        //--Skip tokens.
        while ((! TokenIn(token, pList1)) &&
               (! TokenIn(token, pList2)) &&
               (! TokenIn(token, pList3)) &&
               (token != tcPeriod)       &&
               (token != tcEndOfFile)) {
            GetToken();
        }

        //--Flag an unexpected end of file (if haven't already).
        if ((token == tcEndOfFile) &&
            (errorCode != errUnexpectedEndOfFile)) {
            Error(errUnexpectedEndOfFile);
        }
    }
}
```

Parsing Statements with Error Handling

Figure 6.5 shows a new version of implementation file parser.cpp.

Member function Resync does error synchronization. It can take up to three token lists (if there are fewer than three lists, the default arguments are NULL). The parser calls this function frequently to resynchronize itself. If the current token is *not* in at least one of the token lists, the function flags an unexpected token error, and then it skips tokens in the source program until it reaches one that *is* in one of the lists. The function also checks for and flags an unexpected end of the source file.

Member function Parse is now very short. It calls ParseStatement to parse a single statement (presumably, a compound statement). Upon return, it calls function Resync to synchronize itself at the program end (it may already be there). Parse then calls function CondGetTokenAppend, which either gets the period token or flags the missing period error.

Figure 6.6 Implementation file **parsstmt.cpp** for the Syntax Checker I utility program.

```
//   ****************************************************************
//   *                                                              *
//   *      P A R S E R    (Statements)                             *
//   *                                                              *
//   *      Parse statements.                                       *
//   *                                                              *
//   *      CLASSES: TParser                           *
//   *                                                              *
//   *      FILE:    prog6-1/parsstmt.cpp                           *
//   *                                                              *
//   *      MODULE:  Parser                                         *
//   *                                                              *
//   *      Copyright (c) 1996 by Ronald Mak                        *
//   *      For instructional purposes only.  No warranties.        *
//   *                                                              *
//   ****************************************************************

#include <stdio.h>
#include <string.h>
#include "common.h"
#include "parser.h"


//--------------------------------------------------------------
//  ParseStatement            Parse a statement.
//--------------------------------------------------------------

void TParser::ParseStatement(void)
{
    InsertLineMarker();

    //--Call the appropriate parsing function based on
    //--the statement's first token.
    switch (token) {
        case tcIdentifier:  ParseAssignment();   break;
        case tcREPEAT:      ParseREPEAT();       break;
        case tcWHILE:       ParseWHILE();        break;
        case tcIF:          ParseIF();           break;
        case tcFOR:         ParseFOR();          break;
        case tcCASE:        ParseCASE();         break;
        case tcBEGIN:       ParseCompound();     break;
    }
```

(continues)

```
    //--Resynchronize at a proper statement ending.
    if (token != tcEndOfFile) {
        Resync(tlStatementFollow, tlStatementStart);
    }
}


//----------------------------------------------------------
//  ParseStatementList          Parse a statement list until the
//                              terminator token.
//
//      terminator : the token that terminates the list
//----------------------------------------------------------

void TParser::ParseStatementList(TTokenCode terminator)
{
    //--Loop to parse statements and to check for and skip semicolons.
    do {
        ParseStatement();

        if (TokenIn(token, tlStatementStart)) {
            Error(errMissingSemicolon);
        }
        else while (token == tcSemicolon) GetTokenAppend();
    } while ((token != terminator) && (token != tcEndOfFile));
}


//----------------------------------------------------------
//  ParseAssignment             Parse an assignment statement:
//
//                                  <id> := <expr>
//----------------------------------------------------------

void TParser::ParseAssignment(void)
{
    //--Search for the target variable's identifier and enter it
    //--if necessary.  Append the symbol table node handle
    //--to the icode.
    TSymtabNode        *pTargetNode = SearchAll (pToken->String());
    if (!pTargetNode)  pTargetNode = EnterLocal(pToken->String());

    icode.Put(pTargetNode);
    GetTokenAppend();

    //-- :=
```

```
    Resync(tlColonEqual, tlExpressionStart);
    CondGetTokenAppend(tcColonEqual, errMissingColonEqual);

    //--<expr>
    ParseExpression();
}


//-------------------------------------------------------------
//  ParseREPEAT      Parse a REPEAT statement:
//
//                      REPEAT <stmt-list> UNTIL <expr>
//-------------------------------------------------------------

void TParser::ParseREPEAT(void)
{
    GetTokenAppend();

    //--<stmt-list>
    ParseStatementList(tcUNTIL);

    //--UNTIL
    CondGetTokenAppend(tcUNTIL, errMissingUNTIL);

    //--<expr>
    InsertLineMarker();
    ParseExpression();
}


//-------------------------------------------------------------
//  ParseWHILE       Parse a WHILE statement.:
//
//                      WHILE <expr> DO <stmt>
//-------------------------------------------------------------

void TParser::ParseWHILE(void)
{
    //--<expr>
    GetTokenAppend();
    ParseExpression();

    //--DO
    Resync(tlDO, tlStatementStart);
    CondGetTokenAppend(tcDO, errMissingDO);

    //--<stmt>
    ParseStatement();
}
```

(continues)

```
//------------------------------------------------------------
//  ParseIF          Parse an IF statement:
//
//                          IF <expr> THEN <stmt-1>
//
//                  or:
//
//                          IF <expr> THEN <stmt-1> ELSE <stmt-2>
//------------------------------------------------------------

void TParser::ParseIF(void)
{
    //--<expr>
    GetTokenAppend();
    ParseExpression();

    //--THEN
    Resync(tlTHEN, tlStatementStart);
    CondGetTokenAppend(tcTHEN, errMissingTHEN);

    //--<stmt-1>
    ParseStatement();

    if (token == tcELSE) {

        //--ELSE <stmt-2>
        GetTokenAppend();
        ParseStatement();
    }
}


//------------------------------------------------------------
//  ParseFOR         Parse a FOR statement:
//
//                          FOR <id> := <expr-1> TO|DOWNTO <expr-2>
//                              DO <stmt>
//------------------------------------------------------------

void TParser::ParseFOR(void)
{
    //--<id>
    GetTokenAppend();
    if ((token == tcIdentifier) && (! SearchAll(pToken->String()))) {
```

```
        Error(errUndefinedIdentifier);
    }
    CondGetTokenAppend(tcIdentifier, errMissingIdentifier);

    //-- :=
    Resync(tlColonEqual, tlExpressionStart);
    CondGetTokenAppend(tcColonEqual, errMissingColonEqual);

    //--<expr-1>
    ParseExpression();

    //--TO or DOWNTO
    Resync(tlTODOWNTO, tlExpressionStart);
    if (TokenIn(token, tlTODOWNTO)) GetTokenAppend();
    else Error(errMissingTOorDOWNTO);

    //--<expr-2>
    ParseExpression();

    //--DO
    Resync(tlDO, tlStatementStart);
    CondGetTokenAppend(tcDO, errMissingDO);

    //--<stmt>
    ParseStatement();
}

//----------------------------------------------------------------
//  ParseCASE        Parse a CASE statement:
//
//                      CASE <expr> OF
//                          <case-branch> ;
//                          ...
//                      END
//----------------------------------------------------------------

void TParser::ParseCASE(void)
{
    int caseBranchFlag;  // true if another CASE branch, else false

    //--<expr>
    GetTokenAppend();
    ParseExpression();

    //--OF
    Resync(tlOF, tlCaseLabelStart);
```

(continues)

■■■■■■■■ **Figure 6.6** Implementation file **parsstmt.cpp** for the Syntax Checker I utility program. (*Continued*)

```
        CondGetTokenAppend(tcOF, errMissingOF);

        //--Loop to parse CASE branches.
        caseBranchFlag = TokenIn(token, tlCaseLabelStart);
        while (caseBranchFlag) {
            if (TokenIn(token, tlCaseLabelStart)) ParseCaseBranch();

            if (token == tcSemicolon) {
                GetTokenAppend();
                caseBranchFlag = true;
            }
            else if (TokenIn(token, tlCaseLabelStart)) {
                Error(errMissingSemicolon);
                caseBranchFlag = true;
            }
            else caseBranchFlag = false;
        }

        //--END
        Resync(tlEND, tlStatementStart);
        CondGetTokenAppend(tcEND, errMissingEND);
    }

    //-------------------------------------------------------------
    //  ParseCaseBranch      Parse a CASE branch:
    //
    //                                  <case-label-list> : <stmt>
    //-------------------------------------------------------------

    void TParser::ParseCaseBranch(void)
    {
        int caseLabelFlag;  // true if another CASE label, else false

        //--<case-label-list>
        do {
            ParseCaseLabel();
            if (token == tcComma) {

                //--Saw comma, look for another CASE label.
                GetTokenAppend();
                if (TokenIn(token, tlCaseLabelStart)) caseLabelFlag = true;
                else {
                    Error(errMissingConstant);
```

```
                        caseLabelFlag = false;
                }
            }
        else caseLabelFlag = false;

    } while (caseLabelFlag);

    //-- :
    Resync(tlColon, tlStatementStart);
    CondGetTokenAppend(tcColon, errMissingColon);

    //--<stmt>
    ParseStatement();
}

//------------------------------------------------------------
//  ParseCaseLabel       Parse a CASE label.
//------------------------------------------------------------

void TParser::ParseCaseLabel(void)
{
    int signFlag = false;   // true if unary sign, else false

    //--Unary + or -
    if (TokenIn(token, tlUnaryOps)) {
        signFlag = true;
        GetTokenAppend();
    }

    switch (token) {

        //--Identifier:  Must be defined.
        case tcIdentifier:
            if (! SearchAll(pToken->String())) {
                Error(errUndefinedIdentifier);
            }
            GetTokenAppend();
            break;

        //--Number:  Must be integer.
        case tcNumber:
            if (pToken->Type() != tyInteger) Error(errInvalidConstant);
            GetTokenAppend();
            break;

        //--String:  Must be a single character without a unary sign.
```

(continues)

```
    //--             (Note that the string length includes the quotes.)
    case tcString:
        if (signFlag || (strlen(pToken->String()) != 3)) {
            Error(errInvalidConstant);
        }
        GetTokenAppend();
        break;
    }
}


//------------------------------------------------------------
//  ParseCompound        Parse a compound statement:
//
//                          BEGIN <stmt-list> END
//------------------------------------------------------------

void TParser::ParseCompound(void)
{
    GetTokenAppend();

    //--<stmt-list>
    ParseStatementList(tcEND);

    //--END
    CondGetTokenAppend(tcEND, errMissingEND);
}
```

Figure 6.6 shows a new version of implementation file `parsstmt.cpp`.

Statements and Statement Lists

Member function `ParseStatement` inserts a line marker into the icode and then
calls the appropriate parsing function based on the current token. After the statement has been parsed, the function resynchronizes the parser at a token that can
legitimately follow a statement. This is often a semicolon, but as we can see from the
syntax diagrams in Figure 6.1, it can also be any one of the reserved words END,
ELSE, or UNTIL (and we add a period to the list). In case there is a missing semicolon separating two statements, and to help make sure the parser doesn't skip an
entire statement while attempting to resynchronize, the call to Resync also includes
the list t1StatementStart.

Member function `ParseStatementList` parses a list of statements separated by semicolons, as found in compound and REPEAT statements. In a loop, it calls `ParseStatement` to parse each statement. After each statement, it checks to see if the current token is the start of the next statement. If so, the function flags a missing semicolon error. It skips any semicolons. The loop ends when the current token code matches the `terminator` argument, or it has reached the end of the source file. The terminator will be `tcUNTIL` for a REPEAT statement, or `tcEND` for a compound statement.

Assignment Statements

Member function `ParseAssignment` is similar to the one in the previous chapter. After parsing the target variable identifier, the function resynchronizes at either the `:=` token or the start of the expression. It flags an error if the token is not `:=`.

REPEAT Statements

Member function `ParseREPEAT` parses REPEAT statements. It calls `ParseStatementList` to parse the statement list, passing `tcUNTIL` as the terminator. Afterwards, it looks for the UNTIL reserved word token and flags an error if the word is missing. Before calling `ParseExpression` to parse the expression, it calls `InsertLineMarker` to insert a line marker into the icode so that later if the backend executor encounters a runtime error while evaluating the expression, it can report the source line number of the expression.

WHILE Statements

Member function `ParseWHILE` parses WHILE statements. It first calls `ParseExpression` to parse the expression, and then it resynchronizes at the DO reserved word token or at the start of the statement after the DO. It flags a missing DO if necessary, and finishes by calling `ParseStatement` to parse the statement.

IF Statements

Pascal syntax supports two forms of the IF statement, one with an ELSE branch and one without. Member function `ParseIF` parses both forms of the IF statement. It first calls `ParseExpression` to parse the expression, and then it resynchronizes at the THEN reserved word token or at the start of the statement after the

THEN, flagging a missing THEN if necessary. After calling ParseStatement to parse the statement after THEN, the function checks if the current token is the ELSE reserved word. If so, it calls ParseStatement again to parse the statement after the ELSE.

One potential problem with IF statements is that of the "dangling ELSE." In the Pascal statement

```
IF a = b THEN IF c = d THEN a := c ELSE a := d
```

the THEN branch of an IF statement contains another IF statement. To which IF does the ELSE branch belong? In Pascal, the ELSE always belongs to the immediately preceding IF not already paired with an ELSE, so in this example, it belongs to the second IF. The syntax diagrams in Figure 6.1 follow this rule, and the rule is implemented by member function TParser::ParseIF.

FOR Statements

Member function ParseFOR parses FOR statements. It first parses the control variable identifier, flagging an error if the identifier is missing or undefined. It resynchronizes at the := token (flagging an error if the token is missing) or at the start of the first expression. After calling ParseExpression to parse that expression, the function resynchronizes at the TO or DOWNTO reserved word token (flagging an error if one or the other is not present) or at the start of the second expression. After calling ParseExpression again to parse the second expression, ParseFOR resynchronizes at the DO reserved word token (with another potential error flag) or at the start of the statement after the DO. Finally, the function calls ParseStatement to parse the statement.

CASE Statements

Member function ParseCASE parses the CASE statement, the most complex Pascal control statement. It first calls ParseExpression to parse the CASE expression, and then it resynchronizes at the OF reserved word token (flagging an error if the word is missing) or at the start of the first CASE branch label. The function then repeatedly calls ParseCaseBranch to parse the CASE branches. Local variable caseBranchFlag is set to true whenever there is another CASE branch to parse, otherwise to false. Note that there may no CASE branches at all.

After calling `ParseCaseBranch`, if `ParseCASE` sees a semicolon or the start of another `CASE` label, there will be another `CASE` branch. (It flags a missing semicolon error if necessary.) After the parsing the last `CASE` branch, it drops out of the loop and resynchronizes at the `END` reserved word token (flagging an error if `END` is missing) or at the start of the next statement.

Member function `ParseCaseBranch` parses each `CASE` branch. It first loops to parse the comma-separated list of `CASE` labels by calling `ParseCaseLabel`. Local variable `caseLabelFlag` is set to true whenever there is another label to parse, otherwise to false. After calling `ParseCaseLabel`, `ParseCaseBranch` checks for a comma. If there is one and it is followed by the start of another `CASE` label, there must indeed be another label to parse. If there is a comma but not another label, then the function flags a missing constant error.

After parsing the last `CASE` label, `ParseCaseBranch` resynchronizes at the colon (flagging an error if it is missing) or at the start of the branch statement. It then calls `ParseStatement` to parse the branch statement.

Finally, member function `ParseCaseLabel` parses each `CASE` label. A label can be a defined identifier or an integer number (either can have a unary + or -), or it can be a character. The function flags anything else as an error. (Note that the syntax diagram for `CASE` statements allows any string to be a label.)

Compound Statements

Member function `ParseCompound` parses compound statements. It calls `Parse-StatementList`, passing `tcEND` as the terminator. It then checks for the `END` reserved word token, flagging an error if the token is missing.

Figure 6.7 Implementation file **parsexpr.cpp** of the Syntax Checker I utility program.

```
//  ****************************************************************
//  *                                                            *
//  *    P A R S E R    (Expressions)                            *
//  *                                                            *
//  *    Parse expressions.                                       *
//  *                                                            *
//  *    CLASSES: TParser                                         *
//  *                                                            *
```

(continues)

■■■■■■■ **Figure 6.7** Implementation file **parsexpr.cpp** of the Syntax Checker I
utility program. (*Continued*)

```
// *   FILE:    prog6-1/parsexpr.cpp            *
// *                                            *
// *   MODULE:  Parser                          *
// *                                            *
// *   Copyright (c) 1996 by Ronald Mak         *
// *   For instructional purposes only.  No warranties.  *
// *                                            *
// ************************************************************

#include "common.h"
#include "parser.h"

//------------------------------------------------------------
// ParseExpression      Parse an expression (binary relational
//                      operators = < > <> <= and >= ).
//------------------------------------------------------------

void TParser::ParseExpression(void)
{
    //--Parse the first simple expression.
    ParseSimpleExpression();

    //--If we now see a relational operator,
    //--parse the second simple expression.
    if (TokenIn(token, tlRelOps)) {
        GetTokenAppend();
        ParseSimpleExpression();
    }

    //--Make sure the expression ended properly.
    Resync(tlExpressionFollow, tlStatementFollow, tlStatementStart);
}

//------------------------------------------------------------
// ParseSimpleExpression      Parse a simple expression
//                            (unary operators + or - , and
//                            binary operators + - and OR).
//------------------------------------------------------------

void TParser::ParseSimpleExpression(void)
{
    //--Unary + or -
    if (TokenIn(token, tlUnaryOps)) GetTokenAppend();
```

```
    //--Parse the first term.
    ParseTerm();

    //--Loop to parse subsequent additive operators and terms.
    while (TokenIn(token, tlAddOps)) {
        GetTokenAppend();
        ParseTerm();
    }
}


//----------------------------------------------------------------
//  ParseTerm           Parse a term (binary operators * / DIV
//                      MOD and AND).
//----------------------------------------------------------------

void TParser::ParseTerm(void)
{
    //--Parse the first factor.
    ParseFactor();

    //--Loop to parse subsequent multiplicative operators and factors.
    while (TokenIn(token, tlMulOps)) {
        GetTokenAppend();
        ParseFactor();
    }
}


//----------------------------------------------------------------
//  ParseFactor         Parse a factor (identifier, number,
//                      string, NOT <factor>, or parenthesized
//                      subexpression).
//----------------------------------------------------------------

void TParser::ParseFactor(void)
{
    switch (token) {

        case tcIdentifier: {

            //--Search for the identifier.  If found, append the
            //--symbol table node handle to the icode.  If not
            //--found, enter it and flag an undefined identifier error.
            TSymtabNode *pNode = SearchAll(pToken->String());
            if (pNode) icode.Put(pNode);
            else {
                Error(errUndefinedIdentifier);
```

(continues)

■■■■■ **Figure 6.7** Implementation file **parsexpr.cpp** of the Syntax Checker I
utility program. (*Continued*)

```
            EnterLocal(pToken->String());
        }

        GetTokenAppend();
        break;
    }

    case tcNumber: {

        //--Search for the number and enter it if necessary.
        //--Set the number's value in the symbol table node.
        //--Append the symbol table node handle to the icode.
        TSymtabNode *pNode = SearchAll(pToken->String());
        if (!pNode) {
            pNode = EnterLocal(pToken->String());
            pNode->value = pToken->Type() == tyInteger
                                ? (float) pToken->Value().integer
                                : pToken->Value().real;
        }
        icode.Put(pNode);

        GetTokenAppend();
        break;
    }

    case tcString:
        GetTokenAppend();
        break;

    case tcNOT:
        GetTokenAppend();
        ParseFactor();
        break;

    case tcLParen:

        //--Parenthesized subexpression:  Call ParseExpression
        //--                              recursively ...
        GetTokenAppend();
        ParseExpression();

        //-- ... and check for the closing right parenthesis.
        if (token == tcRParen) GetTokenAppend();
```

```
            else                    Error(errMissingRightParen);

            break;

        default:
            Error(errInvalidExpression);
            break;
        }
    }
```

Parsing Expressions with Error Handling

Figure 6.7 shows the new version of implementation file `parsexpr.cpp`. There are only a few changes from the previous version. The member functions now use the global function `TokenIn` to check the current token code against a list of possible valid values. After parsing an expression, member function `ParseExpression` now resynchronizes at the first token that can follow an expression or a statement, or at a token that can start the next statement. (In the latter case, a missing semicolon error will be flagged later by member function `ParseStatementList`.)

Program 6.1: Syntax Checker I

Our first utility program for this chapter is the initial version of a syntax checker for Pascal programs. This version only does statements and expressions, and variables can only be simple identifiers. Figure 6.8 shows its main file. We'll have better versions later as we learn to parse more of the language.

■■■■■■ **Figure 6.8** The main file **synchek1.cpp** of the Syntax Checker I utility program.

```
//  ***************************************************************
//  *                                                             *
//  *     Program 6-1: Syntax Checker I                           *
//  *                                                             *
//  *     Check the syntax of a "program" consisting of a         *
//  *     compound statement containing simple assignment and     *
//  *     control statements.                                     *
//  *                                                             *
```

(continues)

■■■■■ **Figure 6.8** The main file **synchek1.cpp** of the Syntax Checker I utility
program. *(Continued)*

```
// *    FILE:    prog6-1/synchek1.cpp                          *
// *                                                           *
// *    USAGE:   synchek1 <source file>                        *
// *                                                           *
// *               <source file>  name of the source file     *
// *                                                           *
// *    Copyright (c) 1996 by Ronald Mak                       *
// *    For instructional purposes only.  No warranties.       *
// *                                                           *
// *************************************************************

#include <iostream.h>
#include "error.h"
#include "buffer.h"
#include "parser.h"

//-----------------------------------------------------------
// main
//-----------------------------------------------------------

void main(int argc, char *argv[])
{
    //--Check the command line arguments.
    if (argc != 2) {
        cerr << "Usage: synchek1 <source file>" << endl;
        AbortTranslation(abortInvalidCommandLineArgs);
    }

    //--Create the parser for the source file,
    //--and then parse the file.
    TParser *pParser = new TParser(new TSourceBuffer(argv[1]));
    pParser->Parse();
    delete pParser;
}
```

Figure 6.9 shows sample output.

■■■■■ **Figure 6.9** Sample output from the Syntax Checker I utility program.

```
Page 1   synchek1.in   Thu Oct 26 18:13:01 1995

  1 0: BEGIN
  2 0:    alpha := beta - gamma;
              ^
```

```
*** ERROR: Undefined identifier
                                  ^
*** ERROR: Undefined identifier
    3 0:
    4 0:     IF alpha <> theta THEN BEGIN
                            ^
*** ERROR: Undefined identifier
    5 0:         area := length*width
                            ^
*** ERROR: Undefined identifier
                                     ^
*** ERROR: Undefined identifier
    6 0:         volume := area*height        +
                         ^
*** ERROR: Missing ;
                                     ^
*** ERROR: Undefined identifier
    7 0:     END
              ^
*** ERROR: Invalid expression
    8 0:     ELSE x := ((a - b/c) MOD f;
                         ^
*** ERROR: Undefined identifier
                         ^
*** ERROR: Undefined identifier
                            ^
*** ERROR: Undefined identifier
                                  ^
*** ERROR: Undefined identifier
                                  ^
*** ERROR: Missing )
    9 0:
   10 0:     REPEAT
   11 0:         a := b;
   12 0:         b := c
   13 0:     UNTIL *c;
                   ^
*** ERROR: Invalid expression
   14 0:
   15 0:     FOR a := 1 4 DOWNTO b DO TO WHILE NOT a DO;
                       ^
*** ERROR: Unexpected token
                                  ^
*** ERROR: Unexpected token
                                     ^
*** ERROR: Missing ;
   16 0:
```

(continues)

■■■■■ **Figure 6.9** Sample output from the Syntax Checker I utility program.
(*Continued*)

```
Page 2    synchek1.in    Thu Oct 26 18:13:01 1995

  17 0:      CASE switch OF
                   ^
*** ERROR: Undefined identifier
  18 0:          one, 2, 3.3, '44': z := -123.45;
                   ^
*** ERROR: Undefined identifier
                        ^
*** ERROR: Invalid constant
                           ^
*** ERROR: Invalid constant
  19 0:
  20 0:          '5', -'6':  BEGIN
                        ^
*** ERROR: Invalid constant
  21 0:              n := n + 1;
  22 0:              k := k - 1;
  23 0:        END
  24 0:      END
  25 0:
       ^
*** ERROR: Missing END
    ^
*** ERROR: Unexpected end of file
    ^
*** ERROR: Missing .

            25 source lines.
            25 syntax errors.
```

Table 6.1 shows that we changed the parser and common modules. The backend
and executor modules will reappear with the next utility program.

Executing Compound and REPEAT Statements

Now let's expand the executor in the backend module we began in the previous
chapter. We'll add member functions to execute REPEAT statements and compound

▮▮▮▮▮▮▮ **Table 6.1** Modules and Files of Program 6-1

Module	File	Status	Directory
Main	synchek1.cpp	*new*	prog6-1
Parser	parser.h	*changed*	prog6-1
	parser.cpp	*changed*	prog6-1
	parsstmt.cpp	*changed*	prog6-1
	parsexpr.cpp	*changed*	prog6-1
Intermediate code	icode.h	*unchanged*	prog5-2
	icode.cpp	*unchanged*	prog5-2
Scanner	scanner.h	*unchanged*	prog3-1
	scanner.cpp	*unchanged*	prog3-2
	token.h	*unchanged*	prog4-2
	tknword.cpp	*unchanged*	prog3-2
	tknnum.cpp	*unchanged*	prog3-2
	tknstrsp.cpp	*unchanged*	prog3-2
Symbol table	symtab.h	*unchanged*	prog5-2
	symtab.cpp	*unchanged*	prog5-2
Error	error.h	*unchanged*	prog5-2
	error.cpp	*unchanged*	prog5-2
Buffer	buffer.h	*unchanged*	prog2-1
	buffer.cpp	*unchanged*	prog2-1
Common	common.h	*changed*	prog6-1
	common.cpp	*changed*	prog6-1
	misc.h	*unchanged*	prog3-2

statements containing simple assignment statements. This will give us yet another preview of how an interpreter is put together. Of course, we still have several large tasks ahead of us, including parsing type definitions and variable declarations (Chapter 7), and parsing procedures and functions (Chapter 8).

We can use the header file exec.h from the Simple Executor I utility program in the previous chapter, but we need to add the following private member function prototypes to class TExecutor:

```
    void ExecuteStatementList(TTokenCode terminator);
    void ExecuteREPEAT(void);
    void ExecuteCompound(void);
```

Figure 6.10 shows the new version of implementation file execstmt.cpp. Remember that in the back end, member function GetToken is inherited from class TBackend (see Figure 5.25), and it extracts a token from the icode.

■■■■■■■ **Figure 6.10** Implementation file **execstmt.cpp** of the Simple Executor II utility program.

```
// *****************************************************************
// *                                                               *
// *     E X E C U T O R     (Statements)                          *
// *                                                               *
// *     Execute statements.                                       *
// *                                                               *
// *     CLASSES: TExecutor                                        *
// *                                                               *
// *     FILE:     prog6-2/execstmt.cpp                            *
// *                                                               *
// *     MODULE:   Executor                                        *
// *                                                               *
// *     Copyright (c) 1996 by Ronald Mak                          *
// *     For instructional purposes only.  No warranties.          *
// *                                                               *
// *****************************************************************

#include <iostream.h>
#include "exec.h"


//----------------------------------------------------------------
// ExecuteStatement     Execute a statement.
//----------------------------------------------------------------

void TExecutor::ExecuteStatement(void)
{
    if (token != tcBEGIN) ++stmtCount;

    switch (token) {
        case tcIdentifier:  ExecuteAssignment();  break;
        case tcREPEAT:      ExecuteREPEAT();      break;
        case tcBEGIN:       ExecuteCompound();    break;

        case tcWHILE:
        case tcIF:
```

```
        case tcFOR:
        case tcCASE:
            RuntimeError(rteUnimplementedRuntimeFeature);
            break;
    }
}


//------------------------------------------------------------
//   ExecuteStatementList          Execute a statement list until
//                                 the terminator token.
//
//       terminator : the token that terminates the list
//------------------------------------------------------------

void TExecutor::ExecuteStatementList(TTokenCode terminator)
{
    //--Loop to execute statements and skip semicolons.
    do {
        ExecuteStatement();
        while (token == tcSemicolon) GetToken();
    } while (token != terminator);
}


//------------------------------------------------------------
//   ExecuteAssignment   Execute an assignment statement.
//                       Print the assigned value of the
//                       target variable if it is "output".
//------------------------------------------------------------

void TExecutor::ExecuteAssignment(void)
{
    TSymtabNode *pTargetNode = pNode;

    GetToken();  // :=
    GetToken();  // first token of expression

    //--Execute the expression and pop its value into the
    //--target variable's symbol table node.
    ExecuteExpression();
    pTargetNode->value = runStack.Pop();

    //--If the target variable is "output", print its value
    //--preceded by the current source line number.
    if (pTargetNode == pOutputNode) {
        cout << ">> At " << currentLineNumber << ": output = "
            << pTargetNode->value << endl;
```

(continues)

■■■■■■■ **Figure 6.10** Implementation file **execstmt.cpp** of the Simple Executor II
utility program.

```
    }
}


//----------------------------------------------------------------
//  ExecuteREPEAT      Execute a REPEAT statement:
//
//                         REPEAT <stmt-list> UNTIL <expr>
//----------------------------------------------------------------

void TExecutor::ExecuteREPEAT(void)
{
    int atLoopStart = CurrentLocation();  // location of the loop start

    do {
        GetToken();  // first token after REPEAT

        //--<stmt-list> UNTIL
        ExecuteStatementList(tcUNTIL);

        //--<expr>
        GetToken();
        ExecuteExpression();

        //--Decide whether or not to branch back to the loop start.
        if (runStack.Pop() == 0.0) GoTo(atLoopStart);

    } while (CurrentLocation() == atLoopStart);
}


//----------------------------------------------------------------
//  ExecuteCompound      Execute a compound statement:
//
//                             BEGIN <stmt-list> END
//----------------------------------------------------------------

void TExecutor::ExecuteCompound(void)
{
    GetToken();

    //--<stmt-list> END
    ExecuteStatementList(tcEND);

    GetToken();
}
```

Statements and Statement Lists

Member function ExecuteStatement can now handle assignment, REPEAT, and compound statements. Other statements cause an unimplemented feature runtime error.

Member function ExecuteStatementList loops to call ExecuteStatement for each statement in the list. After each call, it skips the trailing semicolons. The function exits the loop when it reaches the terminator token (reserved word END for a compound statement or UNTIL for a REPEAT statement).

REPEAT Statements

Member function ExecuteREPEAT first records the current location of the icode cursor, which is at the top of the REPEAT loop. Then, it repeatedly calls Execute-StatementList (passing tcUNTIL as the terminator) to execute all the statements in the list, and it calls ExecuteExpression to evaluate the expression after the UNTIL. ExecuteREPEAT pops off the expression's value, and if the value is 0.0 (false), it calls GoTo to reset the cursor to the top of the REPEAT loop so that the statement list can be executed again. Otherwise, it exits its loop, leaving the icode cursor at the first token following the REPEAT statement.

Compound Statements

Member function ExecuteCompound calls ExecuteStatementList to execute all the statements in the list. It passes tcEND as the terminator.

Program 6-2: Simple Executor II

Our second utility program for this chapter, Simple Executor II, knows how to execute REPEAT statements and compound statements containing simple assignment statements and REPEAT statements.

Figure 6.11 shows the main file execute2.cpp of the utility program.

▬▬▬▬▬ **Figure 6.11** Main file **execute2.cpp** of the Simple Executor II utility program.

```
// ****************************************************************
// *                                                              *
// *    Program 6-2: Simple Executor II                           *
```
                                                            (*continues*)

Figure 6.11 Main file **execute2.cpp** of the Simple Executor II utility program. (*Continued*)

```
// *                                                              *
// *    Execute "programs" consisting of a compound statement     *
// *    containing assignment statements and REPEAT statements.   *
// *                                                              *
// *    FILE:    prog6-2/execute2.cpp                             *
// *                                                              *
// *    USAGE:   execute2 <source file>                           *
// *                                                              *
// *                 <source file>  name of the source file       *
// *                                                              *
// *    Copyright (c) 1996 by Ronald Mak                          *
// *    For instructional purposes only.  No warranties.          *
// *                                                              *
// ****************************************************************

#include <iostream.h>
#include "common.h"
#include "error.h"
#include "buffer.h"
#include "symtab.h"
#include "parser.h"
#include "backend.h"
#include "exec.h"

//-------------------------------------------------------------
// main
//-------------------------------------------------------------

void main(int argc, char *argv[])
{
    extern int errorCount;

    //--Check the command line arguments.
    if (argc != 2) {
        cerr << "Usage: execute2 <source file>" << endl;
        AbortTranslation(abortInvalidCommandLineArgs);
    }

    //--Create the parser for the source file,
    //--and then parse the file.
    TParser *pParser = new TParser(new TSourceBuffer(argv[1]));
    pParser->Parse();
    delete pParser;
```

```
//--If there were no syntax errors, convert the symbol tables,
//--and create and invoke the backend executor.
if (errorCount == 0) {
    vpSymtabs = new TSymtab *[cntSymtabs];
    for (TSymtab *pSt = pSymtabList; pSt; pSt = pSt->Next()) {
        pSt->Convert(vpSymtabs);
    }

    TBackend *pBackend = new TExecutor;
    pBackend->Go();

    delete[] vpSymtabs;
    delete   pBackend;
}
}
```

Figure 6.12 shows some sample output.

Figure 6.12 Sample output from the Simple Executor II utility program. (User input is underlined.)

```
Page 1    newton.in   Fri Oct 27 01:35:33 1995

  1 0: BEGIN
  2 0:      epsilon := 1e-12;
  3 0:      maxiter := 20;
  4 0:
  5 0:      REPEAT
  6 0:          number := input;
  7 0:
  8 0:          count  := 0;
  9 0:          root   := number;
 10 0:
 11 0:          REPEAT
 12 0:              prev   := root;
 13 0:              root   := (number/root + root)/2;
 14 0:              output := root;
 15 0:
 16 0:              test   := (prev - root)/root;  {relative difference}
 17 0:              test   := test*test;           {so always positive}
 18 0:              count  := count + 1;
 19 0:          UNTIL (test < epsilon) OR (count >= maxiter)
 20 0:      UNTIL number = 1
 21 0: END.
 22 0:
```

(continues)

■■■■■■ **Figure 6.12** Sample output from the Simple Executor II utility program. (User input is underlined.) *(Continued)*

```
                    22 source lines.
                     0 syntax errors.

>> At 6:  input ? 4096
>> At 14: output = 2048.5
>> At 14: output = 1025.25
>> At 14: output = 514.622
>> At 14: output = 261.291
>> At 14: output = 138.483
>> At 14: output = 84.0305
>> At 14: output = 66.3874
>> At 14: output = 64.0429
>> At 14: output = 64
>> At 14: output = 64
>> At 6:  input ? 0

*** RUNTIME ERROR in line 13: Division by zero
```

Table 6.2 shows that we've modified the parser and executor modules.

■■■■■■ **Table 6.2** Modules and Files of Program 6-2

Module	File	Status	Directory
Main	execute2.cpp	*new*	prog6-2
Parser	parser.h	*unchanged*	prog6-1
	parser.cpp	*unchanged*	prog6-1
	parsstmt.cpp	*unchanged*	prog6-1
	parsexpr.cpp	*unchanged*	prog6-1
Backend	backend.h	*unchanged*	prog5-2
Executor	exec.h	*changed*	prog6-2
	exec.cpp	*unchanged*	prog5-2
	execstmt.cpp	*changed*	prog6-2
	execexpr.cpp	*changed*	prog6-2
Intermediate code	icode.h	*unchanged*	prog5-2
	icode.cpp	*unchanged*	prog5-2
Scanner	scanner.h	*unchanged*	prog3-1
	scanner.cpp	*unchanged*	prog3-2
	token.h	*unchanged*	prog4-2

(continues)

Module	File	Status	Directory
	tknword.cpp	*unchanged*	prog3-2
	tknnum.cpp	*unchanged*	prog3-2
	tknstrsp.cpp	*unchanged*	prog3-2
Symbol table	symtab.h	*unchanged*	prog5-2
	symtab.cpp	*unchanged*	prog5-2
Error	error.h	*unchanged*	prog5-2
	error.cpp	*unchanged*	prog5-2
Buffer	buffer.h	*unchanged*	prog2-1
	buffer.cpp	*unchanged*	prog2-1
Common	common.h	*unchanged*	prog6-1
	common.cpp	*unchanged*	prog6-1
	misc.h	*unchanged*	prog3-2

▬▬▬▬▬

Type Checking

A statement that follows the syntax rules as described by the syntax diagrams is not necessarily correct. For example, the diagrams do not indicate type. Type checking must wait until we learn how to parse type definitions and variable declarations, which we do in the next chapter. Nevertheless, the Syntax Checker I utility program is useful for flagging some of the most common syntax errors.

PARSING

DECLARATIONS

Now that we know how to parse Pascal statements, we're ready to tackle the declarations that precede them in a program. We'll use the word *declarations* somewhat loosely to include not only variable and record field declarations, but also constant definitions and type definitions. (We won't be doing statement labels.) Once we know how to parse declarations, we can then improve the statement and expression parsers to handle variables with subscripts and field designators, and to perform translation-time type checking.

Declaration parsing involves both syntax checking and the semantic actions of building the symbol table structures to represent the information in the declarations. In this chapter, we'll make major modifications to the symbol table and parser modules. We'll see how to:

- Parse declarations and enter the information into the symbol table.
- Print this new information as part of an expanded cross-reference listing.
- Parse variables that have subscripts and field designators.
- Perform translation-time type checking.

This chapter's two utility programs are improvements of two previous ones. The first, Cross-Referencer II, will not only print the line numbers of the statements where an identifier appears, but it will also print information about the identifier's definition and type. The second, Syntax Checker II, will do syntax checking of declarations and statements, and it will also do type checking of the statements and expressions.

Review Figures 1.4 and 1.5 to see how the parser and symbol table objects fit into the overall picture.

Pascal Declarations

Figure 7.1 shows the syntax diagrams for the Pascal declarations that we will be parsing. The declarations consist of a constant definition part, a type definition part, and a variable declaration part. Each part is optional, but they must be in that order, and each part ends with a semicolon. In this book, we will not do statement label declarations, packed types, pointer types, set types, file types, or variant record types.

The constant definition part consists of the reserved word CONST followed by a list of constant definitions. Each definition consists of an identifier followed by an equal sign, a constant, and then a semicolon. The constant may be a number or a string, or a previously defined constant identifier. A unary + or − sign may come before a numeric constant or a constant identifier whose value is numeric. (See Figure 6.1 for the syntax diagram of a constant.)

The type definition part consists of the reserved word TYPE followed by a list of type definitions. Each definition consists of an identifier followed by an equal sign, a type specification, and then a semicolon. The specification can be for an enumeration type, a subrange type, an array type, or a record type, or it can simply be a previously defined type identifier.

The variable declaration part consists of the reserved word VAR followed by a list of variable declarations. Each declaration consists of a comma-separated list of identifiers, a colon, a type specification, and then a semicolon.

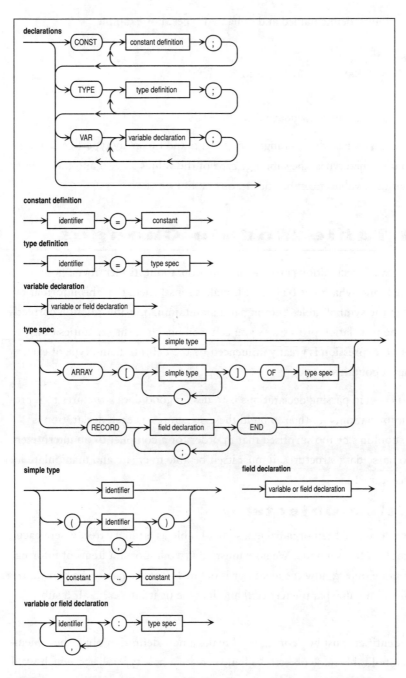

Figure 7.1 Syntax diagrams for Pascal declarations.

Pascal allows you to define named and unnamed types. For example,

```
TYPE
    teens = 11..19;
    list  = ARRAY [1..10] OF real;

VAR
    direction : (north, south, east, west);
```

defines two named types, the subrange type teens and the array type list. There are also two unnamed types, the subrange type of the values 1..10 and the enumeration type with the values north, south, east, and west.

Symbol Table Module Changes

A Pascal program's declarations provide information about its identifiers: how they're defined, and what their types are. It makes sense, then, that this information will be kept in the symbol table. Entering and maintaining this information correctly is crucial to the translation process. As you can well imagine, the semantics of a statement or an expression is greatly influenced by the definition and type of each identifier that it contains.

The key to success in parsing declarations is to design good data structures to represent all the information, and then to build these structures as each declaration is parsed. We shouldn't be too surprised that in order for a compiler or an interpreter to be able to parse data structures, it must itself be able to create and manipulate its own data structures!

Definition Objects

Since Chapter 4, we've been organizing a symbol table as a binary tree, where each identifier's table entry is a node. We now must add two important items of information to each node object: how the identifier is defined (is it the name of a constant? a type? a variable? a value parameter? etc.) and its type (is it integer? real? a subrange? etc.).

Since every identifier must be defined, we'll make a new definition object be a member of the symbol table node object. We'll also create a new type object, which we'll look at later. Each symbol table node can point to a type object, but because some types can be unnamed, we need to keep type objects separate from symbol table node objects. Figure 7.2 shows a class diagram of class `TSymtabNode` and its relationship to the new classes `TDefn` and `TType`.

Class `TDefn` has a public data member how that will indicate whether the identifier was defined as a constant, type, variable, routine, and so on. Depending on the definition, the class's other public data members contain more information about that definition. For example, if an identifier is the name of a constant, then data member `constant` will contain the constant's value.

Class `TType` has many components. The class diagram shows the symbiotic relationship between symbol table node objects and type objects. A symbol table node

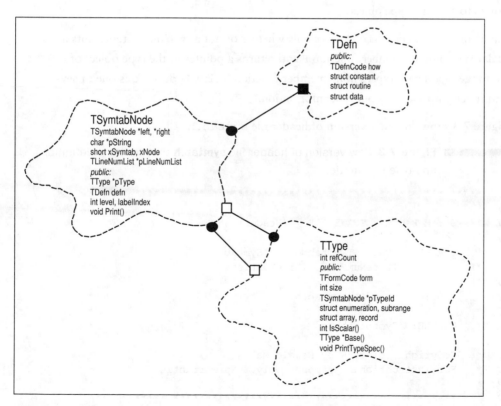

Figure 7.2 Class diagram of classes **TSymtabNode**, **TDefn**, and **TType**.

object's public pType data member points to the type object of the identifier, number, or string. If it represents a named type, a type object's public pTypeId data member points to the symbol table node of its type identifier. pTypeId is null for an unnamed type.

Class TType has a private data member refCount, which will keep track of how many symbol table objects point to a particular type object. We'll see later that this helps us know when to free a type object.

Public data member form indicates whether the type is a scalar, enumeration, subrange, record, or array. Depending on the form, the public data members enumeration, subrange, array, and record contain more information about that form. For example, if a type object represents a subrange, then data member subrange points to the base type object.

Public member function IsScalar tells whether or not a type object represents a scalar type. Public member function Base returns a pointer to the type object of a subrange type's base type. Public member function PrintTypeSpec is one of several functions that print out type information.

Figure 7.3 shows the new version of header file symtab.h.

■■■■■■■ **Figure 7.3** New version of header file **symtab.h** that contains definition and type information.

```
//  ****************************************************************
//  *                                                            *
//  *    S Y M B O L   T A B L E   (Header)                      *
//  *                                                            *
//  *    CLASSES: TDefn, TSymtabNode, TSymtab                    *
//  *             TLineNumNode, TLineNumList                     *
//  *                                                            *
//  *    FILE:    prog7-1/symtab.h                               *
//  *                                                            *
//  *    MODULE:  Symbol table                                   *
//  *                                                            *
//  *    Copyright (c) 1996 by Ronald Mak                        *
//  *    For instructional purposes only.  No warranties.        *
//  *                                                            *
//  ****************************************************************

#ifndef symtab_h
```

```
#define symtab_h

#include <string.h>
#include "misc.h"

extern int currentLineNumber;
extern int asmLabelIndex;
extern int xrefFlag;

class TSymtab;
class TSymtabNode;
class TIcode;

//----------------------------------------------------------------
//  TDefnCode          Definition code: How an identifier
//                                       is defined.
//----------------------------------------------------------------

enum TDefnCode {
    dcUndefined,
    dcConstant, dcType, dcVariable, dcField,
    dcValueParm, dcVarParm,
    dcProgram, dcProcedure, dcFunction,
};

//----------------------------------------------------------------
//  TRoutineCode       Routine code: For procedures, functions,
//                                    and standard routines.
//----------------------------------------------------------------

enum TRoutineCode {
    rcDeclared, rcForward,
    rcRead, rcReadln, rcWrite, rcWriteln,
    rcAbs, rcArctan, rcChr, rcCos, rcEof, rcEoln,
    rcExp, rcLn, rcOdd, rcOrd, rcPred, rcRound,
    rcSin, rcSqr, rcSqrt, rcSucc, rcTrunc,
};

//----------------------------------------------------------------
//  TLocalIds          Local identifier lists structure.
//----------------------------------------------------------------

struct TLocalIds {
    TSymtabNode *pParmIds;      // ptr to local parm id list
    TSymtabNode *pConstantIds;  // ptr to local constant id list
    TSymtabNode *pTypeIds;      // ptr to local type id list
```

(continues)

■■■■■■■ **Figure 7.3** New version of header file **symtab.h** that contains definition
and type information. (*Continued*)

```
    TSymtabNode *pVariableIds;  // ptr to local variable id list
    TSymtabNode *pRoutineIds;   // ptr to local proc and func id list
};


//----------------------------------------------------------------
//  TDefn                 Definition class.
//----------------------------------------------------------------

class TDefn {

public:
    TDefnCode how;  // the identifier was defined

    union {

        //--Constant
        struct {
            TDataValue value;  // value of constant
        } constant;

        //--Procedure, function, or standard routine
        struct {
            TRoutineCode  which;         // routine code
            int           parmCount;     // count of parameters
            int           totalParmSize; // total byte size of parms
            int           totalLocalSize; // total byte size of locals
            TLocalIds     locals;        // local identifiers
            TSymtab       *pSymtab;      // ptr to local symtab
            TIcode        *pIcode;       // ptr to routine's icode
        } routine;

        //--Variable, record field, or parameter
        struct {
            int offset;  // vars and parms: sequence count
                         // fields: byte offset in record
        } data;
    };

    TDefn(TDefnCode dc) { how = dc; }
   ~TDefn(void);
};


//----------------------------------------------------------------
//  TSymtabNode           Symbol table node class.
//----------------------------------------------------------------
```

```
class TLineNumList;
class TType;

class TSymtabNode {
    TSymtabNode   *left, *right;  // ptrs to left and right subtrees
    char          *pString;      // ptr to symbol string
    short         xSymtab;       // symbol table index
    short         xNode;         // node index
    TLineNumList  *pLineNumList; // ptr to list of line numbers

    friend class TSymtab;

public:
    TSymtabNode   *next;    // ptr to next sibling in chain
    TType         *pType;   // ptr to type info

    TDefn defn;             // definition info
    int   level;            // nesting level
    int   labelIndex;       // index for code label

    TSymtabNode(const char *pString, TDefnCode dc = dcUndefined);
    ~TSymtabNode(void);

    TSymtabNode *LeftSubtree (void) const { return left;    }
    TSymtabNode *RightSubtree(void) const { return right;   }
    char        *String      (void) const { return pString; }
    short        SymtabIndex (void) const { return xSymtab; }
    short        NodeIndex   (void) const { return xNode;   }
    void         Convert     (TSymtabNode *vpNodes[]);

    void Print           (void) const;
    void PrintIdentifier (void) const;
    void PrintConstant   (void) const;
    void PrintVarOrField (void) const;
    void PrintType       (void) const;
};

//-------------------------------------------------------------
//  TSymtab            Symbol table class.  The symbol table is
//                     organized as a binary tree that is
//                     sorted alphabetically by the nodes'
//                     name strings.
//-------------------------------------------------------------

class TSymtab {
    TSymtabNode *root;       // ptr to binary tree root
    TSymtabNode **vpNodes;   // ptr to vector of node ptrs
```

(continues)

■■■■■■■ **Figure 7.3** New version of header file **symtab.h** that contains definition
and type information. (*Continued*)

```cpp
    short           cntNodes;   // node counter
    short           xSymtab;    // symbol table index
    TSymtab         *next;       // ptr to next symbol table in list

public:
    TSymtab()
    {
        extern int      cntSymtabs;
        extern TSymtab *pSymtabList;

        root     = NULL;
        vpNodes  = NULL;
        cntNodes = 0;
        xSymtab  = cntSymtabs++;

        //--Insert at the head of the symbol table list.
        next         = pSymtabList;
        pSymtabList = this;
    }

    ~TSymtab()
    {
        delete   root;
        delete[] vpNodes;
    }

    TSymtabNode *Search  (const char *pString) const;
    TSymtabNode *Enter   (const char *pString,
                          TDefnCode dc = dcUndefined);
    TSymtabNode *EnterNew(const char *pString,
                          TDefnCode dc = dcUndefined);

    TSymtabNode *Root(void)          const { return root;           }
    TSymtabNode *Get (short xNode) const { return vpNodes[xNode]; }
    TSymtab     *Next(void)          const { return next;           }
    TSymtabNode **NodeVector(void)   const { return vpNodes;        }
    int          NodeCount (void)   const { return cntNodes;       }
    void         Print     (void)   const { root->Print();          }
    void         Convert   (TSymtab *vpSymtabs[]);
};

//----------------------------------------------------------------
//  TLineNumNode       Line number node class.
//----------------------------------------------------------------
```

```
class TLineNumNode {
    TLineNumNode *next;     // ptr to next node
    const int     number;   // the line number

    friend class TLineNumList;

public:
    TLineNumNode(void)
        : number(currentLineNumber) { next = NULL; }
};

//----------------------------------------------------------------
//  TLineNumList         Line number list class.
//----------------------------------------------------------------

class TLineNumList {
    TLineNumNode *head, *tail;  // list head and tail

public:
    TLineNumList(void) { head = tail = new TLineNumNode; }
    virtual ~TLineNumList(void);

    void Update(void);
    void Print (int newLineFlag, int indent) const;
};

#endif
```

File symtab.h now begins with a list of definition codes that indicate how an identifier is defined. An identifier can be undefined, or it can be the name of a constant, a type, a variable, a record field, a value parameter, a VAR parameter, a program, a procedure, or a function. There is also a list of routine codes that will be used with identifiers that are the names of procedures or functions. Such an identifier can be the name of a declared (programmer-written) routine, a forward routine, or any of the standard Pascal routines such as read and sqrt.

Class TDefn contains a union of public structure data members. If the identifier is a constant name, constant.value is its value (type TDataValue was defined in header file misc.h). If it is a variable or parameter name, data.offset is a sequence count, and if it is a record field name, then data.offset is the byte offset of the field within the record. (The sequence counts and byte offsets will be used starting in the next chapter.) If the identifier is the name of a procedure or a function, data member `routine` contains various items for the routine, including pointers to the routine's local symbol table and to the routine's intermediate code.

Class `TSymtabNode` now has several new public data members: `pType` points to a type object and `defn` is a definition object. For reasons that will be clear later, we will want to link some symbol table nodes into a list, and so `next` will point to the next node object. (We make `next` private so that different parts of the parser can use it to link the nodes together.) Starting in Chapter 8, data member `level` is the current nesting level, and starting in Chapter 12, data member `labelIndex` is used to generate assembly code labels.

Note that the constructor function and public member function `Enter` now take a definition code, which defaults to `dcUndefined`. There is also a new public member function `EnterNew`.

■■■■■ **Figure 7.4** Implementation file **symtab.cpp**.

```
//  ****************************************************************
//  *                                                            *
//  *      S Y M B O L   T A B L E                               *
//  *                                                            *
//  *      Manage a symbol table.                                *
//  *                                                            *
//  *      CLASSES: TDefn, TSymtabNode, TSymtab                  *
//  *               TLineNumNode, TLineNumList                   *
//  *                                                            *
//  *      FILE:    prog7-1/symtab.cpp                           *
//  *                                                            *
//  *      MODULE:  Symbol table                                 *
//  *                                                            *
//  *      Copyright (c) 1996 by Ronald Mak                      *
//  *      For instructional purposes only.  No warranties.      *
//  *                                                            *
//  ****************************************************************

#include <stdio.h>
#include <iostream.h>
#include "common.h"
#include "error.h"
#include "buffer.h"
#include "symtab.h"
#include "types.h"
#include "icode.h"
```

```
int asmLabelIndex = 0;       // assembly label index
int xrefFlag      = false;   // true = cross-referencing on, false = off

//              ****************
//              *              *
//              *  Definition  *
//              *              *
//              ****************


//------------------------------------------------------------
// Destructor     Delete the local symbol table and icode of a
//                program, procedure or function definition.
//                Note that the parameter and local identifier
//                chains are deleted along with the local
//                symbol table.
//------------------------------------------------------------

TDefn::~TDefn(void)
{
    switch (how) {

        case dcProgram:
        case dcProcedure:
        case dcFunction:

            if (routine.which == rcDeclared) {
                delete routine.pSymtab;
                delete routine.pIcode;
            }
            break;

        default:  break;
    }
}


//              **********************
//              *                    *
//              *  Symbol Table Node  *
//              *                    *
//              **********************


//------------------------------------------------------------
// Constructor     Construct a symbol table node by initial-
//                 izing its subtree pointers and the pointer
//                 to its symbol string.
//
```

(continues)

■■■■■■■■■ **Figure 7.4** Implementation file **symtab.cpp**. (*Continued*)

```
//      pStr : ptr to the symbol string
//      dc   : definition code
//------------------------------------------------------------

TSymtabNode::TSymtabNode(const char *pStr, TDefnCode dc)
    : defn(dc)
{
    left = right = next = NULL;
    pLineNumList = NULL;
    pType        = NULL;
    xNode        = 0;
    level        = currentNestingLevel;
    labelIndex   = ++asmLabelIndex;

    //--Allocate and copy the symbol string.
    pString = new char[strlen(pStr) + 1];
    strcpy(pString, pStr);

    //--If cross-referencing, update the line number list.
    if (xrefFlag) pLineNumList = new TLineNumList;
}

//------------------------------------------------------------
// Destructor      Deallocate a symbol table node.
//------------------------------------------------------------

TSymtabNode::~TSymtabNode(void)
{
    void RemoveType(TType *&pType);

    //--First the subtrees (if any).
    delete left;
    delete right;

    //--Then delete this node's components.
    delete[] pString;
    delete   pLineNumList;
    RemoveType(pType);
}

//------------------------------------------------------------
// Print      Print the symbol table node to the list file.
//            First print the node's left subtree, then the
//            node itself, and finally the node's right
```

```
//              subtree.  For the node itself, first print its
//              symbol string, and then its line numbers.
//------------------------------------------------------------

void TSymtabNode::Print(void) const
{
    const int maxNamePrintWidth = 16;

    //--First, print left subtree
    if (left) left->Print();

    //--Print the node:  first the name, then the list of line numbers,
    //--                 and then the identifier information.
    sprintf(list.text, "%*s", maxNamePrintWidth, pString);
    if (pLineNumList) {
        pLineNumList->Print(strlen(pString) > maxNamePrintWidth,
                        maxNamePrintWidth);
    }
    else list.PutLine();
    PrintIdentifier();

    //--Finally, print right subtree
    if (right) right->Print();
}


//------------------------------------------------------------
//  PrintIdentifier        Print information about an
//                         identifier's definition and type.
//------------------------------------------------------------

void TSymtabNode::PrintIdentifier(void) const
{
    switch (defn.how) {
        case dcConstant:    PrintConstant();      break;
        case dcType:        PrintType();          break;

        case dcVariable:
        case dcField:       PrintVarOrField();  break;
    }
}


//------------------------------------------------------------
//  PrintConstant          Print information about a constant
//                         identifier for the cross-reference.
//------------------------------------------------------------
```

(continues)

■■■■■■■■ **Figure 7.4** Implementation file **symtab.cpp**. (*Continued*)

```cpp
void TSymtabNode::PrintConstant(void) const
{
    extern TListBuffer list;

    list.PutLine();
    list.PutLine("Defined constant");

    //--Value
    if ((pType == pIntegerType) ||
        (pType->form == fcEnum)) {
        sprintf(list.text, "Value = %d",
                            defn.constant.value.integer);
    }
    else if (pType == pRealType) {
        sprintf(list.text, "Value = %g",
                            defn.constant.value.real);
    }
    else if (pType == pCharType) {
        sprintf(list.text, "Value = '%c'",
                            defn.constant.value.character);
    }
    else if (pType->form == fcArray) {
        sprintf(list.text, "Value = '%s'",
                            defn.constant.value.pString);
    }
    list.PutLine();

    //--Type information
    if (pType) pType->PrintTypeSpec(TType::vcTerse);
    list.PutLine();
}

//----------------------------------------------------------
//  PrintVarOrField          Print information about a variable
//                           or record field identifier for the
//                           cross-reference.
//----------------------------------------------------------

void TSymtabNode::PrintVarOrField(void) const
{
    extern TListBuffer list;

    list.PutLine();
    list.PutLine(defn.how == dcVariable ? "Declared variable"
```

```
                                     : "Declared record field");

    //--Type information
    if (pType) pType->PrintTypeSpec(TType::vcTerse);
    if ((defn.how == dcVariable) || (this->next)) list.PutLine();
}


//---------------------------------------------------------------
//  PrintType              Print information about a type
//                         identifier for the cross-reference.
//---------------------------------------------------------------

void TSymtabNode::PrintType(void) const
{
    list.PutLine();
    list.PutLine("Defined type");

    if (pType) pType->PrintTypeSpec(TType::vcVerbose);
    list.PutLine();
}


//---------------------------------------------------------------
//  Convert     Convert the symbol table node into a form
//              suitable for the back end.
//
//      vpNodes : vector of node ptrs
//---------------------------------------------------------------

void TSymtabNode::Convert(TSymtabNode *vpNodes[])
{
    //--First, convert the left subtree.
    if (left) left->Convert(vpNodes);

    //--Convert the node.
    vpNodes[xNode] = this;

    //--Finally, convert the right subtree.
    if (right) right->Convert(vpNodes);
}


//              *****************
//              *               *
//              *  Symbol Table  *
//              *               *
//              *****************
```

(continues)

■■■■■ **Figure 7.4** Implementation file **symtab.cpp**. (*Continued*)

```
//--------------------------------------------------------------
//  Search      Search the symbol table for the node with a
//              given name string.
//
//      pString : ptr to the name string to search for
//
//  Return: ptr to the node if found, else NULL
//--------------------------------------------------------------

TSymtabNode *TSymtab::Search(const char *pString) const
{
    TSymtabNode *pNode = root;  // ptr to symbol table node
    int         comp;

    //--Loop to search the table.
    while (pNode) {
        comp = strcmp(pString, pNode->pString);  // compare names
        if (comp == 0) break;                     // found!

        //--Not yet found:  next search left or right subtree.
        pNode = comp < 0 ? pNode->left : pNode->right;
    }

    //--If found and cross-referencing, update the line number list.
    if (xrefFlag && (comp == 0)) pNode->pLineNumList->Update();

    return pNode;  // ptr to node, or NULL if not found
}

//--------------------------------------------------------------
//  Enter       Search the symbol table for the node with a
//              given name string.  If the node is found, return
//              a pointer to it.  Else if not found, enter a new
//              node with the name string, and return a pointer
//              to the new node.
//
//      pString : ptr to the name string to enter
//      dc      : definition code
//
//  Return: ptr to the node, whether existing or newly-entered
//--------------------------------------------------------------

TSymtabNode *TSymtab::Enter(const char *pString, TDefnCode dc)
{
```

```
    TSymtabNode  *pNode;            // ptr to node
    TSymtabNode **ppNode = &root;   // ptr to ptr to node

    //--Loop to search table for insertion point.
    while ((pNode = *ppNode) != NULL) {
        int comp = strcmp(pString, pNode->pString);  // compare strings
        if (comp == 0) return pNode;                  // found!

        //--Not yet found:  next search left or right subtree.
        ppNode = comp < 0 ? &(pNode->left) : &(pNode->right);
    }

    //--Create and insert a new node.
    pNode = new TSymtabNode(pString, dc);  // create a new node,
    pNode->xSymtab = xSymtab;              // set its symtab and
    pNode->xNode   = cntNodes++;           // node indexes,
    *ppNode        = pNode;                // insert it, and
    return pNode;                          // return a ptr to it
}


//-------------------------------------------------------------
//  EnterNew    Search the symbol table for the given name
//              string.  If the name is not already in there,
//              enter it.  Otherwise, flag the redefined
//              identifier error.
//
//      pString : ptr to name string to enter
//      dc      : definition code
//
//  Return: ptr to symbol table node
//-------------------------------------------------------------

TSymtabNode *TSymtab::EnterNew(const char *pString, TDefnCode dc)
{
    TSymtabNode *pNode = Search(pString);

    if (!pNode)  pNode = Enter(pString, dc);
    else         Error(errRedefinedIdentifier);

    return pNode;
}


//-------------------------------------------------------------
//  Convert     Convert the symbol table into a form suitable
//              for the back end.
//
```

(continues)

■■■■■ **Figure 7.4** Implementation file **symtab.cpp**. (*Continued*)

```cpp
//      vpSymtabs : vector of symbol table pointers
//-------------------------------------------------------------

void TSymtab::Convert(TSymtab *vpSymtabs[])
{
    //--Point the appropriate entry of the symbol table pointer vector
    //--to this symbol table.
    vpSymtabs[xSymtab] = this;

    //--Allocate the symbol table node pointer vector
    //--and convert the nodes.
    vpNodes = new TSymtabNode *[cntNodes];
    root->Convert(vpNodes);
}


//              **********************
//              *                    *
//              *  Line Number List  *
//              *                    *
//              **********************

//-------------------------------------------------------------
// Destructor      Deallocate a line number list.
//-------------------------------------------------------------

TLineNumList::~TLineNumList(void)
{
    //--Loop to delete each node in the list.
    while (head) {
        TLineNumNode *pNode = head;  // ptr to node to delete
        head = head->next;           // move down the list
        delete pNode;                // delete node
    }
}


//-------------------------------------------------------------
// Update      Update the list by appending a new line number
//             node if the line number isn't already in the
//             list.
//-------------------------------------------------------------

void TLineNumList::Update(void)
{
    //--If the line number is already there, it'll be at the tail.
```

```
        if (tail && (tail->number == currentLineNumber)) return;

        //--Append the new node.
        tail->next = new TLineNumNode;
        tail       = tail->next;
}


//-------------------------------------------------------------
// Print        Print the line number list.  Use more than one
//              line if necessary; indent subsequent lines.
//
//      newLineFlag : if true, start a new line immediately
//      indent      : amount to indent subsequent lines
//-------------------------------------------------------------

void TLineNumList::Print(int newLineFlag, int indent) const
{
    const int maxLineNumberPrintWidth =  4;
    const int maxLineNumbersPerLine    = 10;

    int           n;        // count of numbers per line
    TLineNumNode *pNode;    // ptr to line number node
    char         *plt = &list.text[strlen(list.text)];
                            // ptr to where in list text to append

    n = newLineFlag ? 0 : maxLineNumbersPerLine;

    //--Loop over line number nodes in the list.
    for (pNode = head; pNode; pNode = pNode->next) {

        //--Start a new list line if the current one is full.
        if (n == 0) {
            list.PutLine();
            sprintf(list.text, "%*s", indent, " ");
            plt = &list.text[indent];
            n   = maxLineNumbersPerLine;
        }

        //--Append the line number to the list text.
        sprintf(plt, "%*d", maxLineNumberPrintWidth, pNode->number);
        plt += maxLineNumberPrintWidth;
        --n;
    }

    list.PutLine();
}
```

Figure 7-4 shows the new version of implementation file `symtab.cpp`.

The `TSymtabNode` constructor function now calls the `TDefn` constructor function. Its destructor function calls function `RemoveType` to (potentially) delete the node's type object. We'll look at `RemoveType` below.

Member function `Print` now calls `PrintIdentifier` after it has printed the identifier name string and its line numbers. `PrintIdentifier` calls the appropriate printing function depending on how the identifier was defined.

Member function `PrintConstant` prints information about a constant identifier for the cross-reference listing. For example, the constant definition `pi = 3.1415926` produces the output

```
Defined constant
Value = 3.14159
Scalar, size 4 bytes.  Type identifier: real
```

The type information is generated by sending the `PrintTypeSpec` message to the type object. We'll look at `PrintTypeSpec` later.

Member function `PrintVarOrField` prints information about a variable or record field identifier. For example, the variable declaration

```
buffer : ARRAY [1..80] OF char
```

produces the output

```
Declared variable
Array, size 80 bytes.  Type identifier: <unnamed>
80 elements
--- INDEX TYPE ---
Subrange, size 2 bytes.  Type identifier: <unnamed>
Minimum value = 1, maximum value = 80
--- Base Range Type ---
Scalar, size 2 bytes.  Type identifier: integer
--- ELEMENT TYPE ---
Scalar, size 1 bytes.  Type identifier: char
```

Again, the type information is generated by sending the `PrintTypeSpec` message to the type object.

Member function `PrintType` prints information about a type definition. For example, the type definition

```
e = (alpha, beta, gamma);
```

generates the output

```
Defined type
Enumeration, size 2 bytes.  Type identifier: e
--- Enumeration Constant Identifiers (value = name) ---
    0 = alpha
    1 = beta
    2 = gamma
```

Each line after the first is generated by sending the `PrintTypeSpec` message to the type object.

Type Objects

Figure 7.5 shows the new header file `types.h`. The file begins with a list of form codes that indicate the type's form: none (used for erroneous type definitions), scalar, enumeration, subrange, array, or record.

■■■■■■ **Figure 7.5** New header file **types.h**.

```
//    ***********************************************************
//    *                                                         *
//    *    T Y P E S    (Header)                                *
//    *                                                         *
//    *    CLASSES: TType                                       *
//    *                                                         *
//    *    FILE:    prog7-1/types.h                             *
//    *                                                         *
//    *    MODULE:  Symbol table                                *
//    *                                                         *
//    *    Copyright (c) 1996 by Ronald Mak                     *
//    *    For instructional purposes only.  No warranties.     *
//    *                                                         *
//    ***********************************************************

#ifndef types_h
#define types_h

#include "error.h"
#include "symtab.h"

extern TType *pIntegerType, *pRealType, *pBooleanType, *pCharType,
             *pDummyType;


//------------------------------------------------------------
// TFormCode          Form code: What form of data structure.
//------------------------------------------------------------
```

(continues)

■■■■ **Figure 7.5** New header file **types.h**. (*Continued*)

```
enum TFormCode {
    fcNone, fcScalar, fcEnum, fcSubrange, fcArray, fcRecord,
};

extern char *formStrings[];

//-------------------------------------------------------------
// TType              Type class.
//-------------------------------------------------------------

class TType {
    int refCount;            // reference count

public:
    TFormCode    form;       // form code
    int          size;       // byte size of type
    TSymtabNode *pTypeId;    // ptr to symtab node of type identifier

    union {

        //--Enumeration
        struct {
            TSymtabNode *pConstIds;  // ptr to list of const id nodes
            int          max;        // max constant value
        } enumeration;

        //--Subrange
        struct {
            TType *pBaseType;  // ptr to base type object
            int    min, max;   // min and max subrange limit values
        } subrange;

        //--Array
        struct {
            TType *pIndexType;         // ptr to index type object
            TType *pElmtType;          // ptr to elmt  type object
            int    minIndex, maxIndex; // min and max index values
            int    elmtCount;          // count of array elmts
        } array;

        //--Record
        struct {
            TSymtab *pSymtab;  // ptr to record fields symtab
        } record;
    };
```

```
    //--General and string type constructors.
    TType(TFormCode fc, int s, TSymtabNode *pId);
    TType(int length);

  ~TType(void);

    int IsScalar(void) const { return (form != fcArray) &&
                                      (form != fcRecord); }

    TType *Base(void) const
    {
        return form == fcSubrange ? subrange.pBaseType : (TType *) this;
    }

    enum TVerbosityCode {vcVerbose, vcTerse};

    void PrintTypeSpec     (TVerbosityCode vc) const;
    void PrintEnumType     (TVerbosityCode vc) const;
    void PrintSubrangeType(TVerbosityCode vc) const;
    void PrintArrayType    (TVerbosityCode vc) const;
    void PrintRecordType   (TVerbosityCode vc) const;

    friend TType *SetType   (TType *&pTargetType, TType *pSourceType);
    friend void   RemoveType(TType *&pType);

    friend void CheckRelOpOperands(const TType *pType1,
                                   const TType *pType2);
    friend void CheckIntegerOrReal(const TType *pType1,
                                   const TType *pType2 = NULL);
    friend void CheckBoolean       (const TType *pType1,
                                   const TType *pType2 = NULL);
    friend void CheckAssignmentTypeCompatible(const TType *pTargetType,
                                              const TType *pValueType,
                                              TErrorCode ec);

    friend int  IntegerOperands(const TType *pType1,
                                const TType *pType2);
    friend int  RealOperands   (const TType *pType1,
                                const TType *pType2);
};

void InitializePredefinedTypes(TSymtab *pSymtab);
void RemovePredefinedTypes(void);

#endif
```

Class `TType` contains different information depending on the type. For an enumeration type, public data member `enumeration.pConstIds` points to a list of the enumeration constant identifiers' symbol table nodes, and `enumeration.max` is the maximum value of the type. For a subrange type, `subrange.pBaseType` points to the type object of the base type, and `subrange.min` and `subrange.max` are the minimum and maximum values of the type.

For an array type, `array.pIndexType` and `array.pElmtType` point to the type objects of its index and element types, respectively. `array.minIndex` and `array.maxIndex` are the minimum and maximum values of the index, and `array.elmtCount` is the element count. For a record type, the type object contains a pointer to a symbol table for its field identifiers.

We'll look at the two constructor functions shortly. Member function `Base` returns either a pointer to the type object itself or, if the type is a subrange type, to the type object of the base type.

Several member functions print type information to the cross-reference listing. The verbosity code controls how much output each printing function generates. There are also several friend functions for initializing, setting, and removing types, plus friend functions for doing type checking.

Before we discuss the implementation of class `TType`, let's take a look at how type objects and symbol table node objects point to each other. Figure 7.6 shows the objects for various sample type definitions.

Note that a type identifier's symbol table node object points to the corresponding type object, and the type object points back to the symbol table node object. However, type objects that represent unnamed types have null symbol table node pointers.

The multidimensional array types are especially interesting. Both of the following type specifications result in the same configuration of symbol table node objects and type objects:

```
ARRAY [1..10, 3..7] of integer
ARRAY [1..10] OF ARRAY [3..7] OF integer
```

This is shown in Figure 7.7.

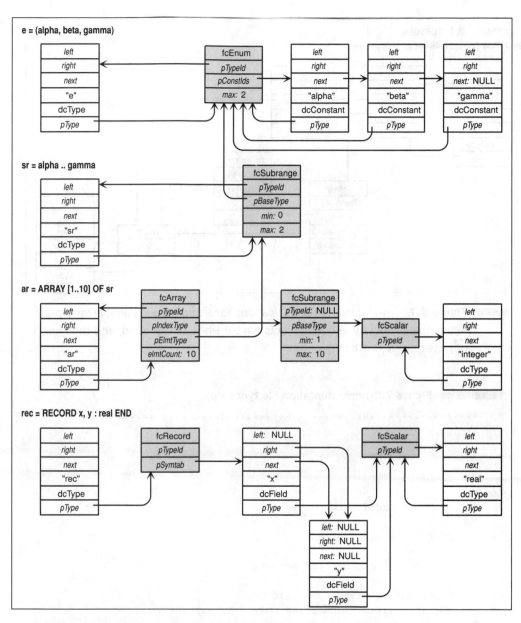

Figure 7.6 Symbol table node objects and type objects for various sample type definitions. Again, we draw the identifier name strings inside of, instead of pointed to by, each node object. The symbol table node objects have a white background, and the type object nodes have a gray background.

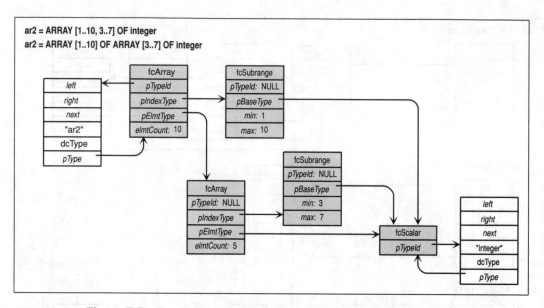

```
ar2 = ARRAY [1..10, 3..7] OF integer
ar2 = ARRAY [1..10] OF ARRAY [3..7] OF integer
```

Figure 7.7 Two equivalent specifications for a multidimensional array type. Again, the symbol table node objects have a white background, and the type objects have a gray background.

■■■■ **Figure 7.8** Implementation file **types.cpp**.

```
//    ****************************************************************
//    *                                                            *
//    *    T Y P E S                                               *
//    *                                                            *
//    *    CLASSES: TType                                          *
//    *                                                            *
//    *    FILE:    prog7-1/types.cpp                              *
//    *                                                            *
//    *    MODULE:  Symbol table                                   *
//    *                                                            *
//    *    Routines to manage type objects.                        *
//    *                                                            *
//    *    Copyright (c) 1996 by Ronald Mak                        *
//    *    For instructional purposes only.  No warranties.        *
//    *                                                            *
//    ****************************************************************

#include <stdio.h>
#include "buffer.h"
```

```
#include "error.h"
#include "types.h"

static char *formStrings[] = {"*** Error ***",  "Scalar", "Enumeration",
                              "Subrange",        "Array",  "Record"};

//--Pointers to predefined types.
TType *pIntegerType = NULL;
TType *pRealType    = NULL;
TType *pBooleanType = NULL;
TType *pCharType    = NULL;
TType *pDummyType   = NULL;


//----------------------------------------------------------------
//  Constructors    General:
//
//      fc    : form code
//      s     : byte size of type
//      pNode : ptr to symbol table node of type identifier
//
//                    String: unnamed string type
//
//      length : string length
//----------------------------------------------------------------

//--General
TType::TType(TFormCode fc, int s, TSymtabNode *pId)
{
    form     = fc;
    size     = s;
    pTypeId  = pId;
    refCount = 0;

    switch (fc) {
        case fcSubrange:
            subrange.pBaseType = NULL;
            break;

        case fcArray:
            array.pIndexType = array.pElmtType = NULL;
            break;

        default:  break;
    }
}
```

(continues)

■■■■■■■■ **Figure 7.8** Implementation file **types.cpp**. (*Continued*)

```cpp
//--String
TType::TType(int length)
{
    form     = fcArray;
    size     = length;
    pTypeId  = NULL;
    refCount = 0;

    array.pIndexType = array.pElmtType = NULL;
    SetType(array.pIndexType, new TType(fcSubrange, sizeof(int), NULL));
    SetType(array.pElmtType,   pCharType);
    array.elmtCount = length;

    //--Integer subrange index type, range 1..length
    SetType(array.pIndexType->subrange.pBaseType, pIntegerType);
    array.pIndexType->subrange.min = 1;
    array.pIndexType->subrange.max = length;
}

//--------------------------------------------------------------
//  Destructor      Delete the allocated objects according to
//                  the form code.  Note that the objects
//                  pointed to by enumeration.pConstIds and by
//                  subrange.pBaseType are deleted along with
//                  the symbol tables that contain their
//                  identifiers.
//--------------------------------------------------------------

TType::~TType(void)
{
    switch (form) {

        case fcSubrange:

            //--Subrange:  Delete the base type object.
            RemoveType(subrange.pBaseType);
            break;

        case fcArray:

            //--Array:  Delete the index and element type objects.
            RemoveType(array.pIndexType);
            RemoveType(array.pElmtType);
            break;
```

```
        case fcRecord:

            //--Record:  Delete the record fields symbol table.
            delete record.pSymtab;
            break;

        default:  break;
    }
}


//----------------------------------------------------------------
//  PrintTypeSpec        Print information about a type
//                       specification for the cross-reference.
//
//      vc : vcVerbose or vcTerse to control the output
//----------------------------------------------------------------

void TType::PrintTypeSpec(TVerbosityCode vc) const
{
    //--Type form and size
    sprintf(list.text, "%s, size %d bytes.  Type identifier: ",
                     formStrings[form], size);

    //--Type identifier
    if (pTypeId) strcat(list.text, pTypeId->String());
    else {
        strcat(list.text, "<unnamed>");
        vc = vcVerbose;  // verbose output for unnamed types
    }
    list.PutLine();

    //--Print the information for the particular type.
    switch (form) {
        case fcEnum:      PrintEnumType     (vc);  break;
        case fcSubrange:  PrintSubrangeType(vc);  break;
        case fcArray:     PrintArrayType    (vc);  break;
        case fcRecord:    PrintRecordType   (vc);  break;
    }
}


//----------------------------------------------------------------
//  PrintEnumType        Print information about an enumeration
//                       type for the cross-reference.
//
//      vc : vcVerbose or vcTerse to control the output
//----------------------------------------------------------------
```

(continues)

■■■■■■■ **Figure 7.8** Implementation file **types.cpp**. (*Continued*)

```cpp
void TType::PrintEnumType(TVerbosityCode vc) const
{
    if (vc == vcTerse) return;

    //--Print the names and values of the enumeration
    //--constant identifiers.
    list.PutLine("--- Enumeration Constant Identifiers "
                 "(value = name) ---");
    for (TSymtabNode *pConstId = enumeration.pConstIds;
         pConstId; pConstId = pConstId->next) {
        sprintf(list.text, "    %d = %s",
                           pConstId->defn.constant.value.integer,
                           pConstId->String());
        list.PutLine();
    }
}

//-----------------------------------------------------------------
//  PrintSubrangeType    Print information about a subrange
//                       type for the cross-reference.
//
//      vc : vcVerbose or vcTerse to control the output
//-----------------------------------------------------------------

void TType::PrintSubrangeType(TVerbosityCode vc) const
{
    if (vc == vcTerse) return;

    //--Subrange minimum and maximum values
    sprintf(list.text, "Minimum value = %d, maximum value = %d",
                       subrange.min, subrange.max);
    list.PutLine();

    //--Base range type
    if (subrange.pBaseType) {
        list.PutLine("--- Base Type ---");
        subrange.pBaseType->PrintTypeSpec(vcTerse);
    }
}

//-----------------------------------------------------------------
//  PrintArrayType       Print information about an array
//                       type for the cross-reference.
//
```

```
//          vc : vcVerbose or vcTerse to control the output
//-------------------------------------------------------------

void TType::PrintArrayType(TVerbosityCode vc) const
{
    if (vc == vcTerse) return;

    //--Element count
    sprintf(list.text, "%d elements", array.elmtCount);
    list.PutLine();

    //--Index type
    if (array.pIndexType) {
        list.PutLine("--- INDEX TYPE ---");
        array.pIndexType->PrintTypeSpec(vcTerse);
    }

    //--Element type
    if (array.pElmtType) {
        list.PutLine("--- ELEMENT TYPE ---");
        array.pElmtType->PrintTypeSpec(vcTerse);
    }
}


//-------------------------------------------------------------
//  PrintRecordType      Print information about a record
//                       type for the cross-reference.
//
//          vc : vcVerbose or vcTerse to control the output
//-------------------------------------------------------------

void TType::PrintRecordType(TVerbosityCode vc) const
{
    if (vc == vcTerse) return;

    //--Print the names and values of the record field identifiers.
    list.PutLine("--- Record Field Identifiers (offset : name) ---");
    list.PutLine();
    for (TSymtabNode *pFieldId = record.pSymtab->Root();
         pFieldId; pFieldId = pFieldId->next) {
        sprintf(list.text, "    %d : %s",
                           pFieldId->defn.data.offset,
                           pFieldId->String());
        list.PutLine();
        pFieldId->PrintVarOrField();
    }
```

(continues)

■■■■■■■ **Figure 7.8** Implementation file **types.cpp**. (*Continued*)

```cpp
}

//----------------------------------------------------------------
//  InitializePredefinedTypes    Initialize the predefined
//                               types by entering their
//                               identifiers into the symbol
//                               table.
//
//      pSymtab : ptr to symbol table
//----------------------------------------------------------------

void InitializePredefinedTypes(TSymtab *pSymtab)
{
    //--Enter the names of the predefined types and of "false"
    //--and "true" into the symbol table.
    TSymtabNode *pIntegerId = pSymtab->Enter("integer", dcType);
    TSymtabNode *pRealId    = pSymtab->Enter("real",    dcType);
    TSymtabNode *pBooleanId = pSymtab->Enter("boolean", dcType);
    TSymtabNode *pCharId    = pSymtab->Enter("char",    dcType);
    TSymtabNode *pFalseId   = pSymtab->Enter("false",   dcConstant);
    TSymtabNode *pTrueId    = pSymtab->Enter("true",    dcConstant);

    //--Create the predefined type objects.
    if (!pIntegerType) {
        SetType(pIntegerType,
                new TType(fcScalar, sizeof(int), pIntegerId));
    }
    if (!pRealType) {
        SetType(pRealType,
                new TType(fcScalar, sizeof(float), pRealId));
    }
    if (!pBooleanType) {
        SetType(pBooleanType,
                new TType(fcEnum, sizeof(int), pBooleanId));
    }
    if (!pCharType) {
        SetType(pCharType,
                new TType(fcScalar, sizeof(char), pCharId));
    }

    //--Link each predefined type's id node to its type object.
    SetType(pIntegerId->pType, pIntegerType);
    SetType(pRealId   ->pType, pRealType);
    SetType(pBooleanId->pType, pBooleanType);
```

```
    SetType(pCharId   ->pType, pCharType);

    //--More initialization for the boolean type object.
    pBooleanType->enumeration.max       = 1;        // max value
    pBooleanType->enumeration.pConstIds = pFalseId; // first constant

    //--More initialization for the "false" and "true" id nodes.
    pFalseId->defn.constant.value.integer = 0;
    pTrueId ->defn.constant.value.integer = 1;
    SetType(pTrueId->pType,  pBooleanType);
    SetType(pFalseId->pType, pBooleanType);
    pFalseId->next = pTrueId;  // "false" node points to "true" node

    //--Initialize the dummy type object that will be used
    //--for erroneous type definitions and for typeless objects.
    SetType(pDummyType, new TType(fcNone, 1, NULL));
}

//-------------------------------------------------------------
// RemovePredefinedTypes       Remove the predefined types.
//-------------------------------------------------------------

void RemovePredefinedTypes(void)
{
    RemoveType(pIntegerType);
    RemoveType(pRealType);
    RemoveType(pBooleanType);
    RemoveType(pCharType);
    RemoveType(pDummyType);
}

//-------------------------------------------------------------
// SetType      Set the target type.  Increment the reference
//              count of the source type.
//
//      pTargetType : ref to ptr to target type object
//      pSourceType : ptr to source type object
//
// Return: ptr to source type object
//-------------------------------------------------------------

TType *SetType(TType *&pTargetType, TType *pSourceType)
{
    if (!pTargetType) RemoveType(pTargetType);

    ++pSourceType->refCount;
```

(continues)

■■■■■■■■ **Figure 7.8** Implementation file **types.cpp**. (*Continued*)

```
    pTargetType = pSourceType;

    return pSourceType;
}


//----------------------------------------------------------------
//  RemoveType   Decrement a type object's reference count, and
//               delete the object and set its pointer to NULL
//               if the count becomes 0.
//
//      pType : ref to ptr to type object
//----------------------------------------------------------------

void RemoveType(TType *&pType)
{
    if (pType && (--pType->refCount == 0)) {
        delete pType;
        pType = NULL;
    }
}


//              ************************
//              *                      *
//              *  Type Compatibility  *
//              *                      *
//              ************************


//----------------------------------------------------------------
//  CheckRelOpOperands  Check that the types of the two operands
//                      of a relational operator are compatible.
//                      Flag an incompatible type error if not.
//
//      pType1 : ptr to the first  operand's type object
//      pType2 : ptr to the second operand's type object
//----------------------------------------------------------------

void CheckRelOpOperands(const TType *pType1, const TType *pType2)
{
    pType1 = pType1->Base();
    pType2 = pType2->Base();

    //--Two identical scalar or enumeration types.
    if (   (pType1 == pType2)
        && ((pType1->form == fcScalar) || (pType1->form == fcEnum))) {
```

```
            return;
        }

        //--One integer operand and one real operand.
        if (   ((pType1 == pIntegerType) && (pType2 == pRealType))
            || ((pType2 == pIntegerType) && (pType1 == pRealType))) {
            return;
        }

        //--Two strings of the same length.
        if (   (pType1->form == fcArray)
            && (pType2->form == fcArray)
            && (pType1->array.pElmtType == pCharType)
            && (pType2->array.pElmtType == pCharType)
            && (pType1->array.elmtCount == pType2->array.elmtCount)) {
            return;
        }

        //--Else:  Incompatible types.
        Error(errIncompatibleTypes);
    }


//--------------------------------------------------------------
//  CheckIntegerOrReal  Check that the type of each operand is
//                      either integer or real.  Flag an
//                      incompatible type error if not.
//
//      pType1 : ptr to the first  operand's type object
//      pType2 : ptr to the second operand's type object or NULL
//--------------------------------------------------------------

void CheckIntegerOrReal(const TType *pType1, const TType *pType2)
{
    pType1 = pType1->Base();
    if ((pType1 != pIntegerType) && (pType1 != pRealType)) {
        Error(errIncompatibleTypes);
    }

    if (pType2) {
        pType2 = pType2->Base();
        if ((pType2 != pIntegerType) && (pType2 != pRealType)) {
            Error(errIncompatibleTypes);
        }
    }
}
```

(continues)

■■■■■■■■■ **Figure 7.8** Implementation file **types.cpp**. (*Continued*)

```
//----------------------------------------------------------------
//   CheckBoolean          Check that the type of each operand is
//                         boolean.  Flag an incompatible type
//                         error if not.
//
//      pType1 : ptr to the first  operand's type object
//      pType2 : ptr to the second operand's type object or NULL
//----------------------------------------------------------------

void CheckBoolean(const TType *pType1, const TType *pType2)
{
    if (   (pType1->Base() != pBooleanType)
        || (pType2 && (pType2->Base() != pBooleanType))) {
        Error(errIncompatibleTypes);
    }
}


//----------------------------------------------------------------
//   CheckAssignmentTypeCompatible    Check that a value's type is
//                                    assignment compatible with
//                                    the target's type.  Flag an
//                                    error if not.
//
//      pTargetType : ptr to the target's type object
//      pValueType  : ptr to the value's  type object
//      ec          : error code
//----------------------------------------------------------------

void CheckAssignmentTypeCompatible(const TType *pTargetType,
                                   const TType *pValueType,
                                   TErrorCode ec)
{
    pTargetType = pTargetType->Base();
    pValueType  = pValueType ->Base();

    //--Two identical types.
    if (pTargetType == pValueType) return;

    //--real := integer
    if (   (pTargetType == pRealType)
        && (pValueType  == pIntegerType)) return;


    //--Two strings of the same length.
    if (   (pTargetType->form == fcArray)
```

```
               && (pValueType ->form == fcArray)
               && (pTargetType->array.pElmtType == pCharType)
               && (pValueType ->array.pElmtType == pCharType)
               && (pTargetType->array.elmtCount ==
                                    pValueType->array.elmtCount)) {
            return;
        }

        Error(ec);
    }

    //-------------------------------------------------------------
    //  IntegerOperands      Check that the types of both operands
    //                       are integer.
    //
    //      pType1 : ptr to the first  operand's type object
    //      pType2 : ptr to the second operand's type object
    //
    //  Return: true if yes, false if no
    //-------------------------------------------------------------

    int IntegerOperands(const TType *pType1, const TType *pType2)
    {
        pType1 = pType1->Base();
        pType2 = pType2->Base();

        return (pType1 == pIntegerType) && (pType2 == pIntegerType);
    }

    //-------------------------------------------------------------
    //  RealOperands         Check that the types of both operands
    //                       are real, or that one is real and the
    //                       other is integer.
    //
    //      pType1 : ptr to the first  operand's type object
    //      pType2 : ptr to the second operand's type object
    //
    //  Return: true if yes, false if no
    //-------------------------------------------------------------

    int RealOperands(const TType *pType1, const TType *pType2)
    {
        pType1 = pType1->Base();
        pType2 = pType2->Base();

        return    ((pType1 == pRealType) && (pType2 == pRealType))
```

(continues)

■■■■■■ **Figure 7.8** Implementation file **types.cpp**. (*Continued*)

```
                || ((pType1 == pRealType) && (pType2 == pIntegerType))
                || ((pType2 == pRealType) && (pType1 == pIntegerType));
}
```

Figure 7.8 shows the new implementation file `types.cpp`. The array `form-Strings` will be used by the type specification printing functions. We also have global pointers to the type objects of the predefined types such as integer and real.

The first constructor function for class `TType` creates and initializes a type object based on the form code, size, and symbol table node pointer arguments. The second constructor function is used to create unnamed string types, and it only takes a string length argument. It creates an array type object whose index type is an unnamed integer subrange type (with values 1 through the string length) and whose element type is the predefined character type. We'll see both constructor functions used during parsing. The destructor function deletes any allocated members of a type object, and it makes several calls to the friend function `RemoveType`.

As we've seen, member function `PrintTypeSpec` is called by the printing functions for constant definitions, type definitions, and variable and record field declarations. It first prints the form of the type using the `formStrings` array, and the type's size in bytes. If the type is named, the function prints the type identifier; otherwise, it prints <unnamed>. Finally, depending on the form, it calls the appropriate type printing function.

The verbosity code `vc` controls how much information to print. We want to print all the information about a type when we're printing the cross-reference entry for the type identifier. We also want to print all the information about an unnamed type. Otherwise, we just need to print the minimum amount of information, which includes the type identifier. Presumably, if you want the complete information about a named type, you can look up the type identifier in the cross-reference listing.

We can look at the type printing functions, each of which prints appropriate information from the type object. Of course, we still haven't yet seen how the information gets *into* the type object. For that, we'll have to wait until we examine the declarations parser.

Member function `PrintEnumType` prints information about an enumeration type specification. We've already seen an example of the output that it generates.

Member function `PrintSubrangeType` prints information about a subrange type specification. It prints the minimum and maximum limit values, and then it calls `PrintTypeSpec` to print information about the subrange's base type. For example, the type specification

```
alpha..gamma;
```

produces the output

```
Minimum value = 0, maximum value = 2
--- Base Type ---
Enumeration, size 2 bytes.  Type identifier: e
```

Member function `PrintArrayType` prints information about an array type specification. It prints the number of elements and information about its index and element types. (Note the recursive calls.) For example, the array type specification

```
ar1 = ARRAY [1..10] OF integer;
```

produces the output

```
10 elements
--- INDEX TYPE ---
Subrange, size 2 bytes.  Type identifier: <unnamed>
Minimum value = 1, maximum value = 10
--- Base Range Type ---
Scalar, size 2 bytes.  Type identifier: integer
--- ELEMENT TYPE ---
Scalar, size 2 bytes.  Type identifier: integer
```

Member function `PrintRecordType` prints information about a record type specification. In a `for` loop, the function prints the offset and name of each field, and then it sends the `PrintVarOrField` message to the field name's symbol table node object to print the field's definition and type information. For example, the record type specification

```
RECORD
    i  : integer;
    x  : real;
    ch : char;
END;
```

produces the output

```
--- Record Field Identifiers (offset : name) ---

    0 : I

Declared record field
Scalar, size 2 bytes.  Type identifier: integer

    2 : x

Declared record field
Scalar, size 4 bytes.  Type identifier: real

    6 : ch

Declared record field
Scalar, size 1 bytes.  Type identifier: char
```

The parser calls friend function InitializePredefinedTypes to initialize Pascal's predefined types, along with the predefined enumeration constants false and true. It also initializes the dummy type, which the parser will use to represent erroneous type specifications. Note that the function calls function SetType to do type object pointer assignments. Friend function RemovePredefinedTypes deletes the predefined type objects.

Friend function SetType sets a type object pointer to point to a particular type object. It increments the reference count of the type object. Friend function RemoveType decrements a type object's reference count. Only if the count becomes zero does the function actually delete the object. We can't simply delete a type object because other type objects or symbol table node objects may still be pointing to it. A type object's reference count keeps track of how many other objects are still pointing to it.

We'll examine the type compatibility checking functions later in this chapter when we learn about translation-time type checking.

■■■■■■■■ **Figure 7.9** Header file **parser.h** for the Cross-Referencer II utility program.

```
//   ****************************************************************
//   *                                                            *
//   *    P A R S E R    (Header)                                 *
//   *                                                            *
```

```
//   *    CLASSES: TParser                                          *
//   *                                                              *
//   *    FILE:    prog7-1/parser.h                                 *
//   *                                                              *
//   *    MODULE:  Parser                                           *
//   *                                                              *
//   *    Copyright (c) 1996 by Ronald Mak                          *
//   *    For instructional purposes only.  No warranties.          *
//   *                                                              *
//   ****************************************************************

#ifndef parser_h
#define parser_h

#include "misc.h"
#include "buffer.h"
#include "error.h"
#include "symtab.h"
#include "types.h"
#include "token.h"
#include "scanner.h"
#include "icode.h"

extern TSymtab globalSymtab;
extern TIcode  icode;

//-------------------------------------------------------------
// TParser              Parser class.
//-------------------------------------------------------------

class TParser {
    TTextScanner *const pScanner;  // ptr to the scanner
    TToken       *pToken;          // ptr to the current token
    TTokenCode    token;           // code of current token

    //--Declarations.
    void ParseDeclarations       (TSymtabNode *pRoutineId);
    void ParseConstantDefinitions(TSymtabNode *pRoutineId);
    void ParseConstant           (TSymtabNode *pConstId);
    void ParseIdentifierConstant (TSymtabNode *pId1, TTokenCode sign);

    void   ParseTypeDefinitions(TSymtabNode *pRoutineId);
    TType *ParseTypeSpec        (void);

    TType *ParseIdentifierType (const TSymtabNode *pId2);
    TType *ParseEnumerationType(void);
```

(continues)

Figure 7.9 Header file **parser.h** for the Cross-Referencer II utility program.
(*Continued*)

```
TType *ParseSubrangeType  (TSymtabNode *pMinId);
TType *ParseSubrangeLimit(TSymtabNode *pLimitId, int &limit);

TType *ParseArrayType (void);
void   ParseIndexType (TType *pArrayType);
int    ArraySize      (TType *pArrayType);
TType *ParseRecordType(void);

void ParseVariableDeclarations(TSymtabNode *pRoutineId);
void ParseFieldDeclarations    (TType        *pRecordType,
                                 int offset);
void ParseVarOrFieldDecls      (TSymtabNode *pRoutineId,
                                 TType        *pRecordType,
                                 int offset);
TSymtabNode *ParseIdSublist    (const TSymtabNode *pRoutineId,
                                 const TType       *pRecordType,
                                 TSymtabNode *&pLastId);

//--Statements.
void ParseStatement     (void);
void ParseStatementList(TTokenCode terminator);
void ParseAssignment    (void);
void ParseREPEAT        (void);
void ParseWHILE         (void);
void ParseIF            (void);
void ParseFOR           (void);
void ParseCASE          (void);
void ParseCaseBranch    (void);
void ParseCaseLabel     (void);
void ParseCompound      (void);

//--Expressions.
void ParseExpression       (void);
void ParseSimpleExpression(void);
void ParseTerm             (void);
void ParseFactor           (void);

void GetToken(void)
{
    pToken = pScanner->Get();
    token  = pToken->Code();
}
```

```
void GetTokenAppend(void)
{
    GetToken();
    icode.Put(token);  // append token code to icode
}

void CondGetToken(TTokenCode tc, TErrorCode ec)
{
    //--Get another token only if the current one matches tc.
    if (tc == token) GetToken();
    else            Error(ec);  // error if no match
}

void CondGetTokenAppend(TTokenCode tc, TErrorCode ec)
{
    //--Get another token only if the current one matches tc.
    if (tc == token) GetTokenAppend();
    else            Error(ec); // error if no match
}

void InsertLineMarker(void) { icode.InsertLineMarker(); }

TSymtabNode *SearchAll(const char *pString) const
{
    return globalSymtab.Search(pString);
}

TSymtabNode *EnterLocal(const char *pString,
                    TDefnCode dc = dcUndefined) const
{
    return globalSymtab.Enter(pString, dc);
}

TSymtabNode *EnterNewLocal(const char *pString,
                       TDefnCode dc = dcUndefined) const
{
    return globalSymtab.EnterNew(pString, dc);
}

TSymtabNode *Find(const char *pString) const
{
    TSymtabNode *pNode = SearchAll(pString);  // look for string

    if (!pNode) {
        Error(errUndefinedIdentifier);        // error if not found
        pNode = globalSymtab.Enter(pString);  // but enter it anyway
```

(*continues*)

Figure 7.9 Header file **parser.h** for the Cross-Referencer II utility program. (*Continued*)

```cpp
        }

        return pNode;
    }

    void CopyQuotedString(char *pString,
                    const char *pQuotedString) const
    {
        int length = strlen(pQuotedString) - 2;   // don't count quotes
        strncpy(pString, &pQuotedString[1], length);
        pString[length] = '\0';
    }

    void Resync(const TTokenCode *pList1,
            const TTokenCode *pList2 = NULL,
            const TTokenCode *pList3 = NULL);

public:
    TParser(TTextInBuffer *pBuffer)
        : pScanner(new TTextScanner(pBuffer))
    {
        InitializePredefinedTypes(&globalSymtab);
    }

    ~TParser(void)
    {
        delete pScanner;
        RemovePredefinedTypes();
    }

    void Parse(void);
};

#endif
```

The Declarations Parser

Figure 7.9 shows header file parser.h that we'll be using for the Cross-Referencer
II utility program. There are prototypes for many new private member functions for
parsing declarations.

Member function `EnterLocal` now takes a definition code argument. New member function `EnterNewLocal` sends the `EnterNew` message to the local symbol table object. New member function `Find` searches all the symbol tables for a given identifier string. If it does not find it, it flags an undefined identifier error and enters the string. The function returns a pointer to the symbol table node, whether it's the node it found or the newly entered one.

New member function `CopyQuotedString` makes a copy of a quoted string, but without the surrounding quotes. New member function `Resync` will resynchronize the parser for error recovery.

The constructor function now calls global function `InitializePredefined-Types`, and the destructor function now calls global function `RemovePredefinedTypes`.

■■■■■■■■■ **Figure 7.10** New version of **TParser::Parse** in implementation file **parser.cpp** of the Cross-Referencer II utility program.

```
//-------------------------------------------------------------
// Parse        Parse the source file.
//-------------------------------------------------------------

void TParser::Parse(void)
{
    //--Create a dummy program identifier symbol table node.
    TSymtabNode dummyProgramId("DummyProgram", dcProgram);
    dummyProgramId.defn.routine.locals.pParmIds     = NULL;
    dummyProgramId.defn.routine.locals.pConstantIds = NULL;
    dummyProgramId.defn.routine.locals.pTypeIds     = NULL;
    dummyProgramId.defn.routine.locals.pVariableIds = NULL;
    dummyProgramId.defn.routine.pSymtab             = NULL;
    dummyProgramId.defn.routine.pIcode              = NULL;

    //--Extract the first token and parse the declarations.
    GetToken();
    ParseDeclarations(&dummyProgramId);

    //--Print the parser's summary.
    list.PutLine();
    sprintf(list.text, "%20d source lines.",  currentLineNumber);
    list.PutLine();
    sprintf(list.text, "%20d syntax errors.", errorCount);
    list.PutLine();
}
```

(continues)

Figure 7.10 shows a new version of member function `TParser::Parse` in implementation file `parser.cpp` that we'll use for the Cross-Referencer II utility program. It first creates a dummy symbol table node for the program identifier. Starting in the next chapter, we'll be able to parse a program header and create a symbol table node for the actual program identifier. For now, though, a dummy one will have to do.

`Parse` calls `ParseDeclarations` to parse the declarations. Afterwards, it prints an annotated cross-reference listing, which will include definition and type information for each identifier. As we've already seen, this information is generated by the various printing member functions of classes `TSymtabNode` and `TType`.

Figure 7.11 New token lists in implementation file **common.cpp**.

```
//--Tokens that can start a declaration.
extern const TTokenCode tlDeclarationStart[] = {
   tcCONST, tcTYPE, tcVAR, tcPROCEDURE, tcFUNCTION, tcDummy
};

//--Tokens that can follow a declaration.
extern const TTokenCode tlDeclarationFollow[] = {
    tcSemicolon, tcIdentifier, tcDummy
};

//--Tokens that can start an identifier or field.
extern const TTokenCode tlIdentifierStart[] = {
    tcIdentifier, tcDummy
};

//--Tokens that can follow an identifier or field.
extern const TTokenCode tlIdentifierFollow[] = {
    tcComma, tcIdentifier, tcColon, tcSemicolon, tcDummy
};

//--Tokens that can follow an identifier or field sublist.
extern const TTokenCode tlSublistFollow[] = {
    tcColon, tcDummy
};

//--Tokens that can follow a field declaration.
extern const TTokenCode tlFieldDeclFollow[] = {
    tcSemicolon, tcIdentifier, tcEND, tcDummy
};
```

```
//--Tokens that can start an enumeration constant.
extern const TTokenCode tlEnumConstStart[] = {
    tcIdentifier, tcDummy
};

//--Tokens that can follow an enumeration constant.
extern const TTokenCode tlEnumConstFollow[] = {
    tcComma, tcIdentifier, tcRParen, tcSemicolon, tcDummy
};

//--Tokens that can follow a subrange limit.
extern const TTokenCode tlSubrangeLimitFollow[] = {
    tcDotDot, tcIdentifier, tcPlus, tcMinus, tcString,
    tcRBracket, tcComma, tcSemicolon, tcOF, tcDummy
};

//--Tokens that can start an index type.
extern const TTokenCode tlIndexStart[] = {
    tcIdentifier, tcNumber, tcString, tcLParen, tcPlus, tcMinus,
    tcDummy
};

//--Tokens that can follow an index type.
extern const TTokenCode tlIndexFollow[] = {
    tcComma, tcRBracket, tcOF, tcSemicolon, tcDummy
};

//--Tokens that can follow the index type list.
extern const TTokenCode tlIndexListFollow[] = {
    tcOF, tcIdentifier, tcLParen, tcARRAY, tcRECORD,
    tcPlus, tcMinus, tcNumber, tcString, tcSemicolon, tcDummy
};

//--Tokens that can start a subscript or field.
extern const TTokenCode tlSubscriptOrFieldStart[] = {
    tcLBracket, tcPeriod, tcDummy
};
```

In order to parse declarations, we need more token lists in implementation file common.cpp. The new ones are shown in Figure 7.11. Also, in header file common.h, we must add:

```
extern const TTokenCode tlDeclarationStart[], tlDeclarationFollow[],
                        tlIdentifierStart[], tlIdentifierFollow[],
                        tlSublistFollow[],   tlFieldDeclFollow[];
```

```
extern const TTokenCode tlEnumConstStart[], tlEnumConstFollow[],
                        tlSubrangeLimitFollow[];

extern const TTokenCode tlIndexStart[], tlIndexFollow[],
                        tlIndexListFollow[];

extern const TTokenCode tlSubscriptOrFieldStart[];
```

Figure 7.12 shows implementation file parsdecl.cpp. In this file, we implement the functions to parse constant definitions, and variable and record field declarations.

■■■■■■■ **Figure 7.12** New implementation file **parsdecl.cpp**.

```
//  +
//  *                                                            *
//  *      P A R S E R    (Declarations)                         *
//  *                                                            *
//  *      Parse constant definitions and variable and record    *
//  *      field declarations.                                    *
//  *                                                            *
//  *      CLASSES: TParser                                       *
//  *                                                            *
//  *      FILE:    prog7-1/parsdecl.cpp                          *
//  *                                                            *
//  *      MODULE:  Parser                                        *
//  *                                                            *
//  *      Copyright (c) 1996 by Ronald Mak                       *
//  *      For instructional purposes only.  No warranties.       *
//  *                                                            *
//  ************************************************************

#include <stdio.h>
#include <string.h>
#include "common.h"
#include "parser.h"

int execFlag = true;     // true for excutor back end,
                         //   false for code generator back end


//------------------------------------------------------------
//  ParseDeclarations   Parse any constant definitions, type
//                      definitions, and variable declarations,
//                      in that order.
//------------------------------------------------------------
```

```
void TParser::ParseDeclarations(TSymtabNode *pRoutineId)
{
    if (token == tcCONST) {
        GetToken();
        ParseConstantDefinitions(pRoutineId);
    }

    if (token == tcTYPE) {
        GetToken();
        ParseTypeDefinitions(pRoutineId);
    }

    if (token == tcVAR) {
        GetToken();
        ParseVariableDeclarations(pRoutineId);
    }
}


//              **************************
//              *                        *
//              *  Constant Definitions   *
//              *                        *
//              **************************


//--------------------------------------------------------------
//  ParseConstDefinitions    Parse a list of constant definitions
//                           separated by semicolons:
//
//                           <id> = <constant>
//
//      pRoutineId : ptr to symbol table node of program,
//                   procedure, or function identifier
//--------------------------------------------------------------

void TParser::ParseConstantDefinitions(TSymtabNode *pRoutineId)
{
    TSymtabNode *pLastId = NULL;  // ptr to last constant id node
                                  //   in local list

    //--Loop to parse a list of constant definitions
    //--seperated by semicolons.
    while (token == tcIdentifier) {
```

(continues)

```
            //--<id>
            TSymtabNode *pConstId = EnterNewLocal(pToken->String());

            //--Link the routine's local constant id nodes together.
            if (!pRoutineId->defn.routine.locals.pConstantIds) {
                pRoutineId->defn.routine.locals.pConstantIds = pConstId;
            }
            else {
                pLastId->next = pConstId;
            }
            pLastId = pConstId;

            //-- =
            GetToken();
            CondGetToken(tcEqual, errMissingEqual);

            //--<constant>
            ParseConstant(pConstId);
            pConstId->defn.how = dcConstant;

            //-- ;
            Resync(tlDeclarationFollow, tlDeclarationStart,
                   tlStatementStart);
            CondGetToken(tcSemicolon, errMissingSemicolon);

            //--Skip extra semicolons.
            while (token == tcSemicolon) GetToken();
            Resync(tlDeclarationFollow, tlDeclarationStart,
                   tlStatementStart);
        }
}


//----------------------------------------------------------
//  ParseConstant        Parse a constant.
//
//      pConstId : ptr to symbol table node of the identifier
//                 being defined
//----------------------------------------------------------

void TParser::ParseConstant(TSymtabNode *pConstId)
{
    TTokenCode sign = tcDummy;  // unary + or - sign, or none

    //--Unary + or -
```

```
if (TokenIn(token, tlUnaryOps)) {
    if (token == tcMinus) sign = tcMinus;
    GetToken();
}

switch (token) {

    //--Numeric constant:  Integer or real type.
    case tcNumber:
        if (pToken->Type() == tyInteger) {
            pConstId->defn.constant.value.integer =
                sign == tcMinus ? -pToken->Value().integer
                                :  pToken->Value().integer;
            SetType(pConstId->pType, pIntegerType);
        }
        else {
            pConstId->defn.constant.value.real =
                sign == tcMinus ? -pToken->Value().real
                                :  pToken->Value().real;
            SetType(pConstId->pType, pRealType);
        }

        GetToken();
        break;

    //--Identifier constant
    case tcIdentifier:
        ParseIdentifierConstant(pConstId, sign);
        break;

    //--String constant:  Character or string
    //--                  (character array) type.
    case tcString:
        int length = strlen(pToken->String()) - 2;  // skip quotes

        if (sign != tcDummy) Error(errInvalidConstant);

        //--Single character
        if (length == 1) {
            pConstId->defn.constant.value.character =
                                        pToken->String()[1];
            SetType(pConstId->pType, pCharType);
        }

        //--String (character array):  Create a new unnamed
        //--                           string type.
```

(continues)

```
            else {
                char *pString = new char[length];
                CopyQuotedString(pString, pToken->String());
                pConstId->defn.constant.value.pString = pString;
                SetType(pConstId->pType, new TType(length));
            }

            GetToken();
            break;
    }
}

//-------------------------------------------------------------
//  ParseIdentifierConstant      In a constant definition of the
//                               form
//
//                                      <id-1> = <id-2>
//
//                               parse <id-2>. The type can be
//                               integer, real, character,
//                               enumeration, or string
//                               (character array).
//
//      pId1 : ptr to symbol table node of <id-1>
//      sign : unary + or - sign, or none
//-------------------------------------------------------------

void TParser::ParseIdentifierConstant(TSymtabNode *pId1,
                                      TTokenCode    sign)
{
    TSymtabNode *pId2 = Find(pToken->String());  // ptr to <id-2>

    if (pId2->defn.how != dcConstant) {
        Error(errNotAConstantIdentifier);
        SetType(pId1->pType, pDummyType);
        GetToken();
        return;
    }

    //--Integer identifier
    if (pId2->pType == pIntegerType) {
        pId1->defn.constant.value.integer =
            sign == tcMinus ? -pId2->defn.constant.value.integer
```

```
                                    :  pId2->defn.constant.value.integer;
        SetType(pId1->pType, pIntegerType);
    }

    //--Real identifier
    else if (pId2->pType == pRealType) {
        pId1->defn.constant.value.real =
            sign == tcMinus ? -pId2->defn.constant.value.real
                            :  pId2->defn.constant.value.real;
        SetType(pId1->pType, pRealType);
    }

    //--Character identifier:  No unary sign allowed.
    else if (pId2->pType == pCharType) {
        if (sign != tcDummy) Error(errInvalidConstant);

        pId1->defn.constant.value.character =
                        pId2->defn.constant.value.character;
        SetType(pId1->pType, pCharType);
    }

    //--Enumeration identifier:  No unary sign allowed.
    else if (pId2->pType->form == fcEnum) {
        if (sign != tcDummy) Error(errInvalidConstant);

        pId1->defn.constant.value.integer =
                        pId2->defn.constant.value.integer;
        SetType(pId1->pType, pId2->pType);
    }

    //--Array identifier:  Must be character array, and
    //                     no unary sign allowed.
    else if (pId2->pType->form == fcArray) {
        if ((sign != tcDummy) ||
            (pId2->pType->array.pElmtType != pCharType)) {
            Error(errInvalidConstant);
        }

        pId1->defn.constant.value.pString =
                        pId2->defn.constant.value.pString;
        SetType(pId1->pType, pId2->pType);
    }

    GetToken();
}
```

(continues)

■■■■■■■ **Figure 7.12** New implementation file **parsdecl.cpp**. (*Continued*)

```
//      *********************************************
//      *                                           *
//      *  Variable and Record Field Declarations   *
//      *                                           *
//      *********************************************


//----------------------------------------------------------------
//  ParseVariableDeclarations    Parse variable declarations.
//
//      pRoutineId : ptr to symbol table node of program,
//                   procedure, or function identifier
//----------------------------------------------------------------

void TParser::ParseVariableDeclarations(TSymtabNode *pRoutineId)
{
    if (execFlag) {
        ParseVarOrFieldDecls(pRoutineId, NULL, 0);
    }
}


//----------------------------------------------------------------
//  ParseFieldDeclarations       Parse a list record field
//                               declarations.
//
//      pRecordType : ptr to record type object
//      offet       : byte offset within record
//----------------------------------------------------------------

void TParser::ParseFieldDeclarations(TType *pRecordType, int offset)
{
    ParseVarOrFieldDecls(NULL, pRecordType, offset);
}


//----------------------------------------------------------------
//  ParseVarOrFieldDecls         Parse a list of variable or
//                               record field declarations
//                               separated by semicolons:
//
//                                   <id-sublist> : <type>
//
//      pRoutineId  : ptr to symbol table node of program,
//                    procedure, or function identifier, or NULL
//      pRecordType : ptr to record type object, or NULL
//      offset      : variable: runtime stack offset
```

```
//                     field: byte offset within record
//-----------------------------------------------------------

void TParser::ParseVarOrFieldDecls(TSymtabNode *pRoutineId,
                                   TType       *pRecordType,
                                   int offset)
{
    TSymtabNode *pId, *pFirstId, *pLastId;   // ptrs to symtab nodes
    TSymtabNode *pPrevSublistLastId = NULL;  // ptr to last node of
                                             //    previous sublist
    int         totalSize = 0;               // total byte size of
                                             //    local variables

    //--Loop to parse a list of variable or field declarations
    //--separated by semicolons.
    while (token == tcIdentifier) {

        //--<id-sublist>
        pFirstId = ParseIdSublist(pRoutineId, pRecordType, pLastId);

        //-- :
        Resync(tlSublistFollow, tlDeclarationFollow);
        CondGetToken(tcColon, errMissingColon);

        //--<type>
        TType *pType = ParseTypeSpec();

        //--Now loop to assign the type and offset to each
        //--identifier in the sublist.
        for (pId = pFirstId; pId; pId = pId->next) {
            SetType(pId->pType, pType);

            if (pRoutineId) {

                //--Variables
                if (execFlag) {
                    pId->defn.data.offset = offset++;
                }
                totalSize += pType->size;
            }
            else {

                //--Record fields
                pId->defn.data.offset = offset;
                offset += pType->size;
            }
```

(continues)

■■■■■■■■ **Figure 7.12** New implementation file **parsdecl.cpp**. (*Continued*)

```
        }

        if (pFirstId) {

            //--Set the first sublist into the routine id's symtab node.
            if (pRoutineId &&
                (!pRoutineId->defn.routine.locals.pVariableIds)) {
                pRoutineId->defn.routine.locals.pVariableIds = pFirstId;
            }

            //--Link this list to the previous sublist.
            if (pPrevSublistLastId) pPrevSublistLastId->next = pFirstId;
            pPrevSublistLastId = pLastId;
        }

        //-- ;   for variable and record field declaration, or
        //-- END for record field declaration
        if (pRoutineId) {
            Resync(tlDeclarationFollow, tlStatementStart);
            CondGetToken(tcSemicolon, errMissingSemicolon);

            //--Skip extra semicolons.
            while (token == tcSemicolon) GetToken();
            Resync(tlDeclarationFollow, tlDeclarationStart,
                   tlStatementStart);
        }
        else {
            Resync(tlFieldDeclFollow);
            if (token != tcEND) {
                CondGetToken(tcSemicolon, errMissingSemicolon);

                //--Skip extra semicolons.
                while (token == tcSemicolon) GetToken();
                Resync(tlFieldDeclFollow, tlDeclarationStart,
                       tlStatementStart);
            }
        }
    }

    //--Set the routine identifier node or the record type object.
    if (pRoutineId) {
        pRoutineId->defn.routine.totalLocalSize = totalSize;
    }
    else {
```

```
            pRecordType->size = offset;
        }
    }


    //-------------------------------------------------------------
    //  ParseIdSublist        Parse a sublist of variable or record
    //                        identifiers separated by commas.
    //
    //      pRoutineId  : ptr to symbol table node of program,
    //                    procedure, or function identifier, or NULL
    //      pRecordType : ptr to record type object, or NULL
    //      pLastId     : ref to ptr that will be set to point to the
    //                    last symbol table node of the sublist
    //-------------------------------------------------------------

    TSymtabNode *TParser::ParseIdSublist(const TSymtabNode *pRoutineId,
                                         const TType       *pRecordType,
                                         TSymtabNode       *&pLastId)
    {
        TSymtabNode *pId;
        TSymtabNode *pFirstId = NULL;

        pLastId = NULL;

        //--Loop to parse each identifier in the sublist.
        while (token == tcIdentifier) {

            //--Variable:  Enter into local  symbol table.
            //--Field:     Enter into record symbol table.
            pId = pRoutineId ? EnterNewLocal(pToken->String())
                             : pRecordType->record.pSymtab->
                                            EnterNew(pToken->String());

            //--Link newly-declared identifier nodes together
            //--into a sublist.
            if (pId->defn.how == dcUndefined) {
                pId->defn.how = pRoutineId ? dcVariable : dcField;
                if (!pFirstId) pFirstId = pLastId = pId;
                else {
                    pLastId->next = pId;
                    pLastId       = pId;
                }
            }

            //-- ,
            GetToken();
```

(continues)

■■■■■■■ **Figure 7.12** New implementation file **parsdecl.cpp**. (*Continued*)

```
        Resync(tlIdentifierFollow);
        if (token == tcComma) {

            //--Saw comma.
            //--Skip extra commas and look for an identifier.
            do {
                GetToken();
                Resync(tlIdentifierStart, tlIdentifierFollow);
                if (token == tcComma) Error(errMissingIdentifier);
            } while (token == tcComma);
            if (token != tcIdentifier) Error(errMissingIdentifier);
        }
        else if (token == tcIdentifier) Error(errMissingComma);
    }

    return pFirstId;
}
```

Member function `ParseDeclarations` looks for the reserved words CONST, TYPE, and VAR, in that order, and calls the appropriate parsing functions.

Parsing Constant Definitions

Member function `ParseConstantDefinitions` loops to parse one or more constant definitions. Since the constant identifier that is being defined must not already be in the symbol table, the function calls `EnterNewLocal`. It links the symbol table nodes of the constant identifiers together, and then points data member `defn.routine.locals.pConstantIds` of the routine name's symbol table node to this list. It parses the equal sign and calls `ParseConstant` to parse the constant. Afterwards, it resynchronizes and parses the semicolon. Note that we delay setting the symbol table node object's `defn.how` member to `dcConstant` until *after* the call to `ParseConstant`.

Member function `ParseConstant` parses the constant in a constant definition. This constant can be a number, a character, a string, or an identifier that has previously been defined to be a constant. Only a numeric constant (either a number or a constant identifier whose value is a number) can be preceded by a unary + or −. The function calls `CopyQuotedString` to make a copy of a string constant, and it creates a new unnamed string type object.

Member function `ParseIdentifierConstant` parses a constant that is an identifier constant. For example, in the definition of `factor` below:

```
CONST
    pi    = 3.1415926;
    factor = pi;
```

uses the identifier constant `pi`.

`ParseIdentifierConstant` first checks that the identifier has indeed been
defined as a constant. Both the value and the type of the identifier constant are used.
Only an identifier constant whose value is numeric can be preceded by a unary sign.

Parsing Variables and Record Field Declarations

As we can see from the syntax diagram in Figure 7.1, variable declarations and
record field declarations share the same syntax. Member function `ParseVarOr-
FieldDecls` parses both. However, the declarations parser first calls member func-
tion `ParseVariableDeclarations` to parse variable declarations, or member
function `ParseFieldDeclarations` to parse record field declarations. Each of
these latter two functions calls `ParseVarOrFieldDecls`, but with different argument values.

`ParseVarOrFieldDecls` builds sublists of symbol table nodes for identifiers that
are declared together. For example, in Figure 7.6, we saw how the node objects for
the record field identifiers x and y are linked together via their `next` pointers. Then
`ParseVarOrFieldDecls` links the sublists together into a single list of all the
local variable identifiers of a routine, or all the field identifiers of a record type.
We'll see in the next chapter that every Pascal routine (program, procedure, or function) each will have its own symbol table for its local variables. For now though,
we'll continue with the single symbol table for all variable identifiers, but we do
need a separate symbol table for the field identifiers of each record type.

`ParseVarOrFieldDecls` loops to parse each sublist of identifiers. It calls function `ParseIdSublist` to do the parsing and return a pointer to the head node of
the symbol table node sublist. After parsing the colon, `ParseVarOrFieldDecls`
calls function `ParseTypeSpec` to parse the type specification. We'll examine this
latter function later, but for now it's enough to know that it returns a pointer to a

type object. A `for` loop then runs over the symbol table node sublist, setting the `pType` data member of each node object. The loop also sets each node's `defn.data.offset` data member. If we're parsing variable declarations, the offset is simply a sequential counter for the local variables of the Pascal routine. If we're parsing record field declarations, then the offset is the byte offset within the record.

`ParseVarOrFieldDecls` next links the current symbol table node sublist to the end of the previous sublist. If it is parsing variable declarations, it also points the `defn.routine.pLocalIds` data member of the routine name's symbol table node to the first sublist. By the time `ParseVarOrFieldDecls` is done, this data member will point to the entire linked list of the routine's local variables.

Finally, `ParseVarOrFieldDecls` resynchronizes the parser. If it is parsing variable declarations, it looks for a semicolon. If it is parsing record field declarations, it looks for either a semicolon or the reserved word END. In either case, another identifier token after the semicolon means more declarations follow. However, encountering END while parsing record fields means we're done parsing the record type.

After `ParseVarOrFieldDecls` is done parsing the declarations, it knows the total size of all the variables or fields. If it was parsing variable declarations, it sets this size into the routine name's symbol table node. If it was parsing record field declarations, it sets the size into the record's type object.

Member function `ParseIdSublist` does all the work of parsing the comma-separated list of variable or field identifiers that are being declared together. In a loop, it builds the symbol table node sublist. If it is parsing a list of variables, the function enters each identifier into the local symbol table (which, starting in the next chapter, will be the separate symbol table for each Pascal routine). If the function is parsing record fields, it enters each identifier into the symbol table of the record type. It also sets each node object's `defn.how` member to either `dcVariable` or `dcField`.

After each identifier, `ParseIdSublist` resynchronizes the parser, and it continues to loop if there is a comma followed by another identifier. Otherwise, the loop terminates, and the function returns a pointer to the head of the sublist.

Parsing Types

Although Pascal type definitions are not as syntactically complex as type definitions in C or C++, parsing them can still be a bit of a challenge. We'll split the parsing functions for type definitions among two implementation files, `parstyp1.cpp` and `parstyp2.cpp`.

Figure 7.13 shows the new implementation file `parstyp1.cpp`.

■■■■■■■■■■ **Figure 7.13** New implementation file **parstyp1.cpp**.

```
//  ****************************************************************
//  *                                                            *
//  *      P A R S E R      (Types #1)                           *
//  *                                                            *
//  *      Parse type definitions, and identifier, enumeration,  *
//  *      and subrange type specifications.                     *
//  *                                                            *
//  *      CLASSES: TParser                                      *
//  *                                                            *
//  *      FILE:     prog7.1/parstyp1.cpp                        *
//  *                                                            *
//  *      MODULE:   Parser                                      *
//  *                                                            *
//  *      Copyright (c) 1996 by Ronald Mak                      *
//  *      For instructional purposes only.  No warranties.      *
//  *                                                            *
//  ****************************************************************

#include "common.h"
#include "parser.h"


//--------------------------------------------------------------
//  ParseTypeDefinitions      Parse a list of type definitions
//                            separated by semicolons:
//
//                                  <id> = <type>
//
//      pRoutineId : ptr to symbol table node of program,
//                   procedure, or function identifier
//--------------------------------------------------------------

void TParser::ParseTypeDefinitions(TSymtabNode *pRoutineId)
{
```

(continues)

Figure 7.13 New implementation file **parstyp1.cpp**. (*Continued*)

```
TSymtabNode *pLastId = NULL;   // ptr to last type id node
                               //    in local list

//--Loop to parse a list of type definitions
//--seperated by semicolons.
while (token == tcIdentifier) {

    //--<id>
    TSymtabNode *pTypeId = EnterNewLocal(pToken->String());

    //--Link the routine's local type id nodes together.
    if (!pRoutineId->defn.routine.locals.pTypeIds) {
        pRoutineId->defn.routine.locals.pTypeIds = pTypeId;
    }
    else {
        pLastId->next = pTypeId;
    }
    pLastId = pTypeId;

    //-- =
    GetToken();
    CondGetToken(tcEqual, errMissingEqual);

    //--<type>
    SetType(pTypeId->pType, ParseTypeSpec());
    pTypeId->defn.how = dcType;

    //--If the type object doesn't have a name yet,
    //--point it to the type id.
    if (! pTypeId->pType->pTypeId) {
        pTypeId->pType->pTypeId = pTypeId;
    }

    //-- ;
    Resync(tlDeclarationFollow, tlDeclarationStart,
           tlStatementStart);
    CondGetToken(tcSemicolon, errMissingSemicolon);

    //--Skip extra semicolons.
    while (token == tcSemicolon) GetToken();
    Resync(tlDeclarationFollow, tlDeclarationStart,
           tlStatementStart);
}
}
```

```
//------------------------------------------------------------
//  ParseTypeSpec        Parse a type specification.
//
//  Return: ptr to type object
//------------------------------------------------------------

TType *TParser::ParseTypeSpec(void)
{
    switch (token) {

        //--Type identifier
        case tcIdentifier: {
            TSymtabNode *pId = Find(pToken->String());

            switch (pId->defn.how) {
                case dcType:      return ParseIdentifierType(pId);
                case dcConstant:  return ParseSubrangeType(pId);

                default:
                    Error(errNotATypeIdentifier);
                    GetToken();
                    return(pDummyType);
            }
        }

        case tcLParen:  return ParseEnumerationType();
        case tcARRAY:   return ParseArrayType();
        case tcRECORD:  return ParseRecordType();

        case tcPlus:
        case tcMinus:
        case tcNumber:
        case tcString:  return ParseSubrangeType(NULL);

        default:
            Error(errInvalidType);
            return(pDummyType);
    }
}

//              ********************
//              *                  *
//              *  Identifier Type  *
//              *                  *
//              ********************
```

(continues)

■■■■■■■■ **Figure 7.13** New implementation file **parstyp1.cpp**. (*Continued*)

```
//------------------------------------------------------------
//  ParseIdentifierType        In a type defintion of the form
//
//                                  <id-1> = <id-2>
//
//                                  parse <id-2>.
//
//        pId2 : ptr to symbol table node of <id-2>
//
//  Return: ptr to type object of <id-2>
//------------------------------------------------------------

TType *TParser::ParseIdentifierType(const TSymtabNode *pId2)
{
    GetToken();
    return pId2->pType;
}


//          ***********************
//          *                     *
//          *   Enumeration Type   *
//          *                     *
//          ***********************


//------------------------------------------------------------
//  ParseEnumerationType       Parse a enumeration type
//                             specification:
//
//                                  ( <id-1>, <id-2>, ..., <id-n> )
//
//  Return: ptr to type object
//------------------------------------------------------------

TType *TParser::ParseEnumerationType(void)
{
    TType        *pType     = new TType(fcEnum, sizeof(int), NULL);
    TSymtabNode *pLastId    = NULL;
    int          constValue = -1;  // enumeration constant value

    GetToken();
    Resync(tlEnumConstStart);

    //--Loop to parse list of constant identifiers separated by commas.
    while (token == tcIdentifier) {
        TSymtabNode *pConstId = EnterNewLocal(pToken->String());
```

```
        ++constValue;

        if (pConstId->defn.how == dcUndefined) {
            pConstId->defn.how = dcConstant;
            pConstId->defn.constant.value.integer = constValue;
            SetType(pConstId->pType, pType);

            //--Link constant identifier symbol table nodes together.
            if (!pLastId) {
                pType->enumeration.pConstIds = pLastId = pConstId;
            }
            else {
                pLastId->next = pConstId;
                pLastId       = pConstId;
            }
        }

        //-- ,
        GetToken();
        Resync(tlEnumConstFollow);
        if (token == tcComma) {

            //--Saw comma.  Skip extra commas and look for
            //--            an identifier.
            do {
                GetToken();
                Resync(tlEnumConstStart, tlEnumConstFollow);
                if (token == tcComma) Error(errMissingIdentifier);
            } while (token == tcComma);
            if (token != tcIdentifier) Error(errMissingIdentifier);
        }
        else if (token == tcIdentifier) Error(errMissingComma);
    }

    //-- )
    CondGetToken(tcRParen, errMissingRightParen);

    pType->enumeration.max = constValue;
    return pType;
}

//            ******************
//            *                *
//            *  Subrange Type  *
//            *                *
//            ******************
```

(continues)

■■■■■■■■ **Figure 7.13** New implementation file **parstyp1.cpp**. (*Continued*)

```
//---------------------------------------------------------------
//  ParseSubrangeType          Parse a subrange type specification:
//
//                                 <min-const> .. <max-const>
//
//       pMinId : ptr to symbol table node of <min-const> if it
//                is an identifier, else NULL
//
//  Return: ptr to type object
//---------------------------------------------------------------

TType *TParser::ParseSubrangeType(TSymtabNode *pMinId)
{
    TType *pType = new TType(fcSubrange, 0, NULL);

    //--<min-const>
    SetType(pType->subrange.pBaseType,
            ParseSubrangeLimit(pMinId, pType->subrange.min));

    //-- ..
    Resync(tlSubrangeLimitFollow, tlDeclarationStart);
    CondGetToken(tcDotDot, errMissingDotDot);

    //--<max-const>
    TType *pMaxType = ParseSubrangeLimit(NULL, pType->subrange.max);

    //--Check limits.
    if (pMaxType != pType->subrange.pBaseType) {
        Error(errIncompatibleTypes);
        pType->subrange.min = pType->subrange.max = 0;
    }
    else if (pType->subrange.min > pType->subrange.max) {
        Error(errMinGtMax);

        int temp = pType->subrange.min;
        pType->subrange.min = pType->subrange.max;
        pType->subrange.max = temp;
    }

    pType->size = pType->subrange.pBaseType->size;
    return pType;
}


//---------------------------------------------------------------
//  ParseSubrangeLimit         Parse a mininum or maximum limit
```

```
//                      constant of a subrange type.
//
//      pLimitId : ptr to symbol table node of limit constant if
//                 it is an identifier (already set for the
//                 minimum limit), else NULL
//      limit    : ref to limit value that will be set
//
//  Return: ptr to type object of limit constant
//-------------------------------------------------------------

TType *TParser::ParseSubrangeLimit(TSymtabNode *pLimitId, int &limit)
{
    TType       *pType = pDummyType;   // type to return
    TTokenCode  sign = tcDummy;        // unary + or - sign, or none

    limit = 0;

    //--Unary + or -
    if (TokenIn(token, tlUnaryOps)) {
        if (token == tcMinus) sign = tcMinus;
        GetToken();
    }

    switch (token) {

        case tcNumber:

            //--Numeric constant:  Integer type only.
            if (pToken->Type() == tyInteger) {
                limit = sign == tcMinus ? -pToken->Value().integer
                                        :  pToken->Value().integer;
                pType = pIntegerType;
            }
            else Error(errInvalidSubrangeType);
            break;

        case tcIdentifier:

            //--Identifier limit:  Must be integer, character, or
            //--                   enumeration type.
            if (!pLimitId) pLimitId = Find(pToken->String());

            if (pLimitId->defn.how == dcUndefined) {
                pLimitId->defn.how = dcConstant;
                pType = SetType(pLimitId->pType, pDummyType);
                break;
            }
```

(continues)

■■■■■■■ **Figure 7.13** New implementation file **parstyp1.cpp**. (*Continued*)

```cpp
            else if ((pLimitId->pType == pRealType)  ||
                     (pLimitId->pType == pDummyType) ||
                     (pLimitId->pType->form == fcArray)) {
                Error(errInvalidSubrangeType);
            }
            else if (pLimitId->defn.how == dcConstant) {

                //--Use the value of the constant identifier.
                if (pLimitId->pType == pIntegerType) {
                    limit = sign == tcMinus
                        ? -pLimitId->defn.constant.value.integer
                        :  pLimitId->defn.constant.value.integer;
                }
                else if (pLimitId->pType == pCharType) {
                    if (sign != tcDummy) Error(errInvalidConstant);
                    limit = pLimitId->defn.constant.value.character;
                }
                else if (pLimitId->pType->form == fcEnum) {
                    if (sign != tcDummy) Error(errInvalidConstant);
                    limit = pLimitId->defn.constant.value.integer;
                }
                pType = pLimitId->pType;
            }

            else Error(errNotAConstantIdentifier);
            break;

        case tcString:

            //--String limit:  Character type only.
            if (sign != tcDummy) Error(errInvalidConstant);

            if (strlen(pToken->String()) != 3) { // len includes quotes
                Error(errInvalidSubrangeType);
            }

            limit = pToken->String()[1];
            pType = pCharType;
            break;

        default:
            Error(errMissingConstant);
            return pType;   // don't get another token
    }
```

```
        GetToken();
        return pType;
}
```

Parsing Type Definitions and Type Specifications

Member function `ParseTypeDefinitions` loops to parse a list of type definitions. For each definition, it parses and enters the identifier being defined into the
local symbol table. It links all the symbol table nodes of a routine's type identifiers
together, and points data member `defn.routine.locals.pTypeIds` of the routine name's symbol table node to the list. After parsing the equal sign, it calls function `ParseTypeSpec`, which parses the type specification and returns a pointer to
the type object, which function `SetType` then sets into the identifier's symbol table
node object. If the type object was newly created and thus still unnamed, `Parse-
TypeDefinitions` points it back to the identifier's node object. The function
resynchronizes the parser at the semicolon. If another identifier follows, then there's
another type definition to parse.

Notice that, as we saw earlier with member function `ParseConstantDefini-
tions`, we delay setting the `defn.how` member of the type identifier's node object
until *after* the call to `ParseTypeSpec`.

Member function `ParseTypeSpec` calls the appropriate functions to parse a type
specification. From the syntax diagrams in Figure 7.1, we see that a type specification can be a part of a type definition, as either a named type or an unnamed type.
(For example, an unnamed subrange type can be the index type or the element type
of an array type definition.) A type specification can also appear as an unnamed
type in a variable declaration.

Consider the following:

```
TYPE
    whole = integer;
    teens = thirteen..nineteen;
```

In the definition of `whole`, the type specification is simply the previously defined
type identifier `integer`. When `ParseTypeSpec` encounters an identifier token, it
calls function `Find` to search all the symbol tables (only one for now) to make sure

that it has indeed already been defined. If the identifier is a type identifier, `Parse-TypeSpec` calls function `ParseIdentifierType`. If, however, the identifier is a constant identifier, as in the definition of `teens` above (assume that `thirteen` and `nineteen` are constants), then `ParseTypeSpec` calls function `ParseSubrangeType`.

If `ParseTypeSpec` encounters a left parenthesis, then it must be the beginning of an enumeration type specification, and so it calls function `ParseEnumerationType`. If instead it parses the reserved word `ARRAY` or `RECORD`, it calls function `ParseArrayType` or `ParseRecordType`, respectively. If `ParseTypeSpec` encounters +, −, a number, or a string, it calls function `ParseSubrangeType`. Anything else it flags as an error.

`ParseTypeSpec` always returns a pointer to a type object, possibly to the dummy type object in the case of an erroneous type specification.

Parsing Identifier Types

Member function `ParseIdentifierType` is simple: It returns a pointer to the type identifier's type object.

Parsing Enumeration Types

Member function `ParseEnumerationType` parses an enumeration type specification. It creates a new enumeration type object, and then it loops to parse the comma-separated list of enumeration constant identifiers. It enters each identifier into the local symbol table and sets the node's data members `defn.how` to `dcConstant` and points `pType` to the new type object. The function assigns each constant its value, and it links their symbol table node objects together. It resynchronizes the parser after each constant identifier, and checks for missing commas or identifiers. It looks for the closing right parenthesis at the end of the constant identifier list.

Parsing Subrange Types

Member function `ParseSubrangeType` creates a new subrange type object, and then it calls function `ParseSubrangeLimit` to parse each of the minimum and maximum limits and return a pointer to each limit's type object. It checks to make sure that both limits are of the same type and that the value of the minimum limit is less than or equal to the value of the maximum limit. If the minimum limit is greater than the maximum limit, the function flags the error and then swaps the values.

Member function `ParseSubrangeLimit` first parses any unary + or – sign. It then parses a subrange limit that can be an integer, a character, or a previously defined constant identifier whose value is an integer, character, or enumeration constant. In each case, the function obtains the value of the limit and returns a pointer to its type object.

▪▪▪▪▪ **Figure 7.14** New implementation file **parstyp2.cpp**.

```
//  ****************************************************************
//  *                                                            *
//  *      P A R S E R    (Types #2)                             *
//  *                                                            *
//  *      Parse array and record type specifications.           *
//  *                                                            *
//  *      CLASSES: TParser                                      *
//  *                                                            *
//  *      FILE:    prog7-1/parstyp2.cpp                         *
//  *                                                            *
//  *      MODULE:  Parser                                       *
//  *                                                            *
//  *      Copyright (c) 1996 by Ronald Mak                      *
//  *      For instructional purposes only.  No warranties.      *
//  *                                                            *
//  ****************************************************************

#include "common.h"
#include "parser.h"

//              ***************
//              *             *
//              *  Array Type  *
//              *             *
//              ***************


//--------------------------------------------------------------
//  ParseArrayType      Parse an array type specification:
//
//                          ARRAY [ <index-type-list> ]
//                              OF <elmt-type>
//
//  Return: ptr to type object
//--------------------------------------------------------------
```

(continues)

```cpp
TType *TParser::ParseArrayType(void)
{
    TType *pArrayType = new TType(fcArray, 0, NULL);
    TType *pElmtType  = pArrayType;
    int    indexFlag;  // true if another array index, false if done

    //-- [
    GetToken();
    CondGetToken(tcLBracket, errMissingLeftBracket);

    //--Loop to parse each type spec in the index type list,
    //--seperated by commas.
    do {
        ParseIndexType(pElmtType);

        //-- ,
        Resync(tlIndexFollow, tlIndexStart);
        if ((token == tcComma) || TokenIn(token, tlIndexStart)) {

            //--For each type spec after the first, create an
            //--element type object.
            pElmtType = SetType(pElmtType->array.pElmtType,
                                new TType(fcArray, 0, NULL));
            CondGetToken(tcComma, errMissingComma);
            indexFlag = true;
        }
        else indexFlag = false;

    } while (indexFlag);

    //-- ]
    CondGetToken(tcRBracket, errMissingRightBracket);

    //--OF
    Resync(tlIndexListFollow, tlDeclarationStart, tlStatementStart);
    CondGetToken(tcOF, errMissingOF);

    //--Final element type.
    SetType(pElmtType->array.pElmtType, ParseTypeSpec());

    //--Total byte size of the array.
    if (pArrayType->form != fcNone) {
        pArrayType->size = ArraySize(pArrayType);
    }
```

```
    return pArrayType;
}

//-------------------------------------------------------------
//  ParseIndexType        Parse an array index type.
//
//      pArrayType : ptr to array type object
//-------------------------------------------------------------

void TParser::ParseIndexType(TType *pArrayType)
{
    if (TokenIn(token, tlIndexStart)) {
        TType *pIndexType = ParseTypeSpec();
        SetType(pArrayType->array.pIndexType, pIndexType);

        switch (pIndexType->form) {

            //--Subrange index type
            case fcSubrange:
                pArrayType->array.elmtCount =
                        pIndexType->subrange.max -
                        pIndexType->subrange.min + 1;
                pArrayType->array.minIndex =
                        pIndexType->subrange.min;
                pArrayType->array.maxIndex =
                        pIndexType->subrange.max;
                return;

            //--Enumeration index type
            case fcEnum:
                pArrayType->array.elmtCount =
                        pIndexType->enumeration.max + 1;
                pArrayType->array.minIndex = 0;
                pArrayType->array.maxIndex =
                        pIndexType->enumeration.max;
                return;

            //--Error
            default:  goto BadIndexType;
        }
    }

BadIndexType:

    //--Error
    SetType(pArrayType->array.pIndexType, pDummyType);
```

(continues)

```
    pArrayType->array.elmtCount = 0;
    pArrayType->array.minIndex  = pArrayType->array.maxIndex = 0;
    Error(errInvalidIndexType);
}


//----------------------------------------------------------------
// ArraySize           Calculate the total byte size of an
//                     array type by recursively calculating
//                     the size of each dimension.
//
//      pArrayType : ptr to array type object
//
// Return: byte size
//----------------------------------------------------------------

int TParser::ArraySize(TType *pArrayType)
{
    //--Calculate the size of the element type
    //--if it hasn't already been calculated.
    if (pArrayType->array.pElmtType->size == 0) {
        pArrayType->array.pElmtType->size =
                            ArraySize(pArrayType->array.pElmtType);
    }

    return (pArrayType->array.elmtCount *
            pArrayType->array.pElmtType->size);
}

//              ****************
//              *              *
//              *  Record Type  *
//              *              *
//              ****************


//----------------------------------------------------------------
// ParseRecordType     Parse a record type specification:
//
//                        RECORD
//                            <id-list> : <type> ;
//                            ...
//                        END
//
// Return: ptr to type object
//----------------------------------------------------------------
```

```
TType *TParser::ParseRecordType(void)
{
    TType *pType          = new TType(fcRecord, 0, NULL);
    pType->record.pSymtab = new TSymtab;

    //--Parse field declarations.
    GetToken();
    ParseFieldDeclarations(pType, 0);

    //--END
    CondGetToken(tcEND, errMissingEND);

    return pType;
}
```

Parsing Array Types

Figure 7.14 shows implementation file `parstyp2.cpp`, which contains the member functions to parse array and record type specifications.

Member function `ParseArrayType` first creates a new array type object. It then loops to parse a comma-separated list of index type specifications.

In Pascal, listing several index type specifications together, as in

```
ARRAY [1..3, 'a'..'z', boolean] OF integer;
```

is just shorthand for

```
ARRAY [1..3] OF
    ARRAY ['a'..'z'] OF
        ARRAY [boolean] OF integer;
```

Therefore, as function `ParseArrayType` parses each index type specification in a list after the first one, it must create a new array type object for the current element type. After it's done parsing all the index type specifications, the final element type is the one after the `OF`. In the above example, that type is `integer`. The final result is a set of chained type objects similar to what we saw in Figure 7.7.

Local pointer variable `pElmtType` keeps track of the current element type object. The variable first points to the initial array type object. Then, as the function loops to parse each index type specification, each comma after the specification causes it to set `pElmtType->array.pElmtType` to point to a newly created array type object. Thus, pElmtType "marches down" the chain of array type objects via the array.pElmtType data member.

After it has parsed all the index type specifications, ParseArrayType parses the] and the reserved word OF, and then it calls ParseTypeSpec to parse the final element type specification. It sets the current value of pElmtType->array.pElmtType to point to the resulting type object, calls function ArraySize to calculate the total size of the array, and then it returns a pointer to the initial array type object.

Member function ParseIndexType parses an index type specification by calling function ParseTypeSpec. An index type can only be a subrange or an enumeration type. Any other type is flagged as an error. ParseIndexType sets the array type object's element count and the minimum and maximum index values accordingly.

Member function ArraySize calculates the total byte size of an array type. If necessary, it calls itself recursively to calculate the array size of the element type. Then, it multiplies the number of elements by the size of the element type to compute the size.

Parsing Record Types

Parsing record type definitions is surprisingly easy, since we've already done most of the work.

Member function ParseRecordType first creates a new record type object and a new symbol table object for the field identifiers. It then calls function ParseFieldDeclarations to parse the field declarations. Afterwards, it returns a pointer to the record type object.

Program 7-1: Cross-Referencer II

So far in this chapter, we've made several major accomplishments: First, we're now able to parse Pascal declarations and represent the information with symbol table node objects, definition objects, and type objects; second, we wrote member functions for classes TSymtabNode and TType to print this information out in the cross-reference listing. A third accomplishment is that we've enabled the statement and expression parsers to do translation-time type checking.

We'll explore type checking shortly. Right now, let's take advantage of the printing functions by expanding the Cross-Referencer I utility program we wrote in Chapter 4. Our new utility will not only print each identifier's name string and source line numbers, but it will also print information about how the identifier was defined and information about its type. Figure 7.15 shows the utility program's main file `xref2.cpp`.

▪▪▪▪▪▪▪▪ **Figure 7.15** Main file **xref2.cpp** of the Cross-Referencer II utility program.

```
//   ****************************************************************
//   *                                                              *
//   *      Program 7-1: Cross-Referencer II                        *
//   *                                                              *
//   *      Generate a cross-reference listing that includes        *
//   *      information about each identifier.                       *
//   *                                                              *
//   *      FILE:    prog7-1/xref2.cpp                              *
//   *                                                              *
//   *      USAGE:   xref2 <source file>                            *
//   *                                                              *
//   *               <source file>  name of the source file         *
//   *                                                              *
//   *                  -x               turn on cross-referencing   *
//   *                                                              *
//   *      Copyright (c) 1996 by Ronald Mak                        *
//   *      For instructional purposes only.  No warranties.        *
//   *                                                              *
//   ****************************************************************

#include <iostream.h>
#include <string.h>
#include "common.h"
#include "error.h"
#include "buffer.h"
#include "symtab.h"
#include "parser.h"


//------------------------------------------------------------
//  main
//------------------------------------------------------------

void main(int argc, char *argv[])
{
    extern int xrefFlag;
```

(continues)

■■■■■ **Figure 7.15** Main file **xref2.cpp** of the Cross-Referencer II utility program. (*Continued*)

```
//--Check the command line arguments.
if ((argc != 2) && (argc != 3)) {
    cerr << "Usage: xref2 <source file> [-x]" << endl;
    AbortTranslation(abortInvalidCommandLineArgs);
}

//--Set the cross-referencing flag.
xrefFlag = (argc == 3) && (strcmp(argv[2], "-x") == 0);

//--Create the parser for the source file,
//--and then parse the file.
TParser *pParser = new TParser(new TSourceBuffer(argv[1]));
pParser->Parse();
delete pParser;

//--Print the cross-reference.
if (xrefFlag) {
    list.PutLine();
    list.PutLine("***** Cross-Reference *****");
    list.PutLine();
    globalSymtab.Print();
}
}
```

Figure 7.16 shows sample output.

■■■■■ **Figure 7.16** Sample output from the Cross-Referencer II utility program.

```
Page 1    xref2.in    Fri Oct 27 22:26:15 1995

 1 0: CONST
 2 0:     ten       = 10;
 3 0:     minusten  = -ten;
 4 0:     hundred   = 100;
 5 0:     maxlength = 80;
 6 0:     pi        = 3.1415926;
 7 0:     ch        = 'x';
 8 0:     hello     = 'Hello, world.';
 9 0:
10 0: TYPE
11 0:     e  = (alpha, beta, gamma);
12 0:     ee = e;
13 0:     sr = alpha..gamma;
```

```
14 0:      cr = 'a'..ch;
15 0:
16 0:      ar1 = ARRAY [1..-minusten] OF integer;
17 0:      ar2 = ARRAY [e, sr] OF real;
18 0:      ar3 = ARRAY [(fee, fye, foe, fum), ten..hundred] OF
19 0:               ARRAY [ee] OF boolean;
20 0:      ar4 = ARRAY [boolean, 'm'..'r'] OF char;
21 0:
22 0:      rec1 = RECORD
23 0:                 i  : integer;
24 0:                 x  : real;
25 0:                 ch : char;
26 0:             END;
27 0:
28 0:      rec2 = RECORD
29 0:                 a  : ar1;
30 0:                 r  : rec1;
31 0:                 rr : RECORD
32 0:                          i : integer;
33 0:                          b : boolean;
34 0:                      END;
35 0:             END;
36 0:
37 0: VAR
38 0:      length, width : integer;
39 0:      radius, circumference : real;
40 0:      b       : boolean;
41 0:      c       : cr;
42 0:      letter : 'a'..'z';
43 0:      r       : rec1;
44 0:      buffer : ARRAY [1..maxlength] OF char;
45 0:      table  : ARRAY [ee, 1..5] OF rec1;
46 0:      a1, a  : ar1;
47 0:      a2      : ar2;
48 0:      a3      : ar3;
49 0:      a4      : ar4;
50 0:      thing  : ARRAY [0..9] OF rec2;
```

Page 2   xref2.in   Fri Oct 27 22:26:15 1995

```
51 0:
        ^
```

*** ERROR: Unexpected end of file

                   51 source lines.
                   1 syntax errors.

(continues)

■■■■■ **Figure 7.16** Sample output from the Cross-Referencer II utility program. (*Continued*)

```
***** Cross-Reference *****

                a   46

Declared variable
Array, size 20 bytes.   Type identifier: ar1

                a1  46

Declared variable
Array, size 20 bytes.   Type identifier: ar1

                a2  47

Declared variable
Array, size 36 bytes.   Type identifier: ar2

                a3  48

Declared variable
Array, size 2184 bytes.   Type identifier: ar3

                a4  49

Declared variable
Array, size 12 bytes.   Type identifier: ar4

            alpha   11   13

Defined constant
Value = 0
Enumeration, size 2 bytes.   Type identifier: e

            ar1  16   29   46

Defined type
Array, size 20 bytes.   Type identifier: ar1
10 elements
--- INDEX TYPE ---
Subrange, size 2 bytes.   Type identifier: <unnamed>
Minimum value = 1, maximum value = 10
--- Base Type ---
Scalar, size 2 bytes.   Type identifier: integer
```

Page 3   xref2.in   Fri Oct 27 22:26:15 1995

--- ELEMENT TYPE ---
Scalar, size 2 bytes. Type identifier: integer

            ar2   17   47

Defined type
Array, size 36 bytes. Type identifier: ar2
3 elements
--- INDEX TYPE ---
Enumeration, size 2 bytes. Type identifier: e
--- ELEMENT TYPE ---
Array, size 12 bytes. Type identifier: <unnamed>
3 elements
--- INDEX TYPE ---
Subrange, size 2 bytes. Type identifier: sr
--- ELEMENT TYPE ---
Scalar, size 4 bytes. Type identifier: real

            ar3   18   48

Defined type
Array, size 2184 bytes. Type identifier: ar3
4 elements
--- INDEX TYPE ---
Enumeration, size 2 bytes. Type identifier: <unnamed>
--- Enumeration Constant Identifiers (value = name) ---
    0 = fee
    1 = fye
    2 = foe
    3 = fum
--- ELEMENT TYPE ---
Array, size 546 bytes. Type identifier: <unnamed>
91 elements
--- INDEX TYPE ---
Subrange, size 2 bytes. Type identifier: <unnamed>
Minimum value = 10, maximum value = 100
--- Base Type ---
Scalar, size 2 bytes. Type identifier: integer
--- ELEMENT TYPE ---
Array, size 6 bytes. Type identifier: <unnamed>
3 elements
--- INDEX TYPE ---
Enumeration, size 2 bytes. Type identifier: e
--- ELEMENT TYPE ---

(continues)

■■■■ **Figure 7.16** Sample output from the Cross-Referencer II utility program. (*Continued*)

```
Enumeration, size 2 bytes.  Type identifier: boolean


          ar4   20   49

Defined type
Array, size 12 bytes.  Type identifier: ar4

Page 4   xref2.in   Fri Oct 27 22:26:15 1995

2 elements
--- INDEX TYPE ---
Enumeration, size 2 bytes.  Type identifier: boolean
--- ELEMENT TYPE ---
Array, size 6 bytes.  Type identifier: <unnamed>
6 elements
--- INDEX TYPE ---
Subrange, size 1 bytes.  Type identifier: <unnamed>
Minimum value = 109, maximum value = 114
--- Base Type ---
Scalar, size 1 bytes.  Type identifier: char
--- ELEMENT TYPE ---
Scalar, size 1 bytes.  Type identifier: char


            b   40

Declared variable
Enumeration, size 2 bytes.  Type identifier: boolean


          beta   11

Defined constant
Value = 1
Enumeration, size 2 bytes.  Type identifier: e


        boolean   1   19   20   33   40

Defined type
Enumeration, size 2 bytes.  Type identifier: boolean
--- Enumeration Constant Identifiers (value = name) ---
    0 = false
    1 = true


          buffer   44
```

```
Declared variable
Array, size 80 bytes.  Type identifier: <unnamed>
80 elements
--- INDEX TYPE ---
Subrange, size 2 bytes.  Type identifier: <unnamed>
Minimum value = 1, maximum value = 80
--- Base Type ---
Scalar, size 2 bytes.  Type identifier: integer
--- ELEMENT TYPE ---
Scalar, size 1 bytes.  Type identifier: char


          c  41


Declared variable
Subrange, size 1 bytes.  Type identifier: cr


Page 5   xref2.in   Fri Oct 27 22:26:15 1995



          ch   7  14


Defined constant
Value = 'x'
Scalar, size 1 bytes.  Type identifier: char


        char   1  20  25  44

Defined type
Scalar, size 1 bytes.  Type identifier: char


   circumference  39

Declared variable
Scalar, size 4 bytes.  Type identifier: real


         cr  14  41


Defined type
Subrange, size 1 bytes.  Type identifier: cr
Minimum value = 97, maximum value = 120
--- Base Type ---
Scalar, size 1 bytes.  Type identifier: char


         e  11  12  17


Defined type
```

(*continues*)

■■■■■■ **Figure 7.16** Sample output from the Cross-Referencer II utility program. (*Continued*)

```
Enumeration, size 2 bytes.  Type identifier: e
--- Enumeration Constant Identifiers (value = name) ---
    0 = alpha
    1 = beta
    2 = gamma


            ee   12   19   45


Defined type
Enumeration, size 2 bytes.  Type identifier: e
--- Enumeration Constant Identifiers (value = name) ---
    0 = alpha
    1 = beta
    2 = gamma


            false    1


Defined constant
Value = 0
Enumeration, size 2 bytes.  Type identifier: boolean


            fee   18


Page 6    xref2.in    Fri Oct 27 22:26:15 1995


Defined constant
Value = 0
Enumeration, size 2 bytes.  Type identifier: <unnamed>
--- Enumeration Constant Identifiers (value = name) ---
    0 = fee
    1 = fye
    2 = foe
    3 = fum


            foe   18


Defined constant
Value = 2
Enumeration, size 2 bytes.  Type identifier: <unnamed>
--- Enumeration Constant Identifiers (value = name) ---
    0 = fee
    1 = fye
```

```
        2 = foe
        3 = fum


            fum   18

Defined constant
Value = 3
Enumeration, size 2 bytes.  Type identifier: <unnamed>
--- Enumeration Constant Identifiers (value = name) ---
        0 = fee
        1 = fye
        2 = foe
        3 = fum


            fye   18

Defined constant
Value = 1
Enumeration, size 2 bytes.  Type identifier: <unnamed>
--- Enumeration Constant Identifiers (value = name) ---
        0 = fee
        1 = fye
        2 = foe
        3 = fum


            gamma   11   13

Defined constant
Value = 2
Enumeration, size 2 bytes.  Type identifier: e


            hello   8
```

Page 7   xref2.in   Fri Oct 27 22:26:15 1995

```
Defined constant
Value = 'Hello, world.'
Array, size 13 bytes.  Type identifier: <unnamed>
13 elements
--- INDEX TYPE ---
Subrange, size 2 bytes.  Type identifier: <unnamed>
Minimum value = 1, maximum value = 13
--- Base Type ---
Scalar, size 2 bytes.  Type identifier: integer
--- ELEMENT TYPE ---
Scalar, size 1 bytes.  Type identifier: char
```

(continues)

■■■■■■■■ **Figure 7.16** Sample output from the Cross-Referencer II utility program.
(*Continued*)

```
          hundred   4  18

Defined constant
Value = 100
Scalar, size 2 bytes.  Type identifier: integer

          integer   1  16  23  32  38

Defined type
Scalar, size 2 bytes.  Type identifier: integer

          length  38

Declared variable
Scalar, size 2 bytes.  Type identifier: integer

          letter  42

Declared variable
Subrange, size 1 bytes.  Type identifier: <unnamed>
Minimum value = 97, maximum value = 122
--- Base Type ---
Scalar, size 1 bytes.  Type identifier: char

       maxlength   5  44

Defined constant
Value = 80
Scalar, size 2 bytes.  Type identifier: integer

          minusten   3  16

Defined constant
Value = -10
Scalar, size 2 bytes.  Type identifier: integer

              pi    6

Page 8   xref2.in   Fri Oct 27 22:26:15 1995

Defined constant
Value = 3.14159
Scalar, size 4 bytes.  Type identifier: real
```

```
          r  43
```

Declared variable
Record, size 7 bytes. Type identifier: rec1

```
          radius  39
```

Declared variable
Scalar, size 4 bytes. Type identifier: real

```
          real   1  17  24  39
```

Defined type
Scalar, size 4 bytes. Type identifier: real

```
          rec1  22  30  43  45
```

Defined type
Record, size 7 bytes. Type identifier: rec1
--- Record Field Identifiers (offset : name) ---

```
    0 : i
```

Declared record field
Scalar, size 2 bytes. Type identifier: integer

```
    2 : x
```

Declared record field
Scalar, size 4 bytes. Type identifier: real

```
    6 : ch
```

Declared record field
Scalar, size 1 bytes. Type identifier: char

```
          rec2  28  50
```

Defined type
Record, size 31 bytes. Type identifier: rec2
--- Record Field Identifiers (offset : name) ---

```
    0 : a
```

Declared record field

(continues)

■■■■■■■■ **Figure 7.16** Sample output from the Cross-Referencer II utility program. *(Continued)*

```
Page 9    xref2.in    Fri Oct 27 22:26:15 1995


Array, size 20 bytes.  Type identifier: ar1


    20 : r


Declared record field
Record, size 7 bytes.  Type identifier: rec1


    27 : rr


Declared record field
Record, size 4 bytes.  Type identifier: <unnamed>
--- Record Field Identifiers (offset : name) ---


     0 : i


Declared record field
Scalar, size 2 bytes.  Type identifier: integer


     2 : b


Declared record field
Enumeration, size 2 bytes.  Type identifier: boolean


            sr   13   17


Defined type
Subrange, size 2 bytes.  Type identifier: sr
Minimum value = 0, maximum value = 2
--- Base Type ---
Enumeration, size 2 bytes.  Type identifier: e


          table   45


Declared variable
Array, size 105 bytes.  Type identifier: <unnamed>
3 elements
--- INDEX TYPE ---
Enumeration, size 2 bytes.  Type identifier: e
--- ELEMENT TYPE ---
Array, size 35 bytes.  Type identifier: <unnamed>
```

```
5 elements
--- INDEX TYPE ---
Subrange, size 2 bytes.  Type identifier: <unnamed>
Minimum value = 1, maximum value = 5
--- Base Type ---
Scalar, size 2 bytes.  Type identifier: integer
--- ELEMENT TYPE ---
Record, size 7 bytes.  Type identifier: rec1


        ten   2   3  18

Page 10    xref2.in   Fri Oct 27 22:26:15 1995


Defined constant
Value = 10
Scalar, size 2 bytes.  Type identifier: integer


        thing  50

Declared variable
Array, size 310 bytes.  Type identifier: <unnamed>
10 elements
--- INDEX TYPE ---
Subrange, size 2 bytes.  Type identifier: <unnamed>
Minimum value = 0, maximum value = 9
--- Base Type ---
Scalar, size 2 bytes.  Type identifier: integer
--- ELEMENT TYPE ---
Record, size 31 bytes.  Type identifier: rec2


        true   1

Defined constant
Value = 1
Enumeration, size 2 bytes.  Type identifier: boolean


        width  38

Declared variable
Scalar, size 2 bytes.  Type identifier: integer
```

Table 7.1 shows the modules and source files for the Cross-Referencer II utility program. The back end will return in Chapter 9.

■■■■■ **Table 7.1** Modules and Files of Program 7-1

Module	File	Status	Directory
Main	xref2.cpp	*new*	prog7-1
Parser	parser.h	*changed*	prog7-1
	parser.cpp	*changed*	prog7-1
	parsdecl.cpp	*new*	prog7-1
	parstyp1.cpp	*new*	prog7-1
	parstyp2.cpp	*new*	prog7-1
Intermediate code	icode.h	*unchanged*	prog5-2
	icode.cpp	*unchanged*	prog5-2
Scanner	scanner.h	*unchanged*	prog3-1
	scanner.cpp	*unchanged*	prog3-2
	token.h	*unchanged*	prog4-2
	tknword.cpp	*unchanged*	prog3-2
	tknnum.cpp	*unchanged*	prog3-2
	tknstrsp.cpp	*unchanged*	prog3-2
Symbol table	types.h	*new*	prog7-1
	types.cpp	*new*	prog7-1
	symtab.h	*changed*	prog7-1
	symtab.cpp	*changed*	prog7-1
Error	error.h	*unchanged*	prog5-2
	error.cpp	*unchanged*	prog5-2
Buffer	buffer.h	*unchanged*	prog2-1
	buffer.cpp	*unchanged*	prog2-1
Common	common.h	*changed*	prog7-1
	common.cpp	*changed*	prog7-1
	misc.h	*unchanged*	prog3-2

Syntax Checking Pascal Declarations

We did not neglect syntax checking, of course, as we wrote the declarations parser. Figure 7.17 shows the parser in action as it handles erroneous declarations.

■■■■■■■■■ **Figure 7.17** Erroneous Pascal declarations.

```
Page 1    declerrs.in    Fri Oct 27 22:39:53 1995

   1 0: CONST
   2 0:      ten       = 10;
   3 0:      pi        = pi;
                         ^
*** ERROR: Not a constant identifier
   4 0:      ch1       = -'y';
                          ^
*** ERROR: Invalid constant
   5 0:
   6 0: TYPE
   7 0:      e  = (alpha, +ten, gamma)
                          ^
*** ERROR: Unexpected token
                               ^
*** ERROR: Redefined identifier
   8 0:      sr = gamma..alpha;
                  ^
*** ERROR: Missing ;
                         ^
*** ERROR: Min limit greater than max limit
   9 0:
  10 0:      ar3 = ARRAY [(fee, fye foe,, fum,) ten..pi, 'm' OF
                          ^
*** ERROR: Missing ,
                                 ^
*** ERROR: Missing identifier
                                    ^
*** ERROR: Missing identifier
                                       ^
*** ERROR: Missing ,
                                         ^
*** ERROR: Invalid subrange type
                                          ^
*** ERROR: Incompatible types
                                            ^
*** ERROR: Missing ..
                                             ^
*** ERROR: Missing constant
                                              ^
*** ERROR: Incompatible types
                                               ^
*** ERROR: Missing ]
```

(continues)

■ ■ ■ Figure 7.17 Erroneous Pascal declarations. (*Continued*)

```
  11 0:                    ARRAY [sr] ar3;
                                       ^
*** ERROR: Missing OF
                                   ^
*** ERROR: Not a type identifier
  12 0:
  13 0:     rec = RECORD
  14 0:             ch : ;

Page 2   declerrs.in   Fri Oct 27 22:39:53 1995

                             ^
*** ERROR: Invalid type
  15 0:
  16 0: VAR
         ^
*** ERROR: Missing END
         ^
*** ERROR: Missing ;
  17 0:     a, a+2 : ar3;
               ^
*** ERROR: Redefined identifier
           ^
*** ERROR: Unexpected token
  18 0:
         ^
*** ERROR: Unexpected end of file

            18 source lines.
            24 syntax errors.
```

Type Checking

Type checking is a semantic action that the parser can perform as it does syntax checking and translation of the source program. Type checking verifies that a program uses types correctly. Common type checks are:

- **Variables:** Does an array variable have the correct number and type of subscripts? Is a record variable's field designator valid?
- **Expressions:** Are the types of the operands of an operator correct? For example, the arithmetic operator + requires integer or real operands, and the boolean operator AND requires boolean operands.

- **Assignment statements:** Can an expression value of one type be assigned to a target variable of a different type? For example, it is legal to assign an integer value to a real variable, but not vice versa.

- **Control statements:** Is the type of expression that appears in a control statement correct? For example, the expression in an IF statement must be boolean.

Now that the symbol table has access to information about each identifier's type, our statement and expression parsers can do type checking. In header file types.h, shown in Figure 7.5, we saw the following prototypes for the type-checking friend functions of class TType:

```
friend void CheckRelOpOperands(const TType *pType1,
                               const TType *pType2);
friend void CheckIntegerOrReal(const TType *pType1,
                               const TType *pType2 = NULL);
friend void CheckBoolean     (const TType *pType1,
                               const TType *pType2 = NULL);
friend void CheckAssignmentTypeCompatible(const TType *pTargetType,
                                          const TType *pValueType,
                                          TErrorCode ec);

friend int  IntegerOperands(const TType *pType1,
                            const TType *pType2);
friend int  RealOperands   (const TType *pType1,
                            const TType *pType2);
```

These functions are implemented in file types.cpp, shown in Figure 7.8.

The type-checking functions are called by new versions of the statement parser and expression parser member functions. We need to make a few changes to header file parser.h. Two of the statement parsing member functions now have an argument:

```
void ParseCaseBranch(const TType *pExprType);
void ParseCaseLabel (const TType *pExprType);
```

All of the expression parsing member functions now return a pointer to a type object, and there are a few new functions:

```
TType *ParseExpression       (void);
TType *ParseSimpleExpression(void);
TType *ParseTerm             (void);
TType *ParseFactor           (void);
TType *ParseVariable   (const TSymtabNode *pId);
TType *ParseSubscripts(const TType *pType);
TType *ParseField      (const TType *pType);
```

■■■■■■■■■■ **Figure 7.18** New version of member function **TParser::Parse** in
implementation file **parser.cpp** for the Syntax Checker II utility program.

```cpp
//------------------------------------------------------------
// Parse        Parse the source file.
//------------------------------------------------------------

void TParser::Parse(void)
{
    //--Create a dummy program identifier symbol table node.
    TSymtabNode dummyProgramId("DummyProgram", dcProgram);
    dummyProgramId.defn.routine.locals.pParmIds    = NULL;
    dummyProgramId.defn.routine.locals.pConstantIds = NULL;
    dummyProgramId.defn.routine.locals.pTypeIds     = NULL;
    dummyProgramId.defn.routine.locals.pVariableIds = NULL;
    dummyProgramId.defn.routine.pSymtab             = NULL;
    dummyProgramId.defn.routine.pIcode              = NULL;

    //--Extract the first token and parse the declarations
    //--followed by a statement.
    GetToken();
    ParseDeclarations(&dummyProgramId);
    ParseCompound();

    //--Resynchronize at the final period.
    Resync(tlProgramEnd);
    CondGetToken(tcPeriod, errMissingPeriod);

    //--Print the parser's summary.
    list.PutLine();
    sprintf(list.text, "%20d source lines.",  currentLineNumber);
    list.PutLine();
    sprintf(list.text, "%20d syntax errors.", errorCount);
    list.PutLine();
}
```

Figure 7.18 shows a new version of member function TParser::Parse in
implementation file parser.cpp. It calls ParseDeclarations and then
ParseCompound. Then it resynchronizes at the final period.

Figure 7.19 shows a new version of file parseexpr.cpp. It now includes type
checking and several new member functions.

■■■■■■■■■ **Figure 7.19** New version of implementation file **parsexpr.cpp**.

```
// *************************************************************
// *                                                           *
// *    P A R S E R    (Expressions)                           *
// *                                                           *
// *    Parse expressions.                                     *
// *                                                           *
// *    CLASSES: TParser                                       *
// *                                                           *
// *    FILE:    prog7-2/parsexpr.cpp                          *
// *                                                           *
// *    MODULE:  Parser                                        *
// *                                                           *
// *    Copyright (c) 1996 by Ronald Mak                       *
// *    For instructional purposes only.  No warranties.       *
// *                                                           *
// *************************************************************

#include <string.h>
#include "common.h"
#include "parser.h"


//-------------------------------------------------------------
// ParseExpression      Parse an expression (binary relational
//                      operators = < > <> <= and >= ).
//
// Return: ptr to the expression's type object
//-------------------------------------------------------------

TType *TParser::ParseExpression(void)
{
    TType *pResultType;    // ptr to result type
    TType *pOperandType;   // ptr to operand type

    //--Parse the first simple expression.
    pResultType = ParseSimpleExpression();

    //--If we now see a relational operator,
    //--parse the second simple expression.
    if (TokenIn(token, tlRelOps)) {
        GetTokenAppend();
        pOperandType = ParseSimpleExpression();

        //--Check the operand types and return the boolean type.
```

(continues)

```
            CheckRelOpOperands(pResultType, pOperandType);
            pResultType = pBooleanType;
        }

        //--Make sure the expression ended properly.
        Resync(tlExpressionFollow, tlStatementFollow, tlStatementStart);

        return pResultType;
    }


    //---------------------------------------------------------------
    //  ParseSimpleExpression        Parse a simple expression
    //                               (unary operators + or - , and
    //                               binary operators + - and OR).
    //
    //  Return: ptr to the simple expression's type object
    //---------------------------------------------------------------

    TType *TParser::ParseSimpleExpression(void)
    {
        TType       *pResultType;       // ptr to result type
        TType       *pOperandType;      // ptr to operand type
        TTokenCode  op;                 // operator
        int         unaryOpFlag = false; // true if unary op, else false

        //--Unary + or -
        if (TokenIn(token, tlUnaryOps)) {
            unaryOpFlag = true;
            GetTokenAppend();
        }

        //--Parse the first term.
        pResultType = ParseTerm();

        //--If there was a unary sign, check the term's type.
        if (unaryOpFlag) CheckIntegerOrReal(pResultType);

        //--Loop to parse subsequent additive operators and terms.
        while (TokenIn(token, tlAddOps)) {

            //--Remember the operator and parse the subsequent term.
            op = token;
            GetTokenAppend();
            pOperandType = ParseTerm();
```

```
        //--Check the operand types to determine the result type.
        switch (op) {

            case tcPlus:
            case tcMinus:

                //--integer <op> integer => integer
                if (IntegerOperands(pResultType, pOperandType)) {
                    pResultType = pIntegerType;
                }

                //--real    <op> real    => real
                //--real    <op> integer => real
                //--integer <op> real    => real
                else if (RealOperands(pResultType, pOperandType)) {
                    pResultType = pRealType;
                }

                else Error(errIncompatibleTypes);
                break;

            case tcOR:

                //--boolean OR boolean => boolean
                CheckBoolean(pResultType, pOperandType);
                pResultType = pBooleanType;
                break;
        }

    }

    return pResultType;
}

//-------------------------------------------------------------
// ParseTerm          Parse a term (binary operators * / DIV
//                    MOD and AND).
//
// Return: ptr to the term's type object
//-------------------------------------------------------------

TType *TParser::ParseTerm(void)
{
    TType       *pResultType;   // ptr to result type
    TType       *pOperandType;  // ptr to operand type
    TTokenCode  op;                 // operator
```

(continues)

■■■■■ **Figure 7.19** New version of implementation file **parsexpr.cpp**. (*Continued*)

```cpp
//--Parse the first factor.
pResultType = ParseFactor();

//--Loop to parse subsequent multiplicative operators and factors.
while (TokenIn(token, tlMulOps)) {

    //--Remember the operator and parse the subsequent factor.
    op = token;
    GetTokenAppend();
    pOperandType = ParseFactor();

    //--Check the operand types to determine the result type.
    switch (op) {

        case tcStar:

            //--integer * integer => integer
            if (IntegerOperands(pResultType, pOperandType)) {
                pResultType = pIntegerType;
            }

            //--real    * real    => real
            //--real    * integer => real
            //--integer * real    => real
            else if (RealOperands(pResultType, pOperandType)) {
                pResultType = pRealType;
            }

            else Error(errIncompatibleTypes);
            break;

        case tcSlash:

            //--integer / integer => real
            //--real    / real    => real
            //--real    / integer => real
            //--integer / real    => real
            if (   IntegerOperands(pResultType, pOperandType)
                || RealOperands    (pResultType, pOperandType)) {
                pResultType = pRealType;
            }
            else Error(errIncompatibleTypes);
            break;

        case tcDIV:
```

```
        case tcMOD:

            //--integer <op> integer => integer
            if (IntegerOperands(pResultType, pOperandType)) {
                pResultType = pIntegerType;
            }
            else Error(errIncompatibleTypes);
            break;

        case tcAND:

            //--boolean AND boolean => boolean
            CheckBoolean(pResultType, pOperandType);
            pResultType = pBooleanType;
            break;
        }
    }

    return pResultType;
}

//----------------------------------------------------------------
//  ParseFactor          Parse a factor (identifier, number,
//                       string, NOT <factor>, or parenthesized
//                       subexpression).
//
//  Return: ptr to the factor's type object
//----------------------------------------------------------------

TType *TParser::ParseFactor(void)
{
    TType *pResultType;   // ptr to result type

    switch (token) {

        case tcIdentifier: {

            //--Search for the identifier.  If found, append the
            //--symbol table node handle to the icode.  If not
            //--found, enter it and flag an undefined identifier error.
            TSymtabNode *pNode = Find(pToken->String());
            if (pNode->defn.how != dcUndefined) icode.Put(pNode);
            else {
                pNode->defn.how = dcVariable;
                SetType(pNode->pType, pDummyType);
            }
```

(continues)

```
        //--Is it a constant or variable identifier?
        if (pNode->defn.how == dcConstant) {
            pResultType = pNode->pType;
            GetTokenAppend();
        }
        else pResultType = ParseVariable(pNode);

        break;
    }

    case tcNumber: {

        //--Search for the number and enter it if necessary.
        TSymtabNode *pNode = SearchAll(pToken->String());
        if (!pNode) {
            pNode = EnterLocal(pToken->String());

            //--Determine the number's type, and set its value into
            //--the symbol table node.
            if (pToken->Type() == tyInteger) {
                pResultType = pIntegerType;
                pNode->defn.constant.value.integer =
                                        pToken->Value().integer;
            }
            else {
                pResultType = pRealType;
                pNode->defn.constant.value.real =
                                        pToken->Value().real;
            }
            SetType(pNode->pType, pResultType);
        }

        //--Append the symbol table node handle to the icode.
        icode.Put(pNode);

        pResultType = pNode->pType;
        GetTokenAppend();
        break;
    }

    case tcString: {

        //--Search for the string and enter it if necessary.
        char        *pString = pToken->String();
```

```
    TSymtabNode *pNode    = SearchAll(pString);
    if (!pNode) {
        pNode    = EnterLocal(pString);
        pString = pNode->String();

        //--Compute the string length (without the quotes).
        //--If the length is 1, the result type is character,
        //--else create a new string type.
        int length = strlen(pString) - 2;
        pResultType = length == 1 ? pCharType
                                  : new TType(length);
        SetType(pNode->pType, pResultType);

        //--Set the character value or string pointer into the
        //--symbol table node.
        if (length == 1) {
            pNode->defn.constant.value.character = pString[1];
        }
        else {
            pNode->defn.constant.value.pString = &pString[1];
        }
    }

    //--Append the symbol table node handle to the icode.
    icode.Put(pNode);

    pResultType = pNode->pType;
    GetTokenAppend();
    break;
}

case tcNOT:

    //--The operand type must be boolean.
    GetTokenAppend();
    CheckBoolean(ParseFactor());
    pResultType = pBooleanType;

    break;

case tcLParen:

    //--Parenthesized subexpression:  Call ParseExpression
    //--                              recursively ...
    GetTokenAppend();
    pResultType = ParseExpression();
```

(continues)

```
            //-- ... and check for the closing right parenthesis.
            if (token == tcRParen) GetTokenAppend();
            else                   Error(errMissingRightParen);

            break;

        default:

            Error(errInvalidExpression);
            pResultType = pDummyType;

            break;
    }

    return pResultType;
}

//-------------------------------------------------------------
//  ParseVariable        Parse a variable, which can be a simple
//                       identifier, an array identifier followed
//                       subscripts, or a record identifier
//                       followed by  fields.
//
//      pId : ptr to the identifier's symbol table node
//
//  Return: ptr to the variable's type object
//-------------------------------------------------------------

TType *TParser::ParseVariable(const TSymtabNode *pId)
{
    TType *pResultType = pId->pType;   // ptr to result type

    //--Check how the variable identifier was defined.
    switch (pId->defn.how) {
        case dcVariable:
        case dcValueParm:
        case dcVarParm:
        case dcFunction:
        case dcUndefined:       break;   // OK

        default:
            pResultType = pDummyType;
            Error(errInvalidIdentifierUsage);
            break;
```

```
        }

        GetTokenAppend();

        //-- [ or . : Loop to parse any subscripts and fields.
        while (TokenIn(token, tlSubscriptOrFieldStart)) {
            pResultType = token == tcLBracket ? ParseSubscripts(pResultType)
                                              : ParseField(pResultType);
        }

        return pResultType;
}


//------------------------------------------------------------
//  ParseSubscripts      Parse a bracketed list of subscript
//                       separated by commas, following an
//                       array variable:
//
//                           [ <expr>, <expr>, ... ]
//
//      pType : ptr to the array's type object
//
//  Return: ptr to the array element's type object
//------------------------------------------------------------

TType *TParser::ParseSubscripts(const TType *pType)
{
    //--Loop to parse a list of subscripts separated by commas.
    do {
        //-- [ (first) or , (subsequent)
        GetTokenAppend();

        //-- The current variable is an array type.
        if (pType->form == fcArray) {

            //--The subscript expression must be assignment type
            //--compatible with the corresponding subscript type.
            CheckAssignmentTypeCompatible(pType->array.pIndexType,
                                      ParseExpression(),
                                      errIncompatibleTypes);

            //--Update the variable's type.
            pType = pType->array.pElmtType;
        }

        //--No longer an array type, so too many subscripts.
```

(continues)

```
        //--Parse the extra subscripts anyway for error recovery.
        else {
            Error(errTooManySubscripts);
            ParseExpression();
        }

    } while (token == tcComma);

    //-- ]
    CondGetTokenAppend(tcRBracket, errMissingRightBracket);

    return (TType *) pType;
}


//-------------------------------------------------------------
//  ParseField          Parse a field following a record
//                      variable:
//
//                          . <id>
//
//      pType : ptr to the record's type object
//
//  Return: ptr to the field's type object
//-------------------------------------------------------------

TType *TParser::ParseField(const TType *pType)
{
    GetTokenAppend();

    if ((token == tcIdentifier) && (pType->form == fcRecord)) {
        TSymtabNode *pFieldId = pType->record.pSymtab->
                                        Search(pToken->String());
        if (!pFieldId) Error(errInvalidField);
        icode.Put(pFieldId);

        GetTokenAppend();
        return pFieldId ? pFieldId->pType : pDummyType;
    }
    else {
        Error(errInvalidField);
        GetTokenAppend();
        return pDummyType;
    }
}
```

Type Checking Expressions

In order to type check an expression, we need to know the types of its constituent parts. We modify the expression parsing member functions ParseExpression, ParseSimpleExpression, ParseTerm, and ParseFactor so that each returns a type in the form of a pointer to a type object.

If there is only a single simple expression, member function ParseExpression simply returns its type. If there are two simple expressions (separated by a relational operator), ParseExpression calls class TType's friend function CheckRelOp-Operands to verify that the types of the two operands are compatible, and then it returns the boolean type. According to the friend function (see Figure 7.8), the operands of a relational operator are type-compatible if both are of the identical scalar or enumeration type, one is integer and the other is real, or both are strings of the same length.

Member function ParseSimpleExpression returns the type of the term if there is only one term. If there is more than one term, then the function has to do type checking and decide what type to return based on the operators. It calls class TType's friend functions CheckIntegerOrReal, IntegerOperands, Real-Operands, and CheckBoolean (see Figure 7.8). CheckIntegerOrReal verifies that each operand is either integer or real. IntegerOperands checks whether both operands are integer. RealOperands checks whether both operands are real, or one is real and the other is integer. CheckBoolean verifies that each operand is boolean. For a + or − operator, ParseSimpleExpression returns the integer type if both operands are integer. It returns the real type if both operands are real, or one is real and the other is integer. It returns the boolean type if the operator is OR and both operands are boolean.

Member function ParseTerm returns the type of the factor if there is only one factor. Just like ParseSimpleExpression, it must do type checking and decide which type to return based on the operators if there is more than one factor. For the * operator, it returns the integer type if both operands are integer. It returns the real type if both operands are real, or one is real and the other is integer. If the operator is /, the function returns the real type for any combination of integer or real operands. For the DIV and MOD operators, it returns the integer type only if both operands are integer. Finally, if the operator is AND, the function returns the boolean type only if both operands are boolean.

Member function ParseFactor returns the type of a constant identifier. It returns the type of a numeric factor (integer or real). It creates and returns a new string type for a string factor. If the factor is NOT followed by an expression, ParseFactor verifies that the expression's type is boolean, and then it returns the boolean type. For a parenthesized subexpression, it returns the type of the subexpression. Parse-Factor can also call function ParseVariable to parse a factor that is a variable, and then it returns the type of the variable.

Type Checking Variables

New member function ParseVariable parses a variable, which can be a simple identifier, or an identifier followed by subscripts, fields designators, or both. It first makes sure that the identifier was defined as a variable, as a value or a VAR parameter, or as a function. (These can all appear in expressions or as the target of an assignment.) Then, it loops as long as the current token is a [or a ., and it calls function ParseSubscripts or ParseField, respectively. Finally, the function returns the type of the variable, which can be the type of an array element or a record field.

Member function ParseSubscripts parses a comma-separated subscript list surrounded by [and]. For each subscript, it verifies that the current type is an array, calls ParseExpression to parse the subscript expression, calls class TType's friend function CheckAssignmentTypeCompatible to verify that the subscript expression type is compatible with the corresponding index type, and sets pType to point to the array's element type object. ParseSubscripts also makes sure that there aren't too many subscripts. After parsing all the subscripts, it returns the final element type. We'll look at function CheckAssignmentTypeCompatible later when we discuss assignment statements.

Member function ParseField parses a field designator. It checks that the variable's type is a record, and then it searches the record type's symbol table to verify that the field name is defined for that record. If all is well, the function returns the field's type. Figure 7.20 shows a new version of file parsstmt.cpp, which includes type checking.

■■■■■■■ **Figure 7.20** New version of implementation file **parsstmt.cpp**.

```
//  ****************************************************************
//  *                                                              *
//  *     P A R S E R     (Statements)                             *
//  *                                                              *
//  *     Parse statements.                                        *
//  *                                                              *
//  *     CLASSES: TParser                                *        *
//  *                                                              *
//  *     FILE:      prog7-2/parsstmt.cpp                          ^
//  *                                                              *
//  *     MODULE:  Parser                                          *
//  *                                                              *
//  *     Copyright (c) 1996 by Ronald Mak                         *
//  *     For instructional purposes only.  No warranties.         *
//  *                                                              *
//  ****************************************************************

#include <stdio.h>
#include <string.h>
#include "common.h"
#include "parser.h"


//------------------------------------------------------------
//  ParseStatement              Parse a statement.
//------------------------------------------------------------

void TParser::ParseStatement(void)
{
    InsertLineMarker();

    //--Call the appropriate parsing function based on
    //--the statement's first token.
    switch (token) {
        case tcIdentifier:  ParseAssignment();  break;
        case tcREPEAT:      ParseREPEAT();       break;
        case tcWHILE:       ParseWHILE();        break;
        case tcIF:          ParseIF();           break;
        case tcFOR:         ParseFOR();          break;
        case tcCASE:        ParseCASE();         break;
        case tcBEGIN:       ParseCompound();     break;
    }

    //--Resynchronize at a proper statement ending.
    if (token != tcEndOfFile) {
```

(continues)

```
        Resync(tlStatementFollow, tlStatementStart);
    }
}

//-----------------------------------------------------------
//  ParseStatementList       Parse a statement list until the
//                           terminator token.
//
//      terminator : the token that terminates the list
//-----------------------------------------------------------

void TParser::ParseStatementList(TTokenCode terminator)
{
    //--Loop to parse statements and to check for and skip semicolons.
    do {
        ParseStatement();

        if (TokenIn(token, tlStatementStart)) {
            Error(errMissingSemicolon);
        }
        else while (token == tcSemicolon) GetTokenAppend();
    } while ((token != terminator) && (token != tcEndOfFile));
}

//-----------------------------------------------------------
//  ParseAssignment          Parse an assignment statement:
//
//                                  <id> := <expr>
//-----------------------------------------------------------

void TParser::ParseAssignment(void)
{
    //--Search for the target variable's identifier and enter it
    //--if necessary.  Append the symbol table node handle
    //--to the icode.
    TSymtabNode *pTargetNode = Find(pToken->String());
    if (pTargetNode->defn.how != dcUndefined) icode.Put(pTargetNode);
    else {
        pTargetNode->defn.how = dcVariable;
        SetType(pTargetNode->pType, pDummyType);
    }

    TType *pTargetType = ParseVariable(pTargetNode);
```

```
        //-- :=
        Resync(tlColonEqual, tlExpressionStart);
        CondGetTokenAppend(tcColonEqual, errMissingColonEqual);

        //--<expr>
        TType *pExprType = ParseExpression();

        //--Check for assignment compatibility.
        CheckAssignmentTypeCompatible(pTargetType, pExprType,
                                      errIncompatibleAssignment);
}


//-------------------------------------------------------------
//  ParseREPEAT      Parse a REPEAT statement:
//
//                        REPEAT <stmt-list> UNTIL <expr>
//-------------------------------------------------------------

void TParser::ParseREPEAT(void)
{
        GetTokenAppend();

        //--<stmt-list>
        ParseStatementList(tcUNTIL);

        //--UNTIL
        CondGetTokenAppend(tcUNTIL, errMissingUNTIL);

        //--<expr> : must be boolean
        InsertLineMarker();
        CheckBoolean(ParseExpression());
}


//-------------------------------------------------------------
//  ParseWHILE       Parse a WHILE statement.:
//
//                        WHILE <expr> DO <stmt>
//-------------------------------------------------------------

void TParser::ParseWHILE(void)
{
        //--<expr> : must be boolean
        GetTokenAppend();
        CheckBoolean(ParseExpression());

        //--DO
```

(continues)

```
        Resync(tlDO, tlStatementStart);
        CondGetTokenAppend(tcDO, errMissingDO);

        //--<stmt>
        ParseStatement();
}

//------------------------------------------------------------
//  ParseIF          Parse an IF statement:
//
//                        IF <expr> THEN <stmt-1>
//
//                  or:
//
//                        IF <expr> THEN <stmt-1> ELSE <stmt-2>
//------------------------------------------------------------

void TParser::ParseIF(void)
{
        //--<expr> : must be boolean
        GetTokenAppend();
        CheckBoolean(ParseExpression());

        //--THEN
        Resync(tlTHEN, tlStatementStart);
        CondGetTokenAppend(tcTHEN, errMissingTHEN);

        //--<stmt-1>
        ParseStatement();

        if (token == tcELSE) {

            //--ELSE <stmt-2>
            GetTokenAppend();
            ParseStatement();
        }
}

//------------------------------------------------------------
//  ParseFOR          Parse a FOR statement:
//
//                        FOR <id> := <expr-1> TO|DOWNTO <expr-2>
//                            DO <stmt>
//------------------------------------------------------------
```

```
void TParser::ParseFOR(void)
{
    TType *pControlType;  // ptr to the control id's type object

    //--<id>
    GetTokenAppend();
    if (token == tcIdentifier) {

        //--Verify the definition and type of the control id.
        TSymtabNode *pControlId = Find(pToken->String());
        if (pControlId->defn.how != dcUndefined) {
            pControlType = pControlId->pType->Base();
        }
        else {
            pControlId->defn.how = dcVariable;
            pControlType = pControlId->pType = pIntegerType;
        }
        if (    (pControlType != pIntegerType)
            && (pControlType != pCharType)
            && (pControlType->form != fcEnum)) {
            Error(errIncompatibleTypes);
            pControlType = pIntegerType;
        }

        icode.Put(pControlId);
        GetTokenAppend();
    }
    else Error(errMissingIdentifier);

    //-- :=
    Resync(tlColonEqual, tlExpressionStart);
    CondGetTokenAppend(tcColonEqual, errMissingColonEqual);

    //--<expr-1>
    CheckAssignmentTypeCompatible(pControlType, ParseExpression(),
                                  errIncompatibleTypes);

    //--TO or DOWNTO
    Resync(tlTODOWNTO, tlExpressionStart);
    if (TokenIn(token, tlTODOWNTO)) GetTokenAppend();
    else Error(errMissingTOorDOWNTO);

    //--<expr-2>
    CheckAssignmentTypeCompatible(pControlType, ParseExpression(),
                                  errIncompatibleTypes);

    //--DO
```

(continues)

```
        Resync(tlDO, tlStatementStart);
        CondGetTokenAppend(tcDO, errMissingDO);

        //--<stmt>
        ParseStatement();
}

//------------------------------------------------------------
//  ParseCASE          Parse a CASE statement:
//
//                         CASE <expr> OF
//                             <case-branch> ;
//                             ...
//                         END
//------------------------------------------------------------

void TParser::ParseCASE(void)
{
        int caseBranchFlag;  // true if another CASE branch, else false

        //--<expr>
        GetTokenAppend();
        TType *pExprType = ParseExpression()->Base();

        //--Verify the type of the CASE expression.
        if (   (pExprType != pIntegerType)
            && (pExprType != pCharType)
            && (pExprType->form != fcEnum)) {
            Error(errIncompatibleTypes);
        }

        //--OF
        Resync(tlOF, tlCaseLabelStart);
        CondGetTokenAppend(tcOF, errMissingOF);

        //--Loop to parse CASE branches.
        caseBranchFlag = TokenIn(token, tlCaseLabelStart);
        while (caseBranchFlag) {
            if (TokenIn(token, tlCaseLabelStart)) {
                ParseCaseBranch(pExprType);
            }

            if (token == tcSemicolon) {
```

```
            GetTokenAppend();
            caseBranchFlag = true;
        }
        else if (TokenIn(token, tlCaseLabelStart)) {
            Error(errMissingSemicolon);
            caseBranchFlag = true;
        }
        else caseBranchFlag = false;
    }

    //--END
    Resync(tlEND, tlStatementStart);
    CondGetTokenAppend(tcEND, errMissingEND);
}

//-------------------------------------------------------------
//  ParseCaseBranch       Parse a CASE branch:
//
//                            <case-label-list> : <stmt>
//
//      pExprType : ptr to the CASE expression's type object
//-------------------------------------------------------------

void TParser::ParseCaseBranch(const TType *pExprType)
{
    int caseLabelFlag;  // true if another CASE label, else false

    //--<case-label-list>
    do {
        ParseCaseLabel(pExprType);
        if (token == tcComma) {

            //--Saw comma, look for another CASE label.
            GetTokenAppend();
            if (TokenIn(token, tlCaseLabelStart)) caseLabelFlag = true;
            else {
                Error(errMissingConstant);
                caseLabelFlag = false;
            }
        }
        else caseLabelFlag = false;

    } while (caseLabelFlag);

    //-- :
    Resync(tlColon, tlStatementStart);
```

(continues)

```
    CondGetTokenAppend(tcColon, errMissingColon);

    //--<stmt>
    ParseStatement();
}

//-------------------------------------------------------------
//  ParseCaseLabel        Parse a CASE label.
//
//       pExprType : ptr to the CASE expression's type object
//-------------------------------------------------------------

void TParser::ParseCaseLabel(const TType *pExprType)
{
    TType *pLabelType;         // ptr to the CASE label's type object
    int    signFlag = false;   // true if unary sign, else false

    //--Unary + or -
    if (TokenIn(token, tlUnaryOps)) {
        signFlag = true;
        GetTokenAppend();
    }

    switch (token) {

        //--Identifier:  Must be a constant whose type matches that
        //--             of the CASE expression.
        case tcIdentifier: {

            TSymtabNode *pLabelId = Find(pToken->String());
            icode.Put(pLabelId);

            if (pLabelId->defn.how != dcUndefined) {
                pLabelType = pLabelId->pType->Base();
            }
            else {
                pLabelId->defn.how = dcConstant;
                SetType(pLabelId->pType, pDummyType);
                pLabelType = pDummyType;
            }
            if (pExprType != pLabelType) Error(errIncompatibleTypes);

            //--Only an integer constant can have a unary sign.
```

```
        if (signFlag && (pLabelType != pIntegerType)) {
            Error(errInvalidConstant);
        }

        GetTokenAppend();
        break;
}

//--Number:  Both the label and the CASE expression
//--         must be integer.
case tcNumber: {

    if (pToken->Type() != tyInteger) Error(errInvalidConstant);
    if (pExprType != pIntegerType) Error(errIncompatibleTypes);

    TSymtabNode *pNode = SearchAll(pToken->String());
    if (!pNode) {
        pNode = EnterLocal(pToken->String());
        pNode->pType = pIntegerType;
        pNode->defn.constant.value.integer =
                                    pToken->Value().integer;
    }
    icode.Put(pNode);

    GetTokenAppend();
    break;
}

//--String:  Must be a single character without a unary sign.
//--         (Note that the string length includes the quotes.)
//--         The CASE expression type must be character.
case tcString: {

    if (signFlag || (strlen(pToken->String()) != 3)) {
        Error(errInvalidConstant);
    }
    if (pExprType != pCharType) Error(errIncompatibleTypes);

    TSymtabNode *pNode = SearchAll(pToken->String());
    if (!pNode) {
        pNode = EnterLocal(pToken->String());
        pNode->pType = pCharType;
        pNode->defn.constant.value.character =
                                    pToken->String()[1];
    }
    icode.Put(pNode);
```

(continues)

■■■■■■■ **Figure 7.20** New version of implementation file **parsstmt.cpp**.
(*Continued*)

```
            GetTokenAppend();
            break;
        }
    }
}


//-------------------------------------------------------------
//  ParseCompound        Parse a compound statement:
//
//                           BEGIN <stmt-list> END
//-------------------------------------------------------------

void TParser::ParseCompound(void)
{
    GetTokenAppend();

    //--<stmt-list>
    ParseStatementList(tcEND);

    //--END
    CondGetTokenAppend(tcEND, errMissingEND);
}
```

Type Checking Assignment Statements

Pascal has a set of assignment type compatibility rules that determine whether a source value of one type can be assigned to a target variable of another type. Member function ParseAssignment calls class TType's friend function Check-AssignmentTypeCompatible (see Figure 7.8). The friend function checks the base source type against the base target type, and deems the assignment to be compatible if

- The source and target types are the same.
- The source type is integer and the target type is real.
- The source and target are strings of the same length.

We've already seen that CheckAssignmentTypeCompatible is not just called by ParseAssignment, but by other functions (such as ParseSubscripts) that also need to check for type compatibility.

Type Checking Control Statements

Member functions ParseREPEAT, ParseWHILE, and ParseIF all call Check-Boolean to verify that its expression is boolean.

Member function ParseFOR checks that its control variable is of type integer, character, or enumeration, and that its initial and final expressions are assignment type compatible with the control variable. Member function ParseCaseLabel makes sure that each CASE label is of the same type as that of the CASE expression.

Program 7-2: Syntax Checker II

Our second utility program, Syntax Checker II, expands upon the utility in the previous chapter. We saw earlier how we can already do syntax checking of declarations, and now we've just added the ability to do translation-time type checking of statements and expressions.

Figure 7.21 shows the main file synchek2.cpp.

■■■■■ **Figure 7.21** Main file **synchek2.cpp** of the Syntax Checker II utility program.

```
//    ***************************************************************
//    *                                                             *
//    *    Program 7-2: Syntax Checker II                           *
//    *                                                             *
//    *    Check the syntax of a "program" consisting of            *
//    *    declarations followed by a statement.                    *
//    *                                                             *
//    *    FILE:    prog7-2/synchek2.cpp                            *
//    *                                                             *
//    *    USAGE:   synchek2 <source file>                          *
//    *                                                             *
//    *                 <source file>  name of the source file      *
//    *                                                             *
//    *    Copyright (c) 1996 by Ronald Mak                         *
//    *    For instructional purposes only.  No warranties.         *
//    *                                                             *
//    ***************************************************************

#include <iostream.h>
```

(continues)

■■■■■■■■ **Figure 7.21** Main file **synchek2.cpp** of the Syntax Checker II utility program. (*Continued*)

```cpp
#include "common.h"
#include "error.h"
#include "buffer.h"
#include "symtab.h"
#include "parser.h"


//----------------------------------------------------------------
//  main
//----------------------------------------------------------------

void main(int argc, char *argv[])
{
    //--Check the command line arguments.
    if (argc != 2) {
        cerr << "Usage: synchek2 <source file>" << endl;
        AbortTranslation(abortInvalidCommandLineArgs);
    }

    //--Create the parser for the source file,
    //--and then parse the file.
    TParser *pParser = new TParser(new TSourceBuffer(argv[1]));
    pParser->Parse();
    delete pParser;
}
```

Figure 7.22 shows sample output.

■■■■■■■■ **Figure 7.22** Sample output from the Syntax Checker II utility program.

```
Page 1    synchek2.in    Sat Oct 28 01:56:44 1995

  1 0: CONST
  2 0:     ten   = 10;
  3 0:     pi    = 3.1415926;
  4 0:     ch    = 'x';
  5 0:     hello = 'Hello, world.';
  6 0:
  7 0: TYPE
  8 0:     e  = (alpha, beta, gamma);
  9 0:     ee = e;
 10 0:     sr = alpha..gamma;
 11 0:
 12 0:     ar1 = ARRAY [1..ten] OF integer;
```

```
13 0:     ar2 = ARRAY [e, sr] OF real;
14 0:     ar3 = ARRAY [(fee, fye, foe, fum), sr] OF
15 0:              ARRAY [ee] OF boolean;
16 0:
17 0:     rec = RECORD
18 0:              i, j, k : integer;
19 0:              x, y    : real;
20 0:              ch      : char;
21 0:              a       : ARRAY [sr] OF e;
22 0:          END;
23 0:
24 0: VAR
25 0:     radius, circumference : real;
26 0:     b      : boolean;
27 0:     letter : 'a'..'z';
28 0:     greek  : ee;
29 0:     list   : ar1;
30 0:     a2     : ar2;
31 0:     a3     : ar3;
32 0:     thing  : rec;
33 0:     a4     : ARRAY [9..15] OF rec;
34 0:
35 0: BEGIN
36 0:     IF (NOT letter) THEN radius := circumference/pi/2 + b;
                           ^
*** ERROR: Incompatible types
                                                              ^
*** ERROR: Incompatible types
37 0:     FOR radius := 1 DOWNTO a2 DO greek := thing.a[beta];
              ^
*** ERROR: Incompatible types
                              ^
*** ERROR: Incompatible types
38 0:
39 0:     b := (ten*radius >= thing.x) AND NOT a3[foe, alpha, beta];
40 0:
41 0:     CASE letter OF
42 0:        ch  : a2[alpha, gamma] := a2[beta][alpha];
```

Page 2   synchek2.in   Sat Oct 28 01:56:44 1995

```
43 0:        pi  : a3[fye] := a3[7];
                  ^
*** ERROR: Incompatible types
                                  ^
*** ERROR: Incompatible types
```

(continues)

■■■■■ **Figure 7.22** Sample output from the Syntax Checker II utility program.
(*Continued*)

```
 44 0:              'q' : thing.what := list[ten, 7, 3];
                                     ^
*** ERROR: Invalid field
                                                   ^
*** ERROR: Too many subscripts
                                               ^
*** ERROR: Too many subscripts
                                                 ^
*** ERROR: Incompatible assignment
 45 0:            14  : thing.x := a4[ten].i DIV thing.y;
                  ^
*** ERROR: Incompatible types
                                                 ^
*** ERROR: Incompatible types
 46 0:      END;
 47 0: END.
 48 0:

              48 source lines.
              12 syntax errors.
```

Table 7.2 shows the modules and source files for this utility program.

■■■■■ **Table 7.2** Modules and Files of Program 7-2

Module	File	Status	Directory
Main	synchek2.cpp	*new*	prog7-2
Parser	parser.h	*changed*	prog7-2
	parser.cpp	*changed*	prog7-2
	parsdecl.cpp	*unchanged*	prog7-1
	parstyp1.cpp	*unchanged*	prog7-1
	parstyp2.cpp	*unchanged*	prog7-1
	parsstmt.cpp	*changed*	prog7-2
	parsexpr.cpp	*changed*	prog7-2
Intermediate code	icode.h	*unchanged*	prog5-2
	icode.cpp	*unchanged*	prog5-2
Scanner	scanner.h	*unchanged*	prog3-1
	scanner.cpp	*unchanged*	prog3-2
	token.h	*unchanged*	prog4-2

■■■■■■■ **Table 7.2** Modules and Files of Program 7-2 (*Continued*)

Module	File	Status	Directory
	tknword.cpp	*unchanged*	prog3-2
	tknnum.cpp	*unchanged*	prog3-2
	tknstrsp.cpp	*unchanged*	prog3-2
Symbol table	types.h	*unchanged*	prog7-1
	types.cpp	*unchanged*	prog7-1
	symtab.h	*unchanged*	prog7-1
	symtab.cpp	*unchanged*	prog7-1
Error	error.h	*unchanged*	prog5-2
	error.cpp	*unchanged*	prog5-2
Buffer	buffer.h	*unchanged*	prog2-1
	buffer.cpp	*unchanged*	prog2-1
Common	common.h	*unchanged*	prog7-1
	common.cpp	*unchanged*	prog7-1
	misc.h	*unchanged*	prog3-2

■■■■■■■

Parsing declarations was a lot of work! But now that that's behind us, we can complete the parser module with the one remaining task: parsing procedures and functions. We take them on in the next chapter.

PARSING PROGRAMS, PROCEDURES, AND FUNCTIONS

In this chapter, we'll add member functions to class `TParser` that parse program, procedure, and function headers, plus procedure and function calls. We already can parse declarations, statements, and expressions, so with the new functions, we'll be able to parse entire Pascal programs. Indeed, our first utility program, Syntax Checker III, will do syntax checking of entire programs.

After this chapter, the parser module and the front end will be nearly complete. We recall that the front end translates a source program's declarations into entries in a symbol table, and it translates the statements and expressions into intermediate code. The symbol table and icode objects are the interface between the front end and the back end (see Figures 1.4 and 1.5).

We are going to further interconnect the symbol table and the icode objects. We've already seen how the intermediate code contains "handles" to symbol table nodes (i.e, the symbol table and the node indexes). We've also seen how a record type identifier's symbol table node can point to another symbol table that contains the record's field identifiers.

To take care of both global and local declarations, we need to create a global symbol table for a Pascal program's global predefined identifiers, such as `integer`, `real`, `true`, and `writeln`. The global symbol table will also contain the program name. The program name's symbol table node will then point to a separate local symbol table that contains the program's local identifiers.

If the program has procedures and functions, then the program's local symbol table will contain their names. The symbol table node of each procedure and function name will point to yet another local symbol table that contains the local identifiers of the procedure or function. Any of the local symbol tables can be empty if there are no local declarations. Obviously, the global symbol table is never empty. (From now on, we'll use the term *routine* to mean a program, procedure, or function, and the term *subroutine* to mean a procedure or a function.)

We'll enter the names of the program's outermost procedures and functions into the program's local symbol table, since they are part of the program's local declarations. Similarly, if one of these subroutines, say a procedure, itself has a nested subroutine, say a function, we'll enter the function name into the procedure's local symbol table. Since each subroutine name's symbol table node points to a local symbol table, the symbol tables will be nested within each other just as the program's procedures and functions are nested.

The symbol table entry for the program name and for each procedure and function name will also point to a separate icode object containing the intermediate code for that routine's statements. Therefore, the icode objects will be accessible only from within the symbol table objects.

Obviously, in order for the back end to work correctly, the front end must properly enter all information about the source program into the symbol table and icode objects. Our second utility program, Pascal Pretty-Printer, reproduces the source program (in a "pretty" format) using only these interface objects, and so it helps ensure that the front end did its job right.

In this chapter, we'll see how to:

- Parse program, procedure, and function headers and enter the information into symbol tables.
- Use a symbol table stack to handle scope.

- Parse procedure and function calls.
- Parse calls to the standard Pascal procedures and functions.
- Reproduce the source program in the back end using information the front end stored into the symbol table and icode objects.

Scope and the Symbol Table Stack

The *scope* of an identifier in a Pascal program is that part of the source program where the identifier can be used—in other words, everywhere the identifier is defined. The scope of a global identifier (such as `writeln`) is the entire program. The scope of a local identifier begins with its declaration (in a constant definition, type definition, variable declaration, or procedure or function declaration) and extends through the last statement of the routine in which the identifier is declared. The scope of a record field identifier is the record type definition that declares the field.

When the parser parses a routine, we can say that it *enters a scope*. This scope refers to the union of all of the individual scopes of the routine's local identifiers. A common analogy is to think of such a scope as a shell within which all the routine's local identifiers are defined. For example, a procedure's scope begins right after the procedure name (thus including the formal parameters but not the procedure name) and extends through its last statement. (To avoid confusion, we'll use *parameters* when talking about Pascal procedures and functions. *Formal parameters* are declared in procedure and function headers, and *actual parameters* are passed in procedure and function calls. We'll use *arguments* when talking about C++ functions.) The parser *exits a scope* after parsing the last statement. Generally, unless we explicitly refer to an identifier's scope, we mean a routine's scope.

An identifier can be redefined within a nested scope. This happens if the same identifier appears in a declaration in a nested subroutine. Then this redefinition is valid inside the nested scope, and the original definition is hidden. Outside the nested scope, but within the original scope, the original definition applies. Pascal allows the same identifier to name different objects (constants, types, variables, fields, formal parameters, or routines) as long as the similarly named objects are in different scopes.

Thus, scopes are nested just as a program's routines are nested. Whenever the parser encounters an identifier, it needs to figure out which object the identifier refers to. For example, if the parser encounters the variable x in a routine, it must first check the local scope by searching for x in the routine's local symbol table. If x isn't in that symbol table, the parser must then check the next enclosing scope by searching the symbol table of the next enclosing routine. This search of symbol tables continues outward through the nested scopes until x is finally found, and the parser uses that definition. The global symbol table is searched last, if necessary. Only if the entire search is unsuccessful can the parser flag x as undefined.

Figure 8.1 The Syntax Checker III utility program flagging scope errors. Note the nesting level number after each line number.

```
Page 1    scopeerr.pas   Mon Nov 28 20:22:47 1994

  1 0: PROGRAM scope (input, output);
  2 1:
  3 1: VAR
  4 1:     i, j, k : integer;
  5 1:
  6 1: FUNCTION f (j : boolean) : real;
  7 2:
  8 2:     VAR
  9 2:         i : real;
 10 2:
 11 2:     BEGIN {f}
 12 2:         i := 1.0;    {local of f}
 13 2:         j := false;  {parm  of f}
 14 2:         k := 3;      {global}
 15 2:
 16 2:         i := 1;  j := 2;  k := 3;  {j ERROR}
                                ^
*** ERROR: Incompatible assignment
 17 2:
 18 2:         f := i;
 19 2:     END {f};
 20 1:
 21 1: PROCEDURE p1 (j : integer);
 22 2:
 23 2:     VAR
 24 2:         i : char;
 25 2:
 26 2:     PROCEDURE p2 (k : boolean);
```

```
27 3:
28 3:        VAR
29 3:           n : integer;
30 3:
31 3:        BEGIN {p2}
32 3:           i := 'x';    {local of p1}
33 3:           j := 5;      {parm  of p1}
34 3:           k := true;   {parm  of p2}
35 3:           n := 7;      {local of p2}
36 3:
37 3:           i := 1;  j := 2;  k := 3;  {i, k ERROR}
                 ^
```

*** ERROR: Incompatible assignment

*** ERROR: Incompatible assignment
```
38 3:        END {p2};
39 2:
40 2:     BEGIN {p1}
41 2:        i := 'z';   {local of p1}
42 2:        j := 7;     {parm  of p1}
43 2:        k := 9;     {global}
44 2:
```

Page 2   scopeerr.pas   Mon Nov 28 20:22:47 1994

```
45 2:        i := 1;  j := 2;  k := 3;  n := 4;  {i, n ERROR}
              ^
```

*** ERROR: Incompatible assignment

*** ERROR: Undefined identifier

*** ERROR: Incompatible assignment
```
46 2:     END {p1};
47 1:
48 1:
49 1: BEGIN {scope}
50 1:    i := 1; {global}
51 1:    j := 2; {global}
52 1:    k := 3; {global}
53 1: END {scope}.
54 0:
```

                    54 source lines.
                    6 syntax errors.

(continues)

Figure 8.1 shows output from the Syntax Checker III utility program that we'll write shortly. It shows how the parser can flag scope errors. In the first error, the assignment j := 2 is incorrect because identifier j refers to the formal boolean parameter j of function f. In the second and fourth errors, the assignment i := 1 is incorrect because i refers to the local character variable i of procedure p1. In the third error, the assignment k := 3 is incorrect because k refers to the formal boolean parameter k of nested procedure p2. The fifth and sixth errors are caused by the reference to n, which is undefined because the local variables of procedure p2 are not accessible by p1's statements.

The listing shows how scopes also provide protection. Nested procedure p2 can access any of procedure p1's local identifiers, except for ones that p2 redefines. However, if p2 declares a local variable n, p1 cannot access it. Any such attempt would result in the undefined identifier error. Back to the shell analogy, nested scopes are like nested shells that allow you to look outward but not inward. In other words, from within a shell, you can look outside for an identifier's definition, but you cannot look into a nested shell.

Each scope is at a *nesting level*. The global scope is at nesting level 0. The main program's scope is at nesting level 1. The scope of each of the outermost procedures and functions is at nesting level 2, and so on. In our source program listings, we display the current nesting level next to the line number. Until now, we've just printed a 0, but beginning in this chapter, we'll print the correct number, as shown in Figure 8.1.

So we see the need for two changes to the way we handle the symbol table. First, we need multiple symbol tables, one for the global identifiers and one for each routine's local identifiers (one symbol table per scope). The same identifier can be defined differently in each symbol table. Second, we need to do symbol table searches in a way that takes scope into consideration.

The way scopes are nested suggests the use of a stack. Figure 8.2 shows the symbol table stack when the statements of function f are being parsed, and the stack when the statements of procedure p2 are being parsed. The bottom of the stack always points to the global symbol table, and the next stack element always points to the program's local symbol table. The topmost element points to the local symbol table of the routine currently being parsed. The index of the stack element is the same as the nesting level.

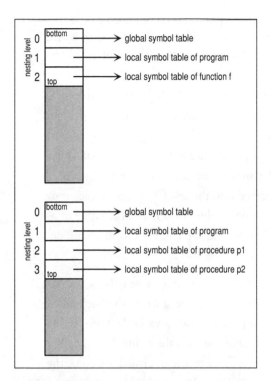

Figure 8.2 The first drawing shows symbol table stack while function **f** (see Figure 8.1) is being parsed. (Note that the stack grows downward in this figure, so that element 2 is the current top of the stack, and element 0 is the bottom.) The second drawing shows the stack while procedure **p2** is being parsed.

The semantic actions the parser must perform when it parses a program, procedure, or function are

1. Parse the routine's name and enter it into the current symbol table.
2. Before parsing the rest of the routine's header, enter a scope by creating a new local symbol table and pushing a pointer to it onto the symbol table stack. Make this the current symbol table, and increment the nesting level.
3. Parse the routine's formal parameters and its declarations, and enter all of the local identifiers into the current symbol table.
4. Parse the routine's statements. When parsing any identifier, search the symbol tables in the order starting from the top of the symbol table stack to the bottom.

5. After parsing the statements, exit the scope by popping the pointer to the current symbol table off the stack. Make the symbol table that is pointed to by the new stack top the current one, which returns us to the enclosing scope. Decrement the nesting level.

As mentioned above, the program name is entered into the global symbol table at nesting level 0. The names of the outermost subroutines are entered into the program's local symbol table at level 1 (and are therefore called *level-1 procedures and functions*). The local identifiers of a level-1 subroutine are entered into the subroutine's local symbol table at level 2. If a level-1 subroutine contains a nested subroutine, then the nested subroutine's name is entered into the level-1 symbol table, and its local identifiers are entered into a level-2 symbol table. In general, the name of a routine is entered into a level-n local symbol table, and the routine's local identifiers are entered into the routine's local symbol table at level $n+1$.

The symbol table stack is used only in the front end. (The interactive debugger that we'll write in Chapter 11 will maintain its own symbol table stack in the back end so that it can parse user commands.) When the parser parses a variable name, it searches the stack to determine which symbol table contains the name. When it appends the handle to the variable's symbol table node to the intermediate code, the handle consists of the symbol table's index number and the node's index number. The back end uses this handle to access the correct symbol table node directly.

As we'll see in the next chapter, the back end uses the nesting level and the offset (stored by the parser in the symbol table node) to access the variable's value on the runtime stack.

Figure 8.3 shows how the parser interacts with the symbol table stack. Whenever the parser sends the `EnterLocal`, `EnterNewLocal`, or `SearchLocal` message to the stack, the stack in turn sends the `Enter`, `EnterNew`, or `Search` message, respectively, to the current local symbol table, the one pointed to by the topmost stack element. The parser sends `EnterScope` and `ExitScope` messages to the stack to enter a new scope or to exit a scope.

Until now, the parser sent the `SearchAll` and `Find` messages to search the single symbol table. Starting in this chapter, whenever the parser sends the `SearchAll` message to the symbol table stack, the stack sends the `Search` message to the symbol tables it points to, in the order from top to bottom, to search the enclosing

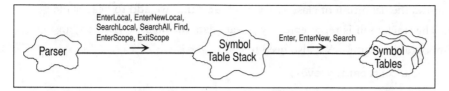

▮▮▮▮▮ **Figure 8.3** Interactions among the parser, symbol table stack, and symbol table objects.

scopes. If the parser sends the `Find` message to the stack, the stack calls `SearchAll` and flags an undefined identifier error if the identifier isn't found.

Figure 8.4 shows the class diagram for class `TSymtabStack`. Since it will only be used by the parser, the symbol table stack object will be allocated as a private data member `symtabStack` of class `TParser`. Each element of the stack will point to a symbol table object.

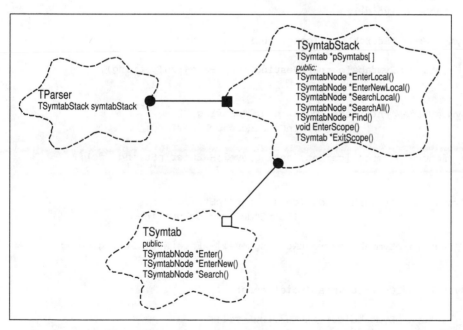

▮▮▮▮▮ **Figure 8.4** Class diagram for class **TSymtabStack**. Only the relevant data members and member functions are shown for classes **TParser** and **TSymtab**.

Figure 8.5 shows the definition of class TSymtabStack that we add to header file symtab.h. The stack itself is represented by private data member pSymtabs, an array of symbol table pointers. We also need to add

```
extern int currentNestingLevel;
```

to the beginning of the file.

■■■■■■■■ **Figure 8.5** The definition of class **TSymtabStack** in header file **symtab.h**.

```
//---------------------------------------------------------------
// TSymtabStack      Symbol table stack class.
//---------------------------------------------------------------

class TSymtabStack {
    enum {maxNestingLevel = 8};

    TSymtab *pSymtabs[maxNestingLevel];  // stack of symbol table ptrs

public:
    TSymtabStack(void);
   ~TSymtabStack(void);

    TSymtabNode *SearchLocal(const char *pString)
    {
        return pSymtabs[currentNestingLevel]->Search(pString);
    }

    TSymtabNode *EnterLocal(const char *pString,
                       TDefnCode dc = dcUndefined)
    {
        return pSymtabs[currentNestingLevel]->Enter(pString, dc);
    }

    TSymtabNode *EnterNewLocal(const char *pString,
                          TDefnCode dc = dcUndefined)
    {
        return pSymtabs[currentNestingLevel]->EnterNew(pString, dc);
    }

    TSymtab *GetCurrentSymtab(void) const
    {
        return pSymtabs[currentNestingLevel];
    }

    void SetCurrentSymtab(TSymtab *pSymtab)
```

```
    {
        pSymtabs[currentNestingLevel] = pSymtab;
    }

    TSymtabNode *SearchAll (const char *pString) const;
    TSymtabNode *Find       (const char *pString) const;
    void         EnterScope(void);
    TSymtab     *ExitScope (void);
};
```

Member function SearchLocal sends the Search message to the current symbol
table pointed to by the top of the symbol table stack. (Recall that global variable
currentNestingLevel keeps track of the current nesting level.) This is the local
symbol table of the routine that is being parsed. Member functions EnterLocal
and EnterNewLocal send the Enter and EnterNew messages, respectively, to
this local symbol table.

▆▆▆▆▆▆▆▆ **Figure 8.6** Implementation of class **TSymtabStack** in file **symtab.cpp**.

```
//-------------------------------------------------------------
//  Constructor      Initialize the global (level 0) symbol
//                   table, and set the others to NULL.
//-------------------------------------------------------------

TSymtabStack::TSymtabStack(void)
{
    extern TSymtab globalSymtab;
    void InitializeStandardRoutines(TSymtab *pSymtab);

    currentNestingLevel = 0;
    for (int i = 1; i < maxNestingLevel; ++i) pSymtabs[i] = NULL;

    //--Initialize the global nesting level.
    pSymtabs[0] = &globalSymtab;
    InitializePredefinedTypes (pSymtabs[0]);
    InitializeStandardRoutines(pSymtabs[0]);
}


//-------------------------------------------------------------
//  Destructor      Remove the predefined types.
//-------------------------------------------------------------

TSymtabStack::~TSymtabStack(void)
{
```

(continues)

```
    RemovePredefinedTypes();
}


//----------------------------------------------------------------
//  SearchAll    Search the symbol table stack for the given
//               name string.
//
//      pString : ptr to name string to find
//
//  Return: ptr to symbol table node if found, else NULL
//----------------------------------------------------------------

TSymtabNode *TSymtabStack::SearchAll(const char *pString) const
{
    for (int i = currentNestingLevel; i >= 0; --i) {
        TSymtabNode *pNode = pSymtabs[i]->Search(pString);
        if (pNode) return pNode;
    }

    return NULL;
}


//----------------------------------------------------------------
//  Find         Search the symbol table stack for the given
//               name string.  If the name is not already in
//               there, flag the undefined identifier error,
//               and then enter the name into the local symbol
//               table.
//
//      pString : ptr to name string to find
//
//  Return: ptr to symbol table node
//----------------------------------------------------------------

TSymtabNode *TSymtabStack::Find(const char *pString) const
{
    TSymtabNode *pNode = SearchAll(pString);

    if (!pNode) {
        Error(errUndefinedIdentifier);
        pNode = pSymtabs[currentNestingLevel]->Enter(pString);
    }
```

```
        return pNode;
}


//--------------------------------------------------------------
//  EnterScope  Enter a new nested scope.  Increment the nesting
//              level.  Push new scope's symbol table onto the
//              stack.
//
//      pSymtab : ptr to scope's symbol table
//--------------------------------------------------------------

void TSymtabStack::EnterScope(void)
{
    if (++currentNestingLevel > maxNestingLevel) {
        Error(errNestingTooDeep);
        AbortTranslation(abortNestingTooDeep);
    }

    SetCurrentSymtab(new TSymtab);
}


//--------------------------------------------------------------
//  ExitScope   Exit the current scope and return to the
//              enclosing scope.  Decrement the nesting level.
//              Pop the closed scope's symbol table off the
//              stack and return a pointer to it.
//
//  Return: ptr to closed scope's symbol table
//--------------------------------------------------------------

TSymtab *TSymtabStack::ExitScope(void)
{
    return pSymtabs[currentNestingLevel--];
}
```

Figure 8.6 shows the implementation of class TSymtabStack in file symtab.cpp. The constructor function initializes the stack and points the bottom element to the global symbol table. It then calls function InitializePredefinedTypes (called by the parser's constructor in the previous chapter) to initialize the predefined types and enter their identifiers into the global symbol table. It also calls function InitializeStandardRoutines to initialize the predefined procedures and functions and enter their identifiers into the global symbol table. We'll look at this function later.

The destructor function calls function `RemovePredefinedTypes` to remove the predefined type objects. In the previous chapter, this was called by the parser's destructor.

Member function `SearchAll` sends the `Search` message to each symbol table pointed to by the symbol table stack, from the stack top to the bottom. It stops as soon as it finds the name string in one of the symbol tables and returns a pointer to the node. Otherwise, it returns null. Member function `Find` calls `SearchAll`. If the name string was not found, the function flags an undefined identifier error and then enters the string into the local symbol table. Whether the string was found or newly entered, the function returns a pointer to the node.

Member function `EnterScope` enters a new nested scope by incrementing (and checking) the nesting level, and then it creates a new symbol table and passes it to member function `SetCurrentSymtab`. Member function `ExitScope` exits the current scope by returning a pointer to the current symbol table, popping it off the symbol table stack, and decrementing the nesting level. We'll call `EnterScope` right after parsing a routine name, and `ExitScope` after parsing the last statement of the routine.

Parsing Declared Routines

The declared routines of a Pascal program include the main program itself and any programmer-written procedures and functions. A program can also call predefined routines, such as `read` and `writeln`.

■■■■■■■■ **Figure 8.7** New version of class **TParser** in header file **parser.h**.

```
//---------------------------------------------------------------
//  TParser           Parser class.
//---------------------------------------------------------------

class TParser {
    TTextScanner *const pScanner;    // ptr to the scanner
    TToken        *pToken;           // ptr to the current token
    TTokenCode     token;            // code of current token
    TSymtabStack  symtabStack;       // the symbol table stack
    TIcode        icode;             // the icode buffer
```

```
//--Routines
TSymtabNode *ParseProgram                (void);
TSymtabNode *ParseProgramHeader          (void);
void         ParseSubroutineDeclarations(TSymtabNode *pRoutineId);
TSymtabNode *ParseSubroutine             (void);
TSymtabNode *ParseProcedureHeader        (void);
TSymtabNode *ParseFunctionHeader         (void);
void         ParseBlock                  (TSymtabNode *pRoutineId);

TSymtabNode *ParseFormalParmList(int &count, int &totalSize);

TType       *ParseSubroutineCall  (const TSymtabNode *pRoutineId,
                                       int parmCheckFlag);
TType *ParseDeclaredSubroutineCall(const TSymtabNode *pRoutineId,
                                       int parmCheckFlag);
TType *ParseStandardSubroutineCall(const TSymtabNode *pRoutineId);
void   ParseActualParmList        (const TSymtabNode *pRoutineId,
                                       int parmCheckFlag);
void   ParseActualParm            (const TSymtabNode *pFormalId,
                                       int parmCheckFlag);

//--Standard subroutines
TType *ParseReadReadlnCall  (const TSymtabNode *pRoutineId);
TType *ParseWriteWritelnCall(const TSymtabNode *pRoutineId);
TType *ParseEofEolnCall               (void);
TType *ParseAbsSqrCall                 (void);
TType *ParseArctanCosExpLnSinSqrtCall(void);
TType *ParsePredSuccCall               (void);
TType *ParseChrCall                    (void);
TType *ParseOddCall                    (void);
TType *ParseOrdCall                    (void);
TType *ParseRoundTruncCall             (void);
void   SkipExtraParms                  (void);

//--Declarations
void ParseDeclarations        (TSymtabNode *pRoutineId);
void ParseConstantDefinitions(TSymtabNode *pRoutineId);
void ParseConstant            (TSymtabNode *pConstId);
void ParseIdentifierConstant (TSymtabNode *pId1, TTokenCode sign);

void   ParseTypeDefinitions(TSymtabNode *pRoutineId);
TType *ParseTypeSpec         (void);

TType *ParseIdentifierType (const TSymtabNode *pId2);
TType *ParseEnumerationType(void);
```

(continues)

■■■■■■■■ **Figure 8.7** New version of class **TParser** in header file **parser.h**.
(*Continued*)

```
TType *ParseSubrangeType (TSymtabNode *pMinId);
TType *ParseSubrangeLimit(TSymtabNode *pLimitId, int &limit);

TType *ParseArrayType (void);
void   ParseIndexType (TType *pArrayType);
int    ArraySize      (TType *pArrayType);
TType *ParseRecordType(void);

void ParseVariableDeclarations(TSymtabNode *pRoutineId);
void ParseFieldDeclarations   (TType       *pRecordType,
                               int offset);
void ParseVarOrFieldDecls     (TSymtabNode *pRoutineId,
                               TType       *pRecordType,
                               int offset);
TSymtabNode *ParseIdSublist   (const TSymtabNode *pRoutineId,
                               const TType       *pRecordType,
                               TSymtabNode *&pLastId);

//--Statements
void ParseStatement     (void);
void ParseStatementList(TTokenCode terminator);
void ParseAssignment    (const TSymtabNode *pTargetId);
void ParseREPEAT        (void);
void ParseWHILE         (void);
void ParseIF            (void);
void ParseFOR           (void);
void ParseCASE          (void);
void ParseCaseBranch    (const TType *pExprType);
void ParseCaseLabel     (const TType *pExprType);
void ParseCompound      (void);

//--Expressions
TType *ParseExpression       (void);
TType *ParseSimpleExpression(void);
TType *ParseTerm             (void);
TType *ParseFactor           (void);
TType *ParseVariable         (const TSymtabNode *pId);
TType *ParseSubscripts       (const TType *pType);
TType *ParseField            (const TType *pType);

void GetToken(void)
{
    pToken = pScanner->Get();
```

```
    token   = pToken->Code();
}

void GetTokenAppend(void)
{
    GetToken();
    icode.Put(token);   // append token code to icode buffer
}

void CondGetToken(TTokenCode tc, TErrorCode ec)
{
    //--Get another token only if the current one matches tc.
    if (tc == token) GetToken();
    else             Error(ec);   // error if no match
}

void CondGetTokenAppend(TTokenCode tc, TErrorCode ec)
{
    //--Get another token only if the current one matches tc.
    if (tc == token) GetTokenAppend();
    else             Error(ec);   // error if no match
}

void InsertLineMarker(void) { icode.InsertLineMarker(); }

TSymtabNode *SearchLocal(const char *pString)
{
    return symtabStack.SearchLocal(pString);
}

TSymtabNode *SearchAll(const char *pString) const
{
    return symtabStack.SearchAll(pString);
}

TSymtabNode *EnterLocal(const char *pString,
                        TDefnCode dc = dcUndefined)
{
    return symtabStack.EnterLocal(pString, dc);
}

TSymtabNode *EnterNewLocal(const char *pString,
                           TDefnCode dc = dcUndefined)
{
    return symtabStack.EnterNewLocal(pString, dc);
}
```

(continues)

■■■■■■ **Figure 8.7** New version of class **TParser** in header file **parser.h**. (*Continued*)

```
TSymtabNode *Find(const char *pString) const
{
    return symtabStack.Find(pString);
}

void CopyQuotedString(char *pString,
                      const char *pQuotedString) const
{
    int length = strlen(pQuotedString) - 2;  // don't count quotes
    strncpy(pString, &pQuotedString[1], length);
    pString[length] = '\0';
}

void Resync(const TTokenCode *pList1,
            const TTokenCode *pList2 = NULL,
            const TTokenCode *pList3 = NULL);

public:
    TParser(TTextInBuffer *pBuffer)
        : pScanner(new TTextScanner(pBuffer)) {}

    ~TParser(void) { delete pScanner; }

    TSymtabNode *Parse(void);
};
```

Figure 8.7 shows the new version of class TParser in header file parser.h. There are two new private data members: symtabStack, the symbol table stack object; and icode, the intermediate code object buffer.

Because each routine will have its own icode object to contain its statements translated into intermediate code, we now need a global icode object. The parser always appends intermediate code for the routine that it is currently parsing into the icode object buffer. When it is done parsing the routine, it creates a new icode object for the routine and copies the contents of the buffer icode object into the new icode object. The parser then resets the buffer icode object to prepare it for the next routine.

Class TParser has many new member functions for parsing routine declarations and for parsing calls to declared and predefined procedures and functions. The member functions SearchLocal, SearchAll, EnterLocal, EnterNewLocal,

Find, EnterScope, and ExitScope all send their corresponding messages to the symbol table stack object. The constructor and destructor functions no longer call InitializePredefinedTypes and RemovePredefinedTypes since these calls are made from the constructor and destructor functions of class TSymtab-Stack (see Figure 8.6). Public member function Parse now returns a pointer to a symbol table node.

▐█████ **Figure 8.8** Member function **Parse** in implementation file **parser.cpp** of the Syntax Checker III utility program.

```
//-------------------------------------------------------------
//  Parse         Parse the source file.
//
//  Return: ptr to the program id's symbol table node
//-------------------------------------------------------------

TSymtabNode *TParser::Parse(void)
{
    //--Extract the first token and parse the program.
    GetToken();
    TSymtabNode *pProgramId = ParseProgram();

    //--Print the parser's summary.
    list.PutLine();
    sprintf(list.text, "%20d source lines.",  currentLineNumber);
    list.PutLine();
    sprintf(list.text, "%20d syntax errors.", errorCount);
    list.PutLine();
    list.PutLine();

    return pProgramId;
}
```

Figure 8.8 shows member function Parse in implementation file parser.cpp for the Syntax Checker III utility program. It calls member function ParseProgram, which parses an entire program and returns a pointer to the program name's symbol table node.

▐█████ **Figure 8.9** New token lists in implementation file **common.cpp**.

```
//--Tokens that can start a procedure or function definition.
extern const TTokenCode tlProcFuncStart[] = {
    tcPROCEDURE, tcFUNCTION, tcDummy
};
```

(continues)

■■■■■■■■ **Figure 8.9** New token lists in implementation file **common.cpp**.
(*Continued*)

```
//--Tokens that can follow a procedure or function definition.
extern const TTokenCode tlProcFuncFollow[] = {
    tcSemicolon, tcDummy
};

//--Tokens that can follow a routine header.
extern const TTokenCode tlHeaderFollow[] = {
    tcSemicolon, tcDummy
};

//--Tokens that can follow a program or procedure id in a header.
extern const TTokenCode tlProgProcIdFollow[] = {
    tcLParen, tcSemicolon, tcDummy
};

//--Tokens that can follow a function id in a header.
extern const TTokenCode tlFuncIdFollow[] = {
    tcLParen, tcColon, tcSemicolon, tcDummy
};

//--Tokens that can follow an actual variable parameter.
extern const TTokenCode tlActualVarParmFollow[] = {
    tcComma, tcRParen, tcDummy
};

//--Tokens that can follow a formal parameter list.
extern const TTokenCode tlFormalParmsFollow[] = {
    tcRParen, tcSemicolon, tcDummy
};
```

Figure 8.9 shows new token lists in implementation file common.cpp. We also need to delete the line

```
    TIcode icode;
```

We need to add the following lines to header file common.h:

```
    extern const TTokenCode tlProcFuncStart[], tlProcFuncFollow[],
                            tlHeaderFollow[];

    extern const TTokenCode tlProgProcIdFollow[],    tlFuncIdFollow[],
                            tlActualVarParmFollow[], tlFormalParmsFollow[];
```

and delete the line

```
extern TIcode icode;
```

■■■■■■■■ **Figure 8.10** Implementation file **parsrtn1.cpp**.

```
//    ************************************************************
//    *                                                          *
//    *     P A R S E R    (Routines #1)                         *
//    *                                                          *
//    *     Parse programs, procedures, and functions.           *
//    *                                                          *
//    *     CLASSES: TParser                                     *
//    *                                                          *
//    *     FILE:    prog8-1/parsrtn1.cpp                        *
//    *                                                          *
//    *     MODULE:  Parser                                      *
//    *                                                          *
//    *     Copyright (c) 1996 by Ronald Mak                     *
//    *     For instructional purposes only.  No warranties.     *
//    *                                                          *
//    ************************************************************

#include <string.h>
#include "common.h"
#include "parser.h"


//--------------------------------------------------------------
//  ParseProgram        Parse a program:
//
//                          <program-header> ; <block> .
//
//  Return: ptr to program id's symbol table node
//--------------------------------------------------------------

TSymtabNode *TParser::ParseProgram(void)
{
    //--<program-header>
    TSymtabNode *pProgramId = ParseProgramHeader();

    //-- ;
    Resync(tlHeaderFollow, tlDeclarationStart, tlStatementStart);
    if (token == tcSemicolon) GetToken();
    else if (TokenIn(token, tlDeclarationStart) ||
            TokenIn(token, tlStatementStart)) {
        Error(errMissingSemicolon);
```

(continues)

```
    }

    //--<block>
    ParseBlock(pProgramId);
    pProgramId->defn.routine.pSymtab = symtabStack.ExitScope();

    //-- .
    Resync(tlProgramEnd);
    CondGetTokenAppend(tcPeriod, errMissingPeriod);

    return pProgramId;
}

//------------------------------------------------------------
//  ParseProgramHeader      Parse a program header:
//
//                              PROGRAM <id>
//
//                          or:
//
//                              PROGRAM <id> ( <id-list> )
//
//  Return: ptr to program id's symbol table node
//------------------------------------------------------------

TSymtabNode *TParser::ParseProgramHeader(void)
{
    TSymtabNode *pProgramId;  // ptr to program id node

    //--PROGRAM
    CondGetToken(tcPROGRAM, errMissingPROGRAM);

    //--<id>
    if (token == tcIdentifier) {
        pProgramId = EnterNewLocal(pToken->String(), dcProgram);
        pProgramId->defn.routine.which                = rcDeclared;
        pProgramId->defn.routine.parmCount            = 0;
        pProgramId->defn.routine.totalParmSize        = 0;
        pProgramId->defn.routine.totalLocalSize       = 0;
        pProgramId->defn.routine.locals.pParmIds      = NULL;
        pProgramId->defn.routine.locals.pConstantIds  = NULL;
        pProgramId->defn.routine.locals.pTypeIds      = NULL;
        pProgramId->defn.routine.locals.pVariableIds  = NULL;
        pProgramId->defn.routine.locals.pRoutineIds   = NULL;
        pProgramId->defn.routine.pSymtab              = NULL;
```

```
        pProgramId->defn.routine.pIcode              = NULL;
        SetType(pProgramId->pType, pDummyType);
        GetToken();
    }
    else Error(errMissingIdentifier);

    //-- ( or ;
    Resync(tlProgProcIdFollow, tlDeclarationStart, tlStatementStart);

    //--Enter the nesting level 1 and open a new scope for the program.
    symtabStack.EnterScope();

    //--Optional ( <id-list> )
    if (token == tcLParen) {
        TSymtabNode *pPrevParmId = NULL;

        //--Loop to parse a comma-separated identifier list.
        do {
            GetToken();
            if (token == tcIdentifier) {
                TSymtabNode *pParmId = EnterNewLocal(pToken->String(),
                                                      dcVarParm);
                SetType(pParmId->pType, pDummyType);
                GetToken();

                //--Link program parm id nodes together.
                if (!pPrevParmId) {
                    pProgramId->defn.routine.locals.pParmIds
                                       = pPrevParmId = pParmId;
                }
                else {
                    pPrevParmId->next = pParmId;
                    pPrevParmId       = pParmId;
                }
            }
            else Error(errMissingIdentifier);
        } while (token == tcComma);

        //-- )
        Resync(tlFormalParmsFollow,
               tlDeclarationStart, tlStatementStart);
        CondGetToken(tcRParen, errMissingRightParen);
    }

    return pProgramId;
}
```

(continues)

■■■■■■ **Figure 8.10** Implementation file **parsrtn1.cpp**. (*Continued*)

```
//-------------------------------------------------------------
//  ParseSubroutineDeclarations      Parse procedures and
//                                   function declarations.
//
//      pRoutineId : ptr to symbol table node of the name of the
//                   routine that contains the subroutines
//-------------------------------------------------------------

void TParser::ParseSubroutineDeclarations(TSymtabNode *pRoutineId)
{
    TSymtabNode *pLastId = NULL;   // ptr to last routine id node
                                   //   in local list

    //--Loop to parse procedure and function definitions.
    while (TokenIn(token, tlProcFuncStart)) {
        TSymtabNode *pRtnId = ParseSubroutine();

        //--Link the routine's local (nested) routine id nodes together.
        if (!pRoutineId->defn.routine.locals.pRoutineIds) {
            pRoutineId->defn.routine.locals.pRoutineIds = pRtnId;
        }
        else {
            pLastId->next = pRtnId;
        }
        pLastId = pRtnId;

        //-- ;
        Resync(tlDeclarationFollow, tlProcFuncStart, tlStatementStart);
        if (token == tcSemicolon) GetToken();
        else if (TokenIn(token, tlProcFuncStart) ||
                 TokenIn(token, tlStatementStart)) {
            Error(errMissingSemicolon);
        }
    }
}


//-------------------------------------------------------------
//  ParseSubroutine         Parse a subroutine:
//
//                              <subroutine-header> ; <block>
//
//                      or:
//
//                              <subroutine-header> ; forward
//
```

```
//   Return: ptr to subroutine id's symbol table node
//-------------------------------------------------------------

TSymtabNode *TParser::ParseSubroutine(void)
{
    //--<routine-header>
    TSymtabNode *pRoutineId = (token == tcPROCEDURE)
                                    ? ParseProcedureHeader()
                                    : ParseFunctionHeader();

    //-- ;
    Resync(tlHeaderFollow, tlDeclarationStart, tlStatementStart);
    if (token == tcSemicolon) GetToken();
    else if (TokenIn(token, tlDeclarationStart) ||
            TokenIn(token, tlStatementStart)) {
        Error(errMissingSemicolon);
    }

    //--<block> or forward
    if (stricmp(pToken->String(), "forward") != 0) {
        pRoutineId->defn.routine.which = rcDeclared;
        ParseBlock(pRoutineId);
    }
    else {
        GetToken();
        pRoutineId->defn.routine.which = rcForward;
    }

    pRoutineId->defn.routine.pSymtab = symtabStack.ExitScope();
    return pRoutineId;
}

//-------------------------------------------------------------
//  ParseProcedureHeader     Parse a procedure header:
//
//                                  PROCEDURE <id>
//
//                           or:
//
//                                  PROCEDURE <id> ( <parm-list> )
//
//  Return: ptr to procedure id's symbol table node
//-------------------------------------------------------------

TSymtabNode *TParser::ParseProcedureHeader(void)
{
```

(continues)

```cpp
TSymtabNode *pProcId;       // ptr to procedure id node
int forwardFlag = false;   // true if forwarded, false if not

GetToken();

//--<id> : If the procedure id has already been declared in
//--        this scope, it must have been a forward declaration.
if (token == tcIdentifier) {
    pProcId = SearchLocal(pToken->String());
    if (!pProcId) {

        //--Not already declared.
        pProcId = EnterLocal(pToken->String(), dcProcedure);
        pProcId->defn.routine.totalLocalSize = 0;
        SetType(pProcId->pType, pDummyType);
    }    ,
    else if ((pProcId->defn.how == dcProcedure) &&
             (pProcId->defn.routine.which == rcForward)) {

        //--Forwarded.
        forwardFlag = true;
    }
    else Error(errRedefinedIdentifier);

    GetToken();
}
else Error(errMissingIdentifier);

//-- ( or ;
Resync(tlProgProcIdFollow, tlDeclarationStart, tlStatementStart);

//--Enter the next nesting level and open a new scope
//--for the procedure.
symtabStack.EnterScope();

//--Optional ( <id-list> ) : If there was a forward declaration,
//--                          there must not be a parameter list,
//--                          but if there is, parse it anyway
//--                          for error recovery.
if (token == tcLParen) {
    int           parmCount;      // count of formal parms
    int           totalParmSize;  // total byte size of all parms
    TSymtabNode *pParmList = ParseFormalParmList(parmCount,
                                                 totalParmSize);
```

```
        if (forwardFlag) Error(errAlreadyForwarded);
        else {

            //--Not forwarded.
            pProcId->defn.routine.parmCount      = parmCount;
            pProcId->defn.routine.totalParmSize  = totalParmSize;
            pProcId->defn.routine.locals.pParmIds = pParmList;
        }
    }
    else if (!forwardFlag) {

        //--No parameters and no forward declaration.
        pProcId->defn.routine.parmCount      = 0;
        pProcId->defn.routine.totalParmSize  = 0;
        pProcId->defn.routine.locals.pParmIds = NULL;
    }

    pProcId->defn.routine.locals.pConstantIds = NULL;
    pProcId->defn.routine.locals.pTypeIds     = NULL;
    pProcId->defn.routine.locals.pVariableIds = NULL;
    pProcId->defn.routine.locals.pRoutineIds  = NULL;

    SetType(pProcId->pType, pDummyType);
    return pProcId;
}


//------------------------------------------------------------
//  ParseFunctionHeader      Parse a function header:
//
//                                  FUNCTION <id>
//
//                       or:
//
//                                  FUNCTION <id> : <type-id>
//
//                       or:
//
//                                  FUNCTION <id> ( <parm-list> )
//                                              : <type-id>
//
//  Return: ptr to function id's symbol table node
//------------------------------------------------------------

TSymtabNode *TParser::ParseFunctionHeader(void)
{
```

(continues)

```
TSymtabNode *pFuncId;      // ptr to function id node
int forwardFlag = false;   // true if forwarded, false if not

GetToken();

//--<id> : If the function id has already been declared in
//--        this scope, it must have been a forward declaration.
if (token == tcIdentifier) {
    pFuncId = SearchLocal(pToken->String());
    if (!pFuncId) {

        //--Not already declared.
        pFuncId = EnterLocal(pToken->String(), dcFunction);
        pFuncId->defn.routine.totalLocalSize = 0;
    }
    else if ((pFuncId->defn.how == dcFunction) &&
             (pFuncId->defn.routine.which == rcForward)) {

        //--Forwarded.
        forwardFlag = true;
    }
    else Error(errRedefinedIdentifier);

    GetToken();
}
else Error(errMissingIdentifier);

//-- ( or : or ;
Resync(tlFuncIdFollow, tlDeclarationStart, tlStatementStart);

//--Enter the next nesting level and open a new scope
//--for the function.
symtabStack.EnterScope();

//--Optional ( <id-list> ) : If there was a forward declaration,
//--                         there must not be a parameter list,
//--                         but if there is, parse it anyway
//--                         for error recovery.
if (token == tcLParen) {
    int          parmCount;      // count of formal parms
    int          totalParmSize;  // total byte size of all parms
    TSymtabNode *pParmList = ParseFormalParmList(parmCount,
                                                 totalParmSize);
```

```
        if (forwardFlag) Error(errAlreadyForwarded);
        else {

            //--Not forwarded.
            pFuncId->defn.routine.parmCount      = parmCount;
            pFuncId->defn.routine.totalParmSize  = totalParmSize;
            pFuncId->defn.routine.locals.pParmIds = pParmList;
        }
    }
    else if (!forwardFlag) {

        //--No parameters and no forward declaration.
        pFuncId->defn.routine.parmCount      = 0;
        pFuncId->defn.routine.totalParmSize  = 0;
        pFuncId->defn.routine.locals.pParmIds = NULL;
    }

    pFuncId->defn.routine.locals.pConstantIds = NULL;
    pFuncId->defn.routine.locals.pTypeIds     = NULL;
    pFuncId->defn.routine.locals.pVariableIds = NULL;
    pFuncId->defn.routine.locals.pRoutineIds  = NULL;

    //--Optional <type-id> : If there was a forward declaration,
    //--                     there must not be a type id, but if
    //--                     there is, parse it anyway for error
    //--                     recovery.
    if (!forwardFlag || (token == tcColon)) {
        CondGetToken(tcColon, errMissingColon);
        if (token == tcIdentifier) {
            TSymtabNode *pTypeId = Find(pToken->String());
            if (pTypeId->defn.how != dcType) Error(errInvalidType);

            if (forwardFlag) Error(errAlreadyForwarded);
            else             SetType(pFuncId->pType, pTypeId->pType);

            GetToken();
        }
        else {
            Error(errMissingIdentifier);
            SetType(pFuncId->pType, pDummyType);
        }
    }

    return pFuncId;
}
```

(continues)

■■■■■■■ **Figure 8.10** Implementation file **parsrtn1.cpp**. (*Continued*)

```
//------------------------------------------------------------
//  ParseBlock        Parse a routine's block:
//
//                         <declarations> <compound-statement>
//
//      pRoutineId : ptr to symbol table node of routine's id
//------------------------------------------------------------

void TParser::ParseBlock(TSymtabNode *pRoutineId)
{
    //--<declarations>
    ParseDeclarations(pRoutineId);

    //--<compound-statement> : Reset the icode and append BEGIN to it,
    //--                        and then parse the compound statement.
    Resync(tlStatementStart);
    if (token != tcBEGIN) Error(errMissingBEGIN);
    icode.Reset();
    ParseCompound();

    //--Set the program's or routine's icode.
    pRoutineId->defn.routine.pIcode = new TIcode(icode);
}
```

Programs

Figure 8.10 shows file `parsrtn1.cpp`, the first of two files that implement class `TParser`'s member functions for parsing routines. Member function `ParseProgram` parses a program, which, as shown in Figure 8.11, contains a program header and a block. Every Pascal routine has a header and a block. A block is simply declarations followed by a compound statement. `ParseProgram` calls member functions

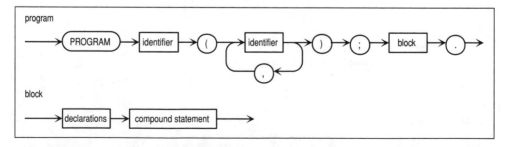

■■■■■■■ **Figure 8.11** Syntax diagrams for a program.

`ParseProgramHeader` and `ParseBlock`. `ParseBlock` will call `EnterScope`, and so `ParseProgram` calls `ExitScope`. This call also sets data member `defn.routine.pSymtab` of the routine name's symbol table node to point to the routine's local symbol table. `ParseProgram` then resynchronizes and returns a pointer to the program name's symbol table node.

Member function `ParseProgramHeader` parses a program header. After parsing the program name, it enters the identifier into the current (global) symbol table and initializes the node. The function calls `EnterScope` to create the program's local symbol table and push a pointer to it onto the symbol table stack, thus entering a new scope at nesting level 1.

If there is a formal parameter list, `ParseProgramHeader` parses the formal parameters and enters each parameter identifier into the program's local symbol table. It links the symbol table nodes together and points data member `defn.routine.locals.pParmIds` of the program name's symbol table node to the head of the list.

Procedure and Function Declarations

Figure 8.12 shows the complete syntax diagram for Pascal declarations that includes procedure and function declarations. Figure 8.13 shows the syntax diagrams for these declarations.

Member function `ParseSubroutineDeclarations` (in Figure 8.10) loops to parse procedure and function declarations. It calls member function `ParseSubroutine` to parse each procedure or function declaration, and it links together the symbol table nodes of all the subroutine names in this set of declarations. Argument `pRoutineId` points to the symbol table node of the routine in which these subroutines are declared, and the function points `pRoutineId->defn.routine.locals.pRoutineIds` to the head of this list.

`ParseSubroutine` parses a procedure or function declaration. It calls either member function `ParseProcedureHeader` or `ParseFunctionHeader` to parse the header (and call `EnterScope`), and it calls `ParseBlock` to parse the subroutine's block. Before returning, the function calls `ExitScope` and points data member `defn.routine.pSymtab` of the subroutine's symbol table node to the local symbol table.

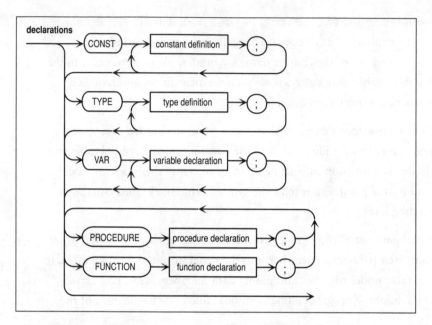

Figure 8.12 Complete syntax diagram for Pascal declarations.

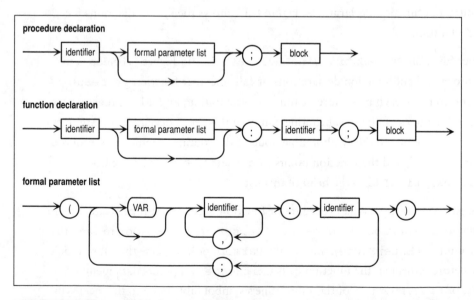

Figure 8.13 Syntax diagrams for procedure and function declarations.

ParseProcedureHeader parses a procedure header. It calls SearchLocal on the local symbol table of the routine in which the procedure is declared to look for the procedure name. If the name is not found, the function enters it into the local symbol table. If the name is found, it must have been defined previously in a forward declaration, or we have a redefinition error. After parsing the procedure name, ParseProcedureHeader calls EnterScope to create a local symbol table for the procedure and to push a pointer to it onto the symbol table stack.

Now ParseProcedureHeader is ready to parse a formal parameter list, if there is one. It calls member function ParseFormalParmList, which returns a pointer to the head of a list of the formal parameter identifiers' symbol table nodes. If there was a forward declaration, there shouldn't be a formal parameter list here, but if there is one, ParseProcedureHeader parses it anyway for error recovery. The function updates the procedure's symbol table node with the count and total size of the formal parameters and points it to the formal parameter symbol table node list. It completes the initialization of the node before returning a pointer to the procedure's symbol table node.

ParseFunctionHeader is similar to ParseProcedureHeader, except that it also parses the function type and points the function's symbol table node to the type object. It also checks that if the function name was in a previous forward declaration, the current declaration does not have a function type.

Finally, member function ParseBlock parses a routine's block by calling ParseDeclarations and ParseCompound. Before parsing the compound statement, it resets the icode object buffer, and after parsing the statement, it calls class TIcode's copy constructor to create a new icode object for the routine and to copy the icode buffer's intermediate code. ParseBlock points data member defn.routine.pIcode of the routine's symbol table node to the new icode object.

■■■■■■■ **Figure 8.14** New version of member function **TParser::ParseDeclarations** in implementation file **parsdecl.cpp**.

```
//--------------------------------------------------------------
//  ParseDeclarations    Parse any constant definitions, type
//                       definitions, variable declarations, and
//                       procedure and function declarations, in
//                       that order.
//--------------------------------------------------------------
```

(continues)

■■■■■■■■ **Figure 8.14** New version of member function **TParser::ParseDeclarations** in implementation file **parsdecl.cpp**. (*Continued*)

```cpp
void TParser::ParseDeclarations(TSymtabNode *pRoutineId)
{
    if (token == tcCONST) {
        GetToken();
        ParseConstantDefinitions(pRoutineId);
    }

    if (token == tcTYPE) {
        GetToken();
        ParseTypeDefinitions(pRoutineId);
    }

    if (token == tcVAR) {
        GetToken();
        ParseVariableDeclarations(pRoutineId);
    }

    if (TokenIn(token, tlProcFuncStart)) {
        ParseSubroutineDeclarations(pRoutineId);
    }
}
```

Figure 8.14 shows the new version of member function ParseDeclarations in implementation file parsdecl.cpp that calls ParseSubroutineDeclarations.

■■■■■■■■ **Figure 8.15** Implementation file **parsrtn2.cpp**.

```cpp
//  ****************************************************************
//  *                                                              *
//  *     P A R S E R    (Routines #2)                             *
//  *                                                              *
//  *     Parse formal parameters, procedure and function calls,   *
//  *     and actual parameters.                                   *
//  *                                                              *
//  *     CLASSES: TParser                                         *
//  *                                                              *
//  *     FILE:    prog8-1/parsrtn2.cpp                            *
//  *                                                              *
//  *     MODULE:  Parser                                          *
//  *                                                              *
//  *     Copyright (c) 1996 by Ronald Mak                         *
//  *     For instructional purposes only.  No warranties.         *
//  *                                                              *
```

```
//    ************************************************************

#include "common.h"
#include "parser.h"

//--------------------------------------------------------------
//  ParseFormalParmList     Parse a formal parameter list:
//
//                              ( VAR <id-list> : <type-id> ;
//                                <id-list> : <type-id> ;
//                                ... )
//
//      count     : ref to count of parameters
//      totalSize : ref to total byte size of all parameters
//
//  Return: ptr to head of parm id symbol table node list
//--------------------------------------------------------------

TSymtabNode *TParser::ParseFormalParmList(int &count, int &totalSize)
{
    extern int execFlag;

    TSymtabNode *pParmId;               // ptrs to parm symtab nodes
    TSymtabNode *pFirstId, *pLastId;
    TSymtabNode *pPrevSublistLastId = NULL;
    TSymtabNode *pParmList  = NULL;     // ptr to list of parm nodes
    TDefnCode    parmDefn;              // how a parm is defined

    count = totalSize = 0;
    GetToken();

    //--Loop to parse a parameter declarations separated by semicolons.
    while ((token == tcIdentifier) || (token == tcVAR)) {
        TType *pParmType;  // ptr to parm's type object

        pFirstId = NULL;

        //--VAR or value parameter?
        if (token == tcVAR) {
            parmDefn = dcVarParm;
            GetToken();
        }
        else parmDefn = dcValueParm;

        //--Loop to parse the comma-separated sublist of parameter ids.
        while (token == tcIdentifier) {
            pParmId = EnterNewLocal(pToken->String(), parmDefn);
```

(continues)

```
            ++count;
            if (!pParmList) pParmList = pParmId;

            //--Link the parm id nodes together.
            if (!pFirstId) pFirstId = pLastId = pParmId;
            else {
                pLastId->next = pParmId;
                pLastId       = pParmId;
            }

            //-- ,
            GetToken();
            Resync(tlIdentifierFollow);
            if (token == tcComma) {

                //--Saw comma.
                //--Skip extra commas and look for an identifier.
                do {
                    GetToken();
                    Resync(tlIdentifierStart, tlIdentifierFollow);
                    if (token == tcComma) {
                        Error(errMissingIdentifier);
                    }
                } while (token == tcComma);
                if (token != tcIdentifier) {
                    Error(errMissingIdentifier);
                }
            }
            else if (token == tcIdentifier) Error(errMissingComma);
        }

        //-- :
        Resync(tlSublistFollow, tlDeclarationFollow);
        CondGetToken(tcColon, errMissingColon);

        //--<type-id>
        if (token == tcIdentifier) {
            TSymtabNode *pTypeId = Find(pToken->String());
            if (pTypeId->defn.how != dcType) Error(errInvalidType);
            pParmType = pTypeId->pType;
            GetToken();
        }
        else {
            Error(errMissingIdentifier);
```

```
            pParmType = pDummyType;
        }

        if (execFlag) {
            //--Loop to assign the offset and type to each
            //--parm id in the sublist.
            for (pParmId = pFirstId; pParmId; pParmId = pParmId->next) {
                pParmId->defn.data.offset = totalSize++;
                SetType(pParmId->pType, pParmType);
            }
        }

        //--Link this sublist to the previous sublist.
        if (pPrevSublistLastId) pPrevSublistLastId->next = pFirstId;
        pPrevSublistLastId = pLastId;

        //-- ; or )
        Resync(tlFormalParmsFollow, tlDeclarationFollow);
        if ((token == tcIdentifier) || (token == tcVAR)) {
            Error(errMissingSemicolon);
        }
        else while (token == tcSemicolon) GetToken();
    }

    //-- )
    CondGetToken(tcRParen, errMissingRightParen);

    return pParmList;
}

//-------------------------------------------------------------
//  ParseSubroutineCall     Parse a call to a declared or a
//                          standard procedure or function.
//
//      pRoutineId    : ptr to routine id's symbol table node
//      parmCheckFlag : true to check parameter, false not to
//
//  Return: ptr to the subroutine's type object
//-------------------------------------------------------------

TType *TParser::ParseSubroutineCall(const TSymtabNode *pRoutineId,
                                    int parmCheckFlag)
{
    GetTokenAppend();

    return (pRoutineId->defn.routine.which == rcDeclared) ||
```

(continues)

■■■■■■ **Figure 8.15** Implementation file **parsrtn2.cpp**. (*Continued*)

```
                (pRoutineId->defn.routine.which == rcForward)  ||
                !parmCheckFlag
                    ? ParseDeclaredSubroutineCall(pRoutineId, parmCheckFlag)
                    : ParseStandardSubroutineCall(pRoutineId);
}


//--------------------------------------------------------------
//  ParseDeclaredSubroutineCall Parse a call to a declared
//                              procedure or function.
//
//      pRoutineId    : ptr to subroutine id's symbol table node
//      parmCheckFlag : true to check parameter, false not to
//
//  Return: ptr to the subroutine's type object
//--------------------------------------------------------------

TType *TParser::ParseDeclaredSubroutineCall
                                (const TSymtabNode *pRoutineId,
                                 int parmCheckFlag)
{
    ParseActualParmList(pRoutineId, parmCheckFlag);
    return pRoutineId->pType;
}


//--------------------------------------------------------------
//  ParseActualParmList      Parse an actual parameter list:
//
//                              ( <expr-list> )
//
//      pRoutineId    : ptr to routine id's symbol table node
//      parmCheckFlag : true to check parameter, false not to
//--------------------------------------------------------------

void TParser::ParseActualParmList(const TSymtabNode *pRoutineId,
                                  int parmCheckFlag)
{
    TSymtabNode *pFormalId = pRoutineId ? pRoutineId->defn.routine.
                                                    locals.pParmIds
                                        : NULL;

    //--If there are no actual parameters, there better not be
    //--any formal parameters either.
    if (token != tcLParen) {
        if (parmCheckFlag && pFormalId) Error(errWrongNumberOfParms);
        return;
    }
```

```
    //--Loop to parse actual parameter expressions
    //--separated by commas.
    do {
        //-- ( or ,
        GetTokenAppend();

        ParseActualParm(pFormalId, parmCheckFlag);
        if (pFormalId) pFormalId = pFormalId->next;
    } while (token == tcComma);

    //-- )
    CondGetTokenAppend(tcRParen, errMissingRightParen);

    //--There better not be any more formal parameters.
    if (parmCheckFlag && pFormalId) Error(errWrongNumberOfParms);
}

//--------------------------------------------------------------
//  ParseActualParm      Parse an actual parameter.  Make sure it
//                       matches the corresponding formal parm.
//
//      pFormalId      : ptr to the corresponding formal parm
//                       id's symbol table node
//      parmCheckFlag  : true to check parameter, false not to
//--------------------------------------------------------------

void TParser::ParseActualParm(const TSymtabNode *pFormalId,
                              int parmCheckFlag)
{
    //--If we're not checking the actual parameters against
    //--the corresponding formal parameters (as during error
    //--recovery), just parse the actual parameter.
    if (!parmCheckFlag) {
        ParseExpression();
        return;
    }

    //--If we've already run out of formal parameter,
    //--we have an error.  Go into error recovery mode and
    //--parse the actual parameter anyway.
    if (!pFormalId) {
        Error(errWrongNumberOfParms);
        ParseExpression();
        return;
    }
```

(continues)

■■■■■■■ **Figure 8.15** Implementation file **parsrtn2.cpp**. (*Continued*)

```
//--Formal value parameter: The actual parameter can be an
//--                        arbitrary expression that is
//--                        assignment type compatible with
//--                        the formal parameter.
if (pFormalId->defn.how == dcValueParm) {
    CheckAssignmentTypeCompatible(pFormalId->pType,
                                  ParseExpression(),
                                  errIncompatibleTypes);
}

//--Formal VAR parameter: The actual parameter must be a
//--                      variable of the same type as the
//--                      formal parameter.
else if (token == tcIdentifier) {
    TSymtabNode *pActualId = Find(pToken->String());
    icode.Put(pActualId);

    if (pFormalId->pType != ParseVariable(pActualId)) {
        Error(errIncompatibleTypes);
    }
    Resync(tlExpressionFollow, tlStatementFollow, tlStatementStart);
}

//--Error: Parse the actual parameter anyway for error recovery.
else {
    ParseExpression();
    Error(errInvalidVarParm);
}
}
```

Formal Parameters

Figure 8.15 shows file parsrtn2.cpp, the second file that implements class
TParser's member functions that parse routines. Member function ParseFormalParmList has an outer loop to parse each sublist of parameters that have the
same definition (value or VAR) and type. The inner loop parses each parameter name
in a sublist. It enters each name into the subroutine's local symbol table with a call
to EnterNewLocal and links the symbol table nodes of the sublist together. After
the inner loop, the outer loop parses the sublist's type, points each symbol table
node in the sublist to the type object, and then links the sublist to the end of the previous one. ParseFormalParmList returns a pointer to the head of the symbol
table node list.

Parsing Procedure and Function Calls

A Pascal program can call both declared and predefined standard procedures and functions. We'll handle calls to standard subroutines in a separate implementation file, since they follow a different set of rules for parameter type and number. Member function `ParseSubroutineCall` decides whether to call member function `ParseDeclaredSubroutineCall` or `ParseStandardSubroutineCall`. Argument `parmCheckFlag` indicates whether or not the actual parameters should be checked. It is false whenever a subroutine call is parsed during error recovery. Figure 8.16 shows the syntax diagram for a call to a declared subroutine.

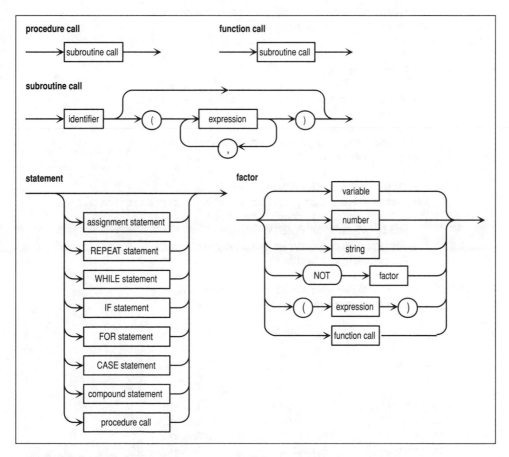

■■■■ **Figure 8.16** Syntax diagrams for a call to a declared procedure or function.

ParseDeclaredSubroutineCall (in Figure 8.15) calls member function
ParseActualParmList to parse the list of actual parameters. It returns a pointer
to the subroutine's type object (which is the dummy type object for a procedure).

■■■■■■■ **Figure 8.17** New version of member function **TParser::ParseStatement** in
implementation file **parsstmt.cpp**.

```
//------------------------------------------------------------
//  ParseStatement          Parse a statement.
//------------------------------------------------------------

void TParser::ParseStatement(void)
{
    InsertLineMarker();

    //--Call the appropriate parsing function based on
    //--the statement's first token.
    switch (token) {

        case tcIdentifier: {

            //--Search for the identifier and enter it if
            //--necessary.  Append the symbol table node handle
            //--to the icode.
            TSymtabNode *pNode = Find(pToken->String());
            icode.Put(pNode);

            //--Based on how the identifier is defined,
            //--parse an assignment statement or a procedure call.
            if (pNode->defn.how == dcUndefined) {
                pNode->defn.how = dcVariable;
                SetType(pNode->pType, pDummyType);
                ParseAssignment(pNode);
            }
            else if (pNode->defn.how == dcProcedure) {
                ParseSubroutineCall(pNode, true);
            }
            else ParseAssignment(pNode);

            break;
        }

        case tcREPEAT:      ParseREPEAT();      break;
        case tcWHILE:       ParseWHILE();       break;
        case tcIF:          ParseIF();          break;
        case tcFOR:         ParseFOR();         break;
```

```
        case tcCASE:        ParseCASE();        break;
        case tcBEGIN:       ParseCompound();    break;
    }

    //--Resynchronize at a proper statement ending.
    if (token != tcEndOfFile) {
        Resync(tlStatementFollow, tlStatementStart);
    }
}
```

Figure 8.17 shows a new version of member function `ParseStatement` in implementation file `parsstmt.cpp`. If the lead token of a statement is an identifier, the function must determine, based on how the identifier was defined, whether to call `ParseAssignment` or `ParseSubroutineCall`. Figure 8.18 shows the new version of `ParseAssignment` in the same file. It now requires an argument, a pointer to the target identifier's symbol table node. Some of the work that it used to do is now done by `ParseStatement`.

■■■■■■ **Figure 8.18** New version of member function **TParser::ParseAssignment** in implementation file **parsstmt.cpp**.

```
//-------------------------------------------------------------
//   ParseAssignment          Parse an assignment statement:
//
//                                  <id> := <expr>
//
//       pTargetId : ptr to target id's symbol table node
//-------------------------------------------------------------

void TParser::ParseAssignment(const TSymtabNode *pTargetId)
{
    TType *pTargetType = ParseVariable(pTargetId);

    //-- :=
    Resync(tlColonEqual, tlExpressionStart);
    CondGetTokenAppend(tcColonEqual, errMissingColonEqual);

    //--<expr>
    TType *pExprType = ParseExpression();

    //--Check for assignment compatibility.
    CheckAssignmentTypeCompatible(pTargetType, pExprType,
                                  errIncompatibleAssignment);
}
```

(continues)

Figure 8.19 shows the identifier case of the new version of member function ParseFactor in implementation file parsexpr.cpp. It now needs to recognize a function call. Depending on how the identifier is defined, it calls either ParseSubroutineCall or ParseVariable.

■■■■■■■■■■ **Figure 8.19** The **identifier** case in the new version of member function **TParser::ParseFactor** in implementation file **parsexpr.cpp**.

```cpp
case tcIdentifier: {

    //--Search for the identifier and enter it if
    //--necessary.  Append the symbol table node handle
    //--to the icode.
    TSymtabNode *pNode = Find(pToken->String());
    icode.Put(pNode);

    if (pNode->defn.how == dcUndefined) {
        pNode->defn.how = dcVariable;
        SetType(pNode->pType, pDummyType);
    }

    //--Based on how the identifier is defined,
    //--parse a constant, function call, or variable.
    switch (pNode->defn.how) {

        case dcFunction:
            pResultType = ParseSubroutineCall(pNode, true);
            break;

        case dcProcedure:
            Error(errInvalidIdentifierUsage);
            pResultType = ParseSubroutineCall(pNode, false);
            break;

        case dcConstant:
            GetTokenAppend();
            pResultType = pNode->pType;
            break;

        default:
            pResultType = ParseVariable(pNode);
            break;
    }

    break;
}
```

Actual Parameters

As shown in Figure 8.15, member function `ParseActualParmList` first verifies that if the call has no actual parameters, then subroutine also has no formal parameters. If there are actual parameters, it loops to parse each parameter by calling member function `ParseActualParm`, passing a pointer to the symbol table node of the corresponding formal parameter. Before returning, the function checks that the number of actual parameters matches the number of formal parameters.

`ParseActualParm` first checks if there are more actual parameters than formal parameters. Then, if the formal parameter is a value parameter, it verifies that the actual parameter is assignment type compatible with the formal parameter. If the formal parameter is a `VAR` parameter, the actual parameter must be a variable of the same type. If there's a problem, `ParseActualParm` calls `ParseExpression` for error recovery.

■■■■■■■■ **Figure 8.20** Implementation file **parsstd.cpp** for the standard procedures and functions.

```
//    ****************************************************************
//    *                                                            *
//    *    P A R S E R    (Standard Routines)                      *
//    *                                                            *
//    *    Parse calls to standard procedures and functions.       *
//    *                                                            *
//    *    CLASSES: TParser                                        *
//    *                                                            *
//    *    FILE:    prog8-1/parsstd.cpp                            *
//    *                                                            *
//    *    MODULE:  Parser                                         *
//    *                                                            *
//    *    Copyright (c) 1996 by Ronald Mak                        *
//    *    For instructional purposes only.  No warranties.        *
//    *                                                            *
//    ****************************************************************

#include "common.h"
#include "parser.h"


//------------------------------------------------------------
//  ParseStandardSubroutineCall     Parse a call to a standard
//                                  procedure or function.
//
```

(continues)

━━━━━━━━ **Figure 8.20** Implementation file **parsstd.cpp** for the standard procedures
and functions. (*Continued*)

```
//      pRoutineId : ptr to the subroutine id's
//                   symbol table node
//
// Return: ptr to the type object of the call
//------------------------------------------------------------

TType *TParser::ParseStandardSubroutineCall
                                (const TSymtabNode *pRoutineId)
{
    switch (pRoutineId->defn.routine.which) {

        case rcRead:
        case rcReadln:  return(ParseReadReadlnCall(pRoutineId));

        case rcWrite:
        case rcWriteln: return(ParseWriteWritelnCall(pRoutineId));

        case rcEof:
        case rcEoln:    return(ParseEofEolnCall());

        case rcAbs:
        case rcSqr:     return(ParseAbsSqrCall());

        case rcArctan:
        case rcCos:
        case rcExp:
        case rcLn:
        case rcSin:
        case rcSqrt:    return(ParseArctanCosExpLnSinSqrtCall());

        case rcPred:
        case rcSucc:    return(ParsePredSuccCall());

        case rcChr:     return(ParseChrCall());
        case rcOdd:     return(ParseOddCall());
        case rcOrd:     return(ParseOrdCall());

        case rcRound:
        case rcTrunc:   return(ParseRoundTruncCall());

        default:        return(pDummyType);
    }
}
```

```
//-------------------------------------------------------------
// ParseReadReadlnCall      Parse a call to read or readln.
//                          Each actual parameter must be a
//                          scalar variable.
//
//      pRoutineId : ptr to the routine id's symbol table node
//
// Return: ptr to the dummy type object
//-------------------------------------------------------------

TType *TParser::ParseReadReadlnCall(const TSymtabNode *pRoutineId)
{
    //--Actual parameters are optional for readln.
    if (token != tcLParen) {
        if (pRoutineId->defn.routine.which == rcRead) {
            Error(errWrongNumberOfParms);
        }
        return pDummyType;
    }

    //--Loop to parse comma-separated list of actual parameters.
    do {
        //-- ( or ,
        GetTokenAppend();

        //--Each actual parameter must be a scalar variable,
        //--but parse an expression anyway for error recovery.
        if (token == tcIdentifier) {
            TSymtabNode *pParmId = Find(pToken->String());
            icode.Put(pParmId);

            if (ParseVariable(pParmId)->Base()->form
                        != fcScalar) Error(errIncompatibleTypes);
        }
        else {
            ParseExpression();
            Error(errInvalidVarParm);
        }

        //-- , or )
        Resync(tlActualVarParmFollow,
               tlStatementFollow, tlStatementStart);
    } while (token == tcComma);

    //-- )
    CondGetTokenAppend(tcRParen, errMissingRightParen);
```

(continues)

■■■■■■■■ **Figure 8.20** Implementation file **parsstd.cpp** for the standard procedures and functions. (*Continued*)

```
        return pDummyType;
}

//--------------------------------------------------------------
//  ParseWriteWritelnCall    Parse a call to write or writeln.
//                           Each actual parameter can be in any
//                           one of the following forms:
//
//                                    <expr>
//                                    <expr> : <expr>
//                                    <expr> : <expr> : <expr>
//
//      pRoutineId : ptr to the routine id's symbol table node
//
//  Return: ptr to the dummy type object
//--------------------------------------------------------------

TType *TParser::ParseWriteWritelnCall(const TSymtabNode *pRoutineId)
{
    //--Actual parameters are optional only for writeln.
    if (token != tcLParen) {
        if (pRoutineId->defn.routine.which == rcWrite) {
            Error(errWrongNumberOfParms);
        }
        return pDummyType;
    }

    //--Loop to parse comma-separated list of actual parameters.
    do {
        //-- ( or ,
        GetTokenAppend();

        //--Value <expr> : The type must be either a non-Boolean
        //--               scalar or a string.
        TType *pActualType = ParseExpression()->Base();
        if (   ((pActualType->form != fcScalar) ||
                (pActualType == pBooleanType))
            && ((pActualType->form != fcArray)  ||
                (pActualType->array.pElmtType != pCharType)) ) {
            Error(errIncompatibleTypes);
        }

        //--Optional field width <expr>
```

```
        if (token == tcColon) {
            GetTokenAppend();
            if (ParseExpression()->Base() != pIntegerType) {
                Error(errIncompatibleTypes);
            }

            //--Optional precision <expr>
            if (token == tcColon) {
                GetTokenAppend();
                if (ParseExpression()->Base() != pIntegerType) {
                    Error(errIncompatibleTypes);
                }
            }
        }
    } while (token == tcComma);

    //-- )
    CondGetTokenAppend(tcRParen, errMissingRightParen);

    return pDummyType;
}


//-------------------------------------------------------------
//  ParseEofEolnCall      Parse a call to eof or eoln.
//                        No parameters => boolean result
//
//  Return: ptr to the boolean type object
//-------------------------------------------------------------

TType *TParser::ParseEofEolnCall(void)
{
    //--There should be no actual parameters, but parse
    //--them anyway for error recovery.
    if (token == tcLParen) {
        Error(errWrongNumberOfParms);
        ParseActualParmList(NULL, 0);
    }

    return pBooleanType;
}


//-------------------------------------------------------------
//  ParseAbsSqrCall       Parse a call to abs or sqr.
//                        Integer parm => integer result
//                        Real parm    => real result
//
```

(continues)

```
//  Return: ptr to the result's type object
//-------------------------------------------------------------

TType *TParser::ParseAbsSqrCall(void)
{
    TType *pResultType;  // ptr to result type object

    //--There should be one integer or real parameter.
    if (token == tcLParen) {
        GetTokenAppend();

        TType *pParmType = ParseExpression()->Base();
        if ((pParmType != pIntegerType) && (pParmType != pRealType)) {
            Error(errIncompatibleTypes);
            pResultType = pIntegerType;
        }
        else pResultType = pParmType;

        //--There better not be any more parameters.
        if (token != tcRParen) SkipExtraParms();

        //-- )
        CondGetTokenAppend(tcRParen, errMissingRightParen);
    }
    else Error(errWrongNumberOfParms);

    return pResultType;
}

//-------------------------------------------------------------
//  ParseArctanCosExpLnSinSqrtCall  Parse a call to arctan, cos,
//                                  exp, ln, sin, or sqrt.
//                                  Integer parm => real result
//                                  Real parm    => real result
//
//  Return: ptr to the real type object
//-------------------------------------------------------------

TType *TParser::ParseArctanCosExpLnSinSqrtCall(void)
{
    //--There should be one integer or real parameter.
    if (token == tcLParen) {
        GetTokenAppend();
```

```
        TType *pParmType = ParseExpression()->Base();
        if ((pParmType != pIntegerType) && (pParmType != pRealType)) {
            Error(errIncompatibleTypes);
        }

        //--There better not be any more parameters.
        if (token != tcRParen) SkipExtraParms();

        //-- )
        CondGetTokenAppend(tcRParen, errMissingRightParen);
    }
    else Error(errWrongNumberOfParms);

    return pRealType;
}


//-------------------------------------------------------------
//  ParsePredSuccCall    Parse a call to pred or succ.
//                       Integer parm => integer result
//                       Enum parm    => enum result
//
//  Return: ptr to the result's type object
//-------------------------------------------------------------

TType *TParser::ParsePredSuccCall(void)
{
    TType *pResultType;  // ptr to result type object

    //--There should be one integer or enumeration parameter.
    if (token == tcLParen) {
        GetTokenAppend();

        TType *pParmType = ParseExpression()->Base();
        if ((pParmType != pIntegerType) &&
            (pParmType->form != fcEnum)) {
            Error(errIncompatibleTypes);
            pResultType = pIntegerType;
        }
        else pResultType = pParmType;

        //--There better not be any more parameters.
        if (token != tcRParen) SkipExtraParms();

        //-- )
        CondGetTokenAppend(tcRParen, errMissingRightParen);
    }
```

(continues)

■■■■■■■■ **Figure 8.20** Implementation file **parsstd.cpp** for the standard procedures
and functions. (*Continued*)

```
        else Error(errWrongNumberOfParms);

        return pResultType;
    }


//----------------------------------------------------------
//  ParseChrCall         Parse a call to chr.
//                       Integer parm => character result
//
//  Return: ptr to the character type object
//----------------------------------------------------------

TType *TParser::ParseChrCall(void)
{
    //--There should be one character parameter.
    if (token == tcLParen) {
        GetTokenAppend();

        TType *pParmType = ParseExpression()->Base();
        if (pParmType != pIntegerType) Error(errIncompatibleTypes);

        //--There better not be any more parameters.
        if (token != tcRParen) SkipExtraParms();

        //-- )
        CondGetTokenAppend(tcRParen, errMissingRightParen);
    }
    else Error(errWrongNumberOfParms);

    return pCharType;
}


//----------------------------------------------------------
//  ParseOddCall         Parse a call to odd.
//                       Integer parm => boolean result
//
//  Return: ptr to the boolean type object
//----------------------------------------------------------

TType *TParser::ParseOddCall(void)
{
    //--There should be one integer parameter.
    if (token == tcLParen) {
```

```
        GetTokenAppend();

        TType *pParmType = ParseExpression()->Base();
        if (pParmType != pIntegerType) Error(errIncompatibleTypes);

        //--There better not be any more parameters.
        if (token != tcRParen) SkipExtraParms();

        //-- )
        CondGetTokenAppend(tcRParen, errMissingRightParen);
    }
    else Error(errWrongNumberOfParms);

    return pBooleanType;
}

//--------------------------------------------------------------
//  ParseOrdCall       Parse a call to ord.
//                     Character parm => integer result
//                     Enum parm      => integer result
//
//  Return: ptr to the integer type object
//--------------------------------------------------------------

TType *TParser::ParseOrdCall(void)
{
    //--There should be one character or enumeration parameter.
    if (token == tcLParen) {
        GetTokenAppend();

        TType *pParmType = ParseExpression()->Base();
        if ((pParmType != pCharType) && (pParmType->form != fcEnum)) {
            Error(errIncompatibleTypes);
        }

        //--There better not be any more parameters.
        if (token != tcRParen) SkipExtraParms();

        //-- )
        CondGetTokenAppend(tcRParen, errMissingRightParen);
    }
    else Error(errWrongNumberOfParms);

    return pIntegerType;
}
```

(continues)

■■■■■■ **Figure 8.20** Implementation file **parsstd.cpp** for the standard procedures and functions. (*Continued*)

```cpp
//----------------------------------------------------------
//  ParseRoundTruncCall       Parse a call to round or trunc.
//                            Real parm => integer result
//
//  Return: ptr to the integer type object
//----------------------------------------------------------

TType *TParser::ParseRoundTruncCall(void)
{
    //--There should be one real parameter.
    if (token == tcLParen) {
        GetTokenAppend();

        TType *pParmType = ParseExpression()->Base();
        if (pParmType != pRealType) Error(errIncompatibleTypes);

        //--There better not be any more parameters.
        if (token != tcRParen) SkipExtraParms();

        //-- )
        CondGetTokenAppend(tcRParen, errMissingRightParen);
    }
    else Error(errWrongNumberOfParms);

    return pIntegerType;
}


//----------------------------------------------------------
//  SkipExtraParms        Skip extra parameters in a call to a
//                        standard procedure or function.
//
//      pSymtab : ptr to symbol table
//----------------------------------------------------------

void TParser::SkipExtraParms(void)
{
    Error(errWrongNumberOfParms);

    while (token == tcComma) {
        GetTokenAppend();
        ParseExpression();
    }
}
```

```
//-------------------------------------------------------------
// InitializeStandardRoutines  Initialize the standard
//                             routines by entering their
//                             identifiers into the symbol
//                             table.
//
//     pSymtab : ptr to symbol table
//-------------------------------------------------------------

static struct TStdRtn {
    char          *pName;
    TRoutineCode  rc;
    TDefnCode     dc;
} stdRtnList[] = {
    {"read",    rcRead,    dcProcedure},
    {"readln",  rcReadln,  dcProcedure},
    {"write",   rcWrite,   dcProcedure},
    {"writeln", rcWriteln, dcProcedure},
    {"abs",     rcAbs,     dcFunction},
    {"arctan",  rcArctan,  dcFunction},
    {"chr",     rcChr,     dcFunction},
    {"cos",     rcCos,     dcFunction},
    {"eof",     rcEof,     dcFunction},
    {"eoln",    rcEoln,    dcFunction},
    {"exp",     rcExp,     dcFunction},
    {"ln",      rcLn,      dcFunction},
    {"odd",     rcOdd,     dcFunction},
    {"ord",     rcOrd,     dcFunction},
    {"pred",    rcPred,    dcFunction},
    {"round",   rcRound,   dcFunction},
    {"sin",     rcSin,     dcFunction},
    {"sqr",     rcSqr,     dcFunction},
    {"sqrt",    rcSqrt,    dcFunction},
    {"succ",    rcSucc,    dcFunction},
    {"trunc",   rcTrunc,   dcFunction},
    {NULL},
};

void InitializeStandardRoutines(TSymtab *pSymtab)
{
    int i = 0;

    do {
        TStdRtn     *pSR       = &stdRtnList[i];
        TSymtabNode *pRoutineId = pSymtab->Enter(pSR->pName, pSR->dc);
```

(continues)

```
        pRoutineId->defn.routine.which                = pSR->rc;
        pRoutineId->defn.routine.parmCount            = 0;
        pRoutineId->defn.routine.totalParmSize        = 0;
        pRoutineId->defn.routine.totalLocalSize       = 0;
        pRoutineId->defn.routine.locals.pParmIds      = NULL;
        pRoutineId->defn.routine.locals.pConstantIds  = NULL;
        pRoutineId->defn.routine.locals.pTypeIds      = NULL;
        pRoutineId->defn.routine.locals.pVariableIds  = NULL;
        pRoutineId->defn.routine.locals.pRoutineIds   = NULL;
        pRoutineId->defn.routine.pSymtab              = NULL;
        pRoutineId->defn.routine.pIcode               = NULL;
        SetType(pRoutineId->pType, pDummyType);
    } while (stdRtnList[++i].pName);
}
```

Standard Procedures and Functions

Pascal has a number of standard subroutines that are predefined at the global nesting level 0 for every program. Figure 8.20 shows implementation file
parsstd.cpp.

The standard subroutines are somewhat *nonstandard* in the way calls are made to
them! Some of them (like read) take a variable number of parameters. Two of
them, write and writeln, have optional colon-separated field width and precision expressions after each parameter. Still others (like abs) take either an integer or
real parameter and return a value of the same type as the parameter. Therefore, we
resort to having a number of *ad hoc* member functions to parse calls to the standard
subroutines.

Recall that the constructor function for the symbol table stack class TSymtab-
Stack calls function InitializeStandardRoutines to enter their names into
the global symbol table (see Figure 8.6). This global function (at the end of file
parsstd.cpp) uses a table to enter the names of all the standard subroutines into
the global symbol table and to initialize their symbol table nodes. Member function
ParseStandardSubroutineCall (at the beginning of the file) calls the appropriate parsing function based on these symbol table nodes.

Member function `ParseReadReadlnCall` parses a call to `read` or `readln`. Any actual parameters must be variables. Member function `ParseWriteWritelnCall`, which parses calls to `write` or `writeln`, is similar, except that the actual parameters can be arbitrary expressions, and each argument can be followed by a field width expression and a precision expression separated by colons.

The remaining member functions are short and fairly straightforward. `ParseAbsSqrCall` returns a value that is the same type as its actual parameter (integer or real), as does `ParsePredSuccCall` (integer or enumeration). `ParseOrdCall` takes either a character or an enumeration actual parameter, and always returns an integer result. Member function `SkipExtraParms` is called by the other functions to flag and skip over any extra actual parameters during error recovery.

Program 8-1: Syntax Checker III

This chapter's first utility program uses our nearly complete front end to syntax-check entire Pascal programs (except for the features that we don't implement in this book, such as pointer types, variant records, statement labels, and GOTO statements). Figure 8.21 shows the main file synchek3.cpp. We already saw an example of its output in Figure 8.1.

▬▬▬ **Figure 8.21** Main file **synchek3.cpp** of the Syntax Checker III utility program.

```
//  *********************************************************
//  *                                                       *
//  *    Program 8-1: Syntax Checker III                    *
//  *                                                       *
//  *    Check the syntax of a complete Pascal program.     *
//  *                                                       *
//  *    FILE:    prog8-1/synchek3.cpp                      *
//  *                                                       *
//  *    USAGE:   synchek3 <source file>                    *
//  *                                                       *
//  *             <source file>  name of the source file    *
//  *                                                       *
//  *    Copyright (c) 1996 by Ronald Mak                   *
//  *    For instructional purposes only.  No warranties.   *
//  *                                                       *
//  *********************************************************
```

(continues)

■■■■■■ **Figure 8.21** Main file **synchek3.cpp** of the Syntax Checker III utility program. (*Continued*)

```cpp
#include <iostream.h>
#include "error.h"
#include "buffer.h"
#include "parser.h"

//------------------------------------------------------------
//  main
//------------------------------------------------------------

void main(int argc, char *argv[])
{
    //--Check the command line arguments.
    if (argc != 2) {
        cerr << "Usage: synchek3 <source file>" << endl;
        AbortTranslation(abortInvalidCommandLineArgs);
    }

    //--Create the parser for the source file,
    //--and then parse the file.
    TParser *pParser = new TParser(new TSourceBuffer(argv[1]));
    pParser->Parse();
    delete pParser;
}
```

Table 8.1 shows the modules and files for the Syntax Checker III utility program.

Program 8-2: Pascal Pretty-Printer

Before we leave the front end and begin work on the interpreter's back end, let's write one more utility program. This utility, Pascal Pretty-Printer, reads in a Pascal source program and prints it out in a "pretty" format, in which all the lines are indented in a consistent way that reflects the structure of the program. (Like beauty, prettiness is in the eye of the programmer. We'll leave it as an exercise for the reader to modify this utility program to attain true prettiness.)

The utility will do all of its reformatting in the back end. In effect, it recreates the source program from the information in the symbol table objects and the icode objects. Therefore, it also helps verify that the front end has done its job correctly, in preparation for our work starting in the next chapter on the back end.

■■■■■■■ **Table 8.1** Modules and Files of Program 8-1

Module	File	Status	Directory
Main	synchek3.cpp	*new*	prog8-1
Parser	parser.h	*changed*	prog8-1
	parser.cpp	*changed*	prog8-1
	parsrtn1.cpp	*new*	prog8-1
	parsrtn2.cpp	*new*	prog8-1
	parsstd.cpp	*new*	prog8-1
	parsdecl.cpp	*changed*	prog8-1
	parstyp1.cpp	*unchanged*	prog7-1
	parstyp2.cpp	*unchanged*	prog7-1
	parsstmt.cpp	*changed*	prog8-1
	parsexpr.cpp	*changed*	prog8-1
Intermediate code	icode.h	*unchanged*	prog5-2
	icode.cpp	*unchanged*	prog5-2
Scanner	scanner.h	*unchanged*	prog3-1
	scanner.cpp	*unchanged*	prog3-2
	token.h	*unchanged*	prog4-2
	tknword.cpp	*unchanged*	prog3-2
	tknnum.cpp	*unchanged*	prog3-2
	tknstrsp.cpp	*unchanged*	prog3-2
Symbol table	types.h	*unchanged*	prog7-1
	types.cpp	*unchanged*	prog7-1
	symtab.h	*changed*	prog8-1
	symtab.cpp	*changed*	prog8-1
Error	error.h	*unchanged*	prog5-2
	error.cpp	*unchanged*	prog5-2
Buffer	buffer.h	*unchanged*	prog2-1
	buffer.cpp	*unchanged*	prog2-1
Common	common.h	*changed*	prog8-1
	common.cpp	*changed*	prog8-1
	misc.h	*unchanged*	prog3-2

■■■■■■

To implement the pretty-printer, we'll create a new proto–back end module in which we introduce the new class `TPrettyPrinter`, derived from the back end class `TBackend`, and the new class `TPrettyListBuffer`, derived from the text output buffer class `TTextOutBuffer`. Table 8.2 shows the new and changed source files.

■■■■■■ **Table 8.2** Modules and Files of Program 8-2

Module	File	Status	Directory
Main	pprint.cpp	*new*	prog8-2
Parser	parser.h	*unchanged*	prog8-1
	parser.cpp	*changed*	prog8-2
	parsrtn1.cpp	*unchanged*	prog8-1
	parsrtn2.cpp	*unchanged*	prog8-1
	parsstd.cpp	*unchanged*	prog8-1
	parsdecl.cpp	*unchanged*	prog8-1
	parstyp1.cpp	*unchanged*	prog7-1
	parstyp2.cpp	*unchanged*	prog7-1
	parsstmt.cpp	*unchanged*	prog8-1
	parsexpr.cpp	*unchanged*	prog8-1
Back end	backend.h	*changed*	prog8-2
	exec.h	*not used*	
	exec.cpp	*not used*	
	execstmt.cpp	*not used*	
	execexpr.cpp	*not used*	
"Proto Back end"	pprint.h	*new*	prog8-2
	pprtn.cpp	*new*	prog8-2
	ppdecl.cpp	*new*	prog8-2
	ppstmt.cpp	*new*	prog8-2
	pretlist.h	*new*	prog8-2
	pretlist.cpp	*new*	prog8-2
Intermediate code	icode.h	*unchanged*	prog5-2
	icode.cpp	*unchanged*	prog5-2
Scanner	scanner.h	*unchanged*	prog3-1
	scanner.cpp	*unchanged*	prog3-2
	token.h	*unchanged*	prog4-2

■■■■■■■ **Table 8.2** Modules and Files of Program 8-2 (*Continued*)

Module	File	Status	Directory
	tknword.cpp	*unchanged*	prog3-2
	tknnum.cpp	*unchanged*	prog3-2
	tknstrsp.cpp	*unchanged*	prog3-2
Symbol table	types.h	*unchanged*	prog7-1
	types.cpp	*unchanged*	prog7-1
	symtab.h	*unchanged*	prog8-1
	symtab.cpp	*unchanged*	prog8-1
Error	error.h	*unchanged*	prog5-2
	error.cpp	*unchanged*	prog5-2
Buffer	buffer.h	*unchanged*	prog2-1
	buffer.cpp	*unchanged*	prog2-1
Common	common.h	*unchanged*	prog8-1
	common.cpp	*unchanged*	prog8-1
	misc.h	*unchanged*	prog3-2

Figure 8.22 shows the class diagrams. Class `TPrettyPrinter` has member functions to pretty-print the various parts of a Pascal program.

Class `TPrettyListBuffer` is derived from class `TTextOutBuffer`. Its private data member `margin` keeps track of the current left margin, in terms of the number of spaces from the left edge, and private data member `textLength` is the length of an output line. Public member functions `Put` and `PutLine` print to the list file. Member functions `Indent` and `Dedent` move the left margin right and left, respectively. Member function `SetMargin` sets the margin at the current print position and returns the previous margin. Member function `ResetMargin` sets the margin to its argument value, which is generally the value returned by an earlier call to `SetMargin`. These latter two functions are useful for keeping text aligned over several lines, such as a long formal parameter list.

Class `TPrettyPrinter` is derived from class `TBackend`. Its private data member `pPretty` points to a `TPrettyListBuffer` object, and it has a number of private member functions to pretty-print a Pascal source program.

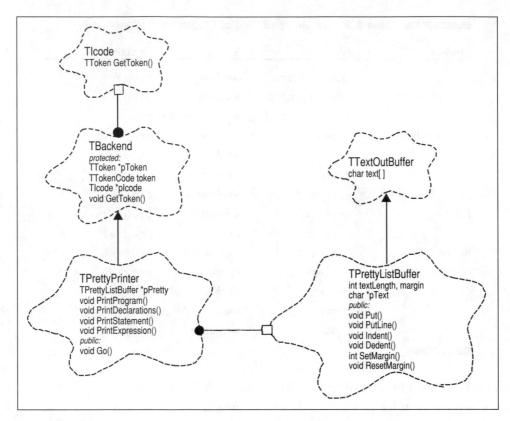

Figure 8.22 Class diagrams for classes **TPrettyPrinter** and **TPrettyListBuffer**.

The runtime relationships of the new pretty-printer and pretty-list buffer objects with each other and with the other objects are shown in the object diagram in Figure 8.23. To extract tokens, the pretty-printer object sends `GetToken` messages to the

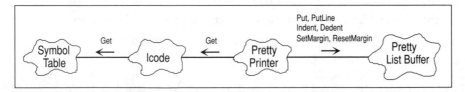

Figure 8.23 The relationships of the pretty-printer and pretty-list buffer objects with each other and with the other objects.

intermediate code object of the routine whose statements it is currently printing. For each identifier, number, and string token, the icode object sends a `Get` message to the symbol table object to obtain a pointer to symbol table node.

The pretty-printer object sends `Put`, `PutLine`, `Indent`, `Dedent`, `SetMargin`, and `ResetMargin` messages to the pretty-list buffer object to move the left margin and to print the reformatted source program lines.

■■■■■■■ **Figure 8.24** Header file **pretlist.h**.

```
//    ****************************************************************
//    *                                                            *
//    *    P R E T T Y   P R I N T   L I S T I N G   (Header)       *
//    *                                                            *
//    *    CLASSES: TPrettyListBuffer                              *
//    *                                                            *
//    *    FILE:    prog8-2/pretlist.h                             *
//    *                                                            *
//    *    MODULE:  Buffer                                         *
//    *                                                            *
//    *    Copyright (c) 1996 by Ronald Mak                        *
//    *    For instructional purposes only.  No warranties.        *
//    *                                                            *
//    ****************************************************************

#ifndef pretlist_h
#define pretlist_h

#include "buffer.h"

//----------------------------------------------------------------
//  TPrettyListBuffer        Pretty print list buffer subclass
//                           of TTextOutBuffer.
//----------------------------------------------------------------

class TPrettyListBuffer : public TTextOutBuffer {
    enum {
        indentSize        =  4,
        maxMargin         = 60,
        maxPrettyTextLength = 80,
    };

    int    textLength;  // length of output text line
    char *pText;        // pointer to end of text
    int    margin;      // left margin (number of spaces)
```

(*continues*)

■■■■■■■■■ **Figure 8.24** Header file **pretlist.h**. (*Continued*)

```cpp
public:
    TPrettyListBuffer(void)
    {
        pText      = text;
        *pText     = '\0';
        textLength = margin = 0;
    }

    void Put(const char *pString);
    virtual void PutLine(void);

    void PutLine(const char *pText)
    {
        Put(pText);
        PutLine();
    }

    void Indent(void) { margin += indentSize; }
    void Dedent(void) { if ((margin -= indentSize) < 0) margin = 0; }

    int SetMargin(void)
    {
        int m  = margin;        // save current margin
        margin = textLength;    // set margin at current position
        return m;               // return old margin
    }

    void ResetMargin(int m) { margin = m; }
};

#endif
```

Figure 8.24 shows the header file `pretlist.h` and Figure 8.25 shows the .implementation file `pretlist.cpp`.

■■■■■■■■■ **Figure 8.25** Implementation file **pretlist.cpp**.

```cpp
//    ****************************************************************
//    *                                                            *
//    *    P R E T T Y    P R I N T    L I S T I N G                *
//    *                                                            *
//    *    Pretty-printing list buffer routines.                   *
//    *                                                            *
//    *    CLASSES: TPrettyListBuffer                              *
```

```
//  *                                                         *
//  *    FILE:    pretlist.cpp                                *
//  *                                                         *
//  *    MODULE:  Buffer                                      *
//  *                                                         *
//  *    Routines to output a pretty printed source listing.  *
//  *                                                         *
//  *    Copyright (c) 1995 by Ronald Mak                     *
//  *    For instructional purposes only.  No warranties.     *
//  *                                                         *
//  ************************************************************

#include <stdio.h>
#include <string.h>
#include "pretlist.h"

//------------------------------------------------------------
// Put       Append a token string to the output record if it
//           fits.  If not, print the current record and
//           append the string to the next record.  If at the
//           beginning of the record, first indent.
//
//     pString : ptr to the token string to append
//------------------------------------------------------------

void TPrettyListBuffer::Put(const char *pString)
{
    int tokenLength = strlen(pString);

    //--Start a new output record if the current one is full.
    if (textLength + tokenLength >= maxPrettyTextLength - 1) PutLine();

    //--Indent if at the beginning of the output record.
    if ((textLength == 0) && (margin > 0)) {
        int m = margin < maxMargin ? margin : maxMargin;
        sprintf(text, "%*s", m, " ");
        pText      = text + m;
        textLength = m;
    }

    strcpy(pText, pString);
    pText      += tokenLength;
    textLength += tokenLength;
}
```

(continues)

■■■■■■ **Figure 8.25** Implementation file **pretlist.cpp**. (*Continued*)

```
//-------------------------------------------------------------
//  PutLine      Print the output record and reset it
//               to the blank line.
//-------------------------------------------------------------

void TPrettyListBuffer::PutLine(void)
{
    if (textLength == 0) return;

    cout << text << endl;

    text[0]    = '\0';
    pText      = text;
    textLength = 0;
}
```

Member function Put appends a token string to the current output record if the string fits; otherwise, it starts a new record. If the current print position is at the beginning of the record, the function appends the appropriate number of spaces to indent the line. Member function PutLine prints the current output record and resets it to the empty line.

■■■■■■ **Figure 8.26** Header file **pprinter.h**.

```
//  ***************************************************************
//  *                                                             *
//  *      P R E T T Y   P R I N T E R    (Header)                *
//  *                                                             *
//  *      CLASSES: TPrettyPrinter                                *
//  *                                                             *
//  *      FILE:    prog8-2/pprinter.h                            *
//  *                                                             *
//  *      MODULE:  Pretty printer                                *
//  *                                                             *
//  *      Copyright (c) 1996 by Ronald Mak                       *
//  *      For instructional purposes only.  No warranties.       *
//  *                                                             *
//  ***************************************************************

#ifndef pprinter_h
#define pprinter_h

#include "misc.h"
```

```
#include "buffer.h"
#include "error.h"
#include "symtab.h"
#include "pretlist.h"
#include "backend.h"

//-------------------------------------------------------------
//  TPrettyPrinter      Pretty printer subclass of TBackend.
//-------------------------------------------------------------

class TPrettyPrinter : public TBackend {

    TPrettyListBuffer *const pPretty;  // ptr to pretty list buffer

    //--Routines.
    void PrintProgram           (const TSymtabNode *pProgramId);
    void PrintSubroutine        (const TSymtabNode *pRoutineId);
    void PrintSubroutineHeader  (const TSymtabNode *pRoutineId);
    void PrintSubroutineFormals (const TSymtabNode *pParmId);
    void PrintBlock             (const TSymtabNode *pRoutineId);

    //--Declarations.
    void PrintDeclarations          (const TSymtabNode *pRoutineId);
    void PrintTypeSpec              (const TType *pType, int defnFlag);
    void PrintConstantDefinitions   (const TSymtabNode *pConstId);
    void PrintTypeDefinitions       (const TSymtabNode *pTypeId);
    void PrintVariableDeclarations  (const TSymtabNode *pVarId);
    void PrintVarsOrFields          (const TSymtabNode *pId);
    void PrintSubroutineDeclarations(const TSymtabNode *pRtnId);
    void PrintEnumType              (const TType *pType);
    void PrintSubrangeType          (const TType *pType);
    void PrintSubrangeLimit         (int limit, const TType *pBaseType);
    void PrintArrayType             (const TType *pType);
    void PrintRecordType            (const TType *pType);

    //--Statements.
    void PrintStatement         (void);
    void PrintStatementList     (TTokenCode terminator);
    void PrintAssignmentOrCall  (void);
    void PrintREPEAT            (void);
    void PrintWHILE            (void);
    void PrintIF               (void);
    void PrintFOR              (void);
    void PrintCASE             (void);
    void PrintCompound          (void);
```

(continues)

■■■■■■■ **Figure 8.26** Header file **pprinter.h**. (*Continued*)

```cpp
    //--Expressions.
    void PrintExpression(void);
    void PrintIdentifier(void);

    void Put         (const char *pString) { pPretty->Put(pString);      }
    void PutLine     (void)                { pPretty->PutLine();         }
    void PutLine     (const char *pString) { pPretty->PutLine(pString);  }
    void Indent      (void)   { pPretty->Indent(); }
    void Dedent      (void)   { pPretty->Dedent(); }
    int  SetMargin   (void)   { return pPretty->SetMargin(); }
    void ResetMargin(int m) { pPretty->ResetMargin(m);      }

public:
    TPrettyPrinter(void)
        : pPretty(new TPrettyListBuffer) {}

    virtual ~TPrettyPrinter(void) { delete pPretty; }

    virtual void Go(const TSymtabNode *pProgramId)
    {
        PrintProgram(pProgramId);
    }
};

#endif
```

Figure 8.26 shows header file pprinter.h. Like the other back end subclasses, TPrettyPrinter has a public member function Go to start the back end. Starting with this chapter, this function now takes an argument, a pointer to the program name's symbol table node. For the Pascal Pretty-Printer utility, this function simply calls PrintProgram.

■■■■■■■ **Figure 8.27** Main file of the Pascal Pretty-Printer utility program.

```cpp
//    ***************************************************************
//    *                                                             *
//    *    Program 8-2: Pascal Pretty Printer                       *
//    *                                                             *
//    *    Reformat and print a Pascal source program in a          *
//    *    "pretty" way.                                            *
//    *                                                             *
//    *    FILE:   prog8-2/pprint.cpp                               *
//    *                                                             *
//    *    USAGE:  pprint <source file>                             *
```

```
//   *                                                           *
//   *              <source file>  name of the source file       *
//   *                                                           *
//   *    Copyright (c) 1996 by Ronald Mak                       *
//   *    For instructional purposes only.  No warranties.       *
//   *                                                           *
//   **************************************************************

#include <iostream.h>
#include "error.h"
#include "buffer.h"
#include "symtab.h"
#include "parser.h"
#include "backend.h"
#include "pprinter.h"

//-------------------------------------------------------------
//  main
//-------------------------------------------------------------

void main(int argc, char *argv[])
{
    extern listFlag;

    //--Check the command line arguments.
    if (argc != 2) {
        cerr << "Usage: pprint <source file>" << endl;
        AbortTranslation(abortInvalidCommandLineArgs);
    }

    //--Create the parser for the source file,
    //--and then parse the file.  Don't list the source.
    listFlag = false;
    TParser    *pParser    = new TParser(new TSourceBuffer(argv[1]));
    TSymtabNode *pProgramId = pParser->Parse();
    delete pParser;

    //--If there were no syntax errors, convert the symbol tables,
    //--and create and invoke the backend pretty-printer.
    if (errorCount == 0) {
        vpSymtabs = new TSymtab *[cntSymtabs];
        for (TSymtab *pSt = pSymtabList; pSt; pSt = pSt->Next()) {
            pSt->Convert(vpSymtabs);
        }

        TBackend *pBackend = new TPrettyPrinter;
        pBackend->Go(pProgramId);
```

(continues)

■■■■■■■■ **Figure 8.27** Main file of the Pascal Pretty-Printer utility program.
        (*Continued*)

```
        delete[] vpSymtabs;
        delete   pBackend;
    }
}
```

Figure 8.27 shows the main file `pprint.cpp` of the utility program. After the front end is done, it converts the symbol tables for the back end, creates the pretty printer back end object, and sends the `Go` message.

■■■■■■■■ **Figure 8.28** Implementation file **pprtn.cpp**.

```
// ****************************************************************
// *                                                              *
// *    P R E T T Y   P R I N T E R    (Routines)                 *
// *                                                              *
// *    Pretty-print program, procedure, and functions.           *
// *                                                              *
// *    CLASSES: TPrettyPrinter                                    *
// *                                                              *
// *    FILE:    prog8-2/pprtn.cpp                                 *
// *                                                              *
// *    MODULE:  Pretty printer                                   *
// *                                                              *
// *    Copyright (c) 1996 by Ronald Mak                          *
// *    For instructional purposes only.  No warranties.          *
// *                                                              *
// ****************************************************************

#include <stdio.h>
#include "pprinter.h"


//---------------------------------------------------------------
// PrintProgram         Pretty-print a program:
//
//                          PROGRAM <id> (<id-1>, <id-2>, ...);
//                              <block>.
//
//      pProgramId : ptr to the program id's symbol table node
//---------------------------------------------------------------

void TPrettyPrinter::PrintProgram(const TSymtabNode *pProgramId)
{
    Put("PROGRAM ");
```

```
    Put(pProgramId->String());   // program name

    //--Print the program parameter list.
    TSymtabNode *pParmId = pProgramId->defn.routine.locals.pParmIds;
    if (pParmId) {
        Put(" (");
        int saveMargin = SetMargin();

        //--Loop to print each program parameter.
        do {
            Put(pParmId->String());
            pParmId = pParmId->next;
            if (pParmId) Put(", ");
        } while (pParmId);

        Put(")");
        ResetMargin(saveMargin);
    }
    PutLine(";");

    //--Print the program's block followed by a period.
    Indent();
    PrintBlock(pProgramId);
    PutLine(".");
    Dedent();
}


//-------------------------------------------------------------
//  PrintSubroutine      Pretty-print a procedure or function.
//
//                              <header>;
//                                 <block>;
//
//      pRoutineId : ptr to the routine id's symbol table node
//-------------------------------------------------------------

void TPrettyPrinter::PrintSubroutine(const TSymtabNode *pRoutineId)
{
    PrintSubroutineHeader(pRoutineId);
    PutLine(";");

    //--Print the routine's block followed by a semicolon.
    Indent();
    PrintBlock(pRoutineId);
    PutLine(";");
    Dedent();
```

(continues)

■■■■■■■■ **Figure 8.28** Implementation file **pprtn.cpp**. (*Continued*)

```
}

//-----------------------------------------------------------
//  PrintSubroutineHeader     Pretty-print a procedure or
//                            function header:
//
//                                   PROCEDURE <id> <formals>
//                                   FUNCTION <id> <formals> : <type>
//
//      pRoutineId : ptr to the routine id's symbol table node
//-----------------------------------------------------------

void TPrettyPrinter::PrintSubroutineHeader
                                (const TSymtabNode *pRoutineId)
{
    PutLine(" ");
    Put(pRoutineId->defn.how == dcProcedure ? "PROCEDURE "
                                            : "FUNCTION " );

    //--Print the procedure or function name
    //--followed by the formal parameter list.
    Put(pRoutineId->String());
    PrintSubroutineFormals(pRoutineId->defn.routine.locals.pParmIds);

    //--Print a function's return type.
    if (pRoutineId->defn.how == dcFunction) {
        Put(" : ");
        PrintTypeSpec(pRoutineId->pType, false);
    }
}

//-----------------------------------------------------------
//  PrintSubroutineFormals  Pretty-print a procedure or
//                          function formal parameter list:
//
//                                  (<id-1>, <id-2>, ... : <type-1>;
//                                   VAR <id-3>, ... : <type-2>)
//
//      pParmId : ptr to the head of the formal parm id list
//-----------------------------------------------------------

void TPrettyPrinter::PrintSubroutineFormals(const TSymtabNode *pParmId)
{
    if (!pParmId) return;
```

```
        Put(" (");
        int saveMargin = SetMargin();

        //--Loop to print each sublist of parameters with
        //--common definition and type.
        do {
            TDefnCode  commonDefn  = pParmId->defn.how;  // common defn
            TType      *pCommonType = pParmId->pType;      // common type
            int        doneFlag;  // true if sublist done, false if not

            if (commonDefn == dcVarParm) Put("VAR ");

            //--Loop to print the parms in the sublist.
            do {
                Put(pParmId->String());

                pParmId  = pParmId->next;
                doneFlag = (!pParmId) || (commonDefn  != pParmId->defn.how)
                                      || (pCommonType != pParmId->pType);
                if (!doneFlag) Put(", ");
            } while (!doneFlag);

            //--Print the sublist's common type.
            Put(" : ");
            PrintTypeSpec(pCommonType, false);

            if (pParmId) PutLine(";");
        } while (pParmId);

        Put(")");
        ResetMargin(saveMargin);
}

//------------------------------------------------------------
// PrintBlock       Pretty-print a program, procedure, or
//                  function block.
//
//      pRoutineId : ptr to the routine id's symbol table node
//------------------------------------------------------------

void TPrettyPrinter::PrintBlock(const TSymtabNode *pRoutineId)
{
    //--First print the definitions and declarations.
    PrintDeclarations(pRoutineId);
    PutLine(" ");
```

(continues)

```
    //--Then print the statements in the icode.
    pIcode = pRoutineId->defn.routine.pIcode;
    PrintCompound();
}
```

Pretty-Printing Programs, Procedures, and Functions

Figure 8.28 shows file pprtn.cpp, which implements the member functions for pretty-printing programs, procedures, and functions.

Member function PrintProgram begins by pretty-printing the program header. If there is a parameter list, it calls SetMargin right after printing the left parenthesis, so that if the parameter list spills over to several lines, each subsequent line lines up with the first parameter. It calls ResetMargin after printing the right parenthesis. Then, it calls Indent to indent the program block's declarations and statements. After calling member function PrintBlock, PrintProgram prints the final period and then calls Dedent.

Member function PrintSubroutine calls member function PrintSubroutine-Header to pretty-print a procedure or function header. Afterwards, like Print-Program, it indents, pretty-prints the routine's block, prints the semicolon, and dedents.

PrintSubroutineHeader calls member function PrintSubroutineFormals to print the formal parameter list. Then, if the subroutine is a function, it prints a colon and calls member function PrintTypeSpec to print the function's type identifier.

PrintSubroutineFormals prints a subroutine's formal parameter list. It calls SetMargin after printing the left parenthesis so that subsequent parameter lines will line up under the first parameter. The outer loop prints each sublist of parameters with a common definition and type, and the inner loop prints each parameter name. PrintSubroutineFormals calls PrintTypeSpec to print the sublist's type.

Both PrintProgram and PrintSubroutine call member function PrintBlock to print the routine's block. This function first calls member function PrintDeclarations to pretty-print the declarations. Then, it points data member pIcode to the routine's icode object before calling PrintCompound to pretty-print the routine's statements.

Some examples of pretty-printed subroutine headers are:

```
FUNCTION random (limit : posint) : posint;

PROCEDURE newlocation (creature : contents;
                       oldrow, oldcol : index;
                       VAR newrow, newcol : index);
```

■■■■■■■■■■ **Figure 8.29** Implementation file **ppdecl.cpp**.

```
// *************************************************************
// *                                                           *
// *    P R E T T Y   P R I N T E R   (Declarations)           *
// *                                                           *
// *    Pretty-print declarations.                             *
// *                                                           *
// *    CLASSES: TPrettyPrinter                                *
// *                                                           *
// *    FILE:     prog8-2/ppdecl.cpp                           *
// *                                                           *
// *    MODULE:   Pretty printer                               *
// *                                                           *
// *    Copyright (c) 1996 by Ronald Mak                       *
// *    For instructional purposes only.  No warranties.       *
// *                                                           *
// *************************************************************

#include <stdio.h>
#include "types.h"
#include "pprinter.h"


//-----------------------------------------------------------
// PrintDeclarations    Pretty-print definitions and
//                      declarations.
//
//      pRoutineId : ptr to the routine id's symbol table node
//-----------------------------------------------------------

void TPrettyPrinter::PrintDeclarations(const TSymtabNode *pRoutineId)
{
    TSymtabNode *pConstId= pRoutineId->defn.routine.locals.pConstantIds;
    TSymtabNode *pTypeId = pRoutineId->defn.routine.locals.pTypeIds;
    TSymtabNode *pVarId  = pRoutineId->defn.routine.locals.pVariableIds;
```
(continues)

```
    TSymtabNode *pRtnId  = pRoutineId->defn.routine.locals.pRoutineIds;

    if (pConstId) PrintConstantDefinitions   (pConstId);
    if (pTypeId)  PrintTypeDefinitions       (pTypeId);
    if (pVarId)   PrintVariableDeclarations  (pVarId);
    if (pRtnId)   PrintSubroutineDeclarations(pRtnId);
}

//-------------------------------------------------------------
//  PrintConstantDefinitions     Pretty-print constant
//                               definitions:
//
//                                       CONST
//                                           <id-1> = <value-1>;
//                                           <id-2> = <value-2>;
//                                           ...
//
//      pConstId : ptr to the head of the constant id list
//-------------------------------------------------------------

void TPrettyPrinter::PrintConstantDefinitions
                            (const TSymtabNode *pConstId)
{
    PutLine(" ");
    PutLine("CONST");
    Indent();

    //--Loop to print constant definitions, one per line.
    do {
        char    text[maxInputBufferSize];
        TType *pConstType = pConstId->pType;

        //--Print the constant identifier followed by = .
        Put(pConstId->String());
        Put(" = ");
        int saveMargin = SetMargin();

        //--Print the constant value.
        if (pConstType->form == fcArray) {  // string
            Put("'");
            Put(pConstId->defn.constant.value.pString);
            Put("'");
        }
        else if (pConstType == pIntegerType) {
```

```
            sprintf(text, "%d", pConstId->defn.constant.value.integer);
            Put(text);
        }
        else if (pConstType == pRealType) {
            sprintf(text, "%g", pConstId->defn.constant.value.real);
            Put(text);
        }
        else if (pConstType == pCharType) {
            sprintf(text, "'%c'",
                           pConstId->defn.constant.value.character);
            Put(text);
        }

        PutLine(";");
        ResetMargin(saveMargin);

        pConstId = pConstId->next;
    } while (pConstId);

    Dedent();
}

//-------------------------------------------------------------
//  PrintTypeDefinitions          Pretty-print type definitions:
//
//                                     TYPE
//                                         <id-1> = <type-spec-1>;
//                                         <id-2> = <type-spec-2>;
//                                         ...
//
//      pTypeId : ptr to the head of the type id list
//-------------------------------------------------------------

void TPrettyPrinter::PrintTypeDefinitions(const TSymtabNode *pTypeId)
{
    PutLine(" ");
    PutLine("TYPE");
    Indent();

    //--Loop to print type definitions, one per line.
    do {
        //--Print the type identifier followed by = .
        Put(pTypeId->String());
        Put(" = ");
        int saveMargin = SetMargin();
```

(continues)

■■■■■ **Figure 8.29** Implementation file **ppdecl.cpp**. (*Continued*)

```
        //--Print the type specification.
        PrintTypeSpec(pTypeId->pType,
                      pTypeId == pTypeId->pType->pTypeId);

        PutLine(";");
        ResetMargin(saveMargin);

        pTypeId = pTypeId->next;
    } while (pTypeId);

    Dedent();
}


//---------------------------------------------------------------
//  PrintVariableDeclarations    Pretty-print variable
//                               declarations:
//
//                                       VAR
//                                           <var-or-fields>
//
//      pVarId : ptr to the head of the variable id list
//---------------------------------------------------------------

void TPrettyPrinter::PrintVariableDeclarations
                                (const TSymtabNode *pVarId)
{
    PutLine(" ");
    PutLine("VAR");
    Indent();
    PrintVarsOrFields(pVarId);
    Dedent();
}


//---------------------------------------------------------------
//  PrintVarsOrFields            Pretty-print variable or record
//                               field declarations:
//
//                      <id-1>, <id-2>, ... : <type-spec-1>;
//                          ...
//
//      pId : ptr to the head of the variable or field id list
//---------------------------------------------------------------

void TPrettyPrinter::PrintVarsOrFields(const TSymtabNode *pId)
```

```
{
    TType *pCommonType = pId->pType;   // ptr to common type of sublist

    //--Loop to print sublists of variables with a common type.
    do {
        Put(pId->String());
        pId = pId->next;

        if (pId && (pId->pType == pCommonType)) Put(", ");
        else {

            //--End of sublist:  Print the common type and begin
            //--                 a new sublist.
            Put(" : ");
            int saveMargin = SetMargin();
            PrintTypeSpec(pCommonType, false);

            PutLine(";");
            ResetMargin(saveMargin);

            if (pId) pCommonType = pId->pType;
        }
    } while (pId);
}


//------------------------------------------------------------
//  PrintSubroutineDeclarations     Pretty-print procedure or
//                                  function declarations.
//
//      pRtnId : ptr to the head of the routine id list
//------------------------------------------------------------

void TPrettyPrinter::PrintSubroutineDeclarations
                            (const TSymtabNode *pRtnId)
{
    do {
        PrintSubroutine(pRtnId);
        pRtnId = pRtnId->next;
    } while (pRtnId);
}


//------------------------------------------------------------
//  PrintTypeSpec        Pretty-print a type specification.  If
//                       the type is being defined as a named
//                       type, or it is unnamed, print it out
//                       completely.  Otherwise, just print the
```

(continues)

■■■■■■■ **Figure 8.29** Implementation file **ppdecl.cpp**. (*Continued*)

```
//                      type identifier.
//
//      pType    : ptr to the type object
//      defnFlag : true if being defined as a named type,
//                 false if not
//-------------------------------------------------------------

void TPrettyPrinter::PrintTypeSpec(const TType *pType, int defnFlag)
{
    //--Named type that is part of a type specification:
    //--Just print the type identifier.
    if (!defnFlag && pType->pTypeId) Put(pType->pTypeId->String());

    //--Otherwise, print the type spec completely.
    else switch (pType->form) {
        case fcEnum:        PrintEnumType     (pType);    break;
        case fcSubrange:    PrintSubrangeType (pType);    break;
        case fcArray:       PrintArrayType    (pType);    break;
        case fcRecord:      PrintRecordType   (pType);    break;
    }
}


//-------------------------------------------------------------
//  PrintEnumType       Pretty-print an enumeration type spec:
//
//                              (<id-1>, <id-2>,
//                               <id-3>, ...)
//
//      pType : ptr to the type object
//-------------------------------------------------------------

void TPrettyPrinter::PrintEnumType(const TType *pType)
{
    TSymtabNode *pConstId = pType->enumeration.pConstIds;

    Put("(");
    int saveMargin = SetMargin();

    //--Loop to print the enumeration constant identifiers.
    do {
        Put(pConstId->String());
        pConstId = pConstId->next;
        if (pConstId) Put(", ");
    } while (pConstId);
```

```
    Put(")");
    ResetMargin(saveMargin);
}

//----------------------------------------------------------
//  PrintSubrangeType   Pretty-print a subrange type spec:
//
//                              <min>..<max>
//
//      pType : ptr to the type object
//----------------------------------------------------------

void TPrettyPrinter::PrintSubrangeType(const TType *pType)
{
    PrintSubrangeLimit(pType->subrange.min, pType->subrange.pBaseType);
    Put("..");
    PrintSubrangeLimit(pType->subrange.max, pType->subrange.pBaseType);
}

//----------------------------------------------------------
//  PrintSubrangeLimit  Pretty-print the minimum or maximum
//                      limit of a subrange type spec.
//
//      limit     : the min or max limit value
//      pBaseType : ptr to the base type object
//----------------------------------------------------------

void TPrettyPrinter::PrintSubrangeLimit(int limit,
                                        const TType *pBaseType)
{
    char text[maxInputBufferSize];

    if (pBaseType == pIntegerType) {
        sprintf(text, "%d", limit);
        Put(text);
    }
    else if (pBaseType == pCharType) {
        sprintf(text, "'%c'", limit);
        Put(text);
    }

    //--Enumeration:  Find the appropriate enumeration constant id.
    else {
        TSymtabNode *pConstId = pBaseType->enumeration.pConstIds;
        while (limit-- > 0) pConstId = pConstId->next;
        Put(pConstId->String());
```

(continues)

```
    }
}

//--------------------------------------------------------------
// PrintArrayType        Pretty-print an array type spec:
//
//                  ARRAY [<type-spec-1>] OF
//                    ARRAY [<type-spec-2>] OF <type-spec-3>
//
//      pType : ptr to the type object
//--------------------------------------------------------------

void TPrettyPrinter::PrintArrayType(const TType *pType)
{
    TType *pIndexType = pType->array.pIndexType;
    TType *pElmtType  = pType->array.pElmtType;

    Put("ARRAY [");
    PrintTypeSpec(pIndexType, false);
    Put("] OF ");

    if ((pElmtType->pTypeId) || (pElmtType->IsScalar())) {
        PrintTypeSpec(pElmtType, false);
    }
    else {

        //--Cascade array of unnamed arrays or records
        //--over multiple lines.
        PutLine();
        Indent();
        PrintTypeSpec(pElmtType, false);
        Dedent();
    }
}


//--------------------------------------------------------------
// PrintRecordType       Pretty-print a record type spec:
//
//                        RECORD
//                            <var-or-fields>
//                        END
//
//      pType : ptr to the type object
//--------------------------------------------------------------
```

```
void TPrettyPrinter::PrintRecordType(const TType *pType)
{
    PutLine("RECORD");

    Indent();
    PrintVarsOrFields(pType->record.pSymtab->Root());
    Dedent();

    Put("END");
}
```

Pretty-Printing Declarations

Figure 8.29 shows file `ppdecl.cpp`, which implements the member functions to pretty-print declarations. Member function `PrintDeclarations` calls member functions `PrintConstantDefinitions`, `PrintTypeDefinitions`, `Print-VariableDeclarations`, and `PrintSubroutineDeclarations` if the corresponding symbol table node lists pointed to by the routine name's symbol table node are not empty.

`PrintConstantDefinitions` prints constant definitions indented under the reserved word CONST. For each definition, it calls `SetMargin` after printing the equal sign so that if a long constant spills over several lines, the subsequent lines will line up under the beginning of the constant. Some examples of pretty-printed constant definitions are:

```
CONST
    ten = 10;
    pi = 3.14159;
    ch = 'x';
    hello = 'Hello, world.';
```

Member function `PrintTypeDefinitions` is similar, except that it calls member function `PrintTypeSpec` to pretty-print the type specification after the equal sign. Depending on the type and whether or not it is being defined, this latter function either prints the type identifier or calls one of the member functions `PrintEnum-Type`, `PrintSubrangeType`, `PrintArrayType`, or `PrintRecordType`.

`PrintEnumType` loops to print the enumeration constant identifiers. If they take up more than one line, each subsequent line lines up under the first identifier. `PrintSubrangeType` calls member function `PrintSubrangeLimit` twice to print the subrange limit values. If the base type is enumeration, `PrintSubrange-Limit` loops over the list of the constant identifiers' symbol table nodes to select the appropriate name to print based on the ordinal value.

`PrintArrayType` calls `PrintTypeSpec` to pretty-print the index type. If the element type is a named type, or it is neither an array nor a record, `PrintArrayType` simply calls `PrintTypeSpec` again to print the element type. However, if the element type is an array or a record, `PrintArrayType` indents, calls `PrintType-Spec`, and then dedents. Thus, a multidimensional array is printed with each dimension indented from the previous one.

Finally, member function `PrintRecordType` calls member function `PrintVarsOrFields` to print the field declarations indented between the reserved words RECORD and END.

Examples of pretty-printed type definitions are:

```
TYPE
    e = (alpha, beta, gamma);
    ee = e;
    sr = alpha..gamma;
    cr = 'a'..'x';
    ar1 = ARRAY [1..10] OF integer;
    array2 = ARRAY [(fee, fye, foe, fum)] OF
                ARRAY [10..100] OF
                    ARRAY [e] OF
                        ARRAY ['m'..'r'] OF
                            ARRAY [e] OF boolean;
    rec = RECORD
            a : ar1;
            rr : RECORD
                    i : integer;
                    b : boolean;
                END;
        END;
```

Member function `PrintVariableDeclarations` calls member function `PrintVarsOrFields` to pretty-print the variable declarations indented under the reserved word VAR. `PrintVarsOrFields` pretty-prints both variable declarations and record field declarations. Its outer loop prints sublists of variables or fields with a common type. The inner loop prints the identifiers in each sublist. After the inner loop, `PrintVarsOrFields` calls `PrintTypeSpec` to pretty-print a sublist's common type.

Examples of pretty-printed variable declarations are:

```
VAR
    radius, circumference : real;
    b : boolean;
    letter : 'a'..'z';
    buffer : ARRAY [1..80] OF char;
```

Finally, member function `PrintSubroutineDeclarations` loops to call `PrintSubroutine` to pretty-print each procedure and function declaration.

■■■■■■■ **Figure 8.30** Implementation file **ppstmt.cpp**.

```
// ****************************************************************
// *                                                            *
// *      P R E T T Y   P R I N T E R    (Statements)           *
// *                                                            *
// *      Pretty-print statements and expressions.              *
// *                                                            *
// *      CLASSES: TPrettyPrinter                               *
// *                                                            *
// *      FILE:    prog8-2/ppstmt.cpp                           *
// *                                                            *
// *      MODULE:  Pretty printer                               *
// *                                                            *
// *      Copyright (c) 1996 by Ronald Mak                      *
// *      For instructional purposes only.  No warranties.      *
// *                                                            *
// ****************************************************************

#include <stdio.h>
#include "pprinter.h"

//              ****************************
//              *                          *
//              *  Pretty-Print Statements  *
//              *                          *
//              ****************************


//------------------------------------------------------------
// PrintStatement      Pretty-print a statement.
//------------------------------------------------------------
```

(continues)

■■■■■ **Figure 8.30** Implementation file **ppstmt.cpp**. (*Continued*)

```
void TPrettyPrinter::PrintStatement(void)
{
    switch (token) {
        case tcIdentifier:  PrintAssignmentOrCall();    break;
        case tcBEGIN:       PrintCompound();            break;
        case tcREPEAT:      PrintREPEAT();              break;
        case tcWHILE:       PrintWHILE();               break;
        case tcIF:          PrintIF();                  break;
        case tcFOR:         PrintFOR();                 break;
        case tcCASE:        PrintCASE();                break;
    }

    while (token == tcSemicolon) {
        Put(";");
        GetToken();
    }
    PutLine();
}


//----------------------------------------------------------------
//  PrintStatementList       Pretty-print a statement list:
//
//                                  <stmt-1>;
//                                  <stmt-2>;
//                                  ...
//----------------------------------------------------------------

void TPrettyPrinter::PrintStatementList(TTokenCode terminator)
{
    while (token != terminator) PrintStatement();
}


//----------------------------------------------------------------
//  PrintAssignmentOrCall       Pretty-print an assignment
//                              statement or a procedure call:
//
//                                      <id>
//                                      <id> := <expr>
//----------------------------------------------------------------

void TPrettyPrinter::PrintAssignmentOrCall(void)
{
    PrintIdentifier();
```

```
    if (token == tcColonEqual) {
        Put(" := ");

        GetToken();
        PrintExpression();
    }
}


//---------------------------------------------------------------
//   PrintREPEAT          Pretty-print a REPEAT statement:
//
//                             REPEAT
//                                 <stmt-list>
//                             UNTIL <expr>
//---------------------------------------------------------------

void TPrettyPrinter::PrintREPEAT(void)
{
    PutLine("REPEAT");
    Indent();

    GetToken();
    PrintStatementList(tcUNTIL);

    Dedent();
    Put("UNTIL ");
    int saveMargin = SetMargin();

    GetToken();
    PrintExpression();
    ResetMargin(saveMargin);
}


//---------------------------------------------------------------
//   PrintWHILE           Pretty-print a WHILE statement:
//
//                             WHILE <expr> DO
//                                 <stmt>
//---------------------------------------------------------------

void TPrettyPrinter::PrintWHILE(void)
{
    Put("WHILE ");
    int saveMargin = SetMargin();
```

(*continues*)

■■■■■ **Figure 8.30** Implementation file **ppstmt.cpp**. (*Continued*)

```
    GetToken();
    PrintExpression();
    ResetMargin(saveMargin);
    PutLine(" DO");

    Indent();
    GetToken();
    PrintStatement();
    Dedent();
}

//------------------------------------------------------------
//  PrintIF            Pretty-print an IF statement:
//
//                          IF <expr> THEN
//                              <stmt-1>
//                          ELSE
//                              <stmt-2>
//------------------------------------------------------------

void TPrettyPrinter::PrintIF(void)
{
    Put("IF ");

    GetToken();
    PrintExpression();
    PutLine(" THEN");

    Indent();
    GetToken();
    PrintStatement();
    Dedent();

    if (token == tcELSE) {
        PutLine("ELSE");

        Indent();
        GetToken();
        PrintStatement();
        Dedent();
    }
}

//------------------------------------------------------------
//  PrintFOR           Pretty-print a FOR statement:
```

```
//
//                          FOR <id> := <expr-1> TO <expr-2> DO
//                              <stmt>
//-----------------------------------------------------------------

void TPrettyPrinter::PrintFOR(void)
{
    Put("FOR ");

    GetToken();
    PrintIdentifier();
    Put(" := ");

    GetToken();
    PrintExpression();
    Put(token == tcTO ? " TO " : " DOWNTO ");

    GetToken();
    PrintExpression();
    PutLine(" DO");

    Indent();
    GetToken();
    PrintStatement();
    Dedent();
}


//-----------------------------------------------------------------
//   PrintCASE            Pretty-print a CASE statement:
//
//                        CASE <expr> OF
//                            <const-1>, <const-2>:
//                                <stmt-1>;
//                            ...
//                        END
//-----------------------------------------------------------------

void TPrettyPrinter::PrintCASE(void)
{
    Put("CASE ");

    GetToken();
    PrintExpression();
    PutLine(" OF ");

    Indent();
```

(continues)

```
        GetToken();

        //--Loop to print CASE branches.
        while (token != tcEND) {

            //--Loop to print the CASE labels of a branch.
            do {
                PrintExpression();
                if (token == tcComma) {
                    Put(", ");
                    GetToken();
                }
            } while (token != tcColon);

            PutLine(":");

            Indent();
            GetToken();
            PrintStatement();
            Dedent();
        }

        Dedent();
        Put("END");

        GetToken();
    }

    //------------------------------------------------------------
    //  PrintCompound        Pretty-print a compund statement:
    //
    //                                BEGIN
    //                                    <stmt-list>
    //                                END
    //------------------------------------------------------------

    void TPrettyPrinter::PrintCompound(void)
    {
        PutLine("BEGIN");
        Indent();

        GetToken();
        PrintStatementList(tcEND);

        Dedent();
        Put("END");
```

```
        GetToken();
}


//              *****************************
//              *                           *
//              *   Pretty-Print Expressions *
//              *                           *
//              *****************************


//----------------------------------------------------------------
//  PrintExpression        Pretty-print an expression.
//----------------------------------------------------------------

void TPrettyPrinter::PrintExpression(void)
{
    int doneFlag = false;   // true if done with expression, false if not

    //--Loop over the entire expression.
    do {
        switch (token) {
            case tcIdentifier:  PrintIdentifier();  break;

            case tcNumber:  Put(pToken->String());  GetToken();  break;
            case tcString:  Put(pToken->String());  GetToken();  break;

            case tcPlus:        Put(" + ");     GetToken();     break;
            case tcMinus:       Put(" - ");     GetToken();     break;
            case tcStar:        Put("*");       GetToken();     break;
            case tcSlash:       Put("/");       GetToken();     break;
            case tcDIV:         Put(" DIV ");   GetToken();     break;
            case tcMOD:         Put(" MOD ");   GetToken();     break;
            case tcAND:         Put(" AND ");   GetToken();     break;
            case tcOR:          Put(" OR ");    GetToken();     break;
            case tcEqual:       Put(" = ");     GetToken();     break;
            case tcNe:          Put(" <> ");    GetToken();     break;
            case tcLt:          Put(" < ");     GetToken();     break;
            case tcLe:          Put(" <= ");    GetToken();     break;
            case tcGt:          Put(" > ");     GetToken();     break;
            case tcGe:          Put(" >= ");    GetToken();     break;
            case tcNOT:         Put("NOT ");    GetToken();     break;

            case tcLParen:
                Put("(");
                GetToken();
                PrintExpression();
                Put(")");
                GetToken();
```

(continues)

■■■■■■■ **Figure 8.30** Implementation file **ppstmt.cpp**. (*Continued*)

```
                break;

            default:
                doneFlag = true;
                break;
        }
    } while (!doneFlag);
}

//------------------------------------------------------------
//  PrintIdentifier        Pretty-print an identifier, possibly
//                         followed by modifiers (subscripts,
//                         actual parameters, or fields):
//
//                              <id>
//                              <id>[<expr-1>, <expr-2>, ...]
//                              <id>(<expr-1>, <expr-2>, ...)
//                              <id-1>.<id-2>
//------------------------------------------------------------

//--Tokens that can start an identifier modifier.
TTokenCode tlIdModStart[] = {tcLBracket, tcLParen, tcPeriod, tcDummy};

//--Tokens that can end an identifier modifier.
TTokenCode tlIdModEnd[]   = {tcRBracket, tcRParen, tcDummy};

void TPrettyPrinter::PrintIdentifier(void)
{
    Put(pToken->String());
    GetToken();

    //--Loop to print any modifiers (subscripts, record fields,
    //--or actual parameter lists).
    while (TokenIn(token, tlIdModStart)) {

        //--Record field.
        if (token == tcPeriod) {
            Put(".");
            GetToken();
            PrintIdentifier();
        }

        //--Subscripts or actual parameters.
        else {
            int saveMargin;
```

```
        //--Set margin for actual parameters.
        if (token == tcLParen) {
            Put("(");
            saveMargin = SetMargin();
        }
        else Put("[");

        GetToken();

        while (!TokenIn(token, tlIdModEnd)) {
            PrintExpression();

            //--Write and writeln field width and precision.
            while (token == tcColon) {
                Put(":");
                GetToken();
                PrintExpression();
            }

            if (token == tcComma) {
                Put(", ");
                GetToken();
            }
        }

        //--Reset actual parameter margin.
        if (token == tcRParen) {
            Put(")");
            ResetMargin(saveMargin);
        }
        else Put("]");

        GetToken();
    }
}
}
```

Pretty-Printing Statements

Figure 8-30 shows file ppstmt.cpp, which implements the member functions to pretty-print statements and expressions. Depending on the statement's lead token, member function PrintStatement calls the appropriate pretty-printing function.

Member function PrintStatementList loops to call PrintStatement to pretty-print each statement in a statement list.

Member function `PrintAssignmentOrCall` pretty-prints either an assignment statement or a procedure call. It calls member function `PrintIdentifier` to pretty-print the statement's leading identifier token, and member function `Print-Expression` to pretty-print an assignment's source expression. (We'll see shortly that `PrintIdentifier` also prints an actual parameter list.)

Member function `PrintREPEAT` pretty-prints a REPEAT statement using the format:

```
REPEAT
    <stmt-1>;
    <stmt-2>;
    ...
    <stmt-n>
UNTIL <expr>
```

Member function `PrintWHILE` pretty-prints a WHILE statement using the format:

```
WHILE <expr> DO
    <stmt>
```

Member function `PrintIF` pretty-prints an IF statement using the format:

```
IF <expr> THEN
    <stmt>
```

or the format:

```
IF <expr> THEN
    <stmt-1>
ELSE
    <stmt-2>
```

Member function `PrintFOR` pretty-prints a FOR statement using the format:

```
FOR <id> := <expr-1> TO <expr-2> DO
    <stmt>
```

(The TO can also be DOWNTO.)

Member function `PrintCASE` pretty-prints a CASE statement using the format:

```
CASE <expr> OF
    <label-list-1>:
        <stmt-1>;
    <label-list-2>:
        <stmt-2>;
    ...
    <label-list-n>:
        <stmt-n>
END
```

Finally, member function `PrintCompound` pretty-prints a compound statement using the format:

```
BEGIN
    <stmt-1>;
    <stmt-2>;
    ...
    <stmt-n>
END
```

Pretty-Printing Expressions

Member function `PrintExpression` treats an expression as a list of identifiers, numbers, strings, and operators. The function loops, calling member function `PrintIdentifier` to pretty-print an identifier, string, number, or operator token. It calls itself recursively to pretty-print a subexpression surrounded by parentheses.

`PrintIdentifier` pretty-prints an identifier followed by modifiers such as subscripts, fields, or an actual parameter list. It calls `PrintExpression` up to three times for each actual parameter, since there could be field width and precision expressions.

We make one small change to member function `Parse` in implementation file `parser.cpp`. For the Pascal Pretty-Printer utility program, if there are no syntax errors, we don't want to print the summary:

```
//--Print the parser's summary.
if (errorCount > 0) {
      list.PutLine();
      sprintf(list.text, "%20d source lines.",  currentLineNumber);
      list.PutLine();
      sprintf(list.text, "%20d syntax errors.", errorCount);
      list.PutLine();
}
```

Figure 8.31 shows sample output from the utility program.

████████ **Figure 8.31** Sample output from the Pascal Pretty-Printer utility program.

```
PROGRAM newton (input, output);

    CONST
        epsilon = 1e-06;

    VAR
        number, root, sqroot : real;
```

(continues)

■■■■■■■ **Figure 8.31** Sample output from the Pascal Pretty-Printer utility program.
(*Continued*)

```
BEGIN
    REPEAT
        writeln;
        write('Enter new number (0 to quit): ');
        read(number);
        IF number = 0 THEN
            BEGIN
                writeln(number:12:6, 0.0:12:6);
            END
        ELSE
            IF number < 0 THEN
                BEGIN
                    writeln('*** ERROR:  number < 0');
                END
            ELSE
                BEGIN
                    sqroot := sqrt(number);
                    writeln(number:12:6, sqroot:12:6);
                    writeln;
                    root := 1;
                    REPEAT
                        root := (number/root + root)/2;
                        writeln(root:24:6, 100*abs(root - sqroot)/sqroot:
                            12:2, '%')
                    UNTIL abs(number/sqr(root) - 1) < epsilon;
                END
    UNTIL number = 0
END.
```

Language Conversion

We can think of the Pretty-Printer as converting "Plain Pascal" to "Pretty Pascal."
Language converters are often used to translate a program from one source language
to another. For example, early C++ compilers actually converted C++ programs into
equivalent (but not very readable) C programs. Indeed, the compiler that we will
write in the third part of this book converts Pascal programs into 8086 assembly
language programs.

CHAPTER

9

INTERPRETING

DECLARED PROCEDURES

AND FUNCTIONS

T his chapter begins the second part of this book, where we start to create an executor object for the back end. We'll complete the executor module in the next chapter, where we combine it with the modules we've written for the front end to achieve a working Pascal interpreter. In Chapter 11, we'll add more capabilities to the executor module, and convert the interpreter into an interactive source-level debugger.

We've already been introduced to the back end. In Chapters 5 and 6, we wrote member functions for class TExecutor to execute Pascal assignment, REPEAT, and compound statements, and Pascal expressions. Objects instantiated from classes TSymtab and TIcode are the interface between the front and back ends. At the end of the previous chapter, we wrote a proto–back end in the form of a pretty-printer to validate these symbol table and intermediate code objects.

In the previous chapter, we saw how, in the front end, the parser processed program, procedure, and function declarations, and procedure and function calls, and how it maintains a symbol table stack. In this chapter, we'll see how, in the back end, the executor handles calls to declared procedures and functions, and how it maintains a

463

runtime stack. We'll take care of the remaining Pascal control statements and calls to the standard subroutines in the next chapter.

This chapter describes how to:

- Allocate the values of a routine's formal parameters and local variables on the runtime stack.
- Use the runtime stack to maintain the current execution state.
- Flag runtime errors.
- Print rudimentary runtime trace information for debugging.

The Runtime Stack

Our earlier use of the executor's runtime stack was limited to keeping track of intermediate values while evaluating expressions. In a complete interpreter, the runtime stack plays a much greater role. At any point during the execution of a program, the stack represents a "snapshot" of the execution state. It contains information about which procedures and functions have been called, their return values and addresses, the current values of all their formal parameters and local variables, and which of these values are accessible according to the scope rules.

Allocating Local Variables and Formal Parameters

We've been keeping the current runtime value of each variable and formal parameter in its symbol table node. This won't do for a Pascal interpreter because procedures and functions can be called recursively. During a recursive subroutine call, the old set of values for the subroutine's formal parameters and local variables must be stored to make way for the new set of values. This new set of values becomes available and is used during the current execution of the subroutine, while the old set of values is unavailable. When the subroutine returns from the recursive call, the new set of values must be discarded and the old set of values must again become available.

It therefore makes sense to keep the values of the parameters and variables not in the symbol table, but on the runtime stack. Whenever we call a subroutine, we allocate space on top of the stack to store these values. Upon return from the call, we pop the values off. If the call is recursive, we allocate a new set of values above the old set, and upon return from the call, we pop off those values to uncover the old values. In this scheme, we consider the global variables to be local to the program itself, and so we allocate their values at the bottom of the stack when we start to execute the program.

So in the symbol table node of each variable and formal parameter, we'll no longer keep its current *value*, but instead the current *location* of its value in the runtime stack. We'll see shortly exactly how to do this.

Stack Frames

So far, we've seen two uses for the runtime stack: to store the current runtime values of a routine's formal parameters and local variables, and to keep track of intermediate values during expression evaluation. An interpreter also uses the runtime stack to keep track of where to return to when the currently executing subroutine returns, and (for a function call) the return value. It also keeps information on the stack that enables it to legitimately access nonlocal values according to Pascal's scope rules. All this information, except for the intermediate expression values, is arranged in *stack frames*.

We allocate a stack frame for the program itself at the bottom of the runtime stack when we first begin to execute the program. Each time we call a subroutine, we push a stack frame for that subroutine onto the stack, and we pop off the frame when we return from the subroutine. A pointer known as the *stack frame base pointer* always points to the base (first component) of the current stack frame. The current stack frame is always the topmost one, and it represents the currently executing routine.

Figure 9.1 shows a routine's stack frame. The first component, the one the stack frame base pointer can point to, is the return value of a function. (A procedure will also allocate the return value item for consistency, but it will not otherwise use it.) This is followed by a static link, a dynamic link, and the return address. These four components make up the *stack frame header*. On top of the header, we allocate stack items to store the current values for each of the routine's formal parameters, and on top of those items, we allocate items for the current values of each of its

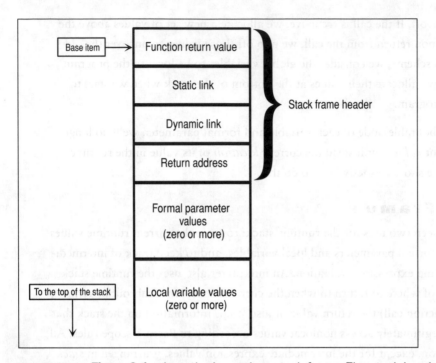

Base item → Function return value

Static link

Dynamic link

Return address

Stack frame header

Formal parameter
values
(zero or more)

To the top of the stack

Local variable values
(zero or more)

Figure 9.1 A routine's runtime stack frame. The stack header consists of the function return value, the static and dynamic links, and the return address. When a routine is currently executing, the stack frame base pointer points to the base item of its stack frame. In this diagram, the stack grows downward, so the top of the stack is toward the bottom.

local variables. Finally, during the routine's execution, we push and pop intermediate expression values on top of the local variable values. The static and dynamic links point back to previous stack frames, as we'll see later.

A routine's stack frame contains the current set of values for its formal parameters and local variables. If we call a routine recursively, we allocate a new stack frame for each call, and so the current set of values is always in its stack frame closest to the top of the stack.

Every stack frame header is the same size. The number of formal parameters and the number of local variables of a particular procedure or function never changes. Therefore, if each time we allocate a stack frame for a routine, we allocate the stack items for the values of its parameters and variables in the same order (which is reasonable to do), then the *offset* from the routine's stack frame base to the item containing the value of a particular parameter or variable is always the same. If we store this offset in each symbol table entry, we will always be able to access the current runtime value of any parameter or variable. To access the value of a variable declared in the currently executing routine, we look up the variable's offset in its symbol table node, add the offset to the frame base pointer, and the result points to the value on the runtime stack. We'll see how to access nonlocal values shortly.

Figure 9.2 shows the stack frame of a subroutine that has several formal parameters and local variables. Each time this particular stack frame is allocated on the runtime stack, the offset from its base to the value of local variable i remains the same.

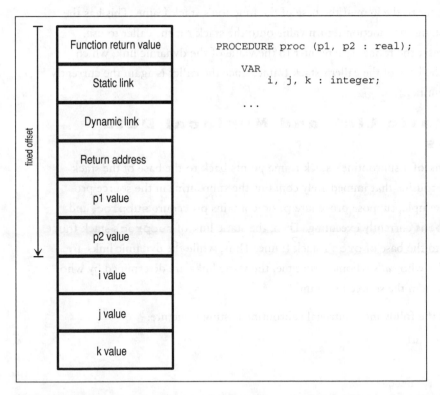

Figure 9.2   The stack frame of a subroutine with two formal parameters **p1** and **p2** and three local variables **i**, **j**, and **k**. The offset from the base of the stack frame to the value of any particular parameter or variable, such as **i**, is always the same.

The Dynamic Link and Subroutine Returns

The dynamic link of a stack frame simply points back to the base of the previous stack frame. In other words, the stack frame of each subroutine points back to the stack frame of its caller.

When we return from a procedure or a function, the dynamic link enables us to restore the stack to its state when the subroutine was about to be called. We pop off the called subroutine's stack frame, so that stack frame of its caller is again on top. When we return from a procedure, we simply reset the top-of-stack pointer to the item just below the procedure's stack frame base. This puts the pointer back to where it was just before the call. When we return from a function, we reset the top-of-stack pointer to the item at the base of the function's stack frame. This has the effect of pushing the function return value onto the stack for the caller to use. Finally, we reset the frame base pointer to the value of the dynamic link, which points it to the base of the caller's stack frame, since the caller is again the currently executing routine.

The Static Link and Nonlocal Data Access

The static link of a subroutine's stack frame points back to the base of the stack frame of the routine that immediately contains the subroutine in the source program. For example, suppose procedure `proc` contains procedure `subproc`, and that `subproc` is currently executing. Then, the static link of `subproc`'s stack frame points back to the base of `proc`'s stack frame. Thus, while the dynamic links are determined by who *calls* whom at runtime, the static links are determined by who *contains* whom in the source program.

Let's look at the following nontrivial subroutine nesting structure:

```
PROGRAM main1;

VAR
      i : integer;

PROCEDURE proc2; forward;

FUNCTION func2 (j : integer);
```

```
            FUNCTION func3(k : integer);
                BEGIN {func3}
                    ...
                    proc2;   {indirect recursion}
                    ...
                END {func3};

            BEGIN {func2}
                ...
                func3;
                ...
            END {func2};

    PROCEDURE proc2;

            PROCEDURE proc3;
                BEGIN {proc3}
                    ...
                    proc3;   {direct recursion}
                    ...
                    func2;
                    ...
                END {proc3};

            BEGIN {proc2}
                ...
                proc3;
                ...
                func2;
                ...
            END {proc2};

    BEGIN {main1}
            ...
            proc2;
            ...
    END {main1}.
```

We've chosen routine names that indicate the nesting level of the routine's formal
parameters and local variables (which, we recall, is one greater than the nesting level
of the routine name itself).

Figure 9.3 shows how the dynamic and static links change as the program's procedures and functions call each other. As you can see, the dynamic links (drawn on the

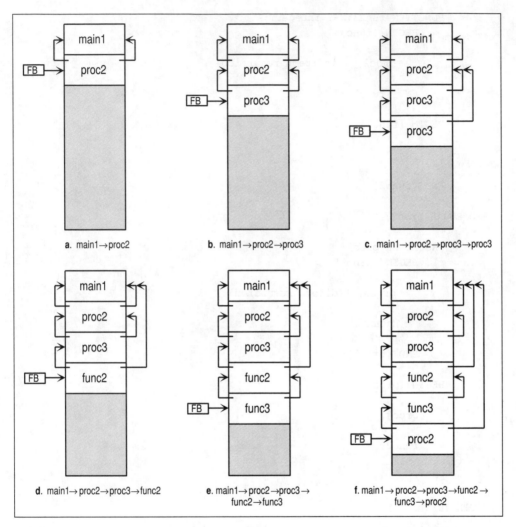

a. main1→proc2

b. main1→proc2→proc3

c. main1→proc2→proc3→proc3

d. main1→ proc2→proc3→func2

e. main1→ proc2→proc3→
   func2→func3

f. main1 → proc2→proc3→func2 →
   func3→proc2

Figure 9.3 How the runtime stack maintains stack frames during the execution of a program with nested procedures and functions, as outlined in the text. In each stack diagram, we draw the dynamic links on the left and the static links on the right. The stack frame base pointer (FB) points to the topmost stack frame, which always belongs to the currently executing routine. (Each link actually points to the base of a stack frame.) The stack grows downward in each diagram, so the top of the stack is at the bottom. The diagrams do not show intermediate expression values, which could appear on top of each stack frame.

▬▬▬▬▬▬ **Table 9.1** Static Links During Subroutine Calls

Figure 9.3a	`main1` calls `proc2`	`proc2`'s static link points back to `main1`'s stack frame, since `main1` immediately contains `proc2`.
Figure 9.3b	`proc2` calls `proc3`	`proc3`'s static link points back to `proc2`'s stack frame, since `proc2` immediately contains `proc3`.
Figure 9.3c	`proc3` calls `proc3` (direct recursion)	The static link in `proc3`'s new stack frame also points back to `proc2`'s stack frame. When `proc3` returns from the recursive call, the runtime stack resets to its previous state (Figure 9.3b).
Figure 9.3d	`proc3` calls `func2`	`func2`'s static link points back to `main1`'s stack frame, since `main1` immediately contains `func2`.
Figure 9.3e	`func2` calls `func3`	`func3`'s static link points back to `func2`'s stack frame, since `func2` immediately contains `func3`.
Figure 9.3f	`func3` calls `proc2` (indirect recursion)	The static link in `proc2`'s new stack frame points back to `main1`'s stack frame.

▬▬▬▬▬▬

left) always point back to the stack frame of the caller. The static links (drawn on the right) are more interesting to watch, as described in Table 9.1.

That's quite a bit of work to maintain the static links, so what are they good for? The static links enable us to access nonlocal values. To access the value of any routine's formal parameters or local variables, we must know the runtime stack location of the base of the routine's stack frame, so that we can add an offset from there to get to the value. Accessing the values of the currently executing routine is easy, since the stack frame base pointer points to its stack frame.

In Figure 9.3e, `func3` is currently executing. We can access the value of its formal parameter k directly, since it is allocated in `func3`'s stack frame, which the stack frame base pointer points to. To access the value of `func2`'s formal parameter j, we must first follow the static link from func3's stack frame back to func2's stack frame. Then we can add j's offset to the base of func2's stack frame to get to j's value.

To access the value of main1's local variable i, we must follow the static link from func3's stack frame back to func2's stack frame, and then the static link from func2's stack frame back to main1's stack frame. From there, we add i's offset to get to its value.

How do we know how many static links to follow to get to a particular value? It's all done with the difference in nesting levels. In the first case, to access k's value, the current nesting level (of currently executing func3's statements) is 3, and k's nesting is also 3. The difference is 0, so we know the value is local and no static links need to be followed. In the second case, j's nesting level is 2, so the difference is 3 - 2 = 1. We must follow one static link to get to j's value. In the third case, i's nesting level is 1, the difference is 3 - 1 = 2, and so we must follow two static links to get to i's value.

Notice that while func3 is executing, we cannot access any of proc3's or proc2's values, even though they are in the call chain. This is in accordance with Pascal's scope rules. Similarly, in Figure 9.3c, during proc3's second invocation, we cannot access the values from its first invocation.

So we see that accessing nonlocal values is slower than accessing local values, since we must follow static links to get to them. How much slower depends on the difference between the current nesting level and the nesting level of the nonlocal parameter or variable.

Return Address

The last component in a stack frame header is the return address. Whenever a routine calls a subroutine (the *callee*), the caller must record the return address on the runtime stack, so that when the callee completes its execution, we know where to return to in the caller's code.

The interpreter executes a routine's statements from its intermediate code, so the return address is a location within that code. Since every object of class TIcode contains a pointer to the current location within its code (data member cursor), we may at first think that the return address can simply be a pointer to the caller routine's icode object. But once again, we need to consider recursion. Each recursive call may have a different return location within the intermediate code. So, the return address that we store in a stack frame header must contain two parts: a pointer to the caller routine's icode object and the return location within the code.

The Runtime Stack Class

Figure 9.4 shows the class diagram for the new version of class `TRuntimeStack`. Class `TExecutor` contains the runtime stack object as private data member run-

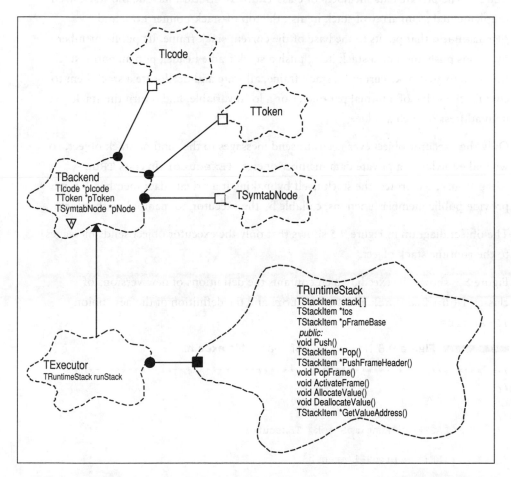

Figure 9.4 Class diagram for the new version of class **TRuntimeStack**.

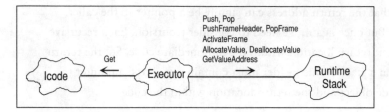

Push, Pop
PushFrameHeader, PopFrame
ActivateFrame
AllocateValue, DeallocateValue
GetValueAddress

Icode ← Get — Executor → Runtime Stack

Figure 9.5 Only the executor object sends messages to the runtime stack object.

Stack. The private data members of class TRuntimeStack include the stack itself (implemented as an array of stack items), the top-of-stack pointer tos, and pFrameBase that points to the base of the current stack frame. Its public member functions push and pop a stack item, push a stack frame header, pop an entire stack frame, activate (make current) a stack frame, allocate and deallocate a stack item to contain the value of a formal parameter or a local variable, and return the stack item address of such a value.

Only the executor object ever needs to send messages to the runtime stack object, so we make the latter a private data member of class TExecutor. In class TRuntimeStack, we protect the stack itself by making it a private data member, but we provide public member functions, callable by the executor, to manipulate the stack.

The object diagram in Figure 9.5 shows that only the executor object sends messages to the runtime stack object.

Figure 9.6 shows file exec.h, which contains the definitions of new versions of classes TRuntimeStack and TExecutor, and the definition of the new union TStackItem.

Figure 9.6 New version of header file **exec.h**.

```
//    ****************************************************************
//    *                                                            *
//    *    E X E C U T O R   (Header)                              *
//    *                                                            *
//    *    CLASSES: TRuntimeStack, TExecutor                       *
//    *                                                            *
//    *    FILE:    prog9-1/exec.h                                 *
//    *                                                            *
//    *    MODULE:  Executor                                       *
//    *                                                            *
```

```
//   *                                                       *
//   *    Copyright (c) 1996 by Ronald Mak                   *
//   *    For instructional purposes only.  No warranties.   *
//   *                                                       *
//   ***********************************************************

#ifndef exec_h
#define exec_h

#include "error.h"
#include "symtab.h"
#include "types.h"
#include "icode.h"
#include "backend.h"

//----------------------------------------------------------------
//  TStackItem          Item pushed onto the runtime stack.
//----------------------------------------------------------------

union TStackItem {
    int     integer;
    float   real;
    char    character;
    void    *address;
};

//----------------------------------------------------------------
//  TRuntimeStack       Runtime stack class.
//----------------------------------------------------------------

class TRuntimeStack {
    enum {
        stackSize       = 128,
        frameHeaderSize =   5,
    };

    //--Stack frame header
    struct TFrameHeader {
        TStackItem functionValue;
        TStackItem staticLink;
        TStackItem dynamicLink;

        struct {
            TStackItem icode;
            TStackItem location;
        } returnAddress;
```

(continues)

Figure 9.6 New version of header file **exec.h**. (*Continued*)

```cpp
    };

    TStackItem  stack[stackSize];  // stack items
    TStackItem *tos;               // ptr to the top of the stack
    TStackItem *pFrameBase;        // ptr to current stack frame base

public:
    TRuntimeStack(void);

    void Push(int value)
    {
        if (tos < &stack[stackSize-1]) (++tos)->integer = value;
        else RuntimeError(rteStackOverflow);
    }

    void Push(float value)
    {
        if (tos < &stack[stackSize-1]) (++tos)->real = value;
        else RuntimeError(rteStackOverflow);
    }

    void Push(char value)
    {
        if (tos < &stack[stackSize-1]) (++tos)->character = value;
        else RuntimeError(rteStackOverflow);
    }

    void Push(void *addr)
    {
        if (tos < &stack[stackSize-1]) (++tos)->address = addr;
        else RuntimeError(rteStackOverflow);
    }

    TStackItem *PushFrameHeader(int oldLevel, int newLevel,
                               TIcode *pIcode);
    void ActivateFrame(TStackItem *pNewFrameBase, int location);
    void PopFrame     (const TSymtabNode *pRoutineId, TIcode *&pIcode);

    TStackItem *Pop(void)       { return tos--; }
    TStackItem *TOS(void) const { return tos;   }

    void AllocateValue  (const TSymtabNode *pId);
    void DeallocateValue(const TSymtabNode *pId);

    TStackItem *GetValueAddress(const TSymtabNode *pId);
```

```
};

//------------------------------------------------------------
//  TExecutor           Executor subclass of TBackend.
//------------------------------------------------------------

class TExecutor : public TBackend {
    long          stmtCount;  // count of executed statements
    TRuntimeStack runStack;   // ptr to runtime stack

    int eofFlag;  // true if at end of file, else false

    //--Trace flags
    int traceRoutineFlag;      // true to trace routine entry/exit
    int traceStatementFlag;    // true to trace statements
    int traceStoreFlag;        // true to trace data stores
    int traceFetchFlag;        // true to trace data fetches

    //--Routines
    void    ExecuteRoutine(const TSymtabNode *pRoutineId);
    void    EnterRoutine  (const TSymtabNode *pRoutineId);
    void    ExitRoutine   (const TSymtabNode *pRoutineId);
    TType *ExecuteSubroutineCall        (const TSymtabNode *pRoutineId);
    TType *ExecuteDeclaredSubroutineCall(const TSymtabNode *pRoutineId);
    TType *ExecuteStandardSubroutineCall(const TSymtabNode *pRoutineId);
    void    ExecuteActualParameters     (const TSymtabNode *pRoutineId);

    //--Statements
    void ExecuteStatement(void);
    void ExecuteStatementList(TTokenCode terminator);
    void ExecuteAssignment(const TSymtabNode *pTargetId);
    void ExecuteREPEAT(void);
    void ExecuteCompound(void);

    //--Expressions
    TType *ExecuteExpression(void);
    TType *ExecuteSimpleExpression(void);
    TType *ExecuteTerm(void);
    TType *ExecuteFactor(void);
    TType *ExecuteConstant  (const TSymtabNode *pId);
    TType *ExecuteVariable  (const TSymtabNode *pId, int addressFlag);
    TType *ExecuteSubscripts(const TType *pType);
    TType *ExecuteField(void);

    //--Tracing
    void TraceRoutineEntry(const TSymtabNode *pRoutineId);
```

(continues)

■■■■ ■■■■ **Figure 9.6** New version of header file **exec.h**. (*Continued*)

```
    void TraceRoutineExit (const TSymtabNode *pRoutineId);
    void TraceStatement(void);
    void TraceDataStore(const TSymtabNode *pTargetId,
                        const void       *pDataValue,
                        const TType       *pDataType);
    void TraceDataFetch(const TSymtabNode *pId,
                        const void       *pDataValue,
                        const TType       *pDataType);
    void TraceDataValue(const void       *pDataValue,
                        const TType       *pDataType);

    void RangeCheck(const TType *pTargetType, int value);

    void Push(int    value) { runStack.Push(value); }
    void Push(float  value) { runStack.Push(value); }
    void Push(char   value) { runStack.Push(value); }
    void Push(void  *addr)  { runStack.Push(addr);  }

    TStackItem *Pop(void)        { return runStack.Pop(); }
    TStackItem *TOS(void) const { return runStack.TOS(); }

public:
    TExecutor(void)
    {
        stmtCount = 0;

        traceRoutineFlag   = true;
        traceStatementFlag = true;
        traceStoreFlag     = true;
        traceFetchFlag     = true;
    }

    virtual void Go(const TSymtabNode *pProgramId);
};

#endif
```

To keep things simpler, we'll assume that all items on the runtime stack are the same size. Union `TStackItem` represents an item, which can contain an integer, real, or character value, or it can contain a generic address. We use a generic (`void *`) address because at times, a stack item can point to data in another stack item or to the separately allocated data area of an array or a record, or a stack item can be part of a return address and point to an icode object.

Public member function TRuntimeStack::Push is overloaded to push an integer, real, character, or address stack item. Each version first checks for a stack overflow. Member function Pop returns the top-of-stack pointer and then decrements it, and member function TOS simply returns the top-of-stack pointer.

We'll look at the definition of the new version of class TExecutor later.

■■■■■■■■ **Figure 9.7** New version of implementation file **exec.cpp**.

```
//   ****************************************************************
//   *                                                              *
//   *    E X E C U T O R                                           *
//   *                                                              *
//   *    Execute the intermediate code.                            *
//   *                                                              *
//   *    CLASSES: TRuntimeStack, TExecutor                         *
//   *                                                              *
//   *    FILE:    prog9-1/exec.cpp                                 *
//   *                                                              *
//   *    MODULE:  Executor                                         *
//   *                                                              *
//   *    Copyright (c) 1996 by Ronald Mak                          *
//   *    For instructional purposes only.  No warranties.          *
//   *                                                              *
//   ****************************************************************

#include "exec.h"

//              *******************
//              *                 *
//              *   Runtime Stack  *
//              *                 *
//              *******************


//----------------------------------------------------------------
// Constructor
//----------------------------------------------------------------

TRuntimeStack::TRuntimeStack(void)
{
    tos       = &stack[-1];  // point to just below bottom of stack
    pFrameBase = &stack[ 0];  // point to bottom of stack

    //--Initialize the program's stack frame at the bottom.
    Push(0);  // function return value
    Push(0);  // static  link
```

(continues)

```
    Push(0);  // dynamic link
    Push(0);  // return address icode pointer
    Push(0);  // return address icode location
}


//------------------------------------------------------------
//  PushFrameHeader      Push the callee subroutine's stack frame
//                       header onto the runtime stack.  (Leave
//                       it inactive.)
//
//      oldLevel : nesting level of the caller routine
//      newLevel : nesting level of the callee subroutine's
//                 formal parameters and local variables
//      pIcode   : ptr to caller's intermediate code
//
//  Return: ptr to the base of the callee's stack frame
//------------------------------------------------------------

TStackItem *TRuntimeStack::PushFrameHeader(int oldLevel, int newLevel,
                                           TIcode *pIcode)
{
    TFrameHeader *pHeader = (TFrameHeader *) pFrameBase;
    TStackItem   *pNewFrameBase = tos + 1;  // point to item just above
                                            //   current TOS item

    Push(0);  // function return value (placeholder)

    //--Compute the static link.
    if (newLevel == oldLevel + 1) {

        //--Callee nested within caller:
        //--Push address of caller's stack frame.
        Push(pHeader);
    }
    else if (newLevel == oldLevel) {

        //--Callee at same level as caller:
        //--Push address of common parent's stack frame.
        Push(pHeader->staticLink.address);
    }
    else /* newLevel < oldLevel */ {

        //--Callee nested less deeply than caller:
        //--Push address of nearest commmon ancestor's stack frame.
        int delta = oldLevel - newLevel;
```

```
        while (delta-- >= 0) {
            pHeader = (TFrameHeader *) pHeader->staticLink.address;
        }
        Push(pHeader);
    }

    Push(pFrameBase);   // dynamic link
    Push(pIcode);       // return address icode pointer
    Push(0);            // return address icode location (placeholder)

    return pNewFrameBase;
}

//-------------------------------------------------------------
//  ActivateFrame      Activate the newly-allocated stack frame
//                     by pointing the frame base pointer to it
//                     and setting the return address location.
//
//      pNewFrameBase : ptr to the new stack frame base
//      location      : return address location
//-------------------------------------------------------------

void TRuntimeStack::ActivateFrame(TStackItem *pNewFrameBase,
                                  int location)
{
    pFrameBase = pNewFrameBase;
    ((TFrameHeader *) pFrameBase)->returnAddress
                                .location.integer = location;
}


//-------------------------------------------------------------
//  PopFrame   Pop the current frame from the runtime stack.
//             If it's for a function, leave the return value
//             on the top of the stack.
//
//      pRoutineId : ptr to subroutine name's symbol table node
//      pIcode     : ref to ptr to caller's intermediate code
//-------------------------------------------------------------

void TRuntimeStack::PopFrame(const TSymtabNode *pRoutineId,
                             TIcode *&pIcode)
{
    TFrameHeader *pHeader = (TFrameHeader *) pFrameBase;

    //--Don't do anything if it's the bottommost stack frame.
    if (pFrameBase != &stack[0]) {
```

(continues)

```
        //--Return to the caller's intermediate code.
        pIcode = (TIcode *) pHeader->returnAddress.icode.address;
        pIcode->GoTo(pHeader->returnAddress.location.integer);

        //--Cut the stack back.  Leave a function value on top.
        tos = (TStackItem *) pFrameBase;
        if (pRoutineId->defn.how != dcFunction) --tos;
        pFrameBase = (TStackItem *) pHeader->dynamicLink.address;
    }
}


//----------------------------------------------------------------
//  AllocateValue        Allocate a runtime stack item for the
//                       value of a formal parameter or a local
//                       variable.
//
//      pId : ptr to symbol table node of variable or parm
//----------------------------------------------------------------

void TRuntimeStack::AllocateValue(const TSymtabNode *pId)
{
    TType *pType = pId->pType->Base();  // ptr to type object of value

    if      (pType == pIntegerType) Push(0);
    else if (pType == pRealType)    Push(0.0f);
    else if (pType == pBooleanType) Push(0);
    else if (pType == pCharType)    Push(0);

    else if (pType->form == fcEnum) Push(0);
    else {

        //--Array or record
        void *addr = new char[pType->size];
        Push(addr);
    }
}


//----------------------------------------------------------------
//  DeallocateValue      Deallocate the data area of an array or
//                       record value of a formal value parameter
//                       or a local variable.
//
//      pId : ptr to symbol table node of variable or parm
//----------------------------------------------------------------
```

```
void TRuntimeStack::DeallocateValue(const TSymtabNode *pId)
{
    if ((! pId->pType->IsScalar()) && (pId->defn.how != dcVarParm)) {
        TStackItem *pValue = ((TStackItem *) pFrameBase)
                                            + frameHeaderSize
                                            + pId->defn.data.offset;

        delete[] pValue->address;
    }
}


//-------------------------------------------------------------
//  GetValueAddress      Get the address of the runtime stack
//                       item that contains the value of a formal
//                       parameter or a local variable.  If
//                       nonlocal, follow the static links to the
//                       appropriate stack frame.
//
//      pId : ptr to symbol table node of variable or parm
//
//  Return:  ptr to the runtime stack item containing the
//           variable, parameter, or function return value
//-------------------------------------------------------------

TStackItem *TRuntimeStack::GetValueAddress(const TSymtabNode *pId)
{
    int functionFlag = pId->defn.how == dcFunction;  // true if function
                                                     //   else false
    TFrameHeader *pHeader = (TFrameHeader *) pFrameBase;

    //--Compute the difference between the current nesting level
    //--and the level of the variable or parameter.  Treat a function
    //--value as if it were a local variable of the function.  (Local
    //--variables are one level higher than the function name.)
    int delta = currentNestingLevel - pId->level;
    if (functionFlag) --delta;

    //--Chase static links delta times.
    while (delta-- > 0) {
        pHeader = (TFrameHeader *) pHeader->staticLink.address;
    }

    return functionFlag ? &pHeader->functionValue
                        : ((TStackItem *) pHeader)
                            + frameHeaderSize + pId->defn.data.offset;
}
```

(continues)

■■■■ **Figure 9.7** New version of implementation file **exec.cpp**. (*Continued*)

```
//              *************
//              *           *
//              *  Executor  *
//              *           *
//              *************


//-------------------------------------------------------------
// Go                   Start the executor.
//-------------------------------------------------------------

void TExecutor::Go(const TSymtabNode *pProgramId)
{
    //--Initialize standard input and output.
    eofFlag = cin.eof();
    cout.setf(ios::fixed, ios::floatfield);
    cout << endl;

    //--Execute the program.
    currentNestingLevel = 1;
    ExecuteRoutine(pProgramId);

    //--Print the executor's summary.
    cout << endl;
    cout << "Successful completion.  " << stmtCount
         << " statements executed." << endl;
}


//-------------------------------------------------------------
// RangeCheck       Range check an assignment to a subrange.
//
//      pTargetType : ptr to target type object
//      value       : integer value to assign
//-------------------------------------------------------------

void TExecutor::RangeCheck(const TType *pTargetType, int value)
{

    if (    (pTargetType->form == fcSubrange)
        && (    (value < pTargetType->subrange.min)
            || (value > pTargetType->subrange.max))) {
        RuntimeError(rteValueOutOfRange);
    }
}
```

Figure 9.7 shows implementation file `exec.cpp`, which implements classes `TRun-timeStack` and `TExecutor`. Class `TRuntimeStack`'s constructor function initializes the pointers `tos` and `pFrameBase`, and allocates the stack frame for the main routine at the bottom of the stack.

The executor object sends the `PushFrameHeader` message to the runtime stack to initiate a subroutine call. The member function allocates a new stack frame header at the top of the stack for the callee. First it pushes a placeholder item for the function return value (allocated but unused by a procedure call). Then it must push the static link, which it computes based on the current nesting level of the caller (`oldLevel`) and the nesting level of the callee (`newLevel`):

- The callee is nested in the caller (for an example, see Figure 9.3b), so that `newLevel` equals `oldLevel + 1`. The static link is a pointer to the caller's stack frame base, which is the current value of the stack frame pointer `pFrameBase`.
- The callee is at the same level as the caller. The static link is a pointer to their common parent routine's stack frame base, the value of `pHeader->staticLink.address`.
- The callee is nested less deeply than the caller, so that `newLevel` is less than `oldLevel` (see Figures 9.3d and 9.3f). The static link is a pointer to their nearest common ancestor routine's stack frame base. This value is obtained by following `oldLevel-newLevel+1` static links from the caller's stack frame.

Next, `PushFrameHeader` pushes the value of `pFrameBase` for the dynamic link. Finally, it pushes the two-part return address. The first part is a pointer to the caller's icode object, and the second part is a placeholder for now.

Note that `PushFrameHeader` does not set `pFrameBase` to point to the newly allocated stack frame. This is done later by member function `ActivateFrame`. The reason for this delay will become clear shortly when we see how actual parameter expressions are evaluated and pushed onto the stack.

Member function `PopFrame` pops off a subroutine's stack frame when it's time to return. First, the return address is obtained from the stack frame header, and then the entire stack frame is cut off the stack via its dynamic link: `pFrameBase` is reset to point to the caller's stack frame.

Member function `AllocateValue` allocates a stack item for the value of a routine's formal parameter or local variable. For a scalar value, it simply pushes a placeholder. (Presumably, its value is set during the routine's execution.) For an array or a record value, `AllocateValue` allocates a separate data area of the appropriate size, and pushes the address of this area onto the stack. Thus, as far as the runtime stack is concerned, the value of a parameter or a variable that is an array or a record is the pointer to its data area. We'll reemphasize this point later when we see arrays and records in expressions and passed as value or `VAR` parameters. A formal `VAR` parameter also has as its value the address of the original data.

When a subroutine returns, we don't need to pop off its parameter and variable values individually, since `PopFrame` removes the entire stack frame all at once. However, member function `DeallocateValue` does need to be called to deallocate the array and record data areas.

Member function `GetValueAddress` returns a pointer to the stack item that contains the value of a formal parameter or local variable. As described earlier, it uses the difference between the current nesting level and the nesting level of the parameter or variable to determine how many static links to follow to the base of the appropriate stack frame. It then adds the offset of the parameter or variable and the size of the stack frame header in order to point to the desired stack item.

`GetValueAddress` can also return a pointer to a function's return value. In this case, it must take into account that a function name's nesting level is one less than that of its parameters and variables. Also, there is no offset, since the return value is at the base of the function's stack frame header.

■■■■■■ **Figure 9.8** New version of member function **ParseVariableDeclarations** in implementation file **parsdecl.cpp**.

```
//-------------------------------------------------------------
//  ParseVariableDeclarations    Parse variable declarations.
//
//      pRoutineId : ptr to symbol table node of program,
//                   procedure, or function identifier
//-------------------------------------------------------------

void TParser::ParseVariableDeclarations(TSymtabNode *pRoutineId)
{
```

```
if (execFlag) {
    ParseVarOrFieldDecls(pRoutineId, NULL,
            pRoutineId->defn.routine.parmCount);
    }
}
```

Figure 9.8 shows the new version of member function `TParser::ParseVari-ableDeclarations` in implementation file `parsdecl.cpp`. It passes the value of `pRoutineId->defn.routine.parmCount` to member function `TParser::ParseVarOrFieldDecls` to properly initialize the offset of the first local variable, since the first local variable is allocated on the runtime stack on top of the last formal parameter. (The offsets of the formal parameter identifiers already properly begin with zero.)

Executing Statements and Expressions

Figure 9.6 also showed the new definition of class `TExecutor`. Figure 9.9 shows its class diagram. Private data member `eofFlag` keeps track of whether the standard

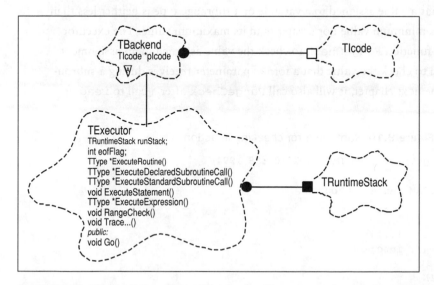

Figure 9.9 Class diagram for the new version of class **TExecutor**.

input file is at the end. This becomes important in the next chapter during calls to the standard procedures read and readln.

Class TExecutor now has new member functions to execute routines and to evaluate constants and variables, and new member functions to do debug tracing and range checking. Several member functions, Push, Pop, and TOS, send messages directly to the runtime stack object. Like their parser counterparts, each of the expression execution member functions now returns a pointer to the type object of the expression.

Figure 9.7 also showed the implementation of the member functions Go and RangeCheck. Go first initializes eofFlag and the standard output file to print all real numbers with the fixed-point notation (for calls to the standard procedures write and writeln in the next chapter). It resets the current nesting level to 1 (the level of the main program's statements), and calls member function ExecuteRoutine to execute the program.

Runtime Range Checking

Runtime range checking is another example of runtime error checking, which we first saw in Chapter 5, where we checked for division by zero. Range checking makes sure that a value assigned to a variable of a subrange type is neither less than the subrange's minimum value nor greater than its maximum value. The executor calls member function RangeCheck to check the value assigned in an assignment statement and to check the value that a formal parameter receives during a subroutine call. In the next chapter, it will also call RangeCheck after a call to read or readln.

■■■■ **Figure 9.10** Runtime error checking in action.

```
Page 1    range.pas    Wed Dec 21 22:03:58 1994


  1 0: PROGRAM range (output);
  2 1:
  3 1: VAR
  4 1:     i : 1..10;
  5 1:     j : integer;
  6 1:
  7 1: BEGIN
  8 1:     j := 12;
  9 1:     i := j;       {range error!}
```

```
10 1: END.
11 0:

                11 source lines.
                 0 syntax errors.
```

```
>> Entering routine range
>>   At 8
>>     j <== 12
>>   At 9
>>     j: 12

*** RUNTIME ERROR in line 9: Value out of range
```

Figure 9.10 shows runtime error checking in action. It also shows some runtime trace output.

Debugging Traces

In Chapter 11, we'll write routines that will allow us to control and monitor the execution of a program. For now, the executor will use several passive debugging routines that print subroutine entry and exit, data values that are fetched or stored, and the line numbers of the statements being executed. Figure 9.11 shows the implementation of these member functions in file tracer.cpp. Trace output will be controlled by several global flags, traceRoutineFlag, traceStatementFlag, traceStoreFlag, and traceFetchFlag.

■■■■■■■ **Figure 9.11** Implementation file **tracer.cpp**.

```
// ***************************************************************
// *                                                             *
// *    T R A C E R                                              *
// *                                                             *
// *    Print debugging runtime trace messages.                 *
// *                                                             *
// *    CLASSES: TExecutor                                       *
// *                                                             *
// *    FILE:    prog9-1/tracer.cpp                              *
// *                                                             *
// *    MODULE:  Executor                                        *
// *                                                             *
// *    Copyright (c) 1996 by Ronald Mak                         *
// *    For instructional purposes only.  No warranties.        *
// *                                                             *
// ***************************************************************
```

(continues)

■■■■■■■■ **Figure 9.11** Implementation file **tracer.cpp**. (*Continued*)

```cpp
#include <stdio.h>
#include <string.h>
#include <iostream.h>
#include "common.h"
#include "buffer.h"
#include "exec.h"


//----------------------------------------------------------------
//  TraceRoutineEntry   Trace the entry into a routine.
//
//      pId : ptr to the routine name's symbol table node
//----------------------------------------------------------------

void TExecutor::TraceRoutineEntry(const TSymtabNode *pRoutineId)
{
    if (traceRoutineFlag) {
        cout << ">> Entering routine " << pRoutineId->String() << endl;
    }
}


//----------------------------------------------------------------
//  TraceRoutineExit    Trace the exit from a routine.
//
//      pId : ptr to the routine name's symbol table node
//----------------------------------------------------------------

void TExecutor::TraceRoutineExit(const TSymtabNode *pRoutineId)
{
    if (traceRoutineFlag) {
        cout << ">> Exiting routine " << pRoutineId->String() << endl;
    }
}


//----------------------------------------------------------------
//  TraceStatement      Trace the execution of a statement.
//----------------------------------------------------------------

void TExecutor::TraceStatement(void)
{
    if (traceStatementFlag) cout << ">>  At " << currentLineNumber
                                 << endl;
}


//----------------------------------------------------------------
//  TraceDataStore      Trace the storing of data into a
```

```
//                       variable or formal parameter.
//
//      pTargetId  : ptr to the target name's symbol table node
//      pDataValue : ptr to the data value
//      pDataType  : ptr to the data's type object
//------------------------------------------------------------

void TExecutor::TraceDataStore(const TSymtabNode *pTargetId,
                               const void        *pDataValue,
                               const TType        *pDataType)
{
    if (traceStoreFlag) {
        TFormCode form = pTargetId->pType->form;

        cout << ">>   " << pTargetId->String();
        if      (form == fcArray)  cout << "[*]";
        else if (form == fcRecord) cout << ".*";
        cout << " <== ";

        TraceDataValue(pDataValue, pDataType);
    }
}


//------------------------------------------------------------
// TraceDataFetch      Trace the fetching of data from a
//                     variable or formal parameter.
//
//      pId        : ptr to the variable name's symbol table node
//      pDataValue : ptr to the data value
//      pDataType  : ptr to the data's type object
//------------------------------------------------------------

void TExecutor::TraceDataFetch(const TSymtabNode *pId,
                               const void        *pDataValue,
                               const TType        *pDataType)
{
    if (traceFetchFlag) {
        TFormCode form = pId->pType->form;

        cout << ">>   " << pId->String();
        if      (form == fcArray)  cout << "[*]";
        else if (form == fcRecord) cout << ".*";
        cout << ": ";

        TraceDataValue(pDataValue, pDataType);
    }
}
```

(continues)

■■■■■■■ **Figure 9.11** Implementation file **tracer.cpp**. (*Continued*)

```cpp
//-----------------------------------------------------------
//  TraceDataValue       Trace a data value.
//
//      pDataValue : ptr to the data value
//      pDataType  : ptr to the data's type object
//-----------------------------------------------------------

void TExecutor::TraceDataValue(const void  *pDataValue,
                               const TType *pDataType)
{
    char text[maxInputBufferSize];  // text for value

    if (pDataType == pRealType) {
        sprintf(text, "%0.6g", ((TStackItem *) pDataValue)->real);
    }
    else if (pDataType == pCharType) {
        sprintf(text, "'%c'", ((TStackItem *) pDataValue)->character);
    }
    else if (pDataType == pBooleanType) {
        strcpy(text, ((TStackItem *) pDataValue)->integer == 0
                                          ? "false" : "true");
    }
    else if (pDataType->form == fcArray) {
        if (pDataType->array.pElmtType == pCharType) {
            int length = pDataType->array.elmtCount;
            memcpy(text + 1, pDataValue, length);
            text[0]          = '\'';
            text[length + 1] = '\'';
            text[length + 2] = '\0';
        }
        else strcpy(text, "<array>");
    }
    else if (pDataType->form == fcRecord) {
        strcpy(text, "<record>");
    }
    else if (pDataType->Base()->form == fcEnum) {
        int count = ((TStackItem *) pDataValue)->integer;
        TSymtabNode *pId = pDataType->Base()->enumeration.pConstIds;
        while (--count >= 0) pId = pId->next;
        strcpy(text, pId->String());
    }
    else {
        sprintf(text, "%d", ((TStackItem *) pDataValue)->integer);
    }

    cout << text << endl;
}
```

Member functions `TraceRoutineEntry` and `TraceRoutineExit` print the name of the routine being called or being returned from, respectively. Member function `TraceStatement` prints the source line number (as determined from the last-encountered line marker in the intermediate code) of the statement currently being executed.

Member functions `TraceDataStore` and `TraceDataFetch` print the name of the formal parameter or variable whose value is being set or accessed, respectively. Each prints an indication that the variable or parameter is an array element or a record field, but does not attempt to print the full subscript expression or field designator. Both call member function `TraceDataValue` to print the value.

▮▮▮▮▮▮▮▮▮▮ **Figure 9.12** New version of member function **ExecuteStatement** in implementation file **execstmt.cpp**.

```cpp
#include <memory.h>
#include "exec.h"

//------------------------------------------------------------
//  ExecuteStatement      Execute a statement.
//------------------------------------------------------------

void TExecutor::ExecuteStatement(void)
{
    if (token != tcBEGIN) {
        ++stmtCount;
        TraceStatement();
    }

    switch (token) {

        case tcIdentifier: {
            if (pNode->defn.how == dcProcedure) {
                ExecuteSubroutineCall(pNode);
            }
            else {
                ExecuteAssignment(pNode);
            }
            break;
        }

        case tcREPEAT:      ExecuteREPEAT();      break;
        case tcBEGIN:       ExecuteCompound();    break;
```

(continues)

■■■■■■■■ **Figure 9.12** New version of member function **ExecuteStatement** in
implementation file **execstmt.cpp**. (*Continued*)

```
        case tcWHILE:
        case tcIF:
        case tcFOR:
        case tcCASE:
            RuntimeError(rteUnimplementedRuntimeFeature);
            break;
    }
}
```

Executing Statements

Figure 9.12 shows the new version of member function ExecuteStatement in the
implementation file. If the statement to be executed is not a compound statement,
the function increments stmtCount and calls TraceStatement to print a statement trace.

If the lead token of the statement is an identifier, ExecuteStatement must now
decide whether the statement is an assignment statement or a procedure call. In the
latter case, it calls member function ExecuteSubroutineCall, which we'll
examine later.

■■■■■■■■ **Figure 9.13** New version of member function **ExecuteAssignment** in
implementation file **execstmt.cpp**.

```
//---------------------------------------------------------------
//  ExecuteAssignment     Execute an assignment statement.
//                        Print the assigned value of the
//                        target variable if it is "output".
//
//      pTargetId : ptr to target's symbol table node
//---------------------------------------------------------------

void TExecutor::ExecuteAssignment(const TSymtabNode *pTargetId)
{
    TStackItem *pTarget;       // runtime stack address of target
    TType      *pTargetType;   // ptr to target type object
    TType      *pExprType;     // ptr to expression type object

    //--Assignment to function name.
    if (pTargetId->defn.how == dcFunction) {
        pTargetType = pTargetId->pType;
        pTarget     = runStack.GetValueAddress(pTargetId);
```

```
        GetToken();
    }

    //--Assignment to variable or formal parameter.
    //--ExecuteVariable leaves the target address on
    //--top of the runtime stack.
    else {
        pTargetType = ExecuteVariable(pTargetId, true);
        pTarget     = (TStackItem *) Pop()->address;
    }

    //--Execute the expression and leave its value
    //--on top of the runtime stack.
    GetToken();
    pExprType = ExecuteExpression();

    //--Do the assignment.
    if (pTargetType == pRealType) {
        pTarget->real = pExprType->Base() == pIntegerType
                            ? Pop()->integer  // real := integer
                            : Pop()->real;    // real := real
    }
    else if ((pTargetType->Base() == pIntegerType) ||
             (pTargetType->Base()->form == fcEnum)) {
        int value = Pop()->integer;
        RangeCheck(pTargetType, value);

        //--integer     := integer
        //--enumeration := enumeration
        pTarget->integer = value;
    }
    else if (pTargetType->Base() == pCharType) {
        char value = Pop()->character;
        RangeCheck(pTargetType, value);

        //--character := character
        pTarget->character = value;
    }
    else {
        void *pSource = Pop()->address;

        //--array  := array
        //--record := record
        memcpy(pTarget, pSource, pTargetType->size);
    }

    TraceDataStore(pTargetId, pTarget, pTargetType);
}
```

Figure 9.13 shows the new version of member function `ExecuteAssignment` in file `execstmt.cpp`. If the target is a function identifier, it sends the `GetValueAddress` to the runtime stack object to get the stack item address of the return value. Otherwise, it calls member function `ExecuteVariable` (described later) to push the stack item address of the variable's value. In either case, local variable `pTarget` will contain the target's stack item address.

After calling member function `ExecuteExpression`, `ExecuteAssignment` is ready to assign the value. It assigns scalar values directly to the target stack item. If the expression evaluated to an array or a record, its value left on the stack is the address of its data area. `ExecuteAssignment` copies this data area into the target's data area. Finally, function `TraceDataStore` is called to print a data store trace.

There is one more small change in file `execstmt.cpp`. In member function `ExecuteREPEAT`, we need to modify the statement that tests the value of the `UNTIL` expression, since a stack item now can contain several types of values:

```
//--Decide whether or not to branch back to the loop start.
if (runStack.Pop()->integer == 0) GoTo(atLoopStart);
```

■■■■■■■ **Figure 9.14** New version of implementation file **execexpr.cpp**.

```
//   ****************************************************************
//   *                                                              *
//   *      E X E C U T O R     (Expressions)                       *
//   *                                                              *
//   *      Execute expressions.                                    *
//   *                                                              *
//   *      CLASSES: TExecutor                                      *
//   *                                                              *
//   *      FILE:    prog9-1/execexpr.cpp                           *
//   *                                                              *
//   *      MODULE:  Executor                                       *
//   *                                                              *
//   *      Copyright (c) 1996 by Ronald Mak                        *
//   *      For instructional purposes only.  No warranties.        *
//   *                                                              *
//   ****************************************************************

#include <string.h>
#include "exec.h"
```

```
//-------------------------------------------------------------
// ExecuteExpression    Execute an expression (binary relational
//                      operators = < > <> <= and >= ).
//
// Return: ptr to expression's type object
//-------------------------------------------------------------

TType *TExecutor::ExecuteExpression(void)
{
    TType       *pOperand1Type;  // ptr to first  operand's type
    TType       *pOperand2Type;  // ptr to second operand's type
    TType       *pResultType;    // ptr to result type
    TTokenCode  op;              // operator

    //--Execute the first simple expression.
    pResultType = ExecuteSimpleExpression();

    //--If we now see a relational operator,
    //--execute the second simple expression.
    if (TokenIn(token, tlRelOps)) {
        op            = token;
        pOperand1Type = pResultType->Base();
        pResultType   = pBooleanType;

        GetToken();
        pOperand2Type = ExecuteSimpleExpression()->Base();

        //--Perform the operation, and push the resulting value
        //--onto the stack.
        if (   ((pOperand1Type == pIntegerType) &&
                (pOperand2Type == pIntegerType))
            || ((pOperand1Type == pCharType) &&
                (pOperand2Type == pCharType))
            || (pOperand1Type->form == fcEnum)) {

            //--integer <op> integer
            //--boolean <op> boolean
            //--char    <op> char
            //--enum    <op> enum
            int value1, value2;
            if (pOperand1Type == pCharType) {
                value2 = Pop()->character;
                value1 = Pop()->character;
            }
            else {
```

(continues)

■■■■ **Figure 9.14** New version of implementation file **execexpr.cpp**. (*Continued*)

```
        value2 = Pop()->integer;
        value1 = Pop()->integer;
    }

    switch (op) {

        case tcEqual:
            Push(value1 == value2);
            break;

        case tcNe:
            Push(value1 != value2);
            break;

        case tcLt:
            Push(value1 <  value2);
            break;

        case tcGt:
            Push(value1 >  value2);
            break;

        case tcLe:
            Push(value1 <= value2);
            break;

        case tcGe:
            Push(value1 >= value2);
            break;
    }
}
else if ((pOperand1Type == pRealType) ||
         (pOperand2Type == pRealType)) {

    //--real    <op> real
    //--real    <op> integer
    //--integer <op> real
    float value2 = pOperand2Type == pRealType ? Pop()->real
                                              : Pop()->integer;
    float value1 = pOperand1Type == pRealType ? Pop()->real
                                              : Pop()->integer;

    switch (op) {
```

```
                    case tcEqual:
                        Push(value1 == value2);
                        break;

                    case tcNe:
                        Push(value1 != value2);
                        break;

                    case tcLt:
                        Push(value1 <  value2);
                        break;

                    case tcGt:
                        Push(value1 >  value2);
                        break;

                    case tcLe:
                        Push(value1 <= value2);
                        break;

                    case tcGe:
                        Push(value1 >= value2);
                        break;
                }
            }
            else {

                //--string <op> string
                char *addr2 = (char *) Pop()->address;
                char *addr1 = (char *) Pop()->address;

                int cmp = strncmp(addr1, addr2, pOperand1Type->size);

                switch (op) {
                    case tcEqual:   Push(cmp == 0);  break;
                    case tcNe:      Push(cmp != 0);  break;
                    case tcLt:      Push(cmp <  0);  break;
                    case tcGt:      Push(cmp >  0);  break;
                    case tcLe:      Push(cmp <= 0);  break;
                    case tcGe:      Push(cmp >= 0);  break;
                }
            }
        }

        return pResultType;
    }
```

(continues)

■■■■■■ **Figure 9.14** New version of implementation file **execexpr.cpp**. (*Continued*)

```
//------------------------------------------------------------
//  ExecuteSimpleExpression      Execute a simple expression
//                               (unary operators + or -
//                               and binary operators + -
//                               and OR).
//
//  Return: ptr to expression's type object
//------------------------------------------------------------

TType *TExecutor::ExecuteSimpleExpression(void)
{
    TType       *pOperandType;     // ptr to operand's type
    TType       *pResultType;      // ptr to result type
    TTokenCode  op;                // operator
    TTokenCode  unaryOp = tcPlus;  // unary operator

    //--Unary + or -
    if (TokenIn(token, tlUnaryOps)) {
        unaryOp = token;
        GetToken();
    }

    //--Execute the first term.
    pResultType = ExecuteTerm();

    //--If there was a unary -, negate the first operand value.
    if (unaryOp == tcMinus) {
        if (pResultType == pRealType) Push(-Pop()->real);
        else                          Push(-Pop()->integer);
    }

    //--Loop to execute subsequent additive operators and terms.
    while (TokenIn(token, tlAddOps)) {
        op = token;
        pResultType = pResultType->Base();

        GetToken();
        pOperandType = ExecuteTerm()->Base();

        //--Perform the operation, and push the resulting value
        //--onto the stack.
        if (op == tcOR) {

            //--boolean OR boolean
```

```
            int value2 = Pop()->integer;
            int value1 = Pop()->integer;

            Push(value1 || value2);
            pResultType = pBooleanType;
        }
        else if ((pResultType  == pIntegerType) &&
                 (pOperandType == pIntegerType)) {

            //--integer +|- integer
            int value2 = Pop()->integer;
            int value1 = Pop()->integer;

            Push(op == tcPlus ? value1 + value2
                              : value1 - value2);
            pResultType = pIntegerType;
        }
        else {

            //--real    +|- real
            //--real    +|- integer
            //--integer +|- real
            float value2 = pOperandType == pRealType ? Pop()->real
                                                     : Pop()->integer;
            float value1 = pResultType  == pRealType ? Pop()->real
                                                     : Pop()->integer;

            Push(op == tcPlus ? value1 + value2
                              : value1 - value2);
            pResultType = pRealType;
        }
    }

    return pResultType;
}


//-------------------------------------------------------------
//  ExecuteTerm         Execute a term (binary operators * / DIV
//                      MOD and AND).
//
//  Return: ptr to term's type object
//-------------------------------------------------------------

TType *TExecutor::ExecuteTerm(void)
{
    TType       *pOperandType;  // ptr to operand's type
```

(continues)

■■■■■■ **Figure 9.14** New version of implementation file **execexpr.cpp**. (*Continued*)

```
TType       *pResultType;    // ptr to result type
TTokenCode  op;              // operator

//--Execute the first factor.
pResultType = ExecuteFactor();

//--Loop to execute subsequent multiplicative operators and factors.
while (TokenIn(token, tlMulOps)) {
    op = token;
    pResultType = pResultType->Base();

    GetToken();
    pOperandType = ExecuteFactor()->Base();

    //--Perform the operation, and push the resulting value
    //--onto the stack.
    switch (op) {

        case tcAND: {

            //--boolean AND boolean
            int value2 = Pop()->integer;
            int value1 = Pop()->integer;

            Push(value1 && value2);
            pResultType = pBooleanType;
            break;
        }

        case tcStar:

            if ((pResultType  == pIntegerType) &&
                (pOperandType == pIntegerType)) {

                //--integer * integer
                int value2 = Pop()->integer;
                int value1 = Pop()->integer;

                Push(value1*value2);
                pResultType = pIntegerType;
            }
            else {

                //--real    * real
```

```
            //--real    * integer
            //--integer * real
            float value2 = pOperandType == pRealType
                                        ? Pop()->real
                                        : Pop()->integer;
            float value1 = pResultType == pRealType
                                        ? Pop()->real
                                        : Pop()->integer;

            Push(value1*value2);
            pResultType = pRealType;
        }
        break;

    case tcSlash: {

        //--real    / real
        //--real    / integer
        //--integer / real
        //--integer / integer
        float value2 = pOperandType == pRealType
                                    ? Pop()->real
                                    : Pop()->integer;
        float value1 = pResultType == pRealType
                                    ? Pop()->real
                                    : Pop()->integer;

        if (value2 == 0.0f) RuntimeError(rteDivisionByZero);

        Push(value1/value2);
        pResultType = pRealType;
        break;
    }

    case tcDIV:
    case tcMOD: {

        //--integer DIV|MOD integer
        int value2 = Pop()->integer;
        int value1 = Pop()->integer;

        if (value2 == 0) RuntimeError(rteDivisionByZero);

        Push(op == tcDIV ? value1/value2
                         : value1%value2);
        pResultType = pIntegerType;
```

(continues)

```
                break;
            }
        }
    }

    return pResultType;
}

//-------------------------------------------------------------
//  ExecuteFactor      Execute a factor (identifier, number,
//                     string, NOT <factor>, or parenthesized
//                     subexpression).  An identifier can be
//                     a function, constant, or variable.
//
//  Return: ptr to factor's type object
//-------------------------------------------------------------

TType *TExecutor::ExecuteFactor(void)
{
    TType *pResultType;  // ptr to result type

    switch (token) {

        case tcIdentifier: {
            switch (pNode->defn.how) {

                case dcFunction:
                    pResultType = ExecuteSubroutineCall(pNode);
                    break;

                case dcConstant:
                    pResultType = ExecuteConstant(pNode);
                    break;

                default:
                    pResultType = ExecuteVariable(pNode, false);
                    break;
            }
            break;
        }

        case tcNumber: {

            //--Push the number's integer or real value onto the stack.
```

```
    if (pNode->pType == pIntegerType) {
        Push(pNode->defn.constant.value.integer);
    }
    else {
        Push(pNode->defn.constant.value.real);
    }
    pResultType = pNode->pType;

    GetToken();
    break;
}

case tcString: {

    //--Push either a character or a string address onto the
    //--runtime stack, depending on the string length.
    int length = strlen(pNode->String()) - 2;  // skip quotes
    if (length == 1) {

        //--Character
        Push(pNode->defn.constant.value.character);
        pResultType = pCharType;
    }
    else {

        //--String address
        Push(pNode->defn.constant.value.pString);
        pResultType = pNode->pType;
    }

    GetToken();
    break;
}

case tcNOT:

    //--Execute boolean factor and invert its value.
    GetToken();
    ExecuteFactor();

    Push(1 - Pop()->integer);
    pResultType = pBooleanType;
    break;

case tcLParen: {
```

(continues)

■■■■■■■ **Figure 9.14** New version of implementation file **execexpr.cpp**. (*Continued*)

```
            //--Parenthesized subexpression:  Call ExecuteExpression
            //--                               recursively.
            GetToken();  // first token after (

            pResultType = ExecuteExpression();

            GetToken();  // first token after )
            break;
        }
    }

    return pResultType;
}

//----------------------------------------------------------------
// ExecuteConstant      Push a constant onto the runtime stack.
//
//      pId : ptr to constant identifier's symbol table node
//
// Return: ptr to constant's type object
//----------------------------------------------------------------

TType *TExecutor::ExecuteConstant(const TSymtabNode *pId)
{
    TType       *pType = pId->pType;
    TDataValue  value = pId->defn.constant.value;

    if      (pType == pRealType)     Push(value.real);
    else if (pType == pCharType)     Push(value.character);
    else if (pType->form == fcArray) Push(value.pString);
    else                             Push(value.integer);

    GetToken();
    TraceDataFetch(pId, TOS(), pType);
    return pType;
}

//----------------------------------------------------------------
// ExecuteVariable      Push a variable's value or address onto
//                      the runtime stack.
//
//      pId           : ptr to variable's symbol table node
//      addressFlag : true to push address, false to push value
//
```

```
//   Return: ptr to variable's type object
//------------------------------------------------------------

TType *TExecutor::ExecuteVariable(const TSymtabNode *pId,
                                   int addressFlag)
{
    TType *pType = pId->pType;

    //--Get the variable's runtime stack address.
    TStackItem *pEntry = runStack.GetValueAddress(pId);

    //--If it's a VAR formal parameter, or the type is an array
    //--or record, then the stack item contains the address
    //--of the data.  Push the data address onto the stack.
    Push((pId->defn.how == dcVarParm) || (! pType->IsScalar())
               ? pEntry->address
               : pEntry);

    GetToken();

    //--Loop to execute any subscripts and field designators,
    //--which will modify the data address at the top of the stack.
    int doneFlag = false;
    do {
        switch (token) {

            case tcLBracket:
                pType = ExecuteSubscripts(pType);
                break;

            case tcPeriod:
                pType = ExecuteField();
                break;

            default:  doneFlag = true;
        }
    } while (!doneFlag);

    //--If addressFlag is false, and the data is not an array
    //--or a record, replace the address at the top of the stack
    //--with the data value.
    if ((!addressFlag) && (pType->IsScalar())) {
        if (pType == pRealType) {
            Push(((TStackItem *) Pop()->address)->real);
        }
        else if (pType->Base() == pCharType) {
```

(continues)

```
                Push(((TStackItem *) Pop()->address)->character);
            }
            else {
                Push(((TStackItem *) Pop()->address)->integer);
            }
        }

        if (!addressFlag) {
            void *pDataValue = pType->IsScalar() ? TOS() : TOS()->address;

            TraceDataFetch(pId, pDataValue, pType);
        }

        return pType;
}

//----------------------------------------------------------------
//  ExecuteSubscripts    Execute each subscript expression to
//                       modify the data address at the top of
//                       the runtime stack.
//
//      pType : ptr to array type object
//
//  Return: ptr to subscripted variable's type object
//----------------------------------------------------------------

TType *TExecutor::ExecuteSubscripts(const TType *pType)
{
    //--Loop to executed subscript lists enclosed in brackets.
    while (token == tcLBracket) {

        //--Loop to execute comma-separated subscript expressions
        //--within a subscript list.
        do {
            GetToken();
            ExecuteExpression();

            //--Evaluate and range check the subscript.
            int value = Pop()->integer;
            RangeCheck(pType, value);

            //--Modify the data address at the top of the stack.
            Push(((char *) Pop()->address) +
                            pType->array.pElmtType->size
```

```
                              *(value - pType->array.minIndex));

                //--Prepare for another subscript in this list.
                if (token == tcComma) pType = pType->array.pElmtType;

        } while (token == tcComma);

        //--Prepare for another subscript list.
        GetToken();
        if (token == tcLBracket) pType = pType->array.pElmtType;
    }

    return pType->array.pElmtType;
}

//-------------------------------------------------------------
//  ExecuteField        Execute a field designator to modify the
//                      data address at the top of the runtime
//                      stack
//
//  Return: ptr to record field's type object
//-------------------------------------------------------------

TType *TExecutor::ExecuteField(void)
{
    GetToken();
    TSymtabNode *pFieldId = pNode;

    Push(((char *) (Pop()->address)) + pFieldId->defn.data.offset);

    GetToken();
    return pFieldId->pType;
}
```

Executing Expressions

As shown in Figure 9.14, the expression evaluation member functions now each
return a pointer to the type object of its expression. Type is important during
expression evaluation. Functions ExecuteExpression, ExecuteSimpleExpression, and ExecuteTerm each have local variables pResultType and
pOperandType. The first variable points to the result type object to be returned by
the function. The second variable points to the type object of each operand after the
first operand. The result type is determined by the operator and by the types of the

operands. Note that whenever an operator takes two operands, the second operand is popped first off the stack, followed by the first operand.

Member function `ExecuteFactor` executes a function call by calling member function `ExecuteSubroutineCall` (described later) if the operand is a function identifier. If the identifier is a constant, it calls member function `ExecuteConstant` to push the constant's value onto the stack. Otherwise, it calls member function `ExecuteVariable`.

`ExecuteVariable` takes a pointer to the symbol table node of a variable or formal parameter identifier, and either pushes the identifier's value, or the stack item address of the value, depending on the `addressFlag` argument and the identifier's type. (Remember that the value of an array or a record is a pointer to its data area.)

- Parameter `addressFlag` is false: The identifier is in an expression. `ExecuteVariable` will push the *value* of the variable.

- Parameter `addressFlag` is true: The identifier is the target of an assignment statement, or it is an actual parameter in a subroutine call corresponding to a formal `VAR` parameter. `ExecuteVariable` will push the *address* of the variable's value.

`ExecuteVariable` starts by sending the `GetValueAddress` message to the run-time stack to get the stack item address of the variable or parameter. It pushes the address, unless the identifier has an array or record type or is a formal `VAR` parameter, in which case `ExecuteVariable` pushes the address contained in the stack item. In any case, the top of the stack now contains the address of some data, whether this data is in some other stack item or in a data area.

If there are any subscripts or a field designators, `ExecuteVariable` then repeatedly calls member functions `ExecuteSubscripts` and `ExecuteField` to modify the address at the top of the stack.

Next, `ExecuteVariable` decides whether to leave the address on top of the stack, or use the address to fetch the data and replace the address with the data value. It leaves the address alone if `addressFlag` is true, or if the data is an array or record. Finally, function `TraceDataFetch` is called to print a data fetch trace.

Function `ExecuteSubscripts` evaluates subscript expressions and modifies the data address at the top of the stack to point to the desired element within the array's data area. First, it does a range check of each subscript value. Then, it subtracts the array index's minimum value from the subscript value, multiplies the result by the byte size of the array element, and adds the product to the data address. Execute-Subscripts also keeps track of and returns a pointer to the final array element type.

Function ExecuteField simply adds the field identifier's offset to the address at the top of the stack, so that the address then points to the desired field within the record's data area. It returns a pointer to the field's type object.

Figure 9.15 shows a Pascal program containing a variety of assignment statements and its trace output.

▬▬▬▬▬▬ **Figure 9.15** A Pascal program containing a variety of assignment statements and its trace output.

```
Page 1    assign.pas    Thu Jan 05 18:07:17 1995

  1 0: PROGRAM assign (output);
  2 1:
  3 1: CONST
  4 1:     ten = 10;
  5 1:     pi  = 3.14159;
  6 1:
  7 1: TYPE
  8 1:     subrange = 5..ten;
  9 1:     enum = (zero, one, two, three, four, five);
 10 1:     arr  = ARRAY [enum] OF real;
 11 1:     rec  = RECORD
 12 1:                 i : integer;
 13 1:                 z : RECORD
 14 1:                         x : real;
 15 1:                         a : arr;
 16 1:                     END;
 17 1:             END;
 18 1:     arec = ARRAY [12..15] OF rec;
 19 1:
 20 1: VAR
 21 1:     i, j, k : subrange;
 22 1:     e1, e2  : enum;
 23 1:     x, y, z : real;
 24 1:     p, q    : boolean;
 25 1:     ch      : char;
 26 1:     r1, r2  : rec;
```

(continues)

```
27 1:      a1, a2  : arec;
28 1:      string1, string2 : ARRAY [1..ten] OF char;
29 1:
30 1: BEGIN
31 1:      i := 7;
32 1:      j := ten DIV 2;
33 1:      k := 4*(i - j);
34 1:      e1 := three;
35 1:      e2 := e1;
36 1:      x := pi/7.2;
37 1:      y := x + 3;
38 1:      z := x - ten + y;
39 1:      p := true;
40 1:      q := NOT (x = y) AND p;
41 1:
42 1:      r1.i := 7;
43 1:      r1.z.x := 3.14;
44 1:      r1.z.a[two] := +2.2;
45 1:      i := r1.i;
46 1:      x := r1.z.x;
47 1:      x := r1.z.a[two];
48 1:
49 1:      a1[14].i := 7;
50 1:      a1[14].z.x := 3.14;
```

Page 2   assign.pas   Thu Jan 05 18:07:17 1995

```
51 1:      a1[14].z.a[two] := +2.2;
52 1:      i := a1[14].i;
53 1:      x := a1[14].z.x;
54 1:      x := a1[14].z.a[two];
55 1:
56 1:      ch := 'x';
57 1:      string1 := 'Hello, you';
58 1:      string2 := string1;
59 1:      p := string1 = string2;
60 1:      string1[ten] := ch;
61 1:      ch := string1[1];
62 1:      p := string1 = string2;
63 1:      p := string1 > string2;
64 1:
65 1:      r2 := r1;
```

```
66 1:     i := r2.i;
67 1:     x := r2.z.x;
68 1:     x := r2.z.a[two];
69 1:
70 1:     a2 := a1;
71 1:     i := a1[14].i;
72 1:     x := a1[14].z.x;
73 1:     x := a1[14].z.a[two];
74 1: END.
75 0:
```

```
                75 source lines.
                0 syntax errors.
```

```
>> Entering routine assign
>>  At 31
>>   i <== 7
>>  At 32
>>   ten: 10
>>   j <== 5
>>  At 33
>>   i: 7
>>   j: 5
>>   k <== 8
>>  At 34
>>   three: three
>>   e1 <== three
>>  At 35
>>   e1: three
>>   e2 <== three
>>  At 36
>>   pi: 3.14159
>>   x <== 0.436332
>>  At 37
>>   x: 0.436332
>>   y <== 3.43633
>>  At 38
>>   x: 0.436332
>>   ten: 10
>>   y: 3.43633
>>   z <== -6.12734
>>  At 39
>>   true: true
>>   p <== true
>>  At 40
>>   x: 0.436332
```

(continues)

▬▬▬▬ **Figure 9.15** A Pascal program containing a variety of assignment
statements and its trace output. (*Continued*)

```
>>    y: 3.43633
>>    p: true
>>    q <== true
>>  At 42
>>    r1.* <== 7
>>  At 43
>>    r1.* <== 3.14
>>  At 44
>>    two: two
>>    r1.* <== 2.2
>>  At 45
>>    r1.*: 7
>>    i <== 7
>>  At 46
>>    r1.*: 3.14
>>    x <== 3.14
>>  At 47
>>    two: two
>>    r1.*: 2.2
>>    x <== 2.2
>>  At 49
>>    a1[*] <== 7
>>  At 50
>>    a1[*] <== 3.14
>>  At 51
>>    two: two
>>    a1[*] <== 2.2
>>  At 52
>>    a1[*]: 7
>>    i <== 7
>>  At 53
>>    a1[*]: 3.14
>>    x <== 3.14
>>  At 54
>>    two: two
>>    a1[*]: 2.2
>>    x <== 2.2
>>  At 56
>>    ch <== 'x'
>>  At 57
>>    string1[*] <== 'Hello, you'
>>  At 58
>>    string1[*]: 'Hello, you'
>>    string2[*] <== 'Hello, you'
>>  At 59
```

```
>>    string1[*]: 'Hello, you'
>>    string2[*]: 'Hello, you'
>>     p <== true
>> At 60
>>    ten: 10
>>    ch: 'x'
>>    string1[*] <== 'x'
>> At 61
>>    string1[*]: 'H'
>>    ch <== 'H'
>> At 62
>>    string1[*]: 'Hello, yox'
>>    string2[*]: 'Hello, you'
>>     p <== false
>> At 63
>>    string1[*]: 'Hello, yox'
>>    string2[*]: 'Hello, you'
>>     p <== true
>> At 65
>>    r1.*: <record>
>>    r2.* <== <record>
>> At 66
>>    r2.*: 7
>>     i <== 7
>> At 67
>>    r2.*: 3.14
>>     x <== 3.14
>> At 68
>>    two: two
>>    r2.*: 2.2
>>     x <== 2.2
>> At 70
>>    a1[*]: <array>
>>    a2[*] <== <array>
>> At 71
>>    a1[*]: 7
>>     i <== 7
>> At 72
>>    a1[*]: 3.14
>>     x <== 3.14
>> At 73
>>    two: two
>>    a1[*]: 2.2
>>     x <== 2.2
>> Exiting routine assign

Successful completion.  38 statements executed.
```

Executing Declared Subroutine Calls and Returns

Figure 9.16 shows implementation file execrtn.cpp, which implements the member functions for executing routines.

■■■■■■■■■ **Figure 9.16** Implementation file **execrtn.cpp**.

```
//  ****************************************************************
//  *                                                              *
//  *     E X E C U T O R    (Routines)                            *
//  *                                                              *
//  *     Execute programs, procedures, and functions, and calls   *
//  *     to declared and standard subroutines.                    *
//  *                                                              *
//  *     CLASSES: TExecutor                                       *
//  *                                                              *
//  *     FILE:     prog9-1/execrtn.cpp                            *
//  *                                                              *
//  *     MODULE:   Executor                                       *
//  *                                                              *
//  *     Copyright (c) 1996 by Ronald Mak                         *
//  *     For instructional purposes only.  No warranties.         *
//  *                                                              *
//  ****************************************************************

#include <memory.h>
#include "exec.h"


//----------------------------------------------------------------
//  ExecuteRoutine        Execute a program, procedure, or
//                        function.
//----------------------------------------------------------------

void TExecutor::ExecuteRoutine(const TSymtabNode *pRoutineId)
{
    EnterRoutine(pRoutineId);

    //--Execute the routine's compound statement.
    ExecuteCompound();

    ExitRoutine(pRoutineId);
}


//----------------------------------------------------------------
//  EnterRoutine          Enter a routine:  Switch to its
```

```
//                         intermediate code and allocate its
//                         local variables on the runtime stack.
//
//      pRoutineId : ptr to routine name's symbol table node
//-------------------------------------------------------------

void TExecutor::EnterRoutine(const TSymtabNode *pRoutineId)
{
    TSymtabNode *pId;  // ptr to local variable's symtab node

    TraceRoutineEntry(pRoutineId);

    //--Allocate the callee's local variables.
    for (pId = pRoutineId->defn.routine.locals.pVariableIds;
         pId;
         pId = pId->next) runStack.AllocateValue(pId);

    //--Switch to the callee's intermediate code.
    pIcode = pRoutineId->defn.routine.pIcode;
    pIcode->Reset();
}


//-------------------------------------------------------------
//  ExitRoutine         Exit a routine:  Deallocate its local
//                      parameters and variables, pop its frame
//                      off the runtime stack, and return to the
//                      caller's intermediate code.
//
//      pRoutineId : ptr to routine name's symbol table node
//-------------------------------------------------------------

void TExecutor::ExitRoutine(const TSymtabNode *pRoutineId)
{
    TSymtabNode *pId;  // ptr to symtab node of local variable or parm

    TraceRoutineExit(pRoutineId);

    //--Deallocate local parameters and variables.
    for (pId = pRoutineId->defn.routine.locals.pParmIds;
         pId;
         pId = pId->next) runStack.DeallocateValue(pId);
    for (pId = pRoutineId->defn.routine.locals.pVariableIds;
         pId;
         pId = pId->next) runStack.DeallocateValue(pId);

    //--Pop off the callee's stack frame and return to the caller's
    //--intermediate code.
```

(continues)

■■■■■■■■ **Figure 9.16** Implementation file **execrtn.cpp**. (*Continued*)

```
    runStack.PopFrame(pRoutineId, pIcode);
}

//------------------------------------------------------------
//  ExecuteSubroutineCall          Execute a call to a procedure or
//                                 or a function.
//
//      pRoutineId : ptr to the subroutine name's symtab node
//
//  Return: ptr to the call's type object
//------------------------------------------------------------

TType *TExecutor::ExecuteSubroutineCall(const TSymtabNode *pRoutineId)
{
    return pRoutineId->defn.routine.which == rcDeclared
                ? ExecuteDeclaredSubroutineCall(pRoutineId)
                : ExecuteStandardSubroutineCall(pRoutineId);
}

//------------------------------------------------------------
//  ExecuteDeclaredSubroutineCall    Execute a call to a declared
//                                   procedure or function.
//
//      pRoutineId : ptr to the subroutine name's symtab node
//
//  Return: ptr to the call's type object
//------------------------------------------------------------

TType *TExecutor::ExecuteDeclaredSubroutineCall
                                (const TSymtabNode *pRoutineId)
{
    int oldLevel = currentNestingLevel;    // level of caller
    int newLevel = pRoutineId->level + 1;  // level of callee's locals

    //--Set up a new stack frame for the callee.
    TStackItem *pNewFrameBase = runStack.PushFrameHeader
                                    (oldLevel, newLevel, pIcode);

    //--Push actual parameter values onto the stack.
    GetToken();
    if (token == tcLParen) {
        ExecuteActualParameters(pRoutineId);
        GetToken();
    }
```

```
    //--Activate the new stack frame ...
    currentNestingLevel = newLevel;
    runStack.ActivateFrame(pNewFrameBase, CurrentLocation() - 1);

    //--... and execute the callee.
    ExecuteRoutine(pRoutineId);

    //--Return to the caller.  Restore the current token.
    currentNestingLevel = oldLevel;
    GetToken();

    return pRoutineId->pType;
}


//---------------------------------------------------------------
//  ExecuteStandardSubroutineCall    Execute a call to a standard
//                                   procedure or function.
//
//      pRoutineId : ptr to the subroutine name's symtab node
//
//  Return: ptr to the call's type object
//---------------------------------------------------------------

TType *TExecutor::ExecuteStandardSubroutineCall
                            (const TSymtabNode *pRoutineId)
{
    RuntimeError(rteUnimplementedRuntimeFeature);
    return pRoutineId->pType;
}


//---------------------------------------------------------------
//  ExecuteActualParameters       Execute the actual parameters of
//                                a declared subroutine call.
//
//      pRoutineId : ptr to the subroutine name's symtab node
//---------------------------------------------------------------

void TExecutor::ExecuteActualParameters(const TSymtabNode *pRoutineId)
{
    TSymtabNode *pFormalId;  // ptr to formal parm's symtab node

    //--Loop to execute each actual parameter.
    for (pFormalId = pRoutineId->defn.routine.locals.pParmIds;
         pFormalId;
         pFormalId = pFormalId->next) {
```

(continues)

■■■■■■■ **Figure 9.16** Implementation file **execrtn.cpp**. (*Continued*)

```
        TType *pFormalType = pFormalId->pType;
        GetToken();

        //--VAR parameter: ExecuteVariable will leave the actual
        //--               parameter's addresss on top of the stack.
        if (pFormalId->defn.how == dcVarParm) {
            ExecuteVariable(pNode, true);
        }

        //--Value parameter
        else {
            TType *pActualType = ExecuteExpression();

            if ((pFormalType == pRealType) &&
                (pActualType->Base() == pIntegerType)) {

                //--real formal := integer actual:
                //--Convert integer value to real.
                float value = Pop()->integer;
                Push(value);
            }
            else if (! pFormalType->IsScalar()) {

                //--Formal parameter is an array or a record:
                //--Make a copy of the actual parameter's value.
                void *addr = new char[pFormalType->size];
                memcpy(addr, Pop()->address, pFormalType->size);
                Push(addr);
            }
            else {

                //--Range check a subrange formal parameter.
                RangeCheck(pFormalType, TOS()->integer);
            }
        }
    }
}
```

Member function ExecuteSubroutineCall calls either member function ExecuteDeclaredSubroutineCall or ExecuteStandardSubroutineCall depending on whether the subroutine is declared or standard, respectively. (The latter function will be completed in the next chapter.)

Function `ExecuteDeclaredSubroutineCall` first sends the `PushFrame-Header` message to the runtime stack. We recall that this allocates the stack frame header for the callee, but does not make the new stack frame active. The stack frame base pointer `pFrameBase` still points to the caller's stack frame. This is so that `ExecuteDeclaredSubroutineCall` can repeatedly call member function `ExecuteActualParameters` to evaluate the actual parameter expressions from within the caller's context—in other words, any identifiers that appear in the parameter expressions are looked up starting from the caller's stack frame. After all, the caller is still executing at this point. After all the actual parameters have been evaluated and their values are pushed on the stack above the callee's stack frame header, `ExecuteDeclaredSubroutineCall` sends the `ActivateFrame` message to the runtime stack to point `pFrameBase` to the callee's stack frame. This message also includes the return location within the caller's intermediate code. It is one less than the current location so the first token after the call can be later extracted again.

Before calling member function `ExecuteRoutine`, `ExecuteDeclaredSubroutineCall` also sets the current nesting level to the level of the callee's statements. After the callee is done executing, the function resets the current nesting level to the caller's level and extracts again the first token after the call.

Function `ExecuteActualParameters` matches each actual parameter with the corresponding formal parameter. If the formal parameter is a `VAR` parameter, it calls `ExecuteVariable` to push the address of the actual parameter on top of the stack. Otherwise, it calls `ExecuteExpression` to push the value of the actual parameter. If an actual parameter evaluates to an array or a record, `ExecuteActualParameters` makes a copy of the data area and replaces, at the top of the stack, the address of the original data area with the address of the copy. If the actual parameter value is a scalar, a range check ensures that its value is proper for the formal parameter.

Function `ExecuteRoutine` calls member functions `EnterRoutine`, `ExecuteCompound`, and `ExitRoutine`. Member function `ExecuteCompound` will execute all of a routine's statements.

Member function `EnterRoutine` allocates the callee's local variables on the runtime stack and switches over to the callee's intermediate code. It calls member function `TraceRoutineEntry` to print a routine entry trace.

Member function `ExitRoutine` repeatedly sends the `DeallocateValue` message to the runtime stack for each of the callee's formal parameters and local variables. It then sends the `PopFrame` message to the runtime stack to pop off the callee's frame. Function `TraceRoutineExit` is called to print a routine exit trace.

Table 9.2 summarizes the various actions involved in calling a declared subroutine, executing it, and then returning to the caller.

Table 9.2 Actions During Subroutine Calls and Returns

Member function	Action
TRuntimeStack::PushFrameHeader	Push the callee's frame header onto the runtime stack, but do not activate it yet.
TExecutor:: ExecuteActualParameters	Evaluate the actual parameters within the caller's context, and push them onto the runtime stack.
TExecutor:: ExecuteDeclaredSubroutineCall	Set the current nesting level to that of the callee.
TRuntimeStack::ActivateFrame	Point pFrameBase to the callee's stack frame, and set the return location of the caller into the stack frame header.
TRuntimeStack::AllocateValue	Allocate the callee's local variables on the runtime stack.
TExecutor::EnterRoutine	Switch to the callee's intermediate code.
TExecutor::ExecuteCompound	Execute the callee's intermediate code.
TExecutor:: DeallocateValue	Deallocate the callee's formal parameters and local variables.
TRuntimeStack::PopFrame	Pop off the callee's stack frame and switch back to the caller's intermediate code.
TExecutor:: ExecuteDeclaredSubroutineCall	Restore the current nesting level to that of the caller, and re-extract the first token after the call.

Program 9-1: Pascal Executor III

We now have everything we need for the third version of our Pascal executor, one that can execute declared subroutines, assignment, REPEAT, and compound statements, and expressions.

Figure 9.17 shows the main file.

▆▆▆▆▆▆▆▆▆ **Figure 9.17** Main file **execute3.cpp** of the Pascal Executor III.

```
//    ************************************************************
//    *                                                          *
//    *    Program 9-1: Pascal Executor III                      *
//    *                                                          *
//    *    Execute a Pascal program containing procedures and    *
//    *    functions, and assignment, compound, and REPEAT       *
//    *    statements.                                           *
//    *                                                          *
//    *    FILE:    prog9-1/execute3.cpp                         *
//    *                                                          *
//    *    USAGE:   execute3 <source file>                       *
//    *                                                          *
//    *                 <source file>  name of the source file   *
//    *                                                          *
//    *    Copyright (c) 1996 by Ronald Mak                      *
//    *    For instructional purposes only.  No warranties.      *
//    *                                                          *
//    ************************************************************

#include <iostream.h>
#include "error.h"
#include "buffer.h"
#include "symtab.h"
#include "parser.h"
#include "backend.h"
#include "exec.h"

//-------------------------------------------------------------
//  main
//-------------------------------------------------------------

void main(int argc, char *argv[])
{
    //--Check the command line arguments.
    if (argc != 2) {
```

(continues)

■■■■■■ **Figure 9.17** Main file **execute3.cpp** of the Pascal Executor III. (*Continued*)

```
        cerr << "Usage: execute3 <source file>" << endl;
        AbortTranslation(abortInvalidCommandLineArgs);
    }

    //--Create the parser for the source file,
    //--and then parse the file.
    TParser     *pParser    = new TParser(new TSourceBuffer(argv[1]));
    TSymtabNode *pProgramId = pParser->Parse();
    delete pParser;

    //--If there were no syntax errors, convert the symbol tables,
    //--and create and invoke the backend pretty-printer.
    if (errorCount == 0) {
        vpSymtabs = new TSymtab *[cntSymtabs];
        for (TSymtab *pSt = pSymtabList; pSt; pSt = pSt->Next()) {
            pSt->Convert(vpSymtabs);
        }

        TBackend *pBackend = new TExecutor;
        pBackend->Go(pProgramId);

        delete[] vpSymtabs;
        delete   pBackend;
    }
}
```

Table 9.3 shows the required modules and source files.

■■■■■■ Table 9.3 Modules and Files of Program 9-1

Module	File	Status	Directory
Main	execute3.cpp	*new*	prog9-1
Parser	parser.h	*unchanged*	prog8-1
	parser.cpp	*unchanged*	prog8-1
	parsrtn1.cpp	*unchanged*	prog8-1
	parsrtn2.cpp	*unchanged*	prog8-1
	parsstd.cpp	*unchanged*	prog8-1
	parsdecl.cpp	*changed*	prog9-1
	parstyp1.cpp	*unchanged*	prog7-1
	parstyp2.cpp	*unchanged*	prog7-1

■■■■■ Table 9.3   Modules and Files of Program 9-1 (*Continued*)

Module	File	Status	Directory
	parsstmt.cpp	*unchanged*	prog8-1
	parsexpr.cpp	*unchanged*	prog8-1
Executor	backend.h	*unchanged*	prog8-2
	exec.h	*changed*	prog9-1
	exec.cpp	*changed*	prog9-1
	execrtn.cpp	*new*	prog9-1
	execstmt.cpp	*changed*	prog9-1
	execexpr.cpp	*changed*	prog9-1
	tracer.cpp	*new*	prog9-1
Intermediate code	icode.h	*unchanged*	prog5-2
	icode.cpp	*unchanged*	prog5-2
Scanner	scanner.h	*unchanged*	prog3-1
	scanner.cpp	*unchanged*	prog3-2
	token.h	*unchanged*	prog4-2
	tknword.cpp	*unchanged*	prog3-2
	tknnum.cpp	*unchanged*	prog3-2
	tknstrsp.cpp	*unchanged*	prog3-2
Symbol table	types.h	*unchanged*	prog7-1
	types.cpp	*unchanged*	prog7-1
	symtab.h	*unchanged*	prog8-1
	symtab.cpp	*unchanged*	prog8-1
Error	error.h	*unchanged*	prog5-2
	error.cpp	*unchanged*	prog5-2
Buffer	buffer.h	*unchanged*	prog2-1
	buffer.cpp	*unchanged*	prog2-1
Common	common.h	*unchanged*	prog8-1
	common.cpp	*unchanged*	prog8-1
	misc.h	*unchanged*	prog3-2

We've already seen some sample output from this program (see Figures 9.10 and 9.15). Figure 9.18 shows output from a Pascal program containing nested procedures and functions.

▇▇▇▇▇▇▇▇ **Figure 9.18** Pascal Executor III output from a program containing nested procedures and functions.

```
Page 1    nested.pas    Wed Dec 21 22:24:26 1994

  1 0: PROGRAM main1 (output);
  2 1:
  3 1:    VAR
  4 1:        i, j : integer;
  5 1:
  6 1:    FUNCTION func2 : integer;
  7 2:        forward;
  8 1:
  9 1:    PROCEDURE proc2;
 10 2:
 11 2:        VAR
 12 2:            i, j : integer;
 13 2:
 14 2:        PROCEDURE proc3;
 15 3:
 16 3:            VAR
 17 3:                i, j : integer;
 18 3:
 19 3:            BEGIN {proc 3}
 20 3:                i := -123;        {-123}
 21 3:                j := func2;       {777}
 22 3:                j := i;           {-123}
 23 3:            END {proc 3};
 24 2:
 25 2:        BEGIN {proc 2}
 26 2:            i := -12;     {-12}
 27 2:            proc3;
 28 2:            j := i;       {-12}
 29 2:        END {proc 2};
 30 1:
 31 1:    FUNCTION func2;
 32 2:
 33 2:        VAR
 34 2:            i, j : integer;
 35 2:
 36 2:        FUNCTION func3 : integer;
 37 3:
 38 3:            VAR
 39 3:                i, j : integer;
 40 3:
 41 3:            BEGIN {func3}
```

```
42 3:                    i := 123;         {123}
43 3:                    func3 := 777;     {777}
44 3:                    j := i;           {123}
45 3:                END {func3};
46 2:
47 2:             BEGIN {func2}
48 2:                i := 12;              {12}
49 2:                func2 := func3;       {33}
50 2:                j := i;               {12}
```

Page 2   nested.pas   Wed Dec 21 22:24:26 1994

```
51 2:             END {func2};
52 1:
53 1:         BEGIN {main1}
54 1:            i := 1;        {1}
55 1:            proc2;
56 1:            j := i;        {1}
57 1:         END {main1}.
58 0:
```

                    58 source lines.
                    0 syntax errors.

```
>> Entering routine main1
>>   At 54
>>    i <== 1
>>   At 55
>> Entering routine proc2
>>   At 26
>>    i <== -12
>>   At 27
>> Entering routine proc3
>>   At 20
>>    i <== -123
>>   At 21
>> Entering routine func2
>>   At 48
>>    i <== 12
>>   At 49
>> Entering routine func3
>>   At 42
>>    i <== 123
>>   At 43
>>    func3 <== 777
>>   At 44
```

(continues)

■■■■ **Figure 9.18** Pascal Executor III output from a program containing nested procedures and functions. (*Continued*)

```
>>   i: 123
>>   j <== 123
>> Exiting routine func3
>>   func2 <== 777
>>  At 50
>>   i: 12
>>   j <== 12
>> Exiting routine func2
>>   j <== 777
>>  At 22
>>   i: -123
>>   j <== -123
>> Exiting routine proc3
>>  At 28
>>   i: -12
>>   j <== -12
>> Exiting routine proc2
>>  At 56
>>   i: 1
>>   j <== 1
>> Exiting routine main1

Successful completion.  15 statements executed.
```

Figure 9.19 shows the results of value and VAR parameters.

■■■■ **Figure 9.19** Pascal Executor III output showing the results of value and **VAR** parameters.

```
Page 1    parms.pas    Fri Jan 06 01:08:19 1995

  1 0: PROGRAM parms (output);
  2 1:
  3 1: TYPE
  4 1:     matrix = ARRAY [1..2, 1..3] OF integer;
  5 1:
  6 1: VAR
  7 1:     j       : integer;
  8 1:     i1, i2 : integer;
  9 1:     m1, m2 : matrix;
 10 1:
 11 1: PROCEDURE proc2 (    pi1 : integer;
 12 2:                  VAR pi2 : integer;
```

```
13 2:                          pm1 : matrix;
14 2:                      VAR pm2 : matrix);
15 2:
16 2:        VAR
17 2:            j : integer;
18 2:
19 2:        PROCEDURE proc3 (    ppi1 : integer;
20 3:                         VAR ppi2 : integer;
21 3:                             ppm1 : matrix;
22 3:                         VAR ppm2 : matrix);
23 3:
24 3:            VAR
25 3:                j : integer;
26 3:
27 3:            BEGIN
28 3:                ppi1      := -3333;
29 3:                ppi2      := -3333;
30 3:                ppm1[2,3] := -3333;
31 3:                ppm2[2,3] := -3333;
32 3:
33 3:                j := ppi1;          {-3333}
34 3:                j := ppi2;          {-3333}
35 3:                j := ppm1[2,2];     {-2222}
36 3:                j := ppm2[2,2];     {-2222}
37 3:                j := ppm1[2,3];     {-3333}
38 3:                j := ppm2[2,3];     {-3333}
39 3:
40 3:                j := pi1;           {-2222}
41 3:                j := pi2;           {-3333}
42 3:                j := pm1[2,2];      {-2222}
43 3:                j := pm2[2,2];      {-2222}
44 3:                j := pm1[2,3];      {   23}
45 3:                j := pm2[2,3];      {-3333}
46 3:
47 3:                j := i1;            {    1}
48 3:                j := i2;            {-3333}
49 3:                j := m1[2,2];       {   22}
50 3:                j := m2[2,2];       {-2222}
```

```
51 3:                j := m1[2,3];       {   23}
52 3:                j := m2[2,3];       {-3333}
53 3:            END;
54 2:
55 2:        BEGIN
```

(continues)

■■■■■ **Figure 9.19** Pascal Executor III output showing the results of value and
VAR parameters. (*Continued*)

```
56 2:           pi1       := -2222;
57 2:           pi2       := -2222;
58 2:           pm1[2,2] := -2222;
59 2:           pm2[2,2] := -2222;
60 2:
61 2:           j := pi1;            {-2222}
62 2:           j := pi2;            {-2222}
63 2:           j := pm1[2,2];       {-2222}
64 2:           j := pm2[2,2];       {-2222}
65 2:           j := pm1[2,3];       {   23}
66 2:           j := pm2[2,3];       {   23}
67 2:
68 2:           j := i1;             {    1}
69 2:           j := i2;             {-2222}
70 2:           j := m1[2,2];        {   22}
71 2:           j := m2[2,2];        {-2222}
72 2:           j := m1[2,3];        {   23}
73 2:           j := m2[2,3];        {   23}
74 2:
75 2:           proc3(pi1, pi2, pm1, pm2);
76 2:
77 2:           j := pi1;            {-2222}
78 2:           j := pi2;            {-3333}
79 2:           j := pm1[2,2];       {-2222}
80 2:           j := pm2[2,2];       {-2222}
81 2:           j := pm1[2,3];       {   23}
82 2:           j := pm2[2,3];       {-3333}
83 2:
84 2:           j := i1;             {    1}
85 2:           j := i2;             {-3333}
86 2:           j := m1[2,2];        {   22}
87 2:           j := m2[2,2];        {-2222}
88 2:           j := m1[2,3];        {   23}
89 2:           j := m2[2,3];        {-3333}
90 2:       END;
91 1:
92 1: BEGIN
93 1:     i1 := 1;
94 1:     i2 := 2;
95 1:
96 1:     m1[1,1] := 11;  m1[1,2] := 12;  m1[1,3] := 13;
97 1:     m1[2,1] := 21;  m1[2,2] := 22;  m1[2,3] := 23;
98 1:
```

```
 99 1:     m2[1,1] := 11;  m2[1,2] := 12;  m2[1,3] := 13;
100 1:     m2[2,1] := 21;  m2[2,2] := 22;  m2[2,3] := 23;

Page 3   parms.pas   Fri Jan 06 01:08:19 1995

101 1:
102 1:     j := m1[2,2];         {22}
103 1:     j := m2[2,2];         {22}
104 1:     j := m1[2,3];         {23}
105 1:     j := m2[2,3];         {23}
106 1:
107 1:     proc2(i1, i2, m1, m2);
108 1:
109 1:     j := i1;              {     1}
110 1:     j := i2;              {-3333}
111 1:     j := m1[2,2];         {    22}
112 1:     j := m2[2,2];         {-2222}
113 1:     j := m1[2,3];         {    23}
114 1:     j := m2[2,3];         {-3333}
115 1: END.
116 0:

                116 source lines.
                  0 syntax errors.

>> Entering routine parms
>>   At 93
>>    i1 <== 1
>>   At 94
>>    i2 <== 2
>>   At 96
>>    m1[*] <== 11
>>   At 96
>>    m1[*] <== 12
>>   At 96
>>    m1[*] <== 13
>>   At 97
>>    m1[*] <== 21
>>   At 97
>>    m1[*] <== 22
>>   At 97
>>    m1[*] <== 23
>>   At 99
>>    m2[*] <== 11
>>   At 99
>>    m2[*] <== 12
```

(continues)

■■■■■■ **Figure 9.19** Pascal Executor III output showing the results of value and **VAR** parameters. (*Continued*)

```
>>   At 99
>>     m2[*] <== 13
>>   At 100
>>     m2[*] <== 21
>>   At 100
>>     m2[*] <== 22
>>   At 100
>>     m2[*] <== 23
>>   At 102
>>     m1[*]: 22
>>     j <== 22
>>   At 103
>>     m2[*]: 22
>>     j <== 22
>>   At 104
>>     m1[*]: 23
>>     j <== 23
>>   At 105
>>     m2[*]: 23
>>     j <== 23
>>   At 107
>>     i1: 1
>>     m1[*]: <array>
>> Entering routine proc2
>>   At 56
>>     pi1 <== -2222
>>   At 57
>>     pi2 <== -2222
>>   At 58
>>     pm1[*] <== -2222
>>   At 59
>>     pm2[*] <== -2222
>>   At 61
>>     pi1: -2222
>>     j <== -2222
>>   At 62
>>     pi2: -2222
>>     j <== -2222
>>   At 63
>>     pm1[*]: -2222
>>     j <== -2222
>>   At 64
>>     pm2[*]: -2222
```

```
>>    j <== -2222
>>  At 65
>>    pm1[*]: 23
>>    j <== 23
>>  At 66
>>    pm2[*]: 23
>>    j <== 23
>>  At 68
>>    i1: 1
>>    j <== 1
>>  At 69
>>    i2: -2222
>>    j <== -2222
>>  At 70
>>    m1[*]: 22
>>    j <== 22
>>  At 71
>>    m2[*]: -2222
>>    j <== -2222
>>  At 72
>>    m1[*]: 23
>>    j <== 23
>>  At 73
>>    m2[*]: 23
>>    j <== 23
>>  At 75
>>    pi1: -2222
>>    pm1[*]: <array>
>> Entering routine proc3
>>  At 28
>>    ppi1 <== -3333
>>  At 29
>>    ppi2 <== -3333
>>  At 30
>>    ppm1[*] <== -3333
>>  At 31
>>    ppm2[*] <== -3333
>>  At 33
>>    ppi1: -3333
>>    j <== -3333
>>  At 34
>>    ppi2: -3333
>>    j <== -3333
>>  At 35
>>    ppm1[*]: -2222
>>    j <== -2222
```

(continues)

■■■■■■ **Figure 9.19** Pascal Executor III output showing the results of value and **VAR** parameters. (*Continued*)

```
>>   At 36
>>    ppm2[*]: -2222
>>    j <== -2222
>>   At 37
>>    ppm1[*]: -3333
>>     j <== -3333
>>   At 38
>>    ppm2[*]: -3333
>>     j <== -3333
>>   At 40
>>    pi1: -2222
>>     j <== -2222
>>   At 41
>>    pi2: -3333
>>     j <== -3333
>>   At 42
>>     pm1[*]: -2222
>>     j <== -2222
>>   At 43
>>     pm2[*]: -2222
>>     j <== -2222
>>   At 44
>>     pm1[*]: 23
>>     j <== 23
>>   At 45
>>     pm2[*]: -3333
>>      j <== -3333
>>   At 47
>>    i1: 1
>>     j <== 1
>>   At 48
>>    i2: -3333
>>     j <== -3333
>>   At 49
>>     m1[*]: 22
>>     j <== 22
>>   At 50
>>     m2[*]: -2222
>>     j <== -2222
>>   At 51
>>     m1[*]: 23
>>      j <== 23
>>   At 52
```

```
>>   m2[*]: -3333
>>    j <== -3333
>> Exiting routine proc3
>>  At 77
>>   pi1: -2222
>>    j <== -2222
>>  At 78
>>   pi2: -3333
>>    j <== -3333
>>  At 79
>>   pm1[*]: -2222
>>    j <== -2222
>>  At 80
>>   pm2[*]: -2222
>>    j <== -2222
>>  At 81
>>   pm1[*]: 23
>>    j <== 23
>>  At 82
>>   pm2[*]: -3333
>>    j <== -3333
>>  At 84
>>   i1: 1
>>    j <== 1
>>  At 85
>>   i2: -3333
>>    j <== -3333
>>  At 86
>>   m1[*]: 22
>>    j <== 22
>>  At 87
>>   m2[*]: -2222
>>    j <== -2222
>>  At 88
>>   m1[*]: 23
>>    j <== 23
>>  At 89
>>   m2[*]: -3333
>>    j <== -3333
>> Exiting routine proc2
>>  At 109
>>   i1: 1
>>    j <== 1
>>  At 110
>>   i2: -3333
>>    j <== -3333
```

(continues)

■■■■■ **Figure 9.19** Pascal Executor III output showing the results of value and **VAR** parameters. (*Continued*)

```
>>  At 111
>>    m1[*]: 22
>>    j <== 22
>>  At 112
>>    m2[*]: -2222
>>    j <== -2222
>>  At 113
>>    m1[*]: 23
>>    j <== 23
>>  At 114
>>    m2[*]: -3333
>>    j <== -3333
>> Exiting routine parms

Successful completion.   76 statements executed.
```

We'll complete this interpreter in the next chapter by writing routines to execute the other control statements, and routines to execute calls to the standard procedures and functions.

10

INTERPRETING CONTROL STATEMENTS AND THE STANDARD PROCEDURES AND FUNCTIONS

We will achieve a major milestone in this chapter: a working Pascal interpreter. To accomplish this feat, we'll write the routines to execute the remaining control statements and the standard procedures and functions.

This chapter describes how to:

- Execute control statements with the aid of location markers inserted into the intermediate code by the parser.
- Execute calls to the standard procedures and functions.

Control Statements and Location Markers

Since Chapter 6, we've been able to execute one Pascal control statement, the REPEAT statement. Figure 10.1 shows the intermediate *code diagram* for that statement.

The code diagram shows how the intermediate code is laid out by the parser in the front end. It's no accident that it resembles the statement's syntax diagram. A code

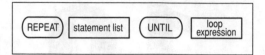

■■■■■ **Figure 10.1**   The intermediate code diagram for the **REPEAT** statement.

diagram helps us to describe what the executor "sees" in the intermediate code at run-time and what actions it takes.

Member function `TExecutor::ExecuteREPEAT` (Figure 6.10) first remembers the location in the intermediate code of the token right after the `REPEAT` token, which is the first token of the statement list. Later, after evaluating the boolean expression after the `UNTIL` token, `ExecuteREPEAT` may need to reset the icode cursor back to the remembered location in order to execute the statement list again.

This all works out fine, since the executor is going back to a location in the icode that it has already encountered. Unfortunately, things are not so simple with the other control statements.

The WHILE, IF, and FOR Statements

Figure 10.2 shows the code diagram for the `WHILE` statement that represents what our parser has been generating up until now. The executor needs to remember the location of the start of the expression so that it can repeatedly go back to evaluate it again and then execute the loop statement, as long as the expression is true. But what happens if the expression is false? We can imagine the executor going into skip mode, during which it extracts tokens of the loop statement but does not actually execute the statement. Then it must revert to execute mode to execute the statement after the `WHILE` statement.

A much cleaner and more efficient technique is for the parser to provide some help as it parses the `WHILE` statement. The parser can place a *location marker* in the intermediate code, as shown in Figure 10.3.

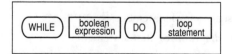

■■■■■ **Figure 10.2**   The original intermediate code diagram for the WHILE statement.

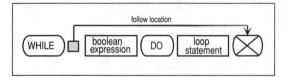

Figure 10.3   The **WHILE** statement's intermediate code diagram with a location marker. The rightmost symbol represents the token that immediately follows the **WHILE** statement.

As the name suggests, a location marker contains the location of some other place in the intermediate code. For the WHILE statement, it is the location of the token that follows the statement. (This token is likely to be a semicolon, but it can also be the reserved word END, ELSE, or UNTIL.) At runtime, the executor extracts and remembers the location stored in the location marker, and if the boolean expression evaluates to false, the executor uses the remembered location to jump past the end of the WHILE statement where it can next extract the following token.

A location marker always points to some location in the intermediate code ahead of itself. Of course, when the parser first emits the location marker for a WHILE statement, it doesn't yet know the location of the first token after the loop statement. Therefore, the parser always first emits a placeholder location marker containing a dummy location, and it must remember where it emitted this placeholder. After it has parsed the loop statement, it knows the location of the first token after that statement, and it can then fix the placeholder location marker by replacing its dummy location with the correct location.

Figure 10.4 shows the intermediate code diagrams for the IF and FOR statements. The location markers in the IF statement enable the executor to jump around the true statement or the false statement. The FOR statement is similar to the WHILE statement—the location marker enables the executor to jump to the end of the statement.

The CASE Statement

The CASE statement is a bit more complex, and we can best illustrate it with a specific example. Figure 10.5 shows the intermediate code diagram for the following outline of a CASE statement:

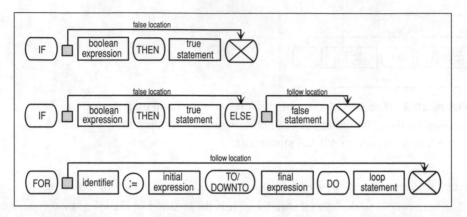

Figure 10.4 Intermediate code diagrams for the **FOR** and **IF** statements.

```
CASE case expression OF
    1    : branch statement;
    2, 3 : branch statement
END
```

As with the WHILE and FOR statements, the first location marker the parser emits points to the token that follows the entire CASE statement. The second location marker points to a branch table that the parser emits after the code for the final

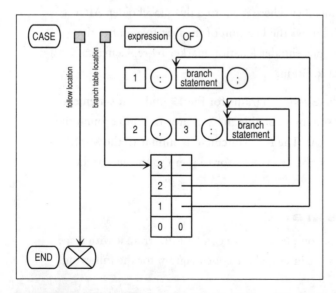

Figure 10.5 The intermediate code diagram for a sample **CASE** statement.

branch statement. (Like all others, both location markers start out as placeholders that the parser later fixes up.)

The branch table has one entry for each CASE label, plus a special entry that marks the end of the table. Each entry contains a label value and the location of the first token of the corresponding branch statement. At runtime, the executor extracts both location markers, evaluates the CASE expression, and uses the second location marker to jump to the branch table. It searches the table for the entry with a label value that matches the CASE expression value and then uses that entry to branch to the appropriate branch statement. After executing the branch statement, the executor uses the location in the first location marker to jump to the end of the entire CASE statement.

▬▬▬▬▬▬ **Figure 10.6** New public member functions of class **TIcode** to handle location markers, as implemented in file **icode.cpp**.

```
//-----------------------------------------------------------
//  PutLocationMarker    Append a location marker to the
//                       intermediate code.
//
//      location : location to mark
//
//  Return: location of the location marker's offset
//-----------------------------------------------------------

int TIcode::PutLocationMarker(void)
{
    if (errorCount > 0) return 0;

    //--Append the location marker code.
    char code = mcLocationMarker;
    CheckBounds(sizeof(char));
    memcpy((void *) cursor, (const void *) &code, sizeof(char));
    cursor += sizeof(char);

    //--Append 0 as a placeholder for the location offset.
    //--Remember the current location of the offset itself.
    short offset    = 0;
    int   atLocation = CurrentLocation();
    CheckBounds(sizeof(short));
    memcpy((void *) cursor, (const void *) &offset, sizeof(short));
    cursor += sizeof(short);

    return atLocation;
}
```

(continues)

```
//-------------------------------------------------------------
//   FixupLocationMarker        Fixup a location marker in the
//                              intermediate code by patching in the
//                              offset of the current token's
//                              location.
//
//       location : location of the offset to fix up
//-------------------------------------------------------------

void TIcode::FixupLocationMarker(int location)
{
    //--Patch in the offset of the current token's location.
    short offset = CurrentLocation() - 1;
    memcpy((void *) (pCode + location), (const void *) &offset,
           sizeof(short));
}


//-------------------------------------------------------------
//   GetLocationMarker          Extract a location marker from the
//                              intermediate code.
//
//   Return: location offset
//-------------------------------------------------------------

int TIcode::GetLocationMarker(void)
{
    short offset;   // location offset

    //--Extract the offset from the location marker.
    memcpy((void *) &offset, (const void *) cursor, sizeof(short));
    cursor += sizeof(short);

    return int(offset);
}
```

Emitting Location Markers in the Front End

Figure 10.6 shows three new public member functions of class TIcode to handle location markers in the intermediate code, as implemented in a new version of file icode.cpp. The parser first calls member function PutLocationMarker to append a placeholder location marker containing the dummy location zero. (Each icode location will be represented by its offset from the beginning of the code segment.) The function returns the location of the placeholder location marker itself, since the parser needs to fix it up later by calling member function `FixupLocationMarker`.

Member function `FixupLocationMarker` patches in the current icode location minus one, which is the location of the current token. (Recall that `CurrentLocation` returns the current position of the icode cursor, which points to the *next* token to be extracted.) Finally, member function `GetLocationMarker` returns the location stored in a location marker.

Figure 10.7 New version of public member function **Get** in implementation file **icode.cpp**.

```
//-----------------------------------------------------------
//  Get                 Extract the next token from the
//                      intermediate code.
//
//  Return: ptr to the extracted token
//-----------------------------------------------------------

TToken *TIcode::Get(void)
{
    TToken *pToken;         // ptr to token to return
    char    code;           // token code read from the file
    TTokenCode token;

    //--Loop to process any line markers
    //--and extract the next token code.
    do {
        //--First read the token code.
        memcpy((void *) &code, (const void *) cursor, sizeof(char));
        cursor += sizeof(char);
        token = (TTokenCode) code;

        //--If it's a line marker, extract the line number.
        if (token == mcLineMarker) {
            short number;

            memcpy((void *) &number, (const void *) cursor,
                    sizeof(short));
            currentLineNumber = number;
            cursor += sizeof(short);
```

(continues)

Figure 10.7 New version of public member function **Get** in implementation file **icode.cpp**. (*Continued*)

```
        }
} while (token == mcLineMarker);

//--Determine the token class, based on the token code.
switch (token) {
    case tcNumber:  pToken = &numberToken;  break;
    case tcString:  pToken = &stringToken;  break;

    case tcIdentifier:
        pToken      = &wordToken;
        pToken->code = tcIdentifier;
        break;

    case mcLocationMarker:
        pToken      = &specialToken;
        pToken->code = token;
        break;

    default:
        if (token < tcAND) {
            pToken      = &specialToken;
            pToken->code = token;
        }
        else {
            pToken      = &wordToken;   // reserved word
            pToken->code = token;
        }
        break;
}

//--Extract the symbol table node and set the token string.
switch (token) {
    case tcIdentifier:
    case tcNumber:
    case tcString:
        pNode = GetSymtabNode();
        strcpy(pToken->string, pNode->String());
        break;

    case mcLocationMarker:
        pNode = NULL;
        pToken->string[0] = '\0';
        break;
```

```
        default:
            pNode = NULL;
            strcpy(pToken->string, symbolStrings[code]);
            break;
    }

    return pToken;
}
```

Figure 10.7 shows the new version of public member function `TIcode::Get`, also
in file `icode.cpp`, which now has to know about location markers. Note that a
location marker is returned as a special symbol token.

In header file `icode.h`, we first need to add the global constant

```
    const TTokenCode mcLocationMarker = ((TTokenCode) 126);
```

and then, in the definition of class `TIcode`, the following prototypes for the new
public member functions:

```
    int  PutLocationMarker  (void);
    void FixupLocationMarker(int location);
    int  GetLocationMarker  (void);
```

In header file `parser.h`, we need to add the following private member functions to
the definition of class `TParser`:

```
    void InsertLineMarker (void) { icode.InsertLineMarker();      }
    int  PutLocationMarker(void) { return icode.PutLocationMarker(); }

    void FixupLocationMarker(int location)
    {
        icode.FixupLocationMarker(location);
    }
```

━━━━━━━━ **Figure 10.8** New versions of class **TParser** member functions to
parse the **WHILE**, **IF**, and **FOR** statements using location markers, as
implemented in file **parsstmt.cpp**.

```
//----------------------------------------------------------------
//  ParseWHILE       Parse a WHILE statement.:
//
//                          WHILE <expr> DO <stmt>
//----------------------------------------------------------------

void TParser::ParseWHILE(void)
```

(continues)

◼◼◼◼◼ **Figure 10.8** New versions of class **TParser** member functions to parse the **WHILE**, **IF**, and **FOR** statements using location markers, as implemented in file **parsstmt.cpp**. (*Continued*)

```
{
    //--Append a placeholder location marker for the token that
    //--follows the WHILE statement.  Remember the location of this
    //--placeholder so it can be fixed up below.
    int atFollowLocationMarker = PutLocationMarker();

    //--<expr> : must be boolean
    GetTokenAppend();
    CheckBoolean(ParseExpression());

    //--DO
    Resync(tlDO, tlStatementStart);
    CondGetTokenAppend(tcDO, errMissingDO);

    //--<stmt>
    ParseStatement();
    FixupLocationMarker(atFollowLocationMarker);
}

//-------------------------------------------------------------
//  ParseIF          Parse an IF statement:
//
//                        IF <expr> THEN <stmt-1>
//
//                or:
//
//                        IF <expr> THEN <stmt-1> ELSE <stmt-2>
//-------------------------------------------------------------

void TParser::ParseIF(void)
{
    //--Append a placeholder location marker for where to go to if
    //--<expr> is false.  Remember the location of this placeholder
    //--so it can be fixed up below.
    int atFalseLocationMarker = PutLocationMarker();

    //--<expr> : must be boolean
    GetTokenAppend();
    CheckBoolean(ParseExpression());

    //--THEN
    Resync(tlTHEN, tlStatementStart);
```

```
        CondGetTokenAppend(tcTHEN, errMissingTHEN);

        //--<stmt-1>
        ParseStatement();
        FixupLocationMarker(atFalseLocationMarker);

        if (token == tcELSE) {

            //--Append a placeholder location marker for the token that
            //--follows the IF statement.  Remember the location of this
            //--placeholder so it can be fixed up below.
            int atFollowLocationMarker = PutLocationMarker();

            //--ELSE <stmt-2>
            GetTokenAppend();
            ParseStatement();
            FixupLocationMarker(atFollowLocationMarker);
        }
    }


//------------------------------------------------------------
//  ParseFOR        Parse a FOR statement:
//
//                      FOR <id> := <expr-1> TO|DOWNTO <expr-2>
//                          DO <stmt>
//------------------------------------------------------------

void TParser::ParseFOR(void)
{
    TType *pControlType;  // ptr to the control id's type object

    //--Append a placeholder for the location of the token that
    //--follows the FOR statement.  Remember the location of this
    //--placeholder.
    int atFollowLocationMarker = PutLocationMarker();

    //--<id>
    GetTokenAppend();
    if (token == tcIdentifier) {

        //--Verify the definition and type of the control id.
        TSymtabNode *pControlId = Find(pToken->String());
        if (pControlId->defn.how != dcUndefined) {
            pControlType = pControlId->pType->Base();
        }
        else {
```

(continues)

■■■■ **Figure 10.8** New versions of class **TParser** member functions to parse the **WHILE**, **IF**, and **FOR** statements using location markers, as implemented in file **parsstmt.cpp**. (*Continued*)

```
            pControlId->defn.how = dcVariable;
            pControlType = pControlId->pType = pIntegerType;
        }
        if (    (pControlType != pIntegerType)
            && (pControlType != pCharType)
            && (pControlType->form != fcEnum)) {
            Error(errIncompatibleTypes);
            pControlType = pIntegerType;
        }

        icode.Put(pControlId);
        GetTokenAppend();
    }
    else Error(errMissingIdentifier);

    //-- :=
    Resync(tlColonEqual, tlExpressionStart);
    CondGetTokenAppend(tcColonEqual, errMissingColonEqual);

    //--<expr-1>
    CheckAssignmentTypeCompatible(pControlType, ParseExpression(),
                                  errIncompatibleTypes);

    //--TO or DOWNTO
    Resync(tlTODOWNTO, tlExpressionStart);
    if (TokenIn(token, tlTODOWNTO)) GetTokenAppend();
    else Error(errMissingTOorDOWNTO);

    //--<expr-2>
    CheckAssignmentTypeCompatible(pControlType, ParseExpression(),
                                  errIncompatibleTypes);

    //--DO
    Resync(tlDO, tlStatementStart);
    CondGetTokenAppend(tcDO, errMissingDO);

    //--<stmt>
    ParseStatement();
    FixupLocationMarker(atFollowLocationMarker);
}
```

The WHILE, IF, and FOR Statements

Figure 10.8 shows part of file `parsstmt.cpp`, which implements new versions of class `TParser`'s private member functions `ParseWHILE`, `ParseIF`, and `Parse-FOR`. These functions now emit the appropriate location markers into the intermediate code for the executor to use at runtime.

Functions `ParseWHILE` and `ParseFOR` each emit a location marker to jump to the token that follows the statement, which it fixes after parsing the statement. Function `ParseIF` emits a location marker to jump around the true statement. If there is an `ELSE` clause, the function emits a second location marker to jump around the false statement. It fixes one or both location markers at the appropriate times while parsing.

Figure 10.9 Definition of class **TCaseItem** in header file **parser.h**.

```
//------------------------------------------------------------
//  TCaseItem            CASE item class.
//------------------------------------------------------------

class TCaseItem {

public:
    TCaseItem *next;
    int labelValue;
    int atBranchStmt;

    TCaseItem(TCaseItem *&pListHead)
    {
        next         = pListHead;  // insert at head of list
        pListHead    = this;
        atBranchStmt = 0;
    }
};
```

The CASE Statement

In order for member function `TParser::ParseCASE` to emit the branch table, it must first build a linked list version of it in memory. Figure 10.9 shows class `TCase-Item` defined in header file `parser.h`. Each `TCaseItem` object will contain the information needed to emit a branch table entry. The constructor function inserts the new object at the head of the linked list.

■■■■■■■■ **Figure 10.10** New class **TIcode** member functions to handle **CASE** items, as implemented in file **icode.cpp**.

```cpp
//-----------------------------------------------------------------
//   PutCaseItem          Append a CASE item to the intermediate
//                        code.
//
//       value   : CASE label value
//       location: location of CASE branch statement
//-----------------------------------------------------------------

void TIcode::PutCaseItem(int value, int location)
{
    if (errorCount > 0) return;

    short offset = location & 0xffff;

    CheckBounds(sizeof(int) + sizeof(short));
    memcpy((void *) cursor, (const void *) &value, sizeof(int));
    cursor += sizeof(int);
    memcpy((void *) cursor, (const void *) &offset, sizeof(short));
    cursor += sizeof(short);
}


//-----------------------------------------------------------------
//   GetCaseItem          Extract a CASE item from the
//                        intermediate code.
//
//       value   : ref to CASE label value
//       location: ref to location of CASE branch statement
//-----------------------------------------------------------------

void TIcode::GetCaseItem(int &value, int &location)
{
    int   val;
    short offset;

    memcpy((void *) &val, (const void *) cursor, sizeof(int));
    cursor += sizeof(int);
    memcpy((void *) &offset, (const void *) cursor, sizeof(short));
    cursor += sizeof(short);

    value    = val;
    location = offset;
}
```

Figure 10.10 shows more new member functions for class TIcode as implemented in file icode.cpp. The parser calls member function PutCaseItem to append a CASE branch table entry to the intermediate code, and the executor calls member function GetCaseItem to extract the label value and the branch statement location from a branch table entry.

Once again, in header file icode.h, we add prototypes for the new private member functions to class TIcode:

```
void PutCaseItem(int value, int location);
void GetCaseItem(int &value, int &location);
```

And in header file parser.h, we add another private function to class TParser:

```
void PutCaseItem(int value, int location)
{
    icode.PutCaseItem(value, location);
}
```

Figure 10.11 New versions of class **TParser** member functions to parse the **CASE** statement using location markers and a branch table, as implemented in file **parsstmt.cpp**.

```
//-------------------------------------------------------------
//  ParseCASE        Parse a CASE statement:
//
//                        CASE <expr> OF
//                            <case-branch> ;
//                            ...
//                        END
//-------------------------------------------------------------

void TParser::ParseCASE(void)
{
    TCaseItem *pCaseItemList;    // ptr to list of CASE items
    int        caseBranchFlag;   // true if another CASE branch,
                                 //    else false

    pCaseItemList = NULL;

    //--Append placeholders for the location of the token that
    //--follows the CASE statement and of the CASE branch table.
    //--Remember the locations of these placeholders.
    int atFollowLocationMarker      = PutLocationMarker();
```

(continues)

Figure 10.11 New versions of class **TParser** member functions to parse the **CASE** statement using location markers and a branch table, as implemented in file **parsstmt.cpp**. (*Continued*)

```cpp
int atBranchTableLocationMarker = PutLocationMarker();

//--<expr>
GetTokenAppend();
TType *pExprType = ParseExpression()->Base();

//--Verify the type of the CASE expression.
if (    (pExprType != pIntegerType)
    && (pExprType != pCharType)
    && (pExprType->form != fcEnum)) {
    Error(errIncompatibleTypes);
}

//--OF
Resync(tlOF, tlCaseLabelStart);
CondGetTokenAppend(tcOF, errMissingOF);

//--Loop to parse CASE branches.
caseBranchFlag = TokenIn(token, tlCaseLabelStart);
while (caseBranchFlag) {
    if (TokenIn(token, tlCaseLabelStart)) {
        ParseCaseBranch(pExprType, pCaseItemList);
    }

    if (token == tcSemicolon) {
        GetTokenAppend();
        caseBranchFlag = true;
    }
    else if (TokenIn(token, tlCaseLabelStart)) {
        Error(errMissingSemicolon);
        caseBranchFlag = true;
    }
    else caseBranchFlag = false;
}

//--Append the branch table to the intermediate code.
FixupLocationMarker(atBranchTableLocationMarker);
TCaseItem *pItem = pCaseItemList;
TCaseItem *pNext;
do {
    PutCaseItem(pItem->labelValue, pItem->atBranchStmt);
    pNext = pItem->next;
```

```
        delete pItem;
        pItem = pNext;
    } while (pItem);
    PutCaseItem(0, 0);  // end of table

    //--END
    Resync(tlEND, tlStatementStart);
    CondGetTokenAppend(tcEND, errMissingEND);
    FixupLocationMarker(atFollowLocationMarker);
}


//------------------------------------------------------------
//  ParseCaseBranch      Parse a CASE branch:
//
//                       <case-label-list> : <stmt>
//
//      pExprType     : ptr to the CASE expression's type object
//      pCaseItemList : ref to ptr to list of CASE items
//------------------------------------------------------------

void TParser::ParseCaseBranch(const TType *pExprType,
                              TCaseItem *&pCaseItemList)
{
    int caseLabelFlag;  // true if another CASE label, else false

    //--<case-label-list>
    do {
        ParseCaseLabel(pExprType, pCaseItemList);
        if (token == tcComma) {

            //--Saw comma, look for another CASE label.
            GetTokenAppend();
            if (TokenIn(token, tlCaseLabelStart)) caseLabelFlag = true;
            else {
                Error(errMissingConstant);
                caseLabelFlag = false;
            }
        }
        else caseLabelFlag = false;

    } while (caseLabelFlag);

    //-- :
    Resync(tlColon, tlStatementStart);
    CondGetTokenAppend(tcColon, errMissingColon);
```

(continues)

■■■■■■■■ **Figure 10.11** New versions of class **TParser** member functions to parse the **CASE** statement using location markers and a branch table, as implemented in file **parsstmt.cpp**. (*Continued*)

```cpp
        //--Loop to set the branch statement location into each CASE item
        //--for this branch.
        for (TCaseItem *pItem = pCaseItemList;
             pItem && (pItem->atBranchStmt == 0);
             pItem = pItem->next) {
            pItem->atBranchStmt = icode.CurrentLocation() - 1;
        }

        //--<stmt>
        ParseStatement();
}

//--------------------------------------------------------------
//  ParseCaseLabel        Parse a case label.
//
//      pExprType     : ptr to the CASE expression's type object
//      pCaseItemList : ref to ptr to list of case items
//--------------------------------------------------------------

void TParser::ParseCaseLabel(const TType *pExprType,
                             TCaseItem *&pCaseItemList)
{
    TType *pLabelType;       // ptr to the CASE label's type object
    int    signFlag = false; // true if unary sign, else false

    //--Allocate a new CASE item and insert it at the head of the list.
    TCaseItem *pCaseItem = new TCaseItem(pCaseItemList);

    //--Unary + or -
    if (TokenIn(token, tlUnaryOps)) {
        signFlag = true;
        GetTokenAppend();
    }

    switch (token) {

        //--Identifier:  Must be a constant whose type matches that
        //--             of the CASE expression.
        case tcIdentifier: {

            TSymtabNode *pLabelId = Find(pToken->String());
            icode.Put(pLabelId);
```

```
    if (pLabelId->defn.how != dcUndefined) {
        pLabelType = pLabelId->pType->Base();
    }
    else {
        pLabelId->defn.how = dcConstant;
        SetType(pLabelId->pType, pDummyType);
        pLabelType = pDummyType;
    }
    if (pExprType != pLabelType) Error(errIncompatibleTypes);

    //--Only an integer constant can have a unary sign.
    if (signFlag && (pLabelType != pIntegerType)) {
        Error(errInvalidConstant);
    }

    //--Set the label value into the CASE item.
    if ((pLabelType == pIntegerType) ||
        (pLabelType->form == fcEnum)) {
        pCaseItem->labelValue = signFlag
                    ? -pLabelId->defn.constant.value.integer
                    :  pLabelId->defn.constant.value.integer;
    }
    else {
        pCaseItem->labelValue = pLabelId->defn.constant
                                            .value.character;
    }

    GetTokenAppend();
    break;
}

//--Number:  Both the label and the CASE expression
//--           must be integer.
case tcNumber: {

    if (pToken->Type() != tyInteger) Error(errInvalidConstant);
    if (pExprType != pIntegerType) Error(errIncompatibleTypes);

    TSymtabNode *pNode = SearchAll(pToken->String());
    if (!pNode) {
        pNode = EnterLocal(pToken->String());
        pNode->pType = pIntegerType;
        pNode->defn.constant.value.integer =
                                    pToken->Value().integer;
    }
    icode.Put(pNode);
```

(continues)

■■■■■■■■ **Figure 10.11** New versions of class **TParser** member functions to parse the **CASE** statement using location markers and a branch table, as implemented in file **parsstmt.cpp**. (*Continued*)

```
    //--Set the label value into the CASE item.
    pCaseItem->labelValue = signFlag
                        ? -pNode->defn.constant.value.integer
                        :  pNode->defn.constant.value.integer;

    GetTokenAppend();
    break;
}

//--String:  Must be a single character without a unary sign.
//--         (Note that the string length includes the quotes.)
//--         The CASE expression type must be character.
case tcString: {

    if (signFlag || (strlen(pToken->String()) != 3)) {
        Error(errInvalidConstant);
    }
    if (pExprType != pCharType) Error(errIncompatibleTypes);

    TSymtabNode *pNode = SearchAll(pToken->String());
    if (!pNode) {
        pNode = EnterLocal(pToken->String());
        pNode->pType = pCharType;
        pNode->defn.constant.value.character =
                                        pToken->String()[1];
    }
    icode.Put(pNode);

    //--Set the label value into the CASE item.
    pCaseItem->labelValue = pToken->String()[1];

    GetTokenAppend();
    break;
    }
  }
}
```

Figure 10.11 shows new versions of class TParser's private member functions that parse the CASE statement, as implemented in file parsstmt.cpp. Member function ParseCASE emits two location markers that it later fixes up: one to jump to the token that follows the CASE statement, and the other to jump to the branch table. Local variable pCaseItemList will point to the head of the list of TCaseItem objects. This variable will be passed by reference to member functions ParseCaseBranch and ParseCaseLabel, which will build the list. After parsing the last CASE branch statement, ParseCASE fixes up the location marker for the branch table, emits the branch table entries, and deletes the list of TCaseItem objects. It emits a dummy entry to mark the end of the table. Note that because the list of TCaseItem objects is built with new objects inserted at the head of the list, the entries of branch table entries have their label values in the order reversed from their order in the CASE statement (see Figure 10.5).

Each TCaseItem object is allocated and linked to the head of the list by function ParseCaseLabel, which also sets the object's label value field. Function Parse-CaseBranch loops over the list to set the branch statement location field of the objects that correspond to the branch statement it is about to parse (which are all the objects at the beginning of the list that don't already have their location fields set).

In header file parser.h, we need to modify the prototypes of the private member functions for parsing CASE statements:

```
void ParseCaseBranch(const TType *pExprType,
                     TCaseItem *&pCaseItemList);
void ParseCaseLabel (const TType *pExprType,
                     TCaseItem *&pCaseItemList);
```

Executing the Control Statements

We're now ready to add the member functions to class TExecutor to execute Pascal control statements at runtime with the aid of the location markers. First, in header file backend.h, we add the following protected member functions to class TBackend:

```
int GetLocationMarker(void)
{
    return pIcode->GetLocationMarker();
}

void GetCaseItem(int &value, int &location)
```

```
    {
        pIcode->GetCaseItem(value, location);
    }
```

■■■■■■■■ Figure 10.12 New version of member function **ExecuteStatement** in implementation file **execstmt.cpp**.

```
//------------------------------------------------------------
//  ExecuteStatement     Execute a statement.
//------------------------------------------------------------

void TExecutor::ExecuteStatement(void)
{
    if (token != tcBEGIN) {
        ++stmtCount;
        TraceStatement();
    }

    switch (token) {

        case tcIdentifier: {
            if (pNode->defn.how == dcProcedure) {
                ExecuteSubroutineCall(pNode);
            }
            else {
                ExecuteAssignment(pNode);
            }
            break;
        }

        case tcREPEAT:    ExecuteREPEAT();        break;
        case tcWHILE:     ExecuteWHILE();         break;
        case tcFOR:       ExecuteFOR();           break;
        case tcIF:        ExecuteIF();            break;
        case tcCASE:      ExecuteCASE();          break;
        case tcBEGIN:     ExecuteCompound();      break;
    }
}
```

Figure 10.12 shows the new version of private member function TExecutor::ExecuteStatement in implementation file execstmt.cpp. This version of the function can now call the member functions to execute the WHILE, FOR, IF, and CASE statements.

▰▰▰▰▰▰▰▰ **Figure 10.13** New class **TExecutor** member functions to execute the
WHILE, **FOR**, **IF**, and **CASE** statements, as implemented in file
execstmt.cpp.

```cpp
//------------------------------------------------------------
//  ExecuteWHILE     Execute a WHILE statement:
//
//                          WHILE <expr> DO <stmt>
//------------------------------------------------------------

void TExecutor::ExecuteWHILE(void)
{
    GetToken();

    //--Get the location of the token that follows the WHILE statement,
    //--and remember the current location of the boolean expression.
    int atFollow = GetLocationMarker();
    int atExpr   = CurrentLocation();

    //--Loop to evaluate the boolean expression and to execute the
    //--statement if the expression is true.
    int doneFlag = false;
    do {
        //--<expr>
        GetToken();
        ExecuteExpression();

        if (Pop()->integer) {

            //--True: DO <stmt>
            //--      Go back to re-evaluate the boolean expression.
            GetToken();
            ExecuteStatement();
            GoTo(atExpr);
        }
        else {

            //--False: Jump out of the loop.
            doneFlag = true;
            GoTo(atFollow);
        }
    } while (!doneFlag);

    GetToken();   // token following the WHILE statement
}
```

(continues)

■■■■■■■■■ **Figure 10.13** New class **TExecutor** member functions to execute the
WHILE, **FOR**, **IF**, and **CASE** statements, as implemented in file
execstmt.cpp. (*Continued*)

```
//-------------------------------------------------------------
//  ExecuteIF        Execute an IF statement:
//
//                       IF <expr> THEN <stmt-1>
//
//               or:
//
//                       IF <expr> THEN <stmt-1> ELSE <stmt-2>
//-------------------------------------------------------------

void TExecutor::ExecuteIF(void)
{
    GetToken();

    //--Get the location of where to go to if <expr> is false.
    int atFalse = GetLocationMarker();

    //--<expr>
    GetToken();
    ExecuteExpression();

    if (Pop()->integer) {

        //--True: THEN <stmt-1>
        GetToken();
        ExecuteStatement();

        //--If there is an ELSE part, jump around it.
        if (token == tcELSE) {
            GetToken();
            GoTo(GetLocationMarker());
            GetToken();  // token following the IF statement
        }
    }
    else {

        //--False: Go to the false location.
        GoTo(atFalse);
        GetToken();

        if (token == tcELSE) {
```

```
                //--ELSE <stmt-2>
                GetToken();
                GetLocationMarker();   // skip over location marker
                GetToken();
                ExecuteStatement();
            }
        }
    }


    //-------------------------------------------------------------
    // ExecuteFOR      Execute a FOR statement:
    //
    //                        FOR <id> := <expr-1> TO|DOWNTO <expr-2>
    //                            DO <stmt>
    //-------------------------------------------------------------

    void TExecutor::ExecuteFOR(void)
    {
        GetToken();

        //--Get the location of the token that follows the FOR statement.
        int atFollow = GetLocationMarker();

        //--Get a pointer to the control variable's type object and
        //--a pointer to its value on the runtime stack item.
        GetToken();
        TSymtabNode *pControlId    = pNode;
        TType       *pControlType  = ExecuteVariable(pControlId, true);
        TStackItem  *pControlValue = (TStackItem *) Pop()->address;

        //-- := <expr-1>
        GetToken();
        ExecuteExpression();
        int integerFlag  = (pControlType->Base() == pIntegerType) ||
                           (pControlType->Base()->form == fcEnum);
        int initialValue = integerFlag ? Pop()->integer : Pop()->character;
        int controlValue = initialValue;

        //--TO or DOWNTO
        int delta = token == tcTO ? 1 : -1;

        //--<expr-2>
        GetToken();
        ExecuteExpression();
        int finalValue = integerFlag ? Pop()->integer : Pop()->character;
```

(continues)

> **Figure 10.13** New class **TExecutor** member functions to execute the **WHILE**, **FOR**, **IF**, and **CASE** statements, as implemented in file **execstmt.cpp**. (*Continued*)

```cpp
    //--Remember the current location of the start of the loop.
    int atLoopStart = CurrentLocation();

    //--Execute the loop until the control value
    //--reaches the final value.
    while (   ((delta ==  1) && (controlValue <= finalValue))
           || ((delta == -1) && (controlValue >= finalValue))) {

        //--Set the control variable's value.
        if (integerFlag) pControlValue->integer   = controlValue;
        else             pControlValue->character = controlValue & 0xFF;
        RangeCheck(pControlType, controlValue);
        TraceDataStore(pControlId, pControlValue, pControlType);

        //--DO <stmt>
        GetToken();
        ExecuteStatement();

        //--Increment or decrement the control value,
        //--and possibly execute <stmt> again.
        controlValue += delta;
        GoTo(atLoopStart);
    }

    //--Jump out of the loop.
    //--The control variable is left with the final value.
    GoTo(atFollow);
    GetToken();  // token following the FOR statement
}


//-------------------------------------------------------------
//  ExecuteCASE      Execute a CASE statement:
//
//                       CASE <expr> OF
//                           <case-branch> ;
//                           ...
//                       END
//-------------------------------------------------------------

void TExecutor::ExecuteCASE(void)
{
    GetToken();
```

```
    //--Get the locations of the token that follows the
    //--CASE statement and of the branch table.
    int atFollow = GetLocationMarker();
    GetToken();
    int atBranchTable = GetLocationMarker();

    //--Evaluate the CASE expression.
    GetToken();
    TType *pExprType = ExecuteExpression();
    int   exprValue = (pExprType->Base() == pIntegerType) ||
                      (pExprType->Base()->form == fcEnum)
                                       ? Pop()->integer
                                       : Pop()->character;

    //--Search the branch table for the expression value.
    int labelValue, branchLocation;
    GoTo(atBranchTable + 1);
    do {
        GetCaseItem(labelValue, branchLocation);
    } while ((exprValue != labelValue) && (branchLocation != 0));

    //--If found, execute the appropriate CASE branch statement,
    //--and go to the statement after the CASE statement.
    if (branchLocation != 0) {
        GoTo(branchLocation);
        GetToken();
        ExecuteStatement();

        GoTo(atFollow);
        GetToken();  // token following the CASE statement
    }
    else RuntimeError(rteInvalidCaseValue);
}
```

Figure 10.13 shows the new class TExecutor member functions to execute the WHILE, FOR, IF, and CASE statements, as implemented in file execstmt.cpp.

Member function ExecuteWHILE first extracts the location marker of the token that follows the WHILE statement, and then it remembers the location of the beginning of the boolean expression. If the expression evaluates to true, the function executes the loop statement and then jumps back to reevaluate the boolean expression. As soon as the expression evaluates to false, ExecuteWHILE jumps to and extracts the token following the WHILE statement.

Member function `ExecuteIF` first extracts the location marker that jumps around the true statement to the false location, and then it evaluates the boolean expression.

- If the expression is true, `ExecuteIF` executes the true statement. If the first token after the true statement is `ELSE`, the function extracts the second location marker and jumps around the false statement. If the token is not `ELSE`, the function is done executing the `IF` statement.

- If the expression is false, `ExecuteIF` jumps around the true statement to the false location. If the token there is `ELSE`, it extracts and ignores the second location marker, and executes the false statement. If the token is not `ELSE`, the function is done executing the `IF` statement.

Member function `ExecuteFOR` first extracts the location marker of the token that follows the `FOR` statement. It then initializes local variables to keep track of the control variable, the current control value, the initial and final values, and the increment (or decrement) value. The function evaluates the initial value and final value expressions only once before it executes the loop statement, whose starting location it remembers.

`ExecuteFOR` then loops once for each valid control value. Each time through the loop, it sets the control variable to the control value. It range checks the control variable and calls `TraceDataStore` before executing the loop statement. As long as the control value hasn't yet gone beyond the final value, the function jumps back to the beginning of the loop statement. Otherwise, the function jumps to and extracts the token following the `FOR` statement, and the control variable is left with the final value.

Member function `ExecuteCASE` first extracts the two location markers that jump to the token that follows the `CASE` statement and to the branch table. It evaluates the `CASE` expression and then jumps to the branch table to search its entries for a matching label value. If it finds a matching entry, it uses its branch statement location to jump to the corresponding branch statement. After executing the branch statement, the function jumps to and extracts the token following the `CASE` statement. Note that it is a runtime error if `ExecuteCASE` fails to find a match in the branch table.

In the definition of class `TExecutor` in header file `exec.h`, we must add prototypes for the above private member functions:

```
//--Statements
void ExecuteStatement(void);
void ExecuteStatementList(TTokenCode terminator);
void ExecuteAssignment(const TSymtabNode *pTargetNode);
void ExecuteREPEAT(void);
void ExecuteWHILE(void);
void ExecuteIF(void);
void ExecuteFOR(void);
void ExecuteCASE(void);
void ExecuteCompound(void);
```

Executing the Standard Subroutines

To complete our interpreter, we need to be able to execute calls to Pascal's standard procedures and functions. Figure 10.14 shows file execstd.cpp, in which we implement new member functions of class TExecutor. This file is analogous to implementation file parsstd.cpp in the front end.

████████ **Figure 10.14** Implementation file **execstd.cpp**.

```
//   ****************************************************************
//   *                                                            *
//   *    E X E C U T O R    (Standard Routines)                  *
//   *                                                            *
//   *    Execute calls to standard procedures and functions.     *
//   *                                                            *
//   *    CLASSES: TExecutor                                      *
//   *                                                            *
//   *    FILE:     prog10-1/execstd.cpp                          *
//   *                                                            *
//   *    MODULE:   Executor                                      *
//   *                                                            *
//   *    Copyright (c) 1995 by Ronald Mak                        *
//   *    For instructional purposes only.  No warranties.        *
//   *                                                            *
//   ****************************************************************

#include <memory.h>
#include <math.h>
#include <iostream.h>
#include <iomanip.h>
#include "buffer.h"
#include "exec.h"
```

(*continues*)

■■■■■■■■ **Figure 10.14** Implementation file **execstd.cpp**. (*Continued*)

```cpp
//-------------------------------------------------------------
//  ExecuteStandardSubroutineCall    Execute a call to a standard
//                                   procedure or function.
//
//      pRoutineId : ptr to the subroutine name's symtab node
//
//  Return: ptr to the call's type object
//-------------------------------------------------------------

TType *TExecutor::ExecuteStandardSubroutineCall
                            (const TSymtabNode *pRoutineId)
{
    switch (pRoutineId->defn.routine.which) {

        case rcRead:
        case rcReadln:    return ExecuteReadReadlnCall(pRoutineId);

        case rcWrite:
        case rcWriteln:   return ExecuteWriteWritelnCall(pRoutineId);

        case rcEof:
        case rcEoln:      return ExecuteEofEolnCall(pRoutineId);

        case rcAbs:
        case rcSqr:       return ExecuteAbsSqrCall(pRoutineId);

        case rcArctan:
        case rcCos:
        case rcExp:
        case rcLn:
        case rcSin:
        case rcSqrt:      return ExecuteArctanCosExpLnSinSqrtCall
                                                  (pRoutineId);

        case rcPred:
        case rcSucc:      return ExecutePredSuccCall(pRoutineId);

        case rcChr:       return ExecuteChrCall();
        case rcOdd:       return ExecuteOddCall();
        case rcOrd:       return ExecuteOrdCall();

        case rcRound:
        case rcTrunc:     return ExecuteRoundTruncCall(pRoutineId);

        default:          return pDummyType;
```

```
    }
}

//-------------------------------------------------------------
//  ExecuteReadReadlnCall        Execute a call to read or
//                               readln.
//
//  Return: ptr to the dummy type object
//-------------------------------------------------------------

TType *TExecutor::ExecuteReadReadlnCall(const TSymtabNode *pRoutineId)
{
    //--Actual parameters are optional for readln.
    GetToken();
    if (token == tcLParen) {

        //--Loop to read each parameter value.
        do {
            //--Variable
            GetToken();
            TSymtabNode *pVarId    = pNode;
            TType       *pVarType  = ExecuteVariable(pVarId, true);
            TStackItem  *pVarValue = (TStackItem *) Pop()->address;

            //--Read the value.
            if (pVarType->Base() == pIntegerType) {
                cin >> pVarValue->integer;
                RangeCheck(pVarType, pVarValue->integer);
            }
            else if (pVarType == pRealType) {
                cin >> pVarValue->real;
            }
            else {
                char ch = cin.get();
                if (cin.eof() || (ch == '\n')) ch = ' ';
                pVarValue->character = ch;
                RangeCheck(pVarType, ch);
            }

            eofFlag = cin.eof();
            TraceDataStore(pVarId, pVarValue, pVarType);

        } while (token == tcComma);

        GetToken();  // token after )
    }
```

(continues)

```
    //--Skip the rest of the input line if readln.
    if (pRoutineId->defn.routine.which == rcReadln) {
        char ch;
        do {
            ch = cin.get();
            eofFlag = cin.eof();
        } while (!eofFlag && (ch != '\n'));
    }

    return pDummyType;
}

//--------------------------------------------------------------
//  ExecuteWriteWritelnCall      Execute a call to write or
//                               writeln. Actual parms can be:
//
//                                       <expr-1>
//                                       <expr-1>:<expr-2>
//                                       <expr-1>:<expr-2>:<expr-3>
//
//  Return: ptr to the dummy type object
//--------------------------------------------------------------

TType *TExecutor::ExecuteWriteWritelnCall(const TSymtabNode *pRoutineId)
{
    const int defaultFieldWidth = 10;
    const int defaultPrecision  =  2;

    //--Actual parameters are optional for writeln.
    GetToken();
    if (token == tcLParen) {

        //--Loop to write each parameter value.
        do {
            //--<expr-1>
            GetToken();
            TType *pExprType = ExecuteExpression()->Base();

            //--Set default width and precision.
            if (pExprType == pIntegerType) {
                cout << setw(defaultFieldWidth);
            }
            else if (pExprType == pRealType) {
                cout << setw(defaultFieldWidth)
```

```
                             << setprecision(defaultPrecision);
        }
        else cout << setw(0);

        //--Optional field width <expr-2>
        if (token == tcColon) {
            GetToken();
            ExecuteExpression();
            cout << setw(Pop()->integer);

            //--Optional precision <expr-3>
            if (token == tcColon) {
                GetToken();
                ExecuteExpression();
                cout << setprecision(Pop()->integer);
            }
        }

        //--Write the value.
        if (pExprType == pIntegerType) {
            cout << Pop()->integer;
        }
        else if (pExprType == pRealType) {
            cout << Pop()->real;
        }
        else if (pExprType == pBooleanType) {
            cout << (Pop()->integer == 0 ? "FALSE" : "TRUE");
        }
        else if (pExprType == pCharType) {
            cout << Pop()->character;
        }
        else if (pExprType->form == fcArray) {
            char text[maxInputBufferSize];
            int length = pExprType->array.elmtCount;
            memcpy(text, Pop()->address, length);
            text[length] = '\0';
            cout << text;
        }

    } while (token == tcComma);

    GetToken();  // token after )
}

//--End the line if writeln.
if (pRoutineId->defn.routine.which == rcWriteln) cout << endl;
```

(continues)

```cpp
    return pDummyType;
}


//----------------------------------------------------------------
//  ExecuteEofEolnCall          Execute a call to eof or eoln.
//
//  Return: ptr to the boolean type object
//----------------------------------------------------------------

TType *TExecutor::ExecuteEofEolnCall(const TSymtabNode *pRoutineId)
{
    if (pRoutineId->defn.routine.which == rcEof) {

        //--eof
        Push(eofFlag ? 1 : 0);
    }
    else {

        //--eoln
        if (eofFlag) Push(1);   // end of line when at end of file
        else {
            char ch = cin.peek();
            Push(ch == '\n' ? 1 : 0);
        }
    }

    GetToken();  // token after function name
    return pBooleanType;
}


//----------------------------------------------------------------
//  ExecuteAbsSqrCall           Execute a call to abs or sqr.
//                              Integer parm => integer result
//                              Real parm    => real result
//
//  Return: ptr to the result's type object
//----------------------------------------------------------------

TType *TExecutor::ExecuteAbsSqrCall(const TSymtabNode *pRoutineId)
{
    int absFlag = pRoutineId->defn.routine.which == rcAbs;

    GetToken();  // (
    GetToken();
```

```
    TType *pParmType = ExecuteExpression()->Base();

    if (pParmType == pIntegerType) {
        TOS()->integer = absFlag ? abs(TOS()->integer)
                                 : TOS()->integer * TOS()->integer;
    }
    else {
        TOS()->real = absFlag ? float(fabs(TOS()->real))
                              : TOS()->real * TOS()->real;
    }

    GetToken();  // token after )
    return pParmType;
}


//-------------------------------------------------------------
//  ExecuteArctanCosExpLnSinSqrtCall    Execute a call to arctan
//                                      cos, exp, ln, sin, or
//                                      sqrt.
//
//                                  integer parm => real result
//                                  real parm    => real result
//
//  Return: ptr to the real type object
//-------------------------------------------------------------

TType *TExecutor::ExecuteArctanCosExpLnSinSqrtCall
                                (const TSymtabNode *pRoutineId)
{
    TRoutineCode which = pRoutineId->defn.routine.which;

    GetToken();  // (
    GetToken();

    //--Evaluate the parameter, and convert an integer value to
    //--real if necessary.
    TType *pParmType = ExecuteExpression()->Base();
    float  parmValue = pParmType == pRealType ? Pop()->real
                                              : Pop()->integer;

    //--Check the parameter value.
    if (   ((which == rcLn)   && (parmValue <= 0.0))
        || ((which == rcSqrt) && (parmValue <  0.0)) ) {
        RuntimeError(rteInvalidFunctionArgument);
    }
```

(continues)

■■■ ■ **Figure 10.14** Implementation file **execstd.cpp**. (*Continued*)

```
    //--Evaluate the function call.
    switch (which) {
        case rcArctan:  Push(float(atan(parmValue)));   break;
        case rcCos:     Push(float(cos (parmValue)));   break;
        case rcExp:     Push(float(exp (parmValue)));   break;
        case rcLn:      Push(float(log (parmValue)));   break;
        case rcSin:     Push(float(sin (parmValue)));   break;
        case rcSqrt:    Push(float(sqrt(parmValue)));   break;
    }

    GetToken();  // token after )
    return pRealType;
}

//------------------------------------------------------------
// ExecutePredSuccCall          Execute a call to pred or succ.
//                              Integer parm => integer result
//                              Enum parm    => enum result
//
// Return: ptr to the result's type object
//------------------------------------------------------------

TType *TExecutor::ExecutePredSuccCall(const TSymtabNode *pRoutineId)
{
    GetToken();  // (
    GetToken();

    TType *pParmType = ExecuteExpression();
    int    parmValue = Pop()->integer;

    if (pRoutineId->defn.routine.which == rcPred) --parmValue;
    else                                          ++parmValue;
    RangeCheck(pParmType, parmValue);
    Push(parmValue);

    GetToken();  // token after )
    return pParmType;
}

//------------------------------------------------------------
// ExecuteChrCall               Execute a call to chr.
//                              Integer parm => character result
//
// Return: ptr to the character type object
//------------------------------------------------------------
```

```
TType *TExecutor::ExecuteChrCall(void)
{
    GetToken();  // (
    GetToken();
    ExecuteExpression();

    TOS()->integer &= 0xff;

    GetToken();  // token after )
    return pCharType;
}

//-------------------------------------------------------------
//   ExecuteOddCall              Execute a call to odd.
//                               Integer parm => boolean result
//
//   Return: ptr to the boolean type object
//-------------------------------------------------------------

TType *TExecutor::ExecuteOddCall(void)
{
    GetToken();  // (
    GetToken();
    ExecuteExpression();

    TOS()->integer &= 1;

    GetToken();  // token after )
    return pBooleanType;
}

//-------------------------------------------------------------
//   ExecuteOrdCall              Execute a call to ord.
//                               Character parm => integer result
//                               Enum parm      => integer result
//
//   Return: ptr to the integer type object
//-------------------------------------------------------------

TType *TExecutor::ExecuteOrdCall(void)
{
    GetToken();  // (
    GetToken();
    ExecuteExpression();

    GetToken();  // token after )
```

(continues)

■■■■■ **Figure 10.14** Implementation file **execstd.cpp**. (*Continued*)

```
    return pIntegerType;
}


//-------------------------------------------------------------
//   ExecuteRoundTruncCall        Execute a call to round or
//                                trunc.
//                                Real parm => integer result
//
//   Return: ptr to the integer type object
//-------------------------------------------------------------

TType *TExecutor::ExecuteRoundTruncCall(const TSymtabNode *pRoutineId)
{
    GetToken();  // (
    GetToken();
    ExecuteExpression();

    float parmValue = TOS()->real;

    if (pRoutineId->defn.routine.which == rcRound) {     // round
        if (parmValue > 0.0) TOS()->integer = int(parmValue + 0.5);
        else                 TOS()->integer = int(parmValue - 0.5);
    }
    else TOS()->integer = int(parmValue);                    // trunc

    GetToken();  // token after )
    return pIntegerType;
}
```

Member function ExecuteStandardSubroutineCall calls the appropriate member function to execute the standard subroutine call. Each function returns a pointer to the type object of the call's result value, which is left on top of the runtime stack. This function implementation replaces the dummy one in file exec-rtn.cpp that we used in the previous chapter.

The I/O Procedures and Functions

Recall that in implementation file exec.cpp, member function Go initializes the runtime standard input and output files:

```
//--Initialize standard input and output.
eofFlag = cin.eof();
cout.setf(ios::fixed, ios::floatfield);
```

Private data member `eofFlag` keeps track of whether or not we're at the end of the standard input. The standard output file is set to print real values using fixed-point notation, the default for Pascal.

Member function `ExecuteReadReadlnCall` reads a value from the standard input into each of the `VAR` parameters. The function calls `RangeCheck` for integer and character parameters, and it calls `TraceDataStore`. After reading a value for each of the parameters, if the call was to `readln`, the function skips the rest of the input line.

For each parameter, member function `ExecuteWriteWritelnCall` first sets the default width and precision, and then it evaluates the parameter expression. It also evaluates the width and precision expressions, if any. It then writes the parameter value to the standard output. After writing all the parameter values, if the call was to `writeln`, the function begins a new output line.

If the call was to `eof`, member function `ExecuteEofEolnCall` pushes either 1 or 0 depending on the value of `eofFlag`. If the call was to `eoln`, the function pushes 1 if `eofFlag` is true. Otherwise, it peeks (looks at but does not fetch) at the next input character and pushes 1 or 0 depending on whether or not the character is the line feed character `'\n'`.

The Math Functions

Member function `ExecuteAbsSqrCall` pushes either the absolute value (for a call to `abs`) or the square (for a call to `sqr`) of the parameter value. The type of the value it pushes is the same as the type, integer or real, of the parameter.

Member function `ExecuteArctanCosExpLnSinSqrtCall` computes and pushes the appropriate value for a call to `arctan`, `cos`, `exp`, `ln`, `sin`, or `sqrt`. The value it pushes is always real.

The Type Functions

Member function `ExecutePredSuccCall` pushes either the value before or the value after the parameter value, depending on whether the call was to `pred` or `succ`. It performs a range check on the value it pushes.

Member function `ExecuteChrCall` pushes the low-order byte of the parameter value, and member function `ExecuteOddCall` pushes the low-order bit of the parameter value. Member function `ExecuteOrdCall` simply pushes the value of the parameter.

Member function `ExecuteRoundTruncCall` pushes the rounded or truncated real value of its parameter, depending on whether the call was to `round` or `trunc`. The value it pushes is always integer.

In the definition of class `TExecutor` in header file `exec.h`, we need to add prototypes for the above private member functions:

```
//--Standard subroutines
TType *ExecuteReadReadlnCall  (const TSymtabNode *pRoutineId);
TType *ExecuteWriteWritelnCall(const TSymtabNode *pRoutineId);
TType *ExecuteEofEolnCall     (const TSymtabNode *pRoutineId);
TType *ExecuteAbsSqrCall      (const TSymtabNode *pRoutineId);
TType *ExecuteArctanCosExpLnSinSqrtCall
                              (const TSymtabNode *pRoutineId);
TType *ExecutePredSuccCall    (const TSymtabNode *pRoutineId);
TType *ExecuteChrCall(void);
TType *ExecuteOddCall(void);
TType *ExecuteOrdCall(void);
TType *ExecuteRoundTruncCall  (const TSymtabNode *pRoutineId);
```

■■■■■■■■ **Figure 10.15** The main file **run.cpp** of the Pascal Interpreter II.

```
// ****************************************************************
// *                                                              *
// *    Program 10-1: Pascal Interpreter                          *
// *                                                              *
// *    Interpret a Pascal program.                               *
// *                                                              *
// *    FILE:   prog10-1/run.cpp                                  *
// *                                                              *
// *    USAGE:  run <source file>                                 *
// *                                                              *
// *              <source file>  name of the source file          *
// *                                                              *
// *    Copyright (c) 1996 by Ronald Mak                          *
// *    For instructional purposes only.  No warranties.          *
// *                                                              *
// ****************************************************************

#include <iostream.h>
#include "common.h"
#include "error.h"
```

```
#include "buffer.h"
#include "symtab.h"
#include "parser.h"
#include "backend.h"
#include "exec.h"

//------------------------------------------------------------
//  main
//------------------------------------------------------------

void main(int argc, char *argv[])
{
    //--Check the command line arguments.
    if (argc != 2) {
        cerr << "Usage: run <source file>" << endl;
        AbortTranslation(abortInvalidCommandLineArgs);
    }

    //--Create the parser for the source file,
    //--and then parse the file.
    TParser     *pParser    = new TParser(new TSourceBuffer(argv[1]));
    TSymtabNode *pProgramId = pParser->Parse();
    delete pParser;

    //--If there were no syntax errors, convert the symbol tables,
    //--and create and invoke the backend pretty-printer.
    if (errorCount == 0) {
        vpSymtabs = new TSymtab *[cntSymtabs];
        for (TSymtab *pSt = pSymtabList; pSt; pSt = pSt->Next()) {
            pSt->Convert(vpSymtabs);
        }

        TBackend *pBackend = new TExecutor;
        pBackend->Go(pProgramId);

        delete[] vpSymtabs;
        delete   pBackend;
    }
}
```

Program 10-2: Pascal Interpreter

Figure 10.15 shows the main file run.cpp. This completes our Pascal interpreter, all of whose modules and source files are in Table 10.1.

■■■■■ **Table 10.1** Modules and Files of Program 10.1

Module	File	Status	Directory
Main	run.cpp	*new*	prog10.1
Parser	parser.h	*changed*	prog10.1
	parser.cpp	*unchanged*	prog9.1
	parsrtn1.cpp	*unchanged*	prog8-1
	parsrtn2.cpp	*unchanged*	prog8-1
	parsstd.cpp	*unchanged*	prog8-1
	parsdecl.cpp	*unchanged*	prog9-1
	parstyp1.cpp	*unchanged*	prog7-1
	parstyp2.cpp	*unchanged*	prog7-1
	parsstmt.cpp	*changed*	prog10-1
	parsexpr.cpp	*unchanged*	prog8-1
Executor	backend.h	*changed*	prog10-1
	exec.h	*changed*	prog10-1
	exec.cpp	*unchanged*	prog9-1
	execrtn.cpp	*changed*	prog10-1
	execstd.cpp	*new*	prog10-1
	execstmt.cpp	*changed*	prog10-1
	execexpr.cpp	*unchanged*	prog9-1
	tracer.cpp	*unchanged*	prog9-1
Intermediate code	icode.h	*changed*	prog10-1
	icode.cpp	*changed*	prog10-1
Scanner	scanner.h	*unchanged*	prog3-1
	scanner.cpp	*unchanged*	prog3-2
	token.h	*unchanged*	prog4-2
	tknword.cpp	*unchanged*	prog3-2
	tknnum.cpp	*unchanged*	prog3-2
	tknstrsp.cpp	*unchanged*	prog3-2
Symbol table	types.h	*unchanged*	prog7-1
	types.cpp	*unchanged*	prog7-1
	symtab.h	*unchanged*	prog8-1
	symtab.cpp	*unchanged*	prog8-1
Error	error.h	*unchanged*	prog5-2
	error.cpp	*unchanged*	prog5-2

■■■■■■■ **Table 10.1** Modules and Files of Program 10.1 (*Continued*)

Module	File	Status	Directory
Buffer	buffer.h	*unchanged*	prog2-1
	buffer.cpp	*unchanged*	prog2-1
Common	common.h	*unchanged*	prog8-1
	common.cpp	*unchanged*	prog8-1
	misc.h	*unchanged*	prog3-2

■■■■■■■

This interpreter is able to parse and execute programs written in the Pascal subset
that we've been using in this book. Figure 10.16 shows an example run. In the next
chapter, we'll add interactive source-level debugging capabilities.

■■■■■■■ **Figure 10.16** Output from parsing and executing a sample Pascal program.

```
Page 1    translat.pas    Sun Nov 05 19:44:40 1995

   1 0: PROGRAM NumberTranslator (input, output);
   2 1:
   3 1: {   Translate a list of integers from numeric form into
   4 1:      words.  The integers must not be negative nor be
   5 1:      greater than the value of maxnumber.  The last
   6 1:      integer in the list has the value of terminator.
   7 1: }
   8 1:
   9 1: CONST
  10 1:     maxnumber  = 30000; {maximum allowable number}
  11 1:     terminator = 0;     {last number in list}
  12 1:
  13 1: VAR
  14 1:     number : integer;   {number to be translated}
  15 1:
  16 1:
  17 1: PROCEDURE Translate (n : integer);
  18 2:
  19 2:     {Translate number n into words.}
  20 2:
  21 2:     VAR
  22 2:         partbefore,     {part before the comma}
  23 2:         partafter       {part after the comma}
  24 2:           : integer;
  25 2:
```

(*continues*)

```
26 2:
27 2:      PROCEDURE DoPart (part : integer);
28 3:
29 3:          {Translate a part of a number into words,
30 3:           where 1 <= part <= 999.}
31 3:
32 3:      VAR
33 3:          hundredsdigit,        {hundreds digit 0..9}
34 3:          tenspart,             {tens part 0..99}
35 3:          tensdigit,            {tens digit 0..9}
36 3:          onesdigit             {ones digit 0..9}
37 3:              : integer;
38 3:
39 3:
40 3:      PROCEDURE DoOnes (digit : integer);
41 4:
42 4:          {Translate a single ones digit into a word,
43 4:           where 1 <= digit <= 9.}
44 4:
45 4:          BEGIN
46 4:              CASE digit OF
47 4:                  1:  write (' one');
48 4:                  2:  write (' two');
49 4:                  3:  write (' three');
50 4:                  4:  write (' four');
```

Page 2   translat.pas   Sun Nov 05 19:44:40 1995

```
51 4:                  5:  write (' five');
52 4:                  6:  write (' six');
53 4:                  7:  write (' seven');
54 4:                  8:  write (' eight');
55 4:                  9:  write (' nine');
56 4:              END;
57 4:          END {DoOnes};
58 3:
59 3:
60 3:      PROCEDURE DoTeens (teens : integer);
61 4:
62 4:          {Translate the teens into a word,
63 4:           where 10 <= teens <= 19.}
64 4:
65 4:              BEGIN
```

```
66 4:                    CASE teens OF
67 4:                        10:  write (' ten');
68 4:                        11:  write (' eleven');
69 4:                        12:  write (' twelve');
70 4:                        13:  write (' thirteen');
71 4:                        14:  write (' fourteen');
72 4:                        15:  write (' fifteen');
73 4:                        16:  write (' sixteen');
74 4:                        17:  write (' seventeen');
75 4:                        18:  write (' eighteen');
76 4:                        19:  write (' nineteen');
77 4:                    END;
78 4:                END {DoTeens};
79 3:
80 3:
81 3:        PROCEDURE DoTens (digit : integer);
82 4:
83 4:            {Translate a single tens digit into a word,
84 4:             where 2 <= digit <= 9.}
85 4:
86 4:            BEGIN
87 4:                CASE digit OF
88 4:                    2:  write (' twenty');
89 4:                    3:  write (' thirty');
90 4:                    4:  write (' forty');
91 4:                    5:  write (' fifty');
92 4:                    6:  write (' sixty');
93 4:                    7:  write (' seventy');
94 4:                    8:  write (' eighty');
95 4:                    9:  write (' ninety');
96 4:                END;
97 4:            END {DoTens};
98 3:
99 3:
100 3:       BEGIN {DoPart}
```

Page 3   translat.pas   Sun Nov 05 19:44:40 1995

```
101 3:
102 3:               {Break up the number part.}
103 3:               hundredsdigit := part DIV 100;
104 3:               tenspart      := part MOD 100;
105 3:
106 3:               {Translate the hundreds digit.}
107 3:               IF hundredsdigit > 0 THEN BEGIN
108 3:                   DoOnes (hundredsdigit);
```

(continues)

```
109 3:                        write (' hundred');
110 3:                 END;
111 3:
112 3:                 {Translate the tens part.}
113 3:                 IF  (tenspart >= 10)
114 3:                 AND (tenspart <= 19) THEN BEGIN
115 3:                     DoTeens (tenspart);
116 3:                 END
117 3:                 ELSE BEGIN
118 3:                     tensdigit := tenspart DIV 10;
119 3:                     onesdigit := tenspart MOD 10;
120 3:
121 3:                     IF tensdigit > 0 THEN DoTens (tensdigit);
122 3:                     IF onesdigit > 0 THEN DoOnes (onesdigit);
123 3:                 END;
124 3:             END {DoPart};
125 2:
126 2:
127 2:     BEGIN {Translate}
128 2:
129 2:         {Break up the number.}
130 2:         partbefore := n DIV 1000;
131 2:         partafter  := n MOD 1000;
132 2:
133 2:         IF partbefore > 0 THEN BEGIN
134 2:             DoPart (partbefore);
135 2:             write (' thousand');
136 2:         END;
137 2:         IF partafter > 0 THEN DoPart (partafter);
138 2:     END {Translate};
139 1:
140 1:
141 1: BEGIN {NumberTranslator}
142 1:
143 1:     {Loop to read, write, check, and translate the numbers.}
144 1:     REPEAT
145 1:         read (number);
146 1:         write (number:6, ' :');
147 1:
148 1:         IF number < 0 THEN BEGIN
149 1:             write (' ***** Error -- number < 0');
150 1:         END
```

Page 4   translat.pas   Sun Nov 05 19:44:40 1995

```
151 1:          ELSE IF number > maxnumber THEN BEGIN
152 1:              write (' ***** Error -- number > ', maxnumber:1);
153 1:          END
154 1:          ELSE IF number = 0 THEN BEGIN
155 1:              write (' zero');
156 1:          END
157 1:          ELSE BEGIN
158 1:              Translate (number);
159 1:          END;
160 1:
161 1:          writeln;   {complete output line}
162 1:      UNTIL number = terminator;
163 1: END {NumberTranslator}.
164 0:

                164 source lines.
                  0 syntax errors.


      5 : five
     73 : seventy three
    125 : one hundred twenty five
    409 : four hundred nine
    -36 : ***** Error -- number < 0
   2001 : two thousand one
   1400 : one thousand four hundred
  10704 : ten thousand seven hundred four
  31337 : ***** Error -- number > 30000
  25694 : twenty five thousand six hundred ninety four
  15911 : fifteen thousand nine hundred eleven
  30000 : thirty thousand
      0 : zero

Successful completion.  336 statements executed.
```

AN INTERACTIVE

SOURCE-LEVEL

DEBUGGER

As we've seen in the past few chapters, an interpreter retains full control of the runtime environment as it executes a program. Because it works with the source program in the intermediate code, an interpreter remains very close to the original Pascal language. Imagine what a powerful development tool we would have if we could interact with the interpreter as it executes a program!

One of the greatest benefits of using an interpreter is indeed how well it can support interactive source-level debugging. With such a debugger, we can monitor and control the execution of a program, and we can examine the program's statements, variables, and data values using Pascal language constructs and the source program's own variable names. A simple debugger command language can allow us to set breakpoints, watch the values of the source program's variables and assign new values to them, print the values of arbitrary Pascal expressions that contain these variables, and trace and single-step the execution of the source program statements.

In this chapter, we'll convert the interpreter that we completed in the previous chapter into an interactive source-level debugger. We'll see how to:

- Interpret a simple interactive debugger command language that uses Pascal constructs.
- Monitor the execution of a Pascal program.
- Manipulate the program's runtime resources that are maintained by the interpreter.

Source-Level Debugging

Two types of software debuggers are used by programmers: machine-level and source-level. Machine-level debuggers allow us to debug a program at a low level that is close to the machine language. With such a debugger, we can execute one machine instruction at a time and monitor such activity as data moving in and out of the machine registers. Machine-level debuggers may have little or no knowledge of the statements or variable names of the original source program. They are often used to debug compiled programs.

A source-level debugger, on the other hand, allows us to debug at the same level as the high-level language the source program is written in. It knows about the statements and variable names of the program, and when we use such a debugger, we can think in terms of the programming language, not the machine instructions. A Pascal source-level debugger, for example, allows us to execute a program one statement at a time and monitor the values of the program's variables. We refer to the statements by their line numbers and to the variables by their names (hence, source-level debuggers are also called *symbolic debuggers*). Source-level debuggers are often used to debug interpreted programs, although source-level debugging of compiled programs is possible if the compiler can generate special debugging information along with the machine code.

The rest of this chapter shows how we can build a credible source-level debugger on top of the interpreter we completed in the previous chapter.

A Simple Debugger Command Language

Our debugger will be interactive, so we must implement a command language. Examples of commands we can give to the debugger are "Set a breakpoint at line 17" and "Show me the current value of `table[index].word/2.3`."

A command language can range in sophistication from one with a very simple and rigid syntax to one that is as flexible and as expressive as a high-level programming language. For our debugger, we will implement a command language that is simple and yet retains a Pascal flavor. It has a small vocabulary of commands, but it uses Pascal syntax for variables, expressions, and assignment statements. Like Pascal, it is insensitive to whether we use uppercase or lowercase letters. For reasons that will become clear later, we must end each debugger command with a semicolon. Figure 11.1 shows a sample interactive session using the debugger command language.

████████ **Figure 11.1** A sample session with the interactive source-level debugger.

```
C:\BOOK\PROGRAMS\PROG11-1>debug newton.pas

Page 1    newton.pas    Fri Feb 17 00:23:46 1995

   1 0: PROGRAM newton (input, output);
   2 1:
   3 1: CONST
   4 1:     epsilon = 1e-6;
   5 1:
   6 1: VAR
   7 1:     number      : integer;
   8 1:     root, sqroot : real;
   9 1:
  10 1: BEGIN
  11 1:     REPEAT
  12 1:         writeln;
  13 1:         write('Enter new number (0 to quit): ');
  14 1:         read(number);
  15 1:
  16 1:         IF number = 0 THEN BEGIN
  17 1:             writeln(number:12:6, 0.0:12:6);
  18 1:         END
  19 1:         ELSE IF number < 0 THEN BEGIN
  20 1:             writeln('*** ERROR:  number < 0');
  21 1:         END
  22 1:         ELSE BEGIN
  23 1:             sqroot := sqrt(number);
  24 1:             writeln(number:12:6, sqroot:12:6);
  25 1:             writeln;
  26 1:
  27 1:             root := 1;
  28 1:             REPEAT
  29 1:                 root := (number/root + root)/2;
  30 1:                 writeln(root:24:6,
```

(continues)

■■■■■■ **Figure 11.1** A sample session with the interactive source-level debugger.
(*Continued*)

```
31 1:                              100*abs(root - sqroot)/sqroot:12:2,
32 1:                                '%')
33 1:               UNTIL abs(number/sqr(root) - 1) < epsilon;
34 1:          END
35 1:      UNTIL number = 0
36 1: END.
37 0:


                    37 source lines.
                     0 syntax errors.


Command? break 16;

Command? ;

Enter new number (0 to quit): 9

Breakpoint
At 16:  if number=0 then begin

Command? ;
          9     3.000000


              5.000000        66.67%
              3.400000        13.33%
              3.023530         0.78%
              3.000092         0.00%
              3.000000         0.00%


Enter new number (0 to quit): 12

Breakpoint
At 16:  if number=0 then begin

Command? assign number := 16;

Command? show sqrt(number);
              ==> 4

Command? show pi/number;
          ^

*** ERROR: Undefined identifier
                ^
```

```
*** ERROR: Incompatible types

Command? where;

At 16:  if number=0 then begin

Command? step;

Command? ;

At 16:  if number=0 then begin

Command? ;

At 19:  if number<0 then begin

Command? ;

At 23:  sqroot:=sqrt(number)

Command? ;

At 24:  writeln(number:12:6,sqroot:12:6)
           16    4.000000

Command? ;

At 25:  writeln


Command? ;

At 27:  root:=1

Command? unstep;

Command? trace;

Command? ;
<28><29><30>                8.500000      112.50%
<29><30>            5.191176      29.78%
<29><30>            4.136665       3.42%
<29><30>            4.002257       0.06%
<29><30>            4.000000       0.00%
<12>
<13>Enter new number (0 to quit): <14>36
```

(continues)

■■■■■■■ **Figure 11.1** A sample session with the interactive source-level debugger.
(*Continued*)

```
Breakpoint
At 16:  if number=0 then begin

Command? untrace;

Command? store root;

Command? watch;
Watching the following variables:
    root          (store)

Command? break;
Breakpoints at the following lines:
      16

Command? ;
         36      6.000000


At 27: Store root <== 1

At 29: Store root <== 18.5
                  18.500000      208.33%

At 29: Store root <== 10.223
                  10.222973       70.38%

At 29: Store root <== 6.87223
                   6.872227       14.54%

At 29: Store root <== 6.05535
                   6.055352        0.92%

At 29: Store root <== 6.00025
                   6.000253        0.00%

At 29: Store root <== 6
                   6.000000        0.00%

Enter new number (0 to quit): 0

Breakpoint
```

```
At 16:  if number=0 then begin

Command? stop;

Program stopped.
```

Breakpoints

A breakpoint is a special tag placed on an executable statement that tells the debugger to suspend the execution of the program just before that statement. When the debugger reaches a statement with a breakpoint, it prints the statement's line number followed by the text of the statement, and then it prompts for and reads a debugger command.

Command: `break` *number;* Place a breakpoint at the statement beginning on line *number*. If there are several statements that begin on that line, place a breakpoint at each one of them.

Command: `break;` Print the line numbers of all the breakpoints.

Command: `unbreak` *number;* Remove the breakpoint from the statement beginning on line *number*. If several statements begin on that line, remove all their breakpoints.

Command: `unbreak;` Remove all the breakpoints.

Statement and Subroutine Tracing

Tracing program execution tells us which statements and which procedures and functions have been executed, and in what order. Our debugger traces statements by printing the line number of each statement just before executing that statement. It traces subroutines by printing a message that a subroutine has just been entered or is just about to be exited.

Command: `trace;` Turn on statement tracing.

Command: `untrace;` Turn off statement tracing.

Command: `routine;` Turn on tracing of procedure and function entries and exits.

Command: `unroutine;` Turn off tracing of procedure and function entries and exits.

Single-Stepping

Single-stepping is executing the program one statement at a time. When the debugger executes a program in single-step mode, it operates as though a breakpoint were placed at every statement. Thus, we can execute a program in "slow motion," and we have an opportunity to enter a debugger command before each statement is executed.

Command: `step;` Turn on single-stepping.

Command: `unstep;` Turn off single-stepping.

During single-stepping mode, the debugger prints out the line number and the text of the statement it is about to execute. We won't allow single-stepping and tracing both to be turned on at the same time, so turning one on automatically turns the other one off.

Watching Variables

Chapter 9 introduced the useful feature of printing the value of a variable each time it is used (a data fetch) and its new value each time it is assigned to (a data store). The debugger allows you to turn this feature on and off for individual variables. You can watch data fetches, data stores, or both.

Commands: `fetch` *variable*; `store` *variable*; `watch` *variable*; Print each data fetch, or each data store, or both fetches and stores of *variable*, respectively. The variable may only be an identifier; it may not be followed by any subscripts or field designators. If we watch an array or record identifier, then we watch all of its elements or fields.

Command: `watch;` Print the names of all the variables being watched, and whether each variable is being watched for fetches, stores, or both.

Command: `unwatch` *variable*; Remove the watch from *variable*.

Command: `unwatch;` Remove all the watches.

Examples: `fetch alpha;` `store beta;` `watch gamma;` `watch;` `unwatch beta;` `unwatch;` The debugger checks to make sure that each variable is a validly defined identifier within the current scope context of the program. In other words, when we enter a `watch` command, the debugger has suspended program execution before a certain statement. Any identifier that we enter must be valid for the program at that point.

Evaluating Expressions

A very useful feature of the debugger is to print the value of an arbitrary Pascal expression containing the source program's variables. The debugger checks the expression both for syntactic correctness and to ensure that all its identifiers are valid with respect to the current program context.

Command: `show` *expression;* Print the value of *expression.*

Examples: `show table[index].word;`
`show (1.0 - sqrt(rho))/(pi*sqr(sigma));`

Assigning Values to Variables

As we're debugging a program, we may want to change the value of a variable. The command language supports a standard Pascal assignment statement, which the debugger checks for validity.

Command: `assign` *variable* `:=` *expression;* Here, *variable* is any valid source program variable, and it may be followed by subscripts and field designators. The *expression* is, as before, any valid Pascal expression.

Example: `assign table[3].count := table[3].count + 1;`

Where Am I?

Sometimes, especially during an intensive debugging session, we can forget where we are in the program.

Command: `where;` Print the line number followed by the text of the statement to be executed next.

Resuming Program Execution

The empty command tells the debugger to resume program execution to completion, or to the next breakpoint, or, if single-stepping, to the next statement.

Command: `;`

Stopping the Program

The stop command immediately terminates the program execution.

Command: stop;

Converting an Interpreter into a Debugger

An interpreter executes a program from start to finish. Consider what an interactive debugger must do at runtime. As it executes a program, if it encounters a breakpoint, it must

1. Suspend the execution of the program,
2. Prompt for, parse, and execute the debugger commands that we enter, and then
3. Resume execution of the program, with the runtime environment possibly modified by the command.

Yet despite all this, converting our interpreter into an interactive source-level debugger is surprisingly straightforward. We designed a very simple command language so that syntax checking will not be a problem. To parse the commands, we'll reuse the front end's parsing routines (by creating another instance of class TParser). To execute the commands, we'll simply invoke the back end's executor routines recursively. We'll need to write some new debugging routines, but none of them is complicated.

Figure 11.2 shows the object diagram of the back end of the interactive debugger. We see several objects that are new instances of objects we previously saw in the front end.

Just as before, the executor object sends messages to the source icode object and the runtime stack object while it executes the source program. It creates breakpoint item objects and watch item objects to keep track of breakpoints and watched variables.

Whenever the executor encounters a breakpoint, it prompts for a debugger command. To parse a command just typed in at the console, the executor object sends GetCommandToken messages to the command parser object, which in turn sends Get messages to the command scanner object to extract the tokens from the command. The command scanner object sends GetChar messages to the console buffer object.

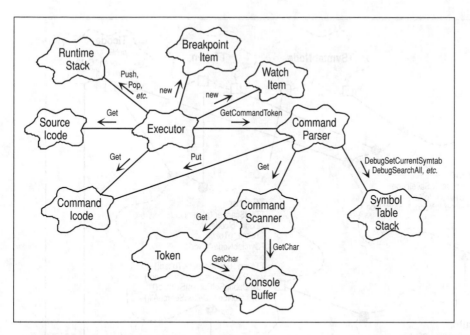

▮▮▮▮▮ **Figure 11.2** Object diagram of the back end of the interactive debugger.

If the command contains source program variables, the command parser object sends DebugSearchAll messages to the runtime symbol table stack object. The command parser maintains this stack by sending it a DebugSetCurrentSymtab message each time it enters a subroutine.

The command parser translates a debugger command into intermediate code, which it appends to the command icode object by sending Put messages. When the command parser is done parsing the command, the executor object executes the command by sending Get messages to the command icode object. When it is done executing debugger commands, the executor resumes executing the source program until the next breakpoint occurs.

As we'll see later, the executor must save and restore the execution state of the source program as it switches from the source program's icode to the command icode, and then back to the source program's icode.

Figure 11.3 shows the class diagram of the classes from which the backend objects are instantiated. The debugger introduces new relationships among the classes.

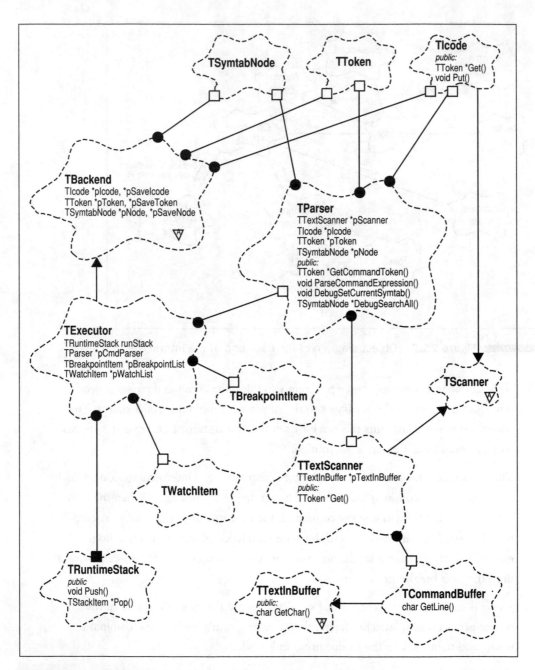

Figure 11.3 Class diagram of the back end of the interactive debugger.

Class TExecutor now has a private data member that points to a TParser object, the parser for the debugger commands. It also has private pointers to objects instantiated from new classes TBreakpointItem and TWatchItem. These objects are managed on linked lists to keep track of breakpoints and watched variables. When the executor object creates the command parser object, it will pass a pointer to the command buffer object to class TParser's constructor function, which in turn passes it to class TTextScanner's constructor function.

Reading Interactive Debugger Commands

Let's start with something very basic—reading debugger commands that have been typed in from the console. Reading text from the console is similar to reading text from the source file, except we don't want to print a copy of each line to the listing.

Figure 11.4 The definition of class **TCommandBuffer** in header file **exec.h**.

```
//--------------------------------------------------------------
//  TCommandBuffer      Command buffer subclass of TTextInBuffer.
//--------------------------------------------------------------

class TCommandBuffer : public TTextInBuffer {
    virtual char GetLine(void);

public:
    TCommandBuffer(void)
        : TTextInBuffer("con", abortSourceFileOpenFailed)
    {
        GetLine();
    }
};
```

Figure 11.4 shows the definition of class TConsole, derived from the base class TTextInBuffer, in header file exec.h. The constructor function passes "con" to the base class's constructor to open the system console for input, and then it reads the first command. Class TCommandBuffer defines its own version of member function GetLine, which is implemented in file exec.cpp, as shown in Figure 11.5.

■■■■■■ **Figure 11.5** Member function **TCommandBuffer::GetLine** in implementation file **exec.cpp**.

```
//-------------------------------------------------------------
//  GetLine           Read the next line from the console.
//
//  Return: first character of the debugger command, or the
//          end-of-file character if at the end of the command
//-------------------------------------------------------------

char TCommandBuffer::GetLine(void)
{
    //--If at the end of the file, return the end-of-file char.
    if (file.eof()) pChar = &eofChar;

    //--Else read the next command line.
    else {
        file.getline(text, maxInputBufferSize);
        pChar = text;    // point to first source line char
    }

    inputPosition = 0;
    return *pChar;
}
```

Saving and Restoring the Execution State

As described above, the debugger must be able to switch from executing the source program to executing a debugger command, and then switch back to the source program. Therefore, it needs to save and restore the execution state of the source program. Figure 11.6 shows the new implementation file backend.cpp, where we define three new member functions for class TBackend.

Both functions SaveState and RestoreState require several new protected data members, which we add to header file backend.h:

```
//--Intermediate code save area
TToken       *pSaveToken;
TTokenCode    saveToken;
char         *pSaveTokenString;
TIcode       *pSaveIcode;
TSymtabNode  *pSaveNode;
```

```
int         saveLocation;
int         saveLineNumber;
```

Of course, we must also add the following protected member function prototypes:

```
void SaveState         (void);
void RestoreState      (void);
void RecreateStatement(void);
```

▬▬▬▬▬▬ **Figure 11.6** New implementation file **backend.cpp**.

```
//     *****************************************************************
//     *                                                               *
//     *     B A C K E N D                                             *
//     *                                                               *
//     *     Common backend routines.                                  *
//     *                                                               *
//     *     CLASSES: TBackend                                         *
//     *                                                               *
//     *     FILE:    prog11-1/backend.cpp                             *
//     *                                                               *
//     *     MODULE:  Back end                                         *
//     *                                                               *
//     *     Copyright (c) 1996 by Ronald Mak                          *
//     *     For instructional purposes only.  No warranties.          *
//     *                                                               *
//     *****************************************************************

#include <string.h>
#include "backend.h"

//----------------------------------------------------------------
//  SaveState           Save the current state of the
//                      intermediate code.
//----------------------------------------------------------------

void TBackend::SaveState(void)
{
    pSaveToken      = pToken;
    saveToken       = token;
    pSaveIcode      = pIcode;
    pSaveNode       = pNode;
    saveLocation    = CurrentLocation();
    saveLineNumber  = currentLineNumber;

    pSaveTokenString = new char[strlen(pToken->String()) + 1];
```

(continues)

```
    strcpy(pSaveTokenString, pToken->String());
}

//---------------------------------------------------------------
//  RestoreState          Restore the current state of the
//                        intermediate code.
//---------------------------------------------------------------

void TBackend::RestoreState(void)
{
    pToken = pSaveToken;
    token  = saveToken;
    pIcode = pSaveIcode;
    pNode  = pSaveNode;
    GoTo(saveLocation);
    currentLineNumber = saveLineNumber;

    strcpy(pToken->String(), pSaveTokenString);
    delete[] pSaveTokenString;
}
```

Hooking into the Original Tracing Routines

We want the debugger to take control of the executor just before each statement. Each time the debugger gets control, it needs to:

- Check whether or not there is a breakpoint at the current statement, and if so, print the line number followed by the statement, and then prompt for a debugger command.
- Print the line number followed by the statement if it is in single-stepping mode, and then prompt for a debugger command.
- Just print the line number if it is in tracing mode.

We also want the debugger to take control each time a variable's value is used or changed, in case the variable is being watched, and each time a subroutine is entered or exited, so that the debugger can maintain a runtime version of the symbol table stack.

The debugger maintains a list of breakpoints and a list of watches. Figure 11.7 shows the definitions of a breakpoint item and a watch item in header file exec.h.

Figure 11.7 Definitions of classes **TBreakpointItem** and **TWatchItem** in header file **exec.h**.

```
//-------------------------------------------------------------
//   TBreakpointItem      Breakpoint item class.
//-------------------------------------------------------------

class TBreakpointItem {

    friend class TExecutor;

    TBreakpointItem *next;         // ptr to next item in list
    int             lineNumber;    // breakpoint line number

    TBreakpointItem(TBreakpointItem *&pbp, int number)
    {
        next = pbp;    // insert before *pbp
        pbp  = this;

        lineNumber = number;
    }
};


//-------------------------------------------------------------
//   TWatchItem           Watch item class.
//-------------------------------------------------------------

class TWatchItem {

    friend class TExecutor;

    TWatchItem   *next;        // ptr to next item in list
    TSymtabNode *pId;          // ptr to watched id's symtab node
    int          fetchFlag;    // true to watch data fetches
    int          storeFlag;    // true to watch data stores

    TWatchItem(TWatchItem *&pw, TSymtabNode *pNode,
               int fFlag, int sFlag)
    {
        next = pw;     // insert before *pw
        pw   = this;

        pId       = pNode;
        fetchFlag = fFlag;
        storeFlag = sFlag;
    }
};
```

Each `TBreakpointItem` object keeps track of a single breakpoint by recording its line number. Its constructor inserts it into a sorted linked list of breakpoint items. Similarly, each `TWatchItem` object keeps track of a single variable by recording a pointer to the variable's symbol table node and flags that indicate whether fetches or stores (or both) are watched. Its constructor inserts it into a sorted linked list of watch items.

In the definition of class `TExecutor` in implementation file `exec.h`, we need to add the following private data members:

```
//--Debugger commands
TParser         *pCmdParser;        // ptr to command parser
TToken          *pCmdToken;         // ptr to current command token
TTokenCode       cmdToken;          // code of current command token
TBreakpointItem *pBreakpointList;   // ptr to head of breakpt list
TWatchItem      *pWatchList;        // ptr to head of watch list

//--Interactive debugging flags
int breakStatementFlag;  // true to break at next statement
int singleSteppingFlag;  // true if single-stepping
```

Data members `pBreakpointList` and `pWatchList` point to the head of the list of breakpoint items and to the head of the list of watch items, respectively. We'll examine the other new data members shortly.

We will add several new private member functions to class `TExecutor` for interactive debugging. Their prototypes are:

```
//--Debugging
void ReadCommand(void);
void DoCommand(void);
void PrintStatement(void);
void PrintLineNumber(void);
void SetBreakpoint(void);
void RemoveBreakpoint(void);
void RemoveBreakpointList(void);
void SetWatch(int fFlag, int sFlag);
void RemoveWatch(void);
void RemoveWatchList(void);
void ShowValue(void);
void DoAssignment(void);
```

■■■■■■ **Figure 11.8** New versions of class **TExecutor**'s constructor and destructor functions in header file **exec.h**.

```
TExecutor(void)
{
    stmtCount        = 0;
    pCmdParser       = NULL;
    pBreakpointList  = NULL;
    pWatchList       = NULL;

    traceRoutineFlag    = false;
    traceStatementFlag  = false;
    traceStoreFlag      = false;
    traceFetchFlag      = false;

    breakStatementFlag  = false;
    singleSteppingFlag  = false;

    listFlag         = false;
    errorArrowOffset = strlen(COMMAND_PROMPT);
}

~TExecutor(void)
{
    delete pCmdParser;

    RemoveBreakpointList();
    RemoveWatchList();
}
```

Figure 11.8 shows new versions of class TExecutor's constructor and destructor functions in header file exec.h. COMMAND_PROMPT is defined at the beginning of the file:

```
#define COMMAND_PROMPT "Command? "
```

The destructor deletes the command parser and the items in the breakpoint and watch lists.

■■■■■■ **Figure 11.9** Definitions of the new member functions of class **TExecutor** in implementation file **exec.cpp**.

```
//-------------------------------------------------------------
//  RemoveBreakpointList        Remove all breakpoints.
//-------------------------------------------------------------
```

(*continues*)

■■■■■■■■ **Figure 11.9** Definitions of the new member functions of class **TExecutor** in implementation file **exec.cpp**. (*Continued*)

```cpp
void TExecutor::RemoveBreakpointList(void)
{
    while (pBreakpointList) {
        TBreakpointItem *next = pBreakpointList->next;
        delete pBreakpointList;
        pBreakpointList = next;
    }
}

//--------------------------------------------------------------
//  RemoveWatchList              Remove all watches.
//--------------------------------------------------------------

void TExecutor::RemoveWatchList(void)
{
    while (pWatchList) {
        TWatchItem *next = pWatchList->next;
        delete pWatchList;
        pWatchList = next;
    }
}
```

Figure 11.9 shows the definitions of class TExecutor's new member functions RemoveBreakpointList and RemoveWatchList in implementation file exec.cpp. Each simply runs down its list and deletes each item.

■■■■■■■■ **Figure 11.10** New versions of the tracing functions for the debugger in implementation file **tracer.cpp**.

```
//   ***************************************************************
//   *                                                             *
//   *    T R A C E R                                              *
//   *                                                             *
//   *    Print runtime debugging trace messages.                  *
//   *                                                             *
//   *    CLASSES: TExecutor                                       *
//   *                                                             *
//   *    FILE:    prog11-1/tracer.h                               *
//   *                                                             *
//   *    MODULE:  Executor                                        *
//   *                                                             *
//   *    Copyright (c) 1996 by Ronald Mak                         *
```

```
// *    For instructional purposes only.  No warranties.       *
// *                                                            *
// *************************************************************

#include <stdio.h>
#include <string.h>
#include <iostream.h>
#include "common.h"
#include "exec.h"

//--------------------------------------------------------------
//  TraceRoutineEntry    Trace the entry into a routine.
//
//      pId : ptr to the routine name's symbol table node
//--------------------------------------------------------------

void TExecutor::TraceRoutineEntry(const TSymtabNode *pRoutineId)
{
    //--Maintain the runtime symbol table stack for debugging.
    pCmdParser->DebugSetCurrentSymtab(pRoutineId->defn.routine.pSymtab);

    if (traceRoutineFlag) {
        cout << endl << "At " << currentLineNumber;
        cout << ": Entering routine " << pRoutineId->String() << endl;
    }
}


//--------------------------------------------------------------
//  TraceRoutineExit     Trace the exit from a routine.
//
//      pId : ptr to the routine name's symbol table node
//--------------------------------------------------------------

void TExecutor::TraceRoutineExit(const TSymtabNode *pRoutineId)
{
    if (traceRoutineFlag) {
        cout << endl << "At " << currentLineNumber;
        cout << ": Exiting routine " << pRoutineId->String() << endl;
    }
}


//--------------------------------------------------------------
//  TraceStatement       Trace the execution of a statement.
//--------------------------------------------------------------

void TExecutor::TraceStatement(void)
```

(continues)

```
{
    //--Check for a breakpoint at this statement.
    for (TBreakpointItem *pbp = pBreakpointList; pbp; pbp = pbp->next) {
        if (currentLineNumber == pbp->lineNumber) {
            cout << endl << "Breakpoint";
            PrintStatement();
            breakStatementFlag = true;
            break;
        }
    }

    //--If break, read a debugger command.
    if (breakStatementFlag) {
        ReadCommand();
        breakStatementFlag = singleSteppingFlag;
    }

    //--If single-stepping, print the current statement.
    //--If tracing statements, just print the current line number.
    if      (singleSteppingFlag) PrintStatement();
    else if (traceStatementFlag) PrintLineNumber();
}


//--------------------------------------------------------------
//  TraceDataStore       Trace the storing of data into a
//                       variable or formal parameter.
//
//      pTargetId  : ptr to the target name's symbol table node
//      pDataValue : ptr to the data value
//      pDataType  : ptr to the data's type object
//--------------------------------------------------------------

void TExecutor::TraceDataStore(const TSymtabNode *pTargetId,
                               const void        *pDataValue,
                               const TType        *pDataType)
{
    traceStoreFlag = false;

    //--Check for a store watch on the target variable.
    for (TWatchItem *pw = pWatchList; pw; pw = pw->next) {
        if ((pTargetId == pw->pId) && (pw->storeFlag)) {
            traceStoreFlag = true;
            break;
```

```
        }
    }

    if (traceStoreFlag) {
        TFormCode form = pTargetId->pType->form;

        cout << endl << "At " << currentLineNumber;
        cout << ": Store " << pTargetId->String();
        if      (form == fcArray)  cout << "[*]";
        else if (form == fcRecord) cout << ".*";
        cout << " <== ";

        TraceDataValue(pDataValue, pDataType);
    }
}

//-------------------------------------------------------------
//  TraceDataFetch        Trace the fetching of data from a
//                        variable or formal parameter.
//
//      pId        : ptr to the variable name's symbol table node
//      pDataValue : ptr to the data value
//      pDataType  : ptr to the data's type object
//-------------------------------------------------------------

void TExecutor::TraceDataFetch(const TSymtabNode *pId,
                               const void        *pDataValue,
                               const TType        *pDataType)
{
    traceFetchFlag = false;

    //--Check for a fetch watch on the variable.
    for (TWatchItem *pw = pWatchList; pw; pw = pw->next) {
        if ((pId == pw->pId) && (pw->fetchFlag)) {
            traceFetchFlag = true;
            break;
        }
    }

    if (traceFetchFlag) {
        TFormCode form = pId->pType->form;

        cout << endl << "At " << currentLineNumber;
        cout << ": Fetch " << pId->String();
        if      (form == fcArray)  cout << "[*]";
        else if (form == fcRecord) cout << ".*";
```

(continues)

■■■■■■ **Figure 11.10** New versions of the tracing functions for the debugger in implementation file **tracer.cpp**. (*Continued*)

```cpp
        cout << ": ";

        TraceDataValue(pDataValue, pDataType);
    }
}

//-------------------------------------------------------------
//  TraceDataValue      Trace a data value.
//
//      pDataValue : ptr to the data value
//      pDataType  : ptr to the data's type object
//-------------------------------------------------------------

void TExecutor::TraceDataValue(const void  *pDataValue,
                               const TType *pDataType)
{
    char text[maxInputBufferSize];   // text for value

    if (pDataType == pRealType) {
        sprintf(text, "%0.6g", ((TStackItem *) pDataValue)->real);
    }
    else if (pDataType == pCharType) {
        sprintf(text, "'%c'", ((TStackItem *) pDataValue)->character);
    }
    else if (pDataType == pBooleanType) {
        strcpy(text, ((TStackItem *) pDataValue)->integer == 0
                                            ? "false" : "true");
    }
    else if (pDataType == pDummyType) {
        sprintf(text, "???");
    }
    else if (pDataType->form == fcArray) {
        if (pDataType->array.pElmtType == pCharType) {
            int length = pDataType->array.elmtCount;
            memcpy(text + 1, pDataValue, length);
            text[0]          = '\'';
            text[length + 1] = '\'';
            text[length + 2] = '\0';
        }
        else strcpy(text, "<array>");
    }
    else if (pDataType->form == fcRecord) {
        strcpy(text, "<record>");
```

```
    }
    else if (pDataType->Base()->form == fcEnum) {
        int count = ((TStackItem *) pDataValue)->integer;
        TSymtabNode *pId = pDataType->Base()->enumeration.pConstIds;
        while (--count >= 0) pId = pId->next;
        strcpy(text, pId->String());
    }
    else {
        sprintf(text, "%d", ((TStackItem *) pDataValue)->integer);
    }

    cout << text << endl;
}
```

The tracing routines introduced in Chapter 9 and implemented in file `tracer.cpp` give us the hooks that we need to allow the debugger to take over at crucial moments. Figure 11.10 shows a new version of the file. In particular, member function `TraceStatement` gives the debugger control just before the executor executes each statement.

The function first checks the breakpoint item list to see if there is a breakpoint at the current line. If there is, it calls member function `PrintStatement` to print the line number and the statement, and later, it calls member function `ReadCommand` to read a debugger command from the console. Since this command could have been a `step` or an `unstep` command, the function sets data member `breakStatement-Flag` to the current value of data member `singleSteppingFlag`. Finally, `TraceStatement` decides whether or not to call member function `PrintState-ment` or `PrintLineNumber` depending on the values of the corresponding flags. (We'll examine each of the above-mentioned new member functions later.)

Member function `TraceRoutineEntry`, as before, prints the name of the routine about to be entered. For the debugger, it also maintains the symbol table stack at runtime by sending the `DebugSetCurrentSymtab` message to the debugger's command parser.

Up until now, the symbol table stack was used only by the front end while parsing the source program. The debugger needs to maintain such a stack at runtime because the commands `show` and `assign` have expressions that can contain variables from the Pascal source program. When the command parser parses these expressions, it must look up the variables within the context of the program statement about to be executed, according to Pascal's scope rules. The debugger will use the symbol table stack that is a private member of the command parser.

Both member functions `TraceDataStore` and `TraceDataFetch` first check the watch item list to see if the variable is being watched for a data fetch or a data store, respectively.

Reusing the Parser for the Debugger Command Language

We'll create a new instance of our tried-and-true parser to parse the debugger command language. We've already seen class `TExecutor`'s new private data members `pCmdParser`, `pCmdToken`, and `cmdToken`. In header file `exec.h`, we add the following private member function to the class:

```
void GetCommandToken(void)
{
    pCmdToken = pCmdParser->GetCommandToken();
    cmdToken  = pCmdToken->Code();
}
```

■■■■■■■■ **Figure 11.11** Public additions to class **TParser** in header file **parser.h**.

```
TToken *GetCommandToken(void)
{
    GetToken();
    return pToken;
}

void ParseCommandExpression        (TIcode     *&pCmdIcode,
                                    TTokenCode  &cmdToken);
TSymtabNode *ParseCommandAssignment(TIcode     *&pCmdIcode,
                                    TTokenCode  &cmdToken);

void DebugSetCurrentSymtab(TSymtab *pSymtab)
{
    symtabStack.SetCurrentSymtab(pSymtab);
}

TSymtabNode *DebugSearchAll(const char *pString) const
{
    return SearchAll(pString);
}
```

The debugger requires a few small additions to class TParser. These public additions, made in header file parser.h, are shown in Figure 11.11.

Public member function GetCommandToken calls GetToken to extract the next token from the console, and it returns the pointer to the token object.

Public member function DebugSetCurrentSymtab sends the SetCurrentSymtab message to the debugger's runtime symbol table stack, which is a private data member of class TParser. We saw earlier how the tracing function TraceRoutineEntry calls this function.

Public member function DebugSearchAll searches the symbol table stack. It gives the debugger access to the parser's private SearchAll member function.

■■■■■■■ **Figure 11.12** The definitions of new member functions of class **TParser** in implementation file **parser.cpp**.

```
//-------------------------------------------------------------
// ParseCommandExpression      Parse the expression part of the
//                             debugger "show" command.
//
//      pCmdIcode : ref to ptr to command icode
//      cmdToken  : ref to current command token
//-------------------------------------------------------------

void TParser::ParseCommandExpression(TIcode     *&pCmdIcode,
                                     TTokenCode  &cmdToken)
{
    icode.Reset();
    GetTokenAppend();  // first token of expression

    //--Parse the expression.
    ParseExpression();
    pCmdIcode = new TIcode(icode);  // copy of expression icode
    cmdToken  = token;              // transfer token to debugger

    //--Convert the current symbol table again in case new nodes
    //--were inserted by the expression.
    TSymtab *pSymtab = symtabStack.GetCurrentSymtab();
    delete pSymtab->NodeVector();
    pSymtab->Convert(vpSymtabs);
}
```

(continues)

Figure 11.12 The definitions of new member functions of class **TParser** in implementation file **parser.cpp**. (*Continued*)

```cpp
//-------------------------------------------------------------
//  ParseCommandAssignment       Parse the assignment statement
//                               part of the debugger "assign"
//                               command.
//
//      pCmdIcode : ref to ptr to command icode
//      cmdToken  : ref to current command token
//
//  Return: ptr to the symbol table node of the target variable
//-------------------------------------------------------------

TSymtabNode *TParser::ParseCommandAssignment(TIcode    *&pCmdIcode,
                                             TTokenCode  &cmdToken)
{
    TSymtabNode *pTargetId = NULL;

    icode.Reset();
    GetTokenAppend();  // first token of target variable

    if (token == tcIdentifier) {
        pTargetId = Find(pToken->String());
        icode.Put(pTargetId);

        //--Parse the assignment.
        ParseAssignment(pTargetId);
        pCmdIcode = new TIcode(icode);  // copy of statement icode
        cmdToken  = token;              // transfer token to debugger

        //--Convert the current symbol table again in case new
        //--nodes were inserted by the assignment expression.
        TSymtab *pSymtab = symtabStack.GetCurrentSymtab();
        delete pSymtab->NodeVector();
        pSymtab->Convert(vpSymtabs);
    }
    else Error(errUnexpectedToken);

    return pTargetId;
}
```

Figure 11.12 shows the definitions of member functions `ParseCommandExpression` and `ParseCommandAssignment` in implementation file `parser.cpp`.

ParseCommandExpression parses the expression part of the show command. This expression can be any valid Pascal expression, and it can contain any source program variables that are defined within the current execution context. ParseCommandExpression calls member function ParseExpression to parse the expression and translate it into intermediate code. It makes a copy of the icode for the debugger and transfers the final command token to the debugger. Finally, because the expression may have introduced new symbol table nodes (such as for a numeric literal), the current routine's symbol table must be converted again for the executor.

Function ParseCommandAssignment parses the assignment statement part of the assign command. This statement can be any valid Pascal assignment statement, and it can contain any source program variables that are defined within the current execution context. ParseCommandAssignment calls member function ParseAssignment to parse the assignment statement and translate it into intermediate code. It makes a copy of the icode for the debugger, transfers the final command token to the debugger, and reconverts the routine's symbol table for the executor. The function returns a pointer to the target variable's symbol table node.

▪▪▪▪▪▪▪ **Figure 11.13** New implementation file **debugger.cpp**.

```
//    ****************************************************************
//    *                                                            *
//    *    D E B U G G E R                                         *
//    *                                                            *
//    *    Runtime debugging routines.                             *
//    *                                                            *
//    *    CLASSES: TExecutor                                      *
//    *                                                            *
//    *    FILE:    prog11-1/debugger.h                            *
//    *                                                            *
//    *    MODULE:  Executor                                       *
//    *                                                            *
//    *    Copyright (c) 1996 by Ronald Mak                        *
//    *    For instructional purposes only.  No warranties.        *
//    *                                                            *
//    ****************************************************************

#include <stdlib.h>
#include <stdio.h>
#include <string.h>
#include <iostream.h>
#include <iomanip.h>
```

(continues)

```cpp
#include "common.h"
#include "exec.h"

//              **************
//              *            *
//              *  Executor  *
//              *            *
//              **************

//--------------------------------------------------------------
//  ReadCommand         Read a debugger command.
//--------------------------------------------------------------

void TExecutor::ReadCommand(void)
{
    //--Loop to prompt for and execute debugger commands
    //--until the null command.
    for (;;) {
        cout << endl << COMMAND_PROMPT;

        //--Create the command parser if it hasn't already been created.
        //--Doing so will cause it to read the first command input line.
        if (!pCmdParser) {
            pCmdParser = new TParser(new TCommandBuffer);
        }

        //--Execute the next debugging command.
        GetCommandToken();
        if      (cmdToken == tcIdentifier) DoCommand();
        else if (cmdToken == tcSemicolon)  break;
        else                               Error(errUnexpectedToken);

        //--The command must end with a semicolon.
        if (cmdToken != tcSemicolon) {
            Error(errUnexpectedToken);
            while (cmdToken != tcSemicolon) GetCommandToken();
        }
    }
}

//--------------------------------------------------------------
//  DoCommand           Execute a debugger command.
//--------------------------------------------------------------

void TExecutor::DoCommand(void)
{
```

```
char *cmdString = pCmdToken->String();
errorCount = 0;

//--Statement trace
if (stricmp(cmdString, "trace") == 0) {
    traceStatementFlag = true;
    singleSteppingFlag = false;
    GetCommandToken();
}
else if (stricmp(cmdString, "untrace") == 0) {
    traceStatementFlag = false;
    GetCommandToken();
}

//--Single stepping
else if (stricmp(cmdString, "step") == 0) {
    traceStatementFlag = false;
    singleSteppingFlag = true;
    GetCommandToken();
}
else if (stricmp(cmdString, "unstep") == 0) {
    singleSteppingFlag = false;
    GetCommandToken();
}

//--Breakpoints
else if (stricmp(cmdString, "break")   == 0) SetBreakpoint();
else if (stricmp(cmdString, "unbreak") == 0) RemoveBreakpoint();

//--Routine entry/exit trace
else if (stricmp(cmdString, "routine") == 0) {
    traceRoutineFlag = true;
    GetCommandToken();
}
else if (stricmp(cmdString, "unroutine") == 0) {
    traceRoutineFlag = false;
    GetCommandToken();
}

//--Watches
else if (stricmp(cmdString, "watch")   == 0) SetWatch(true,  true );
else if (stricmp(cmdString, "fetch")   == 0) SetWatch(true,  false);
else if (stricmp(cmdString, "store")   == 0) SetWatch(false, true );
else if (stricmp(cmdString, "unwatch") == 0) RemoveWatch();

//--Show and assign
else if (stricmp(cmdString, "show")    == 0) ShowValue();
```

(continues)

■■■■■■■■■ **Figure 11.13** New implementation file **debugger.cpp**. (*Continued*)

```cpp
    else if (stricmp(cmdString, "assign") == 0) DoAssignment();

    //--Where
    else if (stricmp(cmdString, "where") == 0) {
        PrintStatement();
        GetCommandToken();
    }

    //--Stop
    else if (stricmp(cmdString, "stop") == 0) {
        cout << endl << "Program stopped." << endl;
        exit(EXIT_SUCCESS);
    }
}

//-----------------------------------------------------------------
//  PrintStatement      Print the current statement.
//-----------------------------------------------------------------

void TExecutor::PrintStatement(void)
{
    cout << endl << "At " << currentLineNumber << ":";
    RecreateStatement();
}

//-----------------------------------------------------------------
//  PrintLineNumber     Print the current line number.
//-----------------------------------------------------------------

void TExecutor::PrintLineNumber(void)
{
    cout << "<" << currentLineNumber << ">";
}

//-----------------------------------------------------------------
//  SetBreakpoint       Set a breakpoint, or print the line
//                      numbers of all the current breakpoints.
//-----------------------------------------------------------------

void TExecutor::SetBreakpoint(void)
{
    GetCommandToken();

    switch (cmdToken) {
```

```
    case tcSemicolon:

        //--No line number: list all breakpoints.
        if (pBreakpointList) {
            cout << "Breakpoints at the following lines:" << endl;
            for (TBreakpointItem *pbp = pBreakpointList;
                 pbp; pbp = pbp->next) {
                cout << setw(10) << pbp->lineNumber << endl;
            }
        }
        else cout << "No breakpoints set." << endl;

        break;

    case tcNumber:

        //--Set a breakpoint at the specified line by allocating a
        //--breakpoint item and inserting it into the sorted list.
        if (pCmdToken->Type() == tyInteger) {
            int number = pCmdToken->Value().integer;
            TBreakpointItem **ppbp = &pBreakpointList;

            //--Search for the insertion point.
            while (*ppbp) {
                if (number <= (*ppbp)->lineNumber) break;
                else ppbp = &(*ppbp)->next;
            }

            //--Insert if not already in list.
            if (!(*ppbp) || (number < (*ppbp)->lineNumber)) {
                new TBreakpointItem(*ppbp, number);
            }
        }
        else Error(errUnexpectedToken);

        GetCommandToken();
        break;

    default:
        Error(errUnexpectedToken);
        break;
    }
}

//-------------------------------------------------------------
//  RemoveBreakpoint       Remove a specific breakpoint, or remove
```

(continues)

■■■■■ **Figure 11.13** New implementation file **debugger.cpp**. (*Continued*)

```cpp
//                       all the current breakpoints.
//------------------------------------------------------------

void TExecutor::RemoveBreakpoint(void)
{
    GetCommandToken();

    switch (cmdToken) {

        case tcSemicolon:

            //--No line number: remove all breakpoints.
            RemoveBreakpointList();
            break;

        case tcNumber:

            //--Remove the breakpoint at the specified line.
            if (pCmdToken->Type() == tyInteger) {
                int number = pCmdToken->Value().integer;
                TBreakpointItem **ppbp = &pBreakpointList;

                //--Search for the line number to delete.
                while (*ppbp) {
                    TBreakpointItem *next = (*ppbp)->next;
                    if (number == (*ppbp)->lineNumber) {
                        delete *ppbp;
                        *ppbp = next;
                        break;
                    }
                    else ppbp = &(*ppbp)->next;
                }
            }
            else Error(errUnexpectedToken);

            GetCommandToken();
            break;

        default:
            Error(errUnexpectedToken);
            break;
    }
}
```

```
//---------------------------------------------------------------
//   SetWatch            Set a watch, or print all the variables
//                       currently watched.
//
//       fFlag : true to watch fetches, else false
//       sFlag : true to watch stores,  else false
//---------------------------------------------------------------

void TExecutor::SetWatch(int fFlag, int sFlag)
{
    GetCommandToken();

    switch (cmdToken) {

        case tcSemicolon:

            //--No variable: list all watches.
            if (pWatchList) {
                cout << "Watching the following variables:" << endl;
                for (TWatchItem *pw = pWatchList;
                     pw; pw = pw->next) {
                    cout << "    " << pw->pId->String() << "\t";
                    if (pw->fetchFlag) cout << " (fetch)";
                    if (pw->storeFlag) cout << " (store)";
                    cout << endl;
                }
            }
            else cout << "No watches set." << endl;

            break;

        case tcIdentifier: {

            //--Set a watch on a specified variable by allocating a
            //--watch item and inserting it into the sorted list.
            TWatchItem  **ppw        = &pWatchList;
            char        *watchString = pCmdToken->String();
            TSymtabNode *pWatchId    = pCmdParser->DebugSearchAll
                                                       (watchString);

            if (pWatchId) {

                //--Search for the insertion point.
                while (*ppw) {
                    int cmp = strcmp(watchString,
```

(continues)

```
                                         (*ppw)->pId->String());
                if (    (cmp < 0)
                     || ( (cmp == 0) &&
                          (pWatchId == (*ppw)->pId) )) break;
                else ppw = &(*ppw)->next;
            }

            //--Insert if not already in list.
            if (!(*ppw) || (pWatchId != (*ppw)->pId)) {
                new TWatchItem(*ppw, pWatchId, fFlag, sFlag);
            }

        } else Error(errUndefinedIdentifier);

        GetCommandToken();
        break;
    }

    default:
        Error(errUnexpectedToken);
        break;
    }
}


//--------------------------------------------------------------
//  RemoveWatch         Stop watching a specific variable, or
//                      stop watching all the variables.
//--------------------------------------------------------------

void TExecutor::RemoveWatch(void)
{
    GetCommandToken();

    switch (cmdToken) {

        case tcSemicolon:

            //--No variable: remove all watches.
            RemoveWatchList();
            break;

        case tcIdentifier: {

            //--Remove the watch of the specified variable.
```

```
            TWatchItem   **ppw      = &pWatchList;
            TSymtabNode  *pWatchId = pCmdParser->DebugSearchAll
                                           (pCmdToken->String());

        if (pWatchId) {

            //--Search for the watched variable to delete.
            while (*ppw) {
                TWatchItem *next = (*ppw)->next;
                if (pWatchId == (*ppw)->pId) {
                    delete *ppw;
                    *ppw = next;
                    break;
                }
                else ppw = &(*ppw)->next;
            }

        } else Error(errUndefinedIdentifier);

        GetCommandToken();
        break;
    }

    default:
        Error(errUnexpectedToken);
        break;
    }
}

//-------------------------------------------------------------
// ShowValue            Print the value of an expression.
//-------------------------------------------------------------

void TExecutor::ShowValue(void)
{
    SaveState();
    pCmdParser->ParseCommandExpression(pIcode, cmdToken);

    //--Execute the command expression and print its value.
    if (errorCount == 0) {
        GetToken();
        TType *pType = ExecuteExpression();
        cout << "                ==> ";
        TraceDataValue((pType->IsScalar()) ? TOS() : TOS()->address,
                    pType);
    }
```

(continues)

```cpp
        delete pIcode;
        RestoreState();
    }

    //------------------------------------------------------------
    //  DoAssignment        Assign a new value to a variable.
    //------------------------------------------------------------

    void TExecutor::DoAssignment(void)
    {
        SaveState();
        TSymtabNode *pTargetId = pCmdParser->ParseCommandAssignment
                                             (pIcode, cmdToken);

        //--Execute the assignment
        if (errorCount == 0) {
            GetToken();
            ExecuteAssignment(pTargetId);
        }

        delete pIcode;
        RestoreState();
    }

    //------------------------------------------------------------
    //  RecreateStatement   Recreate a statement from the
    //                      intermediate code.
    //------------------------------------------------------------

    static const TTokenCode tlStatementRecreateEnd[] = {
        tcSemicolon, tcEND, tcELSE, tcUNTIL, tcDummy
    };

    void TExecutor::RecreateStatement(void)
    {
        const int bufferSize = 60;
        char    buffer[bufferSize];     // buffer for recreated stmt
        int     xBuffer = 0;            // buffer index
        int     currIsDelimiter = false; // true if current token is a
                                        //   delimiter, else false
        int     prevIsDelimiter;        // likewise for previous token

        SaveState();
```

```
//--Loop to get tokens until the end of the statement
//--or the next line marker.
do {
    int len = strlen(pToken->String());  // token string length

    //--Print the buffer if it's full.
    if (xBuffer + len >= bufferSize) {
        buffer[xBuffer] = '\0';
        cout << "\t" << buffer << endl;
        xBuffer = 0;
    }

    //--Append the token string to the buffer.
    strcpy(&buffer[xBuffer], pToken->String());
    xBuffer += len;

    //--Get the next token. Skip over any location markers.
    prevIsDelimiter = currIsDelimiter;
    GetToken();
    while (token == mcLocationMarker) {
        GetLocationMarker();
        GetToken();
    }
    currIsDelimiter = pToken->IsDelimiter();

    //--Append a blank only if both the previous and the
    //--current tokens are not delimiters and we're not
    //--already at the end of the buffer.
    if (!prevIsDelimiter && !currIsDelimiter &&
                            (xBuffer < bufferSize - 1)) {
        buffer[xBuffer] = ' ';
        ++xBuffer;
    }

} while ((currentLineNumber == saveLineNumber) &&
          !TokenIn(token, tlStatementRecreateEnd));

//--Flush the buffer.
if (xBuffer > 0) {
    buffer[xBuffer] = '\0';
    cout << "\t" << buffer << endl;
}

RestoreState();
}
```

The Debugging Routines

Figure 11.13 shows the new file debugger.cpp, in which we implement all of class TExecutor's member functions for debugging.

Member function ReadCommand loops to prompt for and process debugger commands. Just after prompting for the very first command, it creates a new parser object with a new command buffer object. (We create the command parser here instead of in the executor's constructor function because creating the buffer causes an immediate read operation on the console.) If the first token of the command is an identifier, it must be one of the command keywords such as break or step, and so ReadCommand calls member function DoCommand. If the first token is a semicolon, the command is empty. A nonempty command must end with a semicolon to let the parser know that it is at the end of the command.

We want the debugger to prompt for a command before it executes the first statement of the source program. Therefore, in implementation file exec.cpp, we need to add a call to ReadCommand in member function Go:

```
//--Execute the program.
ReadCommand();
currentNestingLevel = 1;
ExecuteRoutine(pProgramId);
```

Member function DoCommand checks the leading identifier token of a command. For trace, untrace, step, unstep, routine, and unroutine, it simply sets and clears the appropriate flags. For the other commands, it calls the appropriate member functions.

Member function PrintStatement calls member function RecreateStatement to print the current source statement. Member function PrintLineNumber prints the current line number during statement tracing.

Member function SetBreakpoint prints the line numbers of all the breakpoints if the break command has no argument. Otherwise, it sets a breakpoint by creating a new break item object and inserting it into the sorted linked list. Member function RemoveBreakpoint calls RemoveBreakpointList to remove all the breakpoints if the unbreak command has no argument. Otherwise, it removes a single breakpoint by deleting its break item object from the linked list.

Member function `SetWatch` prints all the variables being watched if the `watch`, `fetch`, or `store` command has no argument. Otherwise, it sets a watch on a variable by creating a new watch item object and inserting it into the sorted linked list. Member function `RemoveWatch` calls `RemoveWatchList` to remove all watches if the `unwatch` command has no argument. Otherwise, it removes the watch on a single variable by deleting its watch item object from the linked list.

Member function `ShowValue` first calls the base member function `SaveState` to save the current execution state of the source program. It next sends the `ParseCommandExpression` message to the command parser, which returns the intermediate code of the expression and the final command token. `ShowValue` then calls `ExecuteExpression` to evaluate the expression and `TraceDataValue` to print its value. Finally, the function deletes the expression's intermediate code and calls base member function `RestoreState` to restore the source program's execution state.

Member function `DoAssignment` must also save and restore the current execution state of the source program. It sends the `ParseCommandAssignment` to the command parser, and it calls `ExecuteAssignment` to execute the assignment statement.

The debugger often needs to recreate a statement from the intermediate code in order print the statement in its Pascal source form. Member function `Recreate-Statement` does the job in a way similar to what we saw earlier in Chapter 4. This function makes no attempt to make its output "pretty." Notice that it needs to call `SaveState` and `RestoreState` to preserve the executor's current location and token.

Runtime Error Handling

In the previous chapter, whenever our interpreter encountered a runtime error, it printed a message and immediately terminated the execution of the program. With an interactive debugger, a more reasonable action is to suspend the program execution and prompt for a debugger command. We can then examine the values of variables to see why the runtime error occurred, and perhaps even correct or repair the error before resuming the program execution.

Figure 11.14 New member function **RuntimeError** in implementation file **exec.cpp**.

```
//-----------------------------------------------------------
//  RuntimeError          Call the global runtime error routine,
//                        and then read a debugger command.
//-----------------------------------------------------------

void TExecutor::RuntimeError(TRuntimeErrorCode ec)
{
    ::RuntimeError(ec);
    ReadCommand();
}
```

Figure 11.14 shows the new private member function RuntimeError in implementation file exec.cpp. This member function overrides the global function with the same name. In fact, the member function first calls the global function, and then it calls ReadCommand. In header file exec.h, we need to add the following private member function prototype to the definition of class TExecutor:

```
    void RuntimeError(TRuntimeErrorCode ec);
```

Also, we need to make a small change to the global function RuntimeError in implementation file error.cpp. Since we no longer want a runtime error to immediately terminate a program, we must *remove* the following statement:

```
exit(abortRuntimeError);
```

Program 11-1: Interactive Debugger

Figure 11.15 shows the main file debug.cpp. We saw the output from a sample debugging session in Figure 11.1.

██████████ **Figure 11.15** The main file of the interactive debugger.

```
//   ***************************************************************
//   *                                                            *
//   *    Program 11-1: Interactive Debugger                      *
//   *                                                            *
//   *    Interpret a Pascal program with interactive             *
//   *    source-level debugging.                                 *
//   *                                                            *
//   *    FILE:   prog11-1/debug.cpp                              *
//   *                                                            *
```

```
//   *    USAGE:   debug <source file>                            *
//   *                                                            *
//   *                <source file>  name of the source file      *
//   *                                                            *
//   *    Copyright (c) 1996 by Ronald Mak                        *
//   *    For instructional purposes only.  No warranties.         *
//   *                                                            *
//   ************************************************************

#include <iostream.h>
#include "common.h"
#include "error.h"
#include "buffer.h"
#include "symtab.h"
#include "parser.h"
#include "backend.h"
#include "exec.h"


//--------------------------------------------------------------
//  main
//--------------------------------------------------------------

void main(int argc, char *argv[])
{
    //--Check the command line arguments.
    if (argc != 2) {
        cerr << "Usage: debug <source file>" << endl;
        AbortTranslation(abortInvalidCommandLineArgs);
    }

    //--Create the parser for the source file,
    //--and then parse the file.
    TParser     *pParser    = new TParser(new TSourceBuffer(argv[1]));
    TSymtabNode *pProgramId = pParser->Parse();
    delete pParser;

    //--If there were no syntax errors, convert the symbol tables,
    //--and create and invoke the backend pretty-printer.
    if (errorCount == 0) {
        vpSymtabs = new TSymtab *[cntSymtabs];
        for (TSymtab *pSt = pSymtabList; pSt; pSt = pSt->Next()) {
            pSt->Convert(vpSymtabs);
        }

        TBackend *pBackend = new TExecutor;
        pBackend->Go(pProgramId);
```

(continues)

■■■■■■ **Figure 11.15** The main file of the interactive debugger. (*Continued*)

```
        delete[] vpSymtabs;
        delete   pBackend;
    }
}
```

Table 11.1 shows the required modules and source files.

■■■■■■ **Table 11.1** Modules and Files of Program 11-1

Module	File	Status	Directory
Main	debug.cpp	*new*	prog11-1
Parser	parser.h	*changed*	prog11-1
	parser.cpp	*changed*	prog11-1
	parsrtn1.cpp	*unchanged*	prog8-1
	parsrtn2.cpp	*unchanged*	prog8-1
	parsstd.cpp	*unchanged*	prog8-1
	parsdecl.cpp	*unchanged*	prog9-1
	parstyp1.cpp	*unchanged*	prog7-1
	parstyp2.cpp	*unchanged*	prog7-1
	parsstmt.cpp	*unchanged*	prog10-1
	parsexpr.cpp	*unchanged*	prog8-1
Back end	backend.h	*changed*	prog11-1
	backend.cpp	*new*	prog11-1
Executor	exec.h	*changed*	prog11-1
	exec.cpp	*changed*	prog11-1
	execrtn.cpp	*unchanged*	prog10-1
	execstd.cpp	*unchanged*	prog10-1
	execstmt.cpp	*unchanged*	prog10-1
	execexpr.cpp	*unchanged*	prog9-1
	tracer.cpp	*changed*	prog11-1
	debugger.cpp	*new*	prog11-1
Intermediate code	icode.h	*unchanged*	prog10-1
	icode.cpp	*unchanged*	prog10-1
Scanner	scanner.h	*unchanged*	prog3-1
	scanner.cpp	*unchanged*	prog3-2

■■■■■■■■ **Table 11.1** Modules and Files of Program 11-1 (*Continued*)

Module	File	Status	Directory
	token.h	*unchanged*	prog4-2
	tknword.cpp	*unchanged*	prog3-2
	tknnum.cpp	*unchanged*	prog3-2
	tknstrsp.cpp	*unchanged*	prog3-2
Symbol table	types.h	*unchanged*	prog7-1
	types.cpp	*unchanged*	prog7-1
	symtab.h	*unchanged*	prog8-1
	symtab.cpp	*unchanged*	prog8-1
Error	error.h	*unchanged*	prog5-2
	error.cpp	*changed*	prog11-1
Buffer	buffer.h	*unchanged*	prog2-1
	buffer.cpp	*unchanged*	prog2-1
Common	common.h	*unchanged*	prog8-1
	common.cpp	*unchanged*	prog8-1
	misc.h	*unchanged*	prog3-2

■■■■■■■

In the next chapter, we'll begin our compiler by writing a new code generator module to replace the executor module in the back end.

12

MACHINE ARCHITECTURE AND ASSEMBLY CODE

The first part of this book showed how to write a scanner, a parser, and symbol table routines for the Pascal language, and the second part demonstrated how these components can be used in a Pascal interpreter. We now begin the third part of the book, where we write a Pascal compiler that generates code for the 8086-based PC. We'll see that almost all of the work we did in the first part of the book, and much of what we did in the second part, also will be used in the compiler.

This chapter sets the stage with overviews of the architecture of the 8086 processor and its assembly language. We'll start to develop a new backend module with routines to emit assembly code, and we'll create a runtime library based on our interpreter's executor routines. In the next chapter, we'll add backend routines to compile procedures, functions, and assignment statements. Then, in Chapter 14, we'll complete the compiler so that it can compile entire Pascal programs.

Our compiler will translate a Pascal source program into assembly language code instead of directly into machine language code (see the diagram on the right-hand side of Figure 1.1). Thus, the object language for our compiler is assembly language.

(Many commercial compilers, such as some C compilers available on UNIX systems, also generate assembly code. Usually, the assembler is then automatically run to produce the final machine language object file.) We do it this way for several reasons. In order for us to see what the compiler is generating, we must be able to read what it emits. Reading assembly code is *much* easier than deciphering a hexadecimal dump of machine code. An assembler does much useful work, since it is itself a compiler that translates assembly language source programs into machine language programs. The individual bits of a machine language instruction must all be set correctly. Besides the actual code itself, the machine language object file must also contain various tables and other pieces of information to allow the code to be linked and loaded into memory for execution. Producing a proper machine language file is difficult, and the assembler does a very nice job for us. Our compiler will generate assembly language files that can be processed by popular 8086 assemblers, such as those by Borland and Microsoft.

The 8086 Processor Architecture

Let's now take a brief look at the architecture of the 8086 processor. We won't examine the processor in any great detail or thoroughness, but only enough for us to write the compiler. This simplified overview also applies to the successors of the 8086, but our compiler won't generate any instructions beyond a subset of what the 8086 can handle.

At this point, we should also note that we are leaving the somewhat pristine world we inhabited while developing the interpreter. An interpreter is nearly entirely isolated from the real world. On the other hand, a compiler must deal with an actual machine architecture with all of its idiosyncrasies. In our case, we will contend with the 8086 processor architecture and its assembly language.

Of course, some processor architectures are easier than others to work with. Needless to say, one of the challenges a compiler writer faces is that of writing a good compiler *despite* the processor architecture.

Machine Registers and Memory

As shown in Figure 12.1, the 8086 processor has several hardware registers. The 16-bit general-purpose registers are named AX, BX, CX, and DX. Register AX (accu-

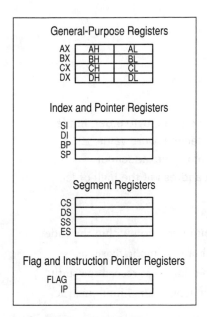

▆▆▆▆▆▆▆ **Figure 12.1** The registers of the 8086 processor.

mulator) is used for most arithmetic and logic operations. Register DX (data) can also participate in these operations. Register BX (base) is used to contain an address for accessing memory indirectly. Register CX (count) is used as a counter by certain iterative instructions.

Each of the general-purpose registers can also be used as two separate 8-bit registers. For example, we can also use the AX register as register AH (A-high) and register AL (A-low).

The index and pointer registers are SI, DI, BP, and SP. Registers SI (source index) and DI (destination index) point to bytes in the source and destination areas of memory for certain string and block instructions, such as string compare and block move. Register BP (base pointer) points to the current stack frame. Register SP (stack pointer) points to the top of the runtime stack. In our interpreter, we had software equivalents of the hardware registers BP and SP.

The segment registers are CS (code segment), DS (data segment), SS (stack segment), and ES (extra segment). These registers point to the start of the various memory segments, as explained below.

```
WORD    [  34  |  12  ]

DWORD   [  78  |  56  ]
DWORD+2 [  34  |  12  ]
```

■■■■■■■■ **Figure 12.2** Data is stored in reversed, or little endian, byte order. In the first example, **WORD** is the address of the hexadecimal word value 1234. In the second example, **DWORD** is the address of the hexadecimal doubleword value 12345678. **DWORD+2** is the address of the high-order half.

The IP (instruction pointer) register points to the current instruction within the code segment. We cannot access it directly from a program, but it is implicitly set as instructions are executed. The flag register contains 1-bit flags that record the status of certain conditions, such as the result of a comparison. Conditional jump instructions are affected by bits in the flag register.

A word in memory is 16 bits (two bytes) wide, and a doubleword is 32 bits (four bytes) wide. The 8086 stores word and doubleword data in memory with their bytes in reversed order. In Figure 12.2, the value of the word at the memory location labeled WORD is 1234 in hexadecimal. The value of the doubleword at the memory location labeled DWORD is 12345678 in hexadecimal. Thus, the high-order half of the doubleword value is at DWORD+2. This method of storing multibyte values is also known as *little endian*, since the value's address points to the byte at the little, or low-order, end of the value.

A word value is usually loaded into register AX to be operated upon, and sometimes into register DX. A doubleword value is loaded into registers with its high-order half in DX and its low-order half in AX (this is known as the DX:AX register pair). A byte value is usually loaded into register AL.

Code and Data Segments

The 8086 processor supports a segmented memory architecture. A segment register points to the start of a segment, which can be up to 64K bytes in size. Segments are a particularly complex feature of the 8086. To keep things simple for our compiler, we will use only two segments, a code segment and a data segment, as shown in Figure 12.3. We'll make the stack segment be the same as the data segment by setting registers DS and SS to the same value. Our compiler will make very limited use of register ES, and when it does, it will set ES to the value of DS.

Our compiler will allocate both the source program's global data and its runtime stack in the data segment, with the global data starting at the segment's lowest address and the stack starting at the segment's highest address. In Figure 12.3, the segments are drawn with their lowest address at the top, so that the stack begins at the bottom of the data segment and grows upward toward lower addresses as data is pushed onto it. Global data begins at the top of the data segment and grows downward toward higher addresses as more data is allocated. Obviously, a serious runtime error occurs if the stack ever runs into the global data.

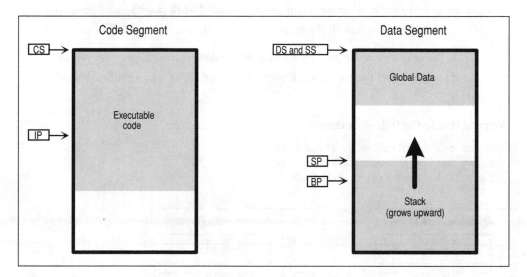

▬▬▬▬ **Figure 12.3** The code and data segments. The stack segment is the same as the data segment. Global data is allocated from the top of the data segment down toward higher addresses, and the stack grows upward from the bottom of the segment toward lower addresses. (In each diagram, the lowest addresses are at the top.)

Register IP points to the current instruction in the code segment. Register SP points to the top of the stack in the data segment, and register BP points to the current stack frame.

Register SP always points to the topmost word of the stack. The 8086 only allows word values to be pushed and popped, so pushing a doubleword value onto the stack requires two pushes, first the high-order half followed by the low-order half.

The Runtime Stack

Just like the software stack of our interpreter, the runtime stack maintained by the 8086 processor stores intermediate results during expression evaluation and the stack frames of active routines.

Figure 12.4 shows the stack frame that is standard for the most popular Pascal compilers on the IBM PC, such as those by Microsoft and Borland. It has the same components as the stack frame we used in our interpreter, only arranged differently. Also, the stack frame base pointer register BP actually points to a word within the frame, instead of to the base of the frame. Thus, we need both positive and negative offsets of register BP to access all the items of the stack frame.

Because the stack grows toward lower address of the data segment, pushing values onto the stack decreases the top of stack pointer register SP, and popping values off increases SP.

We need to add the following constants in header file misc.h:

```
const int procLocalsStackFrameOffset =  0;
const int funcLocalsStackFrameOffset = -4;
const int parametersStackFrameOffset = +6;
```

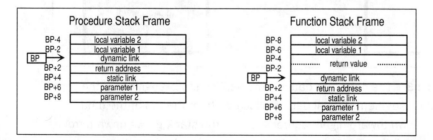

■■■■■■■ **Figure 12.4** Stack frames used by Pascal procedures and functions. These diagrams assume that each subroutine has two word-sized parameters and two word-sized local variables. Notice that register BP points to the dynamic link inside the frame. Remember that the stack grows upward toward lower addresses in these diagrams.

We'll see at the end of this chapter that these constants are used to set the offsets of parameters and local variables, relative to the stack frame base pointer register BP.

The 8086 Assembly Language

The instruction set of a processor is largely determined by the processor's architecture. Assembly language is one step above the machine language, and there is a one-to-one correspondence between assembly instructions and the machine language instructions.

Assembly Language Instructions

The following is the complete list of the instructions that our compiler will generate, along with a brief description of each. We'll use only a small subset of the 8086 instruction set.

mov	*destination,source*	Move a word or a byte from *source* to *destination*.
rep	movsb	Move a block of contiguous bytes. The source address is in register SI, the destination address is in register DI, and the number of bytes to move is in register CX.
lea	*destination,source*	Load the effective address of *source* into *destination*.
cmp	*value1,value2*	Compare *value1* to *value2* and set the flag register accordingly.
repe	cmpsb	Compare *string1* to *string2* and set the flag register accordingly. The address of *string1* is in register SI, the address of *string2* is in register DI, and the number of bytes to compare is in register CX.
push	*source*	Push the *source* word onto the stack.
pop	*destination*	Pop a word from the stack into *destination*.
not	*destination*	*destination* = !*destination*
and	*destination,source*	*destination* = *destination* & *source*
or	*destination,source*	*destination* = *destination*	*source*

`add`	*destination,source*	*destination = destination + source*
`sub`	*destination,source*	*destination = destination - source*
`imul`	*source*	DX:AX = AX * *source*
`idiv`	*source*	AX = DX:AX / *source* (integer quotient)
		DX = DX:AX % *source* (remainder)
`call`	*target*	Call routine *target*.
`ret`	*n*	Return from the current routine and cut the stack back by *n* bytes (by adding *n* to register SP).
`jmp`	*target*	Unconditional jump to *target*.
`jl`	*target*	Jump to target if <
`jle`	*target*	Jump to *target* if <=
`je`	*target*	Jump to *target* if =
`jne`	*target*	Jump to *target* if !=
`jge`	*target*	Jump to *target* if >=
`jg`	*target*	Jump to *target* if >

Assembly Language Operands

An operand of an 8086 assembly instruction is either a memory reference, a register, or an immediate value. If an instruction requires two operands, at most one of the operands can be a memory reference. A memory reference can either be direct, or it can be indirect through register BX or register BP. The data that is referenced is either a single byte or a two-byte word. The compiler will always emit the type operator BYTE PTR or WORD PTR before a memory reference to indicate the type of the operand.

Some examples:

- Move the immediate value 3 into register AX.

    ```
    mov ax,3
    ```

- Move the contents of register DX into register AX.

    ```
    mov ax,dx
    ```

- Move the doubleword value at the memory location labeled avg directly into registers AX (low-order half) and DX (high-order half).

```
mov ax,WORD PTR avg
mov dx,WORD PTR avg+2
```

- Move the byte data pointed to by register BX (indirect reference) into register AL.

```
mov al,BYTE PTR [bx]
```

- Move into register DX the word data located eight bytes from the location pointed to by register BP. (Based on the stack frame format, this data is a parameter passed to a routine.)

```
mov dx,WORD PTR [bp+8]
```

Using a Runtime Library

Some complicated operations, such as input and output and real arithmetic, are difficult for a compiler to generate code for. We can instead write a runtime library, and have the compiler generate calls to the library routines to handle such operations. We can also include library routines to implement the standard Pascal functions.

Since the runtime library is separate from the compiler, we have several options for how to write its routines. An actual library needs to be as small and as fast as possible, so we would want to write it in C or assembly language.

For our compiler, we'll strive for simplicity, so we'll use C routines inspired by the runtime routines of our interpreter. Figure 12.5 shows file `paslib.c`, which contains all the runtime library routines that our compiler will generate calls to. Notice that we also use standard C functions such as `printf`, which, unfortunately, will cause parts of the C runtime library to be dragged in and increase the size of the final object code. Using C functions also introduces a few other perverse complications.

■■■■■■■■ **Figure 12.5** File **paslib.c**, which contains the runtime library routines.

```
// ****************************************************************
// *                                                            *
// *    P A S C A L   R U N T I M E   L I B R A R Y             *
// *                                                            *
// *    Note that all formal parameters are reversed to         *
// *    accomodate the Pascal calling convention of the         *
// *    compiled code.                                          *
```

(continues)

Figure 12.5 File **paslib.c**, which contains the runtime library routines. (*Continued*)

```
//  *                                                              *
//  *    All floating point parameters are passed in as longs      *
//  *    to bypass unwanted type conversions.  Floating point      *
//  *    function values are also returned as longs.               *
//  *                                                              *
//  *    Copyright (c) 1996 by Ronald Mak                          *
//  *    For instructional purposes only.  No warranties.          *
//  *                                                              *
//  **************************************************************

#include <stdlib.h>
#include <stdio.h>
#include <string.h>
#include <math.h>

#define MAX_SOURCE_LINE_LENGTH  256

typedef enum {
    FALSE, TRUE
} BOOLEAN;

union {
    float real;
    long  dword;
} value;

//------------------------------------------------------------
// main                The main routine, which calls
//                     _PascalMain, the "main" of the compiled
//                     program.
//------------------------------------------------------------

void main(void)
{
    extern PascalMain(void);

    PascalMain();
    exit(0);
}


//              *******************
//              *                 *
//              *  Read Routines  *
```

```
//                    *                  *
//              *******************

//-------------------------------------------------------------
// ReadInteger        Read an integer value.
//-------------------------------------------------------------

int ReadInteger(void)
{
    int i;

    scanf("%d", &i);
    return feof(stdin) ? 0 : i;
}


//-------------------------------------------------------------
// ReadReal           Read a real value.
//-------------------------------------------------------------

long ReadReal(void)
{
    scanf("%g", &value.real);
    return feof(stdin) ? 0.0 : value.dword;
}


//-------------------------------------------------------------
// ReadChar           Read a character value.
//-------------------------------------------------------------

char ReadChar(void)
{
    char ch;

    scanf("%c", &ch);
    return (feof(stdin) || (ch == '\n')) ? ' ' : ch;
}


//-------------------------------------------------------------
// ReadLine           Skip the rest of the input record.
//-------------------------------------------------------------

void ReadLine(void)
{
    char ch;

    do {
```

(continues)

■■■■■ **Figure 12.5** File **paslib.c**, which contains the runtime library routines. (*Continued*)

```c
        ch = getchar();
    } while(!feof(stdin) && (ch != '\n'));
}


//          ********************
//          *                  *
//          *  Write Routines  *
//          *                  *
//          ********************


//-----------------------------------------------------------------
//  WriteInteger        Write an integer value.
//-----------------------------------------------------------------

void WriteInteger(int fieldWidth, int i)
{
    printf("%*d", fieldWidth, i);
}


//-----------------------------------------------------------------
//  WriteReal           Write an real value.
//-----------------------------------------------------------------

void WriteReal(int precision, int fieldWidth, long i)
{
    value.dword = i;
    printf("%*.*f", fieldWidth, precision, value.real);
}


//-----------------------------------------------------------------
//  WriteBoolean        Write a boolean value.
//-----------------------------------------------------------------

void WriteBoolean(int fieldWidth, int b)
{
    printf("%*s", fieldWidth, b == 0 ? "FALSE" : "TRUE");
}


//-----------------------------------------------------------------
//  WriteChar           Write a character value.
//-----------------------------------------------------------------

void WriteChar(int fieldWidth, int ch)
```

```
{
    printf("%*c", fieldWidth, ch);
}

//----------------------------------------------------------------
// WriteString          Write a string value.
//----------------------------------------------------------------

void WriteString(int length, int fieldWidth, char *value)
{
    char *pCh       = value;
    int   fillCount = fieldWidth - length;

    //--Write the characters of the string.
    while (length--) putchar(*pCh++);

    //--Pad out the field on the right with blanks if necessary.
    if (fillCount > 0) while (fillCount--) putchar(' ');
}

//----------------------------------------------------------------
// WriteLine            Write a carriage return.
//----------------------------------------------------------------

void WriteLine(void)
{
    putchar('\n');
}

//            ***********************
//            *                     *
//            *  Other I/O Routines  *
//            *                     *
//            ***********************

//----------------------------------------------------------------
// StdEof               Return 1 if at end of file, else 0.
//----------------------------------------------------------------

BOOLEAN StdEof(void)
{
    char ch = getchar();

    if (feof(stdin)) return TRUE;
    else {
        ungetc(ch, stdin);
```

(continues)

■■■■■ **Figure 12.5** File **paslib.c**, which contains the runtime library routines. (*Continued*)

```c
        return FALSE;
    }
}

//----------------------------------------------------------------
//  StdEoln             Return 1 if at end of line, else 0.
//----------------------------------------------------------------

BOOLEAN StdEoln(void)
{
    char ch = getchar();

    if (feof(stdin)) return TRUE;
    else {
        ungetc(ch, stdin);
        return ch == '\n';
    }
}

//              ****************************************
//              *                                      *
//              *   Floating Point Arithmetic Routines  *
//              *                                      *
//              ****************************************

//----------------------------------------------------------------
//  FloatNegate         Return the negated value.
//----------------------------------------------------------------

long FloatNegate(long i)
{
    value.dword = i;

    value.real = -value.real;
    return value.dword;
}

//----------------------------------------------------------------
//  FloatAdd            Return the sum x + y.
//----------------------------------------------------------------

long FloatAdd(long j, long i)
{
```

```
    float x, y;

    value.dword = i;   x = value.real;
    value.dword = j;   y = value.real;

    value.real = x + y;
    return value.dword;
}

//----------------------------------------------------------------
//  FloatSubtract        Return the difference x - y.
//----------------------------------------------------------------

long FloatSubtract(long j, long i)
{
    float x, y;

    value.dword = i;   x = value.real;
    value.dword = j;   y = value.real;

    value.real = x - y;
    return value.dword;
}

//----------------------------------------------------------------
//  FloatMultiply        Return the product x*y.
//----------------------------------------------------------------

long FloatMultiply(long j, long i)
{
    float x, y;

    value.dword = i;   x = value.real;
    value.dword = j;   y = value.real;

    value.real = x*y;
    return value.dword;
}

//----------------------------------------------------------------
//  FloatDivide          Return the quotient x/y.
//----------------------------------------------------------------

long FloatDivide(long j, long i)
{
    float x, y;
```

(continues)

■■■■■■■■ **Figure 12.5**   File **paslib.c**, which contains the runtime library routines.
(*Continued*)

```c
    value.dword = i;  x = value.real;
    value.dword = j;  y = value.real;

    value.real = x/y;
    return value.dword;
}


//-------------------------------------------------------------
//  FloatConvert        Convert an integer value to real and
//                      return the converted value.
//-------------------------------------------------------------

long FloatConvert(int i)
{
    value.real = i;
    return value.dword;
}


//-------------------------------------------------------------
//  FloatCompare        Return -1 if x <  y
//                              0 if x == y
//                             +1 if x >  y
//-------------------------------------------------------------

int FloatCompare(long j, long i)
{
    int   comp;
    float x, y;

    value.dword = i;  x = value.real;
    value.dword = j;  y = value.real;

    if (x < y)        comp = -1;
    else if (x == y)  comp =  0;
    else              comp = +1;

    return comp;
}


//             ***************************************
//             *                                     *
//             *   Standard Floating Point Functions  *
//             *                                     *
//             ***************************************
```

```
//---------------------------------------------------------------
// StdAbs              Return abs of parameter.
//---------------------------------------------------------------

long StdAbs(long i)
{
    value.dword = i;

    value.real = fabs(value.real);
    return value.dword;
}


//---------------------------------------------------------------
// StdArctan           Return arctan of parameter.
//---------------------------------------------------------------

long StdArctan(long i)
{
    value.dword = i;

    value.real = atan(value.real);
    return value.dword;
}


//---------------------------------------------------------------
// StdCos              Return cos of parameter.
//---------------------------------------------------------------

long StdCos(long i)
{
    value.dword = i;

    value.real = cos(value.real);
    return value.dword;
}


//---------------------------------------------------------------
// StdExp              Return exp of parameter.
//---------------------------------------------------------------

long StdExp(long i)
{
    value.dword = i;

    value.real = exp(value.real);
    return value.dword;
}
```

(continues)

■■■■■■ **Figure 12.5** File **paslib.c**, which contains the runtime library routines. (*Continued*)

```c
//-------------------------------------------------------------
//  StdLn                 Return ln of parameter.
//-------------------------------------------------------------

long StdLn(long i)
{
    value.dword = i;

    value.real = log(value.real);
    return value.dword;
}


//-------------------------------------------------------------
//  StdSin                Return sin of parameter.
//-------------------------------------------------------------

long StdSin(long i)
{
    value.dword = i;

    value.real = sin(value.real);
    return value.dword;
}


//-------------------------------------------------------------
//  StdSqrt               Return sqrt of parameter.
//-------------------------------------------------------------

long StdSqrt(long i)
{
    value.dword = i;

    value.real = sqrt(value.real);
    return value.dword;
}


//-------------------------------------------------------------
//  StdRound              Return round of parameter.
//-------------------------------------------------------------

int StdRound(long i)
{
    value.dword = i;
```

```
    value.dword = (int) (value.real + 0.5);
    return (int) value.dword;
}

//------------------------------------------------------------
// StdTrunc          Return trunc of parameter.
//------------------------------------------------------------

int StdTrunc(long i)
{
    value.dword = i;

    value.dword = (int) value.real;
    return (int) value.dword;
}
```

The library routines that have more than one parameter point out a major difference between how C routines and Pascal routines expect parameter values at runtime. Pascal routines expect parameter values to be pushed onto the stack in the order that they are written in the source program, so that the last parameter value is on top of the others on the stack. C functions expect the parameter values to be pushed in reverse order, so that the first parameter value is on top of the others.

For our runtime library, we'll get around this difference with a kludge: we'll simply list the formal parameters of the library routines in reverse order. This way, the compiler can emit the same code sequences to pass parameter values to either Pascal routines or the library routines.

Another difference between C and Pascal routines is the code to return from a routine. We'll cover this in the next chapter.

When a C function has real parameters or returns a real value, it expects its caller to convert these real values to a form suitable for a numeric coprocessor or for floating-point emulation routines. This is beyond the scope of this book, so we'll bypass these conversions by dealing only with integers. Therefore, a library routine that takes real parameters must receive them as long integers, and one that returns a real value must return it as a long integer. We'll use the union type

```
  union {
      float real;
      long  dword;
  } value;
```

Finally, to simplify matters further, we'll compile the main routine of the Pascal source program as though it were a procedure, and we'll always give it the name PascalMain. Then, one of the library routines must be the actual main that calls PascalMain. Starting the execution of a compiled Pascal program with a main routine written in C ensures that the various initializations required by C are done. Then, the library routines will work properly when they are called by the compiled Pascal program.

Each of the input functions ReadInteger, ReadReal, and ReadChar reads a value and then checks for the end of the input file. The function returns the value it read, unless it encountered the end of file, in which case it returns a default value. Functions StdEof and StdEol each first read a character and then check for the end of the input file. (The standard C function feof returns the state of the input file *after* a read operation.) If it is not at the end of the input file, the functions call ungetc so that the character can be read by the next input operation.

The floating point arithmetic functions such as FloatAdd show how real parameters and real return values are passed as long integers. They also show how the formal parameters are reversed. The standard floating point functions such as StdAbs are implemented by calling the equivalent C function for each Pascal function.

Emitting Assembly Code

Our interpreter had an executor module in its back end, which we implemented as subclass TExecutor of class TBackend. For our compiler, we need to replace the executor with a code generator, and so we introduce a new subclass TCodeGenerator. To emit the appropriate assembly language object code, the member functions of TCodeGenerator access (via the member functions of the parent class TBackend) the intermediate code and the symbol table created by the front end. Figure 12.6 shows the class diagram for class TCodeGenerator. We'll examine an object diagram in the next chapter.

The class diagram shows that class TCodeGenerator contains many member functions, only a few of which are shown, that emit assembly code to the output assembly file. The subclass also has a data member pAsmBuffer that points to a

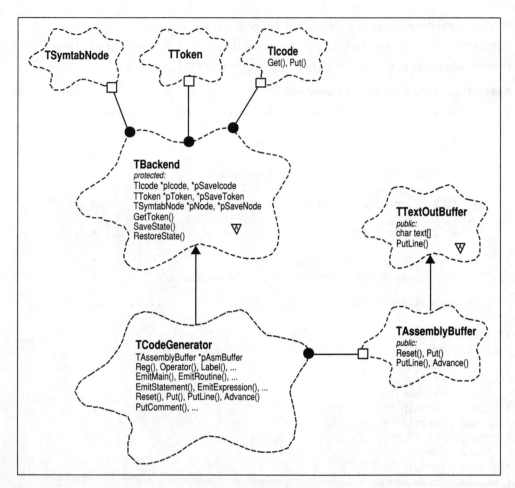

Figure 12.6 Class diagram of the compiler's back end.

`TAssemblyBuffer` object that represents the assembly file. Class `TAssembly-Buffer` is a subclass of `TTextOutBuffer`, and it has member functions that control how the assembly code is written to the assembly file.

Class TAssemblyBuffer and Class TCodeGenerator

Figure 12.7 shows file `codegen.h`, which includes the definition of subclasses `TAssemblyBuffer` and `TCodeGenerator`. The file begins with several `#define` strings that represent assembly language label prefixes, the names of several important items of the runtime stack, and the names of the runtime library routines. These names will appear in the assembly code that our compiler will generate.

■ **Figure 12.7** File **codegen.h**.

```
// *****************************************************************
// *                                                               *
// *    C O D E   G E N E R A T O R   (Header)                      *
// *                                                               *
// *    CLASSES: TAssemblyBuffer, TCodeGenerator                    *
// *                                                               *
// *    FILE:    prog13-1/codegen.h                                 *
// *                                                               *
// *    MODULE:  Code generator                                     *
// *                                                               *
// *    Copyright (c) 1996 by Ronald Mak                            *
// *    For instructional purposes only.  No warranties.           *
// *                                                               *
// *****************************************************************

#ifndef codegen_h
#define codegen_h

#include <string.h>
#include <fstream.h>
#include <iomanip.h>
#include "error.h"
#include "buffer.h"
#include "symtab.h"
#include "types.h"
#include "icode.h"
#include "backend.h"
#include "parser.h"


//------------------------------------------------------------
// Assembly label prefixes
//------------------------------------------------------------

#define STMT_LABEL_PREFIX      "$L"
#define FLOAT_LABEL_PREFIX     "$F"
#define STRING_LABEL_PREFIX    "$S"


//------------------------------------------------------------
// Runtime stack frame items
//------------------------------------------------------------
```

```
#define STATIC_LINK             "$STATIC_LINK"
#define RETURN_VALUE            "$RETURN_VALUE"
#define HIGH_RETURN_VALUE       "$HIGH_RETURN_VALUE"


//-------------------------------------------------------------
//   Names of library routines
//-------------------------------------------------------------

#define FLOAT_NEGATE    "_FloatNegate"
#define FLOAT_ADD       "_FloatAdd"
#define FLOAT_SUBTRACT  "_FloatSubtract"
#define FLOAT_MULTIPLY  "_FloatMultiply"
#define FLOAT_DIVIDE    "_FloatDivide"
#define FLOAT_COMPARE   "_FloatCompare"
#define FLOAT_CONVERT   "_FloatConvert"

#define READ_INTEGER    "_ReadInteger"
#define READ_REAL       "_ReadReal"
#define READ_CHAR       "_ReadChar"
#define READ_LINE       "_ReadLine"

#define WRITE_INTEGER   "_WriteInteger"
#define WRITE_REAL      "_WriteReal"
#define WRITE_BOOLEAN   "_WriteBoolean"
#define WRITE_CHAR      "_WriteChar"
#define WRITE_STRING    "_WriteString"
#define WRITE_LINE      "_WriteLine"

#define STD_EOF         "_StdEof"
#define STD_EOLN        "_StdEoln"
#define STD_ABS         "_StdAbs"
#define STD_ARCTAN      "_StdArctan"
#define STD_COS         "_StdCos"
#define STD_EXP         "_StdExp"
#define STD_LN          "_StdLn"
#define STD_SIN         "_StdSin"
#define STD_SQRT        "_StdSqrt"
#define STD_ROUND       "_StdRound"
#define STD_TRUNC       "_StdTrunc"


//-------------------------------------------------------------
//   Emit0                    Emit a no-operand instruction.
//-------------------------------------------------------------

#define Emit0(opcode)                       \
{                                           \
```

(continues)

■■■■■■ **Figure 12.7** File **codegen.h**. (*Continued*)

```
    Operator(opcode);                       \
    pAsmBuffer->PutLine();                  \
}


//----------------------------------------------------------
//  Emit1              Emit a one-operand instruction.
//----------------------------------------------------------

#define Emit1(opcode, operand1)             \
{                                           \
    Operator(opcode);                       \
    pAsmBuffer->Put('\t');                  \
    operand1;                               \
    pAsmBuffer->PutLine();                  \
}


//----------------------------------------------------------
//  Emit2              Emit a two-operand instruction.
//----------------------------------------------------------

#define Emit2(opcode, operand1, operand2)       \
{                                               \
    Operator(opcode);                           \
    pAsmBuffer->Put('\t');                      \
    operand1;                                   \
    pAsmBuffer->Put(',');                       \
    operand2;                                   \
    pAsmBuffer->PutLine();                      \
}


//----------------------------------------------------------
//  TRegister          Machine registers.
//----------------------------------------------------------

enum TRegister {
    ax, ah, al, bx, bh, bl, cx, ch, cl, dx, dh, dl,
    cs, ds, es, ss, sp, bp, si, di,
};


//----------------------------------------------------------
//  TInstruction       Assembly instructions.
//----------------------------------------------------------

enum TInstruction {
```

```
    mov, rep_movsb, lea, xchg, cmp, repe_cmpsb, pop, push,
    and, or, xor, neg, incr, decr, add, sub, imul, idiv,
    cld, call, ret, jmp, jl, jle, je, jne, jge, jg,
};


//-------------------------------------------------------------
//  TAssemblyBuffer      Assembly language buffer subclass of
//                       TTextOutBuffer.
//-------------------------------------------------------------

class TAssemblyBuffer : public TTextOutBuffer {
    enum {
        maxLength = 72,
    };

    fstream  file;        // assembly output file
    char     *pText;      // assembly buffer pointer
    int      textLength;  // length of assembly comment

public:
    TAssemblyBuffer(const char *pAsmFileName, TAbortCode ac);

    char *Text (void) const { return pText; }

    void Reset(void)
    {
        pText = text;
        text[0] = '\0';
        textLength = 0;
    }

    void Put(char ch) { *pText++ = ch; *pText = '\0'; ++textLength; }
    virtual void PutLine(void) { file << text << endl; Reset(); }

    void PutLine(const char *pText)
    {
        TTextOutBuffer::PutLine(pText);
    }

    void Advance(void);

    void Put(const char *pString)
    {
        strcpy(pText, pString);
        Advance();
    }
```

(continues)

■■■■■ **Figure 12.7** File **codegen.h**. (*Continued*)

```
    void Reset(const char *pString) { Reset(); Put(pString); }

    int Fit(int length) const
    {
        return textLength + length < maxLength;
    }
};


//-------------------------------------------------------------
//  TCodeGenerator        Code generator subclass of TBackend.
//-------------------------------------------------------------

class TCodeGenerator : public TBackend {
    TAssemblyBuffer *const pAsmBuffer;

    //--Pointers to the list of all the float and string literals
    //--used in the source program.
    TSymtabNode *pFloatLitList;
    TSymtabNode *pStringLitList;

    void Reg                (TRegister r);
    void Operator           (TInstruction opcode);
    void Label              (const char *prefix, int index);
    void WordLabel          (const char *prefix, int index);
    void HighDWordLabel     (const char *prefix, int index);
    void Byte               (const TSymtabNode *pId);
    void Word               (const TSymtabNode *pId);
    void HighDWord          (const TSymtabNode *pId);
    void ByteIndirect       (TRegister r);
    void WordIndirect       (TRegister r);
    void HighDWordIndirect  (TRegister r);
    void TaggedName         (const TSymtabNode *pId);
    void NameLit            (const char *pName);
    void IntegerLit         (int n);
    void CharLit            (char ch);

    void EmitStatementLabel(int index);

    //--Program
    void EmitProgramPrologue(void);
    void EmitProgramEpilogue(const TSymtabNode *pProgramId);
    void EmitMain(const TSymtabNode *pMainId);
    void EmitMainPrologue(void);
    void EmitMainEpilogue(void);
```

```
//--Routines
void     EmitRoutine                 (const TSymtabNode *pRoutineId);
void     EmitRoutinePrologue         (const TSymtabNode *pRoutineId);
void     EmitRoutineEpilogue         (const TSymtabNode *pRoutineId);
TType *EmitSubroutineCall            (const TSymtabNode *pRoutineId);
TType *EmitDeclaredSubroutineCall(const TSymtabNode *pRoutineId);
TType *EmitStandardSubroutineCall(const TSymtabNode *pRoutineId);
void     EmitActualParameters        (const TSymtabNode *pRoutineId);

//--Standard routines
TType *EmitReadReadlnCall  (const TSymtabNode *pRoutineId);
TType *EmitWriteWritelnCall(const TSymtabNode *pRoutineId);
TType *EmitEofEolnCall     (const TSymtabNode *pRoutineId);
TType *EmitAbsSqrCall      (const TSymtabNode *pRoutineId);
TType *EmitArctanCosExpLnSinSqrtCall(const TSymtabNode *pRoutineId);
TType *EmitPredSuccCall    (const TSymtabNode *pRoutineId);
TType *EmitChrCall         (void);
TType *EmitOddCall         (void);
TType *EmitOrdCall         (void);
TType *EmitRoundTruncCall  (const TSymtabNode *pRoutineId);

//--Declarations
void EmitDeclarations      (const TSymtabNode *pRoutineId);
void EmitStackOffsetEquate(const TSymtabNode *pId);

//--Loads and pushes
void EmitAdjustBP       (int level);
void EmitRestoreBP      (int level);
void EmitLoadValue      (const TSymtabNode *pId);
void EmitLoadFloatLit   (TSymtabNode *pNode);
void EmitPushStringLit(TSymtabNode *pNode);
void EmitPushOperand    (const TType *pType);
void EmitPushAddress    (const TSymtabNode *pId);
void EmitPushReturnValueAddress(const TSymtabNode *pId);
void EmitPromoteToReal(const TType *pType1, const TType *pType2);

//--Statements
void EmitStatement      (void);
void EmitStatementList(TTokenCode terminator);
void EmitAssignment     (const TSymtabNode *pTargetId);
void EmitREPEAT         (void);
void EmitWHILE          (void);
void EmitIF             (void);
void EmitFOR            (void);
void EmitCASE           (void);
void EmitCompound       (void);
```

(continues)

```
//--Expressions
TType *EmitExpression(void);
TType *EmitSimpleExpression(void);
TType *EmitTerm        (void);
TType *EmitFactor      (void);
TType *EmitConstant    (TSymtabNode *pId);
TType *EmitVariable    (const TSymtabNode *pId, int addressFlag);
TType *EmitSubscripts(const TType *pType);
TType *EmitField       (void);

//--Assembly buffer
char *AsmText(void)            { return pAsmBuffer->Text();  }
void  Reset   (void)          { pAsmBuffer->Reset();        }
void  Put     (char ch)       { pAsmBuffer->Put(ch);        }
void  Put     (char *pString) { pAsmBuffer->Put(pString);   }
void  PutLine(void)           { pAsmBuffer->PutLine();      }
void  PutLine(char *pText)    { pAsmBuffer->PutLine(pText); }
void  Advance(void)           { pAsmBuffer->Advance();      }

//--Comments
void PutComment  (const char *pString);
void StartComment(int n);

void StartComment(void) { Reset(); PutComment("; "); }

void StartComment(const char *pString)
{
    StartComment();
    PutComment(pString);
}

void EmitProgramHeaderComment     (const TSymtabNode *pProgramId);
void EmitSubroutineHeaderComment  (const TSymtabNode *pRoutineId);
void EmitSubroutineFormalsComment (const TSymtabNode *pParmId);
void EmitVarDeclComment           (const TSymtabNode *pVarId);
void EmitTypeSpecComment          (const TType *pType);
void EmitStmtComment              (void);
void EmitAsgnOrCallComment        (void);
void EmitREPEATComment            (void);
void EmitUNTILComment             (void);
void EmitWHILEComment             (void);
void EmitIFComment                (void);
void EmitFORComment               (void);
void EmitCASEComment              (void);
```

```
        void EmitExprComment              (void);
        void EmitIdComment                (void);
public:
        TCodeGenerator(const char *pAsmName)
            : pAsmBuffer(new TAssemblyBuffer(pAsmName,
                                    abortAssemblyFileOpenFailed))
        {
            pFloatLitList = pStringLitList = NULL;
        }

        virtual void Go(const TSymtabNode *pProgramId);
};

#endif
```

We'll use the macros Emit0, Emit1, and Emit2 to emit zero-, one-, and two-operand assembly instructions. Each sends Put and PutLine messages to the assembly buffer object. In the macro calls, the operands opcode, operand1, and operand2 are each replaced by a call to an assembly code emitting routine. We'll look at these routines shortly.

Enumeration type TRegister represents the hardware registers of the 8086 architecture, and enumeration type TInstruction represents the assembly language instructions that our compiler will emit.

Class TAssemblyBuffer is a subclass of TTextOutBuffer, and it defines the object that represents the assembly object file. Its various Reset, Put, and Put-Line member functions append strings of text that are parts of assembly instructions. Member function Advance (defined later in implementation file emitasm.cpp) moves the text pointer pText to the end of what's already in the buffer. Member function Fit determines whether or not another text string can fit.

In the definition of subclass TCodeGenerator, data member pAsmBuffer points to the assembly buffer object. Data members pFloatLitList and pStringLitList point to the heads of lists of the symbol table nodes of real and string constants, respectively. (We'll see how these lists are used in the next chapter.) The member functions Reg through CharLit are all designed to be used with the Emit0, Emit1, and Emit2 macros, and each writes specific parts of an assembly instruction into the assembly buffer.

Member functions AsmText through Advance are covers for the equivalent TAssemblyBuffer member functions. The member functions PutComment through EmitIdComment write comments into the assembly buffer. The remaining private member functions, EmitStatementLabel though EmitField, emit assembly code for various parts of a Pascal program. They will be implemented and described in the following two chapters.

The constructor function initializes pAsmBuffer to point to a new TAssembly-Buffer object. The virtual function Go is called after the front end has created the intermediate code and the symbol table, and it is passed a pointer to the symbol table node of the program name.

■■■■■ **Figure 12.8** Implementation file **emitasm.cpp**.

```
//      ****************************************************************
//      *                                                              *
//      *     E M I T   A S S E M B L Y   S T A T E M E N T S          *
//      *                                                              *
//      *     Routines for generating and emitting                     *
//      *     language statements.                                     *
//      *                                                              *
//      *     CLASSES: TAssemblyBuffer, TCodeGenerator                 *
//      *                                                              *
//      *     FILE:    prog13-1/emitasm.cpp                            *
//      *                                                              *
//      *     MODULE:  Code generator                                  *
//      *                                                              *
//      *     Copyright (c) 1996 by Ronald Mak                         *
//      *     For instructional purposes only.  No warranties.         *
//      *                                                              *
//      ****************************************************************

#include <stdio.h>
#include "buffer.h"
#include "symtab.h"
#include "codegen.h"


//----------------------------------------------------------------
//  Registers and instructions
//----------------------------------------------------------------

char *registers[] = {
    "ax", "ah", "al", "bx", "bh", "bl", "cx", "ch", "cl",
    "dx", "dh", "dl", "cs", "ds", "es", "ss",
```

```
        "sp", "bp", "si", "di",
};

char *instructions[] = {
    "mov", "rep\tmovsb", "lea", "xchg", "cmp", "repe\tcmpsb",
    "pop", "push", "and", "or", "xor",
    "neg", "inc", "dec", "add", "sub", "imul", "idiv",
    "cld", "call", "ret",
    "jmp", "jl", "jle", "je", "jne", "jge", "jg",
};

//              ********************
//              *                  *
//              *  Assembly Buffer  *
//              *                  *
//              ********************

//----------------------------------------------------------------
// Constructor     Construct an assembly buffer by opening the
//                 output assembly file.
//
//      pAssemblyFileName : ptr to the name of the assembly file
//      ac                : abort code to use if open failed
//----------------------------------------------------------------

TAssemblyBuffer::TAssemblyBuffer(const char *pAssemblyFileName,
                                 TAbortCode ac)
{
    //--Open the assembly output file.  Abort if failed.
    file.open(pAssemblyFileName, ios::out);
    if (!file.good()) AbortTranslation(ac);

    Reset();
}

//----------------------------------------------------------------
// Advance         Advance pText to the end of the buffer
//                 contents.
//----------------------------------------------------------------

void TAssemblyBuffer::Advance(void)
{
    while (*pText) {
        ++pText;
        ++textLength;
    }
}
```

(continues)

```
//              ***************************************
//              *                                     *
//              *    Emit parts of assembly statements *
//              *                                     *
//              ***************************************


//------------------------------------------------------------
// Reg                   Emit a register name.  Example:  ax
//
//      r : register code
//------------------------------------------------------------

void TCodeGenerator::Reg(TRegister r)
{
    Put(registers[r]);
}


//------------------------------------------------------------
// Operator              Emit an opcode.  Example:  add
//
//      opcode : operator code
//------------------------------------------------------------

void TCodeGenerator::Operator(TInstruction opcode)
{
    Put('\t');
    Put(instructions[opcode]);
}


//------------------------------------------------------------
// Label                 Emit a generic label constructed from
//                       the prefix and the label index.
//
//                       Example:        $L_007
//
//      pPrefix : ptr to label prefix
//      index   : index value
//------------------------------------------------------------

void TCodeGenerator::Label(const char *pPrefix, int index)
{
    sprintf(AsmText(), "%s_%03d", pPrefix, index);
    Advance();
}
```

```
//----------------------------------------------------------------
//  WordLabel            Emit a word label constructed from
//                       the prefix and the label index.
//
//                       Example:        WORD PTR $F_007
//
//      pPrefix : ptr to label prefix
//      index   : index value
//----------------------------------------------------------------

void TCodeGenerator::WordLabel(const char *pPrefix, int index)
{
    sprintf(AsmText(), "WORD PTR %s_%03d", pPrefix, index);
    Advance();
}


//----------------------------------------------------------------
//  HighDWordLabel       Emit a word label constructed from
//                       the prefix and the label index and
//                       offset by 2 to point to the high Word
//                       of a double Word.
//
//                       Example:        WORD PTR $F_007+2
//
//      pPrefix : ptr to label prefix
//      index   : index value
//----------------------------------------------------------------

void TCodeGenerator::HighDWordLabel(const char *pPrefix, int index)
{
    sprintf(AsmText(), "WORD PTR %s_%03d+2", pPrefix, index);
    Advance();
}


//----------------------------------------------------------------
//  Byte                 Emit a byte label constructed from
//                       the id name and its label index.
//
//                       Example:        BYTE_PTR ch_007
//
//      pId : ptr to symbol table node
//----------------------------------------------------------------

void TCodeGenerator::Byte(const TSymtabNode *pId)
{
    sprintf(AsmText(), "BYTE PTR %s_%03d",
```

(continues)

```
                                pId->String(), pId->labelIndex);
        Advance();
}


//----------------------------------------------------------------
//   Word                 Emit a word label constructed from
//                        the id name and its label index.
//
//                        Example:         WORD_PTR sum_007
//
//      pId : ptr to symbol table node
//----------------------------------------------------------------

void TCodeGenerator::Word(const TSymtabNode *pId)
{
    sprintf(AsmText(), "WORD PTR %s_%03d",
                    pId->String(), pId->labelIndex);
    Advance();
}


//----------------------------------------------------------------
//   HighDWord            Emit a word label constructed from
//                        the id name and its label index and
//                        offset by 2 to point to the high word
//                        of a double Word.
//
//                        Example:         WORD_PTR sum_007+2
//
//      pId : ptr to symbol table node
//----------------------------------------------------------------

void TCodeGenerator::HighDWord(const TSymtabNode *pId)
{
    sprintf(AsmText(), "WORD PTR %s_%03d+2",
                    pId->String(), pId->labelIndex);
    Advance();
}


//----------------------------------------------------------------
//   ByteIndirect         Emit an indirect reference to a byte
//                        via a register.
//
//                        Example:         BYTE PTR [bx]
//
```

```
//       r : register code
//----------------------------------------------------------------

void TCodeGenerator::ByteIndirect(TRegister r)
{
    sprintf(AsmText(), "BYTE PTR [%s]", registers[r]);
    Advance();
}


//----------------------------------------------------------------
//   WordIndirect       Emit an indirect reference to a word
//                      via a register.
//
//                      Example:      WORD PTR [bx]
//
//       r : register code
//----------------------------------------------------------------

void TCodeGenerator::WordIndirect(TRegister r)
{
    sprintf(AsmText(), "WORD PTR [%s]", registers[r]);
    Advance();
}


//----------------------------------------------------------------
//   HighDWordIndirect   Emit an indirect reference to the high
//                       word of a double word via a register.
//
//                       Example:      WORD PTR [bx+2]
//
//       r : register code
//----------------------------------------------------------------

void TCodeGenerator::HighDWordIndirect(TRegister r)
{
    sprintf(AsmText(), "WORD PTR [%s+2]", registers[r]);
    Advance();
}


//----------------------------------------------------------------
//   TaggedName          Emit an id name tagged with the id's
//                       label index.
//
//                       Example:      x_007
//
//       pId : ptr to symbol table node
//----------------------------------------------------------------
```

(continues)

■■■■■■■ **Figure 12.8** Implementation file **emitasm.cpp**. (*Continued*)

```cpp
void TCodeGenerator::TaggedName(const TSymtabNode *pId)
{
    sprintf(AsmText(), "%s_%03d", pId->String(), pId->labelIndex);
    Advance();
}


//-------------------------------------------------------------
//  NameLit             Emit a literal name.
//
//                      Example:        _FloatConvert
//
//      pName : ptr to name
//-------------------------------------------------------------

void TCodeGenerator::NameLit(const char *pName)
{
    sprintf(AsmText(), "%s", pName);
    Advance();
}


//-------------------------------------------------------------
//  IntegerLit          Emit an integer as a string.
//
//      n : integer value
//-------------------------------------------------------------

void TCodeGenerator::IntegerLit(int n)
{
    sprintf(AsmText(), "%d", n);
    Advance();
}


//-------------------------------------------------------------
//  CharLit             Emit a character surrounded by single
//                      quotes.
//
//      ch : character value
//-------------------------------------------------------------

void TCodeGenerator::CharLit(char ch)
{
    sprintf(AsmText(), "'%c'", ch);
    Advance();
}
```

Code Emitting Routines

Figure 12.8 shows the implementation file `emitasm.cpp`. It begins with several string arrays that correspond to the enumeration types `TRegister` and `TInstruction`.

The constructor function for class `TAssemblyBuffer` opens the assembly object file. Member function `Advance` moves the text pointer `pText` to point to the end of the current buffer contents, and it updates `textLength`.

The rest of the file implements class `TCodeGenerator`'s assembly code emitting member functions, which are used with the `Emitx` macros. Member function `Reg` uses string array `registers` to emit a register name such as `ax`. Member function `Operator` uses string array `instructions` to emit an instruction opcode mnemonic such as `add`.

Member function `Label` uses a prefix and an index to emit a generic label such as `$L_007` that is part of an instruction operand that references memory data. Member function `WordLabel` is similar to `Label`, except that it adds the prefix `WORD PTR` before the label, such as `WORD PTR $F_007`. Function `HighDWordLabel` emits a label that refers to the high-order (second) half of a doubleword value, such as `WORD PTR $F_007+2`.

Whenever we emit references to memory data corresponding to variables in the Pascal source program, we'll use labels derived from the variable names to make it easier for us to read the assembly code. Because assembly programs do not have Pascal's scope rules, we must tag each label in the generated code with a unique integer. For example, a Pascal program may have a local variable `count` in a procedure and a global variable `count`. In the generated assembly program, we distinguish the two names with labels like `count_007` and `count_014`. This is the purpose of the global variable `asmLabelIndex` and class `TSymtabNode`'s data member `labelIndex`, which we first saw in Chapter 7.

Member function `Byte` is passed a pointer to a variable's symbol table node, and it emits a byte label constructed from the variable name and its label index, such as `BYTE PTR ch_007`. Member function `Word` is similar, emitting operands like `WORD PTR sum_007`, and member function `HighDWord` emits references to the high word of a doubleword variable, such as `WORD PTR sum_007+2`.

Member functions `ByteIndirect`, `WordIndirect`, and `HighDWordIndirect` emit indirect references via a register, such as `BYTE PTR [bx]`, `WORD PTR [bx]`, and `WORD PTR [bx+2]`, respectively.

Member function `TaggedName` simply emits a variable name tagged with its label index, such as `x_007`. Member function `NameLiteral` emits the literal name that is passed to it, such as `FloatConvert`. Member function `IntegerLiteral` emits an integer value as string, such as `453`. Member function `CharLiteral` emits a character surrounded by single quotes, such as `'x'`.

Because each of the above member functions emits a part of an assembly statement, we need multiple calls, each appending to the results of the previous call, to build an entire statement. The `Emitx` macros that we saw in `codegen.h` help us make these calls. Some examples are:

- `Emit0(cld)` emits

    cld

- `Emit1(call, NameLit(WRITE_CHAR))` emits

    call _WriteChar

- `Emit2(mov, Reg(ax), Word(pId))` emits

    mov ax,WORD PTR gamma_003

(In the last example, we assume that `pId->String()` is gamma and `pId->labelIndex` is 3.)

Figure 12.9 Implementation file **emitsrc.cpp**.

```
//    **************************************************************
//    *                                                          *
//    *    E M I T   S O U R C E   L I N E S                      *
//    *                                                          *
//    *    Emit source lines as comments in the assembly listing. *
//    *                                                          *
//    *    CLASSES: TCodeGenerator                                *
//    *                                                          *
//    *    FILE:    prog13-1/emitsrc.cpp                          *
//    *                                                          *
//    *    MODULE:  Code generator                                *
//    *                                                          *
//    *    Copyright (c) 1996 by Ronald Mak                       *
//    *    For instructional purposes only.  No warranties.       *
```

```
//    *                                                   *
//    ************************************************************

#include <stdio.h>
#include "common.h"
#include "buffer.h"
#include "symtab.h"
#include "codegen.h"

//---------------------------------------------------------------
//  StartComment     Start a new comment with a line number.
//
//      pString : ptr to the string to append
//---------------------------------------------------------------

void TCodeGenerator::StartComment(int n)
{
    Reset();
    sprintf(AsmText(), "; {%d} ", n);
    Advance();
}


//---------------------------------------------------------------
//  PutComment        Append a string to the assembly comment if
//                    it fits.  If not, emit the current comment
//                    and append the string to the next comment.
//
//      pString : ptr to the string to append
//---------------------------------------------------------------

void TCodeGenerator::PutComment(const char *pString)
{
    int length = strlen(pString);

    //--Start a new comment if the current one is full.
    if (!pAsmBuffer->Fit(length)) {
        PutLine();
        StartComment();
    }

    strcpy(AsmText(), pString);
    Advance();
}

//                 ******************
//                 *                *
```

(continues)

■■■■■■■■■■ **Figure 12.9** Implementation file **emitsrc.cpp**. (*Continued*)

```
//                    *   Declarations   *
//                    *                  *
//                    *******************


//---------------------------------------------------------------
//  EmitProgramHeaderComment      Emit the program header as a
//                                comment.
//
//      pProgramId : ptr to the program id's symbol table node
//---------------------------------------------------------------

void TCodeGenerator::EmitProgramHeaderComment
                                    (const TSymtabNode *pProgramId)
{
    PutLine();
    StartComment("PROGRAM ");
    PutComment(pProgramId->String());   // program name

    //--Emit the program's parameter list.
    TSymtabNode *pParmId = pProgramId->defn.routine.locals.pParmIds;
    if (pParmId) {
        PutComment(" (");

        //--Loop to emit each parameter.
        do {
            PutComment(pParmId->String());
            pParmId = pParmId->next;
            if (pParmId) PutComment(", ");
        } while (pParmId);

        PutComment(")");
    }

    PutLine();
}


//---------------------------------------------------------------
//  EmitSubroutineHeaderComment     Emit a subroutine header as
//                                  a comment.
//
//      pRoutineId : ptr to the subroutine id's symtab node
//---------------------------------------------------------------

void TCodeGenerator::EmitSubroutineHeaderComment
                                    (const TSymtabNode *pRoutineId)
```

```
{
    PutLine();
    StartComment(pRoutineId->defn.how == dcProcedure ? "PROCEDURE "
                                                      : "FUNCTION " );
    //--Emit the procedure or function name
    //--followed by the formal parameter list.
    PutComment(pRoutineId->String());
    EmitSubroutineFormalsComment
                    (pRoutineId->defn.routine.locals.pParmIds);

    //--Emit a function's return type.
    if (pRoutineId->defn.how == dcFunction) {
        PutComment(" : ");
        PutComment(pRoutineId->pType->pTypeId->String());
    }

    PutLine();
}

//--------------------------------------------------------------
//  EmitSubroutineFormalsComment    Emit a formal parameter list
//                                  as a comment.
//
//      pParmId : ptr to the head of the formal parm id list
//--------------------------------------------------------------

void TCodeGenerator::EmitSubroutineFormalsComment
                                    (const TSymtabNode *pParmId)
{
    if (!pParmId) return;

    PutComment(" (");

    //--Loop to emit each sublist of parameters with
    //--common definition and type.
    do {
        TDefnCode  commonDefn  = pParmId->defn.how;  // common defn
        TType      *pCommonType = pParmId->pType;     // common type
        int        doneFlag;  // true if sublist done, false if not

        if (commonDefn == dcVarParm) PutComment("VAR ");

        //--Loop to emit the parms in the sublist.
        do {
            PutComment(pParmId->String());

            pParmId  = pParmId->next;
```

(continues)

```
                doneFlag = (!pParmId) || (commonDefn   != pParmId->defn.how)
                                      || (pCommonType != pParmId->pType);
            if (!doneFlag) PutComment(", ");
        } while (!doneFlag);

        //--Print the sublist's common type.
        PutComment(" : ");
        PutComment(pCommonType->pTypeId->String());

        if (pParmId) PutComment("; ");
    } while (pParmId);

    PutComment(")");
}

//-------------------------------------------------------------
//  EmitVarDeclComment       Emit variable declarations as
//                           comments.
//
//      pVarId : ptr to the head of the variable id list
//-------------------------------------------------------------

void TCodeGenerator::EmitVarDeclComment
                             (const TSymtabNode *pVarId)
{
    TType *pCommonType;   // ptr to common type

    if (!pVarId) return;
    pCommonType = pVarId->pType;

    PutLine();
    StartComment("VAR");
    PutLine();
    StartComment();

    //--Loop to print sublists of variables with a common type.
    do {
        PutComment(pVarId->String());
        pVarId = pVarId->next;

        if (pVarId && (pVarId->pType == pCommonType)) PutComment(", ");
        else {

            //--End of sublist:  Print the common type and begin
            //--                 a new sublist.
```

```
            PutComment(" : ");
            EmitTypeSpecComment(pCommonType);
            PutLine();

            if (pVarId) {
                pCommonType = pVarId->pType;
                StartComment();
            }
        }
    } while (pVarId);
}


//--------------------------------------------------------------
//  EmitTypeSpecComment      Emit a type specification as a
//                           comment.
//
//      pType : ptr to the type object
//--------------------------------------------------------------

void TCodeGenerator::EmitTypeSpecComment(const TType *pType)
{
    //--If named type, emit the name, else emit "..."
    PutComment(pType->pTypeId ? pType->pTypeId->String() : "...");
}


//            ***************
//            *             *
//            *  Statements *
//            *             *
//            ***************


//--------------------------------------------------------------
//  EmitStmtComment          Emit a statement as a comment.
//--------------------------------------------------------------

void TCodeGenerator::EmitStmtComment(void)
{
    SaveState();       // save icode state
    StartComment(currentLineNumber);

    switch (token) {
        case tcIdentifier:  EmitAsgnOrCallComment();  break;
        case tcREPEAT:      EmitREPEATComment();       break;
        case tcUNTIL:       EmitUNTILComment();        break;
        case tcWHILE:       EmitWHILEComment();        break;
        case tcIF:          EmitIFComment();           break;
```

(continues)

```
        case tcFOR:         EmitFORComment();          break;
        case tcCASE:        EmitCASEComment();         break;
    }

    RestoreState();  // restore icode state
}

//----------------------------------------------------------------
//  EmitAsgnOrCallComment    Emit an assignment statement or a
//                           procedure call as a comment.
//----------------------------------------------------------------

void TCodeGenerator::EmitAsgnOrCallComment(void)
{
    EmitIdComment();

    if (token == tcColonEqual) {
        PutComment(" := ");

        GetToken();
        EmitExprComment();
    }

    PutLine();
}

//----------------------------------------------------------------
//  EmitREPEATComment    Emit a REPEAT statement as a comment.
//  EmitUNTILComment
//----------------------------------------------------------------

void TCodeGenerator::EmitREPEATComment(void)
{
    PutComment("REPEAT");
    PutLine();
}

void TCodeGenerator::EmitUNTILComment(void)
{
    PutComment("UNTIL ");

    GetToken();
    EmitExprComment();

    PutLine();
```

```
}

//---------------------------------------------------------------
//  EmitWHILEComment     Emit a WHILE statement as a comment.
//---------------------------------------------------------------

void TCodeGenerator::EmitWHILEComment(void)
{
    PutComment("WHILE ");

    GetToken();
    GetLocationMarker();

    GetToken();
    EmitExprComment();

    PutComment(" DO");
    PutLine();
}

//---------------------------------------------------------------
//  EmitIFComment        Emit an IF statement as a comment.
//---------------------------------------------------------------

void TCodeGenerator::EmitIFComment(void)
{
    PutComment("IF ");

    GetToken();
    GetLocationMarker();

    GetToken();
    EmitExprComment();

    PutLine();
}

//---------------------------------------------------------------
//  EmitFORComment       Emit a FOR statement as a comment.
//---------------------------------------------------------------

void TCodeGenerator::EmitFORComment(void)
{
    PutComment("FOR ");

    GetToken();
```

(continues)

```
    GetLocationMarker();

    GetToken();
    EmitIdComment();
    PutComment(" := ");

    GetToken();
    EmitExprComment();
    PutComment(token == tcTO ? " TO " : " DOWNTO ");

    GetToken();
    EmitExprComment();

    PutComment(" DO");
    PutLine();
}

//----------------------------------------------------------------
//  EmitCASEComment      Emit a CASE statement as a comment.
//----------------------------------------------------------------

void TCodeGenerator::EmitCASEComment(void)
{
    PutComment("CASE ");

    GetToken();
    GetLocationMarker();
    GetToken();
    GetLocationMarker();

    GetToken();
    EmitExprComment();

    PutComment(" OF ");
    PutLine();
}


//              ******************
//              *                *
//              *  Expresssions  *
//              *                *
//              ******************


//----------------------------------------------------------------
//  EmitExprComment         Emit an expression as a comment.
//----------------------------------------------------------------
```

```
void TCodeGenerator::EmitExprComment(void)
{
    int doneFlag = false;  // true if done with expression, false if not

    //--Loop over the entire expression.
    do {
        switch (token) {
            case tcIdentifier:  EmitIdComment();  break;

            case tcNumber:  PutComment(pToken->String());  GetToken();
                            break;

            case tcString:  PutComment(pToken->String());  GetToken();
                            break;

            case tcPlus:    PutComment(" + ");    GetToken();  break;
            case tcMinus:   PutComment(" - ");    GetToken();  break;
            case tcStar:    PutComment("*");      GetToken();  break;
            case tcSlash:   PutComment("/");      GetToken();  break;
            case tcDIV:     PutComment(" DIV ");  GetToken();  break;
            case tcMOD:     PutComment(" MOD ");  GetToken();  break;
            case tcAND:     PutComment(" AND ");  GetToken();  break;
            case tcOR:      PutComment(" OR ");   GetToken();  break;
            case tcEqual:   PutComment(" = ");    GetToken();  break;
            case tcNe:      PutComment(" <> ");   GetToken();  break;
            case tcLt:      PutComment(" < ");    GetToken();  break;
            case tcLe:      PutComment(" <= ");   GetToken();  break;
            case tcGt:      PutComment(" > ");    GetToken();  break;
            case tcGe:      PutComment(" >= ");   GetToken();  break;
            case tcNOT:     PutComment("NOT ");   GetToken();  break;

            case tcLParen:
                PutComment("(");
                GetToken();
                EmitExprComment();
                PutComment(")");
                GetToken();
                break;

            default:
                doneFlag = true;
                break;
        }
    } while (!doneFlag);
}
```

(continues)

■■■■■■■■ **Figure 12.9** Implementation file **emitsrc.cpp**. (*Continued*)

```
//-------------------------------------------------------------
//  EmitIdComment              Emit an identifier and its
//                             modifiers as a comment.
//-------------------------------------------------------------

//--Tokens that can start an identifier modifier.
TTokenCode tlIdModStart[] = {tcLBracket, tcLParen, tcPeriod, tcDummy};

//--Tokens that can end an identifier modifier.
TTokenCode tlIdModEnd[]   = {tcRBracket, tcRParen, tcDummy};

void TCodeGenerator::EmitIdComment(void)
{
    PutComment(pToken->String());
    GetToken();

    //--Loop to print any modifiers (subscripts, record fields,
    //--or actual parameter lists).
    while (TokenIn(token, tlIdModStart)) {

        //--Record field.
        if (token == tcPeriod) {
            PutComment(".");
            GetToken();
            EmitIdComment();
        }

        //--Subscripts or actual parameters.
        else {

            //--( or [
            PutComment(token == tcLParen ? "(" : "[");
            GetToken();

            while (!TokenIn(token, tlIdModEnd)) {
                EmitExprComment();

                //--Write and writeln field width and precision.
                while (token == tcColon) {
                    PutComment(":");
                    GetToken();
                    EmitExprComment();
                }
```

```
        if (token == tcComma) {
            PutComment(", ");
            GetToken();
        }
    }

    //--) or ]
    PutComment(token == tcRParen ? ")" : "]");
    GetToken();
        }
    }
}
```

Emitting Pascal Statements as Assembly Comments

Figure 12.9 shows file `emitsrc.cpp`, which implements the member functions of class `TCodeGenerator` that emit Pascal source statements as comments in the assembly object file. Borrowing from the pretty-printer utility in Chapter 8, the statements are recreated from the intermediate code. Each comment will appear just before the statement's assembly code. We won't attempt anything fancy like pretty-printing, or even reproducing the statements in their entirety. Instead, we'll just output enough to help make the assembly code more readable. We'll see several examples of assembly output in the next two chapters.

Stack Frame Offsets for Parameters and Local Variables

Since the stack frames as shown in Figure 12.4 have a different layout from the interpreter, we must change the way offsets are assigned to variables and parameters.

▬▬▬▬▬ **Figure 12.10** A new version of member function **TParser::ParseVariableDeclarations** in file **parsdecl.cpp**.

```
void TParser::ParseVariableDeclarations(TSymtabNode *pRoutineId)
{
    if (execFlag) {
        ParseVarOrFieldDecls(pRoutineId, NULL,
            pRoutineId->defn.routine.parmCount);
```

(continues)

■■■■■■■ **Figure 12.10** A new version of member function
TParser::ParseVariableDeclarations in file **parsdecl.cpp**. (*Continued*)

```
    }
    else {
        ParseVarOrFieldDecls(pRoutineId, NULL,
            pRoutineId->defn.how == dcProcedure
                ? procLocalsStackFrameOffset
                : funcLocalsStackFrameOffset);
    }
}
```

In Chapter 7, we introduced the flag execFlag, which was always true for the
interpreter. Of course, for the compiler, the flag will be false. Figure 12.10 shows a
new version of member function TParser::ParseVariableDeclarations in
file parsdecl.cpp. For the compiler, the function now properly initializes the
stack frame offset for the first local variable, depending on whether the subroutine is
a procedure or a function.

■■■■■■■ **Figure 12.11** New version of member function
TParser::ParseVarOrFieldDecls in file **parsdecl.cpp**.

```
void TParser::ParseVarOrFieldDecls(TSymtabNode *pRoutineId,
                                   TType       *pRecordType,
                                   int offset)
{
    TSymtabNode *pId, *pFirstId, *pLastId;   // ptrs to symtab nodes
    TSymtabNode *pPrevSublistLastId = NULL;  // ptr to last node of
                                             //    previous sublist
    int         totalSize = 0;               // total byte size of
                                             //    local variables

    //--Loop to parse a list of variable or field declarations
    //--separated by semicolons.
    while (token == tcIdentifier) {

        //--<id-sublist>
        pFirstId = ParseIdSublist(pRoutineId, pRecordType, pLastId);

        //-- :
        Resync(tlSublistFollow, tlDeclarationFollow);
        CondGetToken(tcColon, errMissingColon);

        //--<type>
        TType *pType = ParseTypeSpec();
```

```
//--Now loop to assign the type and offset to each
//--identifier in the sublist.
for (pId = pFirstId; pId; pId = pId->next) {
    SetType(pId->pType, pType);

    if (pRoutineId) {

        //--Variables
        if (execFlag) {
            pId->defn.data.offset = offset++;
        }
        else {
            offset -= pType->size;
            pId->defn.data.offset = offset;
        }
        totalSize += pType->size;
    }
    else {

        //--Record fields
        pId->defn.data.offset = offset;
        offset += pType->size;
    }
}

if (pFirstId) {

    //--Set the first sublist into the routine id's symtab node.
    if (pRoutineId &&
        (!pRoutineId->defn.routine.locals.pVariableIds)) {
        pRoutineId->defn.routine.locals.pVariableIds = pFirstId;
    }

    //--Link this list to the previous sublist.
    if (pPrevSublistLastId) pPrevSublistLastId->next = pFirstId;
    pPrevSublistLastId = pLastId;
}

//-- ;   for variable and record field declaration, or
//-- END for record field declaration
if (pRoutineId) {
    Resync(tlDeclarationFollow, tlStatementStart);
    CondGetToken(tcSemicolon, errMissingSemicolon);

    //--Skip extra semicolons.
    while (token == tcSemicolon) GetToken();
```

(continues)

■■■■■ **Figure 12.11** New version of member function
TParser::ParseVarOrFieldDecls in file **parsdecl.cpp**. (*Continued*)

```
            Resync(tlDeclarationFollow, tlDeclarationStart,
                tlStatementStart);
        }
        else {
            Resync(tlFieldDeclFollow);
            if (token != tcEND) {
                CondGetToken(tcSemicolon, errMissingSemicolon);

                //--Skip extra semicolons.
                while (token == tcSemicolon) GetToken();
                Resync(tlFieldDeclFollow, tlDeclarationStart,
                    tlStatementStart);
            }
        }
    }

    //--Set the routine identifier node or the record type object.
    if (pRoutineId) {
        pRoutineId->defn.routine.totalLocalSize = totalSize;
    }
    else {
        pRecordType->size = offset;
    }
}
```

Figure 12.11 shows a new version of member function `TParser::ParseVarOr-`
`FieldDecls`, also in file `parsdecl.cpp`. Inside the `for` loop, the local variable
stack frame offsets are properly assigned for the compiler.

■■■■■ **Figure 12.12** New version of member function
TParser::ParseFormalParmList in file **parsrtn2.cpp**.

```
TSymtabNode *TParser::ParseFormalParmList(int &count, int &totalSize)
{
    extern int execFlag;

    TSymtabNode *pParmId;                 // ptrs to parm symtab nodes
    TSymtabNode *pFirstId, *pLastId;
    TSymtabNode *pPrevSublistLastId = NULL;
    TSymtabNode *pParmList  = NULL;   // ptr to list of parm nodes
    TDefnCode    parmDefn;                 // how a parm is defined
    int          offset = parametersStackFrameOffset;
```

```
count = totalSize = 0;
GetToken();

//--Loop to parse a parameter declarations separated by semicolons.
while ((token == tcIdentifier) || (token == tcVAR)) {
    TType *pParmType;  // ptr to parm's type object

    pFirstId = NULL;

    //--VAR or value parameter?
    if (token == tcVAR) {
        parmDefn = dcVarParm;
        GetToken();
    }
    else parmDefn = dcValueParm;

    //--Loop to parse the comma-separated sublist of parameter ids.
    while (token == tcIdentifier) {
        pParmId = EnterNewLocal(pToken->String(), parmDefn);
        ++count;
        if (!pParmList) pParmList = pParmId;

        //--Link the parm id nodes together.
        if (!pFirstId) pFirstId = pLastId = pParmId;
        else {
            pLastId->next = pParmId;
            pLastId       = pParmId;
        }

        //-- ,
        GetToken();
        Resync(tlIdentifierFollow);
        if (token == tcComma) {

            //--Saw comma.
            //--Skip extra commas and look for an identifier.
            do {
                GetToken();
                Resync(tlIdentifierStart, tlIdentifierFollow);
                if (token == tcComma) {
                    Error(errMissingIdentifier);
                }
            } while (token == tcComma);
            if (token != tcIdentifier) {
                Error(errMissingIdentifier);
            }
```

(continues)

■■■■■ **Figure 12.12** New version of member function
TParser::ParseFormalParmList in file **parsrtn2.cpp**. (*Continued*)

```cpp
        }
        else if (token == tcIdentifier) Error(errMissingComma);
    }

    //-- :
    Resync(tlSublistFollow, tlDeclarationFollow);
    CondGetToken(tcColon, errMissingColon);

    //--<type-id>
    if (token == tcIdentifier) {
        TSymtabNode *pTypeId = Find(pToken->String());
        if (pTypeId->defn.how != dcType) Error(errInvalidType);
        pParmType = pTypeId->pType;
        GetToken();
    }
    else {
        Error(errMissingIdentifier);
        pParmType = pDummyType;
    }

    if (execFlag) {
        //--Loop to assign the offset and type to each
        //--parm id in the sublist.
        for (pParmId = pFirstId; pParmId; pParmId = pParmId->next) {
            pParmId->defn.data.offset = totalSize++;
            SetType(pParmId->pType, pParmType);
        }
    }
    else {
        //--Loop to assign the type to each parm id in the sublist.
        for (pParmId = pFirstId; pParmId; pParmId = pParmId->next) {
            SetType(pParmId->pType, pParmType);
        }
    }

    //--Link this sublist to the previous sublist.
    if (pPrevSublistLastId) pPrevSublistLastId->next = pFirstId;
    pPrevSublistLastId = pLastId;

    //-- ; or )
    Resync(tlFormalParmsFollow, tlDeclarationFollow);
    if ((token == tcIdentifier) || (token == tcVAR)) {
        Error(errMissingSemicolon);
```

```
        }
        else while (token == tcSemicolon) GetToken();
    }

    if (!execFlag) {

        //--Assign the offset to each parm id in the entire
        //--formal parameter list in reverse order.
        ReverseNodeList(pParmList);
        for (pParmId = pParmList;
             pParmId; pParmId = pParmId->next) {
            pParmId->defn.data.offset = offset;
            offset += pParmId->defn.how == dcValueParm
                          ? pParmId->pType->size     // data value
                          : sizeof(void *);          // VAR pointer
            if (offset & 1) ++offset;   // round up to even
        }
        ReverseNodeList(pParmList);

        totalSize = offset - parametersStackFrameOffset;
    }

    //-- )
    CondGetToken(tcRParen, errMissingRightParen);

    return pParmList;
}
```

Figure 12.12 shows a new version of member function `TParser::ParseFormal-`
`ParmList` in file `parsrtn2.cpp`. This version assigns formal parameter stack
frame offsets properly for the compiler. Because a subroutine's parameters are allocated on the runtime stack below where register BP points (see Figure 12.4), one
way to assign the offsets to the parameters is to do it in the reverse order that they
appear in the source program. Therefore, `ParseFormalParmList` calls a new
member function `ReverseNodeList` to reverse the parameter list before it assigns
the offsets. Afterwards, it must call `ReverseNodeList` again to put the list back
into its original order.

▰▰▰▰▰▰▰ **Figure 12.13** New member function **TParser::ReverseNodeList** in file
parser.h.

```
//-------------------------------------------------------------
//  ReverseNodeList      Reverse a list of symbol table nodes.
```

(*continues*)

■■■■■■■■ **Figure 12.13** New member function **TParser::ReverseNodeList** in file **parser.h**. (*Continued*)

```
//
//      head : ref to the ptr to the current head of the list
//-----------------------------------------------------------

void TParser::ReverseNodeList(TSymtabNode *&head)
{
        TSymtabNode *prev = NULL;
        TSymtabNode *curr = head;
        TSymtabNode *next;

        //--Reverse the list in place.
        while (curr) {
            next = curr->next;
            curr->next = prev;
            prev = curr;
            curr = next;
        }

        //--Now point to the new head of the list,
        //--which was formerly its tail.
        head = prev;
}
```

Figure 12.13 shows the new member function `TParser::ReverseNodeList` in file `parsrtn2.cpp`, which reverses a list of symbol table nodes in place. Of course, then in file `parser.h`, we need to add the following private member function declaration to class `TParser`:

```
  void ReverseNodeList(TSymtabNode *&head);
```

With the foundation this chapter has laid for emitting assembly code, we're ready to write the code generator routines to emit code sequences based on a Pascal source program. We'll start in the next chapter.

13

COMPILING PROCEDURES, FUNCTIONS, AND ASSIGNMENT STATEMENTS

In this chapter and the next one, we will complete the code generator in the back end. Like the interpreter's executor, the code generator uses the symbol table and intermediate code that was created by the front end. Thus, both the interpreter and the compiler share the front end and the interface between the front and back ends. We'll have a bit more to say about this latter point in Chapter 15.

As we did with the interpreter, we rely on the front end to have done all the work of scanning, parsing, and checking for syntax and type compatibility errors. The code generator can concentrate solely on emitting correct assembly code. It must contend with the idiosyncrasies of the machine architecture, which, in our case, is that of the 8086 processor.

This chapter covers code generation for:

- The prologue and epilogue of the source program itself, the main routine, and of each subroutine.
- Calls to and returns from Pascal procedures and functions.

- Assignment statements and expressions.
- Calls to the standard procedures `write` and `writeln`.

We'll leave code generation for Pascal control statements for the next chapter. Even so, this chapter covers much ground in great detail. However, all is not as complex as it may appear, especially if you note the parallels between the `TCodeGenerator::Emitxxx` routines and the corresponding `TExecutor::Executexxx` routines of the interpreter.

Organization of the Code Generator

Figure 13.1 shows an object diagram of the code generator back end. (Also review the class diagram in Figure 12.6.)

The code generator object sends `GetToken` messages to the intermediate code object to obtain token and symbol table node objects. Based on what it gets back from the icode object, the code generator object emits assembly code to the object file by sending `Put`, `PutLine`, and other related messages to the assembly buffer object. This process continues until all of the intermediate code has been read.

Assembly Code Sequences

Figure 13.2 shows file `emitcode.cpp`, which implements some of the member functions of class `TCodeGenerator`. (Also see the listing of header file `codegen.h` in Figure 12.7.) These member functions emit declarations of subroutine parameters and local variables, along with code sequences to load values into registers or to push values and addresses onto the runtime stack.

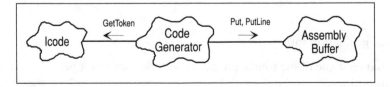

■■■■ **Figure 13.1** Object diagram of the compiler's code generator back end.

■■■■■■■■ **Figure 13.2** Implementation file **emitcode.cpp**.

```
//    *************************************************************
//    *                                                          *
//    *    E M I T    C O D E    S E Q U E N C E S               *
//    *                                                          *
//    *    Routines for generating and emitting various assembly *
//    *    language code sequences.                              *
//    *                                                          *
//    *    CLASSES: TCodeGenerator                               *
//    *                                                          *
//    *    FILE:    prog13-1/emitcode.c                          *
//    *                                                          *
//    *    MODULE:  Code generator                               *
//    *                                                          *
//    *    Copyright (c) 1996 by Ronald Mak                      *
//    *    For instructional purposes only.  No warranties.      *
//    *                                                          *
//    *************************************************************

#include <stdio.h>
#include "types.h"
#include "buffer.h"
#include "symtab.h"
#include "codegen.h"


//--------------------------------------------------------------
//  Go                          Start the compilation.
//--------------------------------------------------------------

void TCodeGenerator::Go(const TSymtabNode *pProgramId)
{
    EmitProgramPrologue();

    //--Emit code for the program.
    currentNestingLevel = 1;
    EmitMain(pProgramId);

    EmitProgramEpilogue(pProgramId);
}


//--------------------------------------------------------------
//  EmitStatementLabel          Emit a statement label constructed
//                              from the label index.
//
//                              Example:  $L_007:
```

(continues)

■■■■■■■■■ **Figure 13.2** Implementation file **emitcode.cpp**. (*Continued*)

```
//
//      index : index value
//-------------------------------------------------------------

void TCodeGenerator::EmitStatementLabel(int index)
{
    sprintf(AsmText(), "%s_%03d:", STMT_LABEL_PREFIX, index);
    PutLine();
}


//              ******************
//              *                *
//              *  Declarations  *
//              *                *
//              ******************


//-------------------------------------------------------------
// EmitDeclarations     Emit code for the parameter and local
//                      variable declarations of a routine.
//
//      pRoutineId : ptr to the routine's symbol table node
//-------------------------------------------------------------

void TCodeGenerator::EmitDeclarations(const TSymtabNode *pRoutineId)
{
    TSymtabNode *pParmId = pRoutineId->defn.routine.locals.pParmIds;
    TSymtabNode *pVarId  = pRoutineId->defn.routine.locals.pVariableIds;

    EmitVarDeclComment(pRoutineId->defn.routine.locals.pVariableIds);
    PutLine();

    //--Subroutine parameters
    while (pParmId) {
        EmitStackOffsetEquate(pParmId);
        pParmId = pParmId->next;
    }

    //--Variables
    while (pVarId) {
        EmitStackOffsetEquate(pVarId);
        pVarId = pVarId->next;
    }
}
```

```
//-------------------------------------------------------------
// EmitStackOffsetEquate        Emit a stack frame offset equate
//                              for a parameter id or a local
//                              variable id.
//
//                              Examples: parm_007 EQU <pb+6>
//                                        var_008  EQU <bp-10>
//
//      pId : ptr to symbol table node
//-------------------------------------------------------------

void TCodeGenerator::EmitStackOffsetEquate(const TSymtabNode *pId)
{
    char   *pName      = pId->String();
    int     labelIndex = pId->labelIndex;
    int     offset     = pId->defn.data.offset;
    TType *pType       = pId->pType;

    if (pType == pCharType) {
        sprintf(AsmText(), "%s_%03d\tEQU\t<BYTE PTR [bp%+d]>",
                           pName, labelIndex, offset);
    }
    else {
        sprintf(AsmText(), "%s_%03d\tEQU\t<WORD PTR [bp%+d]>",
                           pName, labelIndex, offset);
    }

    PutLine();
}


//             **********************
//             *                    *
//             *  Loads and Pushes  *
//             *                    *
//             **********************


//-------------------------------------------------------------
// EmitAdjustBP        Emit code to adjust register bp if
//                     necessary to point to the stack frame
//                     of an enclosing subroutine.
//
//      level : nesting level of enclosing subroutine's data
//-------------------------------------------------------------

void TCodeGenerator::EmitAdjustBP(int level)
```

(continues)

```
{
    //--Don't do anything if local or global.
    if ((level == currentNestingLevel) || (level == 1)) return;

    //--Emit code to chase static links.
    Emit2(mov, Reg(cx), Reg(bp));  // save bp in cx
    do {
        Emit2(mov, Reg(bp), NameLit(STATIC_LINK));  // chase
    } while (++level < currentNestingLevel);
}


//----------------------------------------------------------------
// EmitRestoreBP      Emit code to restore register bp if
//                    necessary to point to the current
//                    stack frame.
//
//     level : nesting level of enclosing subroutine's data
//----------------------------------------------------------------

void TCodeGenerator::EmitRestoreBP(int level)
{
    //--Don't do anything if local or global.
    if ((level == currentNestingLevel) || (level == 1)) return;

    //--Emit code to restore bp.
    Emit2(mov, Reg(bp), Reg(cx));
}


//----------------------------------------------------------------
// EmitLoadValue      Emit code to load a scalar value
//                    into ax or dx:ax.
//
//     pId : ptr to symbol table node of parm or variable
//----------------------------------------------------------------

void TCodeGenerator::EmitLoadValue(const TSymtabNode *pId)
{
    TType *pType = pId->pType;

    EmitAdjustBP(pId->level);

    if (pId->defn.how == dcVarParm) {
        //--VAR formal parameter.
        //--ax or dx:ax = value the address points to
```

```
            Emit2(mov, Reg(bx), Word(pId));
            if (pType == pCharType) {

                //--Character:  al = value
                Emit2(sub, Reg(ax), Reg(ax));
                Emit2(mov, Reg(al), ByteIndirect(bx));
            }
            else if (pType == pRealType) {

                //--Real: dx:ax = value
                Emit2(mov, Reg(ax), WordIndirect(bx));
                Emit2(mov, Reg(ax), HighDWordIndirect(bx));
            }
            else {

                //--Integer or enumeration: ax = value
                Emit2(mov, Reg(ax), WordIndirect(bx));
            }
        }
        else {

            //--Load the value into ax or dx:ax.
            if (pType == pCharType) {

                //--Character:  al = value
                Emit2(sub, Reg(ax), Reg(ax));
                Emit2(mov, Reg(al), Byte(pId));
            }
            else if (pType == pRealType) {

                //--Real: dx:ax = value
                Emit2(mov, Reg(ax), Word(pId));
                Emit2(mov, Reg(dx), HighDWord(pId));
            }
            else {

                //--Integer or enumeration: ax = value
                Emit2(mov, Reg(ax), Word(pId));
            }
        }

    EmitRestoreBP(pId->level);
}


//-------------------------------------------------------------
//  EmitLoadFloatLit    Emit code to load a float literal into
```

(continues)

```
//                         dx:ax. Append the literal to the float
//                         literal list.
//
//       pNode : ptr to symbol table node of literal
//----------------------------------------------------------------

void TCodeGenerator::EmitLoadFloatLit(TSymtabNode *pNode)
{
    TSymtabNode *pf;

    //--dx:ax = value
    Emit2(mov, Reg(ax),
                WordLabel(FLOAT_LABEL_PREFIX, pNode->labelIndex));
    Emit2(mov, Reg(dx),
                HighDWordLabel(FLOAT_LABEL_PREFIX, pNode->labelIndex));

    //--Check if the float is already in the float literal list.
    for (pf = pFloatLitList; pf; pf = pf->next) {
        if (pf == pNode) return;
    }

    //--Append it to the list if it isn't already there.
    pNode->next   = pFloatLitList;
    pFloatLitList = pNode;
}

//----------------------------------------------------------------
//   EmitPushStringLit    Emit code to push the address of a
//                        string literal onto the runtime stack.
//                        Append the literal to the string literal
//                        list.
//
//       pNode : ptr to symbol table node of literal
//----------------------------------------------------------------

void TCodeGenerator::EmitPushStringLit(TSymtabNode *pNode)
{
    TSymtabNode *ps;

    //--ax = addresss of string
    Emit2(lea,  Reg(ax),
                WordLabel(STRING_LABEL_PREFIX, pNode->labelIndex));
    Emit1(push, Reg(ax));
```

```
    //--Check if the string is already in the string literal list.
    for (ps = pStringLitList; ps; ps = ps->next) {
        if (ps == pNode) return;
    }

    //--Append it to the list if it isn't already there.
    pNode->next    = pStringLitList;
    pStringLitList = pNode;
}


//--------------------------------------------------------------
//  EmitPushOperand            Emit code to push a scalar
//                             operand value onto the stack.
//
//      pType : ptr to type of value
//--------------------------------------------------------------

void TCodeGenerator::EmitPushOperand(const TType *pType)
{
    if (! pType->IsScalar()) return;

    if (pType == pRealType) Emit1(push, Reg(dx));
    Emit1(push, Reg(ax));
}


//--------------------------------------------------------------
//  EmitPushAddress            Emit code to push an address
//                             onto the stack.
//
//      pId : ptr to symbol table node of parm or variable
//--------------------------------------------------------------

void TCodeGenerator::EmitPushAddress(const TSymtabNode *pId)
{
    int varLevel  = pId->level;
    int isVarParm = pId->defn.how == dcVarParm;

    EmitAdjustBP(varLevel);

    Emit2(isVarParm ? mov : lea, Reg(ax), Word(pId))
    Emit1(push, Reg(ax));

    EmitRestoreBP(varLevel);
}
```

(continues)

■■■■■■ **Figure 13.2**   Implementation file **emitcode.cpp**. (*Continued*)

```
//--------------------------------------------------------------
//  EmitPushReturnValueAddress        Emit code to push the
//                                    address of the function
//                                    return value in the
//                                    stack frame.
//
//      pId : ptr to symbol table node of function
//--------------------------------------------------------------

void TCodeGenerator::EmitPushReturnValueAddress(const TSymtabNode *pId)
{
    EmitAdjustBP(pId->level + 1);

    Emit2(lea,  Reg(ax), NameLit(RETURN_VALUE));
    Emit1(push, Reg(ax));

    EmitRestoreBP(pId->level + 1);
}


//--------------------------------------------------------------
//  EmitPromoteToReal        Emit code to convert integer
//                           operands to real.
//
//      pType1 : ptr to type of first  operand
//      pType2 : ptr to type of second operand
//--------------------------------------------------------------

void TCodeGenerator::EmitPromoteToReal(const TType *pType1,
                                       const TType *pType2)
{
    if (pType2 == pIntegerType) {            // xxx_1 integer_2
        Emit1(call, NameLit(FLOAT_CONVERT));
        Emit2(add,  Reg(sp), IntegerLit(2));
        Emit1(push, Reg(dx));
        Emit1(push, Reg(ax));                // xxx_1 real_2
    }

    if (pType1 == pIntegerType) {            // integer_1 real_2
        Emit1(pop,  Reg(ax));
        Emit1(pop,  Reg(dx));
        Emit1(pop,  Reg(bx));
        Emit1(push, Reg(dx));
        Emit1(push, Reg(ax));
        Emit1(push, Reg(bx));                // real_2 integer_1

        Emit1(call, NameLit(FLOAT_CONVERT));
```

```
        Emit2(add,  Reg(sp),  IntegerLit(2));   // real_2 real_1

        Emit1(pop,  Reg(bx));
        Emit1(pop,  Reg(cx));
        Emit1(push, Reg(dx));
        Emit1(push, Reg(ax));
        Emit1(push, Reg(cx));
        Emit1(push, Reg(bx));                    // real_1 real_2
    }
}
```

The file begins with member function `TCodeGenerator::Go`, which is called to start up the code generator after the front end has done its job. This function calls other member functions to emit the program prologue code, code for the source program's main routine, and then the program epilogue code.

Member function `EmitStatementLabel` writes a single line to the assembly object file consisting of a statement label constructed from a label index. An example is:

```
$L_007:
```

Allocating Data on the Runtime Stack and in the Global Area

As we saw in the previous chapter, data that is allocated on the runtime stack is accessed via the BP register, which normally points to the current stack frame (see Figure 12.4). Our compiler will emit assembly code to allocate all procedure and function parameters and local variables on the stack. It will also emit code to allocate global variables, real constants, and string constants within the global data area of the data segment (see Figure 12.3).

The compiler will emit an equate for each parameter or local variable. For example, for a parameter p and a local variable v of a procedure, the compiler emits something similar to:

```
p_023  EQU <WORD PTR [bp+6]>
v_024  EQU <WORD PTR [bp-8]>
```

For a global integer variable n, the compiler emits:

```
n_014  DW  0
```

which allocates a word in the global area and initializes it to 0.

This technique allows the compiler to emit uniform code for data references, whether the data is on the stack or in the global area. For example, the following two assembly statements load the value of the parameter into register AX and the value of the global variable into register DX:

```
mov ax,WORD PTR p_023
mov dx,WORD PTR n_014
```

Register BP normally points to the stack frame of the current procedure or function. This is fine for accessing the values of that subroutine's local parameters and variables. However, if an expression in a nested subroutine uses a variable that is declared in some enclosing subroutine—the variable is neither global nor local—then BP must be temporarily adjusted to point to the enclosing subroutine's stack frame in order to access the variable's value. After accessing the value, BP must be restored to point to the current stack frame.

To adjust register BP to point to the stack frame of an enclosing subroutine, our compiler emits code to chase static links on the runtime stack. The number of links to chase is the difference between the current nesting level and the nesting level of the variable declared in the enclosing subroutine. For example, to load the value of a variable `rows` that is declared in the currently executing procedure's *grandparent* (a subroutine two nesting levels lower) the compiler emits:

```
mov cx,bp              ; save current BP in CX
mov bp,$STATIC_LINK    ; BP -> parent's stack frame
mov bp,$STATIC_LINK    ; BP -> grandparent's stack frame
mov ax,WORD PTR rows_026 ; AX = value
mov bp,cx              ; restore current BP
```

We'll see shortly that the compiler emits code to equate $STATIC_LINK to WORD PTR [bp+4].

Declarations of Parameters and Local Variables

Member function `EmitDeclarations` emits declarations for a subroutine's parameters and local variables. It calls member function `EmitStackOffsetE-quate` for each parameter and local variable. As we saw above, each parameter and variable name is tagged with its label index and is equated to its offset from the BP register.

Loads and Pushes

Member function `EmitLoadValue` emits code to load the value of a global or local variable, or of a subroutine parameter, into register AX or the register pair DX:AX. For example:

- For a local character value parameter named ch:

```
sub   ax,ax                      ; clear AX
mov   al,BYTE PTR ch_016         ; AL = value
```

- For a local integer variable named n:

```
mov   ax,WORD PTR n_021          ; AX = value
```

- For a global real variable named x:

```
mov   ax,WORD PTR x_025          
mov   dx,WORD PTR x_025+2        ; DX:AX = value
```

The function needs to obtain the value of a formal VAR parameter indirectly through the address. Examples of the code sequences that it emits are:

- For a character formal VAR parameter named ch:

```
mov   bx,WORD PTR ch_003         ; BX = address
sub   ax,ax                      ; clear AX
mov   al,BYTE PTR [bx]           ; AL = value
```

- For an integer formal VAR parameter named n:

```
mov   bx,WORD PTR n_051          ; BX = address
mov   ax,WORD PTR [bx]           ; AL = value
```

- For a real formal VAR parameter named x:

```
mov   bx,WORD PTR x_071          ; BX = address
mov   ax,WORD PTR [bx]           
mov   dx,WORD PTR [bx+2]         ; DX:AX = value
```

Note the call to member function `EmitAdjustBP` at the beginning and the call to member function `EmitRestoreBP` at the end of `EmitLoadValue`. `EmitRestoreBP` emits code to chase static links as often as necessary (including none for local references), as we saw above, and `EmitRestoreBP` restores BP to point to the current stack frame. These two functions use register CX to save and restore the value of register BX. Needless to say, the compiler cannot emit code that uses register CX between calls to `EmitAdjustBP` and to `EmitRestoreBP`.

Our compiler emits code to allocate in the global area all the real and string constants that appear in the Pascal source program. Member functions `EmitLoad-`

`FloatLit` and `EmitPushStringLit` emit code to load the value of a real constant into DX:AX and to push the address of a string constant onto the runtime stack. Each function also builds lists of the symbol table nodes of all of the Pascal source program's real and string constants. The heads of these lists are pointed to by data members `pFloatLitList` and `pStringLitList`.

For example, to load a real constant whose symbol table node's label index is 56, `EmitLoadFloatLit` emits:

```
mov  ax,$F_056
mov  dx,WORD PTR $F_056+2      ; DX:AX = real value
```

To push the address of a string constant with the label index 63, `EmitPush-StringLit` emits:

```
lea  ax,WORD PTR $S_063        ; AX = string address
push ax                        ; push address onto stack
```

Member function `EmitPushOperand` is called by member function `EmitExpression` while the latter is emitting code for an expression. It emits code to push a scalar operand value that is already in AX or DX:AX onto the runtime stack. For a word-sized value, it emits:

```
push ax
```

and for a doubleword-sized value, it emits:

```
push dx                        ; push high-order half
push ax                        ; push low-order half
```

Member function `EmitPushAddress` pushes the address of a variable or parameter onto the runtime stack. For example, if n is a variable or a formal value parameter, the function emits:

```
lea  ax,WORD PTR n_034         ; AX = address
push ax                        ; push address onto stack
```

If v is a formal `VAR` parameter, v already contains an address, and so the function emits:

```
mov  ax,WORD PTR v_050         ; AX = address
push ax                        ; push address onto stack
```

Just like member function `EmitLoadValue`, `EmitPushAddress` also calls `EmitAdjustBP` at the beginning and `EmitRestoreBP` at the end.

Member function `EmitPushReturnValueAddress` pushes the address of a function return value onto the stack:

```
lea  ax,$RETURN_VALUE          ; AX = address of return value
push ax                        ; push address
```

It also calls `EmitAdjustBP` and `EmitRestoreBP`.

Member function `EmitPromoteToReal` emits code as needed to convert from integer to real the two operand values that have already been pushed onto the runtime stack. Runtime library function `FloatConvert` in `paslib.c` (see Figure 12.5) does the conversion and leaves the real value in DX:AX. If the value of the second operand (the one on top) is integer, the function emits:

```
call _FloatConvert             ; DX:AX = real value of second operand
add  sp,2                      ; pop off the integer operand value
push dx
push ax                        ; and replace it with its real value
```

The code to convert the first operand's integer value to real is a bit more complicated, since it is under the second operand's real value:

```
pop  ax
pop  dx                        ; DX:AX = second operand's real value
pop  bx                        ; BX = first operand's integer value
push dx
push ax                        ; push second operand's value
push bx                        ; push first operand's value
call _FloatConvert             ; DX:AX = real value of first operand
add  sp,2                      ; pop off the integer operand value
pop  bx
pop  cx                        ; CX:BX = second operand's value
push dx
push ax                         ; push first operand's value
push cx
push bx                        ; push first operand's value
```

Prologue and Epilogue Code

The compiler emits a sequence of prologue code at the very beginning of the assembly object file, and a sequence of epilogue code at the very end. It also emits another prologue code sequence for the start of the main routine and epilogue code at the end of the main routine, and yet another sequence of prologue and epilogue code for procedures and functions.

Figure 13.3 shows file emitrtn.cpp, which implements the member functions of class TCodeGenerator that emit the prologue and epilogue code sequences.

■■■■■■■ **Figure 13.3** Implementation file **emitrtn.cpp**.

```
//  ****************************************************************
//  *                                                              *
//  *    C O D E   G E N E R A T O R    (Routines)                 *
//  *                                                              *
//  *    Generating and emit assembly code for declared            *
//  *    procedures and functions.                                 *
//  *                                                              *
//  *    CLASSES: TCodeGenerator                                   *
//  *                                                              *
//  *    FILE:    prog13-1/emitrtn.cpp                             *
//  *                                                              *
//  *    MODULE:  Code generator                                   *
//  *                                                              *
//  *    Copyright (c) 1996 by Ronald Mak                          *
//  *    For instructional purposes only.  No warranties.          *
//  *                                                              *
//  ****************************************************************

#include <stdio.h>
#include "types.h"
#include "buffer.h"
#include "symtab.h"
#include "codegen.h"


//--------------------------------------------------------------
//  EmitProgramPrologue          Emit the program prologue.
//--------------------------------------------------------------

void TCodeGenerator::EmitProgramPrologue(void)
{
    PutLine("\tDOSSEG");
    PutLine("\t.MODEL   small");
    PutLine("\t.STACK   1024");
    PutLine();
    PutLine("\t.CODE");
    PutLine();
    PutLine("\tPUBLIC\t_PascalMain");
    PutLine("\tINCLUDE\tpasextrn.inc");
```

```
        PutLine();

        //--Equates for stack frame components.
        sprintf(AsmText(), "%s\t\tEQU\t<WORD PTR [bp+4]>", STATIC_LINK);
        PutLine();
        sprintf(AsmText(), "%s\t\tEQU\t<WORD PTR [bp-4]>", RETURN_VALUE);
        PutLine();
        sprintf(AsmText(), "%s\tEQU\t<WORD PTR [bp-2]>", HIGH_RETURN_VALUE);
        PutLine();
    }


    //-------------------------------------------------------------
    //  EmitProgramEpilogue        Emit the program epilogue.
    //-------------------------------------------------------------

    void TCodeGenerator::EmitProgramEpilogue(const TSymtabNode *pProgramId)
    {
        TSymtabNode *pId;
        TType       *pType;

        PutLine();
        PutLine("\t.DATA");
        PutLine();

        //--Emit declarations for the program's global variables.
        for (pId = pProgramId->defn.routine.locals.pVariableIds;
             pId; pId = pId->next) {
            sprintf(AsmText(), "%s_%03d\t", pId->String(), pId->labelIndex);
            Advance();

            pType = pId->pType;
            if (pType == pCharType) {
                sprintf(AsmText(), "DB\t0");
            }
            else if (pType == pRealType) {
                sprintf(AsmText(), "DD\t0.0");
            }
            else if (! pType->IsScalar()) {
                sprintf(AsmText(), "DB\t%d DUP(0)", pType->size);
            }
            else {   // integer or enumeration
                sprintf(AsmText(), "DW\t0");
            }

            PutLine();
        }
```

(continues)

■■■■■ **Figure 13.3** Implementation file **emitrtn.cpp**. *(Continued)*

```cpp
    //--Emit declarations for the program's floating point literals.
    for (pId = pFloatLitList; pId; pId = pId->next) {
        sprintf(AsmText(), "%s_%03d\tDD\t%e", FLOAT_LABEL_PREFIX,
                pId->labelIndex, pId->defn.constant.value.real);
        PutLine();
    }

    //--Emit declarations for the program's string literals.
    for (pId = pStringLitList; pId; pId = pId->next) {
        int i;
        char *pString = pId->String();
        int length    = strlen(pString) - 2;  // don't count quotes

        sprintf(AsmText(), "%s_%03d\tDB\t\"", STRING_LABEL_PREFIX,
                                              pId->labelIndex);
        Advance();

        for (i = 1; i <= length; ++i) Put(pString[i]);
        Put('\"');
        PutLine();
    }

    PutLine();
    sprintf(AsmText(), "\tEND");
    PutLine();
}

//----------------------------------------------------------------
//  EmitMain              Emit code for the main routine.
//----------------------------------------------------------------

void TCodeGenerator::EmitMain(const TSymtabNode *pMainId)
{
    TSymtabNode *pRtnId;

    EmitProgramHeaderComment(pMainId);
    EmitVarDeclComment(pMainId->defn.routine.locals.pVariableIds);

    //--Emit code for nested subroutines.
    for (pRtnId = pMainId->defn.routine.locals.pRoutineIds;
         pRtnId; pRtnId = pRtnId->next) {
        EmitRoutine(pRtnId);
    }
```

```
    //--Switch to main's intermediate code and emit code
    //--for its compound statement.
    pIcode = pMainId->defn.routine.pIcode;
    currentNestingLevel = 1;
    EmitMainPrologue();
    EmitCompound();
    EmitMainEpilogue();
}


//----------------------------------------------------------------
//  EmitMainPrologue     Emit the prologue for the main routine.
//----------------------------------------------------------------

void TCodeGenerator::EmitMainPrologue(void)
{
    PutLine();
    PutLine("_PascalMain\tPROC");
    PutLine();

    Emit1(push, Reg(bp));             // dynamic link
    Emit2(mov,  Reg(bp), Reg(sp));    // new stack frame base
}


//----------------------------------------------------------------
//  EmitMainEpilogue     Emit the epilogue for the main routine.
//----------------------------------------------------------------

void TCodeGenerator::EmitMainEpilogue(void)
{
    PutLine();

    Emit1(pop, Reg(bp));        // restore caller's stack frame
    Emit0(ret);                 // return

    PutLine();
    PutLine("_PascalMain\tENDP");
}


//----------------------------------------------------------------
//  EmitRoutine          Emit code for a procedure or function.
//----------------------------------------------------------------

void TCodeGenerator::EmitRoutine(const TSymtabNode *pRoutineId)
{
    TSymtabNode *pRtnId;
```

(continues)

```
    EmitSubroutineHeaderComment(pRoutineId);

    //--Emit code for the parameters and local variables.
    EmitDeclarations(pRoutineId);

    //--Emit code for nested subroutines.
    for (pRtnId = pRoutineId->defn.routine.locals.pRoutineIds;
         pRtnId; pRtnId = pRtnId->next) {
        EmitRoutine(pRtnId);
    }

    //--Switch to the routine's intermediate code and emit code
    //--for its compound statement.
    pIcode = pRoutineId->defn.routine.pIcode;
    currentNestingLevel = pRoutineId->level + 1;  // level of locals
    EmitRoutinePrologue(pRoutineId);
    EmitCompound();
    EmitRoutineEpilogue(pRoutineId);
}

//-------------------------------------------------------------
//  EmitRoutinePrologue        Emit the prologue for a
//                             procedure or function.
//-------------------------------------------------------------

void TCodeGenerator::EmitRoutinePrologue(const TSymtabNode *pRoutineId)
{
    PutLine();
    sprintf(AsmText(), "%s_%03d\tPROC",
            pRoutineId->String(), pRoutineId->labelIndex);
    PutLine();
    PutLine();

    Emit1(push, Reg(bp));               // dynamic link
    Emit2(mov,  Reg(bp), Reg(sp));      // new stack frame base

    //--Allocate stack space for a function's return value.
    if (pRoutineId->defn.how == dcFunction) {
        Emit2(sub, Reg(sp), IntegerLit(4));
    }

    //--Allocate stack space for the local variables.
    if (pRoutineId->defn.routine.totalLocalSize > 0) {
        Emit2(sub, Reg(sp),
```

```
                                    IntegerLit(pRoutineId->defn.routine.totalLocalSize));
        }
}

//----------------------------------------------------------------
//  EmitRoutineEpilogue            Emit the epilogue for a
//                                 procedure or function.
//----------------------------------------------------------------

void TCodeGenerator::EmitRoutineEpilogue(const TSymtabNode *pRoutineId)
{
    PutLine();

    //--Load a function's return value into the ax or dx:ax registers.
    if (pRoutineId->defn.how == dcFunction) {
        Emit2(mov, Reg(ax), NameLit(RETURN_VALUE));
        if (pRoutineId->pType == pRealType) {
            Emit2(mov, Reg(dx), NameLit(HIGH_RETURN_VALUE));
        }
    }

    Emit2(mov, Reg(sp), Reg(bp));        // cut back to caller's stack
    Emit1(pop, Reg(bp));                 // restore caller's stack frame

    Emit1(ret, IntegerLit(pRoutineId->defn.routine.totalParmSize + 2));
                                         // return and cut back stack

    PutLine();
    sprintf(AsmText(), "%s_%03d\tENDP",
            pRoutineId->String(), pRoutineId->labelIndex);
    PutLine();
}

//----------------------------------------------------------------
//  EmitSubroutineCall             Emit code for a call to a
//                                 procedure or a function.
//
//      pRoutineId : ptr to the subroutine name's symtab node
//
//  Return: ptr to the call's type object
//----------------------------------------------------------------

TType *TCodeGenerator::EmitSubroutineCall(const TSymtabNode *pRoutineId)
{
    return pRoutineId->defn.routine.which == rcDeclared
              ? EmitDeclaredSubroutineCall(pRoutineId)
```

(continues)

```
                        : EmitStandardSubroutineCall(pRoutineId);
}

//-------------------------------------------------------------
//  EmitDeclaredSubroutineCall    Emit code for a call to a
//                                declared procedure or function.
//
//      pRoutineId : ptr to the subroutine name's symtab node
//
//  Return: ptr to the call's type object
//-------------------------------------------------------------

TType *TCodeGenerator::EmitDeclaredSubroutineCall
                            (const TSymtabNode *pRoutineId)
{
    int oldLevel = currentNestingLevel;    // level of caller
    int newLevel = pRoutineId->level + 1;  // level of callee's locals

    //--Emit code to push the actual parameter values onto the stack.
    GetToken();
    if (token == tcLParen) {
        EmitActualParameters(pRoutineId);
        GetToken();
    }

    //--Push the static link onto the stack.
    if (newLevel == oldLevel + 1) {

        //--Calling a routine nested within the caller:
        //--Push pointer to caller's stack frame.
        Emit1(push, Reg(bp));
    }
    else if (newLevel == oldLevel) {

        //--Calling another routine at the same level:
        //--Push pointer to stack frame of common parent.
        Emit1(push, NameLit(STATIC_LINK));
    }
    else {        // newLevel < oldLevel

        //--Calling a routine at a lesser level (nested less deeply):
        //--Push pointer to stack frame of nearest common ancestor
        //--(the callee's parent).
        EmitAdjustBP(newLevel - 1);
```

```
            Emit1(push, Reg(bp));
            EmitRestoreBP(newLevel - 1);
        }

        Emit1(call, TaggedName(pRoutineId));

        return pRoutineId->pType;
}

//------------------------------------------------------------
//  EmitActualParameters      Emit code for the actual parameters
//                            of a declared subroutine call.
//
//      pRoutineId : ptr to the subroutine name's symtab node
//------------------------------------------------------------

void TCodeGenerator::EmitActualParameters(const TSymtabNode *pRoutineId)
{
    TSymtabNode *pFormalId;   // ptr to formal parm's symtab node

    //--Loop to emit code for each actual parameter.
    for (pFormalId = pRoutineId->defn.routine.locals.pParmIds;
         pFormalId;
         pFormalId = pFormalId->next) {

        TType *pFormalType = pFormalId->pType;
        GetToken();

        //--VAR parameter: EmitVariable will leave the actual
        //--               parameter's addresss on top of the stack.
        if (pFormalId->defn.how == dcVarParm) {
            EmitVariable(pNode, true);
        }

        //--Value parameter: Emit code to load a scalar value into
        //--                 ax or dx:ax, or push an array or record
        //--                 address onto the stack.
        else {
            TType *pActualType = EmitExpression();

            if (pFormalType == pRealType) {

                //--Real formal parm
                if (pActualType == pIntegerType) {
                    Emit1(push, Reg(ax));
                    Emit1(call, NameLit(FLOAT_CONVERT));
```

(continues)

```
            Emit2(add,  Reg(sp), IntegerLit(2));
        }
        Emit1(push, Reg(dx));
        Emit1(push, Reg(ax));
    }
    else if (! pActualType->IsScalar()) {

        //--Block move onto the stack.  Round the next offset
        //--up to an even number.
        int size   = pActualType->size;
        int offset = size & 1 ? size + 1 : size;

        Emit0(cld);
        Emit1(pop, Reg(si));
        Emit2(sub, Reg(sp), IntegerLit(offset));
        Emit2(mov, Reg(di), Reg(sp));
        Emit2(mov, Reg(cx), IntegerLit(size));
        Emit2(mov, Reg(ax), Reg(ds));
        Emit2(mov, Reg(es), Reg(ax));
        Emit0(rep_movsb);
    }
    else {
        Emit1(push, Reg(ax));
    }
        }
    }
}
```

Program

Member function `EmitProgramPrologue` emits a standard prologue code sequence at the beginning of each assembly object file:

```
        DOSSEG
        .MODEL small
        .STACK 1024

        .CODE

        PUBLIC  _PascalMain
        INCLUDE pasextrn.inc

$STATIC_LINK   EQU  <WORD PTR [bp+4]>
$RETURN_VALUE EQU  <WORD PTR [bp-4]>
$HIGH_RETURN_VALUE   EQU  <WORD PTR [bp-2]>
```

These directives give the assembler useful information. DOSSEG tells the assembler to place the segments in the final machine language file in the conventional order. .MODEL specifies that the program will use the small memory model—one code segment and one data segment, as we saw in Figure 12.3. .STACK states the maximum size of the stack at the bottom of the data segment, and .CODE specifies the start of the code segment. PUBLIC makes the name _PascalMain available to the main routine in the runtime library. (By convention, an underscore is added to the beginning of each public name.) Each of the EQU directives gives name equivalents to three of the stack frame items we saw in Figure 12.4.

INCLUDE causes file pasextrn.inc, shown in Figure 13.4, to be included. This file contains EXTRN directives, one for each library routine.

■■■■ **Figure 13.4** File **pasextrn.inc**.

```
EXTRN     _FloatNegate:PROC
EXTRN     _FloatAdd:PROC
EXTRN     _FloatSubtract:PROC
EXTRN     _FloatMultiply:PROC
EXTRN     _FloatDivide:PROC
EXTRN     _FloatCompare:PROC
EXTRN     _FloatConvert:PROC

EXTRN     _WriteInteger:PROC
EXTRN     _WriteReal:PROC
EXTRN     _WriteBoolean:PROC
EXTRN     _WriteChar:PROC
EXTRN     _WriteString:PROC
EXTRN     _WriteLine:PROC

EXTRN     _ReadInteger:PROC
EXTRN     _ReadReal:PROC
EXTRN     _ReadChar:PROC
EXTRN     _ReadLine:PROC

EXTRN     _StdEof:PROC
EXTRN     _StdEoln:PROC

EXTRN     _StdAbs:PROC

EXTRN     _StdArctan:PROC
EXTRN     _StdCos:PROC
EXTRN     _StdExp:PROC
EXTRN     _StdLn:PROC
```

(continues)

```
EXTRN    _StdSin:PROC
EXTRN    _StdSqrt:PROC

EXTRN    _StdRound:PROC
EXTRN    _StdTrunc:PROC
```

Member function EmitProgramEpilogue emits the epilogue code at the end of each assembly object file. First, it emits

```
.DATA
```

to specify the start of the data segment. Then, as we saw earlier, it emits declarations for each of the Pascal source program's global variables to allocate them in the global data area. More examples of scalar declarations are:

```
ch_012        DB    0                    ; byte
sides_015     DW    0                    ; integer or enumeration
beta_077      DD    0.0                  ; real
```

Note that they're all initialized to zero. Arrays and records are declared and initialized with the DUP modifier. For example:

```
list_065      DB    100 DUP(0)           ; array of 50 integers
```

After the global variables, EmitProgramEpilogue emits declarations for each real and string constant from the source program. Recall that member function Emit-LoadFloatLit links the symbol table nodes of the real constants together into a list pointed to by data member pFloatLitList, and similarly, member function EmitPushStringLit constructs a list of string constant nodes pointed to by data member pStringLitList. EmitProgramEpilogue runs down each linked list to emit the declarations. For example:

```
$F_021 DD    3.141593e+000
$S_026 DB    "Hello, world."
```

Recall that header file codegen.h (see Figure 12.7) defines

```
FLOAT_LABEL_PREFIX to be $F and STRING_LABEL_PREFIX to be $S.
```

Calls and Returns

Chapter 9 described what happens to the interpreter's runtime stack as one procedure or function called another. Our compiler will emit code that follows the calling convention used by the popular Microsoft and Borland compilers. (We are already using the conventional stack frame format.) Table 13.1 describes the sequence of actions as one procedure or function (the caller) calls another (the callee), the callee executes, and then returns to the caller.

████████████ **Table 13.1** Caller and Callee Actions

	Caller actions	Callee actions
1	Push the actual parameter values onto the runtime stack. The last parameter value ends up on top.	
2	Push the static link onto the stack.	
3	Push the return address onto the stack.	
4	Call the callee.	
5		Push the dynamic link onto the stack.
6		Set register BP to point to the callee's stack frame.
7		*Function only:* Allocate space on top of the stack for the return value.
8		Allocate space on top of the stack for the local variables.
9		Execute the callee's code.
10		*Function only:* Load the return value from the stack frame into register AX or into the DX:AX register pair.
11		Cut the stack back to remove the callee's local variables and, for a function, the return value.
12		Use the dynamic link to restore register BP to point to the caller's stack frame.
13		Pop off the return address.
14		Cut the stack back to remove the actual parameter values and the stack link.
15		Return to the caller.
16	Resume executing the caller's code.	

████████

Main Routine

Member function `EmitMain` emits code for the Pascal main routine. It first calls member functions `EmitProgramHeaderComment` and `EmitVarDeclComment`, which we saw in the previous chapter, to emit the source program header and the global variable declarations as assembly comments. It then repeatedly calls member function `EmitRoutine` to emit code for each level-1 procedure and function.

After pointing data member `pIcode` to the main routine's intermediate code and resetting the current nesting level to 1, `EmitMain` calls member functions `Emit-MainPrologue` to emit the prologue code, `EmitCompound` to emit code for the statements, and `EmitMainEpilogue` to emit the epilogue code.

Member function `EmitMainPrologue` emits the following prologue code for the source program's main routine:

```
_PascalMain    PROC

        push bp                 ; dynamic link
        mov  bp,sp              ; point BP to new stack frame
```

Thus, for the main routine as the callee, we do steps 5 and 6 of the above table.

Member function `EmitMainEpilogue` emits the main routine's epilogue code:

```
        pop  bp                 ; restore BP
        ret                     ; return

_PascalMain    ENDP
```

which represents steps 12, 13, and 15. The `ret` instruction also pops off the return address.

Procedures and Functions

Member function `EmitRoutine` emits code for a procedure or a function. It first calls member function `EmitSubroutineHeaderComment` to emit the subroutine header as an assembly comment, and it next calls member function `EmitDeclarations` to emit code for the parameters and local variables. Then, the function calls itself recursively for each nested procedure or function.

After pointing data member `pIcode` to the subroutine's intermediate code and setting the current nesting level to the level of its local data, `EmitRoutine` calls `EmitRou-`

`tinePrologue` to emit the prologue code, `EmitCompound` to emit code for the sub-routine's statements, and `EmitRoutineEpilogue` to emit the epilogue code.

Member function `EmitRoutinePrologue` emits the following prologue code for a subroutine (steps 5 and 6):

```
tagged name     PROC                ; either procedure or function

        push bp                     ; push dynamic link
        mov  bp,sp                  ; point BP to new stack frame
```

If the subroutine is a function, `EmitRoutinePrologue` emits the following to allocate space on the runtime stack for the return value (step 7):

```
sub  sp,4
```

Finally, for either a procedure or a function, `EmitRoutinePrologue` emits the following to allocate space on the stack for all the local variables (step 8):

```
sub  sp,n
```

where n is the total byte size of all the local variables.

Member function `EmitRoutineEpilogue` emits the following epilogue code for a function (step 10):

```
mov  ax,$RETURN_VALUE          ; integer or real value
mov  dx,$HIGH_RETURN_VALUE     ; real value only
```

Then, for either a procedure or a function, it emits (steps 11 through 15):

```
        mov  sp,bp                  ; cut back to caller's stack
        pop  bp                     ; restore BP via dynamic link
        ret  n                      ; cut back stack and return

tagged_name     ENDP
```

where n is the total byte size of all the parameters, plus two more bytes for the static link. When the `ret` instruction has a numeric operand, it also cuts the stack back by that many bytes.

Calling Declared Procedures and Functions

Now we're ready to look at the code that the compiler emits to call a declared procedure or function. Member function `EmitSubroutineCall` calls either member function `EmitDeclaredSubroutineCall` or `EmitStandardSubrou-tineCall`. We'll look at the latter function later.

If there are any actual parameters, `EmitDeclaredSubroutineCall` first calls member function `EmitActualParameters` to push the parameter values onto the stack (step 1). `EmitDeclaredSubroutineCall` then pushes the static link onto the stack (step 2).

The static link always points to the stack frame of the callee's parent. If the callee is nested within the caller, the static link is simply the pointer to the caller's stack frame:

```
push bp
```

If the callee is at the same level as the caller, then the static link is the pointer to their common parent's stack frame:

```
push $STATIC_LINK
```

If the callee is an enclosing subroutine, then `EmitDeclaredSubroutineCall` calls `EmitAdjustBP`, emits code to push the adjusted BP, and then calls `EmitRe-storeBP`. For example, if the callee is the caller's grandparent, then the static link must be the pointer to the great-grandparent's stack frame:

```
mov  cx,bp             ; save current BP in CX
mov  bp,$STATIC_LINK   ; BP -> parent
mov  bp,$STATIC_LINK   ; BP -> grandparent
mov  bp,$STATIC_LINK   ; BP -> great-grandparent
push bp                ; push static link
mov  bp,cx             ; restore BP
```

Finally, `EmitDeclaredSubroutineCall` emits a call to the callee, using the latter's tagged name (steps 3 and 4):

```
call  tagged_name
```

The `call` instruction also pushes the return address onto the stack.

Member function `EmitActualParameters` loops over the list of symbol table nodes of the subroutine's formal parameter to determine how to emit code for each actual parameter.

If the formal parameter is a VAR parameter, `EmitActualParameters` calls member function `EmitVariable` to push the address of the actual parameter onto the stack. For a scalar value parameter, the function calls the member function `Emit-Expression` to emit code that evaluates the actual parameter expression and leaves its value in AX or DX:AX. `EmitActualParameters` then emits code to push the value from AX or DX:AX. It may first need to emit code to call `_FloatConvert` if an integer value must be converted to real:

```
push ax                     ; push integer value
call _FloatConvert          ; DX:AX = real value
add  sp,2                   ; pop off operand
push dx
push ax                     ; push real value
```

Finally, if the value parameter is an array or a record, then `EmitVariable` must emit a block move onto the stack. `EmitExpression`'s emitted code leaves the address of the array or record on top of the stack:

```
cld                         ; clear direction flag (forward move)
pop  si                     ; SI = source address
sub  sp,offset              ; allocate stack space
mov  di,sp                  ; DI = destination address
mov  cx,size                ; CX = number of bytes to move
mov  ax,ds
mov  es,ax                  ; ES = DS
rep  movsb                  ; block move (actually copy)
```

where *size* is the byte size of the source array or record, and *offset* is *size* rounded up if necessary to the next even number. Note that the copy proceeds in the forward direction, starting at the new top of stack and going down the stack.

Register SI normally points to a location in the extra segment. We simply set the segment register ES to point to the data segment. The 8086 processor does not allow a direct move of the contents of DS into ES, so the emitted code uses AX as an intermediary.

▄▄▄▄▄▄ **Figure 13.5** The preliminary version of file **emitstmt.cpp**.

```
// ****************************************************************
// *                                                              *
// *    C O D E   G E N E R A T O R    (Statements)               *
// *                                                              *
// *    Generating and emit assembly code for statements.         *
// *                                                              *
// *    CLASSES: TCodeGenerator                                   *
// *                                                              *
```

(continues)

```
// *    FILE:     prog13-1/emitstmt.cpp              *
// *                                                  *
// *    MODULE:   Code generator                      *
// *                                                  *
// *    Copyright (c) 1996 by Ronald Mak              *
// *    For instructional purposes only.  No warranties.  *
// *                                                  *
// ****************************************************************

#include <stdio.h>
#include "common.h"
#include "codegen.h"

//------------------------------------------------------------
// EmitStatement         Emit code for a statement.
//------------------------------------------------------------

void TCodeGenerator::EmitStatement(void)
{
    //--Emit the current statement as a comment.
    EmitStmtComment();

    switch (token) {

        case tcIdentifier: {
            if (pNode->defn.how == dcProcedure) {
                EmitSubroutineCall(pNode);
            }
            else {
                EmitAssignment(pNode);
            }
            break;
        }

        case tcBEGIN:    EmitCompound();      break;
    }
}


//------------------------------------------------------------
// EmitStatementList    Emit code for a statement list until
//                      the terminator token.
//
//      terminator : the token that terminates the list
//------------------------------------------------------------
```

```
void TCodeGenerator::EmitStatementList(TTokenCode terminator)
{
    //--Loop to emit code for statements and skip semicolons.
    do {
        EmitStatement();
        while (token == tcSemicolon) GetToken();
    } while (token != terminator);
}

//-------------------------------------------------------------
//  EmitAssignment         Emit code for an assignment statement.
//-------------------------------------------------------------

void TCodeGenerator::EmitAssignment(const TSymtabNode *pTargetId)
{
    TType *pTargetType = pTargetId->pType;
                            // ptr to target type object
    TType *pExprType;       // ptr to expression type object
    int    addressOnStack;  // true if target address has been pushed
                            //   onto the runtime stack

    //--Assignment to a function name.
    if (pTargetId->defn.how == dcFunction) {
        EmitPushReturnValueAddress(pTargetId);
        addressOnStack = true;
        GetToken();
    }

    //--Assignment to a nonscalar, a formal VAR parameter, or to
    //--a nonglobal and nonlocal variable. EmitVariable emits code
    //--that leaves the target address on top of the runtime stack.
    else if ((pTargetId->defn.how == dcVarParm) ||
             (! pTargetType->IsScalar()) ||
             ((pTargetId->level > 1)
                    && (pTargetId->level < currentNestingLevel))) {
        pTargetType = EmitVariable(pTargetId, true);
        addressOnStack = true;
    }

    //--Assignment to a global or local scalar. A mov will be emitted
    //--after the code for the expression.
    else {
        GetToken();
        pTargetType = pTargetId->pType;
        addressOnStack = false;
    }
```

(continues)

```cpp
//--Emit code for the expression.
GetToken();
pExprType = EmitExpression();

//--Emit code to do the assignment.
if ((pTargetType->Base() == pIntegerType)
        || (pTargetType->Base()->form == fcEnum)) {
    if (addressOnStack) {
        Emit1(pop, Reg(bx));
        Emit2(mov, WordIndirect(bx), Reg(ax));
    }
    else Emit2(mov, Word(pTargetId), Reg(ax));
}
else if (pTargetType->Base() == pCharType) {

    //--char := char
    if (addressOnStack) {
        Emit1(pop, Reg(bx));
        Emit2(mov, ByteIndirect(bx), Reg(al));
    }
    else Emit2(mov, Byte(pTargetId), Reg(al));
}
else if (pTargetType == pRealType) {

    //--real := ...
    if (pExprType == pIntegerType) {

        //--Convert an integer value to real.
        Emit1(push, Reg(ax));
        Emit1(call, NameLit(FLOAT_CONVERT));
        Emit2(add, Reg(sp), IntegerLit(2));
    }

    //--... real
    if (addressOnStack) {
        Emit1(pop, Reg(bx));
        Emit2(mov, WordIndirect(bx), Reg(ax));
        Emit2(mov, HighDWordIndirect(bx), Reg(dx));
    }
    else {
        Emit2(mov, Word(pTargetId), Reg(ax));
        Emit2(mov, HighDWord(pTargetId), Reg(dx));
    }
}
```

```
    else {

        //--array  := array
        //--record := record
        Emit2(mov, Reg(cx), IntegerLit(pTargetType->size));
        Emit1(pop, Reg(si));
        Emit1(pop, Reg(di));
        Emit2(mov, Reg(ax), Reg(ds));
        Emit2(mov, Reg(es), Reg(ax));
        Emit0(cld);
        Emit0(rep_movsb);
    }
}

//------------------------------------------------------------
//  EmitCompound        Emit code for a compound statement:
//
//                          BEGIN <stmt-list> END
//------------------------------------------------------------

void TCodeGenerator::EmitCompound(void)
{
    StartComment("BEGIN");
    PutLine();

    //--<stmt-list> END
    GetToken();
    EmitStatementList(tcEND);

    GetToken();

    StartComment("END");
    PutLine();
}
```

Assignment Statements

Figure 13.5 shows the preliminary version of file emitstmt.cpp, which implements the member functions of class TCodeGenerator that emit code for Pascal statements. We'll complete this file in the next chapter.

Member function EmitCompound calls member function EmitStatementList, which calls member function EmitStatement.

For now, `EmitStatement` only knows about procedure calls, assignment statements, and compound statements. It first calls member function `EmitStmtComment` to emit the statement itself as an assembly comment.

Member function `EmitAssignment` emits code for an assignment statement. First, it needs to take care of the assignment target. If the target is a function name, it calls member function `EmitPushReturnValueAddress`, which emits code that leaves the address of the return value on top of the stack. If the target is nonscalar, a formal `VAR` parameter, or is a variable that is neither global nor local, `EmitAssignment` calls member function `EmitVariable` (passing true to its `addressFlag` parameter), which emits code that leaves the variable's address on top of the stack.

`EmitAssignment` then calls member function `EmitExpression`, which emits code that either leaves a scalar value in AX or DX:AX, or leaves an array or record address on top of the stack.

Finally, `EmitAssignment` emits code to do the assignment to the target. For example, if the target n is integer and either global or local, the code is simply:

```
mov   WORD PTR n_068,ax
```

Or, if the target address is on the stack, the code is:

```
pop   bx
mov   WORD PTR [bx],ax
```

If an integer value is assigned to a real target, a call to `FloatConvert` is emitted.

If an array is being assigned to an array, or a record to a record, both the target and source addresses are on the stack. `EmitAssignment` emits:

```
mov   cx, size          ; CX = number of bytes to move
pop   si                ; SI = source address
pop   di                ; DI = destination address
mov   ax,ds
mov   es,ax             ; ES = DS
cld                     ; clear direction flag (forward move)
rep   movsb             ; block move (actually copy)
```

where *size* is the byte size of the array or record.

Figure 13.6 shows the complete version of file `emitexpr.c`, which implements the member functions that emit code for expressions.

■■■■■■■ **Figure 13.6** Implementation file **emitexpr.cpp**.

```
//      ************************************************************
//      *                                                          *
//      *    C O D E   G E N E R A T O R    (Expressions)          *
//      *                                                          *
//      *    Generating and emit assembly code for expressions.    *
//      *                                                          *
//      *    CLASSES: TCodeGenerator                               *
//      *                                                          *
//      *    FILE:    prog13-1/emitexpr.cpp                        *
//      *                                                          *
//      *    MODULE:  Code generator                               *
//      *                                                          *
//      *    Copyright (c) 1996 by Ronald Mak                      *
//      *    For instructional purposes only.  No warranties.      *
//      *                                                          *
//      ************************************************************

#include <string.h>
#include "common.h"
#include "codegen.h"

//------------------------------------------------------------
//  EmitExpression   Emit code for an expression (binary
//                   relational operators = < > <> <= and >= ).
//
//  Return: ptr to expression's type object
//------------------------------------------------------------

TType *TCodeGenerator::EmitExpression(void)
{
    TType        *pOperand1Type;  // ptr to first  operand's type
    TType        *pOperand2Type;  // ptr to second operand's type
    TType        *pResultType;    // ptr to result type
    TTokenCode   op;              // operator
    TInstruction jumpOpcode;      // jump instruction opcode
    int          jumpLabelIndex;  // assembly jump label index

    //--Emit code for the first simple expression.
    pResultType = EmitSimpleExpression();

    //--If we now see a relational operator,
    //--emit code for the second simple expression.
    if (TokenIn(token, tlRelOps)) {
        EmitPushOperand(pResultType);
```

(continues)

```
op            = token;
pOperand1Type = pResultType->Base();

GetToken();
pOperand2Type = EmitSimpleExpression()->Base();

//--Perform the operation, and push the resulting value
//--onto the stack.
if (    ((pOperand1Type == pIntegerType) &&
         (pOperand2Type == pIntegerType))
     || ((pOperand1Type == pCharType) &&
         (pOperand2Type == pCharType))
     || (pOperand1Type->form == fcEnum)) {

    //--integer <op> integer
    //--boolean <op> boolean
    //--char    <op> char
    //--enum    <op> enum
    //--Compare dx (operand 1) to ax (operand 2).
    Emit1(pop, Reg(dx));
    Emit2(cmp, Reg(dx), Reg(ax));
}
else if ((pOperand1Type == pRealType) ||
         (pOperand2Type == pRealType)) {

    //--real    <op> real
    //--real    <op> integer
    //--integer <op> real
    //--Convert the integer operand to real.
    //--Call _FloatCompare to do the comparison, which
    //--returns -1 (less), 0 (equal), or +1 (greater).
    EmitPushOperand(pOperand2Type);
    EmitPromoteToReal(pOperand1Type, pOperand2Type);

    Emit1(call, NameLit(FLOAT_COMPARE));
    Emit2(add,  Reg(sp), IntegerLit(8));
    Emit2(cmp,  Reg(ax), IntegerLit(0));
}
else {

    //--string <op> string
    //--Compare the string pointed to by si (operand 1)
    //--to the string pointed to by di (operand 2).
    Emit1(pop, Reg(di));
```

```
                    Emit1(pop, Reg(si));
                    Emit2(mov, Reg(ax), Reg(ds));
                    Emit2(mov, Reg(es), Reg(ax));
                    Emit0(cld);
                    Emit2(mov, Reg(cx),
                              IntegerLit(pOperand1Type->array.elmtCount));
                    Emit0(repe_cmpsb);
                }

                Emit2(mov, Reg(ax), IntegerLit(1));  // default: load 1

                switch (op) {
                    case tcLt:    jumpOpcode = jl;    break;
                    case tcLe:    jumpOpcode = jle;   break;
                    case tcEqual: jumpOpcode = je;    break;
                    case tcNe:    jumpOpcode = jne;   break;
                    case tcGe:    jumpOpcode = jge;   break;
                    case tcGt:    jumpOpcode = jg;    break;
                }

                jumpLabelIndex = ++asmLabelIndex;
                Emit1(jumpOpcode, Label(STMT_LABEL_PREFIX, jumpLabelIndex));

                Emit2(sub, Reg(ax), Reg(ax));       // load 0 if false
                EmitStatementLabel(jumpLabelIndex);

                pResultType = pBooleanType;
        }

    return pResultType;
}


//-------------------------------------------------------------
//  EmitSimpleExpression     Emit code for a simple expression
//                           (unary operators + or -
//                           and binary operators + -
//                           and OR).
//
//  Return: ptr to expression's type object
//-------------------------------------------------------------

TType *TCodeGenerator::EmitSimpleExpression(void)
{
    TType       *pOperandType;      // ptr to operand's type
    TType       *pResultType;       // ptr to result type
    TTokenCode  op;                 // operator
```

(continues)

```
TTokenCode  unaryOp = tcPlus;   // unary operator

//--Unary + or -
if (TokenIn(token, tlUnaryOps)) {
    unaryOp = token;
    GetToken();
}

//--Emit code for the first term.
pResultType = EmitTerm();

//--If there was a unary operator, negate in integer value in ax
//--with the neg instruction, or negate a real value in dx:ax
//--by calling _FloatNegate.
if (unaryOp == tcMinus) {
    if (pResultType->Base() == pIntegerType) Emit1(neg, Reg(ax))
    else if (pResultType == pRealType) {
        EmitPushOperand(pResultType);
        Emit1(call, NameLit(FLOAT_NEGATE));
        Emit2(add,  Reg(sp), IntegerLit(4));
    }
}

//--Loop to execute subsequent additive operators and terms.
while (TokenIn(token, tlAddOps)) {
    op = token;
    pResultType = pResultType->Base();
    EmitPushOperand(pResultType);

    GetToken();
    pOperandType = EmitTerm()->Base();

    //--Perform the operation, and push the resulting value
    //--onto the stack.
    if (op == tcOR) {

        //--boolean OR boolean => boolean
        //--ax = ax OR dx
        Emit1(pop, Reg(dx));
        Emit2(or,  Reg(ax), Reg(dx));
        pResultType = pBooleanType;
    }
    else if ((pResultType  == pIntegerType) &&
             (pOperandType == pIntegerType)) {
```

```
            //--integer +|- integer => integer
            Emit1(pop, Reg(dx));
            if (op == tcPlus) Emit2(add, Reg(ax), Reg(dx))
            else {
                Emit2(sub, Reg(dx), Reg(ax));
                Emit2(mov, Reg(ax), Reg(dx));
            }
            pResultType = pIntegerType;
        }
        else {

            //--real    +|- real    => real
            //--real    +|- integer => real
            //--integer +|- real    => real
            //--Convert the integer operand to real and then
            //--call _FloatAdd or _FloatSubtract.
            EmitPushOperand(pOperandType);
            EmitPromoteToReal(pResultType, pOperandType);

            Emit1(call, NameLit(op == tcPlus ? FLOAT_ADD
                                             : FLOAT_SUBTRACT));
            Emit2(add, Reg(sp), IntegerLit(8));
            pResultType = pRealType;
        }
    }

    return pResultType;
}

//--------------------------------------------------------------
// EmitTerm          Emit code for a term (binary operators
//                     * / DIV tcMOD and AND).
//
// Return: ptr to term's type object
//--------------------------------------------------------------

TType *TCodeGenerator::EmitTerm(void)
{
    TType      *pOperandType;  // ptr to operand's type
    TType      *pResultType;   // ptr to result type
    TTokenCode  op;            // operator

    //--Emit code for the first factor.
    pResultType = EmitFactor();

    //--Loop to execute subsequent multiplicative operators and factors.
```

(continues)

■■■■■■■ **Figure 13.6** Implementation file **emitexpr.cpp**. (*Continued*)

```
while (TokenIn(token, tlMulOps)) {
    op = token;
    pResultType = pResultType->Base();
    EmitPushOperand(pResultType);

    GetToken();
    pOperandType = EmitFactor()->Base();

    //--Perform the operation, and push the resulting value
    //--onto the stack.
    switch (op) {

        case tcAND: {

            //--boolean AND boolean => boolean
            Emit1(pop, Reg(dx));
            Emit2(and, Reg(ax), Reg(dx));
            pResultType = pBooleanType;
            break;
        }

        case tcStar:

            if ((pResultType  == pIntegerType) &&
                (pOperandType == pIntegerType)) {

                //--integer * integer => integer
                //--ax = ax*dx
                Emit1(pop,  Reg(dx));
                Emit1(imul, Reg(dx));
                pResultType = pIntegerType;
            }
            else {

                //--real    * real    => real
                //--real    * integer => real
                //--integer * real    => real
                //--Convert the integer operand to real
                //--and then call _FloatMultiply, which
                //--leaves the value in dx:ax.
                EmitPushOperand(pOperandType);
                EmitPromoteToReal(pResultType, pOperandType);

                Emit1(call, NameLit(FLOAT_MULTIPLY));
                Emit2(add,  Reg(sp), IntegerLit(8));
```

```
                    pResultType = pRealType;
                }
                break;

        case tcSlash: {

                //--real    / real    => real
                //--real    / integer => real
                //--integer / real    => real
                //--integer / integer => real
                //--Convert any integer operand to real
                //--and then call _FloatDivide, which
                    //--leaves the value in dx:ax.
                EmitPushOperand(pOperandType);
                EmitPromoteToReal(pResultType, pOperandType);

                Emit1(call, NameLit(FLOAT_DIVIDE));
                Emit2(add,  Reg(sp), IntegerLit(8));
                pResultType = pRealType;
                break;
            }

        case tcDIV:
        case tcMOD: {

                //--integer DIV|MOD integer => integer
                //--ax = ax IDIV cx
                Emit2(mov,  Reg(cx), Reg(ax));
                Emit1(pop,  Reg(ax));
                Emit2(sub,  Reg(dx), Reg(dx));
                Emit1(idiv, Reg(cx));
                if (op == tcMOD) Emit2(mov, Reg(ax), Reg(dx));
                pResultType = pIntegerType;
                break;
            }
        }
    }


    return pResultType;
}


//-------------------------------------------------------------
// EmitFactor      Emit code for a factor (identifier, number,
//                 string, NOT <factor>, or parenthesized
//                 subexpression).  An identifier can be
//                 a function, constant, or variable.
```

(continues)

■■■■■■■■ **Figure 13.6** Implementation file **emitexpr.cpp**. (*Continued*)

```cpp
//
//  Return: ptr to factor's type object
//------------------------------------------------------------

TType *TCodeGenerator::EmitFactor(void)
{
    TType *pResultType;   // ptr to result type

    switch (token) {

        case tcIdentifier: {
            switch (pNode->defn.how) {

                case dcFunction:
                    pResultType = EmitSubroutineCall(pNode);
                    break;

                case dcConstant:
                    pResultType = EmitConstant(pNode);
                    break;

                default:
                    pResultType = EmitVariable(pNode, false);
                    break;
            }
            break;
        }

        case tcNumber: {

            //--Push the number's integer or real value onto the stack.
            if (pNode->pType == pIntegerType) {

                //--ax = value
                Emit2(mov, Reg(ax),
                      IntegerLit(pNode->defn.constant.value.integer));
                pResultType = pIntegerType;
            }
            else {

                //--dx:ax = value
                EmitLoadFloatLit(pNode);
                pResultType = pRealType;
            }
```

```
        GetToken();
        break;
}

case tcString: {

        //--Push either a character or a string address onto the
        //--runtime stack, depending on the string length.
        int length = strlen(pNode->String()) - 2;   // skip quotes
        if (length == 1) {

            //--Character
            //--ah = 0
            //--al = value
            Emit2(mov, Reg(ax),
                    CharLit(pNode->defn.constant.value.character));
            pResultType = pCharType;
        }
        else {

            //--String
            //--ax = string address
            EmitPushStringLit(pNode);
            pResultType = pNode->pType;
        }

        GetToken();
        break;
}

case tcNOT:

        //--Emit code for boolean factor and invert its value.
        //--ax = NOT ax
        GetToken();
        EmitFactor();
        Emit2(xor, Reg(ax), IntegerLit(1));
        pResultType = pBooleanType;
        break;

case tcLParen: {

        //--Parenthesized subexpression:  Call EmitExpression
        //--                                 recursively.
        GetToken();  // first token after (
        pResultType = EmitExpression();
```

(continues)

```
            GetToken();  // first token after )
            break;
        }
    }

    return pResultType;
}


//----------------------------------------------------------------
//  EmitConstant         Emit code to load a scalar constant into
//                       ax or dx:ax, or to push a string address
//                       onto the runtime stack.
//
//      pId : ptr to constant identifier's symbol table node
//
//  Return: ptr to constant's type object
//----------------------------------------------------------------

TType *TCodeGenerator::EmitConstant(TSymtabNode *pId)
{
    TType *pType = pId->pType;

    if (pType == pRealType) {

        //--Real: dx:ax = value
        EmitLoadFloatLit(pId);
    }
    else if (pType == pCharType) {

        //--Character: ax = value
        Emit2(mov, Reg(ax),
                CharLit(pId->defn.constant.value.character));
    }
    else if (pType->form == fcArray) {

        //--String constant: push string address
        EmitPushStringLit(pId);
    }
    else {

        //--Integer or enumeration: ax = value
        Emit2(mov, Reg(ax),
                IntegerLit(pId->defn.constant.value.integer));
    }
```

```
        GetToken();
        return pType;
}


//-------------------------------------------------------------
// EmitVariable        Emit code to load a variable's value
//                     ax or dx:ax, or push its address onto
//                     the runtime stack.
//
//     pId        : ptr to variable's symbol table node
//     addressFlag : true to push address, false to load value
//
// Return: ptr to variable's type object
//-------------------------------------------------------------

TType *TCodeGenerator::EmitVariable(const TSymtabNode *pId,
                                    int addressFlag)
{
    TType *pType = pId->pType;

    //--It's not a scalar, or addressFlag is true, push the
    //--data address onto the stack. Otherwise, load the
    //--data value into ax or dx:ax.
    if (addressFlag || (! pType->IsScalar())) EmitPushAddress(pId);
    else                                      EmitLoadValue(pId);

    GetToken();

    //--If there are any subscripts and field designators,
    //--emit code to evaluate them and modify the address.
    if ((token == tcLBracket) || (token == tcPeriod)) {
        int doneFlag = false;

        do {
            switch (token) {

                case tcLBracket:
                    pType = EmitSubscripts(pType);
                    break;

                case tcPeriod:
                    pType = EmitField();
                    break;

                default:  doneFlag = true;
            }
```

(continues)

■■■■■■ **Figure 13.6** Implementation file **emitexpr.cpp**. (*Continued*)

```
        } while (!doneFlag);

        //--If addresssFlag is false and the variable is scalar,
        //--pop the address off the top of the stack and use it
        //--to load the value into ax or dx:ax.
        if ((!addressFlag) && (pType->IsScalar())) {
            Emit1(pop, Reg(bx));
            if (pType == pRealType) {

                //--Read: dx:ax = value
                Emit2(mov, Reg(ax), WordIndirect(bx));
                Emit2(mov, Reg(dx), HighDWordIndirect(bx));
            }
            else if (pType->Base() == pCharType) {

                //--Character: al = value
                Emit2(sub, Reg(ax), Reg(ax));
                Emit2(mov, Reg(al), ByteIndirect(bx));
            }
            else {

                //--Integer or enumeration: ax = value
                Emit2(mov, Reg(ax), WordIndirect(bx));
            }
        }
    }

    return pType;
}


//-------------------------------------------------------------
//  EmitSubscripts      Emit code for each subscript expression
//                      to modify the data address at the top of
//                      the runtime stack.
//
//      pType : ptr to array type object
//
//  Return: ptr to subscripted variable's type object
//-------------------------------------------------------------

TType *TCodeGenerator::EmitSubscripts(const TType *pType)
{
    int minIndex, elmtSize;

    //--Loop to executed subscript lists enclosed in brackets.
```

```
    while (token == tcLBracket) {

        //--Loop to execute comma-separated subscript expressions
        //--within a subscript list.
        do {
            GetToken();
            EmitExpression();

            minIndex = pType->array.minIndex;
            elmtSize = pType->array.pElmtType->size;

            //--Convert the subscript into an offset by subracting
            //--the mininum index from it and then multiplying the
            //--result by the element size.   Add the offset to the
            //--address at the top of the stack.
            if (minIndex != 0) Emit2(sub, Reg(ax),
                                          IntegerLit(minIndex));
            if (elmtSize > 1) {
                Emit2(mov,  Reg(dx), IntegerLit(elmtSize));
                Emit1(imul, Reg(dx));
            }
            Emit1(pop,  Reg(dx));
            Emit2(add,  Reg(dx), Reg(ax));
            Emit1(push, Reg(dx));

            //--Prepare for another subscript in this list.
            if (token == tcComma) pType = pType->array.pElmtType;

        } while (token == tcComma);

        //--Prepare for another subscript list.
        GetToken();
        if (token == tcLBracket) pType = pType->array.pElmtType;
    }

    return pType->array.pElmtType;
}

//-------------------------------------------------------------
// EmitField   Emit code for a field designator to modify the
//             data address at the top of the runtime stack.
//
// Return: ptr to record field's type object
//-------------------------------------------------------------

TType *TCodeGenerator::EmitField(void)
```

(continues)

■■■■ **Figure 13.6** Implementation file **emitexpr.cpp**. (*Continued*)

```
{
    GetToken();
    TSymtabNode *pFieldId = pNode;
    int         offset    = pFieldId->defn.data.offset;

    //--Add the field's offset to the data address
    //--if the offset is greater than 0.
    if (offset > 0) {
        Emit1(pop,  Reg(ax));
        Emit2(add,  Reg(ax), IntegerLit(offset));
        Emit1(push, Reg(ax));
    }

    GetToken();
    return pFieldId->pType;
}
```

Variables

Member function `EmitVariable` emits code that either leaves a scalar value in register AX or the DX:AX register pair, or leaves an address on top of the stack. It always leaves an address if `addressFlag` is true, or if the variable is an array or a record. The function first calls either member function `EmitLoadValue` or `Emit-PushAddress`.

If the variable is an array or a record, and there are subscripts or field designators, `EmitVariable` loops to emit code for them by calling member functions `Emit-Subscripts` and `EmitField`. These latter two functions emit code that modifies the address on top of the stack. Then, if `addressFlag` is false and the variable is a scalar, `EmitVariable` emits code to pop the modified address into register BX and indirectly load the value into AX or DX:AX.

Function `EmitSubscripts` emits code that calculates the byte offset represented by a subscript value, and then adds this offset to the address on top of the stack. This calculation is similar to the one done by the interpreter. `EmitSubscripts` first calls `EmitExpression`, which emits code that leaves the subscript value in AX. Then it emits:

```
sub   ax, min          ; subtract minimum subscript value
mov   dx, size         ; DX = dimension byte size
```

```
imul  dx              ; AX = byte offset
pop   dx              ; DX = address
add   dx,ax           ; DX = address + offset
push  dx              ; push modified address
```

where *min* is the minimum subscript value for the dimension, and *size* is the dimension's byte size. The initial sub instruction is not emitted if *min* is zero, and the following mov and imul instructions are not emitted if the *size* is one.

Function EmitField simply adds the field offset to the address on top of the stack. For example, if the field offset is four, the code is:

```
pop   ax              ; AX = record address
add   ax,4            ; AX = address + offset
push  ax              ; push modified address
```

Expressions

The remaining member functions in file emitexpr.c emit code to evaluate expressions. Each of the functions emits code to leave either a scalar value in register AX or in the DX:AX register pair, or an address on top of the stack. If there is more than one operand, functions EmitExpression, EmitSimpleExpression, and EmitTerm all call member function EmitPushOperand to emit code to push a scalar operand onto the stack before emitting code to evaluate a subsequent operand.

Function EmitExpression emits code to do a comparison. If the operands are integer, character, or enumeration, it emits:

```
pop   dx              ; DX = operand 1 value
cmp   dx,ax           ; compare DX to AX
```

If the operands are real, or real and integer, the function calls EmitPushOperand to push the current operand value onto the stack (so both operands are on the stack). If necessary, it also calls member function EmitPromoteToReal to emit code to convert any integer operand to real, and then it emits

```
call  _FloatCompare   ; AX = -1, 0, or 1
add   sp,8            ; pop off operands
cmp   ax,0           ; check result of float compare
```

where _FloatCompare is a runtime library routine in paslib.c (see Figure 12.5) that returns 0 if the two operands are equal, -1 if the first operand is less than the second operand, or 1 if the first operand is greater than the second operand.

If the operands are two strings, both string addresses are on the stack, and so Emit-SimpleExpression emits:

```
pop   di                    ; DI = string 2 address
pop   si                    ; SI = string 1 address
mov   ax,ds
mov   es,ax                 ; ES = DX
cld                         ; clear direction flag (forward comparison)
mov   cx,length             ; CX = string length
repe  cmpsb                 ; compare strings
```

where *length* is the string length.

Following any of the above code sequences, EmitSimpleExpression emits:

```
mov   ax,1                  ; AX = 1 (true)
jump  $L_nnn
sub   ax,ax                 ; AX = 0 (false)
$L_nnn:
```

where *jump* is either jl, jle, je, jne, jge, or jg, depending on whether the comparison operator in the Pascal source was <, <=, =, <>, >=, or >, respectively, and *nnn* is the label index.

Member function EmitSimpleExpression emits the code:

```
neg   ax
```

to negate an integer value that was preceded by a unary minus. If a real value must be negated, it first calls EmitPushOperand to push the value onto the stack, and then it emits:

```
call _FloatNegate
add  sp,4                   ; pop off operand
```

to call the runtime library routine _FloatNegate to negate the value.

With integer operands and the + operator, EmitSimpleExpression emits:

```
pop   dx                    ; DX = operand 1 value
add   ax,dx                 ; AX = AX + DX
```

If the operator is –, it emits instead:

```
pop   dx                    ; DX = operand 1 value
sub   dx,ax                 ; DX = DX - AX
mov   ax,dx                 ; AX = DX
```

With the + operator and real operands, or integer and real operands, the function calls `EmitPushOperand` to push the current operand value onto the stack (so both operands are on the stack). Next, it calls `EmitPromoteToReal` to convert any integer operand to real, and then it emits:

```
call  _FloatAdd        ; DX:AX = real sum
add   sp,8             ; pop off operands
```

to call the runtime library routine `_FloatAdd` to do the addition. If the operator is -, it emits a call to `_FloatSubtract` instead.

Finally, if the operator is OR, `EmitSimpleExpression` emits:

```
pop   dx               ; DX = operand 1 value
or    ax,dx            ; AX = AX | DX
```

With integer operands and the * operator, member function `EmitTerm` emits:

```
pop   dx               ; DX = operand 1 value
imul  dx               ; DX:AX = AX * DX
```

Subsequent code ignores the value in register DX, so if the product exceeds one word in size, an incorrect value is used. If the operator is `div`, the function emits:

```
mov   cx,ax            ; CX = operand 2 value
pop   ax               ; AX = operand 1 value
sub   dx,dx            ; DX = 0
idiv  cx               ; AX = DX:AX / CX
```

If the operator is `mod`, the above code sequence is followed by:

```
mov   ax,dx            ; AX = DX:AX % CX
```

With the * operator and real operands, or integer and real operands, `EmitTerm` calls `EmitPushOperand` to push the current operand value onto the stack (so both operands are on the stack) and `EmitPromoteToReal` to convert any integer operand to real, and then it emits:

```
call  _FloatMultiply   ; DX:AX = real product
add   sp,8             ; pop off operands
```

to call the runtime library routine `_FloatMultiply` to do the multiply. If the operator is /, a call to `_FloatDivide` is emitted instead.

Finally, if the operator is AND, `EmitTerm` emits:

```
pop   dx                    ; DX = operand 1 value
and   ax,dx                 ; AX = AX & DX
```

Member function `EmitFactor` emits the following code for an integer literal:

```
mov   ax,n                  ; AX = integer value
```

where *n* is the literal. If the literal is a character, it emits:

```
mov   ax,'c'    ; AX = character value
```

where *c* is the literal. If the literal is a real number or a string, `EmitFactor` calls `EmitLoadFloatLit` or `EmitPushStringLit`. It calls member function `Emit-Constant` to load the constant's value if the operand is a constant identifier.

Finally, for the `NOT` operator, `EmitFactor` emits:

```
not   ax        ; AX = ! AX
```

■■■■■■ **Figure 13.7** Preliminary version of implementation file **emitstd.cpp**.

```
//    ************************************************************
//    *                                                        *
//    *    C O D E   G E N E R A T O R   (Standard Routines)    *
//    *                                                        *
//    *    Generating and emit assembly code for calls to the  *
//    *    standard procedures and functions.                  *
//    *                                                        *
//    *    CLASSES: TCodeGenerator                             *
//    *                                                        *
//    *    FILE:     prog13-1/emitstd.cpp                      *
//    *                                                        *
//    *    MODULE:   Code generator                            *
//    *                                                        *
//    *    Copyright (c) 1996 by Ronald Mak                    *
//    *    For instructional purposes only.  No warranties.    *
//    *                                                        *
//    ************************************************************

#include <stdio.h>
#include "types.h"
#include "buffer.h"
#include "symtab.h"
#include "codegen.h"


//-----------------------------------------------------------
//  EmitStandardSubroutineCall   Emit code for a call to a
//                               standard procedure or function.
```

```cpp
//
//      pRoutineId : ptr to the subroutine name's symtab node
//
//  Return: ptr to the call's type object
//-------------------------------------------------------------

TType *TCodeGenerator::EmitStandardSubroutineCall
                                (const TSymtabNode *pRoutineId)
{
    return EmitWriteWritelnCall(pRoutineId);
}


//-------------------------------------------------------------
//  EmitWriteWritelnCall        Emit code for a call to write or
//                              writeln.
//
//  Return: ptr to the dummy type object
//-------------------------------------------------------------

TType *TCodeGenerator::EmitWriteWritelnCall
                                (const TSymtabNode *pRoutineId)
{
    const int defaultFieldWidth = 10;
    const int defaultPrecision  =  2;

    //--Actual parameters are optional for writeln.
    GetToken();
    if (token == tcLParen) {

        //--Loop to emit code for each parameter value.
        do {
            //--<expr-1>
            GetToken();
            TType *pExprType = EmitExpression()->Base();

            //--Push the scalar value to be written onto the stack.
            //--A string value is already on the stack.
            if (pExprType->form != fcArray) {
                EmitPushOperand(pExprType);
            }

            if (token == tcColon) {

                //--Field width <expr-2>
                //--Push its value onto the stack.
                GetToken();
```

(continues)

```
        EmitExpression();
        Emit1(push, Reg(ax));

        if (token == tcColon) {

            //--Precision <expr-3>
            //--Push its value onto the stack.
            GetToken();
            EmitExpression();
            Emit1(push, Reg(ax));
        }
        else if (pExprType == pRealType) {

            //--No precision: Push the default precision.
            Emit2(mov, Reg(ax), IntegerLit(defaultPrecision));
            Emit1(push, Reg(ax));
        }
    }
    else {

        //--No field width: Push the default field width and
        //--                 the default precision.
        if (pExprType == pIntegerType) {
            Emit2(mov,  Reg(ax), IntegerLit(defaultFieldWidth));
            Emit1(push, Reg(ax));
        }
        else if (pExprType == pRealType) {
            Emit2(mov,  Reg(ax), IntegerLit(defaultFieldWidth));
            Emit1(push, Reg(ax));
            Emit2(mov,  Reg(ax), IntegerLit(defaultPrecision));
            Emit1(push, Reg(ax));
        }
        else {
            Emit2(mov,  Reg(ax), IntegerLit(0));
            Emit1(push, Reg(ax));
        }
    }

    //--Emit the code to write the value.
    if (pExprType == pIntegerType) {
        Emit1(call, NameLit(WRITE_INTEGER));
        Emit2(add,  Reg(sp), IntegerLit(4));
```

```
            }
            else if (pExprType == pRealType) {
                Emit1(call, NameLit(WRITE_REAL));
                Emit2(add,  Reg(sp), IntegerLit(8));
            }
            else if (pExprType == pBooleanType) {
                Emit1(call, NameLit(WRITE_BOOLEAN));
                Emit2(add,  Reg(sp), IntegerLit(4));
            }
            else if (pExprType == pCharType) {
                Emit1(call, NameLit(WRITE_CHAR));
                Emit2(add,  Reg(sp), IntegerLit(4));
            }
            else {        // string

                //--Push the string length onto the stack.
                Emit2(mov, Reg(ax),
                          IntegerLit(pExprType->array.elmtCount));

                Emit1(push, Reg(ax));
                Emit1(call, NameLit(WRITE_STRING));
                Emit2(add,  Reg(sp), IntegerLit(6));
            }

    } while (token == tcComma);

    GetToken();  // token after )
    }

    //--End the line if writeln.
    if (pRoutineId->defn.routine.which == rcWriteln) {
        Emit1(call, NameLit(WRITE_LINE));
    }

    return pDummyType;
}
```

Write and Writeln

Figure 13.7 shows a preliminary version of file `emitstd.cpp`, which implements the member functions of `TCodeGenerator` that emit code to call the standard Pascal routines. We implemented these routines in the runtime library `paslib.c`.

In order for us to test the assembly code emitted by the backend routines we wrote in this chapter, we need to emit code to write out values. Therefore, we'll first implement member function `EmitWriteWritelnCall`, which for now is the only function that member function `EmitStandardSubroutineCall` will call.

`EmitWriteWritelnCall` loops to emit code for each parameter. It calls `EmitExpression` to emit code for each parameter expression and then, for a scalar value, `EmitPushOperand` to push the value onto the stack. (Recall that `EmitExpression` already leaves a string address on the stack.)

If there is a field width specifier, `EmitWriteWritelnCall` calls `EmitExpression` to emit code to evaluate it, and then emits `push ax` to push the value onto the stack. If there is a precision specifier, there's a third call to `EmitExpression` followed by `push ax`. If any of the field width or precision specifiers are missing, `EmitWriteWritelnCall` emits code to push default values (based on the type of the value to be written) onto the stack.

The function then emits calls to the appropriate runtime library routines, depending on the parameter type.

- Integer:
  ```
  call _WriteInteger
  add  sp,4       ; pop off parameters
  ```

- Real
  ```
  call _WriteReal
  add  sp,8       ; pop off parameters
  ```

- Character
  ```
  call _WriteChar
  add  sp,4       ; pop off parameters
  ```

- String
  ```
  mov  ax,length
  push ax         ; push string length
  call _WriteString
  add  sp,6       ; pop off parameters
  ```

where *length* is the character length of the string. The length must be passed to `_WriteString` because Pascal strings are not null-terminated.

Finally, `EmitWriteWritelnCall` emits

    call _WriteLine

if the call in the Pascal source program was to `writeln`.

Program 13-1: Code Emitter

Figure 13.8 shows the main file of the code emitter utility that will compile a Pascal source program consisting of procedures, functions, assignment statements, and calls to `write` and `writeln` into an assembly language object program.

■■■■■■■ **Figure 13.8** The main file **emit.cpp** of the code emitter utility program.

```
//  ************************************************************
//  *                                                        *
//  *    Program 13-1: Code emitter                          *
//  *                                                        *
//  *    Compile a Pascal program consisting of procedures,  *
//  *    functions, assignment statements, and calls to write*
//  *    and writeln into an assembly language object program.*
//  *                                                        *
//  *    FILE:    prog13-1/emit.cpp                          *
//  *                                                        *
//  *    USAGE:   emit <source file> <assembly file>         *
//  *                                                        *
//  *                <source file>    name of the source file*
//  *                <assembly file>  name of the assembly   *
//  *                                 language object file   *
//  *                                                        *
//  *    Copyright (c) 1996 by Ronald Mak                    *
//  *    For instructional purposes only.  No warranties.    *
//  *                                                        *
//  ************************************************************

#include <iostream.h>
#include "common.h"
#include "error.h"
#include "buffer.h"
#include "symtab.h"
#include "parser.h"
#include "backend.h"
#include "codegen.h"
```

(continues)

```
//--------------------------------------------------------------
// main
//--------------------------------------------------------------

void main(int argc, char *argv[])
{
    extern int execFlag;

    //--Check the command line arguments.
    if (argc != 3) {
        cerr << "Usage: emit <source file> <asssembly file>" << endl;
        AbortTranslation(abortInvalidCommandLineArgs);
    }

    execFlag = false;

    //--Create the parser for the source file,
    //--and then parse the file.
    TParser     *pParser    = new TParser(new TSourceBuffer(argv[1]));
    TSymtabNode *pProgramId = pParser->Parse();
    delete pParser;

    //--If there were no syntax errors, convert the symbol tables,
    //--and create and invoke the backend code generator.
    if (errorCount == 0) {
        vpSymtabs = new TSymtab *[cntSymtabs];
        for (TSymtab *pSt = pSymtabList; pSt; pSt = pSt->Next()) {
            pSt->Convert(vpSymtabs);
        }

        TBackend *pBackend = new TCodeGenerator(argv[2]);
        pBackend->Go(pProgramId);

        delete[] vpSymtabs;
        delete   pBackend;
    }
}
```

Table 13.2 summarizes which source files have been changed or added. The major change is the replacement of the executor with the new code generator in the back end.

▮▮▮▮▮▮ **Table 13.2** Modules and Files of Program 13-1

Module	File	Status	Directory
Main	emit.cpp	*new*	prog13-1
Parser	parser.h	*changed*	prog13-1
	parser.cpp	*unchanged*	prog11-1
	parsrtn1.cpp	*unchanged*	prog8-1
	parsrtn2.cpp	*changed*	prog13-1
	parsstd.cpp	*unchanged*	prog8-1
	parsdecl.cpp	*changed*	prog13-1
	parstyp1.cpp	*unchanged*	prog7-1
	parstyp2.cpp	*unchanged*	prog7-1
	parsstmt.cpp	*unchanged*	prog10-1
	parsexpr.cpp	*unchanged*	prog8-1
Back end	backend.h	*unchanged*	prog11-1
	backend.cpp	*unchanged*	prog11-1
Code generator	codegen.h	*new*	prog13-1
	emitasm.cpp	*new*	prog13-1
	emitsrc.cpp	*new*	prog13-1
	emitcode.cpp	*new*	prog13-1
	emitrtn.cpp	*new*	prog13-1
	emitstd.cpp	*new*	prog13-1
	emitstmt.cpp	*new*	prog13-1
	emitexpr.cpp	*new*	prog13-1
Intermediate code	icode.h	*unchanged*	prog10-1
	icode.cpp	*unchanged*	prog10-1
Scanner	scanner.h	*unchanged*	prog3-1
	scanner.cpp	*unchanged*	prog3-2
	token.h	*unchanged*	prog4-2
	tknword.cpp	*unchanged*	prog3-2
	tknnum.cpp	*unchanged*	prog3-2
	tknstrsp.cpp	*unchanged*	prog3-2
Symbol table	types.h	*unchanged*	prog7-1
	types.cpp	*unchanged*	prog7-1
	symtab.h	*unchanged*	prog8-1
	symtab.cpp	*unchanged*	prog8-1

(continues)

Module	File	Status	Directory
Error	error.h	*unchanged*	prog5-2
	error.cpp	*changed*	prog11-1
Buffer	buffer.h	*unchanged*	prog2-1
	buffer.cpp	*unchanged*	prog2-1
Common	common.h	*unchanged*	prog8-1
	common.cpp	*unchanged*	prog8-1
	misc.h	*changed*	prog13-1

Table 13.2 Modules and Files of Program 13-1 (*Continued*)

Figure 13.9 shows the listing produced by the code emitter utility when it compiles a sample Pascal program. Figure 13.10 shows the generated assembly language object file.

We'll complete the code generator back end in the next chapter, where we implement the member functions of class TCodeGenerator that emit code for the Pascal control statements. Then, we'll have a complete Pascal compiler.

Figure 13.9 The listing of a sample Pascal program.

```
Page 1    simple.pas    Sun Sep 10 21:47:19 1995

  1 0: PROGRAM simple (output);
  2 1:
  3 1:    VAR
  4 1:        n : integer;
  5 1:        x : real;
  6 1:
  7 1:    PROCEDURE proc (i : integer; VAR j : integer);
  8 2:
  9 2:        FUNCTION func (y : real) : real;
 10 3:
 11 3:            BEGIN {func}
 12 3:                j := 5;
 13 3:                func := i + y + 0.5;
 14 3:            END {func};
 15 2:
 16 2:        BEGIN {proc}
 17 2:            j := i DIV 2;
 18 2:            writeln('In proc, the value of j is', j:3);
```

```
19 2:            x := func(3.14);
20 2:              writeln('In proc, the value of j is', j:3);
21 2:          END {proc};
22 1:
23 1:    BEGIN {simple}
24 1:        n := 1;
25 1:        writeln('In simple, the value of n is', n:3);
26 1:        proc(7, n);
27 1:        writeln('In simple, the value of n is', n:3,
28 1:                ' and the value of x is', x:8:4);
29 1:    END {simple}.
30 0:
31 0:
32 0:
```

```
                32 source lines.
                0 syntax errors.
```

■■■■■■■■ **Figure 13.10** The assembly language object file from compiling the
sample Pascal program.

```
    DOSSEG
    .MODEL  small
    .STACK  1024

    .CODE

    PUBLIC _PascalMain
    INCLUDE pasextrn.inc

$STATIC_LINK              EQU     <WORD PTR [bp+4]>
$RETURN_VALUE            EQU     <WORD PTR [bp-4]>
$HIGH_RETURN_VALUE       EQU     <WORD PTR [bp-2]>

; PROGRAM simple (output)

; VAR
; n : integer
; x : real

; PROCEDURE proc (i : integer; VAR j : integer)

i_033   EQU     <WORD PTR [bp+8]>
j_034   EQU     <WORD PTR [bp+6]>

; FUNCTION func (y : real) : real
```

                                                        (*continues*)

■■■■■ **Figure 13.10** The assembly language object file from compiling the sample Pascal program. *(Continued)*

```
y_036      EQU      <WORD PTR [bp+6]>

func_035            PROC

        push     bp
        mov      bp,sp
        sub      sp,4
; {12} j := 5
        mov      cx,bp
        mov      bp,$STATIC_LINK
        mov      ax,WORD PTR j_034
        push     ax
        mov      bp,cx
        mov      ax,5
        pop      bx
        mov      WORD PTR [bx],ax
; {13} func := i + y + 0.5
        lea      ax,$RETURN_VALUE
        push     ax
        mov      cx,bp
        mov      bp,$STATIC_LINK
        mov      ax,WORD PTR i_033
        mov      bp,cx
        push     ax
        mov      ax,WORD PTR y_036
        mov      dx,WORD PTR y_036+2
        push     dx
        push     ax
        pop      ax
        pop      dx
        pop      bx
        push     dx
        push     ax
        push     bx
        call     _FloatConvert
        add      sp,2
        pop      bx
        pop      cx
        push     dx
        push     ax
        push     cx
        push     bx
        call     _FloatAdd
```

```
        add     sp,8
        push    dx
        push    ax
        mov     ax,WORD PTR $F_038
        mov     dx,WORD PTR $F_038+2
        push    dx
        push    ax
        call    _FloatAdd
        add     sp,8
        pop     bx
        mov     WORD PTR [bx],ax
        mov     WORD PTR [bx+2],dx

        mov     ax,$RETURN_VALUE
        mov     dx,$HIGH_RETURN_VALUE
        mov     sp,bp
        pop     bp
        ret     6

func_035        ENDP

proc_032        PROC

        push    bp
        mov     bp,sp
; {17} j := i DIV 2
        mov     ax,WORD PTR j_034
        push    ax
        mov     ax,WORD PTR i_033
        push    ax
        mov     ax,2
        mov     cx,ax
        pop     ax
        sub     dx,dx
        idiv    cx
        pop     bx
        mov     WORD PTR [bx],ax
; {18} writeln('In proc, the value of j is', j:3)
        lea     ax,WORD PTR $S_040
        push    ax
        mov     ax,0
        push    ax
        mov     ax,26
        push    ax
        call    _WriteString
        add     sp,6
```

(continues)

```
        mov     bx,WORD PTR j_034
        mov     ax,WORD PTR [bx]
        push    ax
        mov     ax,3
        push    ax
        call    _WriteInteger
        add     sp,4
        call    _WriteLine
; {19} x := func(3.14)
        mov     ax,WORD PTR $F_042
        mov     dx,WORD PTR $F_042+2
        push    dx
        push    ax
        push    bp
        call    func_035
        mov     WORD PTR x_031,ax
        mov     WORD PTR x_031+2,dx
; {20} writeln('In proc, the value of j is', j:3)
        lea     ax,WORD PTR $S_040
        push    ax
        mov     ax,0
        push    ax
        mov     ax,26
        push    ax
        call    _WriteString
        add     sp,6
        mov     bx,WORD PTR j_034
        mov     ax,WORD PTR [bx]
        push    ax
        mov     ax,3
        push    ax
        call    _WriteInteger
        add     sp,4
        call    _WriteLine

        mov     sp,bp
        pop     bp
        ret     6

proc_032        ENDP

_PascalMain     PROC

        push    bp
```

```
              mov       bp,sp
; {24} n := 1
              mov       ax,1
              mov       WORD PTR n_030,ax
; {25} writeln('In simple, the value of n is', n:3)
              lea       ax,WORD PTR $S_044
              push      ax
              mov       ax,0
              push      ax
              mov       ax,28
              push      ax
              call      _WriteString
              add       sp,6
              mov       ax,WORD PTR n_030
              push      ax
              mov       ax,3
              push      ax
              call      _WriteInteger
              add       sp,4
              call      _WriteLine
; {26} proc(7, n)
              mov       ax,7
              push      ax
              lea       ax,WORD PTR n_030
              push      ax
              push      bp
              call      proc_032
; {27} writeln('In simple, the value of n is', n:3,
; ' and the value of x is', x:8:4)
              lea       ax,WORD PTR $S_044
              push      ax
              mov       ax,0
              push      ax
              mov       ax,28
              push      ax
              call      _WriteString
              add       sp,6
              mov       ax,WORD PTR n_030
              push      ax
              mov       ax,3
              push      ax
              call      _WriteInteger
              add       sp,4
              lea       ax,WORD PTR $S_047
              push      ax
              mov       ax,0
              push      ax
```

(continues)

```
            mov     ax,22
            push    ax
            call    _WriteString
            add     sp,6
            mov     ax,WORD PTR x_031
            mov     dx,WORD PTR x_031+2
            push    dx
            push    ax
            mov     ax,8
            push    ax
            mov     ax,4
            push    ax
            call    _WriteReal
            add     sp,8
            call    _WriteLine

            pop     bp
            ret

_PascalMain     ENDP

        .DATA

n_030   DW      0
x_031   DD      0.0
$F_042  DD      3.140000e+00
$F_038  DD      5.000000e-01
$S_047  DB      " and the value of x is"
$S_044  DB      "In simple, the value of n is"
$S_040  DB      "In proc, the value of j is"

        END
```

14

COMPILING

CONTROL

STATEMENTS

W e complete our compiler in this chapter, enabling it to compile entire Pascal
source programs. We'll implement the remaining TCodeGenerator member
functions in the back end that generate assembly language object code for:

- Pascal control statements.
- Calls to the standard procedures and functions.

Emitting Code for the Control Statements

Chapter 10 introduced code diagrams to show how the control statements' intermediate code is laid out for the interpreter. As we saw in the previous chapter, the
compiler's back end uses the same icode to generate the assembly object code, and
so we'll use the same code diagrams to show how the assembly code is emitted.
This time, we'll annotate the diagrams to show, as the code generator processes
each part of a control statement's icode, exactly what assembly code it emits.

■■■■■ **Figure 14.1** The final version of member function **EmitStatement** in
file **emitstmt.cpp**.

```cpp
void TCodeGenerator::EmitStatement(void)
{
    //--Emit the current statement as a comment.
    EmitStmtComment();

    switch (token) {

        case tcIdentifier: {
            if (pNode->defn.how == dcProcedure) {
                EmitSubroutineCall(pNode);
            }
            else {
                EmitAssignment(pNode);
            }
            break;
        }

        case tcREPEAT:    EmitREPEAT();        break;
        case tcWHILE:     EmitWHILE();         break;
        case tcFOR:       EmitFOR();           break;
        case tcIF:        EmitIF();            break;
        case tcCASE:      EmitCASE();          break;
        case tcBEGIN:     EmitCompound();      break;
    }
}
```

Figure 14.1 shows the final version of the implementation of member function
`TCodeGenerator::EmitStatement` in file `emitstmt.cpp`. It now can call the
appropriate member functions to emit code for the Pascal control statements. Figure
14.2 shows the implementations of these functions.

■■■■■ **Figure 14.2** Implementations of the member functions of class
TCodeGenerator that emit code for Pascal control statements, in file
emitstmt.cpp.

```cpp
//----------------------------------------------------------------
//  EmitREPEAT        Emit code for a REPEAT statement:
//
//                        REPEAT <stmt-list> UNTIL <expr>
//----------------------------------------------------------------

void TCodeGenerator::EmitREPEAT(void)
```

```
{
    int stmtListLabelIndex = ++asmLabelIndex;
    int followLabelIndex   = ++asmLabelIndex;

    EmitStatementLabel(stmtListLabelIndex);

    //--<stmt-list> UNTIL
    GetToken();
    EmitStatementList(tcUNTIL);

    EmitStmtComment();

    //--<expr>
    GetToken();
    EmitExpression();

    //--Decide whether or not to branch back to the loop start.
    Emit2(cmp, Reg(ax), IntegerLit(1));
    Emit1(je,  Label(STMT_LABEL_PREFIX, followLabelIndex));
    Emit1(jmp, Label(STMT_LABEL_PREFIX, stmtListLabelIndex));

    EmitStatementLabel(followLabelIndex);
}


//-------------------------------------------------------------
//  EmitWHILE       Emit code for a WHILE statement:
//
//                      WHILE <expr> DO <stmt>
//-------------------------------------------------------------

void TCodeGenerator::EmitWHILE(void)
{
    int exprLabelIndex   = ++asmLabelIndex;
    int stmtLabelIndex   = ++asmLabelIndex;
    int followLabelIndex = ++asmLabelIndex;

    GetToken();
    GetLocationMarker();     // ignored

    EmitStatementLabel(exprLabelIndex);

    //--<expr>
    GetToken();
    EmitExpression();

    Emit2(cmp, Reg(ax), IntegerLit(1));
```

(continues)

```
        Emit1(je,  Label(STMT_LABEL_PREFIX, stmtLabelIndex));
        Emit1(jmp, Label(STMT_LABEL_PREFIX, followLabelIndex));

        EmitStatementLabel(stmtLabelIndex);

        //--DO <stmt>
        GetToken();
        EmitStatement();

        Emit1(jmp, Label(STMT_LABEL_PREFIX, exprLabelIndex));
        EmitStatementLabel(followLabelIndex);
}

//----------------------------------------------------------------
//  EmitIF          Emit code for an IF statement:
//
//                      IF <expr> THEN <stmt-1>
//
//              or:
//
//                      IF <expr> THEN <stmt-1> ELSE <stmt-2>
//----------------------------------------------------------------

void TCodeGenerator::EmitIF(void)
{
    int trueLabelIndex  = ++asmLabelIndex;
    int falseLabelIndex = ++asmLabelIndex;

    GetToken();
    GetLocationMarker();     // ignored

    //--<expr>
    GetToken();
    EmitExpression();

    Emit2(cmp, Reg(ax), IntegerLit(1));
    Emit1(je,  Label(STMT_LABEL_PREFIX, trueLabelIndex));
    Emit1(jmp, Label(STMT_LABEL_PREFIX, falseLabelIndex));

    EmitStatementLabel(trueLabelIndex);

    StartComment("THEN");
```

```
        PutLine();

        //--THEN <stmt-1>
        GetToken();
        EmitStatement();

        if (token == tcELSE) {
            GetToken();
            GetLocationMarker();      // ignored

            int followLabelIndex = ++asmLabelIndex;
            Emit1(jmp, Label(STMT_LABEL_PREFIX, followLabelIndex));

            StartComment("ELSE");
            PutLine();

            EmitStatementLabel(falseLabelIndex);

            GetToken();
            EmitStatement();

            EmitStatementLabel(followLabelIndex);
        }
        else {
            EmitStatementLabel(falseLabelIndex);
        }
    }

    //-------------------------------------------------------------
    //  EmitFOR          Emit code for a FOR statement:
    //
    //                        FOR <id> := <expr-1> TO|DOWNTO <expr-2>
    //                            DO <stmt>
    //-------------------------------------------------------------

    void TCodeGenerator::EmitFOR(void)
    {
        int testLabelIndex      = ++asmLabelIndex;
        int stmtLabelIndex      = ++asmLabelIndex;
        int terminateLabelIndex = ++asmLabelIndex;

        GetToken();
        GetLocationMarker();     // ignored

        //--Get pointers to the control variable and to its type object.
        GetToken();
```

(continues)

■■■■■■■■ **Figure 14.2** Implementations of the member functions of class
TCodeGenerator that emit code for Pascal control statements, in file
emitstmt.cpp. (*Continued*)

```
TSymtabNode *pControlId   = pNode;
TType       *pControlType = pNode->pType;

int charFlag = (pControlType->Base() == pCharType);

//-- <id> := <expr-1>
EmitAssignment(pControlId);

//--TO or DOWNTO
int toFlag = token == tcTO;

EmitStatementLabel(testLabelIndex);

//--<expr-2>
GetToken();
EmitExpression();

if (charFlag) Emit2(cmp, Byte(pControlId), Reg(al))
else          Emit2(cmp, Word(pControlId), Reg(ax))
Emit1(toFlag ? jle : jge,
      Label(STMT_LABEL_PREFIX, stmtLabelIndex));
Emit1(jmp, Label(STMT_LABEL_PREFIX, terminateLabelIndex));

EmitStatementLabel(stmtLabelIndex);

//--DO <stmt>
GetToken();
EmitStatement();

Emit1(toFlag   ? incr : decr,
      charFlag ? Byte(pControlId) : Word(pControlId));
Emit1(jmp, Label(STMT_LABEL_PREFIX, testLabelIndex));

EmitStatementLabel(terminateLabelIndex);

Emit1(toFlag   ? decr : incr,
      charFlag ? Byte(pControlId) : Word(pControlId));
}

//-------------------------------------------------------------
//  EmitCASE        Emit code for a CASE statement:
//
```

```
//                         CASE <expr> OF
//                             <case-branch> ;
//                             ...
//                         END
//-----------------------------------------------------------------

void TCodeGenerator::EmitCASE(void)
{
    int i, j;
    int followLabelIndex = ++asmLabelIndex;

    struct TBranchEntry {
        int labelValue;
        int branchLocation;
        int labelIndex;
    } *pBranchTable;

    //--Get the locations of the token that follows the
    //--CASE statement and of the branch table.
    GetToken();
    int atFollow      = GetLocationMarker();
    GetToken();
    int atBranchTable = GetLocationMarker();

    //--<epxr>
    GetToken();
    TType *pExprType = EmitExpression();

    int labelValue, branchLocation;
    int charFlag = pExprType->Base() == pCharType;

    //--Loop through the branch table in the icode
    //--to count the number of entries.
    int count = 0;
    GoTo(atBranchTable + 1);
    for (;;) {
        GetCaseItem(labelValue, branchLocation);
        if (branchLocation == 0) break;
        else                        ++count;
    }

    //--Make a copy of the branch table.
    pBranchTable = new TBranchEntry[count];
    GoTo(atBranchTable + 1);
    for (i = 0; i < count; ++i) {
        GetCaseItem(labelValue, branchLocation);
```

(continues)

■■■■■■■ **Figure 14.2** Implementations of the member functions of class **TCodeGenerator** that emit code for Pascal control statements, in file **emitstmt.cpp**. (*Continued*)

```
        pBranchTable[i].labelValue    = labelValue;
        pBranchTable[i].branchLocation = branchLocation;
    }

    //--Loop through the branch table copy to emit test code.
    for (i = 0; i < count; ++i) {
        int testLabelIndex   = ++asmLabelIndex;
        int branchLabelIndex = ++asmLabelIndex;

        Emit2(cmp, charFlag ? Reg(al) : Reg(ax),
                   IntegerLit(pBranchTable[i].labelValue));
        Emit1(jne, Label(STMT_LABEL_PREFIX, testLabelIndex));

        //--See if the branch location is already in the branch table
        //--copy. If so, reuse the branch label index.
        for (j = 0; j < i; ++j) {
            if (pBranchTable[j].branchLocation ==
                                pBranchTable[i].branchLocation) {
                branchLabelIndex = pBranchTable[j].labelIndex;
                break;
            }
        }

        Emit1(jmp, Label(STMT_LABEL_PREFIX, branchLabelIndex));
        EmitStatementLabel(testLabelIndex);

        //--Enter the branch label index into the branch table copy
        //--only if it is new; otherwise, enter 0.
        pBranchTable[i].labelIndex = j < i ? 0 : branchLabelIndex;
    }
    Emit1(jmp, Label(STMT_LABEL_PREFIX, followLabelIndex));

    //--Loop through the branch table copy again to emit
    //--branch statement code that hasn't already been emitted.
    for (i = 0; i < count; ++i) if (pBranchTable[i].labelIndex) {
        GoTo(pBranchTable[i].branchLocation);
        EmitStatementLabel(pBranchTable[i].labelIndex);

        GetToken();
        EmitStatement();
        Emit1(jmp, Label(STMT_LABEL_PREFIX, followLabelIndex));
    }
```

```
        delete[] pBranchTable;

        GoTo(atFollow);
        GetToken();

        StartComment("END");
        PutLine();

        EmitStatementLabel(followLabelIndex);
}
```

REPEAT Statement

Figure 14.3 shows the code diagram for the REPEAT statement, which we first saw in Figure 10.1. This time, we annotate the diagram with two footnotes.

Footnote 1 indicates that after member function EmitREPEAT has processed the REPEAT token, it emits an assembly statement label to mark the beginning of the emitted code for the statement list. Since the label is composed with the value of the local variable stmtListLabelIndex, we show the label in the diagram as $L_*stmtList*.

After emitting the statement label, the function calls EmitStatementList to emit code for the statement list, and then after the UNTIL token, it calls EmitExpression to emit code for the expression. As indicated by footnote 2, after the expression code, EmitREPEAT emits code to test the expression's value and to branch either back to the beginning of the code for the statement list, or forward to the label $L_*follow*,

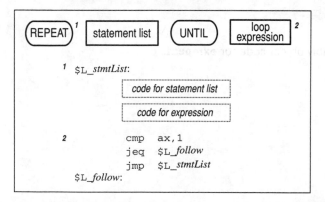

Figure 14.3 Annotated code diagram for the **REPEAT** statement.

which the function emits to mark the beginning of the emitted code for the following statement.

Note that two jump instructions follow the compare instruction, instead of the more straightforward:

```
cmp   ax,1              ; is it true?
jne   $L_stmtlist       ; not yet, so loop again
```

The reason is another idiosyncrasy of the 8086 machine architecture. The conditional jump instruction cannot jump 128 or more bytes, while the unconditional jump instruction can reach any location within the code segment. Thus, the above code won't do for the general case.

Figure 14.4 shows a short Pascal program containing a REPEAT statement, and Figure 14.5 shows the assembly object code.

Figure 14.4   Example Pascal program **exrepeat** containing a **REPEAT** statement.

```
PROGRAM exrepeat (output);

VAR
    i : integer;

BEGIN
    i := 10;
    REPEAT
        writeln(i);
        i := i - 1;
    UNTIL i <= 0;
END.
```

Figure 14.5   Assembly object code for **exrepeat**.

```
      DOSSEG
      .MODEL   small
      .STACK   1024

      .CODE

      PUBLIC _PascalMain
      INCLUDE pasextrn.inc

$STATIC_LINK    EQU      <WORD PTR [bp+4]>
```

```
$RETURN_VALUE          EQU     <WORD PTR [bp-4]>
$HIGH_RETURN VALUE     EQU     <WORD PTR [bp-2]>

; PROGRAM exrepeat (output)

; VAR
; i : integer

_PascalMain      PROC

        push    bp
        mov     bp,sp
; BEGIN
; {7} i := 10
        mov     ax,10
        mov     WORD PTR i_030,ax
; {8} REPEAT
$L_034:
; {9} writeln(i)
        mov     ax,WORD PTR i_030
        push    ax
        mov     ax,10
        push    ax
        call    _WriteInteger
        add     sp,4
        call    _WriteLine
; {10} i := i - 1
        mov     ax,WORD PTR i_030
        push    ax
        mov     ax,1
        pop     dx
        sub     dx,ax
        mov     ax,dx
        mov     WORD PTR i_030,ax
; {10} UNTIL i <= 0
        mov     ax,WORD PTR i_030
        push    ax
        mov     ax,0
        pop     dx
        cmp     dx,ax
        mov     ax,1
        jle     $L_036
        sub     ax,ax
$L_036:
        cmp     ax,1
        je      $L_035
```

(continues)

```
        jmp     $L_034
$L_035:
; END

        pop     bp
        ret

_PascalMain     ENDP

        .DATA

i_030   DW      0

        END
```

WHILE Statement

Figure 14.6 shows the annotated code diagram for the WHILE statement. Member function EmitWHILE emits three statement labels to mark the beginnings of the code for the expression, the code for the loop statement, and the code for the following statement. As above, both a conditional and an unconditional jump instruction are needed after the compare instruction. Note that the function ignores the location marker in the icode.

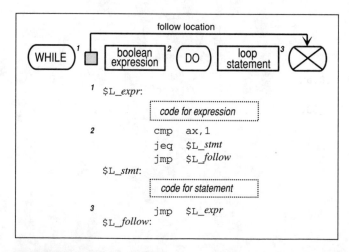

■■■■■■■ **Figure 14.6** Annotated code diagram for the **WHILE** statement.

Figure 14.7 shows a short Pascal program containing a WHILE statement, and Figure 14.8 shows the assembly object code.

▰▰▰▰▰▰▰▰ **Figure 14.7** Example Pascal program **exwhile** containing a **WHILE** statement.

```
PROGRAM exwhile (output);

VAR
    i : integer;

BEGIN
    i := 1;
    WHILE i <= 10 DO BEGIN
        writeln(i);
        i := i + 1;
    END;
END.
```

▰▰▰▰▰▰▰▰ **Figure 14.8** Assembly object code for **exwhile**.

```
        DOSSEG
        .MODEL  small
        .STACK  1024

        .CODE

        PUBLIC _PascalMain
        INCLUDE pasextrn.inc

$STATIC_LINK              EQU     <WORD PTR [bp+4]>
$RETURN_VALUE            EQU     <WORD PTR [bp-4]>
$HIGH_RETURN_VALUE       EQU     <WORD PTR [bp-2]>

; PROGRAM exwhile (output)

; VAR
; i : integer

_PascalMain     PROC

        push    bp
        mov     bp,sp
; BEGIN
; {7} i := 1
        mov     ax,1
```

(continues)

■■■■■■■ **Figure 14.8** Assembly object code for **exwhile**. (*Continued*)

```
        mov     WORD PTR i_030,ax
; {8} WHILE i <= 10 DO
$L_033:
        mov     ax,WORD PTR i_030
        push    ax
        mov     ax,10
        pop     dx
        cmp     dx,ax
        mov     ax,1
        jle     $L_036
        sub     ax,ax
$L_036:
        cmp     ax,1
        je      $L_034
        jmp     $L_035
$L_034:
; BEGIN
; {9} writeln(i)
        mov     ax,WORD PTR i_030
        push    ax
        mov     ax,10
        push    ax
        call    _WriteInteger
        add     sp,4
        call    _WriteLine
; {10} i := i + 1
        mov     ax,WORD PTR i_030
        push    ax
        mov     ax,1
        pop     dx
        add     ax,dx
        mov     WORD PTR i_030,ax
; END
        jmp     $L_033
$L_035:
; END


        pop     bp
        ret

_PascalMain     ENDP

        .DATA
```

```
i_030   DW      0

        END
```

IF Statement

Member function EmitIF emits code for an IF statement, either with or without an ELSE branch. Figure 14.9 shows the annotated code diagrams. If there is no ELSE branch, the function emits two statement labels, $L_*true* to mark the beginning of the code for the statement to execute if the expression is true, and $L_*false* to jump to if the expression is false. If there is an ELSE branch, EmitIF emits yet another statement label, $L_*follow*, to mark the beginning of the code for the following statement. The function also emits THEN and, if appropriate, ELSE assembly comments, and it ignores the location markers.

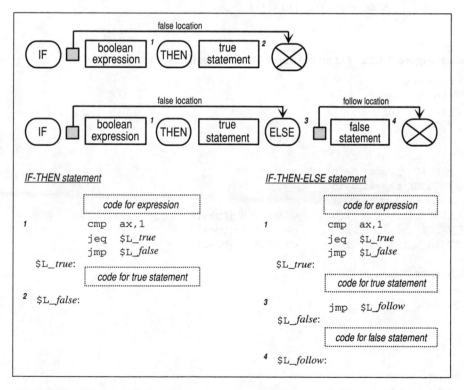

Figure 14.9 Annotated code diagrams for the **IF** statement.

Figure 14.10 shows a short Pascal program containing several IF statements, and Figure 14.11 shows the assembly object code.

■■■■■■■ **Figure 14.10** Example Pascal program **exif** containing **IF** statements.

```
PROGRAM exif (output);

CONST
    one = 1;
    two = 2;

BEGIN
    IF one <> two THEN writeln('true');
    IF one =  two THEN writeln('true');

    IF one <> two THEN writeln('true')
                  ELSE writeln('false');
    IF one =  two THEN writeln('true')
                  ELSE writeln('false');
END.
```

■■■■■■■ **Figure 14.11** Assembly object code for **exif**.

```
        DOSSEG
        .MODEL  small
        .STACK  1024

        .CODE

        PUBLIC  _PascalMain
        INCLUDE pasextrn.inc

$STATIC_LINK            EQU     <WORD PTR [bp+4]>
$RETURN_VALUE           EQU     <WORD PTR [bp-4]>
$HIGH_RETURN_VALUE      EQU     <WORD PTR [bp-2]>

; PROGRAM exif (output)

_PascalMain     PROC

        push    bp
        mov     bp,sp
; BEGIN
; {8} IF one <> two
        mov     ax,1
        push    ax
```

```
            mov     ax,2
            pop     dx
            cmp     dx,ax
            mov     ax,1
            jne     $L_036
            sub     ax,ax
$L_036:
            cmp     ax,1
            je      $L_034
            jmp     $L_035
$L_034:
; THEN
; {8} writeln('true')
            lea     ax,WORD PTR $S_032
            push    ax
            mov     ax,0
            push    ax
            mov     ax,4
            push    ax
            call    _WriteString
            add     sp,6
            call    _WriteLine
$L_035:
; {9} IF one = two
            mov     ax,1
            push    ax
            mov     ax,2
            pop     dx
            cmp     dx,ax
            mov     ax,1
            je      $L_039
            sub     ax,ax
$L_039:
            cmp     ax,1
            je      $L_037
            jmp     $L_038
$L_037:
; THEN
; {9} writeln('true')
            lea     ax,WORD PTR $S_032
            push    ax
            mov     ax,0
            push    ax
            mov     ax,4
            push    ax
            call    _WriteString
```

(continues)

■■■■■■ **Figure 14.11** Assembly object code for **exif**. (*Continued*)

```
        add     sp,6
        call    _WriteLine
$L_038:
; {11} IF one <> two
        mov     ax,1
        push    ax
        mov     ax,2
        pop     dx
        cmp     dx,ax
        mov     ax,1
        jne     $L_042
        sub     ax,ax
$L_042:
        cmp     ax,1
        je      $L_040
        jmp     $L_041
$L_040:
; THEN
; {11} writeln('true')
        lea     ax,WORD PTR $S_032
        push    ax
        mov     ax,0
        push    ax
        mov     ax,4
        push    ax
        call    _WriteString
        add     sp,6
        call    _WriteLine
        jmp     $L_043
; ELSE
$L_041:
; {12} writeln('false')
        lea     ax,WORD PTR $S_033
        push    ax
        mov     ax,0
        push    ax
        mov     ax,5
        push    ax
        call    _WriteString
        add     sp,6
        call    _WriteLine
$L_043:
; {13} IF one = two
        mov     ax,1
        push    ax
```

```
                mov     ax,2
                pop     dx
                cmp     dx,ax
                mov     ax,1
                je      $L_046
                sub     ax,ax
$L_046:
                cmp     ax,1
                je      $L_044
                jmp     $L_045
$L_044:
; THEN
; {13} writeln('true')
                lea     ax,WORD PTR $S_032
                push    ax
                mov     ax,0
                push    ax
                mov     ax,4
                push    ax
                call    _WriteString
                add     sp,6
                call    _WriteLine
                jmp     $L_047
; ELSE
$L_045:
; {14} writeln('false')
                lea     ax,WORD PTR $S_033
                push    ax
                mov     ax,0
                push    ax
                mov     ax,5
                push    ax
                call    _WriteString
                add     sp,6
                call    _WriteLine
$L_047:
; END


                pop     bp
                ret

_PascalMain     ENDP

                .DATA

$S_033  DB      "false"
```

(continues)

■■■■■■■ **Figure 14.11** Assembly object code for **exif**. (*Continued*)

```
$S_032   DB      "true"

         END
```

FOR Statement

Member function EmitFOR emits code for the FOR statement. It emits three statement labels, $L_*test*, $L_*stmt*, and $L_*terminate* to mark the beginning of the code for testing the value of the control variable, the beginning of the code for the loop statement, and the beginning of the termination code, respectively. Figure 14.12 shows the annotated code diagram. The location marker is ignored.

The function emits slightly different code for the TO and the DOWNTO cases. In the TO case, at footnote 3, it emits a jle instruction to jump to the beginning of the loop statement; in the DOWNTO case, it emits a jge instruction. At footnote 4, the function emits an inc instruction to increment the control variable in the TO case,

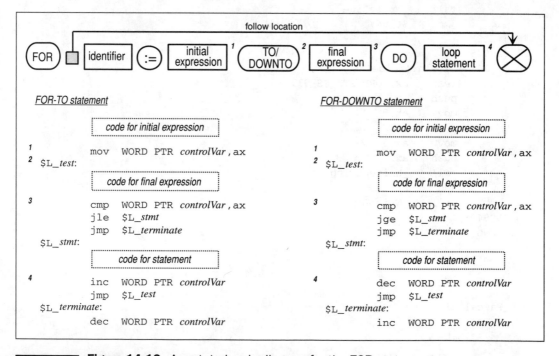

■■■■■■■ **Figure 14.12** Annotated code diagram for the **FOR** statement.

and a dec instruction to decrement the control variable in the DOWNTO case. The very last emitted instruction is executed upon completion of the FOR loop to adjust the control variable so that it has the final expression value: dec in the TO case and inc in the DOWNTO case.

Figure 14.13 shows a short Pascal program containing several FOR statements, and Figure 14.14 shows the assembly object code.

▬▬▬▬ Figure 14.13 Example Pascal program **exfor** containing **FOR** statements.

```
PROGRAM exfor (output);

VAR
    i  : integer;
    ch : char;

BEGIN
    FOR i := 1 TO 5 DO writeln('i = ', i:0);
    writeln;
    FOR i := 5 DOWNTO 1 DO writeln('i = ', i:0);
    writeln;
    FOR ch := 'a' TO 'e' DO writeln('ch = ', ch:0);
END.
```

▬▬▬▬ Figure 14.14 Assembly object code for **exfor**.

```
        DOSSEG
        .MODEL  small
        .STACK  1024


        .CODE

        PUBLIC  _PascalMain
        INCLUDE pasextrn.inc

$STATIC_LINK            EQU     <WORD PTR [bp+4]>
$RETURN_VALUE           EQU     <WORD PTR [bp-4]>
$HIGH_RETURN_VALUE      EQU     <WORD PTR [bp-2]>

; PROGRAM exfor (output)

; VAR
; i : integer
; ch : char
```

(continues)

■■■■■■■■ **Figure 14.14** Assembly object code for **exfor**. (*Continued*)

```
_PascalMain     PROC

        push    bp
        mov     bp,sp
; BEGIN
; {8} FOR i := 1 TO 5 DO
        mov     ax,1
        mov     WORD PTR i_030,ax
$L_039:
        mov     ax,5
        cmp     WORD PTR i_030,ax
        jle     $L_040
        jmp     $L_041
$L_040:
; {8} writeln('i = ', i:0)
        lea     ax,WORD PTR $S_034
        push    ax
        mov     ax,0
        push    ax
        mov     ax,4
        push    ax
        call    _WriteString
        add     sp,6
        mov     ax,WORD PTR i_030
        push    ax
        mov     ax,0
        push    ax
        call    _WriteInteger
        add     sp,4
        call    _WriteLine
        inc     WORD PTR i_030
        jmp     $L_039
$L_041:
        dec     WORD PTR i_030
; {9} writeln
        call    _WriteLine
; {10} FOR i := 5 DOWNTO 1 DO
        mov     ax,5
        mov     WORD PTR i_030,ax
$L_042:
        mov     ax,1
        cmp     WORD PTR i_030,ax
        jge     $L_043
        jmp     $L_044
```

```
$L_043:
; {10} writeln('i = ', i:0)
        lea     ax,WORD PTR $S_034
        push    ax
        mov     ax,0
        push    ax
        mov     ax,4
        push    ax
        call    _WriteString
        add     sp,6
        mov     ax,WORD PTR i_030
        push    ax
        mov     ax,0
        push    ax
        call    _WriteInteger
        add     sp,4
        call    _WriteLine
        dec     WORD PTR i_030
        jmp     $L_042
$L_044:
        inc     WORD PTR i_030
; {11} writeln
        call    _WriteLine
; {12} FOR ch := 'a' TO 'e' DO
        mov     ax,'a'
        mov     BYTE PTR ch_031,al
$L_045:
        mov     ax,'e'
        cmp     BYTE PTR ch_031,al
        jle     $L_046
        jmp     $L_047
$L_046:
; {12} writeln('ch = ', ch:0)
        lea     ax,WORD PTR $S_038
        push    ax
        mov     ax,0
        push    ax
        mov     ax,5
        push    ax
        call    _WriteString
        add     sp,6
        sub     ax,ax
        mov     al,BYTE PTR ch_031
        push    ax
        mov     ax,0
        push    ax
```

(continues)

Figure 14.14 Assembly object code for **exfor**. (*Continued*)

```
        call    _WriteChar
        add     sp,4
        call    _WriteLine
        inc     BYTE PTR ch_031
        jmp     $L_045
$L_047:
        dec     BYTE PTR ch_031
; END

        pop     bp
        ret

_PascalMain     ENDP

        .DATA

i_030   DW      0
ch_031  DB      0
$S_038  DB      "ch = "
$S_034  DB      "i = "

        END
```

CASE Statement

Member function EmitCASE, unlike the others, *does* make use of the location markers in the icode. Figure 14.15 shows the annotated syntax diagram. Besides the $L_*follow* statement label to mark the beginning of the code for the following statement, the function emits assembly statement labels marking each test of the CASE expression's value and the beginning of the code for each CASE branch statement.

The function uses the branch table both to generate code for the value tests and for the branch statements. Because it needs to enter the assembly label index for each branch statement into the table, it makes and uses a copy of the original table, which it obtains using the location marker. For each entry in the table, it emits the compare instruction cmp for the label value followed by two jump instructions. The conditional jne instruction jumps to the next test, and the unconditional jmp instruction jumps to the code for the corresponding branch statement. After the test for the final value, the function emits a jmp to the following statement.

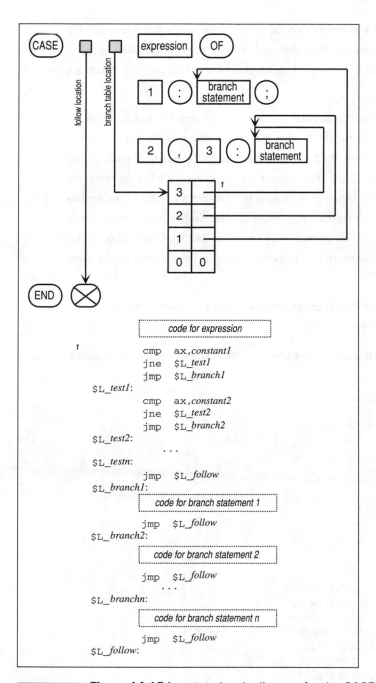

Figure 14.15 Annotated code diagram for the **CASE** statement.

The function also assigns and enters into the table the assembly statement label index for each branch statement. If several table entries refer to the same branch statement, the function enters the label index only into the first entry; it enters a zero into the other entries.

After emitting the test instructions, EmitCASE loops through the branch table again, this time to emit code for the branch statements. It emits the appropriate statement label before the code for each statement, and afterwards, it emits a jump to the following statement. (Note that when it was emitting code for the tests, the function in effect reserved a block of statement label indexes for the branch statements.) After the last branch statement, it emits an END assembly comment. Since the function looks only for table entries with a nonzero branch label index, it emits code for each branch statement only once, even if several entries refer to the same statement.

Figure 14.16 shows a short Pascal program containing a CASE statement, and Figure 14.17 shows the assembly object code.

■■■■■■■ **Figure 14.16** Example Pascal program **excase** containing a **CASE** statement.

```
PROGRAM excase (output);

CONST
    six = 6;

VAR
    i  : integer;
    ch : char;

BEGIN
    FOR i := 1 TO 9 DO BEGIN
        write(i, ' : ');
        CASE i OF
            1:       writeln('one');
            2:       writeln('two');
            3:       writeln('three');
            5,7,4:   writeln('four, five, or seven');
            six:     writeln('six');
            8:       writeln('eight');
            9:       writeln('nine');
        END;
```

```
        END;
END.
```

▬▬▬▬▬▬▬ **Figure 14.17** Assembly object code for **excase**.

```
        DOSSEG
        .MODEL   small
        .STACK   1024

        .CODE

        PUBLIC  _PascalMain
        INCLUDE pasextrn.inc

$STATIC_LINK             EQU        <WORD PTR [bp+4]>
$RETURN_VALUE            EQU        <WORD PTR [bp-4]>
$HIGH_RETURN_VALUE       EQU        <WORD PTR [bp-2]>

; PROGRAM excase (output)

; VAR
; i : integer
; ch : char

_PascalMain       PROC

        push      bp
        mov       bp,sp
; BEGIN
; {11} FOR i := 1 TO 9 DO
        mov       ax,1
        mov       WORD PTR i_031,ax
$L_049:
        mov       ax,9
        cmp       WORD PTR i_031,ax
        jle       $L_050
        jmp       $L_051
$L_050:
; BEGIN
; {12} write(i, ' : ')
        mov       ax,WORD PTR i_031
        push      ax
        mov       ax,10
        push      ax
        call      _WriteInteger
        add       sp,4
```

(continues)

■■■■ **Figure 14.17** Assembly object code for **excase**. (*Continued*)

```
        lea     ax,WORD PTR $S_035
        push    ax
        mov     ax,0
        push    ax
        mov     ax,3
        push    ax
        call    _WriteString
        add     sp,6
; {13} CASE i OF
        mov     ax,WORD PTR i_031
        cmp     ax,9
        jne     $L_053
        jmp     $L_054
$L_053:
        cmp     ax,8
        jne     $L_055
        jmp     $L_056
$L_055:
        cmp     ax,6
        jne     $L_057
        jmp     $L_058
$L_057:
        cmp     ax,4
        jne     $L_059
        jmp     $L_060
$L_059:
        cmp     ax,7
        jne     $L_061
        jmp     $L_060
$L_061:
        cmp     ax,5
        jne     $L_063
        jmp     $L_060
$L_063:
        cmp     ax,3
        jne     $L_065
        jmp     $L_066
$L_065:
        cmp     ax,2
        jne     $L_067
        jmp     $L_068
$L_067:
        cmp     ax,1
        jne     $L_069
```

```
        jmp     $L_070
$L_069:
        jmp     $L_052
$L_054:
; {20} writeln('nine')
        lea     ax,WORD PTR $S_048
        push    ax
        mov     ax,0
        push    ax
        mov     ax,4
        push    ax
        call    _WriteString
        add     sp,6
        call    _WriteLine
        jmp     $L_052
$L_056:
; {19} writeln('eight')
        lea     ax,WORD PTR $S_047
        push    ax
        mov     ax,0
        push    ax
        mov     ax,5
        push    ax
        call    _WriteString
        add     sp,6
        call    _WriteLine
        jmp     $L_052
$L_058:
; {18} writeln('six')
        lea     ax,WORD PTR $S_045
        push    ax
        mov     ax,0
        push    ax
        mov     ax,3
        push    ax
        call    _WriteString
        add     sp,6
        call    _WriteLine
        jmp     $L_052
$L_060:
; {17} writeln('four, five, or seven')
        lea     ax,WORD PTR $S_044
        push    ax
        mov     ax,0
        push    ax
        mov     ax,20
```

(continues)

■■■■■■■■ **Figure 14.17** Assembly object code for **excase**. (*Continued*)

```
        push    ax
        call    _WriteString
        add     sp,6
        call    _WriteLine
        jmp     $L_052
$L_066:
; {16} writeln('three')
        lea     ax,WORD PTR $S_040
        push    ax
        mov     ax,0
        push    ax
        mov     ax,5
        push    ax
        call    _WriteString
        add     sp,6
        call    _WriteLine
        jmp     $L_052
$L_068:
; {15} writeln('two')
        lea     ax,WORD PTR $S_038
        push    ax
        mov     ax,0
        push    ax
        mov     ax,3
        push    ax
        call    _WriteString
        add     sp,6
        call    _WriteLine
        jmp     $L_052
$L_070:
; {14} writeln('one')
        lea     ax,WORD PTR $S_036
        push    ax
        mov     ax,0
        push    ax
        mov     ax,3
        push    ax
        call    _WriteString
        add     sp,6
        call    _WriteLine
        jmp     $L_052
; END
$L_052:
; END
```

```
        inc     WORD PTR i_031
        jmp     $L_049
$L_051:
        dec     WORD PTR i_031
; END

        pop     bp
        ret


_PascalMain     ENDP

        .DATA

i_031   DW      0
ch_032  DB      0
$S_036  DB      "one"
$S_038  DB      "two"
$S_040  DB      "three"
$S_044  DB      "four, five, or seven"
$S_045  DB      "six"
$S_047  DB      "eight"
$S_048  DB      "nine"
$S_035  DB      " : "

        END
```

Calling the Standard Procedures and Functions

Figure 14.18 shows the final version of member function `TCodeGenerator::‐EmitStandardSubroutineCall` in implementation file `emitstd.cpp`. This version now calls other member functions to emit code to call the standard procedures and functions.

▬▬▬▬ **Figure 14.18** Final version of member function **EmitStandardSubroutineCall** in file **emitstd.cpp**.

```
//------------------------------------------------------------
//  EmitStandardSubroutineCall   Emit code for a call to a
//                               standard procedure or function.
//
//      pRoutineId : ptr to the subroutine name's symtab node
//
```

(continues)

Figure 14.18 Final version of member function
EmitStandardSubroutineCall in file **emitstd.cpp**. (*Continued*)

```
//  Return: ptr to the call's type object
//--------------------------------------------------------------

TType *TCodeGenerator::EmitStandardSubroutineCall
                            (const TSymtabNode *pRoutineId)
{
    switch (pRoutineId->defn.routine.which) {

        case rcRead:
        case rcReadln:    return EmitReadReadlnCall(pRoutineId);

        case rcWrite:
        case rcWriteln:   return EmitWriteWritelnCall(pRoutineId);

        case rcEof:
        case rcEoln:      return EmitEofEolnCall(pRoutineId);

        case rcAbs:
        case rcSqr:       return EmitAbsSqrCall(pRoutineId);

        case rcArctan:
        case rcCos:
        case rcExp:
        case rcLn:
        case rcSin:
        case rcSqrt:      return EmitArctanCosExpLnSinSqrtCall
                                                    (pRoutineId);

        case rcPred:
        case rcSucc:      return EmitPredSuccCall(pRoutineId);

        case rcChr:       return EmitChrCall();
        case rcOdd:       return EmitOddCall();
        case rcOrd:       return EmitOrdCall();

        case rcRound:
        case rcTrunc:     return EmitRoundTruncCall(pRoutineId);

        default:          return pDummyType;
    }
}
```

Figure 14.19 shows member function `EmitReadReadlnCall`. It loops over each parameter, emitting code to read the parameter's value. It calls `EmitVariable` to emit code that leaves the address of the parameter on top of the stack, and then it emits a call to the runtime library routine `_ReadInteger`, `_ReadChar`, or `_ReadReal`, according to the type of the parameter. The library routine reads the value and leaves it in register AX or in the DX:AX register pair. `EmitReadReadlnCall` then emits the appropriate `pop` and `mov` instructions to set the value into the parameter. Finally, after all the parameters have been processed, if the call was to `readln`, the function emits a call to the library routine `_ReadLine`.

For example, to read the value of a real parameter x, the function emits:

```
lea   ax,WORD PTR x_077
push  ax                    ; push parameter address
call  _ReadReal             ; DX:AX = real value
pop   bx                    ; BX = parameter address
mov   WORD PTR[bx],ax
mov   WORD PTR[bx+2],dx      ; parameter = value
```

■■■■■■■ **Figure 14.19** Member function **EmitReadReadlnCall** in file **emitstd.cpp**.

```
//------------------------------------------------------------
//  EmitReadReadlnCall          Emit code for a call to read or
//                              readln.
//
//  Return: ptr to the dummy type object
//------------------------------------------------------------

TType *TCodeGenerator::EmitReadReadlnCall(const TSymtabNode *pRoutineId)
{
    //--Actual parameters are optional for readln.
    GetToken();
    if (token == tcLParen) {

        //--Loop to emit code to read each parameter value.
        do {
            //--Variable
            GetToken();
            TSymtabNode *pVarId   = pNode;
            TType       *pVarType = EmitVariable(pVarId, true)->Base();

            //--Read the value.
            if (pVarType == pIntegerType) {
                                                        (continues)
```

Figure 14.19 Member function **EmitReadReadlnCall** in file **emitstd.cpp**.
(*Continued*)

```
            Emit1(call, NameLit(READ_INTEGER));
            Emit1(pop,  Reg(bx));
            Emit2(mov,  WordIndirect(bx), Reg(ax));
        }
        else if (pVarType == pRealType) {
            Emit1(call, NameLit(READ_REAL));
            Emit1(pop,  Reg(bx));
            Emit2(mov,  WordIndirect(bx), Reg(ax));
            Emit2(mov,  HighDWordIndirect(bx), Reg(dx));
        }
        else if (pVarType == pCharType) {
            Emit1(call, NameLit(READ_CHAR));
            Emit1(pop,  Reg(bx));
            Emit2(mov,  ByteIndirect(bx), Reg(al));
        }
    } while (token == tcComma);

    GetToken();  // token after )
}

//--Skip the rest of the input line if readln.
if (pRoutineId->defn.routine.which == rcReadln) {
    Emit1(call, NameLit(READ_LINE));
}

return pDummyType;
}
```

Figure 14.20 shows the remaining member functions implemented in
emitstd.cpp. Member function EmitEofEolnCall emits a call either to
_StdEof or to _StdEoln. Each of the other member functions first calls EmitEx-
pression to emit code that evaluates the actual parameter expression, and then it
emits the appropriate instructions to operate on the expression value in register AX
or the DX:AX register pair.

Figure 14.20 The remaining member functions in file **emitstd.cpp**.

```
//----------------------------------------------------------------
//  EmitEofEolnCall            Emit code for a call to eof or eoln.
//
//  Return: ptr to the boolean type object
//----------------------------------------------------------------
```

```
TType *TCodeGenerator::EmitEofEolnCall(const TSymtabNode *pRoutineId)
{
    Emit1(call, NameLit(pRoutineId->defn.routine.which == rcEof
                            ? STD_EOF
                            : STD_EOLN));

    GetToken();   // token after function name
    return pBooleanType;
}

//---------------------------------------------------------------
//  EmitAbsSqrCall            Emit code for a call to abs or sqr.
//
//  Return: ptr to the result's type object
//---------------------------------------------------------------

TType *TCodeGenerator::EmitAbsSqrCall(const TSymtabNode *pRoutineId)
{
    GetToken();   // (
    GetToken();

    TType *pParmType = EmitExpression()->Base();

    switch (pRoutineId->defn.routine.which) {

        case rcAbs:
            if (pParmType == pIntegerType) {
                int nonNegativeLabelIndex = ++asmLabelIndex;

                Emit2(cmp, Reg(ax), IntegerLit(0));
                Emit1(jge,
                        Label(STMT_LABEL_PREFIX, nonNegativeLabelIndex));
                Emit1(neg, Reg(ax));

                EmitStatementLabel(nonNegativeLabelIndex);
            }
            else {
                EmitPushOperand(pParmType);
                Emit1(call, NameLit(STD_ABS));
                Emit2(add,  Reg(sp), IntegerLit(4));
            }
            break;

        case rcSqr:
            if (pParmType == pIntegerType) {
                Emit2(mov,  Reg(dx), Reg(ax));
```

(continues)

Figure 14.20 The remaining member functions in file **emitstd.cpp**.
(*Continued*)

```
                    Emit1(imul, Reg(dx));
                }
                else {
                    EmitPushOperand(pParmType);
                    EmitPushOperand(pParmType);
                    Emit1(call, NameLit(FLOAT_MULTIPLY));
                    Emit2(add,  Reg(sp), IntegerLit(8));
                }
                break;
            }

    GetToken();  // token after )
    return pParmType;
}


//--------------------------------------------------------------
//  EmitArctanCosExpLnSinSqrtCall      Emit code for a call to
//                                     arctan, cos, exp, ln,
//                                     sin, or sqrt.
//
//  Return: ptr to the real type object
//--------------------------------------------------------------

TType *TCodeGenerator::EmitArctanCosExpLnSinSqrtCall
                                    (const TSymtabNode *pRoutineId)
{
    char *stdFuncName;

    GetToken();  // (
    GetToken();

    //--Evaluate the parameter, and convert an integer value to
    //--real if necessary.
    TType *pParmType = EmitExpression()->Base();
    if (pParmType == pIntegerType) {
        Emit1(push, Reg(ax));
        Emit1(call, NameLit(FLOAT_CONVERT));
        Emit2(add,  Reg(sp), IntegerLit(2));
    }

    EmitPushOperand(pRealType);

    switch (pRoutineId->defn.routine.which) {
```

```
            case rcArctan:   stdFuncName = STD_ARCTAN;   break;
            case rcCos:      stdFuncName = STD_COS;       break;
            case rcExp:      stdFuncName = STD_EXP;       break;
            case rcLn:       stdFuncName = STD_LN;        break;
            case rcSin:      stdFuncName = STD_SIN;       break;
            case rcSqrt:     stdFuncName = STD_SQRT;      break;
    }

    Emit1(call, NameLit(stdFuncName));
    Emit2(add,  Reg(sp), IntegerLit(4));

    GetToken();   // token after )
    return pRealType;
}

//----------------------------------------------------------------
//  EmitPredSuccCall            Emit code for a call to pred
//                              or succ.
//
//  Return: ptr to the result's type object
//----------------------------------------------------------------

TType *TCodeGenerator::EmitPredSuccCall(const TSymtabNode *pRoutineId)
{
    GetToken();   // (
    GetToken();

    TType *pParmType = EmitExpression();

    Emit1(pRoutineId->defn.routine.which == rcPred ? decr : incr,
          Reg(ax));

    GetToken();   // token after )
    return pParmType;
}

//----------------------------------------------------------------
//  EmitChrCall                 Emit code for a call to chr.
//
//  Return: ptr to the character type object
//----------------------------------------------------------------

TType *TCodeGenerator::EmitChrCall(void)
{
    GetToken();   // (
    GetToken();
```

(continues)

■■■■■■■ **Figure 14.20** The remaining member functions in file **emitstd.cpp**.
(*Continued*)

```
    EmitExpression();

    GetToken();  // token after )
    return pCharType;
}


//--------------------------------------------------------------
//  EmitOddCall                    Emit code for a call to odd.
//
//  Return: ptr to the boolean type object
//--------------------------------------------------------------

TType *TCodeGenerator::EmitOddCall(void)
{
    GetToken();  // (
    GetToken();
    EmitExpression();

    Emit2(and, Reg(ax), IntegerLit(1));

    GetToken();  // token after )
    return pBooleanType;
}


//--------------------------------------------------------------
//  EmitOrdCall                    Emit code for a call to ord.
//
//  Return: ptr to the integer type object
//--------------------------------------------------------------

TType *TCodeGenerator::EmitOrdCall(void)
{
    GetToken();  // (
    GetToken();
    EmitExpression();

    GetToken();  // token after )
    return pIntegerType;
}


//--------------------------------------------------------------
//  EmitRoundTruncCall             Emit code for a call to round
//                                 or trunc.
```

```
//
//  Return: ptr to the integer type object
//-----------------------------------------------------------

TType *TCodeGenerator::EmitRoundTruncCall(const TSymtabNode *pRoutineId)
{
    GetToken();  // (
    GetToken();
    EmitExpression();

    EmitPushOperand(pRealType);
    Emit1(call, NameLit(pRoutineId->defn.routine.which == rcRound
                        ? STD_ROUND : STD_TRUNC));
    Emit2(add, Reg(sp), IntegerLit(4));

    GetToken();  // token after )
    return pIntegerType;
}
```

Member function `EmitAbsSqrCall` emits inline code for an integer parameter value. For abs, it emits:

```
        cmp   ax, 0          ; is it negative?
        jge   $L_nonNegative ; no
        neg   ax             ; yes, so negate it
    $L_nonNegative:
```

and for sqr, it emits:

```
    mov   dx, ax
    imul  dx, dx                     ; AX = AX*AX
```

If the parameter value is real, then for abs, `EmitAbsSqrCall` emits:

```
    push dx
    push ax                  ; push real value
    call _StdAbs             ; DX:AX = abs(real value)
    add  sp, 4
```

and for sqr:

```
    push dx
    push ax                  ; push real value
    push dx
    push ax                  ; push again
    call _FloatMultiply      ; DX:AX = value*value
    add  sp, 8
```

Member function `EmitArctanCosExpLnSinSqrtCall` first emits a call to `_FloatConvert` if necessary to convert an integer parameter value to real. It then emits a call to the appropriate runtime library routine `_StdArctan`, `_StdCos`, `_StdExp`, `_StdLn`, `_StdSin`, or `_StdSqrt`.

Member function `EmitPredSuccCall` emits either an `inc` or a `dec` instruction to add 1 to, or subtract 1 from, the integer value in register AX. Member functions `EmitChrCall` and `EmitOrdCall` only call `EmitExpression` and do not emit any more instructions, since the Pascal functions `chr` and `ord` do not change the expression value. Member function `EmitOddCall` simply emits inline:

```
and  ax,1
```

which leaves either 1 (true) or 0 (false) in register AX, depending on whether or not the expression value was odd. Finally, member function `EmitRoundTruncCall` emits a call either to `_StdRound` or to `_StdTrunc`.

Program 14-1: Pascal Compiler

Figure 14.21 shows the main file of the compiler. Table 14.1 shows that we only modified files `emitstmt.cpp` and `emitstd.cpp` from the previous chapter.

■■■■■■■ **Figure 14.21** The main file of the compiler.

```
//  ****************************************************************
//  *                                                              *
//  *    Program 14-1: Compiler                                    *
//  *                                                              *
//  *    Compile a Pascal program into assembly code.              *
//  *                                                              *
//  *    FILE:    prog14-1/compile.cpp                             *
//  *                                                              *
//  *    USAGE:   compile <source file> <assembly file>            *
//  *                                                              *
//  *                 <source file>    name of the source file     *
//  *                 <assembly file>  name of the assembly        *
//  *                                  language output file         *
//  *                                                              *
//  *    Copyright (c) 1996 by Ronald Mak                          *
//  *    For instructional purposes only.  No warranties.          *
//  *                                                              *
//  ****************************************************************
```

```cpp
#include <iostream.h>
#include "common.h"
#include "error.h"
#include "buffer.h"
#include "symtab.h"
#include "parser.h"
#include "backend.h"
#include "codegen.h"

//--------------------------------------------------------------
//  main
//--------------------------------------------------------------

void main(int argc, char *argv[])
{
    extern int execFlag;

    //--Check the command line arguments.
    if (argc != 3) {
        cerr << "Usage: compile <source file> <asssembly file>" << endl;
        AbortTranslation(abortInvalidCommandLineArgs);
    }

    execFlag = false;

    //--Create the parser for the source file,
    //--and then parse the file.
    TParser     *pParser   = new TParser(new TSourceBuffer(argv[1]));
    TSymtabNode *pProgramId = pParser->Parse();
    delete pParser;

    //--If there were no syntax errors, convert the symbol tables,
    //--and create and invoke the backend code generator.
    if (errorCount == 0) {
        vpSymtabs = new TSymtab *[cntSymtabs];
        for (TSymtab *pSt = pSymtabList; pSt; pSt = pSt->Next()) {
            pSt->Convert(vpSymtabs);
        }

        TBackend *pBackend = new TCodeGenerator(argv[2]);
        pBackend->Go(pProgramId);

        delete[] vpSymtabs;
        delete   pBackend;
    }
}
```

Figure 14.22 shows a sample Pascal program, and Figure 14.23 shows the assembly object code generated by the compiler.

■■■■■■■■■■ Figure 14.22 Sample Pascal program **newton**.

```
PROGRAM newton (input, output);

CONST
    epsilon = 1e-6;

VAR
    number, root, sqroot : real;

BEGIN
    REPEAT
        writeln;
        write('Enter new number (0 to quit): ');
        read(number);

        IF number = 0 THEN BEGIN
            writeln(number:12:6, 0.0:12:6);
        END
        ELSE IF number < 0 THEN BEGIN
            writeln('*** ERROR:  number < 0');
        END
        ELSE BEGIN
            sqroot := sqrt(number);
            writeln(number:12:6, sqroot:12:6);
            writeln;

            root := 1;
            REPEAT
                root := (number/root + root)/2;
                writeln(root:24:6,
                        100*abs(root - sqroot)/sqroot:12:2,
                        '%')
            UNTIL abs(number/sqr(root) - 1) < epsilon;
        END
    UNTIL number = 0
END.
```

■■■■■■■■■ Figure 14.23 Assembly object file for program **newton**.

```
        DOSSEG
        .MODEL  small
        .STACK  1024
```

```
                .CODE

                PUBLIC  _PascalMain
                INCLUDE pasextrn.inc

$STATIC_LINK             EQU       <WORD PTR [bp+4]>
$RETURN_VALUE            EQU       <WORD PTR [bp-4]>
$HIGH_RETURN_VALUE       EQU       <WORD PTR [bp-2]>

; PROGRAM newton (input, output)

; VAR
; number, root, sqroot : real

_PascalMain      PROC

        push    bp
        mov     bp,sp
; BEGIN
; {10} REPEAT
$L_046:
; {11} writeln
        call    _WriteLine
; {12} write('Enter new number (0 to quit): ')
        lea     ax,WORD PTR $S_035
        push    ax
        mov     ax,0
        push    ax
        mov     ax,30
        push    ax
        call    _WriteString
        add     sp,6
; {13} read(number)
        lea     ax,WORD PTR number_032
        push    ax
        call    _ReadReal
        pop     bx
        mov     WORD PTR [bx],ax
        mov     WORD PTR [bx+2],dx
; {15} IF number = 0
        mov     ax,WORD PTR number_032
        mov     dx,WORD PTR number_032+2
        push    dx
        push    ax
        mov     ax,0
        push    ax
```

(continues)

```
        call    _FloatConvert
        add     sp,2
        push    dx
        push    ax
        call    _FloatCompare
        add     sp,8
        cmp     ax,0
        mov     ax,1
        je      $L_050
        sub     ax,ax
$L_050:
        cmp     ax,1
        je      $L_048
        jmp     $L_049
$L_048:
; THEN
; BEGIN
; {16} writeln(number:12:6, 0.0:12:6)
        mov     ax,WORD PTR number_032
        mov     dx,WORD PTR number_032+2
        push    dx
        push    ax
        mov     ax,12
        push    ax
        mov     ax,6
        push    ax
        call    _WriteReal
        add     sp,8
        mov     ax,WORD PTR $F_039
        mov     dx,WORD PTR $F_039+2
        push    dx
        push    ax
        mov     ax,12
        push    ax
        mov     ax,6
        push    ax
        call    _WriteReal
        add     sp,8
        call    _WriteLine
; END
        jmp     $L_051
; ELSE
$L_049:
; {18} IF number < 0
```

```
        mov     ax,WORD PTR number_032
        mov     dx,WORD PTR number_032+2
        push    dx
        push    ax
        mov     ax,0
        push    ax
        call    _FloatConvert
        add     sp,2
        push    dx
        push    ax
        call    _FloatCompare
        add     sp,8
        cmp     ax,0
        mov     ax,1
        jl      $L_054
        sub     ax,ax
$L_054:
        cmp     ax,1
        je      $L_052
        jmp     $L_053
$L_052:
; THEN
; BEGIN
; {19} writeln('*** ERROR:  number < 0')
        lea     ax,WORD PTR $S_040
        push    ax
        mov     ax,0
        push    ax
        mov     ax,22
        push    ax
        call    _WriteString
        add     sp,6
        call    _WriteLine
; END
        jmp     $L_055
; ELSE
$L_053:
; BEGIN
; {22} sqroot := sqrt(number)
        mov     ax,WORD PTR number_032
        mov     dx,WORD PTR number_032+2
        push    dx
        push    ax
        call    _StdSqrt
        add     sp,4
        mov     WORD PTR sqroot_034,ax
```

(continues)

```
        mov     WORD PTR sqroot_034+2,dx
; {23} writeln(number:12:6, sqroot:12:6)
        mov     ax,WORD PTR number_032
        mov     dx,WORD PTR number_032+2
        push    dx
        push    ax
        mov     ax,12
        push    ax
        mov     ax,6
        push    ax
        call    _WriteReal
        add     sp,8
        mov     ax,WORD PTR sqroot_034
        mov     dx,WORD PTR sqroot_034+2
        push    dx
        push    ax
        mov     ax,12
        push    ax
        mov     ax,6
        push    ax
        call    _WriteReal
        add     sp,8
        call    _WriteLine
; {24} writeln
        call    _WriteLine
; {26} root := 1
        mov     ax,1
        push    ax
        call    _FloatConvert
        add     sp,2
        mov     WORD PTR root_033,ax
        mov     WORD PTR root_033+2,dx
; {27} REPEAT
$L_056:
; {28} root := (number/root + root)/2
        mov     ax,WORD PTR number_032
        mov     dx,WORD PTR number_032+2
        push    dx
        push    ax
        mov     ax,WORD PTR root_033
        mov     dx,WORD PTR root_033+2
        push    dx
        push    ax
        call    _FloatDivide
```

```
        add     sp,8
        push    dx
        push    ax
        mov     ax,WORD PTR root_033
        mov     dx,WORD PTR root_033+2
        push    dx
        push    ax
        call    _FloatAdd
        add     sp,8
        push    dx
        push    ax
        mov     ax,2
        push    ax
        call    _FloatConvert
        add     sp,2
        push    dx
        push    ax
        call    _FloatDivide
        add     sp,8
        mov     WORD PTR root_033,ax
        mov     WORD PTR root_033+2,dx
; {29} writeln(root:24:6, 100*abs(root - sqroot)/sqroot:12:2, '%')
        mov     ax,WORD PTR root_033
        mov     dx,WORD PTR root_033+2
        push    dx
        push    ax
        mov     ax,24
        push    ax
        mov     ax,6
        push    ax
        call    _WriteReal
        add     sp,8
        mov     ax,100
        push    ax
        mov     ax,WORD PTR root_033
        mov     dx,WORD PTR root_033+2
        push    dx
        push    ax
        mov     ax,WORD PTR sqroot_034
        mov     dx,WORD PTR sqroot_034+2
        push    dx
        push    ax
        call    _FloatSubtract
        add     sp,8
        push    dx
        push    ax
```

(continues)

```
        call    _StdAbs
        add     sp,4
        push    dx
        push    ax
        pop     ax
        pop     dx
        pop     bx
        push    dx
        push    ax
        push    bx
        call    _FloatConvert
        add     sp,2
        pop     bx
        pop     cx
        push    dx
        push    ax
        push    cx
        push    bx
        call    _FloatMultiply
        add     sp,8
        push    dx
        push    ax
        mov     ax,WORD PTR sqroot_034
        mov     dx,WORD PTR sqroot_034+2
        push    dx
        push    ax
        call    _FloatDivide
        add     sp,8
        push    dx
        push    ax
        mov     ax,12
        push    ax
        mov     ax,2
        push    ax
        call    _WriteReal
        add     sp,8
        mov     ax,'%'
        push    ax
        mov     ax,0
        push    ax
        call    _WriteChar
        add     sp,4
        call    _WriteLine
; {29} UNTIL abs(number/sqr(root) - 1) < epsilon
```

```
        mov     ax,WORD PTR number_032
        mov     dx,WORD PTR number_032+2
        push    dx
        push    ax
        mov     ax,WORD PTR root_033
        mov     dx,WORD PTR root_033+2
        push    dx
        push    ax
        push    dx
        push    ax
        call    _FloatMultiply
        add     sp,8
        push    dx
        push    ax
        call    _FloatDivide
        add     sp,8
        push    dx
        push    ax
        mov     ax,1
        push    ax
        call    _FloatConvert
        add     sp,2
        push    dx
        push    ax
        call    _FloatSubtract
        add     sp,8
        push    dx
        push    ax
        call    _StdAbs
        add     sp,4
        push    dx
        push    ax
        mov     ax,WORD PTR $F_031
        mov     dx,WORD PTR $F_031+2
        push    dx
        push    ax
        call    _FloatCompare
        add     sp,8
        cmp     ax,0
        mov     ax,1
        jl      $L_058
        sub     ax,ax
$L_058:
        cmp     ax,1
        je      $L_057
        jmp     $L_056
```

(continues)

■■■■■ **Figure 14.23** Assembly object file for program **newton**. (*Continued*)

```
$L_057:
;  END
$L_055:
$L_051:
; {32} UNTIL number = 0
        mov     ax,WORD PTR number_032
        mov     dx,WORD PTR number_032+2
        push    dx
        push    ax
        mov     ax,0
        push    ax
        call    _FloatConvert
        add     sp,2
        push    dx
        push    ax
        call    _FloatCompare
        add     sp,8
        cmp     ax,0
        mov     ax,1
        je      $L_059
        sub     ax,ax
$L_059:
        cmp     ax,1
        je      $L_047
        jmp     $L_046
$L_047:
;  END


        pop     bp
        ret


_PascalMain     ENDP


        .DATA


number_032      DD      0.0
root_033        DD      0.0
sqroot_034      DD      0.0
$F_031  DD      1.000000e-06
$F_039  DD      0.000000e+00
$S_040  DB      "*** ERROR:  number < 0"
$S_035  DB      "Enter new number (0 to quit): "


        END
```

Table 14.1 shows the modules and source files that make up the compiler.

■■■■■■■ **Table 14.1** Modules and Files of Program 14-1

Module	File	Status	Directory
Main	compile.cpp	*new*	prog14-1
Parser	parser.h	*unchanged*	prog13-1
	parser.cpp	*unchanged*	prog11-1
	parsrtn1.cpp	*unchanged*	prog8-1
	parsrtn2.cpp	*unchanged*	prog13-1
	parsstd.cpp	*unchanged*	prog8-1
	parsdecl.cpp	*unchanged*	prog13-1
	parstyp1.cpp	*unchanged*	prog7-1
	parstyp2.cpp	*unchanged*	prog7-1
	parsstmt.cpp	*unchanged*	prog10-1
	parsexpr.cpp	*unchanged*	prog8-1
Back end	backend.h	*unchanged*	prog11-1
	backend.cpp	*unchanged*	prog11-1
Code generator	codegen.h	*unchanged*	prog13-1
	emitasm.cpp	*unchanged*	prog13-1
	emitsrc.cpp	*unchanged*	prog13-1
	emitcode.cpp	*unchanged*	prog13-1
	emitrtn.cpp	*unchanged*	prog13-1
	emitstd.cpp	*changed*	prog14-1
	emitstmt.cpp	*changed*	prog14-1
	emitexpr.cpp	*unchanged*	prog13-1
Intermediate code	icode.h	*unchanged*	prog10-1
	icode.cpp	*unchanged*	prog10-1
Scanner	scanner.h	*unchanged*	prog3-1
	scanner.cpp	*unchanged*	prog3-2
	token.h	*unchanged*	prog4-2
	tknword.cpp	*unchanged*	prog3-2
	tknnum.cpp	*unchanged*	prog3-2
	tknstrsp.cpp	*unchanged*	prog3-2
Symbol table	types.h	*unchanged*	prog7-1
	types.cpp	*unchanged*	prog7-1

(continues)

■■■■ **Table 14.1** Modules and Files of Program 14-1 (*Continued*)

Module	File	Status	Directory
	symtab.h	*unchanged*	prog8-1
	symtab.cpp	*unchanged*	prog8-1
Error	error.h	*unchanged*	prog5-2
	error.cpp	*unchanged*	prog11-1
Buffer	buffer.h	*unchanged*	prog2-1
	buffer.cpp	*unchanged*	prog2-1
Common	common.h	*unchanged*	prog8-1
	common.cpp	*unchanged*	prog8-1
	misc.h	*unchanged*	prog13-1

This chapter concludes the development of the Pascal compiler.

We began this book by developing a front end consisting of the parser and the scanner. We created an interface layer containing the symbol table and the intermediate code. We then developed an executor back end, and together with the front end and the interface layer, we had a working Pascal interpreter, to which we added interactive symbolic debugging capabilities. Finally, we replaced the executor with a code generator in the back end, and we had a working Pascal compiler that emitted assembly language object files.

In the next and final chapter of this book, we'll take a brief look at some advanced topics and other issues regarding compilers and interpreters.

15

ADVANCED

CONCEPTS:

AN OVERVIEW

We've made major accomplishments in this book: an interpreter, an interactive symbolic debugger, and a compiler. However, we've only examined the basic concepts of writing compilers and interpreters. This chapter contains a brief overview of some of the advanced concepts that you'll encounter if you plan to do further study and do more serious work in this field.

BNF

In this book, we used graphical syntax diagrams to represent the grammar of the Pascal source language. A common textual notation is the Backus-Naur Form, or BNF. As an example, we'll use this notation to describe the syntax of Pascal expressions.

BNF is a *metalanguage*, a language used to describe another language. Each statement of this metalanguage is called a *production rule*. Compare the following two rules to the first syntax diagram in Figure 5.22:

```
<expression> ::=     <simple expression>
                 | <simple expression> <rel op> <simple expression>

<rel op> ::= < | <= | = | <> | >= | >
```

The first rule states that an expression is either a single simple expression or two simple expressions separated by a relational operator. The second rule states that a relational operator is any one of the six tokens that are listed.

The symbols : : = and | are *metasymbols*. They belong to the BNF metalanguage and not to the Pascal source language. (When the same symbol belongs to both languages, a different typeface or type weight can be used to distinguish one usage from another.) The metasymbol : : = separates the left-hand side of a rule (a nonterminal symbol) from its right-hand side (the definition). The metasymbol | separates alternate forms in a definition.

In BNF, *nonterminal symbols* are enclosed by the angle brackets < and >. Nonterminal symbols are defined by other rules. *Terminal symbols* are tokens such as >= and IF. In the syntax diagrams, we used rectangular boxes to represent the nonterminal symbols, and rounded boxes to represent the terminal symbols.

A simple expression is defined by the following rules:

```
<simple expression> ::=     <term>
                        | <sign> <term>
                        | <simple expression> <add op> <term>

<sign>     ::= - | +

<add op> ::= - | + | OR
```

These rules state that a simple expression is one or more terms separated by adding operators. The first term is optionally preceded by a sign. A sign is either – or +, and an adding operator is either –, +, or the reserved word OR. Notice how BNF uses recursion to specify repetition, in this case multiple terms separated by adding operators.

We can now give the rules for a term, for a factor, and for a (simple) variable:

```
<term>     ::= <factor> | <term> <mult op> <factor>

<mult op> ::= * | / | DIV | MOD | AND
```

```
<factor>    ::=    <variable>
                 | <unsigned constant>
                 | <function call>
                 | NOT <factor>
                 | ( <expression> )

<variable> ::= <identifier>
```

We'll see one of the advantages of using a textual notation like BNF when we discuss *compiler compilers* below.

Top-Down versus Bottom-Up Parsing

The parser we wrote in this book uses a *top-down* parsing method known as *recursive descent*. With this method, the parser starts at the topmost nonterminal symbol of the grammar. In our BNF example above, that would be <expression>. The parser then proceeds to work its way down to the terminal symbols, such as <expression> to <simple expression> to <term> to <factor> to NOT. The parsing routines can be recursive.

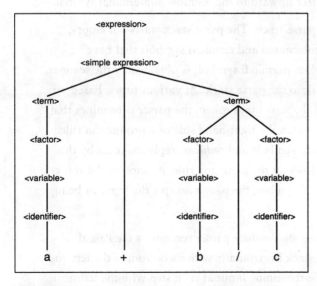

▪▪▪▪ **Figure 15.1** The parse tree for the expression **a + b/c**.

Another way to understand this is to look at the *parse tree* for an expression, as shown in Figure 15.1. (Compare this figure with Figure 5.4.) The parser starts at the top of the tree and, in effect, constructs the tree downward to the terminal symbols at the leaves.

We know we can implement a recursive descent parser by writing a member function to recognize each nonterminal symbol, as defined by the production rule (or syntax diagram) for the symbol. Each function can contain (possibly recursive) calls to member functions to recognize any nonterminal symbols in the definition. We code the semantic actions in these functions.

The advantages of a recursive descent parser are that it is easy to write, and once written, it is easy to read and understand. The main disadvantage is that it tends to be large and slow. If the grammar contains many nonterminal symbols, the parser contains many member functions. Function calls and returns can be relatively slow operations.

Another type of parser uses a *bottom-up* parsing method and is called a *shift-reduce* parser. This parser starts with the terminal symbols and works its way up to the top-most nonterminal symbol. In effect, it starts with the terminal symbols at the bottom of the parse tree and constructs the tree upward to the topmost nonterminal symbol.

A shift-reduce parser works with a parse stack. The parse stack starts out empty, and during the parse, it contains nonterminal and terminal symbols that have already been parsed. Each time a token (terminal symbol) is obtained by the scanner, the parser *shifts* (pushes) the token onto the parse stack. At various times, based on the symbols on top of the stack and the next input token, the parser determines that the symbols on the top of the stack match the right-hand side of a production rule. The parser then pops off the matching symbols and *reduces* (replaces) them by the nonterminal symbol at the left-hand side of the matching rule. As soon as the stack is reduced to the topmost nonterminal symbol, the parser *accepts* the input as being syntactically correct.

For example, Table 15.1 shows how a shift-reduce parser recognizes the Pascal expression `a + b/c`. We show the stack horizontally with its bottom at the left and its top at the right. We also show the remaining input at each step with the leftmost token being the next one to be read by the scanner.

Table 15.1 Shift-Reduce Parsing

Stack (bottom at left, top at right)	Input	Action
	a + b/c	shift
a	+ b/c	reduce
<identifier>	+ b/c	reduce
<variable>	+ b/c	reduce
<factor>	+ b/c	reduce
<term>	+ b/c	shift
<term> +	b/c	shift
<term> + b	/c	reduce
<term> + <identifier>	/c	reduce
<term> + <variable>	/c	reduce
<term> + <factor>	/c	shift
<term> + <factor> /	c	shift
<term> + <factor> / c		reduce
<term> + <factor> / <identifier>		reduce
<term> + <factor> / <variable>		reduce
<term> + <factor> / <factor>		reduce
<term> + <term>		reduce
<simple expression>		reduce
<expression>		accept

A shift-reduce parser uses a parse table that is derived from the grammar. This table determines whether the next action is to shift, reduce, accept, or signal a syntax error. Any semantic actions can also be encoded into this table. If the parse table is well-designed, a shift-reduce parser can be very fast and compact. As we'll see next, a parse table can be created by a program.

Compiler Compilers

One of the advantages of using a textual metalanguage is that we can feed the description of the syntax of a source language into a *compiler compiler*. A compiler compiler reads and compiles such a syntax description and then generates all or part of a compiler for the source language.

A well-known compiler compiler is Yacc ("Yet another compiler compiler"). It reads a syntax description written in a language similar to BNF and generates a shift-reduce parser for the source language. For example, if we described all of Pascal's syntax and fed that into Yacc, it would generate a parser for Pascal. This parser is in the form of a C program. To perform any semantic actions during parsing, we write sequences of C code to perform these operations, and embed these code sequences in the syntax description. When Yacc generates the parser, it includes these code sequences.

For example, suppose we want to write an interpreter for a very simple language consisting of a single expression that has only the add and subtract operators. The following syntax description, along with the embedded semantic code, can be fed into Yacc:

```
%token NUMBER
%left  '+' '-'

expression : expression '+' expression  { $$ = $1 + $3; }
           | expression '-' expression  { $$ = $1 - $3; }
           | '(' expression ')'         { $$ = $2; }
           | NUMBER                     { $$ = $1; }
           ;
```

This description states that NUMBER is a token returned by the scanner, and that the operators + and - are left-associative. In the definition of the expression, expression is a nonterminal symbol, and +, -, (,), and NUMBER are terminal symbols. Note that the metasymbol : is used instead of the ::= of BNF, and that a semicolon terminates each production rule.

Each alternate form of a rule can have semantic actions attached to it. The C code to perform the semantic actions are enclosed in the { and } braces. Within this code, $$ represents the value of the production rule, and $n represents the value of the nth element of the right-hand side. For example, the first semantic action says that the value of parsing and executing an expression plus another expression is the value of the first expression plus the value of the second expression (which is the third element). The fourth semantic action says that whenever the scanner fetches a NUMBER token, the scanner must also specify the token's value (by setting the special variable yylval which is supplied by Yacc).

When Yacc compiles this description, it produces a C routine named yyparse to parse and evaluate an expression. This parser includes the parse stack, a value stack, the parse table, and the semantic code. Within the semantic code, the $$ and n are replaced by references to the value stack to obtain the appropriate values. The parser calls the scanner, which must be named `yylex`, whenever it needs the next input token. When it detects a syntax error, the parser calls an error routine named `yyerror`.

To complete the compiler we must write a C main program that calls `yyparse`. We must also write the scanner `yylex` and the error routine `yyerror`.

A companion to Yacc is Lex, which generates a lexical analyzer (a scanner) named `yylex`. Thus, Yacc and Lex are designed to work together. Lex reads a textual description of the tokens of the source language in order to generate the scanner.

Better Intermediate Code Structures for Compilers

Our compiler and interpreter used intermediate code to represent the source program, and they generated object code or executed the program from the icode. The icode had a simple linear structure that was interspersed with location markers that pointed off to other parts of the icode.

A well-designed icode structure gives the compiler an opportunity to analyze the program in order to generate better object code. When an entire routine (or a substantial portion of a routine) of the source program is available in memory as icode, the compiler can look at each expression and statement within a greater context. By first examining several parts of an expression or statement, the compiler can generate more optimal code. We'll see examples of this later. Figure 15.2 shows a treestructured intermediate code for several Pascal statements that makes it easier for the compiler to look at different parts of the statements.

Code Optimization

As great a challenge as it is for a compiler to generate *correct* code, that is often not enough. We may also want the compiler to generate *optimal* code. Code may be optimal in terms of time (the code should execute as quickly as possible), space (the code should be as small as possible), or both.

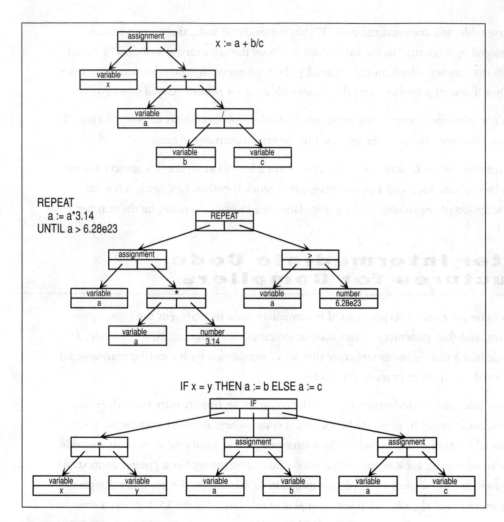

Figure 15.2 Tree-structured intermediate code.

The compiler we wrote is not always able to generate optimal code. This is because of the linear structure of the intermediate code. The code generator sees very little of the program at once, only one or two tokens.

For example, for the Pascal assignment statement:

    count := count + 1

our compiler generates code similar to:

```
mov   ax,WORD PTR count_083
push  ax
mov   ax,1
pop   dx
add   ax,dx
mov   WORD PTR count_083,ax
```

This is generic code that the compiler generates for any addition.

However, if the compiler could analyze the entire statement, it would be able to detect that the constant value 1 is added to the variable count, and that the sum is assigned to the same variable. Such a compiler would then be able to generate much more optimal code:

```
inc   count_083
```

This is an example of a *local optimization* that results from analyzing a small portion of the intermediate code, such as an expression or a statement.

Global optimization requires analysis of larger portions of the intermediate code. Examples of global optimizations include:

- *Dead code elimination.* The compiler simply does not generate code for source statements that can never be reached during execution. (A good compiler would probably issue a warning message when it detects dead code during parsing.)

- *In-line calls.* Sometimes when a procedure or a function is short, the expense of a call and a return can be eliminated if the code for the subroutine itself is inserted in the place of the call.

- *Common subexpressions.* The same subexpression may appear several times in an expression, for example:

  ```
  z := a*(p - q) + b*(p - q) + c*(p - q)
  ```

  To optimize this expression, the compiler can compile the above assignment statement as though it were the following two statements:

  ```
  x := p - q;
  z := a*x + b*x + c*x
  ```

  It might even be able to compile the second assignment statement as though it were written

  ```
  z := x*(a + b + c)
  ```

  to save the cost of two multiplies.

- *Loop-invariant expressions.* An expression in a loop may evaluate to the same value each time through the loop. The compiler can recognize this and move the invariant expression outside of the loop. For example, if the value of limit in the following WHILE loop isn't changed within the loop:

  ```
  WHILE i < limit - 1 DO ...
  ```

  the statement can be compiled as though it were written:

  ```
  x := limit - 1;
  WHILE i < x DO ...
  ```

- *Register allocation.* Unlike the 8086 architecture, some machine architectures offer a number of general-purpose registers that can all participate equally in expression evaluation. For faster execution, the compiler generates code that leaves values in the registers as long as possible to save on moves to and from memory. Of course, the compiler must then keep track of which values are in which registers during runtime.

Although optimization is generally desirable, no compiler must ever change the semantics of a program. Rather than risk computing an answer incorrectly (albeit more quickly), most compilers are conservative when it comes to elaborate optimization techniques.

Common Front Ends and Back Ends

Although high-level languages may differ greatly in syntax, they are often alike in semantics. For example, C and Pascal have FOR statements, and FORTRAN has the DO statement. At runtime, these statements behave very similarly.

One of the most efficient ways to write compilers for different languages is to have the compilers share as much as possible. If we design an intermediate code that can represent source programs written in C, Pascal, and FORTRAN, then we only need to write a single compiler back end consisting of the optimization and code generation modules. Each language would have its own compiler front end consisting of a parser and a scanner. Each front end scans and parses source programs written in the corresponding high-level language and translates the programs to the common icode. Then the common back end takes over to generate the target code.

The converse also works if we need to write compilers for one source language but for several machine architectures. In this case, we have a single front end but a different back end for each architecture.

Where to Go from Here

You may have noticed that we wrote our interpreter and compiler in a very modular fashion. That means that you can substitute routines that work differently but perform the same tasks. For example, you may want to replace the scanner with a faster one, or the parser with one that works bottom-up. The concepts in this chapter might give you some ideas of what you can do to improve what we have written. You should be able to study and understand a more advanced textbook on compiler writing and learn some of the theory behind these concepts.

Of course, you can write a compiler for some high-level language other than Pascal, or improve an existing compiler. A more ambitious project is to invent a new language and then write a compiler or an interpreter (or both) for it. This can be a standalone general-purpose programming language, or it can be a scripting language embedded in an application.

Many compiler writers dream of inventing the ultimate language and then writing the world's best compiler for it.

APPENDIX

A

OBTAINING THE

COMPLETE LISTINGS

You can obtain the complete C++ source file listings for the interactive symbolic debugger (which includes the interpreter), for the compiler, and for all the other programs in this book in two different ways.

Downloading from the Wiley Computer Publishing FTP Site

The source files, including the "make" files and Pascal test programs (and their input files) can be downloaded at no charge from the Wiley Computer Publishing FTP site. The location of the files on the Wiley Computer Publishing FTP site is:

ftp://ftp.wiley.com/public/computer_books/Software_Development/
Mak-Writing_Compilers

Individual files or the entire set may be downloaded using any standard Web browser.

Ordering the files on diskette

If you prefer, you may purchase a 3 1/2" high-density diskette containing the complete files. Please fill out the form below and mail it with a check or money order for $25.00 to:

Apropos Logic

P.O. Box 20884, San Jose, CA 95160

Checks must be drawn on a U.S. bank. Sorry, credit cards are not accepted. California residents must add appropriate local sales tax.

John Wiley & Sons, Inc., is not responsible for order placed with Apropos Logic.

CLASS DIAGRAMS

AND OBJECT

DIAGRAMS

This appendix briefly explains the simplified class diagrams and object diagrams used in this book.

Figure B.1 shows a class diagram and the definitions of the classes it represents.

Base class TBaseClass contains two private data members and a pure virtual private member function (thus making the class abstract), and it also contains a public data member and a public member function. In the diagram, the small A in the triangle indicates that the base class is abstract.

Subclass TSubClass is derived from base class TBaseClass, and this is shown in the diagram by an arrow from the subclass to the base class. The subclass directly contains a class TAlpha object and indirectly contains a class TBeta object as public data members. In the diagrams, containment is shown with a line connecting the container with the containee, with a filled circle at the container end and a rectangle at the containee end. If the containment is direct, the rectangle is filled, and if it is indirect, the rectangle is open.

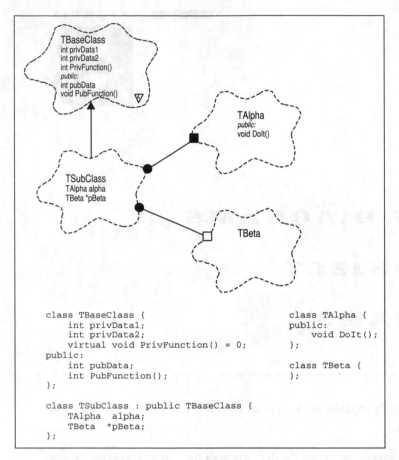

```
class TBaseClass {                           class TAlpha {
    int privData1;                           public:
    int privData2;                               void DoIt();
    virtual void PrivFunction() = 0;         };
public:
    int pubData;                             class TBeta {
    int PubFunction();                       };
};

class TSubClass : public TBaseClass {
    TAlpha  alpha;
    TBeta   *pBeta;
};
```

Figure B.1 A class diagram and the classes it represents.

Figure B.2 shows an object diagram, which represents how objects are related at run time. Here, an object instantiated from class TBeta sends the DoIt message to an object instantiated from class TAlpha. In other words, the TBeta object invokes the public DoIt method of the TAlpha object.

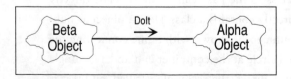

Figure B.2 An object diagram.

INDEX